COURAGE
AND
FEAR

Ukrainian Studies

Series Editor
Vitaly Chernetsky (University of Kansas)

The publication has been financed by the Ministry of Science and Higher Education of the Republic of Poland in the framework of the National Program for the Development of Humanities, project number 0120/NPRH5/H21/84/2017

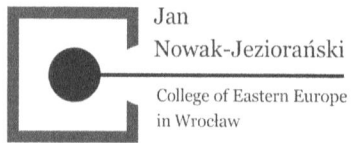

Jan Nowak-Jezioranski College of Eastern Europe in Wroclaw

Harvard Ukrainian Research Institute

COURAGE AND FEAR

OLA HNATIUK

BOSTON
2019

Library of Congress Control Number: 2019947938

English translation Copyright © 2019, Academic Studies Press.

ISBN 9781644692516 (paperback)
ISBN 9781644692523 (adobe pdf)
ISBN 9781644692530 (ePub)

Cover design by Ivan Grave.
Book design by PHi Business Solutions.

Distributed by Academic Studies Press
1577 Beacon Street
Brookline, MA 02446, USA
press@academicstudiespress.com
www.academicstudiespress.com

Contents

Translator's Note	vii
Foreword to English Edition	ix
Preface	xiii
1. Girl with a Dog	1
2. Haven at the Clinic	21
3. Academic Snapshots	91
4. Barbarian in the Garden	181
5. The Great Journey	269
6. Ukrainian Hamlet	301
7. Artists from Café de la Paix	399
Index of Names	451
Bibliography	499
Index	519

Translator's Note

Leopolis, Lwów, Lviv, Lemberg, Lvov—the city functioned under various names in different periods, its transformations reflected in documents, histories, literature as well as non-fiction. This translation uses "Lviv," in keeping with its contemporary Ukrainian nomenclature. The same standard has been applied to other geographic names, except when those toponyms appear in cited sources, or are part of historical terms, such as the Lwów School of Mathematics.

The text and narrative footnotes retain the original orthography of Polish and Jewish first and last names; in the case of Ukrainians, even if they had customarily adopted Polish spellings, the simplified Library of Congress transliteration (LOC) was still applied. By way of example, the Metropolitan of the Greek-Catholic church figures as Andrei Sheptytsky here, and not in the once customarily used Polish rendition—Andrzej Roman Szeptycki. Where English spellings are well established, such as for Archipenko or Babi Yar, the principles of transliteration made room for readers' convenience. However, to assist with research accuracy, the bibliography and all citations apply strict LOC rules, albeit without ligatures.

On a personal note, *Courage and Fear* has proved to be a most gripping translation project. I am deeply indebted to several people in my closest circle, first and foremost the author and my sister Ola Hnatiuk, who cheerfully answered my queries as if we did not live time zones apart. My husband Doug Young rallied behind the translation before anyone thought it plausible and remained its unwavering enthusiast throughout. In the nascent stages of this endeavor, I was lucky to be able to call on my friend and translator John Eyck, who, as always, offered invaluable expert advice.

Foreword to English Edition

Courage and Fear tells the history of Lviv during World War Two. From a North American perspective, it may seem like a region remote in time and space, a relatively insignificant city in a corner of Europe. But Lviv was a rare testing ground for its occupiers—the Soviet Union and the Third Reich. There they carried out some of the most terrifying experiments of the last century. What happened in Lviv then has a resonating significance for our understanding of last century's and today's disputes.

This book examines bonds between local ethnicities, which is instructive of relations among the nations of the region still affected by stereotypes, prejudice, and mutual grievances dating back to those fateful years. One example of such a lasting holdover are the Polish-Ukrainian and, to a lesser extent, the Jewish-Ukrainian memory conflicts. Even more gravely, the legacy of the war years continues to fuel the hostilities between Russia and Ukraine. As Ukrainians defend the territorial integrity of the Ukrainian state and reassert the right to their identity and history, they again face Russia's opposition. Russia's and Germany's imperial designs have often determined the trajectory of world history, and they have left the deepest scars on the populations of Central-Eastern Europe.

In his essay "The Central-Eastern Revision," Yuri Andrukhovych summed up the fates of these countries as a back-and-forth exodus:

> Existence between the Russians and the Germans is the historical destiny of Central Europe. The Central European Fear historically sways between two anxieties: the Germans are advancing, the Russians are advancing. Central European death—this is a prison or concentration camp death, a collective one too, *Massenmord, a purge.* The Central European journey—this is escape. But from and to where? From the Germans or the Russians?[1]

---

1   Yuri Andrukhovych, *My Final Territory*, trans. Michael Naydan (Toronto: University of Toronto Press, 2018), 28–29.

On September 17, 1939, the Red Army marched into the eastern territories of the Second Polish Republic. Soviet leaders claimed this military action was nothing more than "brotherly assistance." A contemporary Soviet poster proclaimed: "we extend our fraternal hand so our brothers can straighten their spines and cast off the lordly yoke." The "liberated" peoples rephrased it as black humor—"they gave us a hand to carry us out feet first." But by the end of that first Soviet occupation, which had lasted twenty-two months, the Polish and Ukrainian population gave up on humor, praying for any change, in the belief that "the Devil himself would be better than the Soviets." The Nazis would prove them wrong.

Until recently, Western readers viewed the war suffering in Europe through the prism of the Western European experience. Timothy Snyder's *Bloodlands: Europe between Hitler and Stalin* widened this perspective, painting a poignant picture of Central-Eastern Europe between 1918 and 1945, where civilian populations fell victim to man-made famines, the Holocaust, and the Stalinist and Nazi terror. But *Bloodlands* did not submit to the national narratives of martyrdom and heroism. Indeed, in a world so saturated with violence that death became unremarkable, acts of active or passive resistance were a rare occurrence.

Snyder's book cast a wider net than mine: the loss of life is counted in tens of millions, and his panorama spans the entire multinational region. *Courage and Fear* views the same history through a micro lens. It directs its focus on one city, zeroing in on the intelligentsia of three ethnicities: Polish, Ukrainian, and Jewish. Its aim is not to conjure the myth of a multicultural, mosaic Central Europe, a lost Atlantis—a project so popular among Polish postwar émigré memoirists (see, e.g., *My Lwow* by Józef Wittlin, published in 1946). In contrast to those wistful narratives, this book draws on archival and printed sources to trace the relationships between select Polish, Ukrainian, and Jewish intellectuals during World War Two. Their relationships are described not from the perspective of ethnic communities, but from individual points of view. A micro focus helps recalibrate our take on this history: the customary, mutually exclusive national narratives recede, making room for a more universal perspective of humanity. The history in *Courage and Fear* aims to escape pathos and bias, and to cross-examine historical verdicts so often mandated by ethnic loyalties.

The book follows the city of Lviv and its region through a period of cataclysmic changes—the Soviet and German occupations, mass reprisals, the Holocaust, and forced deportations after the war. Reviewing the choices my protagonists made in the face of conflict and constant mortal threat, I show instances of heroism and weakness, courage and fear. These stories demonstrate the complexity of human identity and transcend categories of nationality, religion, race, and politics, all of which can distort our understanding and prevent us from truly seeing what motivates solidarity—is it love for thy neighbor or simply human loyalty?

When writing about Lviv intellectuals, we encounter people once well known, who faded into obscurity, not unlike their city. Such was the case in Philippe Sands's *East West Street*, and the same applies to this study. Among my protagonists are Irena Lille, the first female microbiologist in Lviv; Hugo Steinhaus, one of the co-founders of the Lwów School of Mathematics; the historian Mykhailo Marchenko; the singer and actor Eugeniusz Bodo; the literary critic Mykhailo Rudnytsky; and the painter Iaroslava Muzyka. Some of them were acquainted with each other, others would have never guessed that one day they would meet in this book. All belonged to the educated elite, and were selected for this project based on the narratives they left behind. My choice was guided by the accessibility of the sources, as well as the desire to portray a variety of professional milieus—medicine, academia, and art. Almost entirely absent from my study are the Catholic and Greek-Catholic clergy, whose fates merit a separate academic inquiry.

Among these well- or lesser-known figures, the protagonists of the first chapter are an exception. The story of my mother and grandmother serves as a point of departure, an opening to a broader reflection. It may shorten the distance between the author and her readers—especially for those who have Central-Eastern European roots—and find parallels to their family histories.

***

The literature in English regarding Lviv during World War Two is less plentiful than in Polish. But enough has been published to make unnecessary a refresher of the crucial events, developments, and figures of the period. Especially rich in facts and interpretations are the following titles: Jan T. Gross, *Revolution from Abroad. The Soviet Conquest of Poland's Western Ukraine and Western Belorussia* (1988; 2002); Christoph Mick, *Lemberg, Lwów, L'viv, 1914–1947: Violence and Ethnicity in a Contested City* (2015); *Lviv: A City in the Crosscurrents of Culture* (2000) edited by John Czaplicka; and *The Great West Ukrainian Prison Massacre of 1941: A Sourcebook*, edited by Alexander Motyl and Ksenya Kiebuzinsky (2016). The postwar period and contemporary Lviv are the subjects of *The Ukrainian West: Culture and the Fate of Empire in Soviet Lviv* by William Risch (2012), *Ukrainian Intelligentsia in Post-Soviet Lviv: Narratives, Identity and Power* by Eleonora Narvselius (2012), and *The Paradox of Ukrainian Lviv: A Borderland City between*

Stalinists, Nazis, and Nationalists by Tarik Cyril Amar (2015). These studies provide a good sense of Sovietization and mass reprisals, of the Polish and Ukrainian underground resistance, of the pogroms of July 1941, the Holocaust of Lviv's Jews, and the complete overhaul of the city's ethnic structure.

***

In conclusion, I wish to thank everyone to whom I owe the English edition of *Courage and Fear*—above all, my translator and sister Ewa Siwak. She was the first one to insist that the book merited a translation into a language more universal than any of the Central-Eastern European languages, and took on this monumental task with great passion and dedication. Special thanks also go to Serhii Plokhy and Oleh Kotsyuba for supporting the English edition at its every stage and for suggesting Academic Studies Press (ASP) as the co-publisher. I am grateful to the entire editing team at ASP for their editing and graphic work: the project coordinator Kate Yanduganova, academic editor Jodi Greig, copy editor Stuart Allen, series editor Vitalii Chernetsky, and production editor Kira Nemirovsky. Just as importantly, I would like to express my gratitude to Andrzej Dąbrowski, the chairman of Kolegium Europy Wschodniej, and Laurynas Vaičiūnas, the director of its press. They published the Polish original, and without their efforts the present book would not have been possible.

Preface

Every book has its own story. Among its characters are loved ones, friends, and acquaintances, as well as archivists, librarians, editors—people whose help is indispensable to an academic project. Working on my previous books, I had always been conscious of the contributions of these others, but had never perceived them as essential. Somewhat self-importantly I ascribed authorship exclusively to myself. *Courage and Fear* is my most personal book—you would expect that it would not only be my most subjective, but also the one most intimately of my own making. It is, after all, an individual narrative that does not follow the convention of "scholarly objectivity." It steers clear of the tradition of invoking academic authorities. In my perception, however, it is precisely this book that owes the most to friends, with whom I was able to discuss individual chapters, and to others I was lucky to have met and who were willing to share their own perspective on both the present and the past. To mention them all would necessitate a personal second index. Allow me therefore to limit my acknowledgements to the initial readers and critics of the larger sections of my book: Bogumiła Berdychowska, Marta Bohachevsky-Chomiak, Marta Boianivska, Leonid Finberg, Timothy Snyder, Danuta Sosnowska, Stanisław Stępień, Vladyslav Verstiuk, and Kazimierz Wóycicki.

The idea for this project emerged a year after my mom passed away, my mother with whom I spoke too little, especially about the things that most interested me: composite ethnic identities, individual choices, and personal courage. In other words, matters that tend to determine our life's path. No one likes to talk about fear and it is no surprise that my family also avoided the subject, which was painful for both my parents.

My mother was born in Lviv at the start of World War II. She left her hometown in 1946 with the last transport of "repatriates" (Poles who had settled Eastern Galicia and other Eastern territories of the Second Polish Republic annexed by the Soviets in 1939), as Poland's borders shifted west and dramatic population swaps followed. In the fall of 2008, I decided to recruit friends and colleagues and organize an exhibit devoted to the first two years of

World War II in Lviv. The exhibit would depict the experiences of various communities—Polish, Ukrainian, and Jewish—in the face of Soviet occupation. Despite various obstacles and unforeseen circumstances, eventually the project was realized. In July of 2010, after a year of preparations, Lvivians and tourists alike were able to view the first large Ukrainian exhibition hosted in a public space: Lviv's Market Square facing City Hall. Its authors were Oleh Pavlyshyn, of the Institute of Historical Research at the Ivan Franko National University of Lviv, and Mariusz Zajączkowski, of the Lublin branch of the Institute of National Remembrance. Magdalena Śladecka developed the art design, and Iaroslav Hrytsak, Rafał Wnuk, and myself served as academic consultants. The project came about because of the cooperation of the Polish Institute of National Remembrance, the Ukrainian Institute of Remembrance, and the embassy of the Republic of Poland in Kyiv. The Polish Institute's president, Janusz Kurtyka, its director, Agnieszka Rudzińska, and the vice-president of the Ukrainian Institute, Vladyslav Verstiuk, spared no effort in overcoming the obstacles in our path. Polish ambassador Jacek Kluczkowski supported the initiative, at the same time building a foundation for a new kind of dialogue between Polish and Ukrainian historians. Things turned out differently than expected, unfortunately. But discussions and arguments among authors, consultants, and patrons ultimately led to this book. On a personal note—although I had previously known each colleague at least by title—those months nourished our friendships.

A short while after the exhibit, it occurred to me that we barely touched on the issues I had set out to raise. The challenge was too weighty to address in the simplified format of an exhibition. It wanted something. I resolved to find a more adequate format to tell this immeasurably complex story. The work that followed resembled the typical research phase leading up to a book. It differed in one aspect, though: from the start I never intended to focus on unearthing new information, since the historical facts are well established. Recent years have seen the publication of several reference works, which I felt freed me from any duty to reiterate basic information. Moreover, in the course of the past dozen years historians have conducted intense research, substantially deepening our stores of knowledge about wartime Lviv, thus preempting the need to correct assertions and narrow down numbers, dates, or personal information. In this light, even new facts without a strikingly new interpretation do not amount to more than mere supplementation and ultimately cannot alter our current knowledge. Despite the existence of such an impressive body of contemporary scholarship, I chose not to rely exclusively on publications and documents in print. Instead, I delved into archival collections relatively unknown in Poland and underutilized even in Ukraine.

The fundamental goal I set for myself when I began writing was to refocus my story from a national to a personal narrative. Every national narrative dealing with an ethnic community is interested, above all, in the destinies of its "own" protagonists. An "other" may be allotted a limited part, but always under the condition of fitting into the existing canon. If this narrative perceives its "own" to be a victim, and the "other" an enemy, it assigns the respective roles from the start, making the nationalities of positive and negative protagonists easy to predict. No space remains for stories of cooperation, mutual support, or solidarity. National narratives treat each manifestation of those behaviors as exceptions that only prove the rule, without ever reframing the overall image. Even if those less standard stories are in fact exceptional, they deserve all the more attention. They attest to individual courage and to the human will to confront evil, even when faced with the threat of death. To view such actions purely as exceptions to the rule sheds light on our deeply rooted negative stereotypes. My personal experience, as well as my background in national identity studies, suggest that we cannot overcome stereotypes, because they are inherent to how we structure thought. I therefore set a more modest goal for myself: to show divergent patterns.

My choice of the main characters is not personal, albeit nearly all of them played a part in my life, the encounters occurring through family history, readings, films, or songs. What informed my selection above all else was the multifaceted and ambiguous aura these protagonists exude, their ideals and life stories, their survival strategies, and, finally, the accessibility of source materials about them. We can attribute their attitudes and relationships to their individual worldviews or their social origin in the educated elite. They functioned in Lviv's multinational community, which was admittedly ripe with conflict, yet not steeped in hatred. Under different circumstances—in short, had it not been for the abuses by functionaries of totalitarian regimes and by their underlings who in carrying out political visions bear a share of the responsibility for the Shoah and for crimes against humanity—ethnicity would have played only a minor role in their choices and life stories.

My aim was not to write an individual biography or focus on particular figures. Instead, I wanted to paint a picture of relationships among protagonists of different nationalities who happened to coinhabit occupied Lviv during the war. While each chapter has a key character, and the narrative spotlight falls on a particular life story, my main interest lies not in the sum of their biographies, but rather in the bonds tying them to their respective milieus. Hence the narrative does not follow along simple chronological lines of their lives or of the war. Although this more customary narrative frame would make for easier reading, it presents an obstacle when telling stories of intricate relationships. Instead of a linear narrative structure, characteristic for accounts based on chronology, I relied on nested storytelling. In a similar fashion, I chose not to construct my narrative around a simplifying plot. Thus, each chapter seeks not so much to solve a puzzle or ascertain a fact, as to establish the persons, events, and web of circumstances that came to influence a protagonist's strategy. To that end, I draw on a broad variety of documents of a personal nature (*ego-documents*): journals, memoirs, letters, third-person accounts, even interrogation transcripts. Other sources play only a secondary part. I make limited use of memoirs by Karolina Lanckorońska[1] and Aleksander Wat,[2] which are widely known and quoted in Polish scholarship. I applied a similar strategy to established Ukrainian and Jewish sources, such as the writings of poet Ostap Tarnavsky and the librarian and archeologist Larisa Krushelnytska, as well Kurt Lewin[3] and Ignacy Chiger,[4] to create a space for lesser-known or previously unquoted personal accounts.

While this book is not intended as a monograph devoted to Lviv's creative milieus, it was important to me to represent the life stories of representatives of various professions: doctors, scholars, writers, artists, and musicians. In tracing their mutual relationships, I show that they were not necessarily linked through narrow professional interests, and that these connections had a tendency to cross ethnic lines.

The majority of books about Lviv strike a nostalgic tone, which I made an effort to avoid. Yet just to invoke the complexity of this bygone world can evoke nostalgia.

---

1   Karolina Lanckorońska, a well-known art historian from a prominent aristocratic family, was among the first people to give testimony about the massacre of Lviv professors.
2   Aleksander Wat was a noted poet of the Polish avant-garde featured in Marci Shore's study of Polish leftist avant-garde poets *Caviar and Ashes: A Warsaw Generations Life and Death in Marxism, 1918–1968* (New Haven: Yale University Press, 2006).
3   Kurt Lewin, the eldest son of Lviv rabbi Ezekiel Lewin, witness to the Holocaust, author of a number of memoirs.
4   Ignacy Chiger, the father of Krystyna Chiger-Keren, published a memoir *Świat w mroku. Pamiętnik ojca dziewczynki w zielonym sweterku* (Warsaw: PWN, 2011). His daughter's memoir *The Girl in a Green Sweater: A Life in the Holocaust's Shadow* (New York: St. Martin's Press, 2008) was adapted by Agnieszka Holland into a screenplay for the 2011 film *W ciemności* [*In Darkness*].

I would like to express my gratitude to the administration and the employees of the Shevchenko Scientific Society (New York), to the Lviv National Art Gallery, the Manuscript Collection of the National Library of Poland, the Manuscript Collection of the Warsaw University Library, the Central State Historical Archive in Lviv, the Kyiv-Mohyla Academy Archives, the Archive of the National University of Lviv, the State Archives Department of the Security Service of Ukraine, the Archive of the Ukrainian Academy of Arts and Sciences (New York), the Polish Academy of Sciences Archive (Warsaw), the Archive of the United States Holocaust Memorial Museum (Washington), and the Ossolineum Library (Wrocław).

1.   Słupsk, 14.X.57.

Droga Pani!

Naprawdę, bardzo cieszymy się z tego, że odnalazłyśmy adres Państwa. W ciągu minionych lat niejednokrotnie wspominałyśmy Panią, a ja dokładnie wypytywałam Mamusię o wszystko. Teraz, gdy nadarzyła się okazja, Mamusia poprosiła tego pana (który odwiedził Państwo), by, jeśli to będzie możliwe, zdobył adres. Chciałyśmy przesłać przez p. Filipcoka list do Pani, ale wyjechał on niespodziewanie wcześniej, niż pierwotnie zamierzał, więc nie mogłyśmy skreślić nawet kilku słów, za co bardzo przepraszamy.

Mieszkamy teraz w Słupsku. Jest to miasto przeszło 50-tysięczne, położone na Pomorzu Zachodnim, 18 km od morza (województwo koszalińskie, na linii Gdynia – Szczecin). Mamusia pracuje tutaj jako przełożona pielęgniarek szpitala Wojewódzkiego. Placówka jest olbrzymia – przeszło 900 łóżek i do tego położona w dwóch kompleksach gmachów, odległych od siebie o 2 km. Połączenia tramwajowego na tej trasie nie ma, wobec czego traci się dużo czasu na dojazdy sanitarką, kursującą nieregularnie. Wobec takiego stanu rzeczy Mamusia nie odrzywa nawet pracy, nie pozwalającej nawet na prowadzenie korespondencji, więc prosiła, abym ja napisała, co u nas słychać, a sama dopisze parę słów na końcu. Ja ze swej strony przepraszam, że robię to dopiero teraz, ale w związku z egzaminami miałam bardzo dużo pracy i trudno było mi znaleźć chwilę wolną na napisanie listu.

Jeśli chodzi o nas, to nie czujemy się tutaj zbyt dobrze. Nadmorskie powietrze dobrze być nam nie może – obie cierpimy na

Letter from Halina Lewkowska to Iaroslava Muzyka, 1957

CHAPTER 1

Girl with a Dog

My mom, Halina Siwak, née Lewkowska, was born in Lviv on September 18, 1939. Both the date as well as the birthplace are ominous. As a child, for reasons unknown to myself, I would stare at the entry "Place of Birth: Lviv, USSR," on Mom's identity card, examining it again and again. For me, born in Warsaw, this always stirred an unease, a vaguely threatening feeling. It is hard to say today what sparked it, whether this fear had roots in stories I had heard as a young child, or whether it appeared once the date of September 17, 1939 became as significant to me as September 1, 1939.

My school curriculum carefully skipped over September 17, 1939 when the Soviets marched in, focusing instead on the Nazi campaign in Poland that began on September 1, centering on the heroism of the Polish soldier and German bestiality. Certainly, already in elementary school I knew that the Red Army had invaded the eastern territories of the Second Polish Republic. It was officially forbidden knowledge, banned from the school curriculum. I acquired it mostly from family history, though, and in part also via my mom's former dorm roommate and friend, Zofia Błaszczyk. Ms. Błaszczyk had arrived in Poland from the USSR in 1956 (our contact with her broke off after we moved to a different district of Warsaw in the spring of 1969, much in the same way as had contact with Mom's contemporary, Hanna Gnoińska, born into a Polish-Jewish family in Lviv). Much later, in tenth grade in high school, I also learned the truth about Katyn (the 1940 executions of almost 25,000 Polish officers and civil servants ordered by the Soviet Political Bureau and blamed on the Nazis), albeit thanks to my friend Paweł, the grandson of Stanislaw Swianiewicz. Swianiewicz was one of those few fortunate reserve officers who extricated themselves from Soviet imprisonment after that massacre. Being teenagers, we were as unwilling to compromise as we were aggravating. We would frustrate our newest teacher's history classes (he led the Basic Communist Party Organization in our high school), and his lack of reaction would only

Iaroslava Muzyka, *Portrait of a Girl with a Dog*, 1946

cause us to grow increasingly more impudent. In my case, our behavior yielded unwelcome results: my high school diploma bore the evaluation, "Pupil under the influence of foreign propaganda," which could have made it impossible for me to start my adult life. Especially if you wanted to matriculate as a humanities student. But the year was 1980…

Raised in Polish culture and as a Roman Catholic, Mom made a choice out of love for Dad that would result in nothing but problems. First of all, her relationship with her mother and more distant relatives grew colder. This was the end of the 1950s, when family bonds were much stronger than half a century later—not to mention that those bonds made it easier to survive within a system of perennial shortages. To belong to an oppressed Ukrainian minority had its consequences as well, despite their having emerged from the oblivion where they had been condemned by the Political Bureau's decision of forced expatriation and draconian rules of resettlement that all but ensured the community's disintegration. This minority continued to find themselves in a position inferior to other Polish citizens, at the time comparable only to that of a small number of Germans remaining in Poland. The authorities drew an ideological equals sign between those two minorities, a perspective which persisted for decades and has survived as a stereotype ("collaborators," "fascists") to this day.

My mom's choice was unusual in every way. It was a choice not in favor of a *closed identity*, one that was characteristic of an era when nationalisms fought each other. Under the cover of the official international rhetoric a nationally monolithic state was emerging. Only many years later did I become acquainted with the concept of *open identity*, one that is inclusive, and *closed identity*, one that excludes. The slogan, "Who is not with us is against us," commonly evoked in the era of real socialism, was foreign to Mom as well. Not just because she came to belong to the excluded—it so happens that the excluded can use the logic of exclusion too.

Mom, although she had learned Ukrainian only a few years before, taught me the Ukrainian alphabet. Her carefully calligraphed board was prepared according to the dictionary compiled by two linguists from Lviv, Witold Taszycki and Stanisław Jodłowski. With Latin alphabet letters corresponding to the Cyrillic ones, it was supposed to make it easier to read the Roman Catholic catechism. It hung above my bed like a picture of a saint. I have kept both the board and the catechism to this day. The catechism was published in Przemyśl in the fateful year of 1946, the same year in which Soviet authorities delegalized the Uniate Church, and the UB (the Polish Security Office) handed Bishop Iosafat Kotsylovsky over to the NKVD.

In the area of Polish stylistics Mom was my oracle. Her speech, with the characteristic "ł" and voiced "h" resembled prewar pronunciation; she paid careful attention to diction, and tried to impart that care to me. This could seem somewhat ostentatious, smacking of the careful education of a *"girl from a good home."* True, Mom's intelligentsia roots played a very important part in her identity, but she never let others feel like they lacked in education or manners. Through her attention to linguistic formations and social formalities she was fighting her private war. It was a war she had declared against the glut of mediocrity and coarseness (a reflection of those times was the saying "crooked, straight—who cares as long as it's a short-cut"). Doing so, she was expressing her love for her mother tongue, which she strove to share with both her immediate and more distant surroundings.

Many times I would ask myself how it happened, how did this marriage come to be? The Shakespearean topos of Romeo and Juliet can be applied to my parents, but did Shakespeare not sentence his lovebirds to death? Let us try to consider this decision as a social phenomenon: how do you overcome such strong aversion between two nations? These nations are not the feuding

Montague and Capulet clans who can only reconcile over the lovers' grave! On the contrary: the parties to this conflict are fenced off by a "border of friendship," and Romeo and Juliet go on living. Rather, the Shakespearean topos might be compared with another, terror-provoking literary motif: Gogol's Taras Bulba kills his son ("I begot you, and I shall kill you"), because when his son follows his heart, in the father's eyes he is committing apostasy.

Ukrainians considered those Poles who had been repatriated during operation "Vistula" from beyond the Bug River to be their greatest enemies, and those repatriates returned the hostility in kind, at the encouragement of Polish communist authorities. Official propaganda very effectively fomented this negative stereotype, labeling those who had any connection with the Polish underground as "a reactionary force of spittle-bespattered dwarves," and the others as "Bandera's criminals and killers." In this clever way they diverted attention from the real perpetrators of the misery of repatriation. Additionally, a widespread postwar fear, which today we would identify as post-traumatic stress disorder, fueled the mutual hatred between these two ethnic groups. Just how closed both communities remained is shown in the Polish movie *Sami swoi* ("Our Folks"), a film with an exceptionally large viewership in Poland. (This comedy depicted the lives of two village families from the area of Vilnius after they had been resettled in the Recovered Territories. Despite losing their little homeland, they cling to their identity, in part by fiercely cultivating their old property line dispute.) Because the topic of Ukrainians in Poland was taboo, it would be difficult to find a similarly well-known example involving Ukrainian deportees. Ukrainians felt compelled to keep their national identity hidden from neighbors, as well as at work and at school. The resulting Ukrainian community closed itself off from others, and suffered the typical psychological and societal consequences.

During her studies Mom associated herself with a group of "repatriates" who resembled her, and also with arrivals of the "new wave"—the deportees released from Siberia during the Thaw of 1956. Among them were not only Poles, but also citizens of the prewar Republic of Poland who represented other nationalities: Ukrainians, Belarusians, and Jews. Deprived of everything, virtually naked and barefoot, yet with sizeable baggage from the trauma of labor camps and sometimes even prisons, they longed to seize the opportunity to get an education, as afforded by measly government scholarships.

In the 1950s, scattered across all of Poland after operation "Vistula," young Ukrainians found it very difficult to break into academic life and secure university admissions. Not only were those forced expatriates restricted from changing their place of residence, they also lacked Polish educational records (Ukrainian high school certificates were best kept well hidden), and their foreignness was perceived as enmity or even a danger. Some of them saw getting an education as their only chance to cover up the stigma that came with being the subjects of operation "Vistula." To be sure, it would be impossible to escape this taint in small towns, but in a large city they stood a chance. Stubbornly they pursued not so much economic advancement as simply a chance to free themselves from a situation akin to exile, caused by drastically restricted civil rights and economic conditions. After 1956, Ukrainians regained their right to exist as a social group. On account of the thaw, the Ukrainian Socio-Cultural Society (UTSK) was born. To be sure, the organization was thoroughly infiltrated, but at least now Ukrainians were no longer persecuted for simply keeping in touch with one another. Those who found themselves in Warsaw in the mid-1950s created a tightly knit and colorful group of young intelligentsia. Locating other Ukrainians—those from operation "Vistula" and those arriving with the latest wave of "repatriates" in 1956—and building a new microcommunity took much inventiveness and effort. Yet after the terror of Stalinism receded, a new atmosphere permeated civic and private lives.

It was then that Mom met Dad, Eugeniusz Siwak (Ievhen Syvak), born in Masłomęcz near Hrubieszów, forcibly expatriated from his native village in June 1947. He started his studies in the mid-1950s, almost concurrently with Mom, although he was ten years older than his future wife. Earlier, in the fall of 1945 (at that time most Poles from Lviv had already left the city because of the shifting borders), under the impending threat of ethnic cleansing at the hands of the Polish People's Army, his parents succumbed to the "persuasion" of the Polish People's Government. Dad and his father and mother, Teodor and Leoniła Siwak, found themselves on the other side of the border, in the USSR; but once there, they immediately understood that their chances of survival in the Soviet Republic were slim. So Dad and Grandpa illegally made it back across the border, from nearby Volodymyr-Volynsky already in Soviet hands, to the Hrubieszów area (barely thirty kilometers), and then to their familial village. Most of the homes, including the family home they built right before the war, had been set on fire. Grandma Leoniła was able to return only much later, by using Polish documents she purchased in exchange for the rest of their possessions. She left their cow with distant relatives. Many years later when I was in Moscow, those relatives, remembering their debt to our family, brought me a gold chain. I still have it, but I cannot bear to wear it—it weighs too heavily.

Recently I came across some correspondence from the late 1950s between my mom and a well-known Ukrainian painter, Iaroslava Muzyka. Despite the age difference between the two women—over forty years—Mom, who had just graduated from high school, penned very personal letters. The first of her letters was written shortly after the addressee returned from a labor camp, and Mom's writing is steeped in nostalgia. This seems strange considering that Mom left Lviv as a barely seven-year-old girl. What could she remember besides her loved ones? The garden where she could not play because every inch of soil had to produce some sort of crop? Her beloved stuffed dog? Walks in Stryi Park? Kaiserwald, back then a military facility, but now a destination for leisurely Sunday walks? Her letters reverberate with a longing for a lost childhood and for the spell of Lviv, the world's most beautiful city, the city that all the prewar Lviv intelligentsia were writing about. Trauma emanates from these letters; it ensnares happiness and keeps it out of reach.

The next letters date back to Mom's university years and give more insight into her life. In the fall of 1957, she enrolled at Warsaw University. At the dorm on Kicki Street she quickly found a social circle—comprised of "repatriates" and … Ukrainians. One of her last lengthy letters, dating from late 1959, refers to her marriage plans. A key phrase appears: "Most importantly, he is 'one of us.'" So writes a Pole to a Ukrainian, hardly a dozen or so years after the war. A Pole, by choice of her Ukrainian mother and Polish father. To a Ukrainian, who only three years earlier came out of the Siberian labor camps, where she had served a sentence for collaborating with the Ukrainian underground and for contacts with Roman Shukhevych, the commander of the Ukrainian Insurgent Army (UPA).

I read this passage many times, struggling to fully grasp its meaning: "Most importantly he is one of us" is precisely what Ukrainian families living in Poland would say, because for them the possibility of their child's marriage to a Pole meant that their national identity would inevitably fade and "polonization" would occur. Never did I hear of an equivalent argument in a Polish family (one living within the country, not abroad). Why did my mom use this phrase? Until I read it in her letter, I had always considered these words to be a telltale sign of xenophobia. What does "one of us" mean, then? Two communities hostile to each other; and here—"us"! Even if I could ask Mom this question, I doubt that I could formulate it with sufficient clarity.

It seems that the traumatic history, whose witnesses and actors my parents and grandparents had been, should not have left any doubt about how to define "one of us" and "stranger." The labels rested on the concept of ethnicity.

Egoism, pain, or your own history did not allow many people, many communities, even nations, to empathize, or understand the pain of the Other. "He is one of us"? No way!" Impossible. Instead, wouldn't the conclusion be: "She no longer belongs to us"?

Suddenly the shared fate of repressed communities (deported, expatriated, simply torn away from their own home), the collectivity of suffering—individual, but also joint—and the concept of "one of us" regained its proper dimension. Surprising, and yet so logical.

My mom and grandma, Eufrozyna Lewkowska, divested of a roof over their heads, plagued by the specter of deportation to the East, left Lviv forever in June 1946. During the same summer Grandpa and my dad managed to slip through the needle's eye: they illegally crossed the border in great haste. They made it back to "our corner of the world," as Dad used to say, avoiding the adjective "Ukrainian" or, to use a term from a much later era, to his "Homeland." Thirty-four years later I matriculated at Warsaw University as a Ukrainian major. Three more years passed and I found myself for the first time within the territories of the USSR—in the capital of the empire, to be precise. An empire that, despite visible problems (Solidarity and martial law in Poland; military defeats in Afghanistan), did not abandon its dream of power. In March 1983, when I was leaving Moscow, seriously ill, I dreamed not so much of never returning "there," but of simply somehow making it to the Polish border. History had come full circle. Although these were not times of war, but of peace, or rather—to invoke the language of propaganda from those days—"a war for peace"—fear remained the dominant undertone.

Halina Lewkowska in front of the house on Mączna Street, 1943

Mom had an embarrassing habit of biting her nails, which could not be eradicated at all. It contrasted starkly with her perfect manners and the attention she paid to her looks. This habit grew out of wartime, and, as I learned shortly before she died, postwar angst. Not only had she been raised in a constant state of threat, but even her birth occurred under conditions of mortal fear. The pounding of troops marching in from the direction of Łyczakowska

(Lychakivska) Street and the revving of tank engines were some of the first sounds she heard. Soon thereafter her father disappeared, arrested for his role as a secretary at the appellate court in Lviv. He returned to the home he had purchased only two months earlier with bruised kidneys and never left it again. My grandma had no choice—she had to prove herself resourceful, just like her own mother, Oleksandra Fedyk, had once done, rebuilding her house, destroyed during World War I, with money made from sales of baked goods in front of the Pochayiv Lavra monastery complex. Grandma sold what could be sold, and in this manner, so prevalent during the early Soviet occupation, she attempted to support the family. From these times a famous family anecdote originated: at the Krakidaly bazaar nightgowns were purchased to be worn as formal dresses for Soviet wives and mistresses. I would later learn that Lviv's citizens had been eagerly telling this and similar anecdotes as a way of getting even for the systematic humiliation and oppression to which they were subjected.

In contrast to the great majority of Galicia's inhabitants, Grandma spoke Russian. Her Russian was the language of sermons at the interwar Pochayiv Lavra—the church had been using a Russian version of Old Church Slavonic for mass and Russian for sermons. It turned out, however, that the language spoken by those who arrived in 1939 differed so greatly that Grandma found it difficult to understand. This was a lesson learned not only by Poles but also by other nationalities from the eastern territories of the Second Polish Republic.

In the beginning of 1940 Grandma and Grandpa received *Soviet* passports, a fact paradoxically noted on a certified copy of their *church* marriage license. They gained Soviet citizenship, with all its consequences. The inhabitants of Lviv of similar status (an employee of the courthouse, a home owner) typically received a "paragraph 11" stamp in their Soviet identification documents, which meant that one would be forbidden from living in large cities and was required to resettle within a distance of no less than a hundred kilometers away from the border of "German-Soviet friendship." Thus, in comparison with others, my grandparents got quite lucky. Nevertheless, Providence was mediated by circumstance—the house was tiny, its location not particularly attractive for newcomers, and Grandpa worked as a simple clerk, not as a judge.

Clearly there were reasons why the date and place of birth on Mom's identity card caused me concern. Although her ID was issued by the Polish People's Republic, it provoked associations with the USSR and stirred up fears of deportation, a perennial condition under Soviet rule. Together with Mom and Grandma, this fear migrated to the Recovered Territories, dictating necessary

Jan Lewkowski was a simple cannoneer during World War I

strategic behaviors. Grandma, afraid that her Pochayiv family might be forced to relocate to those more distant regions of the USSR if they corresponded with her, had no contact with her sisters at all. It is possible, too, that she wanted to forget, to obscure her origins, not only fearing the stigma but also feeling shame and guilt over the atrocities committed by the UPA, the Ukrainian Insurgent Army, between 1943 and 1944.

Grandpa Jan Lewkowski and Grandma Eufrozyna, née Fedyk, bought the house on Mączna (Muchna) Street a few months before Mom was born. A young couple they were not. Grandpa was a widower (his first wife, Franciszka, née Utzig, died childless) and was approaching sixty. In 1938 he married for the second time, a woman from Pochayiv who was thirty-three years his junior. The ceremony took place in an Orthodox church in Lviv. Their house was

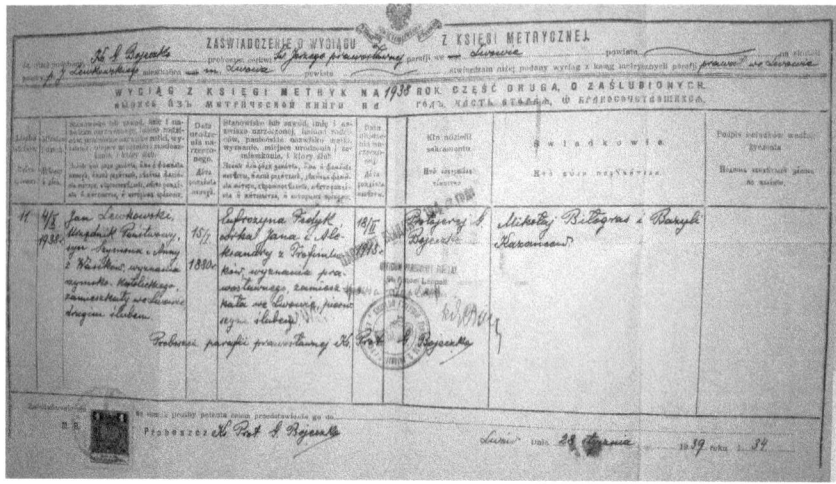

A Soviet stamp on marriage license, 1940. Thus the Lewkowskis became citizens of the USSR

Lewkowski's house on 38 Mączna (Muchna) Street in Lviv, 1939

Wedding photo of Eufrozyna and Jan Lewkowski, 1938

located in a quiet area, near a neighborhood where university faculty lived and a park called Kaiserwald (Shevchenko Park, after the war). The neighborhood was mostly inhabited by Poles, yet there was no shortage of Ukrainians either, though there were relatively few Jews in the district of Łyczaków (Lychakiv).

Mączna Street, lined with low residential buildings on the Łyczaków side, acquired a suburban character farther on. This did not change when a gravestone factory supplying the Łyczakowski (Lychakiv) Cemetery opened there in 1939. During the war, backyard gardens were the residents' salvation; they provided a little food, which, although clearly insufficient for survival, was still better than what was available to folks who lived in the inner city (which was nothing). City people, that is, had to rely exclusively on stores and illegal barter. The nearby train tracks leading to Pidzamche proved to be another lifeline: thanks to the railwaymen one could obtain coal dust, which was in scarce supply.

My grandparents' closest neighbors were Ukrainians, people far from well off, and exceptionally helpful. They were the first ones to lend a hand to Grandma, who in October 1939, after her husband was imprisoned, was left alone with a newborn. Mutual favors were, to be sure, an unwritten rule and in times of war made it easier to survive—so long as one's neighbors had not been paralyzed by fear, swept up by an ideology, or driven to revenge for harm experienced or imagined, or by a common desire to get richer.

In the summer of 1941, after the German-Soviet War broke out, Sara Lille, a Jewish woman past seventy, moved into my grandparents' home. My grandparents gave her one of their two rooms (the house was still unfinished). When Mrs. Lille's son, Jan, wanted to settle the terms of payment, Grandpa did not know what amount to quote as rent, because in the last two years he had been housebound and bedridden. However, he knew exactly what position Jews were in, though he maintained that whatever the Germans were doing had no bearing on the price he would charge for having a boarder. Shortly thereafter, Jan Lille successfully made it through to Lublin, where nobody knew him and where, as Michał Korolewicz, he could carry on as an office worker for a German insurance company, using identification documents he had secured in Lviv. In the meantime, his wife Fryderyka Lille (née Tennenbaum), the first woman microbiologist in Lviv, moved in with "Granny." That is what Sara Lille was called, and despite "visits" from German officers as well as the Ukrainian Auxiliary Police, her cover never came into question. A family legend attributes this luck partly to Grandpa's impeccable German (he had been an Austro-Hungarian gunner), and partly to "Granny." An artillery unit was stationed near Kaiserwald and when Germans would come in looking for accommodations for the unit's officers, they would call Mrs. Lille "Großmutter" and kiss her hand.

Despite such courteous behavior Mom was terrified of Germans and the police knocking on the door. Judging from Fryderyka Lille's memoir, my grandma was equally afraid. Mom had other fearful memories—especially the screams sounding from the next room. Fryderyka's nephew, Marian Landberg, stayed there while sick with typhoid fever. Mom was aware that a little girl was living there as well, although my grandparents continued to deny it. Indeed, Fryderyka (later "Irena") Lille's niece, Hania Gnoińska, lived there in hiding, which Mom eventually confirmed many years later when the two finally met as young women. Dr. Helena Krukowska, who worked at Professor Groër's clinic and was the widow of Professor Włodzimierz Krukowski, murdered with other Lviv professors on Wuleckie (Vuletski) Hills on July 4, provided medical help. Thanks to her care and the fact that sanitary recommendations were painstakingly followed, of the six people occupying two rooms no one else became ill. And the neighbors—despite knowing who lived next door and seeing a few extra persons, including children, come through the house on Mączna Street in 1942—maintained a discreet silence.

Grandpa died on Christmas Day, 1942. He was buried at the Łyczaków (Lychakiv) Cemetery, next to his first wife, Franciszka Utzig. "Granny" remained at the house on Mączna Street. For three more months she watched

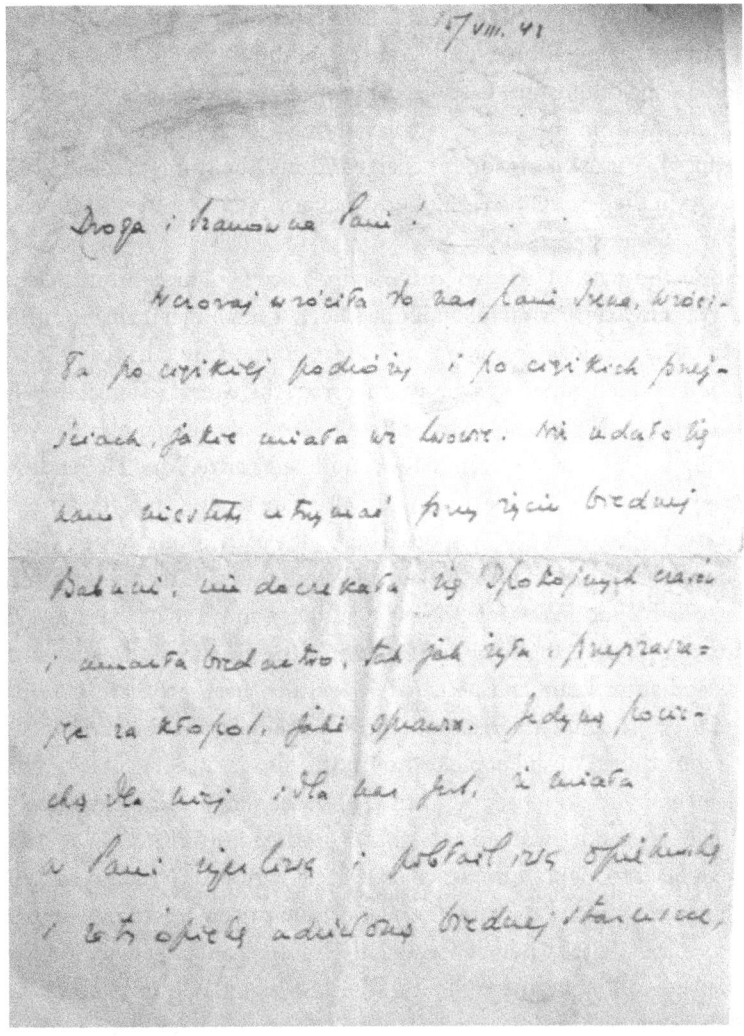

Letter from Jan Lille to Eufrozyna Lewkowska, Lublin, July 15, 1943

the three-year-old girl whose mom, in order to support the three of them, went to work at a preschool. Contact with Lublin, where Fryderyka Lille also found shelter as Irena Szyszkowicz (after the war, Irena Lille), was sporadic. There was not enough money to feed everyone. Only once, in the fall of 1943, a few months after "Granny" passed away, the Lilles sent a small amount. "Granny" was buried at Łyczaków as well, next to Grandpa, under the name of Barbara Mikoś. She received a Catholic burial. Her grave no longer exists. In the 1970s, a Soviet civil servant Iekaterina Ilovaiska was buried in the same plot.

Miraculously, two letters from Lublin have been preserved; in them the Lilles express their gratitude for the care their mother received and suggest that Grandma sell clothing they left with her to recoup her expenses, at least in part. In documents from the trial of Iaroslava Muzyka, her help with selling those belongings became the reason for charges against the painter (this trial will be addressed in the last chapter). Nobody had any intention to call witnesses or clarify the circumstances.

Soon the wife of another of Grandpa's acquaintances from before the Great War moved in. Mr. Hollender had been a small merchant from Bóbrka (Bibrka). His son Józef became a policeman in the Lviv Ghetto, which in all likelihood enabled him to save his mother from the Great Action at the Ghetto in August 1942. My grandparents' home became her hiding place as well. In the spring of 1943, when Grandpa was no longer alive, Mrs. Hollender once again appeared on Mączna Street, with false papers, as Katarzyna Gruszecka. A policeman who lived nearby spotted her in the garden and warned Grandma that she might be turned in by blackmailers or others. At that point Józef Hollender took his mother away. Both she and her son survived. At the very last minute, right before the final destruction of the Ghetto—and after his wife Blanka and sister Klara had perished—Józef fled East, procured false papers and made it through to the region of the Reichskomissariat Ukraine. It is likely that he joined the Polish People's Army at the first chance he got. He returned to Poland as an officer in Berling's army. After the war, under the name of Piotr Smolnicki, Hollender worked as a military prosecutor in Cracow. In 1951 he was sentenced to eight years for collaborating with the Germans. In 1956, in the climate of the thaw and after his release from prison, he attempted to prove his innocence. That is when he located my grandma and asked her to testify in his defense—outlining the content of her testimony. I do not know whether Smolnicki's suggestions did not match the truth or whether there was perhaps another reason (a change in the political situation or his emigration). Suffice it to say that they did not stay in touch.

In 1943, the year so critical to the outcome of World War II, an Austrian officer was moved into the second room on Mączna Street. It is easy to picture how afraid Grandma and Mom must have been of this forcibly assigned tenant. At one time the officer handed his picture to Grandma and asked her (or urged her, really) to carry it in her wallet. It was a time of mass roundups and deportations to labor camps in the Reich. What would have happened to her young child if Grandma had been deported? Grandma, a young, good-looking widow, misunderstood the officer's request and was incensed. Yet he calmly explained to her what she should do in case she was stopped on the street. Soon the officer was sent to the Eastern Front, and she never heard from him again. Our family archive contains his photo album, but his name is unknown.

Starting at the turn of 1941 and 1942, and all the way until the fall of 1942—after the Germans closed the Lviv Ghetto and to enter it meant putting your life at risk—my Grandma, together with Iaroslava Muzyka, delivered food to acquaintances who had been forcibly moved behind the Ghetto walls. Among the people they supplied were the Hollenders, as well as relatives of Fryderyka Lille (her sister Helena, and later the husband of her older sister, Henryka). It is impossible to say who else, as Iaroslava Muzyka left no written recollections. She had so many friends behind the Ghetto walls.

Iaroslava Muzyka, 1940s

The conditions inside the Ghetto deteriorated from month to month: the quarters were unimaginably cramped, food rations utterly insufficient for survival. If you were recognized as a Jew outside the Ghetto, you would be killed, and Lviv, although a city of several hundred thousand inhabitants, had a quality back then that marks it to this day: thanks to gossip, that ever-present companion of Galician life, everybody knew everybody and everything there was to know about them. People who had been forced by German authorities to move to the Ghetto, deprived of their possessions, separated from their loved ones, bereft of their dignity, were dying of illnesses, exhaustion, and hopelessness. They were killed in ad hoc executions, provoked by the most minor suspicions. The occupiers murdered Lviv's Jews in a systematic manner: at the Janowska Camp, at the Piaski Ravine, and in extermination camps, most of all at the nearby Bełżec (Belzec) extermination camp. To share your food rations with the inhabitants of the Ghetto constituted a serious offense in the eyes of the German authorities, and to sell them was a severe crime, punishable by death. Thus it took courage for my Grandma and Iaroslava Muzyka to make their deliveries.

Beside the most obvious danger of being caught by the police or the SS, both women had other reasons to fear for their lives. The most serious one was typhoid fever, which raged in the Ghetto and in the Janowska Camp. Equally strong was their concern with what would happen to their loved ones, were either woman to be arrested or to die. In the case of Iaroslava Muzyka, there were especially incriminating circumstances. In the winter of 1939, her husband, the physician Maksym Muzyka, a well-known microbiologist and a colleague of Fryderyka Lille, was nominated for the position of Deputy Assistant Director of the Medical Institute, which had been created in place of the Medical Department of Lviv University. In late June he was called to duty as an epidemiologist. Although his evacuation was mandatory, the German authorities still regarded Iaroslava Muzyka as a Bolshevik's wife who deserved the same fate as Jews.

How could women like my grandma or Iaroslava Muzyka, who themselves had almost no means of support, who found themselves at the bottom rung of the social ladder, come up with extra provisions during an occupation when food was rationed and very hard to purchase? Risky operations were my grandma's specialty. She would exchange "procured" shoe leather for food with peasants who traded illegally just as she did. Some transactions must have been more difficult: Grandma traded one of the most valuable mementos of her deceased husband, his wedding ring, for a cube of butter. Conversely, Iaroslava Muzyka was in charge of making connections: she would identify the addresses of those who needed the women's help.

Grandma was twenty years younger than her companion. She was brunette with distinct features, who made up what she lacked in life experience with her self-assured manner. This was for show—but Grandma's presence cheered up the painter, a worldly petite blonde who used to frequent the galleries of Lviv and Paris. In contrast to my Grandma's demeanor, the painter's fear must have been quite discernible, because the police would stop her in spite of her "right looks" on the suspicion of being Jewish. At first glance it was Grandma who looked much more suspicious, but whenever Iaroslava Muzyka would be stopped, Grandma would immediately provide a line of defense: "What is wrong with you ... ? Don't you know the most famous Ukrainian painter?"

In July 1944 the German occupiers were driven out of Lviv. However, fear remained: it was, after all, an ever-present companion of Soviet rule. In addition, the Ukrainian and Polish resistance fighters continued their war against each other. Someone like my grandma—who was born in Pochayiv, the heart of Ukrainian Orthodoxy, but chose Polish identity on account of her husband—was seen by ideologues and practitioners of nationalism as a recreant. Such persons were to be mercilessly executed, together with his or her family, which in this case would include her five-year-old daughter. An old acquaintance, a Ukrainian, saved Grandma and Mom from impending danger. That year, 1944, bore witness to a "depolonizing action," as these events are referenced in the documents of the Ukrainian Insurgent Army. Euphemisms aside, this ethnic cleansing spread from Volhynia into Galicia. 1944 was a year lived under the specter of wartime fear, additionally heightened by the threat from one's own people.

Directly after the war Iaroslava Muzyka painted a portrait of my mom, which critics labeled as "a French girl." Their interpretation was not entirely in error; it was in Paris that the artist developed her polished style, so it is not surprising that critics looked to that milieu in order to identify the roots of her work and artistic associations. Well, though the critics spotted French *charme* in the painting, my mom did not like the painting at all. Half a century later she wrote in her reminiscences: "In my portrait Mrs. Slavtsia painted a stain instead of the beautiful white collar, handmade by my mom, that I was wearing." The artist tried everything to console her promising to correct the collar as soon as the painting returned from an exhibition and to give the portrait to Mom as a present. The painting did return, but could be reunited neither with the model nor the artist, as by then they were separated by thousands of miles.

Halina Lewkowska in Iaroslava Muzyka's apartment at Czarniecki Street, 1945

A photo of this portrait has been with me for years, since my Lviv friend Petro Humeniuk, with the help of Vita Susak and Oksana Maksymenko-Kokh, succeeded in locating the original among the archived collection of Iaroslava Muzyka's work at the Lviv National Art Gallery, and took a photo of it. The girl, with jet-black braids, in a slate-colored dress with a white collar, sits with her head slightly bent, clutching a yellowish rag dog and staring at something unknown. A portrait like many others. But for me it has a symbolic dimension: soon thereafter, the girl and her mom truly departed into the unknown.

Initially they stayed with Grandpa's niece and foster child in the village of Ropa in the Sub-Carpathian region. Later however, so as not to be a burden anymore, they moved on, across all of Poland, to Western Pomerania. On their route was Wrocław. There, Grandma made contact with Irena Szyszkowicz (Fryda Lille), who was working with Professor Franciszek Groër. Irena Szyszkowicz wrote an affidavit for Grandma, in which she confirmed Grandma's (quite modest) professional experience as a preschool assistant. But life in Wrocław was not meant to be. When Grandma tried to enter the home allocated to her by the local administration, she was greeted at the threshold by an armed man.

In search of help in securing a job and a place to stay, Grandma then went to Cracow, asking Michał Korolewicz (Jan Lille) for his support. At that time, Korolewicz worked as a director at the Department of Petroleum Industries (he was selected for the post already in the summer of 1944 in Lublin by the Minister of Industry and Commerce, Hilary Minc). Korolewicz declined.

For the next thirty years, until her retirement, Grandma, who in the meantime earned nursing credentials, lived in rooms for hospital personnel. A minor detail reflects how she lived: in her eventual one-room apartment, secured thirty years after she left behind her home in Lviv, she kept metal UNRRA cans.[1] When at the end of the 1970s the Polish government turned to rationing food, Grandma stored sugar in those cans, which previously had been as valuable as gold. In the late 1970s, Irena Lille—who by then had established herself professionally in France (and who in the preceding twenty years had remained in contact with Mom and Grandma)—began sending money to Grandma. Jan Lille (Michał Korolewicz) had passed away. Another few years went by and following a successful antiquarian transaction, Irena Lille—who always favored my mom and was eager to provide support for her—gave her a gold coin, with which

---

1 UNRRA (United Nations Relief and Rehabilitation Administration) was a US food assistance program from the late 1940s. The inhabitants of the Regained Territories viewed its rations as salvation.

Medal recognizing Eufrozyna Lewkowska as "Righteous Among the Nations," awarded on March 16, 2004, twelve years after her death

an apartment in Warsaw was purchased. This occurred forty years after the death of Sara Lille, and forty-two years after chance had entwined the fate of the Lilles and the Lewkowskis, two families from Lviv who, under different circumstances, perhaps never would have met, as they belonged to different layers of the middle class—the lower and the upper. After the war they found themselves far from Lviv. Each felt nostalgic in their own way, wanting to forget their fear, the war, and the postwar years in particular.

In May 1946 Grandma and Mom left Lviv. Their journey to Przemyśl, although barely ninety kilometers away, took no less than two weeks. The heaviest piece of baggage they took along with them was fear. Courage carried no weight.

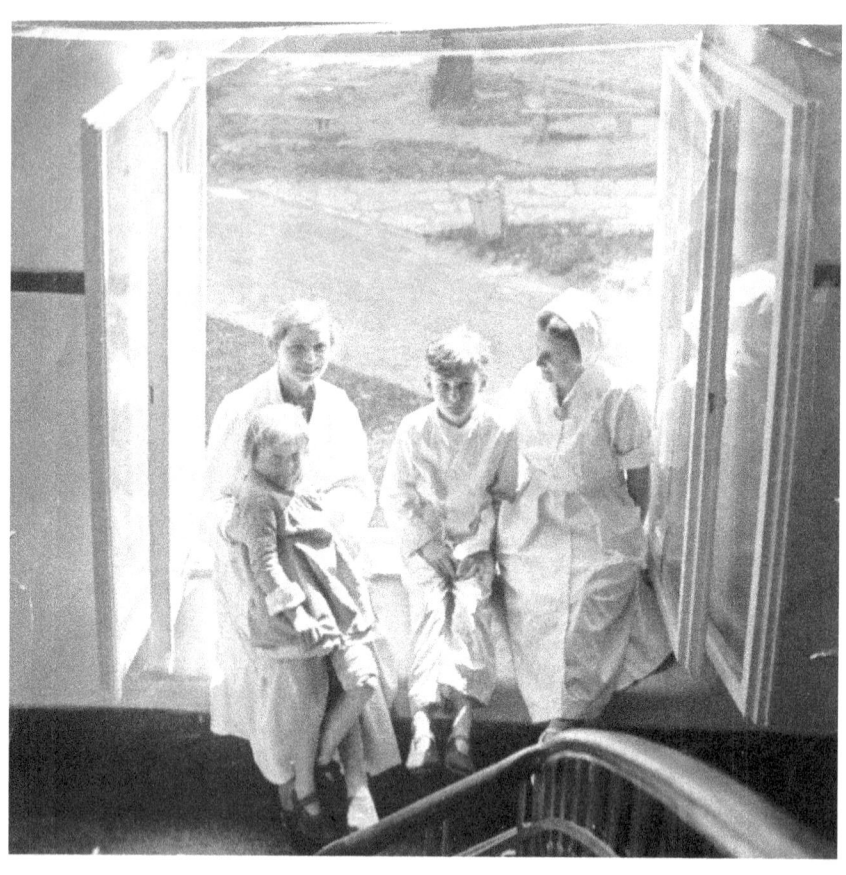
Fryderyka Lille at the pediatric clinic at Głowiński Street

CHAPTER 2
Haven at the Clinic

Fryderyka Lille crossed the Rumanian-Polish border on September 18, 1939, after traveling from France for eleven days. The onset of the war found her in Paris, where professor Robert Debré invited Lille to continue her research on antibodies at Herold Hospital Pediatric Clinic. In early September a letter came from Lviv. Fryda's husband, Jan Lille, described the general mobilization and the bombardment of Lviv; he talked about feeling despondent and powerless. Fryda decided to return to Lviv. To remain in France would be desertion, sheltering in safety, while her loved ones were at the mercy of events. In her

Family Lille in the 1920s

memoir, she explained the decision by saying "I could not live with such guilt on my conscience."[1]

Ludwik Lille, Fryda's brother-in-law, was an avant-garde artist who had moved from Lviv to Paris two years before the war. He bid farewell to his sister-in-law in his atelier on Boulevard Saint-Jacques in the first week of the war. Ludwik was certain they would never see each other again. But both survived the war: he in Paris, Fryda and Jan in the occupied cities of Lviv and Lublin. After the war, the Iron Curtain descended, further impeding their reunion. Fryda and Ludwik did meet again in Paris, where Lille attended a hematology convention in 1952. It was Ludwik's death that caused the Lilles to go to Paris in the mid-1950s; they would remain there for the rest of their lives.

When Jan and Fryda traveled to Paris for Ludwik's funeral in April 1957, they used the names they had assumed during the German occupation and had retained ever since. They did so at the advice of minister Hilary Minc, a powerful figure in the Polish political scene of the late 1940s and the early 1950s. Jan bore the name Michał Korolewicz, and Fryda went by Irena Szyszkowicz. The Lilles-Korolewiczs decided to stay in

Fryderyka Lille

Ludwik Lille. Fryderyka Lille met with her brother-in-law directly before the outbreak of World War II

---

1   Irena Lille, *Moje życie* [*My Life*] (unpublished manuscript, January 1981), 28; typescript in Ola Hnatiuk's collection.

A self-portrait by Ludwik Lille from his formalist period, 1920

France, though Fryda (Irena) briefly returned to Warsaw in May 1957 out of duty towards her nephew/adopted son and to attend to both unfinished hematological research and the couple's assets (their financial resources were quite substantial for the circumstances of Poland at the time). My mom and Hanna Gnoińska, Irena's niece, got to know each other while helping Irena box up her belongings and navigate the procedures of the customs office. Irena Szyszkowicz-Lille was able to leave within just a few weeks, this time under the pretense of attending a hematology convention in Copenhagen. Perhaps she was permitted to travel despite her husband not returning from Paris because the couple had different last names; the authorities didn't catch on and released Irena's passport to her. But just as likely it was the political climate that favored such departures: after the thaw of 1956 the authorities habitually pushed all responsibility for Stalinist crimes onto government functionaries of Jewish background. By doing so Poland was ridding itself of the small fraction of Jews who had survived the Shoah.

VIVE LA FRANCE!

In August of 1939 the specter of war terrified the French public. Newspapers and private conversations alike were dominated by the indignant query: "Mourir pour une ville polonaise?!"[2] People questioned whether the fate of one city (the German ultimatum regarding Danzig/Gdańsk) was worth risking a new war. The media expressed the popular sentiment that France had no reasons at all to

---

2 "Why should we be dying for a Polish city?!"

fulfill the obligations of its alliance treaty. The Polish stance vis-à-vis German demands was "irresponsible." In keeping with this isolationist perspective, the French public generally gave no thought to their country's complicity in the Munich Agreement and its effects.

The Polish population was not aware of the mood among the French public. Ironically, the country pinned its greatest hopes on France. The eventual news that France and England had declared war against Germany triggered widespread enthusiasm. In Lviv, the news prompted a crowd of locals to gather at the French consul's doorsteps singing *La Marseillaise*. The very next day a demonstration of gratitude took place in front of the British and French consulates. Yet the joy was premature: no actual war maneuvers engaging the German forces occurred. The few units on the Siegfried line between France and Germany took no military action. The pretend-game ensued, "phony war"— the *drôle de guerre* or *Sitzkrieg*. Consequently, the entire German military could concentrate on its attack on Poland.

Meanwhile, in the East, a curious alliance emerged. Previously mortal enemies, the Third Reich and the Soviet Union signed the Molotov-Ribbentrop Pact. This treaty of nonaggression and its stipulations turned out to be more binding than the Polish-French or Polish-British alliances. In contrast to the Allies, who declared war but did not act on it, the new ally of the Third Reich sprang into action without declaring war. On the seventeenth day of World War II, the Red Army marched across the USSR's border with the Second Polish Republic. On the first day of this never-declared war, Soviet units reached Ternopil, a town thirty-five kilometers from the border river of Zbruch. They entered Lviv a few days later.

TRAVEL COMPANIONS

Prior to her departure from France in early September 1939, Fryderyka Lille obtained the necessary travel documents from Poland's embassy in Paris (at that time an exit visa was required). In the space for "Religious Creed," she wrote "Roman-Catholic;" the embassy clerk stated that without that declaration travelers could not safely cross borders of countries that were allied with the Third Reich. Her brother-in-law, a well-known avant-garde painter who had, until 1936, worked as a curator at the Jewish Museum in Lviv, did not accompany her to the train station so as not to reveal Fryda's identity and subject her to any danger from other passengers on the international train (who might denounce her as Jewish). In issuing a travel permit despite the war, the embassy made an exception on account of Lille's profession (microbiologist). At the time it was assumed that, beside chemical weapons, which had claimed a horrific toll in the previous war, the coming war would use biological weapons on a large scale.

Coincidentally, Fryda Lille traveled home through Italy, Yugoslavia, and Romania in the company of two engineers who specialized in air defense, and a fellow Lvivian Tadeusz Tomaszewski,[3] a psychologist at the Jan Kazimierz University's Institute of Psychology led by Mieczysław Kreutz. Tomaszewski had been studying abroad, following his 1937 PhD degree from Jan Kazimierz University. He was a friend of Jan Kott, an essay writer and theater scholar living in Paris on a government fellowship. (Subsequent chapters draw on Tomaszewski's journals and Kott's memoirs). After returning to Lviv, Tomaszewki obtained a position as an associate professor of psychology at Ivan Franko National University of Lviv (formerly Jan Kazimierz University—its name was changed in 1940). Later, at the turn of 1944 and 1945, he became a representative of the Polish Committee of National Liberation (PKWN), in charge of repatriation from the Soviet Union.

On September 18, after traveling for eleven days, the foursome reached Sniatyn, a town on the Romanian-Polish border. There they ran into the Skamander poet Kazimierz Wierzyński, and the legendary Lvivian Marian Hemar with his first wife, the actress Maria Modzelewska.[4] Hemar, having spotted Fryda Lille at the border crossing, got out of the car to tell her how grave the situation in the country was, and tried to impress upon her that it would be impossible to get through to Lviv. He suggested she join them and return to Romania. She declined.

That encounter between Fryda Lille and Hemar on September 18, 1939 is barely a flicker in the conflagration of events. Yet one would be remiss to disregard the gravity of the personal choices people made in the context of a catastrophic war. For some, that day meant a flight ridden with obstacles; for others, a no less difficult return; for many, death; for a few, liberation. Alongside civil servants and officers, many representatives of the creative community were

---

3   Tadeusz Tomaszewski's notes from 1940–44 appeared in 1996 in Warsaw as *Lwów 1940–1944. Pejzaż psychologiczny* [*Lviv: A Psychological Landscape*], ed. Zofia Ratajczak (Warsaw: Wydawnictwo Instytutu Psychologii Polskiej Akademii Nauk, 1996). The manuscript (three notebooks) belongs to the collection of the Archiwum Wschodnie Ośrodka Karta (OK AW II/3459). Zofia Ratajczak, who wrote the foreword and served as the academic editor, references an earlier version consisting of loose-leaf journal notes from November 13 through December in her editorial note "Od redakcji" (Tomaszewski, *Lwów. Pejzaż psychologiczny*, 212). This additional source, potentially highly valuable, was not included in the publication nor is it available through the archives.
4   Lille, *Moje życie*, 28. Irena Lille mistakenly refers to Hemar's wife as Modrzejewska, instead of Modzelewska.

making their way towards the Romanian border. Witkacy, the famous writer and artist, was fleeing eastwards from the Germans when he found out about the Soviet advance. As a result, on September 18 Witkacy committed suicide. The greatest of formalists, Witkacy interpreted the Red Army's invasion as a civilizational catastrophe. He had his reasons, having survived the Bolshevik Revolution in Russia. A desire to join their families motivated those who had been abroad and opted to return to Poland. Refugees trying to reach Romania or Hungary had lost all hope for Poland's successful defense against Hitler's Germany, and were counting on opportunities to continue their fight to protect Poland's independence aided by its Western Allies, France and England.

The mass of refugees heading for the border observed with horror and disbelief how Fryda's group went the opposite direction: they voluntarily proceeded to the very hell the onlookers were escaping. Indeed, very soon it became obvious how close the danger was: a German bomb hit the tracks right in front of Fryda's train. The impact ejected passengers into the nearby field. Fryda and her companions did not suffer much harm beyond bruising and shock. The stranded passengers fled to safety in a small town nearby Stanislau (now, Ukrainian Ivano-Frankivsk); it would be impossible to restore train traffic.

Fryda Lille's engineer companions resolved to wait for an opportunity to catch a train and continue their journey. Presumably they realized it no longer made sense to try and reach the military unit where they needed to report. Surely Poland's antiaircraft defense to which they had been assigned had ceased to exist if Germans were able to bomb the only railway suitable for a retreat to allied Romania. Devastated by such instantaneous defeat, both engineers expressed their frustration in an all too common manner: Jews were to blame for the calamity. Cursing Hemar and Wierzyński for abandoning Poland in her misfortune, they promised that Poland would have no place for the Jews after the war. Did they know that the Polish government had just retreated from the country? That the authorities were making arrangements for the safety of Polish creative minds, no matter their ethnic background? (By way of example, Julian Tuwim and his wife were transported straight from the border to Bucharest and placed in the care of the Polish embassy.)[5] That all those cars passing them in Sniatyn, on their way to Romania, belonged to diplomatic missions? Representatives of the French consulate insisted that the group flee with them immediately. Neither man displayed even minimal empathy for the position in which Jews found themselves in the Third Reich, stripped of all rights. The same fate awaited them in occupied Poland. Fryda's accidental

---

5   Shore, *Caviar and Ashes*, 195–6.

companions could not have known how thoroughly the Gestapo was searching for Hemar right then. In that moment of bitterness, the poets Hemar and Wierzyński, and not Poland's government or its military, were the ones who had deserted their country. They bore the blame for the present misery.

Fryda Lille had known Hemar since the early 1920s—they met through her friend Jan Stur, a poet and theorist of expressionism; in 1923, at the end of the young writer's life, she took down a new version of his poem "Człek wędrowny" ["The itinerant fellow"]. After he passed away, Fryda sent Stur's letters and the reworked poem to his friends—Marian Hemar and Stanisław Ignacy Witkiewicz (the given name of the aforementioned Witkacy). (Józef Wittlin, Ludwik Lille, and Aleksander Dan organized a subscription-based posthumous edition of his works through Montsalwat, a small press belonging to Samuel Arem, a cousin on Fryda Tennenbaum's mother's side.) Fryda had close connections with the avant-garde group of formalists, to which her future brother-in-law, Fryderyk Lille, also belonged.

Hemar, probably one of the most popular lyricists of interwar Poland, was the younger brother of Henryk Hescheles, editor in chief of Lviv's Zionist newspaper *Chwila*. A Soviet border patrol captured Hescheles, an eminent Zionist activist, during his attempt to return from Romania, imprisoning him first in Stanislau, then in Lviv. However, they did not charge him with illegal border crossing. The true reason for the arrest was Hescheles's stature in the Zionist movement. The Soviets accused him of betraying the interests of the Jewish minority. This allegation was in reference to a resolution from a Jewish diaspora meeting he published in *Chwila*, which proclaimed loyalty to the Polish state.[6] Hescheles remained in prison for ten months, until his "release" in August 1940.[7] He died in the early days of the Nazi occupation, at the hands of the Germans, much like another recently freed Soviet prisoner from Lviv, the famed internist Roman Rencki. Hescheles was murdered in a pogrom in early July 1941, Rencki—on Wuleckie Hills. His daughter was ten years old at the time. Her memoirs offer the only account of Hescheles's last days.[8]

More fortunate than his brother, Hemar made it out of Romania and farther to the West. In contrast to Hescheles, Hemar did not consider himself

---

6 "Lwowscy Żydzi gotowi są ofiarować swe życie i majątek w obronie Ojczyzny," *Chwila* (August 29, 1939). Member of Parliament Emil Sommerstein who penned the declaration was also arrested. In all probability he was finally able to leave the USSR in July of 1944.
7 Delo po obvineniiu Geshelesa Genryka Ben'iaminovicha, nachato 8 oktiabria 1939—okoncheno 15 dekabria 1939 g., HDA SBU, Delo 941 P.
8 See Janina Hescheles, *Oczyma dwunastoletniej dziewczynki* (Cracow: Wojewódzka Żydowska Komisja Historyczna, 1946).

Henryk Hescheles was arrested as he attempted to return to Lviv in the fall of 1939

a Polish Jew, but rather a Pole; he was baptized in 1935. Active in Warsaw's bohème, he wrote for the most popular prewar cabaret Qui Pro Quo, excelling at political satire along with Julian Tuwim and Antoni Słonimski. Some of his songs became longtime staples in Polish cabaret repertoire, for instance "Ten wąsik" ["That mustache"] as interpreted by Marian Opania. Hemar penned the lyrics to the melody of "Titina," a widely popular song from the first sound movie by Charlie Chaplin, *Modern Times* (1936). The last stanza of Hemar's song, in the distinctive parody by Ludwik Sempoliński, created unmistakable associations with the *Führer*, resulting in protests by the German embassy. As a side note, as the Hemar-Sempoliński parody took Warsaw by storm in 1939 via Mira Zimińska's revue performance "Orzeł czy rzeszka?" ("heads or tails," but also a pun on the eagle—*orzeł*—the symbol of Poland, and *rzeszka* as a diminutive form for the *Reich*), Chaplin was working on the film *The Great Dictator*, a merciless parody of Hitler. After overcoming a number of obstacles, his film reached screens in 1940.

As German agents were searching for Hemar, he got to Romania. Eventually Hemar made it to the Middle East where he served in the Polish Independent Carpathian Brigade for a year. Later he settled in London. His work on the radio show *Wesoła Lwowska Fala* [*Lviv's Merry Wave*], broadcast from London after the war, cemented Hemar's status as the quintessentially Lvivian writer.

On September 19, 1939 the two engineers and reserve officers gave up on further travels, while Fryda Lille and Tadeusz Tomaszewski resolved to continue on foot. The route they chose led through Ternopil, which was controlled by the Red Army. Two days later they reached Lviv by train. The same train was transporting Soviet soldiers.

After returning from Paris to occupied Lviv, Tadeusz Tomaszewski kept a journal

AMONG COLLEAGUES: GROËR'S LVIV PEDIATRIC INSTITUTE

At the end of September, Fryda Lille showed up at 5 Głowiński Street at the pediatric clinic led by Franciszek Groër. Her presence stunned the professor; he believed she was sheltering in the safety of Paris. After all, he had personally recommended her for the research fellowship in France and it did not even cross his mind that she might return. Soon he was able to hire Fryda Lille at the clinic, given how strategically important microbiologists were in the eyes of the Soviets. The new administrator, Hnat Trehub, hired Lille and her friend Giza Dickman to work at the laboratory. Various sources and reminiscences show that Trehub arrived in Lviv in the second half of November. He was promoted from assistant chief to chief of the District Health Care Division, instead of Marian Panchyshyn.[9] From 1940 Trehub served as director of the Lviv Scientific

Franciszek Groër was not only an excellent pediatrician, but also a photography enthusiast

---

9   Roman Osinchuk, "Orhanizatsia okhorony zdorov'ia u l'vivs'kii oblasti (1939–1941)," *Likars'kii zbirnyk. Medytsyna i biolohiia. Nova seriia* 18 (2010): 197.

Ludwik Fleck, microbiologist and philosopher of science

Research Institute for Healthcare and Maternity, retaining the position until he evacuated in June 1941. In her memoir, Lille only made a brief reference to this episode; either she was hired not in the fall, but later, in early 1940, or Groër made the hiring decision in the fall, with Trehub approving it at a later date.

While at the institute, Lille continued her research on white cell serology. She embarked on the topic before the war, together with her senior colleague and longtime acquaintance from the Social Insurance Fund hospital, now director of the institute's bacteriological and chemical laboratory, Ludwik Fleck. A distinguished microbiologist and philosopher of science, Fleck published his first contribution to the discipline in Basel in the mid-1930s.[10] For decades his ideas only reached narrow circles of scientists. Eventually, after Thomas Kuhn published *The Structure of Scientific Revolutions* in Chicago in 1962, acknowledging in the foreword that Fleck's book was his inspiration, Fleck's work attained more prominence. A contemporary researcher compares Fleck's thought with Popper's.[11] Before the war, Fleck rubbed shoulders with the Lwów School of Mathematics, remaining close on the one hand to the circle of Leon Chwistek and Kazimierz Ajdukiewicz, on the other—of Stefan Banach and Hugo Steinhaus. With the latter Fleck collaborated both before and

---

10 See Ludwik Fleck, *Entstehung und Entwicklung einer wissenschaftlichen Tatsache* (Basel: Benno Schwabe & Co., 1935).
11 Jadwiga Wiertlewska-Bielarz and Ludwik Fleck, *Polska szkoła filozofii medycyny. Przedstawiciele i wybrane teksty źródłowe*, ed. Michał Musielak and Jan Zamojski (Poznań: Wydawnictwo Naukowe Uniwersytetu Medycznego im. K. Marcinkowskiego w Poznaniu, 2010); Robert S. Cohen and Thomas Schnelle, eds., *Cognition and Fact—Materials on Ludwik Fleck* (Dordrecht: D. Reidel Publishing Company, 1986).

after the war. Steinhaus devised a statistical method specifically for Fleck that enabled his microbiologist colleague to track the increase in white blood cells during infections.

Ludwik Fleck was a representative of acculturated Polish Jews. He participated in the defense of Lviv against the Bolsheviks. When in the mid-1930s he was no longer permitted to work at the university because of his ethnic origin, Fleck, as did Fryda Lille, earned a living from running a private lab at 8 Ochronka Street. Following the efforts of Maksym Muzyka, the university rehired Fleck in early 1940 to lead the Faculty of Microbiology. The Soviets appointed Muzyka assistant director of the Medical Institute, which replaced the Medical Faculty of Lviv. Both Fleck and Lille met him while working at the Social Insurance Fund hospital (Fryda Lille cowrote her first scientific publication with Dr. Maksym Muzyka,[12] and her next—with Fleck). Fleck was also simultaneously directing the laboratory in Groër's clinic. In Lublin, immediately after Poland's "liberation" by the Soviet Union, Lille and Fleck carried on with their research, which the war had interrupted. As before 1939, Fleck would map out the empirical results in tandem with Hugo Steinhaus (Fleck did not leave behind journals from the Soviet occupation, but we know of their cooperation from Lille's and Steinhaus's memoirs).[13] Groër helped them pass their research results on to a US scientific journal through a contact in Switzerland.

Ludwik Fleck spent the German occupation in the Lviv ghetto. Fryda Lille did not see him again until after the war. At first, the scientist worked in the ghetto laboratory, and subsequently at the Institute for the Study of Typhus and Virology whose director was Rudolf Robert Weigl. Surprisingly, the institute survived the Soviet occupation almost intact. NKVD documents reveal that it employed almost five hundred people. Informants cautioned the authorities that the facility lacked Soviet management. They warned of potential dangers, should the institute fall prey to "bacteriological sabotage." A memo by the NKVD's Ukrainian Commissar Ivan Serov shows that he tried to convince the authorities to relocate the institute deep in the USSR.[14] This happened after

---

12 Maksym Muzyka and Fryderyka Lille, "Sprawa związku pomiędzy szybkością opadania krwinek a grupami krwi," *Wiadomości Lekarskie* 12 (1932): 3–6.

13 Hugo Steinhaus, *Mathematician for All Seasons: Recollections and Notes*, trans. Abe Shenitzer (Cham: Birkhäuser, 2015), 218.

14 Spetssoobshcheniia i dokladnye zapiski o vskrytykh i likvidirovannykh organami NKVD USSR k/r [kontrrevolutsionnykh] organizatsiiakh pol'skikh natsionalistov, 1940 g., HDA SBU, f. 16, op. 33, spr. 58, k. 144–6.

the NKVD analyzed Leszek Czarnik's testimony; they suspected Czarnik of having contacts within Weigl's institute. It was concluded that Czarnik was plotting biological subversion and the NKVD elevated the matter to exceptionally urgent. Czarnik, a physician and scoutmaster who organized the Polish underground, was charged with preparing an insurrection against the Soviets in the spring of 1940.[15] Nevertheless, for the institute, no extraordinary measures followed; most likely its strategic importance was tied to its location near the border, given the likelihood of a war with the Germans. Additionally, official coverage of Weigl's achievements by the Soviet press may have also allowed his facility to retain its relatively independent status.[16]

During the German occupation, Weigl attempted to rescue Fleck, his former assistant, as he did with many others—his colleague Stefan Banach and Banach's son, the aforementioned psychologist Mieczysław Kreutz and his assistant Tadeusz Tomaszewski, Dr. Bolesław Jałowy, Polish literature scholar Stefania Skwarczyńska, Maria Groër (the daughter of professor Franciszek Groër), and Zbigniew Herbert. Although his Institute for the Study of Typhus and Virology had been honored by many commemorative publications,[17] it was not until 2003 that Weigl was named Righteous Among the Nations. The delay resulted from a controversy surrounding his work with the Germans, which prompted some to accuse him of collaboration (same charges were made against Fleck).

The institute, though under tight German control, produced the typhus vaccine, which then would find its way, illegally of course, into the ghettos of Lviv and Warsaw and save the lives of Polish, and even Ukrainian, underground fighters. Since the vaccine was a strategic issue for the occupiers, they tolerated Poles and Ukrainians at the institute. However, obtaining permission to hire a person of Jewish ethnicity would have bordered on the miraculous. Nazi propaganda disparaged Jews for spreading the typhus epidemic (in addition to all other alleged blames). Zhanna Kovba writes:

---

15 Oskar Stanisław Czarnik, "Leszek Czarnik—jeden z 'Argonautów'. Z dziejów konspiracji na Ziemiach Wschodnich, 1939–1941," *Zeszyty Historyczne* 141 (2002): 177–92. Also see Oskar Stanisław Czarnik, "Wspomnienia" (1991), OK AW 11/1100, k. 1–19.
16 I. Shpekht, "Podvyh uchenoho (pro Waihla ta ioho doslidzhennia)," *Vil'na Ukraïna*, no. 186, August 10, 1940.
17 See, in particular, Zbigniew Stuchły, ed., *Zwyciężyć tyfus. Instytut Rudolfa Weigla we Lwowie. Dokumenty i wspomnienia* (Wrocław: Sudety, 2001).

As the director of the Typhus Institute, Rudolf Weigl saved thousands of lives

> in December [of 1941] posters appeared warning the population against contacts with the Jews, who spread the typhus epidemic. One of these posters especially stuck out in the memory of Lvivians: against a dark background the bearded face of a Jewish man wearing a hat, and from underneath his raised arms huge white lice crawl out. At the top, a caption in Ukrainian or Polish "Beware of typhus!" and at the bottom "Avoid Jews!"[18]

Despite these obstacles, Weigl succeeded in employing not just Ludwick Fleck, but also a married couple by the name of Meisel, whose entire family

---

18 Zhanna Kovba, *Liudianist' u bezodni pekla. Povedinka mistsevoho naselennia Skhidnoï Halychyny v roky "ostatochnoho rozviazannia ievreis'koho pytannia"* (Kyiv: Biblioteka Instytutu Iudaiky, 2000), 93.

lived at the institute. Both Henryk and Paula Meisel were distinguished Jewish bacteriologists. Before the war, Henryk Meisel led the State Institute of Hygiene, during the Soviet occupation—the Institute of Hygiene. Later, in 1943, Fleck and Meisel were deported to Auschwitz and forced to labor at the Waffen-SS laboratory, and from there they were transported to Buchenwald, where they continued their typhus vaccine research. Both survived. Their work in camp laboratories provoked accusations that they had collaborated with the Nazis and was the source of their political troubles after the war. Nevertheless, Fleck served as an expert at the Nuremberg trials.[19]

Immediately after the war, Fryda Lille began working (under the name Irena Szyszkowicz) at the Maria Curie-Skłodowska University in Lublin, as did Ludwik Fleck. Both continued their prewar research; now, however, they worked under the guidance of professor Ludwik Hirszfeld. In 1944 Hirszfeld was given the mission of creating a university in Lublin and subsequently became its vice president. As other Jews who survived the Holocaust by hiding, Hirszfeld greeted the arriving Soviet army with enthusiasm. During the occupation, the Hirszfelds ended up in the Warsaw ghetto. He treated those ill with typhus, using the vaccine that had originated in Weigl's institute. Hirszfeld's wife, the pediatrician Hanna Hirszfeld, née Kasman, treated children. In July of 1942 the couple fled to the "Aryan side" and escaped the Shoah thanks to people who sheltered them in the countryside. In 1945 Ludwik Hirszfeld wrote: "I kept bumping into people I knew who greeted me with the words: 'My goodness, you're still alive? We were all sure you had perished.'"[20]

Despite the ambivalence those words must have triggered, Hirszfeld's testimony, borne in the memoirs he published directly after the war (and which were reprinted multiple times), never condemns the actions of Poles vis-à-vis the Holocaust. On the contrary, in many instances he emphasizes that help for Jews also came from people who had been anti-Semites before the war.

After the war, Ludwik Fleck headed the Institute of Medical Microbiology at the Maria Curie-Skłodowska University in Lublin. Subsequently, he

---

19   Ludwik Fleck, "Pathology of the Holocaust," http://www.ludwik-fleck-kreis.org/upload-files/documents/2801_002803_070404-LF-PathologyoftheHolo(3).pdf; Maria Ciesielska, "Ludwick Fleck—profesor mikrobiologii i filozof (1896–1961)," http://lwow.eu/fleck/fleck.html.
20   Ludwik Hirszfeld, *The Story of One Life* (Rochester: University of Rochester Press, 2010), 349.

After the war Ludwik Hirszfeld first led a medical clinic in Lublin, then in Wrocław

worked at the Institute of Mother and Child in Warsaw, as did Fryda Lille, under the leadership of their common advisor and mentor from their Lviv years, Franciszek Groër. Owing to the support of high-ranking persons, Fleck and Lille traveled to international hematological conventions in the mid-1950s, including one in Rio de Janeiro. There Fleck suffered his first heart attack, and Szyszkowicz-Lille was the only friend who visited him in the hospital. On their way back, they stopped in Paris at Ludwik Lille's home to recover from this stressful trip. Upon returning to Warsaw, they learned that a political reshuffle had taken place at the highest levels of the Polish government. Its ripple effects reached the Lilles; when Minc was relieved of his duties in 1956, Jan Lille felt threatened and weighed the possibility of joining his brother in Paris, but he was denied permission to travel.

Three years after the memorable trip to Rio de Janeiro, Fleck accompanied Fryda Lille to the train station (in the spring of 1956 she decided to emigrate). A year earlier Fleck had been diagnosed with leukemia—the same disease for which Fryda had promised her dying mother to find a cure back in 1915. Shortly thereafter Fleck emigrated too and died in Israel in 1961. His fame as a philosopher of science only came posthumously.

PHYSICIAN, ENTHUSIAST, PROTECTOR

During the Soviet occupation, professor Franciszek Groër provided protection to colleagues, giving them work at the institute he directed or recommending them to other employers. He also tried to assist with seemingly more minor aggravations, such as protecting colleagues from forcibly assigned tenants.[21] Though the Soviets required many apartment dwellers to accept tenants from the East, the status of a research scientist carried the right to additional square footage—in particular to a private study. Those and similar housing decisions were made at the highest levels. Only Nikita Khrushchev's signature, who at the time served as the First Secretary of the Communist Party of Ukraine and the Commissar of Western Ukraine, could protect residents from uninvited guests.

Groër's pediatric clinic in Lviv, where Fryderyka Lille, Giza Dickman, Ludwik Fleck and many others found employment in the fall of 1939, became their haven. Beyond providing an opportunity to work, it also protected them against abuses by the Soviet administration. For years the hospital had enjoyed a stellar reputation. Its director, professor Franciszek Groër, was a prominent pediatrician and a man of the world. Of Austrian descent and a Pole by choice, Groër was born in Bielsko-Biała. He went on to study in Vienna and took his first professional steps there. Always seeking to broaden his expertise, he often visited medical clinics in the Russian Empire—in Kyiv and St. Petersburg. Groër married Cecylia Cuming, a British citizen, and if his testimony is to be believed, Cecylia's nationality saved her husband's life at the start of the German occupation. Franciszek Groër came from a long line of medical professionals (his grandfather, also Franciszek Groër, was one of the first surgeons and chief of surgery at the Hospital of the Holy Spirit in Warsaw). The younger Groër obtained a high school diploma (*matura*) in St. Petersburg and in 1906 went on to study medicine in Wrocław. In 1912 he had his diploma recognized in St. Petersburg, and in 1915 began lecturing in Vienna at the University Children's Clinic, under professor Clemens von Pirquet. Soon afterward, in 1918, Groër took a position at the Jan Kazimierz University in Lviv (now Ivan Franko National University of Lviv). As a music aficionado, the pediatrician chaired the

---

21   Lille, *Moje życie*, 31.

A German questionnaire filled out by Franciszek Groër, 1941

Society of Friends of Music and Opera in Lviv between 1932–33. During the occupation he continued at the pediatric clinic in Lviv. After the war, in 1948, the naturalized Lvivian first worked at the Silesian Medical Academy, then, in 1951, moved to become the head of the Tuberculosis Institute at Otwock, and finally directed the Institute of Mother and Child in Warsaw. After his death Hugo Steinhaus wrote to the widowed Cecylia:

> If not for him, I never would have learned about the connection between medicine and mathematics, if not for him, the advancement of Polish medicine would have proceeded on an entirely different path and been delayed in comparison with the advancements in medical science elsewhere.[22]

The Lvivians knew and valued Groër not only as a physician, but also as a sponsor of the city's cultural life and a member of its elite. An enthusiast of both photography and music, Groër even held a position as the administrative director of the Lviv Opera for two years. He had his weaknesses; Polish authors mention that he would introduce himself as *von* Groër, aspiring to aristocracy.[23] Rank and file clinical personnel viewed this as pretentious. The clinic's head accountant Ivan Prokopiv shared detailed impressions from the occupation years; in the spring of 1941 he accompanied Franciszek Groër on a business trip to Kyiv, where they reported on the activities of Lviv's Okhmadyt (Institute of Mother and Child) for the People's Health Commissariat: "I don't know what lies Groër told when it came to his academic research, but he was a sly fox, a graduate of the Medical Institute in Petersburg. They saw him as a force to be reckoned with at the People's Health Commissariat."[24]

The two men stayed at the best hotel in Kyiv, Intourist on Karl Marx Street (today Horodetsky Street, before the revolution—Mykolaivska Street). Prokopiv accompanied the director at the ministry and everywhere else, learning that he had no choice but to fall in line. "We dined together at the hotel restaurant. Groër ordered expensive dishes, caviar etc." The accountant quoted Groër: "'I used to come here during the time of tsarist Russia. This was the best and the most expensive hotel Imperial. Here aristocracy, the upper class, nobility, industrialists and merchants came together. Land owners, industrialists, and merchants signed contracts here.'"[25]

---

22 Helena Krukowska, ed., *Franciszek Groer. Życie i działalność. Zbiór wspomnień* (Warsaw: PZWL, 1973), 39.
23 See Tomaszewski, *Lwów. Pejzaż psychologiczny*, 96; see also Bogusław Malinowski's essay in Krukowska, *Franciszek Groer*, 32.
24 Ivan Prokopiv, "Spohady. V drukarni Iu. Ias'kova u Lvovi. Druha svitova viina, hitlerivs'ka okupatsiia (1934–1944)," LNB, Prok. 475, p. 7, k. 59.
25 Ibid.

In 1929 Groër became the head of the Faculty of Medicine Children's Clinic at 5 Głowiński. When in the mid-1930s anti-Semitic behavior became rampant among university students in Lviv, he had the courage to oppose it. The professor supported research assistants of Jewish ethnicity, giving them work, and even personally protecting them from attacks. In his reminiscences about the pediatrician, Stanisław Kubicz asserts that no segregation ever occurred in the lecture hall of the children's clinic.[26] Yet the circumstances were difficult. Fryda Lille recalls All Souls' Day (November 2) in 1935, when right-wing attackers armed with clubs (*pałkarze*) beat up a number of Jewish students at the Lviv Polytechnic. Despite it being a holiday, Groër came in his car to pick up Lille and Dr. Fryderyk Redlich and drove them home. The next day, when, despite Groër's warnings, Lille arrived at the clinic's lab to finish an experiment she had begun, a few students present at the professor's lecture demanded that Jewish assistants leave the lecture hall. They meant Drs. Lille, Helena Ehrlich, and Zygfryd Bretschneider.

> We got up to leave the lecture hall, but the prof[essor] stood up to it, he slammed his fist on the desk and shouted: "This is a clinic, here are sick children, this is no place for brawls, whoever does not like my assistants is free to leave!" The room fell silent, and some students from the back rows left. After finishing the lecture, our prof[essor] led us out through the back door of the laboratory, fearing we might be attacked as we exited.[27]

In 1996 Eleasar J. Feuerman published his recollection of the events that took place at the Medical Faculty of Lviv's Jan Kazimierz University and at the Lviv Polytechnic. His reports show that both the college administration and the city authorities refused to take measures against the anti-Semitic violence. The voivode Alfred Biłyk rebuked a delegation of parents of Jewish university students, saying: "'What do you actually want us to do, arrest our own children?'"[28]

---

26 Stanisław Kubicz, "Franciszek Groër—kierownik Kliniki Dziecięcej UJK we Lwowie oraz Dyrektor Instytutu Matki i Dziecka w Warszawie," in Krukowska, ed., *Franciszek Groer*, 50.
27 Lille, *Moje życie*, 19–20. See also Jolanta Żyndul, "Zajścia antyżydowskie w Polsce w latach 1935–37: geografia i formy," *Biuletyn Żydowskiego Instytutu Historycznego* 3 (1991): 159.
28 Eleasar J. Feuerman and Laurence Weinbaum, "My lost professors of medicine in Lvov: Remembering the early victims of the Nazis," *Dermatopathology: Practical & Conceptual* 7, no. 4 (2001), https://www.derm101.com/dpc-archive/october-december-2001-volume-7-no-4/dpc0704a07-my-lost-professors-of-medicine-in-lvov-remembrance-of-early-victims-of-the-nazis/.

Soon it became impossible to stand up to the rampant anti-Semitism and Groër did what he could to help his Jewish assistants obtain work outside of the clinic. At the start of the war he refused to leave for Romania, although he had a car, gasoline, a passport with a visa, and even an order to evacuate.[29] Initially he retained his high-level position as a physician and the clinic's director. Tomasz Cieszyński, who had just finished his first year of medical school, alleges that at the first meeting organized by the new authorities in Rudolf Weigl's institute Groër declared: "'The red thread of communism has run through my entire life.'"[30] While Cieszyński's recollection is not beyond doubt, one thing is: Groër, faithful to the Hippocratic oath, treated all children, even those of NKVD functionaries.[31] To repay him, the authorities allowed him what some saw as privileges: "As for the liberal professions, the doctors were most well off at the beginning. Their housing was protected. The Russians went to them for treatment, especially for Soviet children, who were frequently in a life-threatening condition. The incidence of bone tuberculosis was exceptionally high."[32]

Groër and Maksym Muzyka exercised their influence to help many people find employment at the clinic and in pediatric care facilities. During the first few months of the occupation, Tadeusz Boy-Żeleński worked as a pediatrician at the clinic, under his own name. He turned up at Groër's institute by way of his brother-in-law, Jan Grek, who was Groër's friend and neighbor from the apartment building at Romanowicz (now Sakashanskyi) Street. Boy-Żeleński worked under professor Stanisław Progulski, the long-term president of the Lviv chapter of the Polish Medical Association. Prior to the war, Progulski had conducted the first blood transfusion on a child, and Fryderyka Lille had assisted with the procedure and donated the blood. Three days after taking over the city, on July 3, 1941, the Nazis arrested Progulski, Boy-Żeleński, Grek, and many other Lviv physicians and professors.[33]

---

29 Krukowska, ed., *Franciszek Groer*, 16.
30 Tomasz Cieszyński, "O profesorze Jakubie Parnasie na tle Lwowa z lat 1938 do 1945," *Archiwum Historii i Filozofii Medycyny* 61, no. 2 (1997): 133–46.
31 Lille, *Moje życie*, 31.
32 Karolina Lanckorońska, *Michelangelo in Ravensbruck: One Woman's War against the Nazis* (New York: Da Capo, 2008), 15.
33 The body of literature on the topic of the Nazi massacre of Lviv professors Wuleckie Hills is too vast to list here. Among the most important publications are: in Polish, Zygmunt Albert and Karol Fiedor, eds., *Kaźń profesorów lwowskich—lipiec 1941 / studia oraz relacje i dokumenty zebrane i opracowane przez Zygmunta Alberta* (Wrocław: Wydawnictwo Uniwersytetu Wrocławskiego, 1989) and Włodzimierz Bonusiak, *Kto zabił Profesorów Lwowskich?* (Rzeszów: Krajowa Agencja Wydawnicza, 1989). A more recent source (this time in

THE MASSACRE OF LVIV PROFESSORS

In the first two years of German occupation, Nazi terror against the civilian population of Poland, especially against the educated class, turned into an everyday occurrence. Though those reports made their way to Lviv, the city's inhabitants still insisted that nothing could be worse than what they were subjected to under Soviet rule. The massacre of Lviv's professors sent shock waves through the city: as former imperial and royal Habsburg subjects, Lvivians could not fathom that Germans would have committed such atrocities.

Over time various scenarios emerged, identifying the perpetrators and their motivations, though the basic facts seemed clear from the get-go: the German occupiers were intent on murdering the local intelligentsia, whom they assumed to be potential leaders of the resistance movement. Subsequently historians pursued several lines of inquiry, but ultimately their research fell into four basic narratives, which we will label as "nationalist," "Soviet," "Nazi," and "criminal." The first interpretation gained the most traction; it purported that the Lviv-affiliated members of OUN (Organization of Ukrainian Nationalists), who at the start of the occupation and until 1941 were living in Cracow, compiled a list of persons to be detained and provided it to the Nazis. Those detained were later murdered. Soviet writer Vladimir Beliaev, whose literary and journalistic work focused on combatting Ukrainian nationalism, was the first person to propose this thesis.[34] After the government commissioned Beliaev to write those pieces, a political court in the German Democratic Republic repeated Beliaev's accusation at the initiative of the KGB, convicting the battalion "Nachtigall" of the massacre at a trial in absentia. The court declared Theodor Oberländer, then a minister in Konrad Adenauer's West German government, directly responsible. Mass media in the Polish People's Republic joined the chorus in blaming Oberländer. Many years later the backstories of these and similar Soviet efforts to discredit the Federal Republic of

---

German) is Dieter Schenk's *Der Lemberger Professorenmord und der Holocaust in Ostgalizien* (Bonn: J. H. Dietz, 2007). By comparison, the Ukrainian publication by Andrii Bolianovs′kyi, *Ubyvstvo pols′kykh uchenykh u L′vovi v lypni 1941 roku: fakty, mify, rozsliduvannia* (Lviv: Vydavnytstvo Lvivs′koï politekhniky, 2011), is derivative. Some of the most important testimonies naming the specific participants in the mass murder are: Karolina Lanckorońska's memoir (see note 32 above) and a report by Maria Kulczyńska—"Raport Karli Lanckorońskiej," *Odra* 4 (1977): 7–18.

34 His first publications were: "Losy uczonych lwowskich," *Nowe Widnokręgi* 23–4 (1944): 11 and "Uczeni płoną na stosach," *Czerwony Sztandar*, no. 80, December 2, 1944.

Haven at the Clinic | **43**

Soviet authorities declared the monument to Lviv professors designed by
Emmanuil Mysko ideologically incorrect and had it destroyed

Germany and its leaders came to light.³⁵ Immigrant communities representing varied interests attempted to counteract these politically motivated efforts, as evident on the one hand in the publications in the Ukrainian *Suchasna Ukraina*, and on the other in the Polish-Parisian *Kultura*. A regular contributor to the Paris monthly, Borys Levytsky who called for the nationalists to account for their wartime past, speculated in the light of subsequent mass crimes in Volhynia and Galicia that it was plausible that OUN had assisted in the murder of the Lviv professors.³⁶ In the Polish People's Republic, the leadership made sure that this version would become permanent; a quarter century after the attempt to discredit Adenauer, Edward Prus, a Polish writer whose work took aim at Ukrainian nationalism, resurrected the issue. In his book *Herosi spod znaku tryzuba* [*Heroes of the Trident*],³⁷ Prus ascribes complicity in the massacre to two members of OUN, Ievhen Wreciona and "Lehenda" (Ivan Klymiv's nom de guerre), who allegedly compiled the list using a pre-1939 phone book. His explanation for the "errors" made by the Gestapo during the roundup was that those OUN members, though originally from Lviv, were using outdated information. Thus the Gestapo searched for persons who had died between 1939–41 (among them the director of Ossolineum Ludwik Bernacki). In Prus's mind, these outdated addresses provide proof that the two prewar Lvivians and OUN members abetted in the professor massacre.

Other testimonies whose authors blame OUN for aiding in the murder carry more credibility at first glance. Roman Wolczuk, a student at the Lviv Polytechnic at the time, referred in his memoirs to a meeting at 20 Ruska Street, during which, at the orders of Mykola Lebed, the OUN students were given until the evening to supply a list of professors they knew. Wolczuk was determined to warn his favorite professor, but ultimately failed:

> I knew that Bartel lived somewhere on Kadecka Street [in actuality at 5 Herburtów, a street parallel to Kadecka]. I went there but could not locate

---

35 HDA SBU, f. 1, op. 4 (1964 r.), spr. 3, t. 5, k. 195. Rozsekrecheno: 24/376 vid 5.02.2008. Andry Bolianovsky provides details of the "legend" generated by the KGB to discredit both Adenauer and Ukrainian nationalists in *Ubyvstvo pols'kykh uchenykh u L'vovi v lypni 1941 roku: fakty, mify, rozsliduvannia* (Lviv: Vydavnytstvo Lvivs´koï politekhniky, 2011).

36 Levytsky and Stakhiv debated each other in: Borys Lewickyj, "Einsatzgruppen der Sicherheitspolizei," *Kultura* 4 (1960): 87–90, and Volodymyr Stakhiv's articles in *Suchasna Ukraina*, July 21, 1959; February, 7 1960.

37 Edward Prus, *Herosi spod znaku tryzuba* (Warsaw: Instytut Wydawniczy Związków Zawodowych, 1985).

him. Meanwhile it was almost evening, I needed to get back to Ruska Street. I decided to announce that I did not find any addresses and that was it. But there were other people there and they did not ask unnecessary questions. I was told later to get in the car with two uniformed Germans and show them Grodzickich Street. It was already dark when we got there, the car with the driver stopped by some entrance, and after a while Germans led an older man out of there. They drove him to the military barracks at Kadecka Street and let me go home. In this way I inadvertently contributed to the massacre.[38]

But Bartel had already been arrested by the Germans—on July 2, 1941. Supposing Wolczuk had known his professor's address, it would still have been too late to warn him. Grodzickich Street (today Drukarska) is located 200 yards away from 20 Ruska, so it seems improbable that Wolczuk's help in finding the address was indispensable. Even less likely is it that the car was on the road long enough for it to become dark (it was early July!). Lastly, the Gestapo transported all arrested professors to a boarding house for orphans at 5 Abrahamowiczów (today Boy-Zhelensky Street), and not to the barracks on an adjacent street, as Wolczuk writes. While I did not succeed in tracking down all the addresses of the murdered professors—a few of the Polytechnic addresses are missing—none of the university faculty or physicians lived on Grodzickich Street, with the exception of Leopold Biber, who was not arrested. In fact, residences on Grodzickich Street belonged mostly to Jewish merchants and industrialists. Thus a testimony so initially convincing turns out to be unreliable. We must also remember that in early July the Nazis arrested and shot not only several dozen professors, but many representatives of the Jewish intelligentsia too. Among them were Marian Auerbach, Paweł Ostern, and Salomon Czortkower.[39] In sum: if Wolczuk really played a part in this "operation," the victim he references was not one of the professors on the list, but a member of the Jewish intelligentsia.

To be sure we cannot entirely reject the "nationalist" explanation, because OUN did plot to "cleanse the territory of the Polish element." Still, this scenario

---

38 Roman Wolczuk, *Spomyny z peredvoiennoho Lvova ta voiennoho Vidnia* (Kyiv: Krytyka, 2002), 89.
39 Z memorandumu pro znyshchennya nimets′kymy fashystamy inteligentsii m. L′vova 1941, 1944 r., Derzhavnyi Arkhiv L′vivs′koï Oblasti (DALO) f. P. 3, op. 1, spr. 278, k. 28–9, in *Kul′turne zhyttia v Ukraïni. Zakhidni zemli 1939–1953*, vol. 1 (Kyiv: Naukova dumka, 1995–96), 236. The document gives some names incorrectly.

aligns rather neatly with state propaganda and undoubtedly presents certain ideological advantages. Beliaev's paymasters capitalized on those opportunities and popularized this version of events with the purpose of discrediting OUN. It is telling that the "nationalist" narrative emerged during a period when the Ukrainian underground resistance was creating serious issues for Soviet authorities.

Historian and lawyer Władysław Żeleński put forward a different hypothesis to explain the reason behind the massacre. I will label it "Soviet," as this narrative argues that the list contained names of particular professors who had participated in public life during the Soviet occupation.[40] According to the Paris historian (and Boy-Żeleński's nephew), the Germans compiled their list on the basis of the Soviet Lviv publication *Czerwony Sztandar*, which covered the travels of Polish scholars to the Kremlin and their participation in city and district local governments. Indeed, Germans closely watched the shift in Soviet tactics vis-à-vis Poles in the second half of 1940. In July 1941, German propaganda accused Polish Prime Minister Kazimierz Bartel of cooperating with the Soviets. In constructing his hypothesis, Żeleński appears to follow the information trail which the Germans themselves put together immediately after the massacre, as evidenced by an interview with Dr. Hans Joachim Beyer, published in a Ukrainian daily newspaper on July 5, 1941. Beyer was advisor to Reinhard Heydrich, member of the SS-Einsatzkommando C, an individual directly responsible for the murders. Referencing the victims of mass murders in Lviv prisons discovered just a few days earlier, he attributes complicity to Jews and, partly, to Poles: "Jews participated in these murders, in the sense that they escorted the 'suspect' Ukrainians to the NKVD. Other elements took part as well, and one should note that a segment of the Polish intelligentsia, under the leadership of former Prime Minister Bartel, was favorably inclined towards the Soviets."[41]

However, a look at the case of professor Stefan Banach suffices to challenge the "Soviet" scenario. The Nazis did not search for him, though he too was a member of the city council, university dean, and, like the others, traveled to Moscow. The tragic story of professor Roman Rencki belies Żeleński's argumentation as well: he was among those executed on Wuleckie Hills. Earlier, Rencki had spent over a year in a Soviet prison, miraculously avoiding death in

---

40 Władysław Żeleński, "Podróże lwowskich profesorów do Moskwy w r. 1940," *Wiadomości* 23 (1975): 4.
41 "Podii v Zakhidnii Ukraïni. Rozmova z dotsentom dr Hansom Joachimom Beyerom," *Krakivs'ki visti*, July 5, 1941.

the mass murder of prisoners by the retreating Soviets (Erwin Axer recounted Rencki's story: when the shots were fired, Rencki fell; later he made it out from under the pile of corpses and was able to break free from prison the next morning).[42] Similarly, the fate of the eighty-four-year-old professor Adam Sołowij, a distinguished obstetrician of Ukrainian descent, to no extent involved in political life during the Soviet occupation, does not fit Żeleński's hypothesis.

Paradoxically, the third narrative, which we will call "Nazi," has found little traction in the literature on the subject. It is worth noting that in a similar case—the Nazi roundup of faculty from the Jagiellonian University and the University of Mining and Metallurgy in Cracow (later referred to as *Sonderaktion Krakau*)—historians did not try to identify any further "criminal motives." But in their interpretation of this analogous operation in Lviv, which also targeted the intelligentsia, researchers attribute partial blame to Ukrainian nationalists. In search of additional motivations and perpetrators of these Nazi crimes, the scholarship goes so far as to draw a connection between the mass execution and the engagement of the scholar-victims in Soviet political life.

Shortly after the Red Army marched into Lviv, a commission was formed to investigate Nazi crimes. The commission's report from 1944, written on the basis of investigations and the testimonies of surviving witnesses, names the Nazis as the sole perpetrators of the Wuleckie Hills massacre. During the Nuremberg trials, the USSR chief prosecutor Roman Rudenko concluded that the murders were committed not by random criminal groups consisting of German officers and rank-and-file soldiers, but by units especially prepared for the task, who acted according to a plan formulated in advance, and utilized a list.[43] It is worth remembering that the Nazis, and not Ukrainian nationalists, were most "interested" in eliminating the Polish intelligentsia. Karolina Lanckorońska, the main witness, recounts that the leaders of the Third Reich sought to "successfully solve the problem" (in contrast to the November 6, 1939 operation, deemed ineffective, which targeted the faculty of the Jagiellonian University and the University of Mining and Metallurgy in Cracow, ending with their imprisonment at the concentration camp in Sachsenhausen). Similarly, Stefan Banach's article about the Lviv atrocity named Nazis as the perpetrators, although he was most certainly familiar with Beliaev's narrative. In fact, the

---

42 Erwin Axer, *Z pamięci* (Warszawa: Iskry, 2006), 131.
43 *Niurnbergskii protsess. Sbornik materialov v 8 tomakh*, vol. 5 (Moscow: Iuridicheskaia Literatura, 1991): 118.

mathematician's story, published a week after Beliaev's, can be read as a hidden polemic with the Soviet writer.[44]

The fourth scenario of "crime and plunder" does not conflict with the "nationalist" or the "Nazi" narratives, but in effect cancels the "Soviet" connection. It purports that the Nazis aimed to arrest above all persons of high and very high social standing in order to deprive the Lviv community of authority figures. While achieving this objective—and this motive should receive greater consideration—the plan was to "reward" direct participants in the massacre (that is, the German officers) with the assets of those executed. The following premise speaks in favor of this hypothesis: the majority of the apprehended professors resided at Romanowicz Street (now Saksahansky), one of the wealthiest streets in central Lviv, directly adjacent to the Lviv Corso—Akademicka Street (now Shevchenko). The specific victims were: Roman Rencki, Jan Grek and brother-in-law Tadeusz Boy-Żeleński, Tadeusz Ostrowski, Franciszek Groër, Adam Sołowij, and Władysław Dobrzaniecki.

When evaluating the probability of those four theories, we should take a closer look at an inhabitant of prewar Lviv who befriended the local business people and the elite, the art collector and schemer, Dutchman Pieter Nicolaas van Menten. Before the war he purchased works of art; during the war, he simply looted them. Thanks to a certain arrangement, he made it out of the Soviet and into the German zone. Thereafter he was nominated asset manager of a few Jewish antique stores and liquidator of twenty bookstores in Cracow; in addition, he plundered the collection of Professor Ostrowski. At the start of the German-Soviet war he did not waste any opportunities; while recovering his estate near Stryi, he and his underlings murdered Jewish and Polish residents of Pidhorodtsi and Urych so he could "recompense" himself for losses incurred during the Soviet occupation. Later Menten insisted that in the summer of 1941, after the Germans took Lviv, he served as a mere translator with the Einsatzkommando under Schöngarth's command. Schöngarth was the man who bore direct responsibility for the Lviv massacre.[45]

Except for Franciszek Groër, who survived the arrest, the other professors apprehended by the Gestapo were murdered. This circumstance made many Lvivians suspicious. Pelagia Łozynska (Kazimiera Poraj), of Ukrainian descent

---

44 Stefan Banach, "Uczeni polscy zamordowani przez hitlerowców. Antoni Łomnicki—Włodzimierz Stożek," *Czerwony Sztandar* 87 (1944).

45 Compare Schenk, *Der Lemberger Professorenmord und der Holocaust in Ostgalizien*, 135–41, and Hans Knoop, *The Menten Affair*, trans. M. Rudnik (New York: Macmillan, 1978), 70.

Pieter Nicolaas Menten, a war criminal, one of the people directly responsible for the massacre of Lviv professors

and married to a Jew, and who provided an emotionally riveting testimony of the German occupation's early days, spoke of Groër in an extraordinarily blistering manner.[46] Groër was most often accused of having represented himself as German in order to survive the roundup. Tadeusz Tomaszewski also suggested this, adding the acerbic comment: "He is riding the wave again" (in reference to Groër's prominent position during the Soviet occupation).[47] However, in his publication devoted to the Lviv professors, Zygmunt Albert categorically rejected the accusations. In light of testimony by German administrators of the clinic where Groër worked, Albert argued that Groër was not considered German, which meant that the physician never signed the *Volksliste* and should remain above suspicion.

---

46 "Zbiór pamiętników Żydów Ocalałych z Zagłady," 302/217, k. 7, Archiwum Żydowskiego Instytutu Historycznego AŻIH, partly published in Kazimiera Poraj, "Dziennik lwowski," *Biuletyn Żydowskiego Instytutu Historycznego* 52 (October–December 1964) : 76–106.
47 Tomaszewski, *Lwów. Pejzaż psychologiczny*, 95.

Five years later Groër became a member of the Extraordinary Commission for the Investigation of Nazi Crimes, and one of the two main witnesses for the prosecution of the Lviv professor massacre. His role was unambiguous. As Zygmunt Albert asserts, Groër vouched for Menten at the trial, even though the Dutchman had participated in the arrests. Thanks to Groër's testimony, Menten went on trial after the war only as a collaborator, a mere translator, but not a war criminal. After serving an eight-month sentence, he quickly returned to the regular life of a well-off citizen. In fact, he felt safe enough to organize an exhibition of the art he had plundered.

But in reality, Menten played a part, perhaps not key to the massacre (the orders came not from him or even from the commander of the Lviv Gestapo Eberhard Schöngarth, but from Himmler himself), yet clearly sinister. Archival documents located in the Netherlands, first made public by the Dutch journalist Hans Knoop in his 1977 book *De zaak Menten* (*The Menten Affair*, 1978), confirm his involvement. It appears that Polish scholars, specifically Zygmunt Albert and Włodzimierz Bonusiak, were not familiar with Knoop's work. A Ukrainian journalist summarizes *The Menten Affair*:

> According to Dutch researchers, Menten, while in Soviet-occupied Lviv [in fact Menten was able to leave the Soviet zone; in fall of 1939 he was already in Cracow], was gathering information about local art collectors. Maria Groër, the physician's daughter, may have unwittingly assisted him. We know from the documents compiled by researchers that she worked for Menten from January till June of 1942 (De affaire Menten 1945–76, Band 2, p. 678 aanmerking 118). This prompts the conjecture that out of gratitude for saving their lives, the professor did not name Menten before the Extraordinary Commission in 1944.[48]

The dates leave no doubt: Maria Groër worked with Menten during the period in which the collector amassed the most items. Testimony in support of Menten came also from Józef Stiglitz, a Cracow dealer of antique books, whom Menten helped get to Hungary. While Stiglitz escaped with (only) his life, Menten took over his assets.

The matter of Menten, who, on the strength of Groër's and Stiglitz's testimonies, was sentenced to just eight months in prison after the war, resurfaced

---

48 Iaroslav Dovhopolyi, "Piter Menten i lvivs'ki rozstril'ni spysky," zaxid.net, https://zaxid.net/piter_menten_i_lvivski_rozstrilni_spiski_n1272557.

after Hans Knoop published his discoveries in the newspaper *De Telegraf* on May 22, 1976. The investigation was resumed. Mara Cygielstrejch (Mina Pistyner) testified in court. The court initially sentenced Menten to fifteen years, but on appeal reduced his sentence to ten. It emerges from Pistyner's testimony that Menten and his people, having executed the villagers in Urycz and Podhorodce (where Menten's estate was located before the war), showed up to settle accounts with Pistyner's family. The entrepreneur, already in Nazi uniform, decided to take revenge on the Pistyners for prewar disagreements. Menten and Mina's father had been friends and worked together for a few years, but thereafter fought in court over a property named Sopot near Stryi. At the start of the German-Soviet war, Menten forcibly obtained the address of Mina's parents, Izaak and Fryda Pistyner. He appeared in Nazi uniform with a group of subordinates in the Pistyners' modest apartment in Lviv, where they moved after the Soviets evicted them from their property in Pidhorodtsi. Menten intended to shoot everyone in the apartment. Mina Pistyner, who was in exile in Kazakhstan at the time, returned to Lviv after the war and learned of the deaths of her loved ones. Two of the persons present in the apartment during the murders miraculously survived, only to perish later in the ghetto. Pistyner had twice tried to testify, the first time before her 1949 emigration to Palestine, and then again in Paris. Twenty years later, her efforts finally paid off.[49]

MEDICAL FACULTY AND PROFESSIONAL MEDICAL COURSE INSTRUCTORS

In January 1940, the clinic managed by Franciszek Groër before the war became part of the Medical Institute, created to replace the Medical Faculty at Jan Kazimierz University.[50] The Medical Institute reported to the Ministry of Health, and not the Ministry of Education, which turned out to be of consequence. Though communist ideology was omnipresent, it affected the health

---

49 Mara Cygielstrejch's (Mina Pistyner's) recollections in the Menten case are located in the archives of the United States Holocaust Memorial Museum ("Maria Cygielstrejch Reminiscences," *Survivor Testimonies* [Permanent exhibition]. United States Holocast Memorial Museum, Washington DC). I am grateful to the museum librarian Vincent Slatt and the archive director Vadim Altskan for their assistance with my inquiries.
50 For more information about the war period, see Bolesław Popielski and Wanda Wojtkiewicz-Rok, "Dzieje Wydziału Lekarskiego Uniwersytetu Jana Kazimierza we Lwowie 1939–1944," in *Lwowskie środowisko naukowe w latach 1939–1945*, ed. Irena Stasiewicz-Jasiukowa (Warsaw: Polska Akademia Nauk, 1994), 58–71.

professions less than it did schools or universities. Nevertheless, the unification of health services with the Soviet system was underway. The institute automatically absorbed the pediatric clinic, whose name was changed to the acronymic Okhmadyt, in accordance with Soviet coinage standards: **Ok**horona **ma**teri i **dyt**yny. Poland adopted this institutional pattern after the war. Professor Franciszek Groër would become the architect, and, subsequently, director of the Institute of Mother and Child in Warsaw. In the early 1950s, Ludwik Fleck and Irena Szyszkowicz (Lille) would find work there.

Oleksandr Makarchenko, a neurologist from Mariupol in the Donetsk district, became the director of the Lviv Medical Institute. After the war broke out, he worked as director of the Institute for the Improvement of Medical Qualifications in Kharkiv, thus more in an administrative role, and was likely an active party member (people without communist affiliations were not eligible for such prominent positions). He did not obtain an academic degree until 1941. After the war he went on to enjoy a successful career, becoming the Vice President of the Academy of Sciences of the USSR. Polish memoirists shrug off Makarchenko, in his case eagerly parroting Soviet rhetoric (calling him a "shepherd's son," for instance) they otherwise distrust. Adam Krechowiecki (1913–91), at the time a senior assistant in the Anatomy Department, recalled in August of 1990: "A few professors and associate professors, imported from the other side of Zbruch, introduced themselves as 'boor by birth, master by education. ...' The director did not need to publicly confess his 'shepherd' past—'as a boy I used to herd cows,' he would say—because his mug betrayed his pastoral social origin as did every sentence he uttered."[51] Other commentaries on government representatives and employees who arrived from beyond Zbruch display a similar contempt of the upper class for the lower.

At the recommendation of Marian Panchyshyn, the People's Commissar nominated the Lviv bacteriologist Maksym Muzyka as Makarchenko's deputy for scientific and educational matters. Muzyka had served as interim director at the institute until Makarchenko's arrival. Initially the scientist worked at the university;[52] after the decision to restructure the Medical Faculty into a separate entity,[53] he became its interim director.[54] Muzyka's older colleague, the well-known Ukrainian physician and social activist Marian Panchyshyn—they had

---

51   Adam Krechowiecki, "Okupacja sowiecka we Lwowie. Wspomnienia," OK AW II/1585/1, k. 78.
52   Nakaz rektora no. 10, 24.10.1939, R-119, op. 1, spr. 3.
53   *Vil'na Ukraïna*, no. 57, November 30, 1939: 3.
54   TSDIA, f. 362 op. 1, spr 62, ark. 3.

Oleksandr Makarchenko, president of the Medical Institute

worked together in Lviv in the early 1920s[55]—was appointed shortly thereafter as director of the Faculty of Internal Medicine. Earlier, he had been chief of the health department in the Lviv district, a position conferred by Ivan Lukianchikov, the Deputy People's Commissar of Health. However, he only lasted a few months and was quickly replaced by Hnat Trehub, who was sent from Kharkiv.[56]

Once these local Galician Ukrainians had fulfilled whatever the Soviet authorities tasked them with, they were moved to positions of less responsibility where they could no longer exert influence over the shape of their institutions. Panchyshyn and Muzyka, despite the difference in their ages, had similar life trajectories: born in Lviv into Ukrainian families of rather modest means, they succeeded professionally, lived through the Great War, completed medical service in the Austro-Hungarian army, and fought typhus, also during the

---

[55] Roman Osinchuk, "Mar'ian Panchyshyn i Maksym Muzyka—profesory ukrains'koho (taiemnoho) universytetu (1920–1924)," *Likars'kyi zbirnyk. Nova seriia* 4 (1996): 138–40.

[56] Prokopiv, "Spohady," k. 39. See also Osinchuk, "Orhanizatsia okhorony zdorov'ia u l'vivs'kii oblasti (1939–1941)," 197.

Polish-Ukrainian war. After the war they taught at the Ukrainian Underground University in Lviv, and then found themselves—due to their engagement in the Ukrainian national cause—on the outside of Lviv's academic circles. When both men were promoted to important positions at the start of the Soviet occupation, their contemporaries, colleagues and prewar professors, eagerly (and hypocritically) rubbed this lack of academic experience in their faces.

Initially the new authorities favored Marian Panchyshyn and other well-known participants in the People's Assembly in Lviv, especially Kyrylo Studynsky, at the same time compelling them to participate in Soviet rituals. Studynsky and Panchyshyn joined the executive committee, together with Semyon Timoshenko and Nikita Khrushchev; later, they traveled to Moscow as delegates. The media reported on their speeches at the assembly and at a session of the Supreme Soviet of the USSR.[57] At the November 1, 1940 session of the Supreme Soviet, it fell to Marian Panchyshyn to read the People's Assembly resolution requesting that Western Ukraine be incorporated into the USSR. The purpose behind the request was to create the appearance that it was legal to annex this territory of the Second Polish Republic. As a result, Panchyshyn, along with other deputies of the state authorities, became collaborators in the eyes of Lviv's Poles.[58] Tomaszewski characterizes Panchyshyn as a Soviet paper pusher, who also got on well with the Germans a little later.[59] Conversely, Ivan Prokopiv, who in the fall of 1939 began to work as an accountant at the district health department, shows Panchyshyn in a different light. He recalls a conversation with Panchyshyn on the eve of the People's Assembly:

> Dr. Marian Panchyshyn was elected a delegate to the People's Assembly. He prepared his speech and gave it to Kunynets [a secretary] to type up. He then handed it to the Provisional Administration to review, as they had requested. They crossed out fifty percent of the speech, adding quite a bit, too. "Take a look at what they did with my speech"—he showed me the typescript. "They are making me change it and only say at the assembly what they have blessed. What's to do? One must do what one must"—he said and handed the speech to his typist.[60]

---

57 "Promova M. Panchyshyna na Narodnykh Zborakh Zakhidnoï Ukraïny," *Vil'na Ukraïna*, no. 31, October 28, 1939, 3; Mar'ian Panchyshyn, "Rozvyvaiet'sia i kvitne radians'ka medytsyna," *Vil'na Ukraïna*, no. 52, November 2, 1939, 1.
58 Prokopiv, "Spohady," k. 38.
59 Tomaszewski, *Lwów. Pejzaż psychologiczny*, 90, 95.
60 Prokopiv, "Spohady," k. 38.

"A Meeting of Brothers," propaganda drawing from the front page of *Vilna Ukraina*

In his memoir, Mykhailo Ostroverkha described similar circumstances behind Kyrylo Studynsky's speech, also prepared and supplied by a Soviet official.[61]

Among his Polish colleagues, Panchyshyn's standing only worsened when he became the main organizer of Professional Medical Courses during the German occupation. However, as early as in the fall, the German command appointed a few other noted Lviv physicians, among them Adam Gruca, Franciszek Groër, and Bolesław Jałowy, to equivalent positions. But they were not Ukrainians. Regardless of their colleagues' negative opinion of them, it was Marian Panchyshyn and Kyrylo Studynsky that people turned to for help during the Soviet occupation if their family members were arrested by the NKVD. Panchyshyn never refused to help, even if it meant getting into serious trouble, as happened when he intervened with Roman Rudenko, the chief prosecutor of the Ukrainian Soviet Socialist Republic, on behalf of girls whom the NKVD had accused of belonging to OUN and sentenced to death.[62]

In the interwar period Panchyshyn acquired the nickname "the People's Doctor." People knew him not only as an excellent specialist of internal

---

61 Mykhailo Ostroverkha, "Na krutomu zvoroti istorii Ievropy" (unpublished manuscript), Ostroverkha Papers, box 6, folder 1, k. 150, Shevchenko Scientific Society Archive.
62 Osinchuk, "Orhanizatsiia okhorony zdorov'ia u l'vivs'kii oblasti (1939–1941)," 217.

medicine (he was Metropolitan Bishop Andrei Sheptytsky's personal physician), but also as a man who never refused to help those in need, regardless of their ability to pay. Long lines, including farm wagons, would form in front of his villa at 3 Kłuszyńska.

Panchyshyn, who fought in the Polish-Ukrainian conflict of 1918–19, and who had served as an army doctor during World War I, belonged to the ranks of the patriotic Ukrainian intelligentsia. After the Polish-Ukrainian war, there was no place for him at Jan Kazimierz University. He declined a move to Warsaw, even though his prewar teacher, professor Antoni Gluziński, made him an offer. Instead he became dean of the Medical Faculty at the Ukrainian Underground University. For many decades, his students, Roman Osinchuk among them, reminisced about his courses.[63] Panchyshyn's villa housed his private practice (today a museum devoted to the physician), and he also worked as head of the Internal Medicine Ward at the Sheptytsky People's Clinic. Soviet authorities favored him, as they did other educated Ukrainians. Thanks, in part, to his standing, and a clever disappearing act, he avoided forced evacuation. In early July, after conferring with colleagues, he decided to plead with the German authorities for permission to resume the activities of the Medical Institute.

Ukrainian and Polish memoirs and studies by historians of medicine offer divergent accounts of Panchyshyn's activities during Lviv's German occupation. The former ethnic group elevates his merits and blames his death on the Polish Home Army (AK) and terrorist acts against Ukrainian intelligentsia (Andry Lastovetsky, director of the physics faculty, and Oleksandr Podolynsky, Panchyshyn's closest coworker at the People's Clinic before 1939, and head of the obstetrical clinic, were both murdered). The latter group, indirectly (Zygmunt Albert) or directly (Tomasz Cieszyński) accuse Panchyshyn of collaboration. However, the fact that during the German occupation Zygmunt Albert himself was an associate professor at the Professional Medical Courses, formally directed by Karl Schulze, and that Tomasz Cieszyński was not admitted to the program merits attention; instead, Cieszyński acquired his credentials by taking underground courses.[64] In his publication on the history of the medical faculty, Cieszyński states that Panchyshyn and Lastovetsky rejected his application because he was a Pole. He goes on to describe Lastovetsky's murder and

---

63 Ibid., 191–226.
64 Tomasz Cieszyński, "Działalność Wydziału Lekarskiego UJK we Lwowie w czasie II wojny światowej od września 1939 do sierpnia 1944 roku," *Archiwum Historii i Filozofii Medycyny* 58, no. 2 (1995): 141–9.

revels in its unbecoming details. By his account, Lastovetsky's death was a criminal case rather than an act of nationalism. Here, Cieszyński's take aligns with a common perspective: only social scum commit atrocities, never are they committed by one's own community. Besides citing third party accounts—said the testimony of a building watchman—Cieszyński does not invoke any other sources. It is not irrelevant that Tomasz Cieszyński is the son of Antoni Cieszyński, who perished in the Wuleckie Hills massacre. This close familial connection likely informs his absolute judgment of Jakub Parnas, Franciszek Groër, and Lastovetsky, as well as his allegations that OUN members played a part in the massacre of the professors.

In his reminiscences, Tadeusz Tomaszewski takes a more dispassionate view of the death of Andriy Lastovetsky, which was followed by threats against Dr. Bolesław Jałowy, professor Adam Gruca, and, finally by the death of Marian Panchyshyn in 1943.[65] A Soviet commission headed by Mykola Bazhan looked into the circumstances of Panchyshyn's death, since he was a USSR deputy, and delivered a report directly to Nikita Khrushchev. According to the commission's findings, Panchyshyn died of a heart attack after the nervous shock he suffered as a result of threats he received from the Polish underground.[66]

Over the course of 1940, newcomers from the USSR had gradually been taking over lead posts at the Medical Institute. Soon they pushed out the few local Ukrainian specialists, who only recently had been placed in positions of responsibility and who were now demoted. Petro Melnychuk and Eustachy Struk became assistants to Maksym Muzyka. Struk, initially employed at the university president's office,[67] quickly moved to a safer—or so it seemed—place, the Medical Institute. But the NKVD arrested him on suspicion of belonging to OUN and executed him in 1941.[68] Other Ukrainians also found themselves in new positions. Petro Melnychuk, who as assistant director was in charge of the students' living conditions, was transferred to the Faculty of

---

65 Tomaszewski, *Lwów. Pejzaż psychologiczny*, 165.
66 "Lyst M. Bazhana i K. Lytvyna do M. Khrushchova pro prychyny smerti M. Panchyshyna," 3.08.1944, *Kul'turne zhyttia v Ukraïni. Zakhidni zemli*, vol. 1, 195–6.
67 Nakaz rektora no. 32, 3.11.1939. ALU, R-119, op. 3, spr. 3, k. 26.
68 Milena Rudnyts'ka, ed., *Zakhidnia Ukraïna pid bol'shevykamy. Zbirnyk* (New York: Shevchenko Scientific Society in the United States, 1958), 477–9. The press printed a list of victims identified by family members in *Ukraïns'ki shchodenni visti*, July 5, 1941, July 10, 1941. Recently published NKVD documents show that Struk was shot on June 26, 1941 (Vasyl' Tron'ko, ed., *Reabilitovani istorieiu. L'vivs'ka oblast'*, vol. 1 [NANU-SBU, Kyiv-Lviv: Tsentr "Astroliabiia," 2009], 628).

Pharmacy. It was there that Dean Jakub Parnas saved his life.[69] A coworker of Maksym Muzyka from the laboratory of the nationalized People's Clinic, Iulian Kordiuk, became the district health inspector. Oleksandr Barvinsky became a physician at the city health department, and Marian Panchyshyn's assistant Roman Osinchuk was nominated his deputy at the district health department (he had served as the chief physician at the Medical Institute since April 1940).[70] The obstetrician Sofia Parfanovych was tasked with directing the midwifery school.[71] In place of Andry Lastovetsky the Soviets installed Victor Zhuravliov from Stalino (today Donetsk) as the physics faculty director,[72] and Pavlo Holoborodko from Kharkiv took over as director of the Faculty of Surgery and Anatomy.

Andry Lastovetsky (1902–43), a junior colleague of Marian Panchyshyn and Maksym Muzyka, studied physics at Jan Kazimierz University, and worked as a research assistant to Stanisław Loria. In fall 1939 he served as a member of the entrance examination committee for physics, together with professor Loria and Wojciech Rubinowicz.[73] Since he specialized in radiology, after the university was restructured and the Medical Institute became a separate institution, he transferred there and took over the Faculty of Physics. During the German occupation he served as dean of Professional Medical Courses. Kedyw (the Polish Home Army's Directorate of Diversion) sentenced him to death under the false charge of not admitting Poles to the German-led academy, most likely after one of the rejected applicants complained.

The Soviets aimed to generate impressive statistics: in comparison with 1939, during the academic year of 1940/1941, the number of employees at the medical academy grew by a factor of 2.5, and the student body increased trifold. Ukrainians and Jews had preferential status in admissions. On the downside, sometimes persons who had never studied medicine turned up in advanced courses, and some dishonest candidates abused the system. In early 1940, the Medical Institute opened the Faculty of Marxism-Leninism (as did

---

69 See Iaroslav Hanitkevych, *Istorychni etapy naistarshoho v Ukraïni L'vivs'koho Natsional'noho medychnoho universytetu im. Danyla Halyts'koho*, ntsh.org, http://ntsh.org/content/ganit-kevich-yaroslav-istorichni-etapi-naystarshogo-v-ukrayini-lvivskogo-nacionalnogo.
70 Osinchuk, "Orhanizatsiia okhorony zdorov'ia u l'vivs'kii oblasti (1939–1941)," 212.
71 Mykhailo Pavlovskyi, Stepan Kuhkta, *Na skhreshchenykh dorohakh zhyttia Sofiï Parfanovych. Do 100-richchia ULT u L'vovi* (Lviv: KOS, 2010).
72 Grzegorz Motyka and Rafał Wnuk, *Pany i rezuny. Współpraca AK-WiN i UPA 1945–1947* (Warsaw: Volumen, 1997), 78.
73 Nakaz rektora no. 72, 23.11.1939, ALU, R-119, op. 3, spr. 3, k. 60.

the university), led by Nikita Kachanov from the Mykolaiv district. The job of personnel manager—that is, chief of the institution's NKVD unit, a key post in Soviet institutions—went to U. Pavlenko (first name unknown). He left a bad impression.[74]

Similar staffing changes occurred in clinics reporting to the Medical Institute as well, including the pediatric clinic which Franciszek Groër had led. The new director, Hnat Trehub, contrary to Fryda Lille's pejorative mention of him in her memoirs, was a multifaceted figure.[75] A collection of reminiscences devoted to the pediatrician mentions good relations between Groër and Trehub.[76] In daily life, Trehub turned out to be a decent person, though his appearance fully matched the stereotype of a Soviet man. Like most civil servants who arrived from the USSR, he was not well off, and thus valued the privileges that came with his position. Ivan Prokopiv, at first the chief accountant at the Department of Health, and then at Okhmadyt, describes Trehub's manner in detail, referring to him as a Ukrainian (not Russian, as Fryda Lille writes) from Kharkiv who consistently spoke Ukrainian, cultivated good relations with his subordinates, and provided assistance to people facing arrest. Prokopiv reminisced that

> the administrative manager and manager of Hladko's office, a former administration member of the "Złoty kłos" Bakers' Cooperative, accommodated Trehub in the apartment left behind by Sheparovych, director of "Tsentrosoyuz," who had registered as a German (Reichsdeutsch) and emigrated to the Reich. In this way Trehub took up residence on a side street that fed into Potocki Street. Sheparovych possibly also sold him the furniture, but I don't know where Trehub got that kind of money.[77]

It is hard to believe that Trehub really purchased the furnishings. Iulian Sheparovych, ataman of the Ukrainian Galician Army UHA, who also was working

---

74 See: Krechowiecki, I konkurs, k. 76–7; Osinchuk, "Orhanizatsiia okhorony zdorov'ia u l'vivs'kii oblasti (1939–1941)," 219; Myroslaw Charkewycz's (much less reliable) testimony diverges from those two sources. Allegedly, Pavlenko warned him against spreading nationalist propaganda in the publication *Radians'kyi medyk* (see Myroslaw Charkewycz, *Ia vas ne zabuv. Spomyny 1939–1945* [New York: Ukrains'ko-amerykans'ka fundatsia "Volia," 1997], 63–4).
75 Osinchuk, "Orhanizatsiia okhorony zdorov'ia u l'vivs'kii oblasti (1939–1941)," 197–204.
76 Krukowska, ed., *Franciszek Groer*, 16.
77 Prokopiv, "Spohady," k. 39.

for Roman Shukhevych's advertising agency Fama, left in secrecy, trying to escape with his life. To sell his possessions would have lowered his chance of survival. Thus Hnat Trehub came to occupy a small, well-furnished villa in the same way as the rest of the newly arrived administration—by taking over properties and possessions left behind by persons leaving the city. Initially Trehub replaced Marian Panchyshyn as director in the District Health Care Division in the Lviv district, and then assumed management of the clinic. (Interestingly, after the war he returned to this position and remained there until the purge of 1948.)

As mentioned before, microbiologist and epidemiologist Maksym Muzyka became the assistant director of the Medical Institute. He succeeded in retaining the basic lineup of the prewar Medical Faculty, including its dean, even though the Soviets were forcing personnel changes in leadership positions.[78] A new twist was the hiring of a few Galician Ukrainians; among them were, beside Petro Melnychuk and Eustachy Struk, Ivan Poliuha as chairman of the faculty (Poliuha also fought in the Polish-Ukrainian war and belonged to the Ukrainian Military Organization [UVO] in the early 1920s),[79] Oleksandr Koval as the head of the dental clinic, and the hematologist Stepan Martyniv.[80] Refugees from central Poland also succeeded in finding employment, though Soviet authorities viewed this group with suspicion. As a result, Jakub Parnas worked with two chemists, Heppner (first name unknown) and Kazimierz Lindenfeld, a biochemist called Janina Opieńska-Blauth, and his prewar colleague, the dermatologist and venereologist Mykhailo Dubovy (the NKVD arrested the latter on April 13, 1940 and sent him to Uzbekistan in 1941).

---

78 At first the designation of Medical Faculty was retained and Maksym Muzyka was appointed as dean (Nakaz rektora no. 11, 24.10.1939, ALU, R-119, op. 3, spr. 3, k. 8). Witold Nowicki (1878–1941), president of the Medical Association (he served in the Polish-Ukrainian and Polish-Bolshevik wars as a military doctor), elected as dean for the 1939/1940 academic year, remained as a professor and joined Jakub Parnas and Maksym Muzyka in the three-person admission committee (Nakaz rektora no. 12, 24.10.1939, ALU, R-119, op. 3, spr. 3, k. 9). He was murdered on Wuleckie Hills.

79 Ivan Poliuha was hired as chairman of the Medical Faculty on October 27, 1939, thus three days after Maksym Muzyka.

80 Stepan Martyniv (1910–96) also served as the head of the clinic. See Zygmunt Albert, *Lwowski wydział lekarski w czasie okupacji hitlerowskiej, 1941–1944* (Wrocław: Zakład Narodowy im. Ossolińskich, 1975), 108; Anatolii Mahl'ovanyi and Vasyl' Novak, "Do 100-richchia vid dnia narodzhennia profesora Stepana Mykhailovycha Martyniva," *Zhurnal Akademiï medychnych nauk Ukraïny* 16, no. 1 (2010): 177–80.

The noted biochemist, member of the Polish Academy of Arts and Sciences and former dean of the Medical Faculty Jakub Karol Parnas, and the histologist and dermatologist Bolesław Jałowy, became deans of the pharmacy and the medical faculties. During World War I Parnas had returned to Lviv and, after 1920, founded the School of Biochemistry. Because of his leftist leanings, the Soviets considered him to be the right candidate. His Jewish background may have also played a part—it fit nicely into the propaganda: only the Soviet Union opened career opportunities to all citizens, regardless of social or national origin. The Soviets evacuated Parnas and his family on June 26, 1941, first to Kyiv, then to Ufa. From 1943, after a breakthrough on the war front, he worked in Moscow, where he died or was murdered at the Lubianka prison in 1949. His death probably occurred on the tide of an anti-Semitic campaign to crack down on members of the Jewish Antifascist Committee (including the infamous assassination of Salomon Mikhoels). The political purge culminated in the murders of Jewish doctors, whom Soviet propaganda then labeled "murderers in white coats," so as to invoke an association with the Nazis.

Academic circles had no favorable comments about Parnas's prominent position, his membership on the City Council, and his subsequent evacuation. Tomasz Cieszyński intimated that Jakub Parnas had other reasons to evacuate together with Soviet authorities, more pressing than his Jewish background alone. Speculating on the subject of Parnas's speech at the opening of the January 8, 1941 city council session, Cieszyński noted emphatically:

> With this political act, Jakub Parnas made the Soviet Union his home country, breaching loyalty to the Polish Republic, which since 1921 had given him a position as a professor at the UJK, creating the conditions for his fruitful scientific career and rewarding him with the respect of the community. There is something particularly puzzling about this political act. Notwithstanding the moral judgment, we could not understand at the time what the professor was thereby trying to achieve. Did he foresee the war between Germany and the Soviet Union, and, not identifying as a Pole, he opted for what he saw as the safest choice? Did he seriously contemplate a political career within the Soviet regime?[81]

---

81 Tomasz Cieszyński, "O profesorze Jakubie Parnasie na tle Lwowa z lat 1938 do 1945," *Archiwum Historii i Filozofii Medycyny* 61, no. 2 (1997).

It warrants attention that when Tomasz Cieszyński makes accusations of close cooperation with the Soviets, he reserves them exclusively for persons of non-Polish background, in particular for the Austrian Franciszek Groër and the Jew Jakub Parnas. Although Tomaszewski maintains that the community found more fault with Groër as a Pole than with Parnas as a Jew,[82] that does not detract from my claim. As for Ukrainians, Poles generally presumed them to be collaborators—either Soviet or German, depending on circumstances. Cieszyński's bias is typical. In reality, the Soviets pulled many more people into their orbit, but Cieszyński only mentions this once, and only in passing. The allegation of apostasy, which hovers close to high treason ("not identifying as a Pole"), only applies to the disloyal Jew. Others from the same medical community (Groër, Ostrowski, Grek) did not experience similar accusations, although they too, like Parnas, served as city council representatives.

In December of 1940, a number of professors from the institute, among them Franciszek Groër, Jakub Parnas, Jan Grek, Tadeusz Ostrowski, and Maksym Muzyka, became deputies to the City Council or the District Council. It may be that by gaining the status of an official they were acquiring a measure of protection, not only for themselves, but also for their coworkers. Some colleagues from their academic milieu saw this as evidence of collaboration. The charge was selective: more often than not it applied to persons who had been or became "others,"—above all, to Parnas, whose Jewish background was brought up again and again, and to Muzyka, whom Poles never considered "one of their own" to begin with. It follows that the opinion-shaping elites perceived persons of (ethnic) identities other than Polish as collaborators.

The Soviet administration assigned Bolesław Jałowy to the position of second dean of the Medical Institute, probably in recognition of his lower-class origin. Barely thirty-four years old, Jałowy specialized in histology and dermatology. During the German occupation, he retained his position as the director of the Histology Unit; he was simultaneously involved in the underground Medical Faculty Council. Ukrainian resistance fighters shot him on October 1, 1943. Many Polish authors (Tomasz Cieszyński among them) assert that the son of Marian Panchyshyn was Jałowy's killer. They do so on the basis of a statement made by Jan Chmiel, a medical student and witness to the murder. In the fall of 1943, a climate of abject distrust and hatred between Poles and Ukrainian reached its zenith. Rarely did the churning rumor mill fail to sway the opinions

---

82 Tomaszewski, *Lwów. Pejzaż psychologiczny*, 37.

of others. Jałowy's assassination shook Lviv's population; the town's medical community was first decimated at the start of the German occupation by the Wuleckie Hills massacre and in the subsequent years by systematic murders of Jews, physicians among them (only a handful survived). Now, in the fall of 1943, it stood face-to-face with the terrorist acts of the Ukrainian underground and Polish resistance, the latter killing people as prominent in the community as Andriy Lastovetsky, then dean of Professional Medical Courses, and Dr. Oleksandr Podolynsky.

Once the German-Soviet war broke out, as a doctor and bacteriologist, Muzyka was drafted. So was Dr. Iulian Kordiuk, the head of the District Health Care Division, another local who worked in health administration.[83] Muzyka left Lviv in late June 1941. During his evacuation far into the USSR, he worked, among other places, in the town of Frunze, and in Przhevalsk (now Karakol) he headed a branch of the Institute of Microbiology. In late July 1944 he returned to Lviv, tasked by the Soviets with a mission to resume the activities of the Medical Institute. He worked as assistant director there until 1948, when his wife Iaroslava Muzyka was arrested (the NKVD intended to deport him from Lviv into the depths of the USSR). In the recollections of an émigré who visited Muzyka toward the end of his life, we find that the physician was convinced the evacuation in 1941 allowed him to escape death.[84] Two weeks before, both the institute's director Oleksandr Makarchenko and the president of Lviv University were called to Kyiv. Muzyka then assumed the president's responsibilities and, before being mobilized, he managed to pass on his duties to the clinic's chief physician, Roman Osinchuk.[85] Osinchuk remained in this function until the German administration took over.[86] He avoided being forcibly evacuated thanks to the coolheaded advice from his Soviet colleague—"be everywhere and nowhere."[87] When the Soviets evacuated Jakub Parnas, dean of the

---

83 Prokopiv, "Spohady," k. 67.
84 M. Kuzyk, "Vidvidyny u d-ra Maksyma Muzyky," Likars'kyi visnyk 21, no. 2 (April 1974): 67–70.
85 Osinchuk, "Orhanizatsiia okhorony zdorov'ia u l'vivs'kii oblasti (1939–1941)," 222–3.
86 Roman Osinchuk was a cabinet minister in the government formed by Iaroslav Stetsko between July 1 and August 1 of 1941. Iaroslav Stetsko's decree relieving Osinchuk of his duties upon his replacement by Lev Rebet was preserved (see Rozporiadzhennia Holovy Ukraïns'koho Derzhavnoho Pravlinnia v Berlini Stets'ka Iaroslava pro zvil'nennia chlena Pravlinnia Romana Osinchuka i peredachu ioho povnovazhen' Levu Rebetu, Tsentral'nyi Derzhavnyi Istorychnyi Arkhiv, f. 380, op. 1, spr. 6, k. 1).
87 Osinchuk, "Orhanizatsiia okhorony zdorov'ia u l'vivs'kii oblasti (1939–1941)," 224.

A manuscript of Irena (Fryderyka) Lille's memoir

faculty, he somehow managed to send word to Osinchuk (Parnas's son delivered his father's regards, which the acting director considered a gesture of exceptional kindness.)[88] As for Marian Panchyshyn, he outmaneuvered the

---

88 Ibid., 226.

NKVD agents. Assigned to guard him, they hid in the basement during bombardment. Meanwhile, the physician disappeared into one of the many hospital nooks. ...[89]

MY LIFE BY IRENA LILLE

Irena Lille finished her memoir in January 1981 in the town of Saint Cloud, near Paris. More than forty years had passed since the beginning of the war. The unpublished memoir presents all the advantages and disadvantages common to ego-documents. For Lille and other authors of such documents, subsequent experiences and knowledge overlap with the events described and distort perspectives, influencing authors' opinions and explications. Reminiscences lose the qualities that accompany independent thinking, and instead adjust to conform to the main currents and the most common interpretations of events. Details and moods, and the sharpness of perspective only seemingly reflect the atmosphere of a bygone period. In actuality, they have been reformatted by a variety of stereotypes.

And yet the world of Irena Lille's memoir pulls us in with a magical force. Her Lviv is not the mythical, lost Atlantis, so prevalent in the nostalgic memories of many former Lvivians; nevertheless, hers is a deeply personal account. Subjective, at times unfair in its judgments, it shows strange gaps, is ripe with errors and contradictions, but remains incredibly valuable, because the author did not attempt to write *history*, even of her own life. She simply wanted to leave behind a *testimony*, and titled it *My Life*. I do not know whom she had in mind when writing these reminiscences, beside her niece Hanna Gnoińska,[90] my grandmother, and my mom. The nephew of Irena Lille, Marian Landberg (Zbigniew Isalski), left this world before Irena penned her story. Perhaps her Paris girlfriends were her readers as well. The memoirs did not make it to Israel, where Lille's sister emigrated after the war. In January 1984, my mom, returning from her first trip behind the Iron Curtain, brought back a Xerox copy of the manuscript. Another thirty years have gone by since that moment.

---

89 For similar accounts regarding the circumstances that allowed Panchyshyn to dodge the evacuation orders, see ibid., 225 and Prokopiv, "Spohady," k. 66.
90 For information about the families Tennenbaum and Lille, compare: AŻIH, 2606, k. 1–2; letter to the director of the Department of the Righteous Yad Vashem, Dr. Mordecai Paldiel, AŻIH, YV-93/02/2606.

A CHILD'S PLEDGE

Fryderyka Tennenbaum was born in Lviv in 1903, into the Jewish family of Izaak Tennenbaum and Chaja Urim, née Arem.[91] Her father was a small merchant; her mother died of leukemia, leaving behind four daughters—teenagers Helena, Henryka, and Fryderyka, as well as four-year-old Regina. A noted internist, Dr. Roman Rencki, issued the diagnosis, explaining to the distraught husband that even if the patient had been the Empress Elisabeth herself, he could not save her. Habsburg subjects worshipped Sisi, the wife of Franz Joseph, who had died twenty years before, and whose legend still lived on. As for the Tennenbaums, they were a typical Lviv Jewish family of modest means. Rencki's words, though they sounded like a death sentence, were meant to

The internist Roman Rencki, who miraculously escaped from Soviet prison, was captured by the Nazis and executed on Wuleckie Hills

---

91 Copy of Regina Tennenbaum's birth certificate, AŻIH 2606, k. 1.

make it clear to the patient's loved ones that there would be no saving Chaja Tennenbaum. Not because the family could not afford the cure, but because the illness was terminal.

More than sixty years later, Irena Lille begins her memoir with this very scene and the decision she made then and there: to discover a treatment for this incurable disease. An aunt led the other sisters away, but the author—then still Fryderyka Tennenbaum—stayed by her mother's side until the end. That is when she swore to devote her life to medicine and to invent a cure for leukemia, because "no mother should die, leaving behind young children, we must learn how to fight leukemia." She stuck to her resolve despite exceptionally unfavorable circumstances: a difficult family situation, the reluctance of her closest relatives (who opposed the young woman's ambitions), admission caps for Jewish students (*numerus clausus*), her lack of connections in Lviv's relatively closed-off medical community, the necessity of giving up her academic career because of anti-Semitic excesses in the later 1930s, and finally her traumatic war experiences and forced emigration from Poland.[92]

RH DISEASE

During the interwar period, women rarely practiced the hard sciences, let alone biochemistry. In Lviv, Fryderyka Lille was the only female hematologist. Jakub Parnas saw talent in the young woman, and on his recommendation she found work in Groër's clinic. This recognition gave her wings and she flung herself into research. Together with professor Stanisław Progulski she administered a blood transfusion to a baby born with Rh disease. At that time, she coauthored a number of studies with Maksym Muzyka and Stanisław Progulski, among others.

Forced to give up her academic career because of the increasing antisemitism, Lille opened a private laboratory at 4 Fredro Street with a former colleague from the Social Insurance Fund hospital, Dr. Olga Balik (married name Gürtler). She did so on the advice of her boss Franciszek Groër. The lab was located nearby Groër's residence, and Groër would send his patients to the two physicians. My mom's godmother, Zofia Gierczycka, was a lab technician there

---

92 By way of comparison: Ignacy Chiger, from a well-off Lviv family, was not able to attain a medical education. He was the father of Krystyna Chiger, author of the memoir *The Girl in a Green Sweater*. Agnieszka Holland based her screenplay for the 2011 film *W ciemności* on Chiger's book.

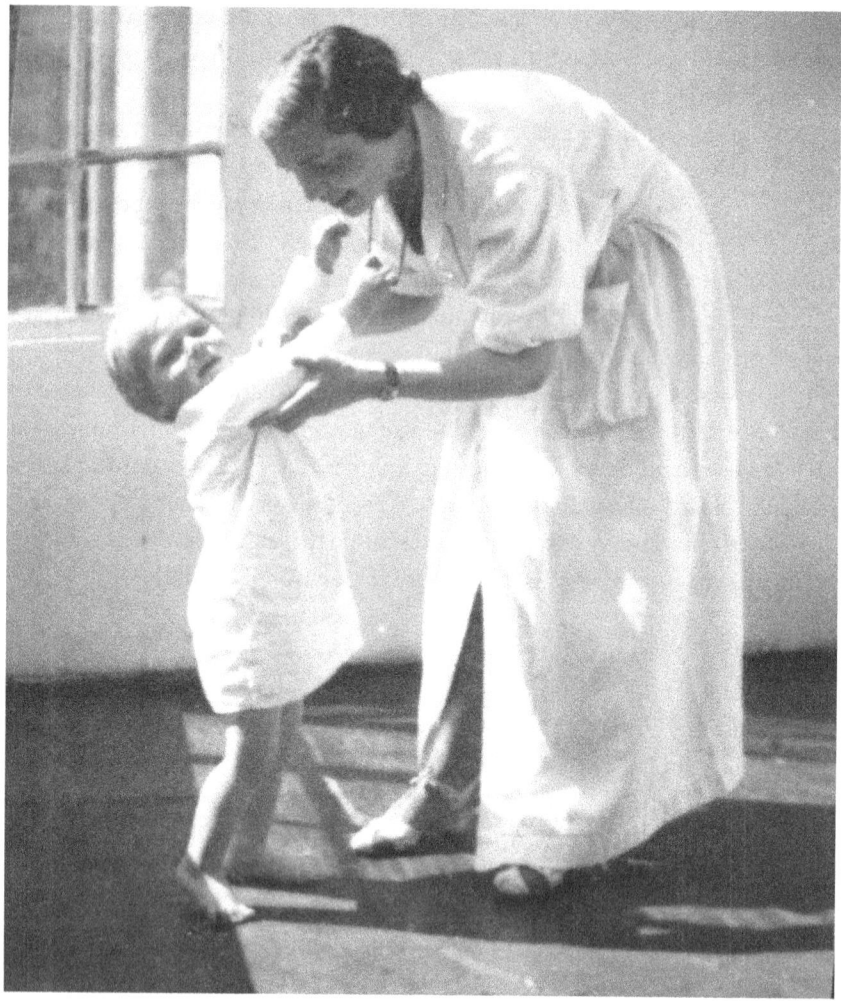

Fryderyka Lille at the pediatric clinic

as well. Despite giving up her job at the clinic, Fryda Lille continued working together with professor Franciszek Groër, who secured for her a research scholarship underwritten by Tespa, a producer of potassium salt. Thanks to him, in the mid-1930s Lille interned in Zurich at the clinic of professor Otto Naegeli, and then, in August 1939, in Paris with professor Robert Debré. She returned to Lviv in late September, at the very last moment a return was even possible. In the following weeks, most people attempting to cross the border were arrested.

"POLISH LORDS" OF JEWISH DESCENT

For the first two years of the war, Fryda lived with husband Jan and mother-in-law Sara Lille in their seven-room apartment at the elegant 3 Maja Street (now Sichovykh Striltsiv). The large apartment building belonged to Count Michał Baworowski. The Lilles moved there in the early 1930s, after their financial status had improved considerably. Both Jan Lille, a man from a prosperous family that temporarily had fallen on hard times when his father became ill, and the ambitious Fryderyka Lille, born into a household of modest means, had high aspirations. They socialized with artists they met through Ludwik Lille, as well as with an affluent circle of attorneys and judges (Jan Lille had studied law). To apply today's categories, they belonged to the upper middle class.

At the start of the first Soviet occupation, popular opinion held that Jewish families had a lower chance of being arrested by the NKVD. Thus for two days, Alojzy Gürtler, the husband of Irena Lille's lab partner, hid in the Lille residence.[93] He feared death, since as a prosecutor there were times when he had brought charges against communists. He also served as a prosecutor in the trial against members of the UVO, who attempted to assassinate Józef Piłsudski in Lviv in 1921.[94] His wife, Dr. Gürtler, obtained permission from the authorities to emigrate to the Reich for herself as a Ukrainian and for her husband as a person of German descent.

In fall of 1939 the authorities assigned two tenant families of representatives of the civil and military administrations to the enormous apartment of the "Polish lords"—that is, the Lilles. Additionally, the Soviets converted those rooms where Jan Lille had practiced law into a dormitory for mining school pupils and closed his law office. At first Jan Lille was put to work as both a truck driver and a porter. The Lilles experienced a sudden loss of economic and social standing. But soon their status was somewhat improved when, thanks to Groër's protection, Mr. Lille obtained employment in a preschool as an administrator and supplies purchaser. Also after Groër's intervention, the family was able to get rid of their most burdensome tenants—the young aspiring miners. "Only" two additional families remained: a Jewish Soviet civil servant from Vinnytsia with a wife and child, and a young colonel by the name Boloboiarinov, with his wife and two children. Lille's mother took care of the Vinnytsia

---

93 Lille, *Moje życie*, 32.
94 Grzegorz Mazur "Zamach na marszałka Józefa Piłsudskiego," *Annales Universitatis Mariae Curie-Skłodowska* LX (Sectio F, Historia, 2005): 407–17.

couple's infant. The colonel soon departed for the Finnish front[95] and his elder son grew attached to Jan Lille. This new life was far from idyllic; in addition to constant interactions with their forcibly assigned tenants, the Lilles lived in never-ending fear of being sent into exile. In April 1940 the Soviets conducted massive deportations, which mostly affected the city's residents. What criteria the NKVD applied in selecting the deportees was not readily apparent to most Lvivians.[96] Exiled friends sent back horrifying news. In all likelihood, the Lille's tenants must have lived in just as much fear as the locals.

Ultimately, real danger arrived from an entirely different direction. In late June 1941 the German-Soviet war broke out. The authorities issued evacuation orders for all civil servants and NKVD functionaries. The Lilles split any food stores with their departing tenants to help them survive their journey into the unknown.

Though terror was an inseparable companion of the communist regime, the Lilles did not experience any major threats in the first two years of the war. Their drama was yet to unfold. We do not learn much about the Soviet occupation from Irena Lille's memoirs, which she wrote in a terse manner, typical for reminiscences by Holocaust survivors. Because the latter trauma obscured those earlier war experiences, Jewish survivors tended to either leave out the Soviet occupation altogether or describe it merely in passing.

THE NATIONALITY YARDSTICK

The start of the German occupation marked the beginning of the most difficult period for the Lilles. Here the reminiscences are rich in detail, though some known encounters remain outside of the writer's scope. This includes Sara Lille's life between 1942–43, when, under the name Barbara Mikoś, she stayed with the Lewkowskis. During this time, my grandparents had almost no contact with the Lilles, who had since moved to Lublin. Other threads are also missing from the memoir, for example, assistance for acquaintances who were ordered to move to the ghetto, or Fryderyka and Jan's work with the underground Home Army in Lublin.

But let us return to the start of the German-Soviet war as Irena Lille remembers it. Years later the author described June 30, 1941, the day the German army marched into Lviv:

---

95 Lille, *Moje życie*, 32.
96 Ibid., 95.

Young, beautiful, looking like athletes, they wore unbuttoned shirts with rolled-up sleeves, joyfully singing "heili heilo." Some civilians embrace them, women throw bunches of flowers, in sum, a jubilant mood everywhere. Among the crowd I spot the couple who take care of our building, they wear yellow-blue armbands, Ukrainians!!! Before today they always passed as Polish, and always spoke Polish to each other, Count Baworowski would not have hired Ukrainians as caretakers of his property.[97]

Barely two weeks later Lille and her mother-in-law found shelter in the home of a mixed Polish-Ukrainian couple.

Interestingly, the author rarely uses national categories in her memoir; we tend not to see members of the same social class in terms of a particular nationality. As an example, the author and Dr. Maksym Muzyka cultivated close ties

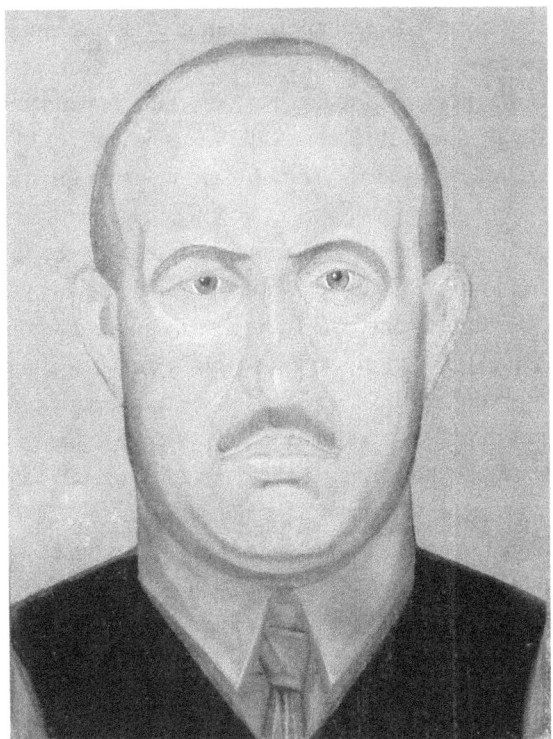

Portrait of Maksym Muzyka, painted by Iaroslava Muzyka, 1924

---

97   Ibid., 34.

in which nationality played little to no part. A physician and microbiologist, older than Fryderyka Lille by more than a dozen years, he was able to pursue an education thanks to his exceptional talent. The same was true of Fryderyka. Muzyka received a scholarship, which he had to work off as a military doctor in the Austrian army once he graduated from medical school (these events directly preceded the outbreak of World War I). In 1919, the Health Minister of the short-lived Western Ukrainian People's Republic, Ivan Kurovets, nominated Muzyka as director of the Institute of Bacteriology in Stanislau. In 1924 he began lecturing at the Medical Faculty of the Ukrainian Underground University. His parents were simple people, caretakers of an apartment building at Reytana Street, where Poles and Jews rented flats. They spoke Polish at home. Although Polish was Muzyka's first language, he made a conscious political choice to embrace a Ukrainian identity.

It was with Maksym Muzyka that Fryda Lille published her first scholarly article. Her memoir makes no reference to Muzyka's nationality. Not once does she mention his wife, the Ukrainian painter Iaroslava Muzyka, a friend of Ludwik Lille's, who—as the author was surely aware—together with my grandmother provided assistance to their ghetto-dwelling acquaintances, including the family of Fryda's sister. Whenever Lille refers to her closest colleague and lab partner, Dr. Olga Balik-Gürtler, she again sidesteps the question of nationality. A different standard applies to the newcomers from the USSR, whom Lille presumes to have come from the lowest social classes and who, in her eyes, have one thing in common—they are culturally primitive people. To illustrate, "a Russian, a very primitive man, Dr. Trehub" makes the decision to hire Lille. At all levels of the Soviet administration (and in Soviet society overall) Lille sees ordinary and vulgar people. These traits seem especially prominent in the Jewish man from Vinnytsia, who was forcibly assigned to her apartment.[98] The wives of officers and civil servants, and Soviet women overall, lack moral norms when it comes to sexuality (Michał Brystygier voices a similar sentiment in his conversation with Teresa Torańska, referring to "the sex life of savages," though he leaves out this detail in a parallel interview published in a Ukrainian periodical.)[99] In Lille's eyes, her Soviet "tenant" was a woman of loose morals ("Colonel Boloboiarinov was fighting in Finland and rarely received a few days of leave

---

98 Ibid., 31, 30.
99 Teresa Toranska, *Śmierć spóźnia się o minutę, Trzy rozmowy Teresy Torańskiej. Michał Brystygier. Michał Głowiński. Adam Daniel Rotfeld* (Warsaw: Agora, 2010), 42; "Mykele, Maikl, Michel', Mykhel' … Beseda Nykolaia Rasheeva s Mykhalom Brystyherom," *Iehupets'* 22 (2013): 393–5.

to come home, and his wife gladly took advantage of it, spending nights with the neighbor Grishchenko").[100]

Ukrainians appear only intermittently in Irena Lille's memoirs; more often than not they belong to the lowest class. Among them are a nameless maid from Sygniówka (now Syhnivka), who offers the Lilles a place to stay so they can wait out the worst period. There were also the building caretakers from 3 Maja Street, whose blue-yellow armbands frightened Lille. Lastly there is the driver Slavko Bilewicz, who undertakes the dangerous mission of driving Jan Lille to Lublin when Jan's closest Polish relatives refuse to. The Lewkowskis' next-door neighbors are also Ukrainians, of course "terrible anti-Semites." Beyond references to persons of "the lower classes," a mention of a Ukrainian national appears once more, in a poignant context. She makes a reference to a Ukrainian who implemented new German orders at the clinic, thus confirming a deeply rooted preconception: Ukrainians collaborate with Germans.[101]

WELCOMED WITH FLOWERS

The image of a gleeful welcome, familiar from Lille's recollection, appears in many other testimonies as well. When Polish and Jewish authors reminisce, specific elements are repeated: Lviv's Ukrainians greeted Germans with joy, suddenly revealed their previously hidden Ukrainian identity, and proudly took to wearing blue-yellow armbands. Multiple studies describe that day in a similar manner. It may seem as though these writers faithfully capture the two moods that filled Lvivians on June 30, 1941: Polish and Jewish majorities were terrified, and the Ukrainian minority was overjoyed. Yet doubts creep in when we read about jubilant crowds and compare those reports against statistical data. Let us recall Lviv's ethnic makeup: about 160,000 Jews and a similar number of Poles lived in the city,[102] whereas before the war about 50,000 Ukrainians lived in Lviv, putting them at just sixteen percent of the population. Although in the summer of 1941 approximately 60,000 Ukrainians resided in Lviv, they still amounted to sixteen percent.[103]

---

100 Lille, *Moje życie*, 32.
101 Irena Lille mentions a Dr. Kotsyubiak (ibid., 37). I did not come across this or a similar name in materials related to the Medical Institute.
102 Eliyahu Yones, *Smoke in the Sand: The Jews of Lvov in the War Years 1939–1944* (Jerusalem: Gefen, 2004), 131.
103 According to German data, in December 1941 150,000 Poles and over 60,000 Ukrainians lived in Lviv. Numbers supplied by the Ukrainian occupation newspaper *L'vivs'ki visti*,

Lviv welcomes the Germans, late June 1941

Let us hear from Ukrainian authors for a moment. The young writer Ostap

---

October 5, 1941 are close: "Lviv's population is around 319,606, among them 4,441 Germans, 60,544 Ukrainians, 145,446 Poles, 111,467 Jews, 2,441 Volksdeutsche." Grzegorz Hryciuk, an authority on this issue, shows these statistics to be biased; they intentionally inflate the overall numbers while deflating the number of Poles (Grzegorz Hryciuk, *Przemiany narodowościowe i ludnościowe w Galicji Wschodniej i na Wołyniu w latach 1931–1948* [Toruń: Wydawnictwo Adam Marszałek, 2005], 236, figure 30). Starting in 1942, Olena Stepaniv led the statistics department in Lviv. See Iaroslav Dashkevych, *Postati* (Lviv: Piramida, 2007), 580. Stepaniv was one of the best-known Ukrainian figures of prewar Lviv and had fought in the Ukrainian Galician Army. In 1943 she published the statistical data collection *Suchasnyi L'viv*. Zhanna Kovba asserts that this sort of publication, as well as materials on the history of Galician towns that Stepaniv printed, were meant to challenge the occupiers. See Zhanna Kovba, *Liudianist' u bezodni pekla*, 160–63. At the turn of the 1930s and 1940s, Olena Stepaniv was in contact with Volodymyr Kubiiovych, author of *Atlas of Ukraine and Neighboring Countries*, a polemic against the findings of Eugeniusz Romer and critical of Romer's method of data collection from the 1931 population census. Per this census there were almost 100,000 Jewish inhabitants in Lviv. In 1939 the number increased to nearly 120,000. Iakov Honigsman asserts the following statistics for Lviv's population in the summer of 1941: 160,000 Jews, 156,000 Poles, and 52,000 Ukrainians (*Katastrofa evreistva Zapadnoi Ukrainy* [Lviv: n.p., 1998], 94). Despite an influx of Jews in fall 1939, we can assume that the percentages did not change significantly until mid-1941, as Soviet deportations and repressions plagued Lvivians across all nationalities, though in different waves. An influx of OUN activists, and the return of refugees from 1939, who, as Ukrainians, now held a privileged status, helps explain the increased numbers of Ukrainians in Lviv in the summer of 1941.

Tarnavsky did not hide his enthusiastic reaction to the change in occupiers because now the streets displayed Ukrainian national symbols. But he also noted a pogrom:

> Blue-yellow flags appeared on buildings. Streets were filling with Lviv lowlifes. Immediately the persecution of Jews began. I myself almost got beaten up because I was not wearing the blue-yellow armband, which guaranteed that no one would touch you. Various characters procured those armbands; they did not even know Ukrainian but were now reacting to everything they lived through under Soviet rule.[104]

The author's intent is clear—to blame the pogrom of early July on Lviv's lowlifes misrepresenting themselves as Ukrainians. Myroslav Semchyshyn writes in a similar vein, omitting, however, some vital details.[105] Ievhen Nakonechny, as a young boy, witnessed Germans marching into a suburb of Lviv. He recalls women welcoming the "Nachtigall" battalion with flowers and cheering: "Slava Ukraini!"[106] Accordingly, it turns out that Ukrainian sources corroborate the image of a warm welcome. Should we then trust those diaries since they tell the same story? Should we allow that a minority of sixteen percent would be able to organize a mass demonstration in order to gain an actual or a delusional advantage?

Yet other testimonies exist and they compel us to scrutinize the scene of mass welcome and flowers for the marching German units. Ignacy Chiger, father of the "girl in the green sweater," writes that Poles in Lviv greeted the Germans no less enthusiastically than Ukrainians did and justified their reactions with *Schadenfreude*: "now not only Poland, but the boastful, imperial Russia has fallen as well."[107] His words raise a suspicion: what if, when authors recall the ethnic makeup of those jubilant crowds, they are guided by their own identifications?

It is important to remember that, in contrast to Chiger's recollection, a different picture dominates accounts by other Polish writers: the joy of traitorous

---

104 Ostap Tarnavs'kyi, *Literaturnyi L'viv* (Lviv: Prosvita, 1995), 67.
105 Myroslav Semchyshyn, *Z knyhy Leva: Ukraïns'kyii L'viv dvadsiatykh-sorokovykh rokiv: spomyny* (Lviv: Naukove tovarystvo im. Shevchenka, 1998), 97.
106 Ievhen Nakonechnyi, *"Shoa" u L'vovi* (Lviv: Piramida, 2006), 95.
107 Ignacy Chiger, *Świat w mroku*, 81.

Ukrainians who had long been awaiting this event, and the horror of everyone else. Relatively rare are divergent testimonies, such as the reminiscences by the physician Adam Krechowiecki and mathematician Stanisław Hartman, who also recall a celebratory welcome, but one given by the Polish population.[108] Their words against yours. Majority against minority. Once we take a look at testimonies more immediate than those penned many decades later, the image changes. The more recent accounts conform to the dominant narrative: during the German occupation Polish society formed a unified front and resisted the occupier. But sources from the time contradict this accepted formula; the mood among Polish Lvivians was indeed joy, or at least satisfaction that change was coming. According to a report for the Headquarters of the Home Army from October 1941 about the situation in Lviv, Bolshevik terror was "incomparably more intense than German terror." As a result, Poles widely "consider the current times blessed in comparison to the Bolsheviks; this explains the favorable attitude Poles display towards Germans as a whole, and toward the German military in particular."[109]

In his diary, Tadeusz Tomaszewski offers a similar account of the atmosphere among Lviv's inhabitants. The psychologist depicts the enthusiasm with which Lvivians greeted the Nazi army, focusing on the psychology of the crowd. His observations, as he recreates the sequence of events in detail, are spot on: the rabble first takes to robbing stores, then participates in destroying Soviet emblems, and ends by actively joining in an anti-Jewish pogrom.[110] The news of NKVD atrocities—while retreating from the city, the NKVD still made sure to murder thousands of prisoners—triggered horror and a wave of outrage. The conclusion is self-evident: "It's good that we are rid of these savages."[111] The psychologist catalogues the reasons why people are pleased with the German seizure of Lviv:

---

108 Stanisław Hartman, "Wspomnienia," OK AW II/639, k. 15; Krechowiecki, "Okupacja sowiecka we Lwowie," k. 100. "[A]lmost everyone who was watching the constant stream of Hitler's tank armada driving through the city, which lasted several days, was happy! [The Nazis] were greeted as saviors. Saviors from an evil far worse!"

109 "Report from 28–29.10.1941," Gabinet Rękopisów. Archiwum Biura Informacji i Propagandy Komendy Głównej Armii Krajowej (Biblioteka Uniwersytecka w Warszawie, n.d.), k. 2.

110 Tomaszewski, *Lwów. Pejzaż psychologiczny*, esp. 61–2.

111 Ibid., 65.

1. Antisemitism, persecution, and humiliation of Jews fulfill a primitive sense of justice, a need for revenge for life's misfortunes. Of this opinion are janitors, impoverished intelligentsia, ... and priests. ... Others rejoice, because once Jews are removed from their positions, there will be more posts for Aryans.
2. An end of the war on religion. ... People are moved by the sound of church bells, which ring again after a long silence.
3. A higher cultural polish of the Germans, neatly dressed, clean, intelligent looking ...
4. Order. Everyone talks about how order will soon reign.[112]

Tomaszewski's notes refer here almost exclusively to Lviv's Poles. The psychologist also noted a radical shift in mood that occurred in late July: people expected Soviet victory and hoped for a miraculous rescue by Great Britain.[113]

The sociologist and philosopher of culture Stanisław Ossowski left a highly interesting, though thus far unpublished testimony. Ossowski came from Warsaw; he had been a reserve officer, and after the defeat of September 1939 found himself a refugee in Lviv. In the fall he began working at the Lviv Ossolineum, in its manuscript collection, alongside a well-known librarian and researcher named Mieczysław Gębarowicz. His diary is more fragmentary than Tomaszewki's and is of a more personal nature. It reflects the attitudes of only one milieu: the intelligentsia. As a sociologist, this author also takes note of a favorable attitude towards Germans. He describes the behavior of an Ossolineum librarian: to welcome the Nazis, the man dressed up as if for church, and greeted the stretched-out colonnades with a raised arm (but was supposedly unsure which arm to raise):

> "Go ahead, sir, take a look at the street: it is like Easter. Yes, I am a Pole, and these are Germans, but I tell you, Hitler is a Godsend."—Indeed, after yesterday, the street makes an unexpected impression. Despite the early hour, plenty of people watch the motorcade drive by; from time to time a round of applause; for the most part the soldiers get flowers. Łącka Street is already closed, they will be filming the massacre victims. I return home, running on the way into Ukrainian women with flowers for the soldiers.[114]

---

112 Ibid., 67.
113 Ibid., 96.
114 "Dziennik Stanisława Ossowskiego, podporucznika WP w 1939 roku. 27.08.1939–2.07.1941," OK AW II/3301, k. 46.

Lviv cinemas began showing a documentary about the victims of the massacre in early August, once Lviv was incorporated into the General Government. The press printed numerous materials devoted to atrocities the Soviets had committed in prisons. Soon new strands emerged: the NKVD had carried out mass executions in Kyiv and in Vynnytsia. Eventually, the Katyn massacre came to light as well. From the point of view of German propaganda, such news coverage would secure unconditional loyalty among the locals in the conquered territories of Eastern Europe. Whether that actually happened is an entirely different story.

In late June, Lviv greeted the marching Germans with flowers. Especially joyful were those who had no clue about German policies regarding Jews, or those whom such policies left feeling indifferent. The testimonies I referred to above leave no doubt: not only Ukrainians, but Poles too, rejoiced. A later revision, necessary to fit the dominant patriotic canon, successfully shifted the narrative: the jubilant majority shrank into the Ukrainian minority.

Subsequent events, especially the pogrom and mass persecutions of Lviv's Jews, have only recently become the subject of careful research, and of heated disputes. I do not intend to quote either the accounts or the arguments. What is beyond doubt is that in July 1941 2,000 Jews lost their lives, regardless of their

German soldiers film a pogrom. Lviv, early July 1941.

age, gender, or social status. The only factor that mattered was their ethnic origin. The Nazis carried out their Holocaust mission in Lviv as they did in other cities and towns. Nonetheless, it would have been significantly more difficult for the Nazis to achieve their murderous goal without participation of the community, frightened and demoralized by recent Soviet terror.

UNSUNG HEROES

But the Nazis were not able to terrorize everyone, nor were they able to immediately force Lvivians to assist in their atrocities. On June 30, 1941, a former Ukrainian maid came to the Lilles' apartment. She lived just outside of Lviv, in Syhnivka, and proposed putting them up at her home in order to ensure their safety. The Lilles did not accept her help for various reasons, though just one of them suffices: Sara Lille was partly paralyzed and, given the circumstances, it was not only dangerous, but downright unrealistic to transport her anywhere. The next offer of assistance came from Mrs. Kugel, the wife of the building administrator, herself a Polish Jew, who offered to take the Lilles in.

The social roles are significant here: persons from the lower strata of society step forward ready to help, in particular a Ukrainian servant and the Jewish administrator of a building owned by a Polish aristocrat. Lille declines the first opportunity, but takes advantage of the second, far less safe option. We can attribute her decision to the poor condition of the elder Mrs. Lille and the perilous situation in town, which made transporting a sick person impossible. Her choice probably also reflects a subconscious desire to preserve their prestigious position. Lastly, it is conceivable that the Lilles did not realize how grave a danger they were facing.

After the Germans marched into Lviv, Fryda Lille reported to work at the clinic, following an order issued by Lviv's new commander, posted in the city on July 1, 1941. It is July 2, 1941. Her boss, Franciszek Groër, reports in detail what he saw and heard.[115] He also informs his staff that Ukrainians, favored by Germans, have taken over key positions in the clinic, but have suggested that the professor continue overseeing the research. But it quickly became obvious that no academic work could take place. The occupiers prohibited lectures, though the clinics had to continue their work. Thus any favoritism, if it took place at all, was fleeting.

Marian Panchyshyn, the former director of the District Health Care Division, was able to evade Soviet evacuation orders, unlike the Medical Institute's assistant

---

115 Zygmunt Albert quotes a detailed account by Franciszek Groër in *Kaźń profesorów lwowskich*, http://www.lwow.com.pl/albert/albert-pl.html.

director, Maksym Muzyka. On June 30, 1941, Panchyshyn was nominated as the health minister in the "government" of Iaroslav Stetsko, and Dr. Roman Osinchuk (his former assistant) and Oleksandr Barvinsky as deputy ministers. In early July, Panchyshyn brought in Dr. Tyt Burachynsky as well and called a meeting. There, the quorum decided to propose resuming the activities of the Medical Institute to the Germans:

> Dr. M. Panchyshyn and R. Osinchuk initiated the reactivation of the Medical Institute. They took up the matter immediately after the Germans marched into Lviv. "Historically" it occurred during a meeting of four physicians: prof. M. Panchyshyn, Dr. T. Burachynsky, Dr. O. Barvinsky, and R. Osinchuk. At that time, they also divided the responsibilities: prof. M. Panchyshyn and R. Osinchuk would reactivate the institute, Dr. O. Barvinsky would head the Health Department of the city of Lviv, and Dr. T. Burachynsky would lead the Medical Association as well as the Ukrainian People's Clinic in Lviv. One and a half months later the institute hired Dr. L. Maksymonko and Ol. Podolynsky from Cracow, who, thanks to their contacts with the German authorities in the capital of the so-called General Government, contributed to reactivating the institute.[116]

Simultaneously, the Ukrainian Red Cross began its operation under the leadership of Dr. Leonid Kurchaba, whom the Germans arrested only a few weeks later in August 1941.

As Prokopiv mentions, Panchyshyn had not served as Lviv's chief of the Health Protection Department since at least since July 12, 1941.[117] After eliminating Stetsko's government (the Gestapo arrested Bandera, as well as Stetsko and a few other members of his cabinet—all OUN activists), on July 4, 1941 the temporary German administration appointed Marian Panchyshyn to provisional administrator of the Medical Institute (the prewar Medical Faculty). He continued in this function until Karl Schulze, an associate professor sent from Berlin, made changes among some of the Panchyshyn-nominated clinic directors, promoting Adam Gruca, Franciszek Groër, Zygmunt Albert, and Bolesław Jałowy, among others.[118] German became the language of instruction, which

---

116 Dr. Iulian Movchan, "Dvadtsat' piat' rokiv tomu (u 25-ti rokovyny smerty d-a M. Panchyshyna," *Likars'kyi visnyk* 15, no. 4 (October 1968): 51.
117 Prokopiv, "Spohady," k. 71.
118 Ievhen Stets'kiv, "Studiï u L'vivs'komu Medychnomu Instytuti v roky Druhoï svitovoï viiny 1939–1945," *Narodne zdorov'ia* 11–12 (2009): 248–9.

the faculty accepted without complaint.[119] A climate of denunciations about who played what role under the Soviets poisoned the institute. But no harm came to Groër, Jałowy, or Panchyshyn.[120]

"NEW ORDER"

At the beginning of July, Fryda Lille was still working at the laboratory in Groër's clinic. The day after the execution of Lviv's professors, Groër showed up in the clinic. He looked unrecognizable. He told her of his arrest and release, of the torture and deaths of those who were arrested alongside him. We know his account from another source:

> Upon arriving at the clinic, professor Groër learned about the arrests of additional physician colleagues, whom he did not see that night. They were: professor of pediatrics Stanisław Progulski and his son Andrzej; furthermore, the professor of dentistry Antony Cieszyński; professor of surgery Dobrzaniecki; professor of medicine Włodzimierz Sieradzki; head of the Ophthalmological Clinic Dr. Jerzy Grzędzielski; prof. Witold Nowicki with his son Jerzy. [121]

Of his physician friends, Roman Rencki, the most notable internist in Lviv, also perished. It was Rencki who a quarter of a century earlier had diagnosed Fryda's mother. A few days prior to his execution, Rencki was one of the few persons who miraculously escaped Soviet prison, together with the priest Rafał Kiernicki. The NKVD arrested him for hiding his income from a sanitarium in Morshyn, which he had established and led for many years. The Soviets turned it into a political charge, accusing Rencki of using the money to provide support to the Polish resistance. All interventions on his behalf were fruitless; even a delegation of professors headed by Marian Panchyshyn did not achieve his release.[122]

After the horrors of the night before, Franciszek Groër was in shock. He reported to the hospital in the morning but was not able to work. Irena Lille walked him from the clinic at Głowiński Street to his home at 8 Romanowicza.

---

119 Iulian Movchan, "Studiï medytsyny u L´vovi za nimetskoï okupatsiï," *Likars´kii zbirnyk: Medytsyna i biolohia. Nova seriia* 17 (2010): 235.
120 Prokopiv, "Spohady," k. 71.
121 Schenk, *Der Lemberger Professorenmord und der Holocaust in Ostgalizien*, 132.
122 Spetssoobshchenie o khode pereseleniia iz zapadnykh oblastei v vostochnye, 13.04.1949, HDA SBU, f. 16, op. 3, spr. 55, k. 115.

His physician colleagues who were also his next-door neighbors or lived down the street—professor Jan Grek, Tadeusz Boy-Żeleński, Adam Sołowij (who lived at number 7), Witold Grabowski (number 3), and Tadeusz Ostrowski (number 5)—had already left this world.

The Lviv Ghetto was fenced off with barbed wire

That day the Lilles resolved to leave Lviv, which was easier said than done. To not report to work at the hospital would mean being charged with sabotage—so stated the promulgation. To go to work could mean death because of her Jewish background. How to escape from Lviv when you are caring for a half-paralyzed mother? How to obtain permission to move when you have been stripped of all rights as a Jew? In mid-July, the occupiers prohibited Lvivians from changing their residences or leaving the region. In late July, the mandatory ousting of Jews from their residences began. In the following months limitations imposed on Jews were becoming increasingly more restrictive: in the fall the ghetto borders were drawn, and in 1942 it was no longer permissible to cross its borders.

The next day, July 5, 1941, brought no less turmoil: German authorities ordered administrators of the clinic group at Głowiński Street to transport all employees of Jewish background to the Gestapo headquarters at Łącki Street, a building which had already earned a terrifying reputation. Fryda Lille was the only Jew in the pediatric clinic; from the other clinics several dozen people were grouped together. A truck brought them there. This form of transport speaks volumes; they were not treated as physicians, nor as normal people, or even as *Untermenschen*, subhumans. A Gestapo officer's whim would decide their life or death. In the prison courtyard, the Gestapo man demanded that the group name the surgeon who had operated on German soldiers while smoking a pipe. Silence was the only answer, and this enraged him. He threatened to shoot them all. The news of what happened to Lviv's professors, the majority of them physicians, had already made the rounds in Lviv and certainly reached the clinics where those executed doctors had worked. None of the arrested had any doubt that they would meet a similar fate.

Fifty years later, Irena Lille reconstructs that day in detail:

> Squeezing a vial with cyanide in my hand, I muster up the courage to say in German that what he is asking is impossible, because in Poland every surgeon must wear a surgical mask, so it would be impossible for him to smoke a pipe. The Gestapo man gave me a hostile look, I thought he would beat me, and I placed the ampule in my mouth. He approached me and instead of hitting me, he shouted: "Schweig, silence!" He turned around with disgust and I carefully took the ampule out of my mouth, keeping it in my hands at the ready, in case they started beating me. The evening was near, we are still standing in rows against the wall of the prison courtyard, waiting for what was to come. Suddenly, as if he got bored with the wait, he shouted for the driver to take us back. Quickly, we get in the car, afraid they may change their minds, and we drive back to the hospital.[123]

After those events, Fryda Lille's return to the clinic was out of the question. In mid-July the city's commander issued a new order: all Jews must wear white armbands with the blue star of David. This is when Fryda Lille poured all her inventiveness and connections into saving her husband and mother-in-law.

THE END OF ALL ILLUSIONS

Meanwhile, in early July, Jan Lille had initially decided to return to the insurance agency which he managed before the war, since Germans reinstated private enterprise. During the Soviet occupation, thanks to Groër's intervention, Lille found work in a preschool as an administrator and supplies purchaser. His decision proves once more how strongly the Lilles were beholden to their status. There is no doubt that at first the couple did not quite grasp the

---

123 Lille, *Moje życie*, 38.

harm they faced as Jews. Neither belonged to the Jewish community or was religious (Jan Lille, in contrast to his brother Ludwik, left the community and converted to Protestantism), and they were married in a civil ceremony. The Lilles were Jews with Polish and European identities, as were many Lvivians of that generation. They were reminded of their Jewish roots only when others insisted on pointing it out or tried to limit their opportunities for advancement. Two years of Soviet rule, which officially condemned anti-Semitism and intentionally promoted "equal opportunities" (while persecuting "the lords"), probably dimmed their awareness. Moreover, the Lilles did not own property and rented the very spacious apartment at 3 Maja Street. It had belonged to Count Baworowski, and since the fall of 1939 was city-owned.

Additionally, the two allies, the Soviet Union and Hitler's Germany, carried out similar information policies among the populations of the territories they occupied. They took great care to prevent the spread of incriminating news; the two governments even signed an agreement to cooperate in pursuing political crimes. Thus the only knowledge of what went on in the German-occupied territories and their official policy of extermination of Jews had to come from direct reports. But in the spring of 1940 the border was closed and most refugees from the General Government ended up in NKVD prisons. Lvivians who did not have contact with people fleeing east probably had not yet heard about the mass murders of Jews, although they knew that in larger cities Germans were creating ghettos.

During the first period of the occupation, the mood in Lviv fluctuated. This depended not only on ethnicity or social standing, but also on personal experience. Many people who previously lived in USSR-occupied areas nurtured illusions about the Germans. As Soviets intensified their punitive measures, the sentiment that "Satan himself will be better than Stalin" gained popularity:

> People had various ideas of the Satan who was supposed to show up, and not all of them looked like the Devil. They knew very little about the persecution in the General Government, which was occurring on a large scale. I myself did not learn about Oświęcim [Auschwitz] until several months later. That is not to say that I had any illusions. But there were many Lvivians who still associated Germanness with the Schönbrunn palace rather than with the chancellery of the Reich. Regardless of how people imagined the approaching second invader, they rejoiced in the reversal of fortunes: two of the powers who had partitioned Poland, yesterday friends, today were at war. The feeling was also that the Germans would come and go, while Russians had looked like they would stay forever. Jews could not

expect anything good—that much was obvious. And Ukrainians? There is probably a lot to clarify here, but I am not the one to do that.[124]

The author of this historical account, Stanisław Hartman, had fled from Warsaw to Lviv, and was thus much more in the know than most Lvivians. It was self-evident to him what the Jews ought to assume. However, even if Lviv's inhabitants were familiar with reports from the General Government, the older generation especially believed that things would go differently in Galicia. Still alive was the memory of Galicia as a crownland of Austria-Hungary, and it provided reassurance that Lviv the province would enjoy a more autonomous status.

By the time the "new order" had been in place for a month, the atmosphere in Lviv deteriorated. People had barely gotten a chance to shake off the horrific discovery of the mass murders in Soviet prisons when the new occupier began dealing fresh blows: arrests, executions, pogroms. Ukrainians who were pro-German had hoped to attain an autonomous status, but their aspirations were shattered when on August 1, 1941 the District of Galicia was incorporated into the General Government. And any remaining delusions that the fate of Galician Jews would be different vanished in the first week of the new regime.

The Lille family likely reasoned this out in the ways outlined by Hartman. Jan Lille was familiar with German culture, spoke the language fluently, and was an experienced attorney. He opted to resume work at the insurance firm "Silesia," whose owner was a Silesian German. The new director, a Czech German by the name Giżycki, initially hired Mr. Lille, but once he found out Lille's ethnicity, he advised him to join a branch office in a different town where people would not know him as well as they did in Lviv. At the advice of another agent in the same firm, the Lilles decided to procure so-called "Aryan papers," take on new names, and move to Lublin, where "Silesia" was just about to open a new branch office. Lille's former secretary arranged for a Catholic priest to offer Jan the birth certificate of his deceased brother. Jan was the first to move to Lublin, already under his new name: Michał Korolewicz. His former driver, the Ukrainian Stanisław Bilewicz, drove him there. It was mid-July 1941. A year later, Jan saw "Silesia's" director, an Austrian named Otto Juhn, in Warsaw. Juhn asked Korolewicz point-blank whether he was Jan Lille from Lviv. Lille could

---

124 Stanisław Hartman (1914–92), a professor of mathematics and physics from Wrocław, born into an assimilated Jewish family in Warsaw, wrote his account of the war years in the winter of 1979. Between 1939–41 Hartman studied in Lviv. In 1942 he was imprisoned in Pawiak Prison (Warsaw); in the 1970s he developed ties to the anti-communist opposition in Poland (Hartman "Wspomnienia," k. 12). Also see his posthumous publication: Stanisław Hartman, *Wspomnienia (lwowskie i inne)* (Wrocław: Leopoldinum, 1994).

not deny it. He experienced a moment of horror as Juhn lifted the telephone receiver. The director was calling his wife and inviting Lille to dinner.[125]

LITTLE HOUSE ON MĄCZNA STREET

In late July of 1941, Fryda and her mother-in-law vacated their residence in the apartment building formerly belonging to Count Baworowski. The location had become too dangerous: an elegant street, one of the most representative buildings, with Luftwaffe officers assigned to the same floor. The Lilles' furniture was gradually requisitioned. Fryda was certain that the occupiers would not stop at furniture and that both Mrs. Lilles must vanish from sight. And so Fryda and her mother-in-law moved into a room in my grandparents' (the Lewkowskis') small house at 38 Mączna Street. Fryda's former lab technician, Zofia Gierczycka, godmother of the infant Halina Lewkowska, helped her find the room. Both Lille women already had Catholic birth certificates, naming them as Irena Szyszkowicz and Barbara Mikoś, procured with the help of Dr. Wanda Ciepielowska.

The Lewkowskis were a married couple of mixed ethnicity: she of Ukrainian origin, he a Pole who cultivated the memories of "the good old times" of Austria-Hungary, where he had served as a cannoneer and then went on to become a clerk at an appellate court. Fryda Lille, who as recently as June 30 had panicked when she saw the administrators of her building display Ukrainian armbands, found a safe shelter at Mączna Street. Shelter for herself, her mother-in-law, and in the coming terrifying months, also for her sisters and nephew.

Dr. Helena Krukowska frequented the house at Mączna Street, and in the evenings professor Groër came from time to time as well. They brought increasingly terrifying news. In early September 1941 Eufrozyna Lewkowska, who together with Iaroslava Muzyka delivered food to close and distant acquaintances in the ghetto, ran into Stanisław Landberg, Fryda Lille's brother-in-law. He pleaded with her to get his wife Henryka and son Marian out of the ghetto. Once again, though this time with difficulty, two birth certificates were obtained. By then the process was much more problematic than in July 1941, because the Nazi administration had cracked down on sources of fake birth certificates, and the local Nazi propaganda paper *Gazeta Lwowska* published denunciations of priests who baptized people (issuing a false birth certificate carried the death penalty).[126] Equipped with new documents, Henryka and Marian traveled to a health resort in Rymanów at the suggestion of a physician friend. Later, the

---

125   Lille, *Moje życie*, 45.
126   *Gazeta Lwowska*, November 8, 1941.

Nazis conducted a manhunt at the resort. Many of those who came there to hide were arrested, including Henryka Tennenbaum (Maria Kwiatkowska). Henryka's sister Helena, also staying in Rymanów, was able to save little Marian Landberg from immediate detention (his name according to the false birth certificate was Zbigniew Isalski) by bribing a policeman. She herself evaided the raid not only thanks to her papers, but also on account of what back then people called "the right looks." But for Henryka and Marian, papers were not sufficient, because their appearance, according to Nazi measurements, was "non-Aryan." Helena took the boy back to Lviv. Marian returned to his father in the ghetto, and was then sent to a labor camp on Janowska Street. Again, the child was rescued from hell. Naturally he turned up at Mączna, where in addition to the two Mrs. Lilles, Helena Lipl (neé Tennenbaum), now known as Maria Różycka, moved in. Dr. Helena Krukowska from Groër's clinic cared for little Marian, who fell ill with typhus. In the little two-room house with a kitchen lived seven or eight people. How Eufrozyna Lewkowska was able to feed three women, a gravely ill child, and her own family—a bedridden husband and a two-year-old daughter—when in the fall of 1941 Lviv was almost entirely devoid of provisions, will remain her secret. After the boy recovered, Fryda Lille sent her nephew and her other sister, Helena, to Warsaw. Both survived, though they were separated.

THE FLIGHT

In the fall of 1941, Irena Szyszkowicz (Fryda Lille) found work as a secretary at the Lublin branch office of "Silesia," managed by her husband. Officially nobody knew that they were married. Every month Irena took a perilous trip on the Lublin-Warsaw train to deliver money to the Bakals, a couple who were sheltering Marian in the Warsaw neighborhood of Żoliborz. According to her memoir, she and her husband began aiding the underground Lublin Home Army, as Irena Szyszkowicz and Michał Korolewicz.[127] In July 1944, made wiser by her Lviv experiences at the start of the Soviet occupation, they prevailed upon their commander to not hang up the banner "Headquarters of the Polish Home Army" on the gates of a home where they lived. (Operation "Tempest" or *Plan "Burza"* was a strategy ordered by the Polish government-in-exile in London, which required that the Polish Home Army take control of any territory of the former Second Republic of Poland which the Soviets were about to "liberate," no matter what the

---

127 Lille, *Moje życie*, 56–7.

human cost.) If the account is accurate, the Lilles' wisdom from their time in Lviv helped not just them, but their entire underground cell, avoid Soviet retribution.

In August 1944 Michał Korolewicz and Irena Szyszkowicz enthusiastically greeted the new government. It is not clear how they first came in contact with Hilary Minc. Minc was an important figure in the Union of Polish Patriots, coauthor of the Polish Committee of National Liberation (PKWN) manifesto, chief of the economic office of this quasi-government, later the Minister of Industry and Commerce, an architect of centralized economic planning, and finally the man responsible for the apparatus of political repression. It is not likely that they met him during Minc's short stay in Lviv during the Soviet occupation. Perhaps Hanna Hirszfeld, a pediatrician and professor of the newly founded Maria Curie-Skłodowska University in Lublin, where Irena Szyszkowicz worked in the clinic of Ludwik Hirszfeld, helped establish the connection. Hanna Hirszfeld (née Kasman) might have used her influence on Leon Kasman, who at the time lived in Lublin and led the propaganda department of the Central Committee of the Polish Workers Party (KC PPR). It is also possible that the puppet government was urgently searching for loyal and competent appointees. Either way, Jan Lille owed the high position he held until the mid-1950s to Minc. In 1944, Minc proposed that Lille come work for him and … that he'd best retain the Polish name he adopted during the occupation.

As Irena reminisces, Lille/Korolewicz assumed an influential post, directing the Cracow Center for Petroleum Products (CPN) until 1950. Subsequently he transferred to Warsaw, to the State Commission for Economic Planning, where he worked directly with Hilary Minc. Both he and his wife were party members. At the turn of the 1940s and 1950s they feared repercussions, as a purge swept the party ranks. Disguised as a fight against cosmopolitanism, it ran "very much counter to what I imagined as the main line of the party's work."[128] However, Korolewicz avoided sanctions and major problems, even though the party removed his mentor from the post of chairman of the State Commission for Economic Planning (PKPG) in March of 1954. Until his departure for Paris to attend his brother's funeral in April of 1957, Lille lived with the constant expectation of arrest.

In the spring of 1957, Irena Szyszkowicz had to once more conquer her anxiety about being separated from her husband. In May 1957 she returned to Warsaw to hastily close a chapter of her life—the era of Stalinism, and the years of her biggest scientific successes. Moving to Paris, where she lived until her death, allowed her to finally abandon fear.

---

128 Ibid., 73.

Opening ceremony at the beginning of the academic year 1929-30, Jan Kazimierz University in Lviv

CHAPTER 3

Academic Snapshots

As a teenager, I was passionate about mathematics. Among my favorite readings were *Lilavati* by Szczepan Jeleński, and somewhat later, *Mathematical Snapshots* (*Kalejdoskop matematyczny*) by Hugo Steinhaus. One of the best Polish books on popular mathematics, it continues to garner interest among readers today, awakening the scientist in the child, and the child in the scientist. In contrast to their engaging puzzles, the authors themselves did not interest me much. In my youthful arrogance I elevated mathematics to the queen of all sciences, and truly believed that I would succeed in untangling those puzzles the *Snapshots*' author could not solve. It never even crossed my mind that in the future I might follow the call of the humanities. Now, as an adult, I sometimes receive dubious compliments such as "the best mathematician among Polish scholars of Ukrainian literature." As Steinhaus once said: "That is how it goes in our country: to praise, for instance, a mathematician, you would say 'What a true humanist!' and to knock down a humanist, shrug your shoulders and say, 'Oh well, a humanist!'"

Back in the mid-1970s, I had no knowledge of the Lwów School of Mathematics and Philosophy, or about its creators. Nor did I know that the first edition of *Snapshots* came out in Lviv in 1939 and was, at least in part, a "side product" of mathematician gatherings at Scottish Café (*Kawiarnia Szkocka*). For the Lviv mathematicians and philosophers, this café, located at the corner of Fredro and Akademicka streets, became the nexus of their world. Neither had I heard of the legendary, almost secret *Scottish Book* (*Księga Szkocka*)—a collection of mathematical problems along with their solutions.

Much has been written about *Scottish Book*. Its first edition appeared through the efforts of Stanisław Ulam, a professor at Harvard University, who received the manuscript Steinhaus handwrote in 1956. *Mathematical Snapshots* was thus the author's version of *Scottish Book*. As it turned out, it was Steinhaus who made the last entry in *Scottish Book*, dated May 31, 1941, barely four weeks

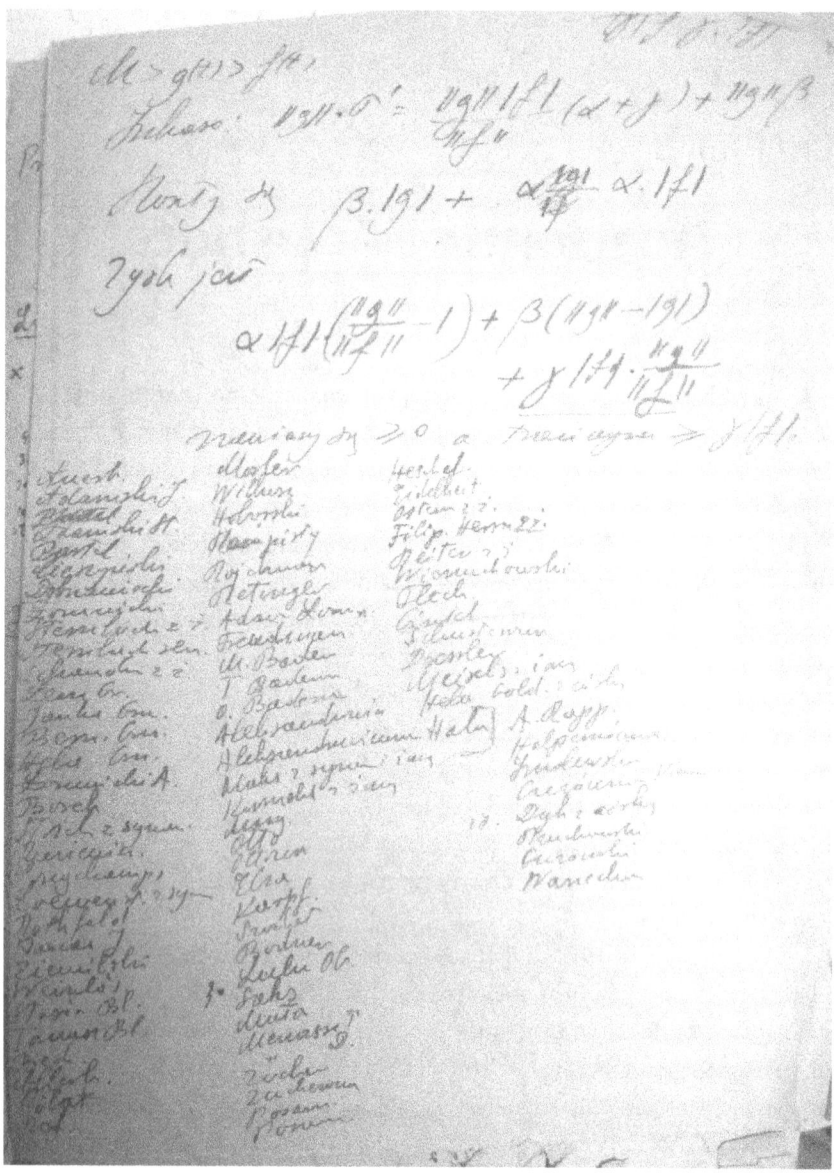

Hugo Steinhaus's notes with names of Lviv professors, 1942

before the German military marched into Lviv. My own copy of *Kalejdoskop/Snapshots* from 1956 keeps silent about the first, prewar edition, published by the Lviv press "Atlas." The People's Republic of Poland avoided references to pre-1945 private ownership, and even more so to prewar Polish borders which had included Lviv. Another detail I could not have known then is that the

Hugo Steinhaus

mathematical bestseller's Russian translation assured the Steinhauses' financial survival in the second year of the Soviet occupation.

Hugo Steinhaus, born into an affluent Jewish family in the Galician town of Jasło, served in the Polish Legions at the start of the Great War. In 1920, after becoming a professor of analysis at Jan Kazimierz University, Steinhaus began to gather outstanding mathematicians around him. We cannot overstate the indispensable role he played in the emergence of the Lwów School of Mathematics and Philosophy. An unprecedented and consequential hire occurred at Steinhaus's prescient recommendation: Jan Kazimierz University engaged Stefan Banach, even though Banach had not finished his degree. Overall, Steinhaus held an exceptionally prominent position among academics. In a society where ethnic background played a decisive part in one's scientific career, universities did not typically select non-Poles as institute directors. Yet Steinhaus, in addition to leading his own institute, also enjoyed extraordinary authority.

At the start of the German occupation, the Steinhaus family vacated their Lviv residence at 14 Kadecka Street after Gestapo officers ransacked the apartment and beat up its owner on July 4, 1941. They ordered the family to pack up valuables of interest and announced they would return the next day. Steinhaus immediately decided they should flee. The couple snuck out of the apartment building through the courtyard into the garden of an adjacent villa. From there, undisturbed, they set off into the unknown. They walked together at a leisurely pace, she with a rose picked from the garden as a goodbye, as if it were a regular afternoon stroll and nothing disturbing was happening around them.[1] The next week signaled the beginning of the end for Lviv's Jews. The Steinhauses found shelter in apartments belonging to Lviv's intelligentsia—with the Blumenfelds, Indruchs, Witkowskis, and finally in the villa of professor Benedykt Fuliński, a biologist, at 82 Tarnawski Street. Steinhaus befriended Fuliński, who propped up his guests with advice and uplifting forecasts about the end of the war and the mathematician's future fortune. Steinhaus claims that those predictions turned out to be 100 percent accurate. The biologist, however, did not survive the war—he died in 1942, suffering from severe depression.

The Steinhauses remained in Lviv until fall of 1941. Though the Fulińskis' villa was quiet and secluded, they were afraid that the neighbors might denounce them. For the remainder of the occupation the couple hid together with Stefania Steinhaus's mother, who used the birth certificate of Benedykt Fuliński's mother. Initially they stayed at Zimna Woda near Lviv, and later moved to Berdechów by Stróże. After the war, Steinhaus founded the Department of Mathematics at the University of Wrocław, once again attracting a group of distinguished academics. Years later his achievements were condensed in a manner as poignant as it was laconic: Thanks to Steinhaus, Polish mathematics rose from the ashes of World War II. This recognition was long overdue, as the prewar period of Polish mathematics had been fading into obscurity for a long time, and its war years had fallen into complete oblivion.

HOLIDAYS ON THE RIVER PRUT

In July 1939, Hugo Steinhaus and his wife Stefania were relaxing in the Carpathian Mountains, in the resort town of Iaremche, and in August they

---

1 This is how Hugo Steinhaus remembered it; Tadeusz Tomaszewski offers a different memory (Tomaszewski, *Lwów. Pejzaż psychologiczny*, 76). I was not able to locate the manuscript of Steinhaus's memoir from the war period and compare the original version from the 1940s against the 1990 edition published in London. The five-volume typescript of his memoirs from the turn of the 1960s and 1970s, preserved in the Ossolineum manuscript division, differs from the published edition in only a few, relatively unimportant details. The Archive of the Polish Academy of Sciences, home to the Steinhaus bequest, contains but a fraction of his pre-World War I reminiscences, edited in the early 1970s for the periodical *Znak*. This and subsequent chapters rely on Abe Shenitzer's English translation of Steinhaus's memoirs (Steinhaus, *Mathematician for All Seasons: Recollections and Notes*, 292–4).

moved to the nearby villa of the Krzemickis in Kamień Dobosza (in Ukrainian, Kamin Dovbusha, today part of Iaremche). A few train stations away in Vorokhta, Hugo Steinhaus's most notable disciple, Stefan Banach, was on holiday too. In contrast to the escalating international tensions, the August weeks on the river Prut passed in a bucolic atmosphere. The resort's climate, mountain hikes, and Chornohora's landscapes allowed for an illusory peace, at least for someone not familiar with the rhythms of Hutsul life, determined by herding sheep and cows in the *polonyny*, or mountain pastures. It was then that the Steinhauses went on their last trek through Chornohora, from Kostrych to Żabie (now Verkhovyna), with their daughter Lidia and son-in-law Jan Kott, Ewa and Irena, the daughters of the Lviv Polytechnic professor Antoni Łomnicki, and the university attorney Stanisław Hubert. At the same time Stanisław Vincenz and his friends also were hiking up to the mountains. Usually gregarious, this time the shepherds herded their animals down in silence. It was a month earlier than their custom dictated, no doubt effecting huge losses on their already poor households. But they had no choice: the authorities ordered that the border zone be vacated. Putting out camp fires and closing their shanties, they filled casks with milk and cheese and descended to their homesteads. The mountains were deserted. Barely a month later, new hosts appeared. Instead of the traditional Hutsul greeting "Slava Isu!" ("Glory to Jesus!") and the reply "Slava na viky Bohu Sviatomu, i Vam,

Hugo Steinhaus and Wacław Sierpiński after the war

panochku" ("Eternal glory to Holy God, to you as well, sir"), any hikers now would now hear the Russian "Stoi, kto idet?" ("Freeze, who is there?").

In Kamin Dovbusha, the Steinhauses conversed with Hugo's two colleagues—Wacław Sierpiński from Warsaw and Stanisław Ruziewicz, at the time president of the Lviv Academy of Foreign Trade. Despite the holiday and the general atmosphere of unease, their discussions returned to mathematics. Though both men considered Steinhaus a scientific authority, behind his back they called into question the Polish identity of this former soldier of the Legions,[2] as well as his idea that assimilated Jews should play a part in propagating allegiance to Polish cultural tradition. In a letter from September 18, 1938, Wacław Sierpiński expressed his outrage at Tadeusz Hollender, whose article suggested that Jews had a claim to Polish culture:

Stanisław Ruziewicz was executed on Wuleckie Hills

---

2   Marek Gałęzowski, *Na wzór Berka Joselewicza. Żołnierze i oficerowie pochodzenia żydowskiego w Legionach Polskich* (Warsaw: Instytut Pamięci Narodowej, 2010), 594.

"'Until recently Jews represented Polish nationality just as well as Poles themselves' (Congratulations!). ... Is this Hollender what *he seems to be* or maybe he is *of the same religion as Hugo*?"³

Steinhaus belonged to a relatively large group of Galician Jews educated in Polish secondary schools in the era of Galician autonomy, who were ardent enthusiasts of Polish culture. The future mathematician came of age during the period of modernity or the era called Young Poland (*Młoda Polska*) and was a member of a semi-legal library in Jasło; he especially enjoyed the prose of Stefan Żeromski and Władysław Reymont. About the famous nineteenth-century author Henryk Sienkiewicz, however, he expressed ambivalence—on the one hand he valued him as a writer, on the other felt that his books subscribed to the cult of the Szlachta, or Polish nobility: "Żeromski, Reymont, and Tetmajer, did not need to struggle to win our hearts—we were overcome at once. ... Although we liked Sienkiewicz, we regarded him as a reactionary and were ashamed that we read him. ...."⁴

Steinhaus's colleagues displayed a fairly typical attitude towards other ethnicities; they viewed their national community in ethnic terms and, consequently, excluded non-Poles. They did not see anything untoward in it and allowed those attitudes to guide their everyday lives, such as finding the "right" bed and breakfast, which meant "Christian." In his last letter to Ruziewicz, from June 19, 1939, Sierpiński writes about a planned stay in Kamin Dovbusha: "The matter of Kamienica [Kamień] Dobosza has me worried. Eight złoty per day is too much for me. When do you leave? Do you already have confirmation that *the bed and breakfast is Christian and good*?"⁵ [emphasis mine]

The hostess in Kamin Dovbusha was a Lviv historian named Zofia Krzemicka (from an assimilated Jewish family), a friend of Ivan Kedryn and Mykhailo Ostroverkha. Kedryn was staying next door, and Ostroverkha was taking care of the neighboring property. The two were Ukrainian journalists, connected not just through their profession, but also their past—both had fought for Ukraine's independence. Yet their political views differed fundamentally: Kedryn belonged to the liberal wing of the Ukrainian National Democratic Alliance UNDO, which promoted the "organic development" of Ukrainian society, and Ostroverkha favored the circle of Dmytro Dontsov and

---

3   Witold Więsław, "Listy Wacława Sierpińskiego do Stanisława Ruziewicza," *Roczniki Polskiego Towarzystwa Matematycznego, Seria 2: Wiadomości Matematyczne* 40 (2004).
4   Steinhaus, *Mathematician for All Seasons: Recollections and Notes*, 29–30.
5   Więsław, "Listy Wacława Sierpińskiego."

the OUN, which accepted violence as a means for political change. Steinhaus refers to Kedryn as well informed, and explains the circumstances of his friendship "with the Ruthenian"—he was related to the villa's resident and socialized with the owners, the Krzemickis, as did "another Ruthenian, Mr. Ostroverkha." The scientist carefully emphasizes the distance between him and the two Ukrainians and highlights the circumstantial character of their relationship, but does not forget to note that when the police came to arrest Ostroverkha, Mrs. Steinhaus supplied him with some provisions.[6] In contrast to Steinhaus's colleagues, Ostroverkha, though undoubtedly prejudiced against Jews, considered their Judaism as a virtue. About the professor's family he wrote:

Mykhailo Ostroverkha left prison just before the Soviet army marched in, and barely two months later fled to the German side

"honest people, not converts."[7] It did not cross his mind, as it did not occur to Steinhaus's colleagues, that these judgements reflected anti-Semitism. In this odd (yet typical for the time) manner, he was voicing respect for people who retained allegiance to their traditions and ancestral faith.

Ostroverkha's memoirs, written in Rome in the first half of 1940, depict his September 1 arrest in minute detail, yet they make no mention of Stefania Steinhaus's empathetic gesture.[8] Perhaps her behavior did not fit Ostroverhkha's stereotype of others? The journalist published his recollections almost twenty years later, with apparently only minor editorial changes.[9] While a similar interaction did make it into Ostroverkha's 1940 manuscript, the specifics differed from what we hear from Steinhaus. Ostroverkha recalls that "The commandant

---

6   Steinhaus, *Mathematician for All Seasons: Recollections and Notes*, 223.
7   Ostroverkha, Ostroverkha Papers, k. 10.
8   Mykhailo Ostroverkha, *Na zakruti. Osin' 1939 r.* (New York: self-published, 1958).
9   Ibid., 14–20.

agreed that I could leave my watch and money with Mrs. Zofia Krzemicka. He brought those to her. She then sent back some bread and tomatoes."[10] These minor discrepancies would not merit attention if they did not underscore the ethnic relations so well: one side positions itself as superior, the other downplays a gesture of human solidarity, excising it altogether from later reminiscences.

In Kamin Dovbusha, all conversations focused on the geopolitical situation and the looming war. Hardly anyone doubted the threat, especially since Hitler's address on April 28 and Polish Foreign Minister Józef Beck's speech at the Sejm on May 5, 1939. Beck announced that Polish diplomacy would do all in its power to assure peace. Yet he also made this poignant proclamation: "We in Poland do not know the concept of peace at any price. There is only one thing in the lives of men, nations, and countries that is without price. That thing is honor." Steinhaus, overly critical of Beck's diplomatic achievements, griped that a simple Hutsul could predict more about the international situation than the Polish foreign minister, eager to put on airs as a statesman.

Drawing parallels between mathematics and world politics, Steinhaus likened the war to a competition which could be analyzed using the theory of probability.[11] His interlocutors applied categories applicable to political prognoses, far from the perfection of mathematical formulas. Their predictions varied, but in the last week of August, after Ribbentrop's visit to Moscow, confidence gradually gave way. Worried Ukrainian peasants brought their fears to Steinhaus: "(S)ir, if there will be … [war], we shall all perish."[12] Newspapers had to stay optimistic and on message, and local authorities prosecuted anyone disseminating news that could spark panic.

Among the vacationers, Ivan Kedryn was a particularly sharp critic of Europe's political situation, and of Poland's vulnerabilities. Like Steinhaus, he too had served in the Austro-Hungarian army in 1915 and fought on the Russian front. In 1916, after Steinhaus's mother intervened with the military administration, her son was able to return from the Volhynia front to Cracow. There—in his own words—he made his greatest scientific discovery by meeting Banach. Kedryn, a half-orphan (his father died when Kedryn was eleven) from a mixed Jewish-Ukrainian family, was wounded in 1916 in a battle by his hometown of Berezhany. He spent the rest of the war in Russian captivity, in a camp near the Russian-Mongolian border. After the Bolshevik Revolution,

---

10 Ostroverkha, Ostroverkha Papers, k. 16.
11 Steinhaus, *Mathematician for All Seasons: Recollections and Notes*, 221.
12 Ibid., 220.

together with Roman Dashkevych who later became director of the *Luhy* (a paramilitary fitness and firefighting society), they made it to Kyiv and began working for newspapers of the Ukrainian People's Republic. During the Bolshevik offensive, he joined Petliura's army and, after the Polish-Ukrainian offensive broke, left Greater Ukraine alongside the remaining military units of the Ukrainian People's Republic. In subsequent years, which he spent as an immigrant in Vienna, Kedryn developed a close affiliation with colonel Ievhen Konovalets. As a member of the executive committee of UNDO, he served as a liaison officer between his party and the UVO, led by the colonel. At Konovalets's recommendation, after returning to Lviv in the mid-1920s, Kedryn worked as a journalist for *Dilo*, the most influential of Ukrainian newspapers. In 1926 he became *Dilo*'s Warsaw correspondent, and then, in 1928, press secretary of the Ukrainian Parliamentary Representation in Warsaw. One of the few Galician Ukrainians who supported the Ukrainian-Polish dialogue, Kedryn remained in touch with the exiled Prime Minister of the Ukrainian People's Republic. In the 1930s, as a declared supporter of the policy of Polish-Ukrainian reconciliation, the journalist participated in semi-official negotiations between representatives of UNDO and the Polish government. Additionally, he took part in unofficial meetings with the political elite, initiated by the former Lviv voivode, Count Piotr Dunin-Borkowski.

As the head of the department of politics at the *Dilo*, Ivan Kedryn-Rudnytsky would not have survived the Soviet occupation. How he made it through the German occupation remains a mystery

The newsman represented Lviv's Ukrainian elite; he belonged to the closed executive committee of UNDO, and as deputy editor in chief he determined *Dilo*'s politics. Through his connections with the journalistic world and with political elites of the Republic of Poland, Kedryn kept quite well informed. Not surprisingly, he was the first to notify the Lvivians vacationing in Kamin Dovbusha that the British Chief of the Imperial General Staff Sir Edmund Ironside deemed Poland's defenses incapable. Though Ironside's statements during his visit and the official communication in its aftermath communicated optimism, unofficial pronouncements show that Ironside did not think it possible for the Polish Republic to make up for the deficiencies in its armament. His proposal to provide an immediate unconditional loan was meant to prove that Great Britain viewed its ally duties toward Poland seriously, in hopes of discouraging Hitler from declaring war.[13] But—as we well know—this diplomatic maneuver had no bearing on German politics: the Reich was moving full steam towards war.

Curiously, Kedryn himself, as he acknowledged in his memoirs, did not think the war would come. A colleague from the newspaper, Ivan Nimchuk, remembers Kedryn's mood: "He wrote to us [the editorial team] carefree letters, in no way believing in the impeding war."[14] Perhaps the information he received from Warsaw forced Kedryn to adjust his perspective. Yet when he shared the grim news, the Lvivians vacationing on the Prut dismissed it as sensationalist. It contrasted sharply with the propaganda slogans widely publicized in newspapers and on posters: "strong—united—ready" and "we shall not give up even a single button," and with the official statements by Marshal Rydz-Śmigły: "If anyone in our country counts on moments of weakness, once again he will be sorely mistaken. And anyone abroad betting on such an opportunity should know that we do not reach for what is not ours, but we will not hand over what is. Not only shall we not hand over our entire uniform, but shall not give up even a single button. And let it be known that this is the decision of our entire nation."[15]

Six months later, already during the Nazi occupation, Kedryn wrote in his *Prychyny upadku Polshchi* [*The Causes of Poland's Fall*]: "When a future historian of the Polish nation looks through annals of periodicals and compares what was written then against what actually occurred, he will arrive at terrible conclusions."[16]

---

13 Edmund Ironside, *Time Unguarded: The Ironside Diaries* (New York: McKay, 1963), 77–81.
14 Ivan Nimchuk, *595 dniv soviets'kym viaznem* (Toronto: Vydavnytstvo i drukarnia oo. Vasyliian, 1950), 6.
15 The press and government propaganda communications frequently invoked this quote from a speech Poland's Marshal Edward Rydz-Śmigły gave at the XII Legionnaires Reunion at Sowiniec on August 6, 1935.
16 Homo Politicus [Ivan Kedryn-Rudnyts'kyi], *Prychyny upadku Pol'shchi* (Cracow: Ukraïns'ke vydavnytstvo, 1940), 242.

Bitterness about Poland's defeat and about the government's conduct in the face of the war dominated the public mood. In the streets of Lviv one often heard locals ridicule the Polish propaganda effort by distorting the slogan of "strong—united—ready" as "strong—against the weak; united—by the trough; ready—to flee."[17] Both occupiers skillfully tapped into this disillusionment in their own propaganda, with the aim of recruiting ethnic minorities to their cause.

Politics being his greatest passion, during the German occupation Ivan Kedryn adopted the pen name Homo Politicus. In his foreword to *The Causes of Poland's Fall*, the journalist assured his readers he did not intend to "kick a man when he is down," nor did he act out of *Schadenfreude*, even if Ukrainians in Poland had good reason to feel it. In fact, he ranked the ethnic policy of the fallen Polish Republic as "political mockery." His true motive—Kedryn asserted—was to arrive at the "historical truth," to establish an accurate picture of political and social life in interwar Poland, and to understand the true, internal causes of Poland's defeat. Later, the author stated that his book was branded as "'anti-Polish libel,' written either at the directive of the Germans, or at least in order to curry favor with them." Without a doubt, Kedryn, as well as the entire UNDO leadership, judged Poland's policy toward the Ukrainian minority as egregious. Published and unpublished sources alike reveal that Ukrainian political leaders remained equally embittered in subsequent years. Ivan's sister, Milena Rudnytska, a well-known politician and social activist of the interwar period and president of the Ukrainian Women's Union, was an editor of a (never published) study indicting Poland's pre-World War II policies, titled *Dvadtsiat rokiv polskoyi svavoli na Zakhidniy Ukraini* [*Twenty Years of Polish Lawlessness in Western Ukraine*].[18] Whatever the assessment of Polish interwar politics may have been, it must have outraged his former colleagues for Kedryn to publish *The Causes of Poland's Fall* in the direct aftermath of Poland's defeat. After the war, Kedryn maintained that he wrote the book solely out of a desire to come to terms with the past, so that in the future the errors would not be repeated.[19] His assurances notwithstanding, it is impossible to read it without cringing.

---

17 Zdzisław Zieliński, "Lwowskie okupacje. Wspomnienia," OK AW II/1501/2, k. 3.
18 "Zhyttiepys Mileny Rudnyts'koï," *Vidnova* 1 (1984): 126.
19 Ivan Kedryn, *Zhyttia—podii—liudy. Spomyny i komentari* (New York: Chervona Kalyna, 1976), 169–70.

In later publications, written in exile, Kedryn tried to justify why some of the Ukrainian political elite in Galicia harbored a pro-German sentiment: "We were not the only naïve ones. Polish officers fled from the Germans to the Soviet Union, supposedly an ally, only to perish in the Katyn Forest."[20] Here, Kedryn draws a parallel between the strategic error of Ukrainian leadership and the flight of Polish officers to the Soviet zone, which ended in the Katyn atrocity. In my opinion, this assessment proves that he failed to understand that OUN's leadership and the Ukrainian Central Committee activists made a strategic error when aligning themselves with the Germans. Its gravity would weigh heavily on future judgements of the Ukrainian independence movement. Kedryn's anti-Soviet attitude further clouds his analysis; clearly, when the Polish military and its commanders retreated east, they were not following a political strategy, rather they simply found themselves at a desperate dead end. Lastly, it will be remembered that prior to September 17, Polish eastern territories were not part of the USSR, thus Kedryn's stipulation that the officers fled into the embrace of an "ally" is downright false.

Hugo Steinhaus's second Ukrainian interlocutor, Mykhailo Ostrverkha, a would-be opera singer, journalist, and translator, managed the villa of the Ukrainian Society of Writers and Journalists in Kamin Dovbusha. He correctly predicted that the treaty signed on August 23, 1939 signaled a German-Soviet pact at Poland's expense.[21] Earlier, persons spreading such news had to face the court; Steinhaus recalls a news report from a trial against a Hutsul who reportedly said over a drink at the tavern: "You will soon see Russia making a deal with Germany against Poland." The charges against him were hastily dropped once the Polish Telegraphic Agency officially announced the Molotov-Ribbentrop treaty.[22] It may be true that the authorities released a person or two on the eve of the war, yet at that very time they certainly imprisoned many more than they let out (communists, representatives of Ukrainian and German minorities), under the suspicion of disloyalty to the Polish state.

The police came for Ostroverkha on September 1, 1939, as they did for other educated Ukrainians, wielding a decree by the Minister of Justice and general prosecutor Witold Grabowski. Most likely they targeted the journalist

---

20 Ivan Kedryn, "Pol'shcha vpala i nas zadavyla," *Novyi shliakh*, September 29, 1979, quoted in Ivan Kedryn, "U mezhakh zatsikavlennia," *Biblioteka ukrainoznavstva NTSh* 53 (1986): 97.
21 Ostroverkha, *Na zakruti. Osin' 1939 r.*, 18.
22 Steinhaus, *Mathematician for All Seasons: Recollections and Notes*, 220.

because of his close contact with the circle of Dontsov's *Visnyk*. The accused suggested that a woman staying at the Krzemicki villa had denounced him, but he did not provide details. His published memoirs remain silent about the copies of *Visnyk* he was hiding in the attic.[23]

The journalist chronicled his last few days of freedom and the first day of the war in detail. The day ended in a walk along the Prut with Steinhaus's daughter and wife, followed by dinner and conversation at the Krzemicki villa. His written record of the chat on September 1 shows that Ostroverkha made sure to keep his political opinions close to his chest:

> "Well, we have a war with the Germans!" she [Krzemicka] exclaimed.
> "Well, well!" I replied enigmatically.
> "Oh, sir! That's not good! It won't be easy with the Germans!" professor Haustein [Steinhaus] chimed in, walking out onto the terrace.
> I stayed quiet. I knew who was who. Besides, the smartest thing a Ukrainian could do in a war between Poland and Germany was to remain silent and do his best to turn things to our advantage.[24]

In the book edition, Ostroverkha abbreviates this conversation; in that version, Steinhaus simply predicted that "terrible times" would come "that we cannot yet imagine."[25] The published book and its manuscript differ ever so slightly, yet the discrepancy reveals that the Ukrainian author (who by that time was living in New York) did not want to fall out of step with the dominant discourse of World War II.

We can glean the most details from Ostroverkha's account of the time he spent in jail in Delyatyn and then in prison in Stanislau, which he left with several dozen Ukrainian prisoners on September 19, 1939.[26] Given the circumstances, it is hardly a surprise that anti-Polish statements abound in those passages as well.

Steinhaus claimed that Ostroverkha preferred the Soviets to the Nazis.[27] When we take into account the journalist's biography, this assertion becomes dubious: he was in Russian captivity during World War I, and had a subsequent

---

23 Ostroverkha, Ostroverkha Papers, n.d. k. 13; Ostroverkha, *Na zakruti. Osin' 1939 r.*, 17.
24 Ostroverkha, Ostroverkha Papers, k. 14.
25 Ostroverkha, *Na zakruti. Osin' 1939 r.*, 18.
26 Ibid., 14, 18–55.
27 Steinhaus, *Mathematician for All Seasons: Recollections and Notes*, 173.

fascination with Italian Fascism, evident from his publishing record at the time.[28] The foreword to his book, published more than a dozen years after the war, contextualizes his perspective on Poles, Russians, and Germans: "I thank God for allowing me to wrestle out of Polish factiousness, Muscovite nihilistic obscurantism, and the German loathing of other races."[29]

In his notes from 1940, Ostroverkha takes an even sharper aim at the Polish policy toward Ukrainians, and at the Polish state.[30] The published version also preserves his negative attitude about the Soviet Union. However, passages in which Ostroverkha accused Mykhailo Rudnytsky, the brother of Ivan Kedryn, of collaborating with the Soviets (which the author blamed on the family's Jewish roots), are gone.[31] If we compare the 1940 manuscript against the 1958 book version, Ostroverkha's take on the geopolitical situation in Eastern Europe remained decidedly anti-Polish and anti-Soviet. However, he walked back his once favorable attitude towards Germans: in the manuscript, Germans are considered allies in the Ukrainian fight for independence, but the book pronounces them yet another occupier and oppressor.

Another author who reminisces about escaping from the areas invaded by the Red Army is Osyp Nazaruk. Unlike Ostroverkha's account, Nazaruk's last volume from the winter of 1939/1940 begins with a lamentation: "I was fleeing my homeland ... my country,"[32] which becomes a leitmotif in the memoirs of this Catholic journalist. Evidently he and other Ukrainian politicians reacted to the demise of the Polish Republic with mixed feelings. His description of the journey from Lviv to Warsaw provides many such examples: on the one hand, Nazaruk wholeheartedly sympathizes with victims of the war and mourns deeply as he makes his way through the ravaged country, and on the other, he muses that with Poland's defeat God has punished the country for its indifference towards its Ukrainian citizens and for the violence to which it subjected them.[33] In contrast, Ostroverkha shows no sympathy. He focuses on acts of brutality that the Polish civil and military administration perpetrated in early September 1939 on Ukrainians. Later, in the 1960s, he notes curtly: in

---

28 Mykhailo Ostroverkha, *Nova imperiia: Italiia i fashyzm* (Lviv: Dorohy, 1938).
29 Ostroverkha, *Na zakruti. Osin' 1939 r.*, 6.
30 Ostroverkha, Ostroverkha Papers, k. 3, 17, k. 97–9.
31 Ostroverkha, *Na zakruti. Osin' 1939 r.*, 105.
32 Osyp Nazaruk, *Ucieczka ze Lwowa do Warszawy. Wspomnienia ukraińskiego konserwatysty z pierwszej połowy października 1939 r.* (Przemyśl: Południowo-Wschodni Instytut Naukowy, 1999), 33.
33 Ibid., 60–110, esp. 86–7, 108.

November 1939, "I tore myself out of Soviet claws"—meaning he crossed over to German-occupied territories.

Later in October, seeking companions for the escape from the Soviet territories that he was plotting, Ostroverkha saw the Steinhauses once again. They met after the People's Assembly convened, but before the USSR formally incorporated Western Ukraine. There he also spoke with Zofia Krzemicka, who despite her Jewish ethnicity contemplated fleeing to Warsaw along with Polish officers. However, Ostroverkha deemed this option too risky for himself. For one, the NKVD was conducting intensive hunts for officers of the Polish Army, secondly, he was afraid that the Poles might turn on him because of his Ukrainian ethnicity.[34] His later fate was shared by many Galician escapees (though his six-month stay in Rome was an exception); the journalist spent the remaining years of the occupation in Cracow and Lviv. Although he maintains that the Gestapo was looking for him, this assertion lacks credibility, given that he was then continuously writing for *Krakivski visti* and *Lvivski visti* under his own name. In line with the efforts of other Ukrainians, Ostoverkha published poetic reports from Lemkivshchyna.[35] Ukrainian intellectuals who found themselves (unwillingly) in the General Government sought to brand Lemkivshchyna (as well as Kholmshchyna and Pidliasshia) as lands that were ethnically Ukrainian. This strategy brought the practical advantage of awarding a comparably higher status to the Ukrainian population in those areas in the eyes of the Nazi administration. In 1943, the Military Board of the Ukrainian Central Committee, led by Volodymyr Kubiiovych, offered Ostroverkha the editorial seat in *Do peremohy*, a weekly published by the Division Galizien (Halychyna).[36] After overcoming tedious permit procedures and technical issues, its first issue appeared in December 1943.[37] German authorities fully financed the magazine, even providing an editorial office at 5 Plac Smolki. In summer 1944, Ostroverkha was evacuated. He followed the German administration, as did other Ukrainians who had held official functions during the German occupation. In 1945 Soviet agencies characterized him as a nationalist

---

34 Ostroverkha, *Na zakruti. Osin' 1939 r.*, 124.
35 Mykhailo Ostroverkha, "Vidletily zhaivoronky u vyrii," *L'vivs'ki visti* no. 44, September 28–29, 1941, 2.
36 The Military Board Halychyna published its weekly *Do peremohy* for the riflemen division "Halychyna" between December 21, 1943 and December 30, 1944.
37 Mykhailo Ostroverkha, *Z khroniky redaktsii "Do peremohy"* (manuscript in Ostroverkha, Ostroverkha Papers, box 6, folder 5, k. 1–25).

activist known for his anti-Soviet views[38] (but did not incriminate him of being an OUN member). After the war, Ostroverkha emigrated to the United States and settled in New York.

Unlike the Steinhauses and Ostroverkha, Kedryn managed to return to Lviv right before mobilization, probably on August 30. The following month, he witnessed and participated in significant events, among them a September 1 meeting of activists who pleaded with the Sejm Vice Marshal Vasyl Mudry and the Metropolitan Andrei Sheptytsky to call on the Ukrainian population to remain loyal to the Polish state. He was also privy to all stages of the September defeat. In early September, a major of the Polish Army was assigned to move into Kedryn's apartment; the journalist witnessed the officer gradually losing his poise. On September 17, 1939, both men—the host and his tenant—realized that the Polish Republic had ended. At that moment they each resolved to flee, though in separate directions: the officer toward Romania, and the journalist, who in 1917–20 had fought for Ukrainian independence—into the German-occupied territories (yet again, based on this and other personal experiences, Kedryn should have realized the hopeless position Polish officers faced, yet later pinned pro-Soviet sentiments on them).

An improvised assembly of political activists, in which Rudnytsky also participated, took place on September 17. Two opposing stances emerged there: to stand by one's community, regardless of the danger, or to flee? Kedryn found himself part of the smaller faction which opted to leave Lviv, in his words, "to save our bare skins." Clearly not everyone condoned this decision, in any case not Ostroverkha: "not only squeaky-clean politicians, but also the common political and moral speculator or worse, ran to the Germans. Suffice it to name Zenon Poray-Pelensky, Ivan Kedryn—brother of the famous Mykhailo R."[39] It seems that in Ostroverkha's eyes only nationalists appeared as knights without blemish, but those who sought compromise and attempted to negotiate with the authorities were collaborators.

At the last moment, on September 22, less than a day before the NKVD was to pay him a "visit," Kedryn managed his way out of besieged Lviv. His first escape attempt, towards the Carpathian Mountains, from where he had returned just three weeks ago, failed. Even a pass personally issued by General

---

38 Spravka A. M. Leont'eva nachal'niku 1 Upravleniia NKGB SSSR P. M. Fitinu o zarubezhnoi deiatel'nosti i sviaziakh OUN 15 avgusta 1945 g., in *Dokumenty XX veka. Vsemirnaia istoriia v Internete*, http://doc20vek.ru/node/2301.

39 Ostroverkha, Ostroverkha Papers, k. 106.

Władysław Langner, the commander of Lviv's defense, did not help; he and his companions were told to turn back from the suburbs. Who knows what would have had happened if he, like thousands of Polish refugees, had made it to Romania instead of Cracow. However, the group realized that they were trapped. Staying was not an option because of the danger from the Soviets, but successfully leaving the city would have bordered on miracle. Early in the morning of September 23, the escapees made their way to the German positions, having bypassed a Polish post. Perhaps a contract officer of the Polish Army, himself an immigrant from the Dnipro region, assisted with this miracle, as Osyp Nazaruk suggests.[40]

The German officers who allowed our five Ukrainian refugees to cross the front line could not hide their bewilderment: "Why would you flee? Your people are entering Lviv, your government!"[41] Neither Kedryn nor his companions bothered to clarify, though all spoke German fluently. Experience told Kedryn: in times like these, every minute is of the essence. He had faced the Bolsheviks twenty years before, while fighting for an independent Ukraine. Arrested in 1920 by the *Cheka* (the first Soviet secret police force), he owed his release to a string of lucky circumstances. In contrast to many Galician activists, Kedryn harbored no illusions about the goals and methods of the Soviet authorities. As *Dilo*'s political commentator, he was well familiar with the interior politics of the USSR, and especially with their policy toward the Ukrainian intelligentsia: "'Liberation' of Ukrainians (Belarusians, Lithuanians) from the Polish yoke was a bluff, its goal to pull the wool over your eyes and to hide their true objective: eliminating the center of Ukrainian anti-Soviet 'irredenta,' Eastern Galicia. …"[42] Of course, the author made this pronouncement in hindsight. While we cannot know if he really felt that way back in September 1939, his prior experience (both personal and political, as reflected in his journalistic pieces for *Dilo*) suggests he did.

Thus Kedryn, despite the threat posed by his ethnic origin (his mother was Jewish), set off with his old friend, leader of the *Luhy* society Roman Dashkevych, his brother-in-law Dr. Pavlo Lysiak, a *Plast* (scout) activist named Atanazy Figol, and the leading Ukrainian Promethean, professor Roman Smal-Stotsky, to cross the river San and reach an area controlled by Hitler's army. He only brought a small briefcase, leaving his wife as well as a valuable

---

40 Nazaruk, *Ucieczka ze Lwowa do Warszawy*, 35.
41 Kedryn, *Zhyttia—podii—liudy*, 44.
42 Kedryn, "Pol'shcha vpala i nas zadavyla," 96.

archive—correspondence, notes, and official documents—behind in Lviv. The archive could have provided exceptionally useful sources related to interwar political life. Regrettably, only one notebook was preserved. Kedryn penned his memoirs drawing on this notebook and the plentiful sources housed by the New York Public Library. However, today the notebook is no longer accessible, not having been included in the archives with his bequest.

In late September Kedryn reached Cracow. At first he worked as a translator in the German press office. In early 1940, he began writing for *Krakivski visti*, a periodical published in occupied Cracow by the Ukrainian Central Committee.[43] The editor in chief, a junior colleague from *Dilo* named Mykhailo Chomiak, commissioned a series of articles on prewar Polish policy (the topic was of current interest to German propaganda). Kedryn's book *The Causes of Poland's Fall* is comprised of the pieces he published in the weekly. If we are to believe Kedryn's memoirs, he translated it into Polish with the assistance of Kazimierz Bukowski, a journalist working for Cracow's most popular newspaper *Wiek Nowy*. Before and during the war, Kedryn remained in close contact with Piotr Dunin-Borkowski, and it was supposedly Dunin-Borkowski who wrote the foreword. In the end, the translation was not published. Interestingly, Borkowski, the former voivode, who in the first weeks of the occupation had been hiding from the Soviets at the home of the Lviv attorney Maurycy Axer, also made his way to the German zone. He frequently visited with the Rudnytskys in their Cracow apartment (Ivan Kedryn-Rudnytsky and Mrs. Rudnytska lived with his brother and his brother's wife). Their friendship lasted until they lost touch in 1943. Dunin-Borkowski hid from the Nazis at his friends' property in Wójcza and stopped coming to Cracow after his closest classmate from secondary school Mieczysław Rettinger died at the hands of the Gestapo. Together, Rettinger and Borkowski had sought to establish ties between the Polish and the Ukrainian underground. Father Iosyf Kladochnyi, who served as a liaison between the Polish resistance and the Metropolitan Sheptytsky, was falsely accused of denouncing members of the Polish underground.

Several memoirists blamed Kladochny for the arrests of Rettinger and of General Stefan "Grot" Rowecki. A number of scholars followed this assertion without consulting additional sources. Dunin-Borkowski's close friend, Aleksander Bocheński, attempted to dispel the accusations against father Kladochny by writing to the author Maria Dąbrowska, who was connected with

---

43 Kedryn, *Zhyttia—podii—liudy*, 342–5.

the Polish underground.[44] The events surrounding Rettinger's death prompted Borkowski to fear that, as a known proponent of Polish-Ukrainian cooperation, he had become an easy target and OUN was likely aware of his contacts with Kedryn.[45]

The conversations taking place in August among the vacationing Lviv elite hint at hidden animosities, which stemmed not so much from divergent politics as from deep-seated ethnic prejudice. On the one hand, Polish university colleagues expressed reservations toward the assimilated Jew Hugo Steinhaus; on the other—a Polish Jew openly expressed his animus toward a Ukrainian, a sentiment he shared with many representatives of the Polish elite; lastly—the Ukrainian intelligentsia harbored a deep distrust toward other ethnicities. The latter attitude we witnessed with Kedryn, and even more so with Ostroverkha, as they hid their aversion toward the "titular nation" and concealed their own pro-German sympathies. Such mutual distrust among the elites soon hastened the disintegration of social ties in Eastern Galicia.

In the second month of their vacation, the Steinhauses were joined by their daughter Lidia and her husband Jan Kott. They married in late June in Paris, where she was studying at the Sorbonne, and he was on a scholarship granted by the National Culture Foundation (*Fundusz Kultury Narodowej*). On August 30, posters advertising general mobilization appeared everywhere. The Steinhauses and their daughter remained at the holiday resort, but Kott, a resident of Warsaw, had to go to the capital to report to his unit. At the tiny train station in Kamin Dovbusha, mothers and wives bid farewell to Kott and other recruits.

Hugo Steinhaus sought advice from a friend, Jerzy Stempowski, a man of both literary talent and an uncommon understanding of politics. He did so through Stanisław Vincenz, with whom he often socialized at the Lviv salon of Ignacy and Stanisława Blumenfeld. Stempowski, who was staying at Vincenz's property in Słoboda Runguska, advised against departing for Romania—he thought that country could fall any day, too. It turned out very differently: despite having lost part of its territory in 1940, Romania retained its neutral status for another two years, giving shelter to tens of thousands of Polish refugees. Romania's wartime losses were on par with Hungary's, a country that had joined the Axis at the very beginning of World War II.

---

44 Letter from Aleksander Bocheński to Maria Dąbrowska / List Aleksandra Bocheńskiego do Marii Dąbrowskiej, Kolekcja korespondencji Marii Dąbrowskiej, Dział Rękopisów, Biblioteka Uniwersytecka w Warszawie (BUW), sygn. 1385, k. 108–10.

45 Ola Hnatiuk, "Piotr Dunin-Borkowski," *Zeszyty Historyczne* 155, no. 534 (2006): 188–225.

On September 17, Stanisław Vincenz, together with his older son (also Stanisław), Jerzy Stempowski, as well as captain Adam Miłobędzki, with whom Vincenz had served during the Polish-Soviet War of 1920, set out from Słoboda towards the border. Before departure, Vincenz, despite his wife's protests, burned some of his library collection, rich in Ucrainica, including foreign editions. The writer knew that every volume forbidden in the USSR could become grounds for arrest, and later be used as material evidence to indict him of counterrevolutionary activities.

After the reconnaissance mission, Vincenz intended to get the rest of his family over (his octogenarian father, his wife and younger son, and two foster daughters), and Jerzy Stempowski was planning the same for his terminally ill friend Ludwika Rettinger. Taking stock of the situation on the Romanian border in Kuty, through which most of the Polish government fled the country, they continued towards Hungary and spent the night in the Hutsul capital Żabie, at a friendly inn owned by Lejzor Gertner. (Gertner, the man responsible for the logistics of the Second Polish Republic's largest investment in the Hutsul region—the observatory on the Pip Ivan mountain—was later executed, meeting the fate of other Galician Jews. Two years later Vincenz saw Gertner's sons in Hungary and managed to supply them with "Aryan" documents.) Barely a month later the travelers came back to Żabie, this time not to the inn, but to the Hutsul museum, temporarily converted into a NKVD jail. However, on the morning of September 18, the four friends crossed the border at the Tatar Pass, where thousands of refugees were headed. Women from the nearby village of Iablunytsia) rushed to the pass, bringing bread, milk, and cheese to the waiting crowds.

It was from Vorokhta, near the border, that the Banachs with their son were planning to get through to Hungary. In a letter to Stanisław Ulam, Banach's son Stefan recalled:

> Thus in [19]39 the war found us in Worochta, which because of border changes was two hours away from the Hungarian border at the time. We had a few thousand złoty from the Rychter-Mościcka award (20,000). The rest disappeared in the P. K. O. [a bank—translator's note]. I advised my parents to cross the Hungarian border, and from there to make our way to the USA. Yet back then the decision was not simple, and so we went to Lviv, where bombs were already falling.[46]

---

46 *Wortal Stefana Banacha*, http://kielich.amu.edu.pl/Stefan_Banach/jpg/wystawa/nbp7.pdf.

Initially, at their daughter's suggestion, the Steinhauses also thought to escape to the West via Hungary. For this purpose, they switched their lodging arrangements from Kamin Dovbusha for a location closer to the Hungarian border, Tatariv. They stayed at the Villa Teresa which belonged to Karol Kossak, grandson of Juliusz and nephew of Wojciech. Karol was also a painter, fascinated with Hutsulshchyna (from his cycle of Hutsul watercolors only a postcard series, published in 1939 by Atlas in Lviv, survived the ravages of the war). At the last minute, when they had already reached the Tatar Pass, an officer they knew from Lviv convinced them that their Jewish ethnicity made it dangerous to cross because there were SS observers among the Hungarian commission. "'Go back to Lwów,' said the officer, 'The Bolsheviks idolize professors. They won't harm you.'"[47] As it turned out, he was partly right.

And thus the Steinhauses remained in Tatariv. For a few days they watched as refugees, carrying only backpacks, attempted to slip across the border to Hungary. They also witnessed the Red Army's arrival in the village and its first moves. There was another reason to give up on their risky flight; if they separated, Steinhaus's mother would be left without caretakers and Lidia without a husband. Instead, they opted to return to Lviv, to the house at Kadecka Street, soon to fall into the hands of the Soviets. The NKVD officials occupying the property attempted to play charades with the host, not realizing that they were dealing not just with a distinguished specialist in game theory, but its actual practitioner, who was an exceptionally keen observer. The NKVD approached Steinhaus, the owner, asking how much the apartment they occupied would cost. Had Steinhaus named a price, without a doubt the "landlord" and his family would have been deported.

Once trains started running again, Hugo and Stefania Steinhaus returned to their home. On the same day, September 26, 1939, Mykhailo Ostroverkha made it back as well. Four days before, the Red Army seized Lviv. At home they found several family members: mother Ewelina née Lipschitz, sister Irena with her daughter, and the daughter's fiancé. In late fall, their son-in-law Jan Kott arrived. After fighting in the September campaign, he left Warsaw and made his way to Lviv through Małkinia and Białystok to join his wife. Kott reached Lviv utterly exhausted and famished, though on the last stretch of his journey he joined Władysław Broniewski, who was returning from a literary gathering in Białystok in the comfort of a separate train compartment. It took a while for Kott to get involved in what in normal times we would refer to as literary pursuits.

---

47   Steinhaus, *Mathematician for All Seasons: Recollections and Notes*, 224.

In his recollections from half a century later, he downplayed his activities in Soviet-occupied Lviv. As for Broniewski, by 1940 he was already in prison. Among the most serious charges the Soviets brought against him was that he had penned "nationalistic poems." After the war those same poems became required reading in Polish schools and were recited at every event commemorating World War II. Following Kott, Stanisław Saks and Bronisław Knaster, two mathematicians from Warsaw, showed up at the Steinhaus residence. The latter brought news that the Nazis had executed Jews in Ostrów Mazowiecka. Both Warsaw academics found employment at the university and thus avoided deportation in June 1940.

In fall 1939 many would-be refugees, some better, some lesser known in academic circles, returned to their Lviv homes. Among the first group was professor Stanisław Głąbiński, a doyen among Polish national activists, soon thereafter arrested as he attempted to cross the border. While I was not able to access his investigation records, what documents were preserved allow for a precise reconstruction of the circumstances of his arrest. Those records include references to a Soviet agent's alias ("Petrov") and the remuneration received for a successful operation: 500 rubles.[48] The NKVD kept track of Głąbiński's activities as well as spying on other would-be escapees. The agents were tailing Głąbiński's group as they headed from Lviv toward the border via Slavske, where they stopped at the bed and breakfast of Maria Witkowska. The NKVD closed in on Głąbiński via two simultaneous operations: "Falangisty" and "Legionery." Other persons under surveillance were Stanisław Skrzypek—an economist at Jan Kazimierz University, former member of the All-Polish Youth (*Młodzież Wszechpolska*), and active in the National Party (*Stronnictwo Narodowe*), who many years later authored the first study focused on the People's Assembly—as well as Maria Witkowska, the bed and breakfast owner. The Soviets arrested Głąbiński for organizing resistance among right-leaning youth affiliated with the prewar *Falanga* National Radical Camp.

Among the lesser known would-be refugees were younger university lecturers such as the geographer Alfred Jahn, as well as students, for instance Kazimierz Żygulski, who later (in the mid-1980s) became Minister of Culture in the People's Republic of Poland. Former Lvivians were returning as well. Two years before, Władysław Nikliborc, one of the founders of the Lwów School of Mathematics, had transferred from the Lviv Polytechnic to the Polytechnic in Warsaw. At the beginning of the war he made it from Warsaw to Lviv

---

48   Spravka po agenturnomy delu "Falangisty," HDA SBU, f. 16, op. 32, spr. 70, k. 57.

and worked at the Polytechnic again. Though as a refugee he was subject to deportation, the university administration was nevertheless able to shield him from that fate. During the German occupation Nikliborc remained in Lviv and taught at the Staatliche Technische Fachkurse. He gave shelter to a Lviv colleague Juliusz Paweł Schauder, the former head of the Mechanics Faculty (in 1943 Schauder was identified on the street as a Jew and shot). As Banach's son recalls, Nikliborc also took care of Stanisław Banach in the last months of his life. After coming to Warsaw in 1945, he returned to teaching at the Warsaw Polytechnic. He took his own life after being interrogated by the Polish communist state security UB (*Urząd Bezpieczeństwa*).

The NKVD arrested many refugees, among them one of the most dynamic right-wing university activists, the associate professor Zdzisław Stahl, as they attempted to cross the border. Others still, despite having reached safety, returned to Poland for various reasons and were arrested then. The lucky two, Stanisław Vincenz and his son Stanisław Aleksander, were released from prison within less than two months after his Ukrainian friends appealed to Petro Panch, president of the local Soviet Society of Writers, who had the courage to plead the Vincenz case with the NKVD.

As he recalled the riveting circumstances of their arrest in *Dialogi z Sowietami* [*Dialogues with the Soviets*], Vincenz quoted an anecdote popular during the 1905 revolution. Two hares meet up at the border. In terror, one shares the news that "they" are currently hunting for camels, to which the other merrily cheers, as the hunt for hares is finally over. Clearly worried, the first replies: "But they will catch you, keep you forever, and good luck proving you are no camel."[49]

Soon the same fear spread everywhere—not only among those imprisoned, but even those still "free." In the eyes of the Soviet Union all citizens of the Republic of Poland were under suspicion.

"WE ARE NO VEGETARIANS"

The day after his return to Lviv, Hugo Steinhaus directed his first steps to the university campus, which was guarded, as he writes, by members of the (Polish) ONR—the National Radical Camp, dressed up as Soviet police (an inconsistency crept in here: in Lviv, it was the All-Polish Youth—*Młodzież Wszechpolska*—that took on the role of ONR). In the same vein, OUN

---

49 Stanisław Vincenz, *Dialogi z Sowietami* (Cracow: Oficyna Literacka, 1986), 57.

members also disguised themselves as Soviet police; Ostroverkha recalls that Bohdan Kravtsiv fled to the German side after a former communist friend recognized him in the disguise.⁵⁰

Steinhaus was critical of the extreme right and its stance toward the new political system, for obvious reasons; until 1939, the right had dominated Lviv's political life, and exerted a strong influence on the university campus. Under the pretext that teaching activities could not resume in a charged atmosphere, the nationalists forced the introduction of "ghetto benches." They strove to exclude lecturers of Jewish ethnicity from academic life (Ukrainian professors posed no threat—they were not permitted to teach at the university back in 1919 and this status quo remained in place until the Second Republic of Poland ceased to exist). Steinhaus writes with distaste about the hypocrisy of certain professors who demanded "ghetto benches," allegedly to calm the volatile mood and focus on teaching.⁵¹ Eleasar J. Feuerman, writing from a student's point of view, argued that "ghetto benches" had the opposite effect: they turned Jewish students into easy targets for right-wing thugs.⁵²

At the university president's office, Steinhaus heard a lengthy account of the past two weeks from those present at the Faculty Senate meeting. The president, Roman Longchamps de Berier, whose start of term coincided with the beginning of the war, directed the faculty to begin preparations for entrance exams. In response, Soviet authorities (the Interim Committee) ordered the administration to call a rally for September 28, 1939. It was to take place in the auditorium.

Iakiv Khomenko, leader of the Komsomol of Ukraine, chaired the meeting. The memoirists erroneously state his name and position as Fedir Ieremenko, the city commander. Ieremenko was indeed the city commander, but it was Khomenko who presided over the gathering, as an official press release published on the front page of *Vilna Ukraina* on September 29, 1939 indicates. In the council chairs sat the "visitors," along with president and deans. The assembly ended according to a classic Soviet scenario: a telegram declaring loyalty was sent to Stalin. Karolina Lanckorońska recalls that after the telegram was read, city commander Fedir Ieremenko (in fact, Iakiv Khomenko) asked who

---

50 Ostroverkha, Ostroverkha Papers, k. 111.
51 Steinhaus, *Mathematician for All Seasons: Recollections and Notes*, 219.
52 Feuerman and Weinbaum, "My lost professors of medicine in Lvov: Remembering the early victims of the Nazis."

was in favor: "… only a few dozen raised their hands. 'And who is against?' Not surprisingly, not a single hand went up. Then, with a broad smile he declared: 'The motion to send a telegram is approved unanimously.'"[53]

Yet, it was not the scripted meeting which made the biggest imprint on people's memory, though it would have seemed peculiar to anyone unfamiliar with Soviet rituals, but a poignant presentation by Oleksandr Korniichuk. Directly after Khomenko opened the meeting, the president of the Writers' Union stepped up to give a speech, in military uniform. While he did not exactly receive a warm reception, authors of several reports are aligned in their praise: Korniichuk was an excellent orator. Steinhaus thought Korniichuk's presentation well thought out, and it certainly hit a soft spot—the Polish government had deserted its country. Indeed, Polish citizens were doubly shaken—first by their leaders' desertion, and now by the uncertainty they faced. Korniichuk hinted at changes, but also promised to support the university along with the academic community. His declaration of openness elicited positive reactions, though in reality this standard propaganda move aimed to create an illusion of normalcy and to coax those present into accepting their situation and embracing the *status quo*. The pledge to educate everyone, regardless of their social standing or ethnic origin, was intended to draw those whose right to education the Polish Republic had continuously denied.

Clearly, Korniichuk was the new administration's calling card. The Polish, and especially the Ukrainian intelligentsia, greeted his numerous appearances with ambivalence. Later, writing in exile, they distanced themselves from Korniichuk, criticizing the falsehoods so rampant in Soviet speeches, and extolling their own courage. Yet only some of these statements merit our belief. For instance, three days before this function, on September 25, 1939, another meeting took place at 10 Rynok, in the headquarters of the most influential Ukrainian newspaper *Dilo*. Commissar Chekaniuk, appointed by the Soviets as interim editor in chief of the daily *Vilna Ukraina*, attacked UNDO and its organ *Dilo* for acquiescing to the Polish administration. His foray aimed to intimidate the nearly seventy Ukrainian journalists present. As *Dilo*'s editor Ivan Nimchuk wrote, a heated discussion ensued; someone posed the question why the USSR, aware of the plight of Ukrainians in Poland, never filed any formal protests.[54] Two days later the Soviets arrested Nimchuk.

---

53   Lanckorońska, *Michelangelo in Ravensbruck: One Woman's War against the Nazis*, 6.
54   Nimchuk, *595 dniv soviets'kym viaznem*, 26.

Karolina Lanckorońska's employment questionnaire, December 24, 1939

Korniichuk's role was to provide a contrast to the terrifying commissar; he dazed and bewildered more than he frightened. A similar scenario unfolded on the days previous to the big meeting: on September 26 at a composers' meeting, and on September 27 at an artists' meeting. *Vilna Ukraina* informed extensively about all functions attended by the president of the Writers' Union.[55] Yet Korniichuk's campus speech sounded a warning bell: appealing to the intelligentsia to support the changes unconditionally, the speaker cautioned against any resistance. The declaration "my ne vegetariantsy" ("we are no vegetarians") stuck out in Steinhaus's mind—the ominous message rang crystal clear in all languages of the region. It hinted at the regime's bloodthirsty essence and its ability to thwart "anyone wishing to continue with nationalistic and reactionary political activity."[56] Nevertheless both Lanckorońska and Steinhaus reminisce that Korniichuk's presentation sowed seeds of hope for the university's survival. Lviv's literati received his appearances with a similar dose of optimism.

Both memoirists were destined to get to know the Soviet authorities better. In spring 1940, Lanckorońska managed to avoid arrest; wanted by the NKVD, she crossed the border illegally and reached Cracow. Steinhaus chose not to write about the fear that dominated the first months of the occupation, but we learn about it from Soviet agents' reports on Lviv professors. An informer recruited by the NKVD wrung his hands at the mass deportations and their disastrous effect on the morale of the academic community, which the authorities clearly intended to solicit. A secret agent writes about widespread fears of deportation and a sudden spike in the interest to move to German-occupied territories; the names Ganszyniec, Taszycki, Ehrlich, and Steinhaus come up. While it is doubtful that the mathematician, well aware of the fate of Jews in the General Government, gave it serious consideration (the same goes for Ehrlich, who was a *bezhenets*, a Russian term applied to all refugees from German-occupied territories), in the cases of Ganszyniec or Taszycki it was certainly possible. The secret collaborator tried to suggest that a German commission had already expressed an interest in the scientists and the Soviets risked losing them. He maintained that but for the climate of fear, their work could be far more beneficial to the Soviet authorities.[57] We know from other sources that in

---

55 *Vil'na Ukraïna* 2 (September 1939): 2.
56 Steinhaus, *Mathematician for All Seasons: Recollections and Notes*, 231.
57 Spetssoobshchenie narodnomu kommissaru vnutrennikh del tov. Serovu ot 11.05.1940, in Spetssoobshcheniia o khode pereseleniia spetskontingenta iz zapadnykh oblastei USSR v vostochnye, f. 16, op. 33, spr. 55, k. 115.

May 1940, three weeks after the mass deportations, a researcher as well known as Kazimierz Bartel registered with the German commission.[58]

Though Steinhaus does not write about his efforts to leave occupied Lviv, Ostroverkha's memoir shows that the Steinhauses intended to break away, at least as of late October 1939. But once refugees from Warsaw (his son-in-law and colleagues) showed up at the Steinhaus residence, the mathematician came to realize that fleeing to German-occupied areas was out of the question; they would have to find an alternative. Correspondence between Maurycy Bloch and Zygmunt William Birnbaum, both of whom came to the US shortly before the war, confirms Steinhaus's quandary. On January 22, 1940 Bloch sent a telegram to Birnbaum warning that Hitler might take Lviv (he nicknamed Hitler "Lojzio") and informed him of a relative's flight; he advised that Birnbaum's family should seek a way out via Vilnius and cautioned against attempting to cross the border with Romania. Lastly, he sounded alarm bells in the matter of Steinhaus: "LOJZIO TAKES LVIV STOP DORUSIA FLED VILNIUS REST UKNOWN STOP TELL YOURS VILNIUS IMMEDIATELY STOP ROMANIA NO GO STOP STEINHAUS ASKS TO EVACUATE FROM KADECKA."[59]

On the same day, in a lengthy letter to Bloch, Birnbaum mentioned that professors of Polish origin were organizing to assist colleagues back home. In his response from January 28, Bloch depicted the situation in occupied Lviv, identifying Germans as the biggest threat (they were supposedly stationed outside of Lviv, which in January 1940 was actually not the case). In subsequent letters, Bloch told of attempts by Henri Léon Lebesgue, a French colleague who held an honorary doctorate from Jan Kazimierz University, to extricate Steinhaus from Lviv. However, once the Nazis seized France and the Soviets Vilnius in June 1940, these paths of escape were cut off as well.

In February 1940, Birnbaum telegrammed his Lviv family from Seattle, this time openly stating that Vilnius was an easier destination than Romania. The Soviets could have thought the telegram sufficient reason for sanctions against the family. All foreign correspondence was subject to inspection, based

---

58 Sławomir Kalbarczyk, "Kazimierz Bartel pod okupacją sowiecką we Lwowie," *Przegląd Historyczny* 82, no. 2 (1991): 285. The author refers to memoirs of Alicja Dorabialska *Jeszcze jedno życie* (Warszawa: PAX, 1972).
59 Zygmunt William Birnbaum Papers, University Libraries, University of Washington, acc. 5266-00 (http://archiveswest.orbiscascade.org/ark:/80444/xv09585/pdf; http://www.lib.washington.edu/specialcollections/collections/exhibits/spotlight-on-zygmunt-william-birnbaum-papers/images/19TELEGRAMsml.jpg).

on its contents, the NKVD leadership selected individuals or groups to monitor, investigate, or arrest.⁶⁰

Maurycy Bloch, a friend of Steinhaus's daughter, came from an affluent merchant family and emigrated to the United States in 1938. On Steinhaus's behalf, he endeavored (succeeding only after the war) to patent a device that Steinhaus had invented—the "introvisor"—which made it possible to locate foreign objects inside the human body. Zygmunt Birnbaum, a member of the Lwów School of Mathematics, having acquired the designation of press correspondent for *Ilustrowany Kurier Codzienny* through the journalist Ludwik Rubel, moved to the United States in July 1937. He joined the faculty of the University of Washington in Seattle in 1939. Both Bloch and Birnbaum worked tirelessly to extricate family members, friends, and colleagues from the occupied territories, though their correspondence reveals that they had little knowledge of the realities of Soviet occupation.⁶¹

One of Steinhaus's and Banach's disciples, Stanisław Ulam, co-creator of the nuclear bomb, also came to the United States. He and his brother Adam Ulam, who after the war worked as a notable Sovietologist at Harvard University, began their journey to New York on August 16, 1939, on the transatlantic ship the "Batory" (at the same time Fryda Lille traveled on the "Kościuszko" from Gdynia to Boulogne). Stanisław's widowed father Józef, and his sister with her husband, remained in Lviv. Only Stanisław's cousin survived the war. The Ulams did not succeed in bringing any family members over from the occupied regions; they could only help those who had escaped Poland at the start of the war. When it came to the USSR's territory, the attempts of private persons, gestures of collegial solidarity, even efforts at high levels all proved fruitless.

No one present at the university rally in late August foresaw what was to come. There was the general belief that these were not the same Bolsheviks as in 1920 and that the Soviet regime's weakness and absurdity would necessarily cause it to self-destruct. People assumed the geopolitical situation would shift and Poland would soon regain her independence. Meanwhile, Soviet authorities were pursuing their agenda, gradually imposing the new order and its inseparable companion—terror.

---

60 Compare the correspondence between the NKVD and the KP(b)U: Perepiska s TsK KP(b)U, HDA SBU, f. 16, op. 84, spr. 9, k. 277–80.
61 Zygmunt William Birnbaum Papers (see note 59).

Indeed, as Korniichuk's metaphor foreshadowed, the reprisal apparatus turned out to be quite carnivorous. The Soviets scoured the academic community to a much greater extent than his propagandist presentation had insinuated. Even so, scientists did retain some of their privileges ("Bolsheviks idolize professors"). Korniichuk, the creator of social realist dramas and a high-level player on the Soviet political scene, had an excellent feel for politics, coupled with an instinctive understanding of how to appeal to an audience. In front of the Ukrainian intelligentsia, he announced a complete Ukrainization of the public sphere, contradicting his earlier university speech. Little did those assembled suspect—he had no intention to keep either promise.

A DREAM COME TRUE. ...

Upon examining official publications and declarations by representatives of the Soviet government, one could surmise that the Soviets initially planned to create a separate Ukrainian university, so as to win over the Ukrainian intelligentsia. In early October, notwithstanding a wave of arrests among political and social activists, the former professors of the Underground Ukrainian University still assumed they would get their own institution of higher learning. A certificate preserved in the Lviv University Archive indicates just that. It bore the signature of the last president of the Underground University, Ievhen Davydiak, and was issued to the attorney Stanislav Starosolsky, a professor at the Ukrainian Underground University.[62] It suggests that Starosolsky meant to apply for a position at this would-be institution. The document's semi-official format implies that the faculty of the former Underground University had formed a body to represent their interests to the Soviet authorities.

The story of Stanislav Starosolsky mirrors the fate of the entire community: the Soviets removed him from the university in April 1940, ostensibly because he failed to provide a doctor's sick note in the correct format. Dean Petro Nedbailo did not support his request for his rehiring, claiming that Starosolsky lacked adequate preparation for scientific work.[63] This could only mean one thing: the authorities had developed serious ideological reservations about Starosolsky. As a matter of fact, on Christmas day of 1939, the NKVD arrested his brother Volodymyr Starosolsky, a well-regarded attorney and socialist party

---

62 Lichnoe delo Starosol'skogo Stanislava Konstantinovicha, ALU, R-119, op. 1, spr. 582.
63 Ibid.

activist who had defended OUN members in political trials. Volodymyr's family (wife and two children) were deported to Kazakhstan in April 1940. Those close blood ties could have triggered Starosolsky's termination from the university. During the German occupation, Starosolsky worked as a judge in the district court and as the director of the office of Stadthauptmann. As with many Ukrainian intellectuals who took the gamble of staying in Lviv after the war, Starosolsky too would suffer Soviet reprisals.

Meanwhile, the Ukrainian intelligentsia believed their goal was within reach. A Ukrainian university in Lviv would affirm their separate national identity and legitimize national aspirations. The long-standing efforts to create a Ukrainian institution of higher learning had nearly paid off before World War I, but, in the end, the war thwarted this chance. After 1918, the Polish government consistently nixed the idea. Popular opinion held that a Ukrainian university would hinder the interests of the Polish state. It is difficult to understand today why the Polish political and intellectual elites opposed it so stubbornly. If they acted out of a deep-seated conviction that Ukrainians were culturally immature, certainly the Polish administration could have agreed to a makeshift college which would have posed no threat to their flagship Jan Kazimierz University. Polish scholar Danuta Sosnowska proposes the following explanation of this mystery: to establish a Ukrainian university in Lviv would have challenged Poles' cultural superiority and hindered the possibility that ethnic minorities might "voluntarily" assimilate, thus undermining the founding myth of the modern Polish state.[64]

In early October 1939, Soviet authorities duped Ukrainians with the prospect of a university, at the same time warning that all Ukrainians aspiring to professorships would have to submit to a dense set of ideological criteria: "Some of the professors who taught fifteen years ago—nationalists and clericalists of all sorts—should realize that they lack preparation for university work, where Marxism-Leninism occupies such a prominent position in the university curriculum."[65] Such allusions clearly implicated those who had taught at the Underground University. Indeed, a large group were clericalists, whether they came from the Greek-Catholic clergy or held religious views. All who had lectured at the Ukrainian Underground University were nationalists. Everyone immediately understood the hidden motive behind this press announcement:

---

64 Danuta Sosnovs'ka, *Universytet na rozdorizhzhi istorii* (Kyiv: Smoloskyp, 2011), 22–3.
65 H. [first name unknown] Antoniuk, "Maibutnii ukraïns'kii universytet maie buty zrazkovym naukovym tsentrom," *Vil'na Ukraïna*, no. 11, October 6, 1939.

to elicit a prompt stream of "loyalty oaths" from persons interested in obtaining an academic position.

This future Ukrainian university—if we choose to play the article's game—would serve as an example for the existing Polish university to follow: "The Ukrainian university, which will be established in Lviv, must become a powerful center of science, and set an example for the existing Polish university for how to transition from scientific methodologies endemic to a bourgeois society to a new world view—the world view of those who created a new state model, the USSR."[66]

If this plan came to fruition, the changes would have been slow and gradual: a two-step Sovietization, first carried out as an experiment at the Ukrainian university—"national in form, socialist in meaning"—and then applied to Polish institutions. But even if this scenario did exist independently of propaganda stories in *Vilna Ukraina*, the Soviets abandoned it. The communist administration was bent on the fastest and most comprehensive implementation of Soviet models. For one, a two-step restructuring would have given the elites time to brace themselves and resist. Secondly, it would have created a precedent dangerous to the supranational unilateral system of Soviet government. And that system was already under threat from the "nationalist faction," as we will read in the next chapter.

As soon as late September a new plan was conceived to transform the university into an institution fully compliant with Soviet norms. As its first agenda item, the Soviets set out to eliminate the Faculty of Theology and to restructure the Medical Faculty into a Medical Institute, reporting to the Health Ministry instead of the Ministry of Education. Another change was to create separate (Polish and Ukrainian) courses of study in four out of the five faculties (philology, history, natural sciences, and physics-mathematics). Law degrees in Polish would no longer be offered.[67] The plan to establish those separate faculties was only partially realized (and only within the Philological Faculty). Thus, in practice, Polish remained the language of instruction, even though as early as November 1939 the Soviets demanded that professors lecture in Ukrainian and introduced "mandatory-voluntary" Ukrainian language instruction for the faculty. Steinhaus writes that it was a point of honor to not attend those courses. In addition to Amvrosii Androkhovych, a seasoned instructor of Ukrainian,

---

66 Ibid.
67 "Informatsiina zapyska zastupnyka narodnoho komisara osvity dlia TsK KP(b)U ta RNK URSR vid 30 veresnia 39 roku," in *Kul'turne zhyttia v Ukraïni*, vol. 1, 56.

the Soviets hired recent philology graduates to teach Ukrainian. One of them, Myroslav Semchyshyn, recalls the ease with which he obtained his university position and the satisfaction he felt:

> At the university I reported to my professor [Vasyl] Simovych, as always exceptionally kind, who already had started his term as dean of humanities and was working on the course program. He announced that it would be imperative to teach some Ukrainian to the Polish-language department. … Yes, I thought, only recently the doors of Jan Kazimierz University in Lviv were closed to some, yet today not only are they open for everyone, but from now on the oldest university on Ukrainian territory will bear the name of the great Ivan Franko.[68]

As mentioned previously, the plan to restructure the university system emerged in late September 1939. Though Korniichuk must have been in the know, he continued to make promises for a separate university so that he could convincingly campaign on behalf of the Soviet administration among the Ukrainian intelligentsia. A few days later, a representative of that community, Kyrylo Studynsky, visited Moscow, although his trip was not public knowledge. Together with Panchyshyn, the scholar participated in the October 4 assembly of the All-Soviet Committee for Higher Educational Affairs, organized by its vice chairman Aleksei Gagarin. Studynsky presented the issues facing Lviv's intelligentsia and its university to the assembled professors and commissariat employees.[69] While neither a draft of his presentation nor a list of requests have been preserved among Studynsky's papers, we can surmise that he brought up the matter of a Ukrainian university as one of the most important stipulations. During another, more official visit to Moscow a month later, the specifics of reorganization were discussed.[70]

The promises Korniichuk made to the Polish and Ukrainian intelligentsia, as well as the hopes Moscow instilled in Studynsky and Panchyshyn, fed into a larger strategy. From the moment they violated the borders of the Second Republic of Poland, the Soviets immediately began to put into practice the same policy of divide and conquer they had effectively utilized as a main instrument of directing social behaviors for the previous two decades. The false

---

68 Semchyshyn, *Z knyhy Leva*, 68.
69 TsDIA, f. 362, op. 1, spr. 43, k. 6.
70 Ibid., k. 8.

notes of socialist realism, certainly audible from the start, soon emerged as an obvious lie. Kost Levytsky, head of the Ukrainian delegation to the civilian town authorities, hesitated in his evaluation of the Soviet regime: the words sound promising, and we must wait for the actions.[71] For the sage of Ukrainian politicians (at the time Levytsky was eighty years old) the wait was not all that long; he was arrested by the end of the first week of Soviet rule in Lviv. Only the savviest observers immediately noticed that the new order was based on a lie:

> What had been most interesting for me at this meeting was the easygoing and super-enlightened attitude of these Soviet notables towards matters we would have considered difficult and sensitive. Thus they said that the language of instruction could be whatever was convenient: Polish, Russian, Ukrainian, or even Yiddish, this representing no real problem for them. They expected scientific articles and books to be published literally by the wagonload, now that all administrative and other difficulties had been swept aside—at one blow! Everybody was now to be admitted to university, tuition would be free, and if space be lacking, then a second, third, or even fourth university would quickly be established. Cost would be no object.[72]

Needless to say, Steinhaus was not familiar with Soviet plans regarding the university. He took the populist promises as intentional deceit, and those spreading the slogans—as deliberate liars.

With less precision and more bluntness, a Lviv joke from late 1939 lampoons the propaganda fabrications of Soviet ethnic policy. The Soviets helped to "fulfill" Polish, Ukrainian, and Jewish stereotypes and dreams:

> Now Poles, who used to complain that Jews kept them away from retail, are frantically selling their effects at the "Krakidaly" [bazaar] in order to survive. Jews, who lamented that Poles would not admit them to well-paid positions as civil servants, now receive salaries as *sluzhashchii* [officials], on which it is impossible to survive. And Ukrainians, always fighting for independent Ukraine, can get their *Vilna Ukraina* for 5 kopeks at every newsstand.[73]

---

71 Nazaruk, *Ucieczka ze Lwowa do Warszawy*, 39.
72 Steinhaus, *Mathematician for All Seasons: Recollections and Notes*, 232.
73 Quoted in Nakonechnyi, *"Shoa" u L'vovi*, 40.

That is how the son of a Ukrainian printer remembers the occupation. Polish public opinion stubbornly asserted that Jews welcomed the Red Army jubilantly and were disappointed only later. Such opinions display an utter lack of empathy; there was no doubt that Jews should be afraid of the Nazis and from that perspective a Soviet Lviv simply seemed like the lesser of two evils. This too became the subject of jokes, as Zdzisław Zieliński relates:

> Somehow the enthusiasm on which the Soviet propaganda liked to engorge itself was hard to spot. It must be that not everyone greeted the arriving army quite effusively. Maybe somewhere Ukrainians of a certain political orientation. … A Lviv anecdote soon summarized the matter pointedly. Supposedly as the Soviets marched in, the Jews were kissing their tanks. But now they would gladly kiss their a … if only the Soviets would leave, but they won't![74]

The author of these reminiscences boasts that such "humor" helped the nation embark on a fight against the occupier … his words seem to imply to the reader that it was the Jews who brought the Soviet calamity onto the Poles, who hardly endorse the Soviets. (The memoirist sees Lviv's Ukrainian population as inconsequentially marginal and thus not worth his attention.) The above passage helps us trace how ethnic attitudes towards the Soviets became stereotyped. Not until 2000, when Jan Tomasz Gross's widely publicized book *Neighbors* (*Sąsiedzi*) came out, did Poles begin to reckon with those stereotypes.

People's actual outlooks differed significantly from Zieliński's description. To be sure, Lviv initially seemed "a pretty good spot to wait out the war,"[75] especially to refugees from central Poland, most of them Jewish. However, at the turn of 1939 and 1940, within just a few months, all Lvivians, from Ukrainians to Poles to Jews, got a chance to experience Soviet terror directly. Announcements and promises from 1939 turned out to be a smoke screen for the Soviets' true political objectives: full and fast integration of the occupied territories, with the appearance of legality. It was a peculiar characteristic of the system that it went to great lengths to ascertain legal formalities of the annexation (as it did with reprisals). Literature published in the USSR devoted to the "reunification" of Ukrainian territories between 1939–41 is too plentiful to discuss

---

74 Zieliński, "Lwowskie okupacje," k. 12.
75 Such opinions are cited by Tadeusz Tomaszewski (*Lwów. Pejzaż psychologiczny*, 49).

here. Beginning in 1939, the dominant agenda was to legally, historically, and morally justify an act of aggression, and this political outlook has survived the collapse of the USSR. Even today, some Russian scholars muse, in all seriousness, about the legal status of areas incorporated into the USSR after the Molotov-Ribbentrop Pact.[76] To legitimize such undertakings became an essential element of Soviet policy.

---

76 Ukrainian studies written in a similar vein exist as well. Journalistic and academic publications by Dmytro Tabachnyk are the starkest example. Tabachnyk served as Minister of Education and Science between 2010 and 2014. He achieved infamy by restoring the term "the Great Patriotic War" to Ukrainian textbooks and editing out references to the Ukrainian independence movement. The following article joins in the spirit of many anti-Polish Russian publications of the time, which sought to deprecate the tributes commemorating the outbreak of World War II in Gdańsk and on the Hel Peninsula. Tabachnyk's article took aim not so much at Poland as at the Ukrainian political opponent of the time (its publication occurred less than four months prior to the 2010 presidential elections):

> In September 1939 the Soviet military crossed Poland's eastern border and after entering the territory of Western Ukraine and Western Belarus took those populations under its wing. Later, in October of the same year, the People's Assembly of Western Ukraine turned to the Soviet government asking that their country be incorporated into the Soviet Union and united with the Ukrainian Soviet Socialist Republic. The request was honored. ... From the standpoint of ethics or the diplomatic practice of the time, the USSR was the last to sign a nonaggression treaty with the Germans, finding itself in almost complete diplomatic isolation. Moscow de facto followed a general European practice, or, to apply a contemporary term, 'shared European values.' Precisely for the same reasons we must not treat the Soviet army's entry into eastern Poland as an 'act of aggression, a direct result of the Molotov-Ribbentrop pact,' though Ukrainian nationalists delight in characterizing it that way. For one, to consider a territory part of the sphere of one's priority interests does not qualify as an automatic and inevitable occupation of said territory (Dmitrii Tabachnik, "Ot Ribbentropa do maidana," *Izvestiia*, September 23, 2009, izvestia.ru/news/353329).

The article, printed on the occasion of the seventieth anniversary of the annexation of Poland's eastern territories by the USSR, maintains that current Ukrainian issues would not have emerged if history had taken a different turn and an alternate legal solution had been applied: "Well, though history does not know the conditional mode, the majority of today's problems could have been avoided if in 1939 Galicia had been annexed by USSR on an autonomous basis. Not to mention that back in 1945 it could have painlessly been returned to Poland" (ibid.).

There are also contemporary Ukrainian authors who warn that Ukraine needs to defend its territorial integrity in the face of threats posed, allegedly, by Polish territorial claims. Compare Vladimir Makarchuk, *Gosudarstvenno-territorial'nyi status zapadno-ukrainskikh zemel' v period Vtoroi mirovoi voiny. Istoriko-pravovoe issledovanie* (Moscow: Fond sodeistviia aktual'nym istoricheskim issledovaniiam, 2010), 6–7.

"A NEW LIFE BEGINS. ..."

To aid in the swift unification of the newly occupied territory with the USSR, the Soviets relentlessly recruited the local population, at first through political officers or *polituks*, then via civilian party activists and Komsomol members. Within a few days, two newspapers with the propagandist titles *Czerwony Sztandar*[77] and *Vilna Ukraina* began appearing. Similarly, Soviet radio—all-Soviet broadcasts as well as the local station—served as propaganda mouthpieces. To establish the Ukrainian-language newspaper *Vilna Ukraina*, the Soviets seized the daily *Dilo* along with its printshop. They apprehended its editor in chief Ivan Nimchuk on September 26. Clearly he was a priority, as his arrest followed immediately after judicial and executive representatives such as the city's mayor Stanisław Ostrowski, and before Lviv's vice mayor Wiktor Chajes.

The front page of issue number five featured a report from a meeting at the university, titled "Pochynaietsia nove zhyttia bez paniv-pomishchykiv, bez hnitu i nasylstva" ["A new life begins, without lords or land owners, without oppression or violence"].[78] In addition to summarizing speeches by representatives of the authorities, it conveyed the university president's presentation and listed students who spoke at the assembly—Dudykevych, Rosenberg, Morgenstein, Handzy, and Janczak.[79] The president expressed hope that the university would become a nexus scholarship; its research would radiate throughout the entire region, making knowledge accessible to all. According to the news story, Jan Czekanowski, an anthropologist who had served as university president between 1934–36, allegedly thanked the Soviet government: "Former university president Jan Czekanowski expressed to the Soviet government his deepest gratitude for their brotherly assistance, provided in these difficult times to the people of Western Ukraine. The speaker asked Korniichuk to send his regards to the Soviet intelligentsia."[80]

Years later, Czekanowski's daughter recalled how distressed her father, a noted anthropologist, was by how "the new authorities distorted his statements

---

77 Since several analyses have been devoted to this title—among them Bogusław Gogol, *"Czerwony Sztandar." Rzecz o sowietyzacji ziem Małopolski Wschodniej* (Gdańsk: Wydawnictwo Uniwersytetu Gdańskiego, 2000) and Agnieszka Cieślikowa, *Prasa okupowanego Lwowa* (Warsaw: Neriton, 1997).
78 Semen Tymoshenko, "Pochynaiet'sia nove zhyttia bez paniv-pomishchykiv, bez hnitu i nasyl'stva," *Vil'na Ukraïna*, no. 5, September 29, 1939: 1.
79 Steinhaus, *Mathematician for All Seasons: Recollections and Notes*, 223; Tymoshenko lists the names, see "Pochynaiet'sia nove zhyttia," 1.
80 Ibid.

at the university," and incited resentment among his colleagues.[81] As Oleksandr Dombrovsky pointed out, this allegedly loyalist appearance contrasted with Czekanowski's actual political views (along with his closest neighbor and friend Jerzy Kuryłowicz, the anthropologist identified with the right-wing national democrats). At the time, Dombrovsky worked as an assistant in the Philological Faculty and was a friend of Omelian Pritsak, whom he had met at a seminar on early Ukrainian history, taught by Ivan Krypakievych at the Shevchenko Scientific Society.[82] Another source of information in this matter is Klemens Rudnicki, then a colonel, who was captured by the NKVD while attempting to cross the border. Eight years later he sought to recreate the atmosphere among Lviv's population in the fall of 1939, but the passage of time makes his account necessarily less precise. According to him, colleagues commonly downplayed the missteps of particular professors, and voiced their disregard for Soviet authorities:

> they are reporting just now about a meeting of Polish professors at Jan Kazimierz University, where they have unanimously adopted a servile cable to Stalin. The cable's content is revolting in its kowtowing to the easterners. Nearly all professors have signed. I run into two of them, H. and Longchamps. "How could you have signed something like that?"—I ask. "We ourselves only found out about the meeting, the cable, and our signing it from the newspaper"—was their answer. They are defenseless anyway. There is nowhere to send your corrections. What would be the use anyway? Why, this is all so stupid and naïve—it will self-destruct in no time.[83]

When reminiscing about this period, Czekanowski's university colleagues remained silent about his presentation, perhaps out of embarrassment. Curiously, the official report failed to mention that Seweryn Krzemieniewski, a distinguished botanist, university president from 1931–32, gave a statement arguing that science rises above ethnic or national origin, and that the university was

---

81 Anna Czekanowska, *Świat rzeczywisty—świat zapamiętany. Losy Polaków we Lwowie 1939–1941* (Lublin: Norbertinum, 2010), 62.
82 Oleksandr Dombrovs'kyi, "Do istoriï l'vivs'koho universytetu v 1939–1941 rr. (spohad u 20-ti rokovyny)," *Kyiv* 59, no. 2 (1960): 32.
83 Klemens Rudnicki, *Na polskim szlaku* (London: Gryf, 1957), quoted in http://www.cracovia-leopolis.pl/index.php?pokaz=art&id=1282.

never a site of reactionary views and oppression. Memoirists account for this address at length, celebrating it as an act of courage.[84]

There is no doubt that Krzemieniewski wanted to refute the attempts to besmirch the university and its professors. He stood up to defend the honor of the academic community. Yet his assertion that neither ethnic nor national origin played a role in the university environment very obviously deviated from the truth. In the 1930s a *numerus clausus* limited the number of Jews to ten percent, and Ukrainians made up only seventeen percent of the student body.[85]

In his memoir, Hugo Steinhaus highlighted Krzemieniewski's statement, in which the botanist called on the authorities to respect the university's values and refuted their allegations (Karolina Lanckorońska gives a similar report of this address). However, Steinhaus makes no mention of loyalist declarations made by other professors and omits details of students' speeches. Instead, he attends to Korniichuk's reaction: "The leaders of the Soviet force occupying Lwów completely ignored the speeches and posturing of the students; for them the professors' attitude was paramount. Kornijczuk later said that he'd been unable to sleep the following night because he had been so tremendously irritated by the fact that none of the Polish professors had spoken in a conciliatory manner to the Ukrainians."[86] How did Steinhaus know of Korniichuk's reaction? From Wanda Wasilewska's memoirs we can only surmise that the Ukrainian writer spoke about it with one of the professors during the many "private" conversations he was conducting at the time.[87] The mathematician's account did not include references to members of the academic community who behaved dishonorably.

Newspapers did not mention the statement by Stanisław Mazur, a mathematician, part of a small circle of campus leftists. Similarly silent are Polish journal writers. The only reference comes from the Ukrainian historian

---

84 Steinhaus, *Mathematician for All Seasons: Recollections and Notes*, 232; Lanckorońska, *Michelangelo in Ravensbruck: One Woman's War against the Nazis*, 6. One contemporary journal author attributes this statement to the economist Wincent Styś, and maintains that only two professors delivered a statement. See Jerzy Chodorowski, "Lwowskie zderzenie cywilizacji. Ze wspomnień o Profesorze Wincentym Stysiu," *Nowy Przegląd Wszechpolski* 11–12 (2005).
85 Hilary Schramm, *Kronika Uniwersytetu Jana Kazimierza we Lwowie za rok akademicki 1929/30* (Lviv: Uniwersytet Jana Kazimierza, 1931), 132.
86 Steinhaus, *Mathematician for All Seasons: Recollections and Notes*, 232.
87 Wanda Wasilewska, *Wspomnienia Wandy Wasilewskiej*, vol. 7 (Warsaw: Archiwum Ruchu Robotniczego, 1981), 344.

Dombrovsky,[88] who, on the other hand, has nothing to say about Krzemieniewski's speech—it was too defiant in comparison with the other meek proclamations. At the same time, Dombrovsky emphasized that the Ukrainians present at the meeting acted with restraint. Their speeches did not threaten revenge on Polish colleagues; Ukrainian professors stopped at innocent—in the opinion of the author—clichés about "lordly Poland."[89]

Although it is not feasible to reconstruct this late-September campus-wide assembly in precise detail, we can do so to an extent by comparing witness reports against the press coverage. Either group of sources skips over essential details: journal writers avoid noting actions loyal to the occupying forces, while the press silences any trace of protest, since government propaganda required that all of the Soviet population endorse the administration. In the 1930s, the USSR had generated scripts for such rallies and templates for media coverage and continued implementing them in the occupied territories. The preceding issue of *Vilna Ukraina* had printed letters that Ukrainian composers and artists addressed to their Soviet colleagues,[90] expressing joy at the Soviet liberation; the same news issue that reported on the campus assembly also published a resolution approved by the Ukrainian Medical Association.[91] Subsequent editions repeated further loyalty oaths by Ukrainian intelligentsia, resembling one another like peas in a pod. After writers and journalists met, a letter to Soviet Ukrainian writers and journalists was published in the name of the Writers' and Journalists' Association (TOPIZh) and signed by Mykhailo Rudnytsky and Roman Kupchynsky.[92] Mykhailo Ostroverkha described the circumstances and named the quorum present, summing up: "After the signing,

---

88 Dombrovs'kyi, "Do istorii l'vivs'koho universytetu v 1939–1941 rr.," 32.
89 Ibid.
90 The composers' resolution "Narod Zakhidnoiï Ukraïny palko vitaie svoikh vyzvolyteliv. Pryvit kompozytoriv" listed the signatures of Stanyslav Liudkevych, Professor Vasyl Barvinsky, and Dr. Nestor Nyzhankivsky; the artists' resolution "Narod Ukraïny palko vitaie svoikh vyzvolyteliv. Do robitnykiv mystetstva Radians'koiï Ukraïny" featured the signatures of Olena Kulchytska, Iaroslava Muzyka, Mykhailo Osinchuk, Mykola Holubets, Serhy Lytvynenko, Ivan Ivanets, Volodymyr Havryluk, Volodymyr Lasovsky, and Edvard Kozak (*Vil'na Ukraïna*, no. 4, September 28, 1939).
91 The resolution bore the signatures of officers of the association: President Marian Panchyshyn, Secretary Oleksandr Lavrivskyi, Maksym Muzyka, Roman Osinchuk, Mykhailo Dubovyi, Iulian Kordiuk, and Sofiia Parfanovych ("Spovneni lubov´iu do vyzvoleliv. Ukraïns'ke likars'ke tovarystvo z radistiu zustrilo prykhid do nashoho mista Chervonoi Armii," *Vil'na Ukraïna*, no. 5, September 29, 1939, 2).
92 "Novi perspektyvy plodotvorchoi pratsi (na naradi zhurnalistvi L'vova)," *Vil'na Ukraïna*, no. 4, September 28, 1939, 4.

our association disbanded. Simultaneously we penned a 'voluntary statement of congratulations,' addressed to the Soviets and our leader Stalin."[93] A news column titled "Word from Jewish Writers" depicted the Soviet invasion of Eastern Poland as "a joyous morning in our lives," which superseded "the nightmare of bondage."[94]

Other equivalent declarations featured the signatures of public figures as well as lesser-known persons. Soon a few of them were to play important, though never essential, roles in several institutions, including the university, which now operated under new conditions. We simply cannot ascertain who really signed off on such documents and under what pressures. Likely some did it out of a conviction that a historic unification of the Ukrainian nation was occurring. Others, out of fear, since when it comes to obtaining signatures, Soviets certainly had their ways. Aleksander Wat reminisced how one day at the Writers' Association the authorities coerced him and Władysław Broniewski to sign a resolution expressing joy that the USSR had finally incorporated Western Ukraine.[95]

If we were to rely exclusively on memoirs, we might conclude that the faculty of Jan Kazimierz University reacted very negatively to the changes at their institution, bristling in particular at the suddenly privileged position of Galician Ukrainians. They accused this group of loyalism and resorted to personal attacks: Ukrainian faculty members allegedly lacked academic knowledge and preparation for scholarly work. It is difficult to accept such opinions as objective given the university's policies during the interwar period, especially knowing that after 1918 Ukrainian lecturers were barred from returning to Jan Kazimierz University in Lviv. Clearly, the hypocrisy of those enjoying systemic privilege compromised any ability they would have to objectively evaluate the professional qualifications of their competitors.

Nevertheless, the prewar academic community left traces that allow us to look past the pretense of principled faculty, unified in their anti-Soviet attitudes. By criticizing others for loyalty to the Soviets and extoling one's own steadfastness, they distract from their own ambiguous actions. The current chapter continues to follow Polish perspectives on Sovietization, while Chapter Four will present parallel Ukrainian perspectives.

---

93 Ostroverkha, Ostroverkha Papers, k. 106.
94 Srul Ashendorf, "Schaslyvyi ranok zhyttia," *Vil'na Ukraïna*, no. 9, October 4, 1939, 3; Sania Fridman, "Mynula nevolia i zhakh," ibid.
95 Aleksander Wat, *Mój wiek. Pamiętnik mówiony*, vol. 1 (Warsaw: Czytelnik, 1998), 284.

"CADRES DECIDE EVERYTHING"[96]

As part of the new order at the university, Steinhaus mentions that the Soviets created an office of the commissar. Iakiv Levchenko, an informal representative of the NKVD, took on this function. At first Steinhaus believed that Levchenko might take up negotiations on behalf of those arrested, especially of professor Stanisław Grabski, for whose release a delegation of professors pleaded with the commissar, pointing to the advanced age of their colleague. The mathematician recalls how Levchenko instantly scoped out the situation by phone, and then communicated clearly that a release was out of the question: "He is old, but he did young things."[97] According to a statement by Vsevolod Merkulov, the People's Deputy Commissar, a store of weapons was found in the courtyard of Grabski's residence,[98] which the delegation could not have known. After intervening with Levchenko to recover experimental equipment left behind in the hospital, Steinhaus concluded that any contact with the Commissar's office spelled danger. The unit would take advantage of any opportunity to extract useful information from a supplicant.

The scientist found that the Soviets conducted personnel changes with a jarring bluntness, for example by letting go the geographer and dean of the Faculty of Mathematics and Natural Sciences, professor August Zierhoffer,[99] and replacing him with the Ukrainian Stefan Biskupsky, a mere adjunct in the Department of Minerology. Initially Biskupsky had studied at the Ukrainian Underground University; after it dissolved, he continued at Jan Kazimierz University, then went on to work at the Lviv Polytechnic, and finally came to the university.[100]

---

96 This phrase draws on a quote from Stalin's 1935 address to the graduates of the military academy. Soon thereafter, a massive purge began.
97 Steinhaus, *Mathematician for All Seasons: Recollections and Notes*, 244.
98 "Spetspovidomlennia zastupnyka narkoma vnutrishnikh sprav L. Berii pro robotu operatyvnykh chekists'kykh hrup u Zakhidnii Ukraïni. Pislia 28 veresnia 1939 r.," in *Radians'ki orhany derzhavnoï bezpeky u 1939–1941 r. Dokumenty HDA SB Ukraïny*, ed. Vasyl' Danylenko and Serhii Kokin (Kyiv: Vydavnychyi dim "Kyievo-Mohylians'ka Akademiia," 2009), 203.
99 Steinhaus, *Mathematician for All Seasons: Recollections and Notes*, 233–4. See also the university president's decree (Nakaz rektora no. 29, 1.11.1939, ALU, R-119, op. 3, spr. 3, k. 23). Similar accounts appear in Lanckorońska, *Michelangelo in Ravensbruck: One Woman's War against the Nazis*; Kazimierz Żygulski, *Jestem z lwowskiego etapu* (Warsaw: Instytut Wydawniczy PAX, 1994), lwow.home.pl/zygulski/zygulski.html; and Zdzisław Stieber, *Wspomnienia Lwowskie*, ZNIO sygn. 16209/II, k.2, published as Dorota Rembiszewska, ed., *Zdzisław Stieber (1903–1983). Materiały i wspomnienia* (Warsaw: Slawistyczny Ośrodek Wydawniczy, 2013).
100 Lichnoe delo profesora mineralogii i petrografii Biskupskogo Stepana Mikhailovicha, ALU, R-119, op. 1, spr. 16.

Swapping Biskupsky for Zierhoffer certainly violated the rules of an academic institution. Notably, the university president's next decree created an admissions committee within the Faculty of Mathematics and Natural Sciences consisting of Stefan Biskupsky as the new dean, the botanist and professor Stanisław Kulczyński (a former university president; he surveyed the student body about "ghetto benches" and was able to demonstrate that those who demanded the separation of Jewish classmates represented a minority, at which point he was forced to resign), as well as Fedir Derkach (assistant to the dean, a functionary, that is, a political commissar). By drawing on both the new and the old cadres and involving them in matters most vital to the university, the Soviets made an attempt, albeit a minimal one, to preserve some continuity in the university processes.

Steinhaus noted the standard fashion in which the Soviets assumed power at an institution that had enjoyed autonomy, a result of having been governed by the academic community. The new university president would show up and announce: "You are no longer Rector. I am now Rector."[101] The telltale attributes of the new institutional climate come through not just in the facts of unceremonious Soviet power-grabbing, but also in the manner in which journal authors account for it. Their narratives depersonalize the enemy, using a common strategy in the struggle for domination, even if that power was only symbolic. In their notes, the outgoing university president is a person widely known and distinguished, but the new president is a nameless "Soviet."[102] Steinhaus writes about a reshuffle at the Lviv Academy of Foreign Trade, one of the best schools of economics. In 1940 it was transformed into the Lviv Institute of Soviet Trade, to mirror other Soviet schools of economics,[103] and its first president Ivan Khimenko was soon replaced by a Soviet functionary. Parallel changes affected other institutions of higher education, with the exception of the Medical Institute. As a rule, those who had been teaching before the war could continue working at their institutions, but the same was not true for higher education administration.

The freshly hired Ukrainian academics faced disrepute because they were overly active in their cooperation to Sovietize the campuses. The new constellation of power affected Galician Ukrainians positively, not only in terms of their

---

101 Steinhaus, *Mathematician for All Seasons: Recollections and Notes*, 234.
102 Ibid.
103 Postanova Rady narodnykh komisariv URSR No. 842 vid 11 chervnia 1940 r., www.lac.lviv.ua/akademija/history/.

personal status, but also by elevating their culture and nation, which the Second Polish Republic had treated like a stepchild. This sudden shift elicited much *Schadenfreude* among local Ukrainians, a reaction which by most accounts, Polish as well as Ukrainian, became common place. Yet this is only partially true, for when facing oppression, the Ukrainian intelligentsia tended to close ranks in solidarity instead of cooperating with the authorities.

One way to court Ukrainians was to spread anti-Polish propaganda. It touched a raw nerve among Ukrainian citizens oppressed by the Polish administration, and the Soviets capitalized on that resentment. The press of the time swarms with depictions of inhumane struggles suffered by ethnic minorities. Thankfully, the Red Army appeared and freed them from the oppressor's yoke. When central national newspapers (*Pravda, Izvestiia*) relate the events of September 1939, less extensively than the regional media, but still in ample detail, they focus on two elements: the joyful welcome the locals prepared for the Red Army and the misery those same locals had endured before.[104] The media repeatedly emphasized how Poland had economically handicapped the Ukrainian and Jewish populations, stirring up hatred for the oppressors as well as hope for a change of fortunes. A simplistic juxtaposition—"this was then—this is now—this will be" became permanently embedded in Soviet mass propaganda.

Not just Soviet journalists, but a local cadre too, penned such publications. Iaroslav Halan, a Ukrainian writer with communist leanings, a member of the Communist Party of Western Ukraine (KPZU), which was disbanded as part of a 1938 purge (his wife was murdered at the same time after moving to the USSR to study), proclaimed on the pages of *Vilna Ukraina* the birth of a new kind of life. He painted a picture of fresh prospects for Jewish university students, and did not shy away from recounting the gruesome details of a pogrom that had been organized a few years before at the Lviv Polytechnic. A party comrade of Iaroslav Halan from the KPZU, Fryderyk Toperman (Topolski), became one of the practitioners of this innovative propaganda within a curious journalistic genre—a feature story that combats an already defeated regime.[105] Toperman had been a communist youth activist and worked directly with the president

---

104 For example, just one issue of the daily *Vil'na Ukraïna*—no. 7, October 1, 1939, 3–4—printed the following items: "Strakhitlyvi zlodiiannia pol'skoï shlakhty" ["Terrible Deeds of the Polish Nobles"]; Robitnytsia z Mykolaieva, "Zviriacha rozprava" ["Animal-Like Atrocities"]; "Inkvizytsia" ["The Inquisition"], Petro Kozlaniuk, Kuz´ma Pelekhatyi, "Vbyvstva, pozhary i morduvannia" ["Killings, Arsons, Murders"]; and their "Zhertvy skazheniloho pols'koho teroru" ["Victims of Rabid Polish Terror"].

105 Iaroslav Halan, "Pochynaiet'sia spravzhnie zhyttia," *Vil'na Ukraïna*, no. 28, October 1, 1939, 3.

of the International Red Aid Julia Brystygier ("Luna"), an activist of the Youth Legion named Jarosław Żaba, and with Bronisław Bochenek.[106] At a 1935 rally at the Lviv Polytechnic, Toperman propagated slogans that were not directly connected with communist ideology, yet were socially catchy: end tuition, remove *numerus clausus*, eliminate ghetto benches.[107] In a letter to Toperman, a fellow member from the organization "Życie" ["Life"] at the Lviv Polytechnic criticized such demagoguery: "these were slogans advised by the communist party, which thought that no matter how objectively possible it may be to realize these ideas, such proclamations and other actions would help assure the population's affinity and support, so as to attain strategic goals (to obtain power, or rather to incorporate the territories into the Soviet Union), regardless of any casualties."[108]

In order to attract the local population, the Soviets reenlisted old slogans and the established crew of professors (except those who had already been arrested in the first months of the occupation). Some former members of the KPZU began recruiting and organizing. The October elections to the People's Assembly of Western Ukraine took place with the support of both Soviet and local cadres. With boundless energy Wanda Wasilewska threw herself into the electoral campaign. A historian from a later era of the Polish People's Republic explained Wasilewska's dedication to installing Soviets in power: "she was the first to grasp that the liberation of Poland could only occur with the assistance of the Soviet Union and therefore sought its help, actively participating in political efforts in the territories of Western Ukraine."[109]

Not much is known about the involvement of other communist activists; even memoir writers remain vague on the subject or leave it out altogether. I am familiar with reports by two persons who gave details: Fryderyk Toperman and Jarosław Rudniański. We can only guess at the extent of Toperman's involvement in Sovietization, judging from the comrades he brings up, for example Jarosław Żaba, Bronisław Bochenek, and Maria Kikh (representative to the Supreme

---

106 For information about the roles Bochenek and Żaba played in the new political system, see *Politechnika Lwowska 1844–1945* (Wrocław: Wydawnictwo Politechniki Wrocławskiej, 1994), 56. Mykhailo Ostroverkha references a Bochenek-instigated murder at the Polytechnic (Ostroverkha, *Na zakruti. Osin' 1939 r.*, 111).
107 Fryderyk Topolski, manuscript, Toronto, 1984, OK AW II/3289, t. 1, k. 19–20.
108 Zygmunt Bogusz's [actually Józef Horoszowski's] letter to Topolski from Caracas, May 30, 1986, OK AW II/3289, t. 2, k. 23.
109 Eleonora Syzdek, "Foreword," in *Wanda Wasilewska we wspomnieniach*, ed. Eleonora Syzdek (Warsaw: Książka i Wiedza, 1982), 18.

Soviet of the Ukrainian SSR). The author barely mentions misunderstandings with those who "had arrived from the East," and "tried to cool my faith and my trust in the Soviet system."[110] But Jarosław, the son of Stefan Rudniański, who became a member of the Komsomol and a propagandist, described how the NKVD pressured his father to denounce his comrades.[111] Adam Schaff's memoirs sidestep any information that could blemish his reputation later. In the 1930s, Schaff had joined the Socialist Youth International. While he offers a thorough, if affected, account of the prewar and postwar years, he only has this to say about the occupation of Lviv: "The Red Army had seized Lviv and thus began my epic saga. But I won't go into that, lest it take up an entire volume."[112]

Upon consulting Toperman's journals, we learn that in 1943 Schaff and his wife lived in Samarkand, which means that they had been evacuated from Lviv, as was Toperman. Of the three memoirists, Rudniański was the only one to perish, most likely at the hands of the NKVD after his departure from Lviv.

"LVIV WILL BECOME A CITY OF SOCIALIST CULTURE AND SCIENCE"

A reliable tactic of Soviet propaganda in Western Ukraine was to conjure deeply painful experiences from the interwar period: anti-Semitic excesses, *numerus clausus*, ghetto benches, physical violence against youth aspiring to learn, limited access to education for Ukrainians and Jews, and the harassment of Ukrainian professors. In one of the first issues of *Vilna Ukraina*, the propagandist Emelian Iaroslavsky poked fun at "cultured" Poland: "Beatings at school. ... This is the European civilization that Polish lords bestowed on Poland, Western Ukraine, and Western Belarus."[113] In official appearances, Jews and Ukrainians were obligated to emphasize the blessing of equal rights that the new administration had restored to them. In *Czerwony Sztandar*, Leon Pasternak wrote of a dark night of reactionary forces, which only drew back when confronted by the strength of the Red Army:

> Until the Red Army arrived on the territory of former [sic] Western Ukraine, the university in Lviv was a fortress, an infamous base of Polish reactionaries. ... It was here, at the university campus, that corpses of

---
110 Topolski, k. 42.
111 Relacja Jarosława Rudniańskiego z 2000 roku, OK AW I/1193, k. 7.
112 Adam Schaff, *Pora na spowiedź* (Warsaw: BGW, 1993), 47.
113 E. Iaroslavskii, "Komu my jdem na dopomohu," *Vil'na Ukraïna*, no. 3, September 27, 1939.

students of Jewish nationality most often fell, here accounts were settled with Ukrainian youth in the most savage ways. A few reactionary professors assisted those unruly lordly brats. Today all this belongs in the past.[114]

In a more measured tone, Stefan Biskupsky mused in *Vilna Ukraina* about the university's future and celebrated the new opportunities for Ukrainians: "Not even in my dreams could I ever picture myself as the dean of the Faculty of Mathematics and Natural Sciences at Lviv University. During the twenty years of the Polish noble state there was not a single Ukrainian professor here who could lecture in the Ukrainian language."[115] On the day the new university charter was adopted and one day before the signing of Stalin's constitution was commemorated, an article entitled "Our Dream Has Come True," by Kyrylo Studynsky, appeared, its title in lockstep with the obligatory poetics. The piece focused on the past wrongs and on the unfulfilled quest of Ukrainians, if not to achieve their own institution of higher education, then at least to recreate the *antebellum status quo*: "among thirty-five hundred students there were no more than one hundred and fifty Ukrainians. ... Within the Polish Republic's first twenty years, its government did not allow a single Ukrainian professor at Lviv University."[116]

The numbers above do not match data provided by university chronicles. In the second half of the 1920s, the total student population grew to over 6,000; among them were over 1,000 Ukrainians, or approximately seventeen percent.[117] According to statistics from September 1939, of the 4860 students, 665 were Ukrainians and 385 were Jews.[118] But Ukrainian publications had adopted the line that once the Underground University was eliminated, Galician Ukrainians preferred to study abroad over studying in Lviv. Studynsky himself had helped etch this narrative in stone and would not choose to paint a more favorable picture now, given the new ideological pressures. Interestingly, his article used

---

114 Leon Pasternak, "W pracowniach pisarzy," *Czerwony Sztandar*, no. 70 (1939). "Western Ukraine" referred to the prewar period. After November 1, 1939 the term "western regions of the USSR" was adopted.
115 Stepan Biskups'kyi, "Novi shlakhy buinoho rozkvitu nauky," *Vil'na Ukraïna*, no. 49, November 21, 1939, 3.
116 Kyrylo Studyns'kyi, "Zbulasia nasha mriia," *Vil'na Ukraïna*, no. 61, December 5, 1939, 3.
117 Compare Józef Siemiradzki, *Kronika Uniwersytetu Jana Kazimierza we Lwowie za rok akademicki 1926/27* (Lviv: Uniwersytet Jana Kazimierza, 1928), 172; Schramm, *Kronika Uniwersytetu Jana Kazimierza we Lwowie za rok akademicki 1929/30*, 32.
118 "Dopovidna zapuska narkomatu osvity URSR TsK KP(b)U i Radnarkomu URSR pro systemu shkil v Zakhidnii Ukraïni," in *Kul'turne zhyttia v Ukraïni*, vol. 1, 56.

the official name "Polish Republic," instead of the expected insult "Polish noble state," coined by Soviet propagandists.

Meanwhile, the official propaganda employed symbolic violence, defacing Poland's coat of arms and its flag on posters and in media cartoons, debasing its national traditions and even the very notion of a sovereign Polish state. Most familiar is a poster drawing of a Red Army soldier piercing the Polish white eagle with a bayonet. On stage this symbolic violence was enacted in the production of Oleksandr Korniichuk's play *Bohdan Khmelnytsky*; in the last scene Cossacks tear up Polish flags. The tableau had a propagandist parallel: allegedly the locals, so eager to great the Red Army, decked the exterior of their homes with red flags, crafted from Polish flags torn in half.

Such propaganda often had the opposite effect from what was intended, making a mockery of Soviet tools of mind control. For instance, the promise of a bright future right before New Year's day—"Lviv will become a city of socialist culture and science"—flew in the face of what everyone knew: prior to the war, the city had been a wealthy nexus of culture and education, second only to Warsaw, but it became impoverished and lost its significance as soon as it fell under Soviet control. An unknown author announced the joyous news on the paper's front page: "Lviv, far from the city of debauchery and barbarity it was in the times of noble Poland, will become a city of socialist culture and science."[119]

Irrespective of official optimism, direct state violence became common place, even on college campuses. During a meeting at the Lviv Polytechnic in the fall of 1939, prewar fraternity activists, the alleged leaders of anti-Semitic brawls, were assailed.[120] Meanwhile, Soviet authorities sought to win over the

---

119 "Lviv bude mistom kul'tury i nauky. Rishennia Radnarkomu URSR I TsK KP(b)U pro orhanizatsii teatriv, muzychnykh kolektyviv", *Vil'na Ukraïna*, no. 79, December 28, 1939, 1.
120 See Zbysław Popławski's account of a meeting at the Lviv Polytechnic which put an end to the student aid organization *Towarzystwo Bratniej Pomocy*, or Bratniak. In addition to the political commissar, several young activists, among them Janek Krasicki, Jan Bochenek, and Jarosław Żaba, played vital roles there. On the later fortunes of Żaba in Anders' Army and Bochenek as provost at the Warsaw Polytechnic, see Zbigniew Olesiak, "O lwowskim środowisku akademickim podczas wojny," *Kwartalnik Historii Nauki i Techniki* 46, no. 2 (2001): 44; Zygmunt Bogusz in the May 30, 1986 letter to Fryderyk Topolski, k. 23. Zbysław Popławski provided the most precise account of the events at the Lviv Polytechnic. During the meeting, one by one the alleged leaders of the anti-Semitic incidents were pointed out: Henryk Różakolski (vice president of Bratniak), Ludwik Płaczek (director of the First House of Technicians, member of the Scythia fraternity), as well as Jan Płończak (who also belonged to Bratniak). See Zbysław Popławski, "Okupanci na Politechnice Lwowskiej. Społeczność uczelni w latach 1939–1945," in *Wspomnienia Zbysława Popławskiego*, OK AW, typescript

Ukrainian and Jewish communities by emphasizing that all citizens were equal. According to Soviet propaganda, in the new Soviet family all nationalities lived together in accord. Although many Jewish students, refugees among them, criticized the new political system, they (above all the prewar communists) recalled the past—both their own lot as well as the policies of the Polish state—even more critically:

> Especially among Jewish youth from the lowest socioeconomic strata, there were plenty of cases of exceptional perseverance. Anything to be able to study, to erase at least in one respect the stigma of the ghetto and the debasement of a pariah. Before the war, despite the rackets, the bestial anti-Semitism at universities on the part of both the students as well as most professors, we listened to lectures standing up, sometimes behind the door, not permitted to enter the classrooms. Each time we attended classes, we risked being crippled, beaten. Having no money to pay tuition, we begged "charitable" institutions for money and took on loans. For what purpose? What could we attain even through graduation, the happiest of possible outcomes? You could not even dream of a paid position. Every year, the Jewish intelligentsia shrank. Jews were pushed out of most institutions. Yet this did not scare us away at all. Mere survival, near starvation awaited us. We were sort of suspended in the air, without any room for fulfillment, detached from the ground. It was quite difficult to escape utter discouragement, demoralization, extreme cynicism in those conditions. No wonder that when the Bolshevik administration assured us of so-so material conditions, we were almost happy, knowing that after we finish our studies, each of us will be able to work in their field, an engineer in a factory, a doctor in a clinic, hospital, a teacher in a school. We will be able to joyfully pour all our dormant energy into working for the good of society[,] ... arm in arm in a grand race of muscles and brains through factories, mines, schools, *kolkhozes*, and *sovkhozes*. It is not enthusiasm for the Soviet system that speaks through me. I kept my eyes open and saw many defects, flaws. More than once we had to fight against various narrow-minded, ignorant, even stupid Soviet bureaucrats, party members, who used their party ticket like a ladder to a career. Those people placed absolutely no trust in us, no matter that we yearned with exuberance to

---

entered into the 1990 Ośrodek Karta contest. Excerpts are published online at http://www.lwow.home.pl/politechnika/politechnika.html.

contribute to the Soviet system. To us socialism meant 100 times more than a bureaucrat's party ticket or touting cookie-cutter slogans, mouthing assurances of one's "straightforward" agenda. For that, they smelled "counterrevolutionaries," "Trotskyists," "fascist spies" in us. There was a certain lecturer of Marxism-Leninism at our institute, who simultaneously held the position of the secretary of our organization party cell. Only party members could teach the tenets of Marxism-Leninism. At his first lecture this man immediately declared us to be a ring of "counterrevolutionaries." He announced that more than one of us deserved the noose, that Soviet authorities do not tolerate enemies of the system and parasites, and that whether we want to or not, we must obey party orders etc. Such was his first lecture.[121]

This mass brainwashing had a specific purpose: to create an illusion that the population embraced the new order. It also had specific addressees: the former ethnic minorities, who in fact amounted to a majority (approximately sixty-five percent) in the Soviet-occupied areas. According to official propaganda, when the Soviet Union seized fifty-one percent of the area of the Second Republic of Poland, it did not commit an act of aggression, but rather a good deed, bestowed on the population by the Red Army. The people had better show gratitude and flaunt their enthusiasm.

"THEY HAVE LIBERATED US, AND NOTHING CAN BE DONE ABOUT IT"

A month after seizing Lviv, the occupiers called up the People's Assembly of Western Ukraine. Its delegates unanimously adopted a request to the Supreme Soviet of the USSR to incorporate Western Ukraine into the Soviet Union.[122] This step created the appearance that the annexation was legal. Several meetings preceded this People's Assembly session. Attendance at such meetings was required; the consecutive declarations did not differ from each other—proof of supposed unanimity.

There is no doubt that the prewar professor community would never have voted for adopting this request of their own free will. Rather, participants in

---

121 "Anonymous report of a young escapee from Warsaw," in *Archiwum Ringelbluma. Konspiracyjne Archiwum Getta Getta Warszawy*, vol. 3: *Relacje z Kresów*, ed. Andrzej Żbikowski (Warsaw: Żydowski Instytut Historyczny, 2000), 518.

122 See a separate study on this topic: Jan Tomasz Gross, *Studium zniewolenia. Wybory październikowe 22.X.1939* (Cracow: Universitas, 1999).

those assemblies and meetings felt that everything was outside of their control, and indeed, this was the basic goal behind organizing massive shows of support. In late September, during the first meeting, a dress rehearsal occurred where a "unanimous" decision was made to send the standard cable to Stalin. Subsequent assemblies took place according to the same script, which by then was no longer surprising to anyone. Directly after the People's Assembly, another rally occurred to support the declarations adopted at the Assembly, at which the new university president Mykhailo Marchenko, as well as Ilarion Svientsitsky, Zenon Horodysky, Adam Rysiewicz, and Rajszer (first name unknown) gave speeches.[123] It was no longer enough to participate; those gathered had to also voice enthusiasm about the "liberation of the Ukrainian people."

At the time, fear of being arrested was not yet omnipresent, and some still dared to express their opinions. One example is Stanisław Fryze's speech during an election rally at the Polytechnic. A memoirist recalls Fryze's words: "We know that the invader will not stop at our current border, and its historic 'Drang nach Osten' will undoubtedly push it to further aggression. Then, when the Red Army counters the invasion and hangs up victorious flags in Berlin—stated the professor—we will shout 'Long live the victorious Red Army, long live Stalin!'"[124] The memoir's author confused the first meeting, led by the managing commissar Iusimov, with an electoral assembly that took place a month later. He also had significantly altered Fryze's statements, framing it with postwar rhetoric. An agent's report comes closer to the actual content: "If the Red Army moves toward Germany, then Poles will send its delegation to Moscow and join in enthusiastically. … However, I cannot express joy at the liberation of the Ukrainian people, because Poland has not been liberated from the Germans yet."[125] Though the Soviets did not arrest professor Fryze then, after "liberating" Poland in 1944 they promptly put him in prison. He was released after the Union of Polish Patriots (ZPP) intervened on his behalf.[126]

---

123 "Velykyi mitynh w universyteti," *Vil'na Ukraïna*, no. 32, October 29, 1939, 4.
124 Robert Szewalski, "Politechnika Lwowska w latach wojny i okupacji (1939–1945)," in *Lwowskie środowisko naukowe w latach 1939–1945*, ed. Irena Stasiewicz-Jasiukowa (Warsaw: Polska Akademia Nauk, Instytut Historii Nauki i Techniki. Zakład Historii Nauk Społecznych IHNOIT, 1994). The report repeats Zbysław Popławski's (1913–2007) account word for word ("Okupanci na Politechnice Lwowskiej. Społeczność uczelni w latach 1939–1945," k. 7–8). It is possible that Zbysław Popławski is an alias of the author Robert Szewalski.
125 Report of the USRS narkom Ivan Serov addressed to Lavrentii Beria about the progress of investigations from October 13, 1939: O khode razrabotki operativno-chekistkikh grupp Zapadnoi Ukrainy, HDA SBU, f. 16, op. 32. spr. 32, k. 132.
126 *Reabilitovani istoriieiu. L'vivs'ka oblast'*, 196.

Stanisław Fryze was arrested after the second "liberation" of Lviv

In fall 1939, people still assumed that it was all right to strategize how to best face the regime as long as they were speaking within their own circles. Hugo Steinhaus did not hide his outrage at the attitude of newly hired Ukrainian colleagues, "all of whom were in favor of the annexation. When I explained that voting on the resolution would not guarantee that it would carry, they responded by saying that it didn't matter since Ukrainian affairs were not our concern. When I then asked them why, if the issue didn't concern us, we were forced to vote, they were at a loss to answer me." [127]

This account sketches the positions of both camps—the Polish, until now dominant and still deaf to the claims of minority fellow citizens, and the Ukrainian, allegedly avenging its prewar subjugation. However, Steinhaus neglects to acknowledge the new administration's powerful presence: the Soviets dictated not just the overall conditions, but even the norms of behavior among the academic community and the entirety of this occupied society, no matter

---

[127] Steinhaus, *Mathematician for All Seasons: Recollections and Notes*, 233.

how divided. We know how it looked in practice from Mykhailo Ostroverkha, who was staying with Kyrylo Studynsky at the time. The honorary president received a prepared and already typed speech, which he was to give the next day at the opening of the assembly.[128]

While the mathematician realized (with a few exceptions) that the professors at Jan Kazimierz University had little say in the university developments, he would not cut the new, local personnel any slack. This assessment lives on in later interpretations; memoir authors as well as historians maintained than at least until fall 1940 the Soviet authorities favored local Ukrainians and played them against the Poles. Grzegorz Hryciuk offers a more judicious evaluation, pointing to cases of reprisal against Ukrainians.[129]

A curt summary, attributed to the composer Stanislav Liudkevych, states: "They have liberated us, and nothing can be done about it." These words reflect how ambivalent Galician Ukrainians were about the annexation of eastern Poland, on the one hand thrilled that Ukrainian territories were now unified, on the other upset that Sovietization was afflicting all aspects of society. Official language made people realize they were now powerless in a different way, as it referred to the Soviet Union as an "undefeated force," this language standing in for an act of acquiescence or capitulation.[130]

It goes without saying that Ukrainian press and radio statements contain no trace of Galician Ukrainians' reluctance towards the Soviet authorities. Similarly, no official printed record exists of critical reactions or speeches by Poles. The resolutions of the "progressive intelligentsia" at meetings declared that it was a matter of honor to participate in preparing and conducting the elections to the People's Assembly and to send their best representatives. It is possible that some among the Ukrainian intelligentsia really converted, yet no documents substantiate this assertion. It merits emphasis that official documents cannot serve as sufficient proof; if we were to take them at face value, we would have to extend the same trust to the official declarations printed in *Czerwony Sztandar*. Ostroverkha, constrained not by censorship, only by his own ideology, wrote that the Bolsheviks were hostile toward local Ukrainians, who "mocked them to their faces."[131] The NKVD archives confirm this, at least

---

128 Ostroverkha, Ostroverkha Papers, k. 150.
129 Grzegorz Hryciuk, "Całkiem dobre miejsce na przetrwanie wojny," in *Ukraiński polonofil. Pamięci Bohdana Osadczuka*, ed. Bogumiła Berdychowska and Ola Hnatiuk (Lublin: UMCS, 2012), 111–22.
130 Kyrylo Studyns'kyi, "Peremozhna syla," *Vil'na Ukraïna*, no. 44, November 15, 1939, 2.
131 Ostroverkha, Ostroverkha Papers, k. 103.

in part. Those UNDO activists not already in Soviet custody appealed to the community to sit out the election.[132]

However, official celebratory expressions of happiness abounded. An obsequious letter to Khrushchev bears the signatures of the director of the Shevchenko Scientific Society, Ivan Rakovsky, and its members: Kyrylo Studynsky, Ivan Krypiakevych, Volodymyr Levytsky, director of the NTSh library Volodymyr Doroshenko, archeologist Iaroslav Pasternak, Roman Harasymchuk, geographer Iury Poliansky, and Iosyp Chaikivsky.[133] To no avail; three months later the NTSh leadership had to adopt a resolution dissolving their own organization. And so the Soviets abolished the oldest Ukrainian scientific organization, the pride of the Ukrainian intelligentsia, and nationalized its assets. Certainly Galician Ukrainians could not have considered this a necessary sacrifice in exchange for reuniting Ukrainian territories.

Any illusions some educated Ukrainians might have harbored in the fall of 1939 disappeared within a few weeks, or a few months at the most. By fall 1940 nobody was fooled. Twenty years later Oleksandr Dombrovski recalled the disenchantment: "After the initial few months of the honeymoon, our lives were turning gloomy and uncertain. Ukrainian signage on street corners and at the university, the half-official status of Ukrainian (next to the official Muscovite language), somehow failed to entice. We saw that it was not the Ukraine we aspired to.[134]

If we read memoirs side by side with official publications on the one hand, and with secret service documentation on the other, broad support for the Soviet authorities no longer appears unequivocal. It turns out that the Lviv community did not trust even its most prominent figures such as Studynsky or the writer Wanda Wasilewska and considered them government minions. As early as the end of 1939, the NKVD began investigating, as separate cases, well-known persons who had just signed loyalty oaths, deeming them "nationalists." Against Studynsky they applied special measures. As part of the

---

132 In a note from October 13, 1939, the People's Commissar (*narkom*) Ivan Serov informed Lavrentii Beria about a denunciation by the agent "Zhuk," which pertained to an attempt to stop Galician Ukrainians from voting, initiated by the former UNDO secretary Frants Svistel and Father (rev.) Leontii Kunyts'kyi (O khode raboty operativno-chekistkikh grupp Zapadnoi Ukrainy, Dokladnye zapiski ob operativnoi rabote, provedennoi NKVD USSR pri prisoedinenii zapadnykh oblastei USSR, f. 16, op. 32, spr. 33, k. 132).
133 "Peredova inteligentsiia. Rezoliutsiia naukovykh pratsivnykiv" and "Lyst do M. S. Khrushchova," *Vil'na Ukraïna*, no. 17, October 13, 1939, 1–2.
134 Dombrovs'kyi, "Do istorii l'vivs'koho universytetu v 1939–1941 rr.," 35.

operation "Zapadnye," in December 1939, the NKVD assigned agents to cover Galician activists, and placed Studynsky in the center of their investigation. On February 17, 1940, People's Commissar Ivan Serov impatiently demanded from his subordinates that they improve their reporting on Kyrylo Studynsky, since he was a principal suspect.[135] In summer 1940, almost two months after Wasilewska spoke with Stalin, and after Stalin sent his encrypted telegram ordering a softer policy toward Poles in the Western districts and Khrushchev issued a directive about "the abuses committed by local authorities against the Poles,"[136] the NKVD continued to investigate Wasilewska, prompted by a tip they received about attempts to set up a radio transmitter. Allegedly it was the Polish Military Organization POW that tasked Wasilewska with this assignment (the myths surrounding this organization merit a separate study; although twenty years had passed since it was disbanded, still the Soviets continued to battle the POW). On August 20, 1940, narkom Serov ordered an urgent surveillance of Wasilewska, at the same time warning his subordinates not to make more careless errors, "repeating known mistakes which resulted in difficult consequences."[137]

Serov's nebulous reference is most likely a euphemism for the murder of Marian Bogatko, Wasilewska's husband, committed by the NKVD. Bogatko was shot in front of his wife, in a home where they were staying at the time. Hardly two months had passed since Wasilewska had become a delegate to the Supreme Soviets of the USSR. In contrast, Bogatko espoused a sober outlook on Soviet reality (though otherwise he was quite prone to drinking). In his memoir, Aleksander Wat mentions that Wasilewska and Bogatko had differences of opinion, and as a simple, straightforward worker he ridiculed the reigning hypocrisy. He could not stand the unscrupulous lies his wife served to participants of a rally that took place after their first Kyiv trip together.

---

135 Soobshchenie nachal'niku oblastnogo upravleniia NKVD kapitanu Krasnovu, g. L'vov, o rezoliutsii narkoma Serova na dokladnoi po Studins'komu, 19.02.1940, in Svedeniia o sostoianii operativnoi raboty UNKVD L'vovskoi oblasti 1940 g., f. 16, op. 33, spr. 71, k. 52.

136 This document was preserved in several archives. More on the subject in Sergei Filippov, *Deiatel'nost' organov VKP(b) v zapadnykh oblastiakh Ukrainy i Belorussii v 1939–1941 gg.*, vol. 1: *Repressii protiv poliakov i pol'skikh grazhdan. Istoricheskie sborniki "Memoriala"* (Moscow: Zven'ia, 1997), 55. The first researcher to cover the subject was Grzegorz Hryciuk: Grzegorz Hryciuk, "Polacy we Lwowie pod okupacją radziecką i niemiecką," PhD diss., Instytut Historii Uniwersytetu Wrocławskiego, 1993, summary in *Dzieje Najnowsze* 3 (1997): 179–82.

137 HDA SBU, f. 16, op. 33, spr. 71, k. 356–7.

> Afterwards Bogatko tells me and Broniewski: "Let's go to the tavern!" And he dragged us to the tavern, he was a terrible drunkard. Imagine, taverns are full of Soviet officers and right after the rally this Bogatko does not just say, but booms in his deep voice various things. I recall, for instance, this sentence: "Just remember, when you go to Kyiv, first step from the train car, grab on—keep one hand on the suitcases, and the other on your cap, because they will swipe it off your head."[138]

If it is not a product of the poet's imagination, this encounter must have taken place at the turn of 1939 and 1940, since on January 23, 1940 the NKVD arrested both Wat and Broniewski, along with a few other writers. Four months later they murdered Bogatko. Wasilewska states she went to Kyiv on January 24, 1940, if she was not mistaken about the dates. Thus we can only consider Wat's account plausible if we assume either that in January she traveled to Kiev twice (which she does not say) or that she gave the incorrect date of her departure for Kyiv (which, in turn, would mean that this was not the reason for her delayed intervention on Broniewski's behalf, as she claimed). No matter if all the details behind the story of Wanda Wasilewska and her husband Marian Bogatko are believable, this much is certain: the NKVD leadership did not trust Wasilewska. As we now know, they were wrong.

According to Khrushchev's memoirs, he asked Korniichuk and Bazhan to tell Wasilewska the truth about her husband's murder: "We told Wanda Lwowna the whole truth and asked for her understanding. Wasilewska believed that the killing was not premeditated and continued her active work, remaining positively disposed towards us."[139] For the time being though, official statements pinned the blame for the murder on Ukrainian nationalists.

It emerges then that when the Soviets favored Ukrainians, they were skillfully playing a game of appearances to obscure their actual goal, so accurately recognized by Kedryn: to eliminate "Ukrainian irredentism" in Eastern Galicia. By the mid-1930s, Soviet security agencies made this political objective known, and presented it expressly to Polish diplomats. Jacek Bruski researched documentation related to the Polish diplomatic reaction to the Holodomor, the Great Famine in Ukraine. He states that the Soviets were especially irritated that the Polish administration would tolerate on its territories the activities

---

138 Wat, *Mój wiek. Pamiętnik mówiony*, 301.
139 N. S. Chruszczow, "Fragmenty wspomnień N. S. Chruszczowa," *Zeszyty Historyczne* 132 (2000): 140.

A saying circulated about Wanda Wasilewska and Oleksandr Korniichuk: "less a couple, more a squad"

of Ukrainian organizations, especially those entities which during this tragic period "led an anti-Soviet campaign." In the fall of 1933, a year after the USSR and the Second Polish Republic signed a mutual nonaggression agreement, the Soviets expected Poland to coordinate their efforts against "nationalists," which was to lay the groundwork for a new era of mutual relations.[140]

GO ALONG, GET ALONG?

Hugo Steinhaus wrote the parts of *Mathematician for All Seasons* (*Wspomnienia i zapiski*) that concerned the beginning of the war while he and his wife were

---

140 Jan Jacek Bruski, "Nieznane polskie dokumenty na temat Hołodomoru. Efekty rekonesansu archiwalnego w Moskwie," *Nowa Ukraina* 5–6 (2008): 64–76, esp. 69, 74.

Hugo Steinhaus

in hiding in Berdechów by Stróże between 1943–44. His account, the postwar memoir by Karolina Lanckorońska,[141] as well as the journals Tadeusz Tomaszewski kept at the time, are all valuable as direct testimonies. They reflect events and climate far more accurately than memoirs written several decades later, like that of Jan Kott, Steinhaus's son-in-law and a distinguished critic,[142] or narratives relating to the academic community authored by Maria Bartlowa,[143] Oleksandr Dombrovsky, Alfred Jahn,[144] Stanisław Hartman[145] or Kazimierz Żygulski.[146] When Steinhaus remarks about certain people, he can be quite harsh, and while also being rather lenient with others, especially with people close to him. Persons who cooperated with the regime were subjected to his particularly unforgiving judgement. In that category he only spared Jan Kott, who actively participated in official literary activities in occupied Lviv, and Stefan Banach. About Banach's involvement Steinhaus writes in a roundabout manner: "Stefan Banach was wrong when he said to me 'This is a system run by the intelligentsia.' It was a system where the intelligentsia was tightly controlled by the Kremlin."[147]

---

141 Karolina Lanckorońska states in her "Prologue" that she penned her reminiscences after the war ended in 1945 and did not change much in the printed edition (*Michelangelo in Ravensbruck: One Woman's War against the Nazis*, 25).
142 Jan Kott, *Still Alive: An Autobiographical Essay* (New Haven: Yale University Press, 1994).
143 M. Bartlowa, "Pamiętnik Marii Bartlowej," *Zeszyty Historyczne* 81 (1987): 34–65. For a detailed discussion of the incaccuracies in Bartlowa's journal, see Kalbarczyk, "Kazimierz Bartel pod okupacją sowiecką we Lwowie," 279–80.
144 Alfred Jahn, *Z Kleparowa w świat szeroki* (Wrocław: Ossolineum, 1991). His memoirs, written in the early 1980s, abound in inaccuracies, in cases when later events overshadow earlier ones: the author talks about his return from the Romanian border; he got to Lviv on September 17, 1939 through Ternopil, where he supposedly ran into several of the Lviv professors; he mentions Steinhaus and Chwistek by name, but neither was in Ternopil at that time. When describing a rally at the university, he states that next to Oleksandr Korniichuk sat Wanda Wasilewska. Yet Wasilewska was not in Lviv yet, and her fascination with Korniichuk (in which she was not alone) began no earlier than late 1939. They did not know each other before, which multiple sources confirm. Based on Włodzimierz Sokorski's and Maria Sokorska's remembrances about Wanda Wasilewska, we can determine the approximate date of her arrival in Lviv—it was the first half of October. Compare Syzdek, "Foreword," 159. We know from Wasilewska's letter to the Moscow Gosizdat in which she requests her overdue remuneration that on October 8, 1939 she and her husband were in Kovel. Compare Vasilii Tokarev, "Stalin i Vanda Vasilevskaia: limitirovannyi dialog (1940)," *Przegląd Rusycystyczny* 1, no. 117 (2007): 43; the author cites a letter preserved in the Russian State Archive of Literature and Arts (Rossiiskii Gosudarstvennyi Arkhiv Literatury i Iskusstva, f. 2550, op. 2, d. 116, l. 1).
145 Hartman, "Wspomnienia."
146 Żygulski, *Jestem z lwowskiego etapu*.
147 Steinhaus, *Mathematician for All Seasons: Recollections and Notes*, 238.

Stefan Banach

Predictably, the Soviets and the Nazis alike score the worst in Steinhaus's memoir, but he does not spare his former (Ukrainian) fellow citizens either. The author judges them harshly for their roles in installing both regimes—the Soviet and the Nazi, and leaves no room for any shades of grey, although he did so for his Jewish colleagues. With Ukrainians, Steinhaus only condemns, taking aim at specific persons, and stretching the blame over an entire community: "Our university was renamed after him [Ivan Franko] in an effort to win over the Ukrainian intelligentsia to the Bolshevik cause. However grateful the Ukrainian intellectuals may have been for such concessions, many of them continued to look in anticipation to Germany to liberate them from the Bolshevik yoke."[148]

---

148 Ibid., 251.

The view of Ukrainian intelligentsia as collaborators became prevalent as early as the second half of 1941. At that time, a few educated Ukrainians, who under the Soviet occupation held relatively high positions (though short of reaching the leadership level), acquired similar status at the start of the German occupation. Typical in this respect are Tomasz Tomaszewski's remarks about Ukrainians and the "nationwide *wallenrodyzm*" (a term derived from a famous drama by Mickiewicz that over time came to signify treacherous revenge), "a historical precedent."[149] In the eyes of Hugo Steinhaus, Iury Poliansky[150] exemplified this stand, and perhaps a few other professors at Lviv University: mathematician Myron Zarytsky, historian Ivan Krypiakevych, linguist Vasyl Simovych, or physician Marian Panchyshyn. The same prejudice persisted among most Galician Poles. In this regard, the opinion of the educated class was quite unoriginal, conforming to a widely accepted stereotype.

A clear-cut assessment of the roles those scholars played during both occupations is difficult to make. Many Ukrainian memoirists avoid passing judgement on their compatriots' involvement with the occupying authorities, and instead go to great lengths to emphasize examples of selfless actions for the benefit of the Ukrainian community. Steinhaus reproduces stereotypes common among Polish authors, who rushed to ascribe to Ukrainians (pretend) pro-Soviet and (actual) pro-German and anti-Polish sentiments.

Vasyl Simovych, who stepped in as acting university president during Bychenko's trip to Kyiv, by coincidence was made accountable by the Germans for the university's assets. Though the announcement of a temporary closure of the university bears his signature, this distinguished scholar and teacher turned down a minister position in Stetsko's Nazi-backed government.[151] On the other

---

149 Tomaszewski, *Lwów. Pejzaż psychologiczny*, 91.
150 Iury Poliansky (1892–75) fought in the Polish-Ukrainian war, was interned after World War I, and between 1920–22 was state commandant of the Ukrainian Military Organization. A geographer, he taught at a Ukrainian high school before World War II; he was a member of the Shevchenko Scientific Society; between September and December of 1939 he served as vice minister of education; after December director and professor at the Faculty of Geography; and after January 1940 university vice president (personnel form, ALU, R. 119, op. 1, spr. 149, k. 6–8), as well as academic secretary of the Academic Council and dean of the Department of Geography. At the start of the German occupation, Poliansky was appointed interim mayor of Lviv; by July 22 a German, Hans Kujath, took over the post, becoming Stadthauptmann.
151 Kost' Pan'kivs'kyi, *Vid Derzhavy do Komitetu (Lito 1941 roku u L'vovi)* (New York: Kliuchi, 1970), 46–7, Iurii Shevel'ov, "Zhyttia i pratsia Vasylia Simovycha," *Slovo* 23 (1991); also confirmed by Iaroslav Stetsko: Iaroslav Stets´ko, *30 chervnia 1941. Proholoshennia vidnovlennia derzhavnosty Ukraïny* (Toronto: Liga Vyzvolennia Ukrainy, 1967).

hand, he succeeded, with Iury Poliansky, in arranging at the end of the first month of the German occupation for payments of salaries to university professors, even though the authorities did not plan on reactivating the university. Yet this gesture met with indignation on the part of some professors. As Tadeusz Tomaszewski recalls, Jerzy Manteuffel, upon hearing that the Ukrainian City Council issued the payments, became outraged: "What Ukrainian [Council]? … We consider it to be the Lviv City Council overall."[152] Apparently Poles could not stomach a gesture of solidarity from Ukrainian academics. Tomaszewski is the only Polish author to even take note of this occurrence. In November 1941, the linguist Zdzisław Stieber obtained a document from Simovych confirming his employment at the university, but his journals omit both incidents: the salary payment and the obtained affidavit, which Simovych issued although he was not supposed to—the university had a German property administrator at the time.[153]

Reading Tomaszewski's journals, we come across details highly relevant to our understanding how the academic community responded to the new occupation. German reprisals against the intelligentsia and the fate of Jagiellonian University were common knowledge. In reference to how the Germans beat Steinhaus and expelled him from his home at Kadecka Street, the psychologist noted: "and he was so glad to get rid of the Bolsheviks!"[154] The remark refers to Steinhaus's initial reaction to the retreat of the Soviet occupier in late June 1941; on a personal level he also hoped to regain partial ownership of the apartment building taken by NKVD officers, of course without compensation. The psychologist describes the circumstances in which Steinhaus left his house somewhat differently: he moved out gradually, and nobody bothered him.[155]

When analyzing the reactions to the start of the German occupation, Tomaszewski writes that the professors were very worried about opportunities to generate income, but they insisted that their "place is at the university." In this context he mentions two Ukrainian women, former students, who offered rational advice suggesting that the faculty immediately begin looking for work, before not just the university, but schools too, have closed.[156]

---

152 Tomaszewski, *Lwów. Pejzaż psychologiczny*, 112.
153 See Rembiszewska, ed., *Zdzisław Stieber (1903–1983). Materiały i wspomnienia*, 243–64, especially the document reproduction on p. 245.
154 Tomaszewski, *Lwów. Pejzaż psychologiczny*, 67.
155 Ibid., 76.
156 Ibid., 65.

The psychologist was one of the few people alert to differences in attitudes among the Ukrainian intelligentsia. In his opinion the older generation displayed a distance towards the German authorities and condemned their Jewish policies. They also held those Ukrainians, who—to invoke Ilarion Svientsitsky—"lick the Germans' boots"[157] in low regard. One could not expect resistance to the new occupier who governed by terror, however, the older generation provided active assistance to the community. The Metropolitan Sheptytsky offered to shelter the rabbi Jecheskiel Lewin. When the Germans demanded that Lviv's Jews collect a sum of twenty million rubles, the Metropolitan contributed a large amount as well.[158] Filip Friedman wrote about similar expressions of solidarity among Poles, although he did not give any specifics.[159]

A well-known figure among the Ukrainian intelligentsia, Iury Poliansky, sought to find a *modus vivendi* during the Soviet occupation. Alfred Jahn, then an assistant in the geography department, praised Poliansky who had just been nominated by the new university president for the position of department director:

> The new Institute [of Geography] director was kind to Poles. ... He hated the new system and the newcomers just as we did, but he had to hide it more than the Poles did. In moments of candor he would tell us that it was hard for him to play his role and protect an almost exclusively Polish institute (they added just one Ukrainian assistant Lewicki [Levytsky], by the way a man also well-disposed towards us, and one Russian Jew from Kyiv, Silber, with whom we soon reached an understanding).[160]

In addition to directing the Institute of Geography, Yury Poliansky served in the important function of academic secretary in the Academic Council. The new system gave him the authority to initiate the process of confirming academic ranks. The university archive stores a number of documents signed by him, which provided a basis for further official procedures. Moscow was reluctant to confirm prewar ranks, yet that did not discourage either the vice

---

157 Ibid., 143.
158 Ibid., 111. Tomaszewski writes about rumors circulating among Ukrainians that the Metropolitan offered money, and references a sum of 30,000, but it is not clear if these were rubles.
159 Filip Friedman, *Zagłada Żydów lwowskich*, vol. 4 (Wydawnictwa Centralnej Żydowskiej Komisji Historycznej przy Centralnym Komitecie Żydów Polskich, 1945).
160 Jahn, *Z Kleparowa w świat szeroki*, 110; also see Tomaszewski, *Lwów. Pejzaż psychologiczny*, 52.

president of academic affairs Kyrylo Studynsky or his subordinate Iury Poliansky from submitting requests to recognize the academic status of university colleagues. The two undertook such efforts regardless of the national origin of their coworkers.[161]

Poliansky behaved similarly during the German occupation when, in July 1941, he served as an interim mayor of Lviv for three weeks. Though German notices bore his signature, he did not execute directives and orders blindly. As Tadeusz Tomaszewski writes, during both occupations his attitude towards Poles was conciliatory: "The Poles considered Poliansky 'a very decent nationalist.'"[162] After he was relieved of his duties as "mayor," he became director of the Nature Museum. Still he continued to assist or even reverse the misfortunes of one or another person when he could. The last chapter of this book follows Poliansky's efforts to help Lviv's Jews.

During the German occupation, Marian Panchyshyn and Ivan Krypiakevych found themselves in much better circumstances compared to most local academics, yet they had no say in decisions concerning more than the few dozen people they oversaw. The institution led by Ivan Krypiakevych emerged relatively late and was not, contrary to the intentions of its founders, an academic institute akin to the prewar Shevchenko Scientific Society or even to a chapter of the Soviet Academy of Sciences. Still, at least it was authorized. Professional Medical Courses, like Professional Technical Courses, provided employment for Ukrainians and Poles, although at first Ukrainians occupied the more important positions. In sum: whatever the German authorities denied to Polish Lvivians, they often permitted Ukrainian Lvivians. For many Polish authors this offered proof sufficient to accuse Ukrainians of collaborating with Germans.

---

161 See, for example, an opinion regarding the Polonist Juliusz Kleiner, with signatures by Studyns'kyi and Polians'kyi (Lichnoe delo professora Kliainera Iuliusha Germanovicha, ALU, R-119, op. 1, spr. 80, 23.12.1939–11.01.1941, k. 56, 59); an excerpt from the minutes of the Academic Council meeting of December 30, 1940 adopting the resolution to request the confirmation of the rank of professor for Stefan Banach (ALU, R-119, op. 1, spr. 11, k. 3, Banakh Stepan Stepanovich, 30.12.1940–10.1.1941); an opinion on Germanist and literary theorist Roman Ingarden (Lichnoe delo professora kafedry nemetskoi literatury, Ingardena Romana Romanovicha, ALU, R-119, op. 1, spr. 73, k. 22); an opinion on Polonists Władysław Floryan (ALU, R-119, op. 1, spr. 195, k. 65) and Kazimierz Kolbuszewski [in fact Kazimierz Kobzdaj] ("Lichnoe delo Kol'bushevskogo Kazimira Tadeusha Antonovicha," ALU, R-119, op. 1, spr. 85); and an opinion on Cracow attorney Stanisław Ehrlich (Lichnoe delo Stanislava Solomonovicha Erlikha, ALU, R-119, op. 1, spr. 217, k. 128). All of these documents established a basis for further procedures.

162 Tomaszewski, Lwów. Pejzaż psychologiczny, 75.

It was likely this opinion that later prompted Steinhaus to fully distance himself from Ukrainians and their approach to the Soviet administration. In turn, the prejudice deepened his dislike for Ukrainian culture and language:

> A language is not just a code for communicating between people, but provides a well-rounded picture of the very soul of the people whose native tongue it is. The Ukrainian language is a peasant language; whenever anybody speaks Ukrainian he feels in his heart that he is playing at being a peasant. My reluctance to deliver my lectures in Ukrainian did not at all derive from a dislike of Ukrainians; had I been told to lecture in the Masurian dialect or that of Polish uplanders, I would still have refused. … A Polish speaker who doesn't habitually speak in peasant argot will never learn to speak Ukrainian. But please do not think that I am here giving voice to a mere nationalistic bias. In many ways the relation of Ukrainian to Polish is analogous to that of *Wasserpolnisch* to German in Silesia, or Slovak to Czech, or Breton to French, or Yiddish to Hebrew.[163]

It is worth noting that although the author draws on Romantic notions of language and nation, he harbors a deep bias against the lower classes, not just Ukrainians, but also Jews, and Poles too. According to Steinhaus, their way of expressing themselves precluded precision, attributable only to the language of the educated class. It appears that his dislike for Ukrainian stems from Polish acculturation, and from his dislike for Yiddish and the culture of the Galician shtetl.

The author's choice of the adjective to reference the Ukrainian language merits a lengthier commentary. The above quote, from Abe Shenitzer's English translation, sidesteps any discrepancies and relies on the modern standard descriptor of "Ukrainian," but in the Polish original Steinhaus used the adjective "ruski." In the 1930s a perplexing discussion was taking place in the Second Republic of Poland about the proper name for the Ukrainian language and nation. In accordance with an administrative decision the use of qualifiers "Rusin" (for today's Ukrainian, equivalent to "Ruthenian") and "ruski" (as the related adjective) was to become the norm in the Second Republic, though in colloquial language it carried a negative connotation. Earlier in the book, Steinhaus relates his preference for this term to actual linguistic usage and invokes an analogy to the Germans, for whom it would not be reasonable "to insist

---

163 Steinhaus, *Mathematician for All Seasons: Recollections and Notes*, 251–2.

that people of other nations call them 'Deutsche.'"¹⁶⁴ Language users themselves, especially the educated class, unequivocally supported the designation "Ukrainian," which connoted an aspiration to national independence. Meanwhile, in the Polish language, "ukraiński" and "Ukraina," as derived from the notion of "ziemie ukrainne" or "frontier lands," were at the time reserved—in keeping with the ideas of the pre-partition Polish Commonwealth—exclusively for the Dnipro region. Thus by arbitrarily imposing this particular name ("Rusin" and "ruski") on Ukrainian language and nationality, the administration implicitly continued its fight against political aspirations of Galician Ukrainians, and reinforced its own longing for the past prowess of the Polish Commonwealth—a state representing an all-Polish legacy.

The "nationalization" of the notion of the Polish Commonwealth (which occurred in the era of modern nationalisms, in the case of Poland—the second half of the nineteenth and first half of the twentieth centuries) established the Polish primacy to inherit the state's traditions and its symbols. Poles achieved this aim all the faster and more effectively because Belarusians, Lithuanians, and Ukrainians took a less political route to nation building, instead reaching back to their folk traditions. Following years of lively debates about the lexical transition from "Ruthenian" to "Ukrainian" at the turn of the nineteenth and twentieth centuries, by the interwar period Galician Ukrainians regarded the process as concluded. Yet the Polish state administration insisted on the outdated form "Ruthenian," and made it obligatory in official use. Naturally, Ukrainian patriots considered it offensive, especially because it was only recently that Ukrainians had lost the 1918–19 war against Poland.

Steinhaus's antipathies extended to the Cyrillic alphabet. He tells a story about a Soviet journalist who came for an interview. When the professor handed him a business card, the journalist inquired how to transcribe Steinhaus's name in Cyrillic. The mathematician replied condescendingly that it was the journalist's problem and commented in his diary: "The poor man didn't seem to be able to grasp that the Roman alphabet suffices for us."¹⁶⁵ One can understand if Steinhaus was unwilling to use Ukrainian if forced, however, his statement about that language's inferior status is perplexing. A saying popularized by the distinguished linguist Max Weinreich could serve as an automatic counterpoint: "A shprakh iz a dialekt mit an armey un flot" ("A language is a dialect with an army and navy"). More than one prewar intellectual in the

---

164 Ibid., 50.
165 Ibid., 275.

Polish Republic espoused and spread views similar to Steinhaus's. One's relationship to language serves as a litmus test of our readiness to recognize other nations' claims to sovereignty. To be fair, the mathematician was a stickler for precise usage of Polish, and thus his sentiment barred not only users of Ukrainian (or, his term, Ruthenian), but also of Yiddish from the intellectual community. Kedryn may have been right when he wrote:

> in the twentieth year of having his own state "an average Pole" knew more or less as much about Ukrainians as about bushmen. And upon hearing that there are more than forty million Ukrainians in the world, of whom six million live in Poland, he would regard his interlocutor with suspicion, seeing in him an enemy of the Polish state, who with these base fabrications undermines faith in the mighty Polish nation.[166]

Steinhaus persisted in inventing all kinds of reasons to avoid participating in Soviet academic life. He declined business trips, even when the Soviets applied flattery in place of threats. Despite such open resistance, he led the Faculty of Analysis until June 1941[167] and served on the admissions committee.[168] He also worked at the Banach-led Lviv branch of the Institute of Mathematics, Academy of Sciences of the USSR.[169] To keep his engagement in public life to a minimum, he only participated in meetings he absolutely could not avoid, such as union meetings. Union membership was required; the application process, regardless of the specific professional community, resembled—as Mieczysław Jastrun commented on similar occasion—mudslinging.

It is no use looking through Steinhaus's memoirs for information that could illuminate the actions of his close friends or family members at the time. Even a moment of emotional upheaval—the arrest of his son-in-law Jan Kott—is treated quite succinctly (though Steinhaus's account still makes it easier to reconstruct the events than Kott's reminiscences, which are filled with fictional elements). During this period Steinhaus mentions Banach only twice and says almost nothing about his brother-in- law Leon Chwistek, founder of

---

166 Homo Politicus [Ivan Kedryn-Rudnyts'kyi], *Prychyny upadku Pol'shchi*, 240.
167 See university president's directive regarding faculty directors (Nakaz rektora no. 307, 29.10.1940, ALU, R-119, op. 3, spr. 31, k. 241–2) and directives confirming the vacation schedule in 1940 and 1941 (Nakaz rektora no. 197, 24.6.1940, ALU, R-119, op. 3, spr. 31, k. 218–21; Nakaz rektora no. 164, 7.6.1940, ALU, R-119, op. 3, spr. 51, k. 282–8).
168 Nakaz rektora no. 72, 23.11.1939, ALU, R-119, op. 3, spr. 3, k. 60
169 Steinhaus, *Mathematician for All Seasons: Recollections and Notes*, 253.

Formism and the most distinguished Polish logician. Only in passing do his readers learn that Chwistek evacuated with the Soviets; a second mention appears as Steinhaus chronicles his family's fate in the early days of the German occupation. After leaving their house at Kadecka Street, they moved into the upper story of the villa of professor Benedykt Fuliński, until then occupied by Steinhaus's sister and brother-in-law. The couple feared the Gestapo would come to the apartment because of Chwistek's association with the authorities during the Soviet occupation.

In the rather traditional Galicia the logician Chwistek never developed a following; his leftist politics coupled with his efforts to popularize avantgarde art made sure of that. He was a close friend of Bruno Jasieński and a group of Futurists known for being communist activists, which Lvivians disapproved of. In 1930, the scholar-artist with his wife and daughter moved from Cracow to Lviv because he could not get hired at the Jagiellonian University. Here, at Jan Kazimierz University, he led the Faculty of Logic until the Soviets removed him. In contrast to Hugo Steinhaus, he did not avoid public appearances; in fact, at the intelligentsia assembly he supported candidates for representatives to the Supreme Soviet of the USSR he knew from Cracow: his former teacher Studynsky and Wanda Wasilewska.[170] Many considered the pieces he published in *Czerwony Sztandar* to cross the line of collaboration,[171] as was the case with public appearances by Boy-Żeleński. When Chwistek switched to lecturing in Ukrainian, he invited a social boycott by the community.[172]

The dislike for the Ukrainian language among former professors did not simply reflect national prejudice; it also expressed their opposition to the policy of Ukrainization introduced by the Soviets. As we have seen already, such Sovietization was initially implemented by forcing the use of the Ukrainian

---

170 Leon Chwistek, "Głos uczonego," *Czerwony Sztandar*, no. 153, March 24, 1940; Ukrainian version of the text is published as "Zbory tvorchoii inteligentsii. Vystup Leona Chwisteka," *Vil'na Ukraïna*, no. 65, March 19, 1940, 3.
171 The first text by Chwistek, titled "Twórcza prawda" ["Creative Truth"], appeared in *Czerwony Sztandar*, no 61, December 5, 1939; the issue was devoted to the anniversary of the adoption of Stalin's constitution. On that day the university approved a change in its statute, introducing far reaching structural changes. Jacek Trznadel assesses Chwistek's role very harshly (*Kolaboranci. Tadeusz Boy-Żeleński i grupa komunistycznych pisarzy we Lwowie 1939–1941* [Komorów: Antyk, 1998], 475). Bohdan Urbankowski's book treats him more gently ("a distinguished, albeit naïve in life matters, philosopher"—*Czerwona msza, czyli uśmiech Stalina* [Warsaw: Alfa, 1998], 509).
172 Tomaszewski, *Lwów. Pejzaż psychologiczny*, 56. The author also recalls the reaction of Roman Ingarden, who turned his back on Boy-Żeleński when they ran into each other (ibid., 27).

language, which carried the benefit of driving a wedge between the local populations. A contemporary researcher, Vladyslav Hrynevych, described it as "de-Ukrainization with the help of the Ukrainian language," so much so that even Galician Ukrainians reacted negatively to this thinly disguised strategy.

For Steinhaus, the hardest to accept was—as he referred to it—"the betrayal of the learned;" a section of Lviv's intelligentsia that tolerated Soviet propaganda or even took part in it. Yet he wrote about it very curtly, perhaps because the issue involved his community. Conversely, when talking about outsiders—communist activists, Ukrainian intelligentsia—the scientist spared no details. If he considered Soviet agitators to be half-witted creatures, the entire system seemed to him well thought out, founded by "fathers of the untruth." He mercilessly attacked the Polish right, which, in his opinion, immediately rebranded itself as pro-Soviet: "Thus it was that in the space of a few weeks these young people went, chameleonlike, through a succession of political stripes—from national radicalism, through democracy, to Bolshevism."[173] He also tears into assistants-turned-activists who believed in the system unquestioningly, though he only mentions two by name: "the young Polish Jews who had become infected by Marxism were so blinded by the apparent fulfillment of their cherished socialist dream, that there was no lie issuing from the Soviets, no matter how nonsensical, that they could not swallow. People like Herzberg and Wojdysławski believed everything the Soviets told them—so they even believed in the Molotov-Ribbentrop Pact!"[174]

Steinhaus described the Soviets' arrival and the reaction of Lviv's poorest Jews based on what he knew from Stanisław Kulczyński, the former university president: "the mass of poor people living in the district behind the theater had turned out in force, decked out in red stars and knotted red kerchiefs, to greet the Bolsheviks, causing some mirth among the Soviet officers. … Clearly, such episodes were more than anything else mere expressions of joy and relief at what seemed like a miraculous salvation from Hitler, and the overthrow of an interwar regime that had been rapidly becoming more fascist."[175] Still in Tatariv, the mathematician witnessed how the impoverished inhabitants responded to the Soviets, and later recounted it virulently, to the point of caricature. The passage exposes Steinhaus's dislike for the lower classes, by definition comprised of "Ruthenians," as well as poor Jews.

---

173 Steinhaus, *Mathematician for All Seasons: Recollections and Notes*, 230.
174 Ibid., 233.
175 Ibid., 230.

When the last police detachments had passed through, Tatarów was left in a temporary political vacuum. The peasants suddenly began decking themselves out in the colors of the Ukrainian nationalist movement, the local Jews pronounced the community communist, and a struggle for power erupted. One Jew, a pauper, more a boot patcher than a real shoemaker, who had spent several years in total behind bars for professing communism between the wars, exclaimed at a meeting: "I have been waiting ten years for this day!" They hung a red flag outside the Tatarów Community Administrative Center, and declared it communist territory, occupying it day and night. They were unbudgeable. But when these self-described atheists all repaired to the synagogue on the sabbath, Ruthenian peasants moved in and took over the building. However, having no idea as to what working in an office as an administrator might entail, they had to compromise by admitting a few Jews back in as "office workers."[176]

Though Steinhaus passes a harsh judgement on prewar communists for their support in installing the new regime, he finds compassion for his assistant, who came from Lviv's impoverished Jewish bourgeoisie, Marceli Stark. As the professor stated, Soviet reality quickly disabused this former member of the Communist Party of Western Ukraine (KPZU) of any illusions about communism. Stark did survive the war, but lost his entire family. After fleeing Lviv he found himself in the Warsaw Ghetto, where he fought in the 1943 uprising and then went through labor camps in Majdanek, Płaszów, Ravensbrück, Sachsenhausen, and Oranienburg.[177] In July 1945 he returned to Poland, but not without difficulties from the Soviet repatriation committee, which considered him a Soviet citizen because of his birthplace. Stark fled; he located Steinhaus in Berdechów by Stróże and tried to convince him to emigrate to Palestine. According to Steinhaus, Stark did not intend to legalize his stay in Poland and avoided any contacts with former friends, likely fearing deportation to the USSR. He decided to get to Palestine through Italy—a prospect not entirely unrealistic, since, as we know from the letters of Piotr Dunin-Borkowski, the consular office in Rome dealt with many such cases at the time. In the end, Marceli Stark remained in Wrocław; what probably eased his decision

---

176 Ibid., 226. In 1939, the Rosh Hashanah holiday fell on September 14–15, and Yom Kippur, a holiday celebrated even by those who were not religious, on September 23.
177 Stark's journal provides a moving account of his war years: Marceli Stark, *A jednak żyję i czuję …* (Warsaw: Instytut Pamięci Narodowej, 2013).

was that in the academic year of 1945/1946 Hugo Steinhaus was hired as a dean at Wrocław University. The two Lvivians continued working together. Though Stark joined the PZPR (Polish United Workers' Party), he did not last long as a member.[178] It is possible that when Steinhaus edited his memoir after the war, he purposely applied a gentler tone to passages related to a disciple he was so close to.

It caught the mathematician's attention that those among his assistants who before the war had served prison sentences for communist activities, such as Stark, as well as Jan Herzberg (Steinhaus judges the latter much more severely), gained no privileges with the new authorities. He took a decided dislike to Stefan Rudniański, a communist who arrived in Lviv from Warsaw and got hired at the university almost immediately. As it turned out, Rudniański did not get to play a more important part—despite his grand ambitions[179]—which Steinhaus noted with satisfaction:

> Stefan Rudniański [was] a Marxist Jew from Warsaw, and possibly a member of the Comintern, who wore a little pointed mephistophelean beard. He looked like a surety to become head of the department of economics, but the most they would do for him was to appoint him lecturer in some specialized subject of little significance. This was a prime illustration of the fact that communists who had not been trained in the Soviet school were not considered to have absorbed the Soviet orthodoxy, and were therefore of little use to the Soviets, while non-party—even rightist—professors who were accomplished in an appropriately useful field might be given special treatment.[180]

Steinhaus was hardly alone in his dislike for Rudniański. As Tadeusz Tomaszewski, a student of Mieczysław Kreutz, recalls, the university community did not care much for the Marxist, as evidenced by voting results: in open voting, his candidacy always passed, but in secret ballots it never did.[181] Moreover, even though he served as chairman of the International Red Aid university chapter,

---

178   Ibid., 35.
179   Authors of a monograph devoted to Rudnianski stated that the position of a university lecturer fulfilled the long-held dreams of this teacher and Marxist; Stanisław Michalski, Seweryn Dziamski, *Filozof i pedagog. Poglądy Stefana Rudniańskiego* (Warsaw: Książka i Wiedza, 1980), 105.
180   Steinhaus, *Mathematician for All Seasons: Recollections and Notes*, 254.
181   Tomaszewski, *Lwów. Pejzaż psychologiczny*, 30.

he was able to obtain neither a professorship, nor his own division. Both Soviet-appointed university presidents treated Rudniańsky with much reserve, and Heorhy Bychenko told him directly that he would not achieve the rank of a professor because … he did not hold the title before the war.[182] As we can see, in some ways the new authorities did heed the prewar academic hierarchy. Both Rudniańsky and Herzberg perished in similar circumstances: during an evacuation from Lviv in 1941, likely murdered by the NKVD.

Steinhaus had a decidedly negative opinion of Jakub Parnas and his academic function. Parnas became dean of the Medical Institute, made public speeches, and in December 1940 was elected to the city council, as was Stefan Banach. He also accepted invitations to scholarly conferences deep in the USSR. The Soviet *Pravda* published a report from a meeting between Parnas and Marchenko on October 20, only two days after the new university president was appointed. The title sends shockwaves: "Vragi v sutanakh i riasakh" ("Enemies in cassocks and frocks"). The piece was printed as the Soviets went about eliminating the Theological Faculty. The mention of Parnas's visit was supposed to legitimize the overall changes at the university and to sort the community into "proponents of changes" and "reactionaries." In a lengthy document from 1943, Mykhailo Marchenko recalls his struggle, as he first started in an administrative capacity, to stave off the constant stream of professors who rushed to introduce themselves to the president, as well as of other intelligentsia, who hoped that the political changes might open opportunities for them to work at the university.[183] It would seem that although the university establishment considered Parnas's travels to the Soviet heartland a disgrace, in reality Parnas was not the black sheep, but rather one among the many who sought favor with the authorities.

In the second half of 1940 and in 1941 a new column commenced in the newspaper *Vilna Ukraina*, keeping the public abreast of "what the Lviv intelligentsia is working on." The subjects of those columns were Parnas as well as other Lviv scholars, including the dean of the Medical Institute Bolesław Jałowy, Banach, Steinhaus, and former university presidents Stanisław Kulczyński

---

182 Ibid., 46.
183 Mykhailo Marchenko, Moia rabota vo L'vove 1939–1940 gg. i vzgliady na prichiny moego aresta, HDA SBU, spr. 31982 FP. Published in Oleksandr Rubl'ov, "Malovidomi storinky biohrafii ukrains'koho istoryka. Mykhailo Marchenko," *Ukraïns'kyi istorychnyi zhurnal* 1–2 (1996): 98 (document 8, Protokol dopytu v'iaznia M. I. Marchenka v Upravlinni NKVS SRSR po Novosybirs'kii oblasti, 1943).

Підготовка до зимових сесій у львівському держуніверситеті ім. Івана Франка. На знімку: професор Г. Б. Штайнгауз консультує студентку IV курсу математичного факультету Ф. Бергрин.
Фото Л. Шульмана.

After the war, Hugo Steinhaus wanted to recreate the school of mathematics in Wrocław

and Seweryn Krzemieniewski.[184] But in Steinhaus's opinion, it was Parnas, the famous Lviv biochemist, who was the authorities' favorite: "Parnas was one of our professors who came in for much praise from the Soviets. He had a dozen or so people at the professorial level working in his Institute for Medical Chemistry, as well as several assistants, was generously funded, and was invited to Kiev,

---

184 "Rozkvit nauky," *Vil'na Ukraïna*, no. 292, December 15, 1940 (interview with Banach); "V kabinetakh vchenykh," *Vil'na Ukraïna*, no. 305, December 30, 1940 (Steinhaus); "Nad chym pratsiuie inteligentsiia L´vova," *Vil'na Ukraïna*, no. 434, February 26, 1941 (interview with Parnas); "Nad chym pratsiuie inteligentsiia L´vova," *Vil'na Ukraïna*, no. 446, March 12, 1941 (interview with Kulczynski); "Nad chym pratsiuie inteligentsiia L´vova," *Vil'na Ukraïna*, no. 449, March 15, 1941 (interview with Krzemieniewski).

Kharkov, and Moscow to expound his institute's findings and attend scientific meetings."[185]

It should be noted that at that time Steinhaus himself worked not just at the university, but also at the Banach-led branch of the Academy of Sciences, where he and a group of colleagues who used to frequent Scottish Café formed a serious and not at all insubstantial unit, which was relatively well compensated out of the Academy's budget. Persons employed by both institutions earned about 2,000 rubles, thus approximately ten times as much as an average salary, and twenty times higher than a pension. Steinhaus recalled this experience in postwar Poland, as he came to realize that academics would not earn as much as they did in the USSR. In his mind this was why Parnas made the decision to remain in Moscow.

The following denouncement shows Parnas in a different light. An NKVD informer recruited from amongst the university community wrote about the distractions the dean and director of this key scientific institution dealt with in an attempt to persuade his superiors against the policy of reprisals: "The biochemist Parnas, instead of working, intervened on behalf of an employee of the institute who was forcibly moved out of Lviv because she owned part of a house consisting of two apartments."[186] The report shows that the scholar used his rank when it was necessary to plead for those arrested or deported, as we read in the previous chapter "Haven at the Clinic." After the Soviets seized Lviv again, he tried to help former coworkers and friends, vouching for them. Such endorsements carried much importance in a region where the authorities treated every resident of territories recently occupied by Germans as a potential collaborator or traitor.[187]

---

185 Steinhaus, *Mathematician for All Seasons: Recollections and Notes*, 274.
186 Agents "Supiński," "Jankowski," "Filozof," "Geber-Janowicz" kept tabs on the campus climate. The latter also reported on his conversations with Steinhaus (HDA SBU, f. 16, op. 33, spr. 55, k. 114–16). These documents reveal that the NKVD intended to recruit the urologist Stanisław Laskownicki.
187 In a letter from September 1, 1944, addressed to the secretary of the Lviv district committee, Major General Ivan Hrushetsky, Parnas spoke out in support of his former coworkers:

> I turn to you with a request to care for these people, as well as my coworkers, senior associate professors Boun-Sobczuk, associate professor Włodzimierz Szapkowski, professor Kazimierz Gostkowski, senior preparer Józef Nuckowski and Jan Nuckowski. In the case of engineer Szankowski and Jan Nuckowski, I must emphasize that they helped save and move to a safe place and safe conditions persons affiliated with the lab who were persecuted by the Germans and would have undoubtedly been sentenced to death. My laboratories

If we assess Jakub Parnas's role in the light of available sources, setting aside the sentiment of the academic community, it appears that his function was no different from that of Stefan Banach, dean at Lviv University. Yet when it comes to Banach, Steinhaus blames him only for a certain political naiveté. In another passage, criticizing Soviet philosophy and the notion of "revolutionary scientific thought," he writes about a favorite trick of communist academic bureaucracy: *duo cum faciunt idem, non est idem* ("if two say the same, it is not the same").

As I mentioned previously, in the fall of 1939 the Soviets nominated Stefan Biskupsky as dean of the Department of Mathematics and Natural Sciences, replacing August Zierhoffer. In doing so they followed a personnel policy which ostensibly favored Ukrainians. In December, barely a month later, the university underwent a thorough restructuring in accordance with the Soviet matrix: the Department of Mathematics and Natural Sciences was eliminated and in its place two departments emerged: Physics-Mathematics and Natural Sciences. For a brief period, Myron Zarytsky served as dean. In early 1940 further changes occurred, and Banach replaced Zarytsky as dean.[188] Most mathematicians, including Steinhaus,[189] retained their positions, albeit in somewhat different configurations:[190] not all were offered their own divisions,

---

and coworkers are in need of the following: a guarantee that the apartments of employees, which irresponsible persons are eyeing, are untouchable; a faster payout of salaries, because people have almost no means to live; provisions appropriate to their academic rank and positions. Additionally, I request that the persons mentioned above be compensated for securing state property as well as my possessions (*Kul'turne zhyttia v Ukraïni*, vol 1, 201).

188 Lichnoe delo Stefana Banakha, ALU R-119, op. 1, spr. 11, k. 1–3. The Banach file contains a questionnaire and a copy of a request by the university's academic council to the Ministry of Education to confirm the rank of associate professor and position as professor, signed by the academic secretary Iury Poliansky, along with a description of Banach's scientific achievements.

189 After the first restructuring in early December 1939, Steinhaus became the director of the physics division, as evidenced by an entry in the list of positions he occupied (Trudovaia knizhka zaveduiushchego kafedroi fiziko-matematicheskogo fak. Shteinhausa Gugo Boguslavovicha, ALU, R-119, op. 1, spr. 394, k. 3): "7.12.1939 naznachen na dolzhnost' zaveduiushchego kafedroi fiziki fakul'teta, prikaz 86."

190 The directors of divisions at the Department of Physics and Mathematics at the university were: Stefan Banach, Hugo Steinhaus, Juliusz Schauder, Eustachy Żyliński, Myron Zarytsky, Stanisław Mazur, Stanisław Loria, and Wojciech Rubinowicz; professors without their own division were: Stanisław Saks, Bronisław Knaster, Leon Chwistek, Mojżesz Jacob, Herman Auerbach, and Władysław Orlicz; associate professors were: Meier Edelheit, Edward

and Leon Chwistek in particular, in spite of his leftist views, was not allowed to continue leading the Faculty of Logic. Thanks to the joint efforts of two deans, Myron Zarytsky and Stefan Banach, a number of Steinhaus's former colleagues—refugees from Warsaw—found work at the university, making it possible to legalize their stay: professors Bronisław Knaster, Stanisław Saks, Edward Szpilrajn, and assistant Menachem Wojdysławski. This saved them from deportation, to which the Soviets subjected all persons without employment and refugee passports. A list of persons removed from deportation

Thanks to the close cooperation between Myron Zarytsky and Stefan Banach, the Lwów School of Mathematics survived the Soviet occupation

---

Szpilrajn, and Menachem Wojdysławski. In the following months the number of divisions increased, as it did at the Medical Institute. The number of full-time employees went up as well (Nakaz rektora no. 307, 29.10.1940, ALU, R-119, op. 3, spr. 31, k. 241–2). Drawing on documentation in the State Archive of the Lviv District, Roman Duda lists the full composition of each division in the chapter "Ukrainizacja po sowiecku" of his monograph *Lwowska Szkoła Matematyczna* (Wrocław: Wydawnictwo Uniwersytetu Wrocławskiego, 2007), 153–4.

includes two of Steinhaus's acquaintances: Stanisław Saks, and Bronisław Knaster.[191] A special unit put together for this purpose was in charge of obtaining documents and resident registrations, though of course it operated under the NKVD's strict oversight. Without the dean's recommendation, and perhaps also special interventions, it was impossible to either obtain a passport without the "paragraph 11" designation that obligated one to leave Lviv, or to avoid deportation in June 1940.

Similarly, students escaping the German occupation would be allowed to stay in Lviv if admitted to the university. In late 1939, when entrance exams began (the committee consisted of professors Hugo Steinhaus, Eustachy Żyliński, and Stefan Banach),[192] many candidates applying for admission came from backgrounds that earlier had stood no chance (too poor, "wrong" ethnicity). The authorities supported such applicants, championing free education to elicit endorsement among impoverished youth. Many non-student refugees sought student status as well, simply for a chance to register as residents of Lviv and survive the war. They, however, did not receive the authorities' support. Far from it: they were treated as potential spies. Both the admissions committee and other faculty members, especially Bronisław Knaster, tried to help at least some of the refugee students. In the eyes of those escapees, Lviv looked very promising, although of course only by comparison. The lineup in the department of Physics and Mathematics, studded with the most distinguished scholars, remained almost unchanged since prewar times. In contrast, territories under German occupation offered no educational options, and, in fact, little chance of survival, especially for intelligentsia of Jewish background. [193]

A mere admission to college did not guarantee one's safety; only a passport issued by the Soviet police gave refugees the right to stay in Lviv. Meanwhile, the NKVD hunted for persons without such documents. Some students—escapees from central Poland, who were able to jump over the college admission hurdle—still could not obtain passports for several months. Kazimierz Szałajko recalls that Banach assisted him with obtaining resident registration in Lviv. Stanisław Hartman had graduated with a degree in mathematics from

---

191 Spetsoobshcheniia o khode pereseleniia spetskontingenta iz zapadnykh oblastei USSR v vostochnye, 9.03–26.12.1940, HDA SBU, f. 16, op. 33, spr. 55, k. 190.
192 The exams took place between November 26 and December 3, 1939 (Nakaz rektora no. 72, 23.11.1939, ALU, R-119, op. 3, spr. 3, k. 60).
193 Kazimierz Szałajko, "Wspomnienia o Stefanie Banachu na tle Lwowa i lwowskiej szkoły matematycznej," *Zeszyty Naukowe Akademii Górniczo-Hutniczej im. S. Staszica* 1522: *Opuscula Mathematica*, no. 13 (1993): 51.

Warsaw University. He applied for admission to the physics department in Lviv, and received help from his former professor Bronisław Knaster. Knaster, himself an escapee, "reclaimed" or removed from the deportation list through the efforts of his colleagues, sheltered evacuees in his apartment[194] during the period of the most concentrated attempts to deport them.[195] But many escapees were not as lucky or lacked adequate protection to be admitted to the university. For example, Jerzy Wolski suffered a myriad of adversities; at the time he was a second-year student of medicine at Jagiellonian University in Cracow, yet could not secure university admission in Lviv. He survived a few months thanks to Józef Ulam, the father of Adam and Stanisław Ulam. Ten days after leaving Ulam's apartment at Kościuszko Street, Wolski was arrested by the NKVD and sent to a camp. In summer of 1941, benefitting from the Sikorski-Maysky agreement, he was released and initially joined the Anders' Army, and later the British Air Force. Unlike those members of the Ulam family who remained in Lviv, Wolski survived the war. Many years later, in a letter to Adam Ulam, he gave a thorough account of the support he received from Ulam's father in the early days of the Soviet occupation.[196]

Compared with other university departments, the Faculty of Physics and Mathematics had to withstand relatively few adversities under the Soviet occupation. Of its mathematicians, only Edward Szpilrajn was arrested during this period, for attempting to flee to Hungary.[197] Two weeks later he was released, possibly because the university vouched for him. In contrast to the Soviets, the Nazis decimated the ranks of Lviv mathematicians between 1941–43.[198] As it turned out, the officer who told Steinhaus, as the latter was

---

194 Hartman, *Wspomnienia (lwowskie i inne)*, 42.
195 Ibid., 42. See also Bolesław Gleichgewicht, *Widziane z oddali* (Wrocław: Wydawnictwo Dolnośląskie, 1993), and "Anonymous report of a young escapee from Warsaw," 516–18.
196 I am grateful to Serhii Plokhii of Harvard University who directed me to this interesting source. See Adam B. Ulam, *Understanding the Cold War: A Historian's Personal Reflections* (New Brunswick: Transaction Publishers, 2002), 91.
197 Hartman, *Wspomnienia (lwowskie i inne)*, 63.
198 The first list of higher education employees killed during the German occupation was compiled after the Red Army entered Lviv in mid-August 1944. On orders from the authorities, those serving as university presidents or institute directors collected preliminary data. The list of those who worked at the Department of Physics and Mathematics is the longest: Herman Auerbach, Maks (Meier) Eidelheit, Juda Kreisler, Józef Mosler, Józef Pepis, Stanisław Saks, Juliusz Szauder, Maurycy Sperling, Marceli Stark, and Ludwik Sternbach. However, the information was not always verified and thus in some cases it turned out inaccurate: for example, Marceli Stark did survive (Spysok zamordovanykh nimtsiami naukovykh robitnykiv

about to cross the Hungarian border, that "the Bolsheviks idolize professors," and no harm would come to him, was not entirely mistaken. While liberal arts scholars were subjected to far greater ideological pressures, academics working in hard sciences, especially if their research had practical applications, were protected. A telltale example is Weigl's institute, whose fate during the occupation deserves a separate study. The NKVD leaders proposed to move the institute deep into the USSR because of the potential for "biological sabotage."[199] Yet their recommendation was never followed, most likely not just because the Soviets wanted to protect the geographical frontier where the war was expected to play out and access to immunizations would be most urgent, but also because the esteemed workforce and the institute itself would be difficult to resettle.

It is hard to sort out to what extent Lviv mathematicians owed their relatively good standing to their professional privilege, and how much weight the stance of the department's leadership—Banach, Zarytsky, and President Marchenko—carried. Certainly, solidarity among these longtime colleagues, who had worked closely together for more than a decade, played a part as well. Equally importantly perhaps, they were able to find common ground with colleagues in the discipline and with university administration and educational authorities. Yet Banach's strategy to make the best out of the situation by cooperating with the Soviets met with a tepid reaction from Steinhaus, his former professor.

In addition to serving as dean, by mid-1940 Stefan Banach became a corresponding member of the Academy of Sciences of the USSR, and in December 1940, a Lviv city council member in charge of education and culture. He also

---

n.d., f. 119, op. 1, spr. 4, k. 1). In a comprehensive article based on records of interrogations performed on Stefan Banach, as well as on archival queries, Lech Maligranda and Jarosław Prytuła were able to painstakingly reconstruct the lot of Lviv scholars—see their "Przesłuchania Stefana Banacha z 1944," *Wiadomości Matematyczne*, no. 48 (2012): 51–72. See also the list of victims prepared by Jan Draus: *Uniwersytet Jana Kazimierza we Lwowie 1918–1946. Portret kresowej uczelni* (Cracow: Księgarnia Akademicka, 2007), 91–110; Sławomir Kalbarczyk, *Polscy pracownicy nauki ofiary zbrodni sowieckich w latach II wojny światowej. Zamordowani, więzieni, deportowani* (Warsaw: Instytut Pamięci Narodowej, 2001). In actuality, between 1942 and 1944 the following scholars were either murdered or died: Herman Auerbach, Juliusz Szaude, Stanisław Saks, and Bruno Winawer (a physicist and writer, member of the Soviet Writers' Union, who worked at the university as Stanisław Loria's assistant).

199 Commissar Ivan Serov, informational note from April 15, 1940, HDA SBU, f. 16, op. 33, spr. 71, k. 144–46. The note pointed to a serious oversight: "The institute employs five hundred people, yet not a single assigned Soviet worker" (ibid., k. 145).

Stefan Banach and Stanisław Mazur became deputies to the Lviv city council in December of 1940

directed the Lviv chapter of the Department of Functional Analysis of the Institute of Mathematics (AN USRS), where his colleagues from the university and the polytechnic (Hugo Steinhaus, Stanisław Mazur, Władysław Orlicz, and Juliusz Szauder) worked. The chapter was formed following Banach's participation in a functional analysis conference in Kyiv in June 1940.[200] By all accounts, the mathematician played an active role in Soviet scholarly life: he joined university delegations to Kyiv,[201] Moscow,[202] and Tbilisi,[203] hosted Soviet professors and academics, Nikolai Bogoliubov, Pavel Aleksandrov, Sergei Sobolev, and Lazar Liusternik among others. Although we know very little about their entries in *Scottish Book*, clearly the scholars, including the director of the Institute of Mathematics in Moscow, held Banach and the entire circle of Lviv mathematicians in high esteem.[204]

As dean, Banach was responsible for organizing a conference to showcase the scientific achievements of those employed in the department.[205] He

---

200 In January 1940 the Soviets established six departments of the Lviv chapter of the Academy of Sciences (Ukrainian history, Ukrainian literary history, linguistics, archeology, folklore, and economics), but no department of mathematics and physics ("Nauka u L′vovi", *Vil′na Ukraïna*, no. 15, January 19, 1940, 6)

201 For information on work trips of professors Banach, Mazur, and Zarytsky see Nakaz rektora no. 345, 8.12.1940, ALU, R-119, op. 3, spr. 31, k. 366 and Nakaz rektora no. 48, 24.02.1941, ALU, R-119, op. 3, spr. 52, k. 106. Banach's last departure to Kyiv occurred on June 18, 1941; he returned to Lviv right before the Germans entered the city (Nakaz rektora no. 168, 12.06.1941, ALU, R-119, op. 3, spr. 52, k. 295). A visit to Kyiv's Academy of Sciences of the Ukrainian SSR, scheduled for June 19–26, 1941, fell exactly at the start of the German-Soviet war.

202 University president's disposition (Nakaz rektora no. 164, 30.04.1940, ALU, R-119, op. 3, spr. 31, k. 141) sent Stefan Banach, Vasyl Simovych, Iury Poliansky, Andry Brahinets, Ivan Krypiakevych, and others to an anniversary conference (a prestigious academic event) at Moscow University. Another disposition (Nakaz rektora no. 320, 11.11.1940, ALU, R-119, op. 3, spr. 31, k. 289) sent mathematicians to a mathematics convention organized by the AN USSR on November 13–17, 1940 (Banach along with Myron Zarytsky, Juliusz Szauder, and Stanisław Mazur).

203 For information about the trip of Professors Stefan Banach and Myron Zarytsky, University Vice President Andry Brahinets, and student Mariia Solak, to sign an agreement of socialist competition see Nakaz rektora no. 48, 24.02.1941, ALU, R-119, op. 3, spr. 52, k. 106.

204 Many years later, Sergei Sobolev, writing to Kazimierz Kuratowski, remembered Banach with appreciation: "In those [war] years Banach and I got to know each other well; I saw him repeatedly in Lviv and in Moscow, where more than once I had the honor to host him in my home" (quoted in Roman Kałuża, *Stefan Banach* [Warsaw: Wydawnictwo GZ, 1992], 115). See also Siergiej Sobolew, "Przemówienie wygłoszone na uroczystości ku uczczeniu pamięci Stefana Banacha," *Wiadomości Matematyczne* 4 (1961): 261–64.

205 Nakaz rektora no. 318, 6.11.1940, ALU, R-119, op. 3, spr. 31, k. 283. The university-wide conference planned for January 29 to February 3, 1941, in which fifteen persons

was also a member of the recruitment committee[206] as well as the doctoral admissions committee (*aspirantura* in the Soviet system), both formed in the academic year 1940/1941.[207] In the Soviet context, putting Banach in charge of educating new scholars signaled that the combination of his academic stature and a low socioeconomic origin had earned him the authorities' trust.

Among the rituals of Soviet bureaucracy were awards given out to employees on the anniversary of the October (Bolshevik) Revolution and distinctions handed out on May 1 for conscientious fulfillment of duties and for successes achieved. The university was no exception; here too, employees received awards on the anniversaries, and the Soviets were careful to primarily honor the local personnel,[208] including Banach. In those occupation years, such distinctions carried a double meaning and could easily spark misunderstandings in one's ethnic and professional communities.

---

from the department participated (among them Steinhaus, Mazur, Knaster, Auerbach, Chwistek, and Saks) later served as the basis of accusations thrown against the university administration that alleged subpar academic research at the institution. Of course, in the first year of the occupation, conditions for scholarly work were hardly favorable. Hugo Steinhaus, though overall an unusually productive scholar, wrote only one study during the occupation. Under Banach's leadership, the department resumed the publication of *Studia Mathematica*. It was the only volume of studies published during the Soviet occupation of Lviv. A collection of historical studies edited by Marchenko was never printed.

206 The admissions committee of the Department of Physics and Mathematics, consisting of Stefan Banach, Stanisław Mazur, and Myron Zarytsky, was formed by the university president's directive no. 185, dated June 12, 1940 (ALU, R-119, op. 3, spr. 31, k. 185). Stefan Banach as dean was a member of the university-wide committee, along with Zenovy Khraplyvy (acting vice president of instruction), Vasyl Simovych (dean of the Philological Faculty), Petro Nedbailo (dean of the Law Department), Andry Brahinets (dean of History), Omelian Terletsky (acting dean of Natural Sciences), full member of the Soviet Academy of Sciences Vasyl Shchuraty, and Professor Stanisław Kulczyński (Nakaz rektora no. 188, 15.06.1940, ALU, R-119, op. 3, spr. 31, k. 190).

207 The doctoral admissions committee consisted of: Vasyl Simovych, Andry Brahinets (1903–63, dean of History, university vice president), Petro Nedbailo (1906–74, dean of Law), Stefan Banach, Stefan Biskupsky, Iury Poliansky (geographer, university vice president), and Reznikov (first name unknown) (Nakaz rektora no. 295, 21.10.1940, ALU, R-119, op. 3, spr. 31, k. 211).

208 See university president's directive regarding awards on the occasion of the twenty-third anniversary of the October Revolution (Nakaz rektora no. 318, 6.11.1940, ALU. R-119, op. 3, spr. 31, k. 283–4). In the Department of Physics and Mathematics, awards went to Dean Stefan Banach, Professors Myron Zarytsky, Stanisław Mazur, Stanisław Saks, and Juliusz Schauder, and assistants Jan Herzberg and Menachem Wojdysławski.

In spring 1940, the mathematician signed a contract with the publisher "Radianska shkola" to bring out a Ukrainian translation of his book.[209] This arrangement is a testament to Banach's high academic authority, and to the Soviets' resolve to win him over. They applied the same strategy when dealing with Kazimierz Bartel, though that offer was even better: a Russian translation, meaning a much larger edition, and, consequently, a higher honorarium. Tto put the level of such compensations in context, in 1941 Wasilewska and Korniichuk combined their honoraria to purchase a tank.

Soviet manifestations of admiration for select distinguished scholars were a touchy subject among Lviv's intelligentsia. We learn about it not only from the few contemporaneous accounts, but also from postwar discussions that dragged on for years and scrutinized the conduct of Kazimierz Bartel and Tadeusz Boy-Żeleński.[210] In defense of Bartel's name, his widow emphasized in her memoir that her husband was unhappy about traveling to Moscow and the publication of his textbook.[211] Various sources indicate that Włodzimierz Krukowski, at the time vice president at the Polytechnic, accompanied professor Bartel on this trip. Krukowski enjoyed the trust of both the authorities and his academic community.[212] This was not the only time professors of that school traveled on Soviet business; at the turn of August and September, thus after Stalin had signaled a change of strategy towards Poles, a group of the most distinguished scientists from the Lviv Polytechnic was invited to Moscow. After their return, newspapers (among them *Czerwony Sztandar*) reported on the trip in the vein of "Our state bestows special care on the Soviet scientist." The former Polish Prime Minister Bartel's trip to Moscow gave rise to speculations that the Soviets might propose Bartel as head of the Polish government. But rumors of a political offer for Bartel are unfounded,[213] although his stay in Moscow and the special treatment of a Polish politician as well known

---

209 The translation of Banach's *Kurs analizy funkcjonalnej* appeared after the war, in 1948. For more on this subject, see Anatolii Plichko and Iaroslav Prytula, "Do 60-richchia publikatsii ukrains'koho perekladu knyhy S. Banakha," *Matematychni studii* 30, no. 1 (2008).
210 Tadeusz Tomaszewski, when quoting university professors on the subject of Soviet publications by Polish academics, invokes Roman Ingarden, who was of the opinion that "one should not write scholarly publications for the Soviets if one does not have to." See Tomaszewski, *Lwów. Pejzaż psychologiczny*, 37.
211 M. Bartlowa, "Pamiętnik Marii Bartlowej," 58.
212 See, for instance, reminiscences of Zbysław Popławski (Okupanci na Politechnice Lwowskiej, k. 22–3).
213 Kalbarczyk, *Polscy pracownicy nauki ofiary zbrodni sowieckich*, 285–6

as Bartel certainly raised eyebrows. Lviv and émigré communities bristled at the thought that the attitude of Lviv's Polish community towards the Soviets might be changing. Some journal authors with ties to National Democracy, in particular the previously mentioned Stanisław Skrzypek,[214] did not shy away from accusing Bartel of collaboration. Skrzypek was an activist for the All-Polish Youth, and later joined the National Party, those very groups which before the war organized disgraceful actions against Bartel because he opposed displays of anti-Semitism on campus (to mention one, a pig wearing the name "Bartel" was let loose in the campus buildings). If Skrzypek's account drew from his own observations, those should have been limited to the first month of the occupation only. Any later "revelations" he based on unverified hearsay, as after November 19, 1939 he went to prison. His comments revive the prewar political fights and a dislike for the Prime Minister's consistent stance on Jewish matters, tarnishing postwar judgements of the murdered politician who could no longer defend his reputation.

To return to the textbook offers, which the Soviets made to a small number of academics—Steinhaus, Banach, and Bartel—all three signed their contracts: Steinhaus to translate his *Kalejdoskop matematyczny*; Banach for a translation of his *Analiza funkcjonalna*; and Kazimierz Bartel to write a geometry textbook for a Moscow publisher by the end of 1941. His translator, Liuger Shkliarskiy, was transferred from Moscow to the Lviv Polytechnic, where he received the rank of associate professor.[215] Banach's university colleague, Associate Dean Myron Zarytsky, translated *Analiza funkcjonalna*. Zarytsky, a disciple of Wacław Sierpiński and teacher of the science fiction writer Stanisław Lem, had a highly unconventional personality. His students remember him as an instructor with rather nonstandard teaching methods. Zarytskyi's grandson Bohdan Soroka, himself one of the most colorful members of the Lviv underground and samizdat of the 1960s, gave an inventory of these methods in his memoir.[216] Dean Zarystky and Banach had known each other since the second half of the 1920s and embarked on a close collaboration after the first Congress of Mathematicians, which took place in Lviv on September 7–19, 1927. Myron Zarytsky did not finish his translation on time, probably because of grave personal circum-

---

214 Stanisław Skrzypek, *Rosja, jaką widziałem. Wspomnienia z lat 1939–1942* (Newtown: Montgomeryshire Printing, 1949), 25.
215 See Popławski, Okupanci na Politechnice Lwowskiej, k. 23.
216 Bohdan Soroka, *Hrafika* (Lviv: Kolir-PRO, 2011), 5–7.

stances: the Soviets arrested his pregnant daughter Kateryna Zarytska[217] and son-in-law Mykhailo Soroka. The book appeared after the war. Banach was already dead, and though his translator was still alive, his name was omitted.

Zarytsky stepped in as dean once Banach fell ill. After the war he could no longer work in this capacity, once his daughter was arrested again. At the time, the Soviets were just finishing up with Lviv; under the allegation of supporting Ukrainian nationalism even the most prominent persons were arrested, among them Stefan Banach's doctor Oleksandr Barvinsky, who was sentenced to ten years in the labor camps (the formal reason for his arrest might have been his position as director of the Health Department during the German occupation, but his real "offense" was that he was Metropolitan Sheptytsky's personal physician). The few remaining members of the prewar intelligentsia were forced to make various concessions, renouncing their convictions, their past, even family members and friends who found themselves on the "wrong side."

In the early days of the Soviet occupation, Stefan Banach, often in Zarytsky's company, participated in several academic conferences; in Lviv he also met up with mathematicians from Moscow, Kyiv, and Odessa. As Tomaszewski recalls, on October 22, 1940, the radio transmitted a program reporting on Banach's praise of the exceptional work conditions the Soviets had created for Lviv's mathematicians, far superior to what they had experienced in "lordly Poland."[218] Since this is not a primary record, but rather a report based on an interview that Banach gave, its validity as a source remains questionable. However, reading *Vilna Ukraina* makes clear that participation in official events certainly necessitated concessions, among them public declarations of loyalty.[219]

---

217 Kateryna Zarytska (1914–86) and Mykhailo Soroka (1911–71) were members of the OUN. Kateryna, the only daughter of Volodymyra and Myron Zarytsky, was found guilty of aiding Minister Bronisław Pieracki's assassin and served a prison sentence from 1935 till 1938. She married Mykhailo Soroka in November 1939. In June 1941, Zarytska was released from Brygidki prison. During the German occupation she founded the Ukrainian Red Cross, and between 1945 and 1947 served as liaison officer to Supreme Commander of the Ukrainian Insurgent Army Roman Shukhevych. Arrested in 1947, and sentenced to twenty-five years of labor camps, she was released in 1972. The Polish government arrested Mykhailo Soroka, director of the State Executive of the OUN, in 1937. He left the Bereza Kartuska detention camp in September 1939. Arrested by the NKVD, he was first detained in a prison in Zamarstyniv, then in a camp in Vorkuta. In 1954 he organized the political prisoner uprising in Kengir.
218 Tomaszewski, *Lwów. Pejzaż psychologiczny*, 33.
219 Stepan Banakh, "Rozkvit nauky," *Vil'na Ukraïna*, no. 292, December 15, 1940, 5; Oleksandr Radin, "Stepan Banakh," *Vil'na Ukraïna*, no. 524, June 13, 1941, 3.

According to Mykhailo Marchenko's testimonies, Banach also attended informal meetings with the newly nominated university president.[220]

When the German-Soviet war began, Banach and Heorhy Bychenko, university president at the time, were in Kyiv. Both managed to return to Lviv at the last moment: the mathematician to his family, Bychenko—to his duties. Banach survived the German occupation thanks to Weigl's institute, where first his son found work until he escaped from Lviv, and then Banach Sr. replaced him in feeding lice. As we read in the chapter "Haven at the Clinic," during the German occupation the institute employed many members of the Polish intelligentsia; these jobs provided sustenance and helped avoid deportation to labor camps in the Reich. In August 1944, the scholar got involved in the reactivation of the university, but soon his poor health caused him to hand the dean's responsibilities over to Zarytsky. Banach published an article devoted to the massacre of the Lviv professors in *Czerwony Sztandar*.[221] His account of the occupation years, given to the prosecutor, has been preserved in the State Archives of Lviv Oblast, alongside Banach's personal files.[222]

In the last year of his life Banach suffered from lung cancer, remaining in care of Dr. Oleksandr Barvinsky, who in 1943–44 stepped in as Metropolitan Andrei Sheptytsky's personal physician after Marian Panchyshyn died. On the pages of *Czerwony Sztandar*, Banach's widow Łucja thanked Barvinsky for his "continuous dedication and attentive care" to her husband.[223] Banach's son was convinced that they owed their survival to his father's Ukrainian friends: "I think that father was protected by Ukrainians themselves because of his tolerant attitude towards them before the war. Mom did not encounter any 'actual misfortunes,' except that some people stopped greeting her in the street (Taszycki). Kulczyński himself produced false papers for Mother."[224] Though

---

220 Interrogation statement of Mykhailo Marchenko from May 30, 1943: Mykhailo Marchenko, Moia rabota vo L'vove 1939–1940 gg. i vzgliady na prichiny moego aresta, HDA SBU, spr. 31982, FP (quoted in Rubl'ov, "Malovidomi storinky biohrafii ukraïns'koho istoryka. Mykhailo Marchenko," 108).
221 Stefan Banach, "Uczeni polscy zamordowani przez hitlerowców. Antoni Łomnicki—Włodzimierz Stożek," *Czerwony Sztandar*, no. 87, December 12, 1944.
222 DALO, f. 26, op. 5, spr. 58.
223 *Czerwony Sztandar*, no. 176, September 5, 1945.
224 From Stefan Banach Jr.'s letter to Stanisław Ulam, *Wortal Stefana Banacha*, http://kielich.amu.edu.pl/Stefan_Banach/zyciorys.html. Łucja Banach, née Braus, came from a Jewish family; she met Banach through Steinhaus, for whom she worked as a secretary. Their son's letter suggests that despite her Jewish ethnicity she was not in hiding during the war; her husband's friends assured her safety.

we cannot with certainty confirm Banach Jr.'s assumptions about the role of his father's Ukrainian friends, "the genius of Lviv" enjoyed tremendous respect within and beyond his own community. Barvinsky was one of the best doctors of internal medicine still in Lviv, and his devotion to Banach shows that in spite of the most difficult experiences of war, when it came to human relations some members of the local intelligentsia retained goodwill and trust for one another, although these principles could come at a high price.

At Banach's funeral, his loved ones, friends who remained in Lviv, and colleagues, especially Ukrainian and Russian mathematicians, bid him farewell. As we see from the obituaries, as well as entries in *Scottish Book* from 1940 and spring 1941, his fellow scientists came to regard him as a close colleague and a true authority. That Lviv mathematicians allowed Soviet mathematicians into their elite club speaks to the quality of their cooperation.

When it comes to Steinhaus, his memoirs remain silent about any closer contact with Soviet mathematicians or their partaking in the "circle of the initiated" by adding to *Scottish Book*. As the author of the very last note, Steinhaus was no doubt aware of those previous entries. Even if he was not present at certain meetings, as a mathematician he must have taken an interest in the problems his Soviet colleagues entered into the prized notebook.

Certainly, Soviet occupation made Steinhaus feel imprisoned. But he could still work, retain his status as a professor, and even enjoy modest privileges: a membership in the Academy of Sciences or an honorarium from the Russian translation of his *Kalejdoskop matematyczny*, prepared by Bronisław Knaster. Although the book constitutes one of the best volumes on popular math, it needed to be adjusted to Soviet conditions, or, to put it bluntly, censored. Some examples Steinhaus incorporated, such as proportional elections, were not well suited for the Soviet edition. Despite many attempts to persuade Steinhaus to cooperate more closely with the Soviet scientific community, even in the face of frequent flattery, he chose to remain on the sidelines of academic life in those years. Steinhaus quoted Parnas's anecdote from a visit to Kharkiv. In a conversation with the director of the Institute of Radiology, the biochemist made a passing remark. "We have a person in Lwów"—only to have the director finish, "… Professor Steinhaus, who has made it possible to see objects hidden from direct view."[225] The exchange referred to Steinhaus's invention of the introvisor, a device used for the surgical removal of foreign objects from the human body that were not visible on x-ray images. Yet the device also symbolizes Steinhaus's

---

225 Steinhaus, *Mathematician for All Seasons: Recollections and Notes*, 274.

keen sense of observation, which allowed him to swiftly grasp the essence of both totalitarian regimes.

It is common practice to appraise the conduct of others but spare your own circle, as Tadeusz Tomaszewski aptly observed in *Pejzaż psychologiczny*. These very judgements—expressions of our powerlessness in the face of totalitarian violence—helped shape later narratives of the Soviet occupation, distorting the picture of events and attitudes. At the university, every professor and student became a passive participant in Sovietization (though the term "collaborator" is out of place here), to varying degrees. Nationality did not determine one's culpability in advance. Each case reflected a personal choice. As it turns out, even those who carried out Soviet policies have a complicated legacy.

"Moia rabota vo L'vovskom universitete," manuscript of
Mykhailo Marchenko's testimony, 1943

CHAPTER 4

Barbarian in the Garden

The chapter borrows its title from Zbigniew Herbert's first essay collection (*Barbarzyńca w ogrodzie / Barbarian in the Garden*). The name of Herbert's volume taps into the writer's self-irony, while also giving expression to his protest against the Western view of him as an entrant from Eastern Europe—that is, "not-quite Europe," as the Ukrainian author Mykola Riabchuk puts it, invoking the perception of Eastern Europe's lesser status that was first expressed in the Enlightenment. Following this track, I sketch the lives of Ukrainian professors nominated to academic positions at Jan Kazimierz University by Soviet authorities and take a closer look at their relations with Polish academics. A comparison between the Soviet newcomers and savages emerges as a prevalent trope in Lviv memoirs. As for Ukrainians, the Polish attitude of cultural superiority only grew stronger at the start of the occupation, fueled by a perception that by and large Ukrainians collaborated with the occupier. Once the Soviet administration placed Ukrainians in positions previously held by Polish scholars, Poles took to approaching the Ukrainian academics in the same manner as they treated the Soviets. On their end, Ukrainian memoirists extolled the achievements of their ethnic group, juxtaposing these new conditions with prewar years, and challenging recent Polish policies, especially the widespread discrimination against ethnic Ukrainians and Jews. When it comes to Jewish memoirists, though they approached the new order quite skeptically, they enthusiastically agreed with Ukrainians on one issue—they welcomed the removal of restrictions on university admissions for students of other ethnicities.

This chapter presents a divergent picture of the relationships between those communities, which surfaced once I compared postwar reminiscences against ego-documents from the war period. How memoirists remember ethnic relations at the university in retrospect deviates from stories told by contemporaneous sources. As it turns out, the picture familiar to us has been largely altered over time. At its root lie popular stereotypes. My impish invocation of one of them, Herbert's "barbarian in the garden," is an attempt to reconstruct a different image of a Soviet representative and his relations with the academic community.

A PORTRAIT: SIDE VIEW AND FULL FACE

In mid-October 1939, two weeks after the first meeting organized by Soviet authorities, Lviv University already had a new president. On October 16, 1939 the Politburo of the Central Committee of the Communist Party of Ukraine issued its decision, with the actual transfer of authority occurring two days later. Accordingly, Roman Longchamps de Berier, Jan Kazimierz University's longtime president, no longer would exercise his duties (by statute he had resumed his function on September 1, 1939, after his June reelection). His very first regulation under Soviet rule decreed that Mykhailo Marchenko take over those responsibilities. Until September 1939, Marchenko[1] had led the feudal period division at the Institute of History of the Ukrainian SSR Academy of Sciences in Kyiv. The next regulation directed that president Roman Longchamps return to the Department of Law.[2] Professor Longchamps was not the only one to forfeit his rank; within a month the lineup in the president's office changed, and within two months the entire university administration was switched out. In early December an assembly of university employees formally accepted those first structural and administrative moves, and the USSR Committee for Higher Education Affairs confirmed a new statute, modeled after a Soviet standard. From now on, the Ukrainian SSR People's Commissar of Education would nominate university provosts, deans and associate deans. The senate's name changed to "academic council," in keeping with Soviet nomenclature, and its

---

1   Ukrainian historians have focused much attention on Mykhailo Marchenko. Among the most important publications are studies are Oleksandr Rubl'ov's "Malovidomi storinky biohrafii ukrains'koho istoryka. Mykhailo Marchenko," *Ukraïns'kyi istorychnyi zhurnal* 1–2 (1996): 116–17; and "Ternystyi shliakh ukrains'koho vchenoho-patriota: M. I. Marchenka," in Mykhailo Marchenko, *Kyïvs´ka Rus´ u borot´bi z kochovykamy do monhol'skoi navaly; Monohrafiia* (Kyiv: Promin', 2012), 144–90. See also the extensive biographical entry prepared by Leonid Zashkil'niak in "Mykhailo Marchenko," *Istorychnyi fakul´tet L´vivs´koho natsional´noho universytetu im. Ivana Franka (1940–2000). Iuveleina knyha do 60-ty richchia istorychnoho fakul´tetu* (Lviv: Vydavnychyi tsentr L´vivs´koho universytetu, 2000), 131. Iryna Zakrynychna put together a bibliography of analyses devoted to Marchenko in *Istoriohrafiia vyvchennia naukovoï tvorchosti Mykhaila Marchenka*, vol. 13, part 2: *Spetsial'ni istorychni dystsypliny: Pytannia teoriï ta metodyky. Zbirnyk naukovykh prats'* (Kyiv: Instytut istoriï Ukraïny NAN Ukraïny, 2006).
2   Nakaz rektora no. 3, 18.10.1939, ALU, R-119, op. 3, spr. 3, k. 2.

Mykhailo Marchenko was arrested on June 23, 1941.
After three years he was released from the Tomsk prison

Mykhailo Marchenko was appointed as university president in mid-October 1939.

authority shrank to merely an advisory body to the president. Similarly, departmental councils lost their powers. With one sweep the Soviets eliminated the university's autonomy, effecting a centralized governance system that was prevalent in the entire Soviet Union.

Faculty members held the new president of Jan Kazimierz University in decidedly low regard. They faulted him for arbitrarily forcing the campus to "Ukrainize," in particular for obligating the faculty to lecture in Ukrainian and for introducing mandatory Ukrainian language courses for students and professors, for immediately creating a number of Ukrainian departments, and staffing high posts with Ukrainians. Likewise, they assumed Marchenko's initiative was behind the implementation of Soviet norms, from organizational conversions that atrophied intellectual life to political changes. Most jarringly, the Theological Faculty as well as certain departments in the Division of Humanities were eliminated, lectures in Polish history and Polish law disappeared from the course schedule, employees were terminated, and the university's name was changed from Jan Kazimierz to Ivan Franko University of Lviv (in the beginning of 1940, a sign "Ivan Franko Ukrainian University" hung on the building for a few weeks). The broad scope of these transformations only reaffirmed to the faculty that the university president wielded much power.

Not surprisingly, when Mykhailo Marchenko was released from his duties on September 22, 1940, the academic community welcomed this change with relief. And although the new president's policies did not differ from Marchenko's, the prewar cadre declared Marchenko anti-Polish, and his successor, Heorhy Bychenko,[3] Polish-friendly (Anna Kowalska's statement excepted).[4] This sentiment prevailed even as Bychenko made cuts to work hours, terminated, demoted, or removed individuals from the university (especially members of the OUN who were arrested)[5] and introduced draconian measures, for instance a requirement to sign out when leaving the premises.[6] The community credited the new president with a change in rhetoric, which in reality did not come from him. Like his predecessor, Bychenko simply abided by directives from the top, and those instructions changed (the previous chapter refers to the apparent turn in Soviet policies towards the Polish population). His later role seems even more nebulous. Hardly anyone in the academic community took note, but Bychenko returned to Lviv from a work trip to Kyiv just after the

---

3   Heorhy Bychenko began taking over Marchenko's responsibilities on September 23, 1940, based on the decree of the People's Commissariat for Education from September 10, 1940 (ALU, R-119, op. 3, spr. 31, k. 151). Mykhailo Marchenko finished transferring his duties on September 30, 1940 (ALU, R-119, op. 3, spr. 31, k. 169).
4   Anna Kowalska, *Dzienniki 1927–1969* (Warszawa: Iskry, 2008), 45.
5   In particular, Bychenko reduced Roman Lonchamps de Berier to half time (Nakaz rektora no. 320, 11.11.1940, ALU, R-119, op. 3, spr. 3, k. 289) and dismissed Henryk Raabe (Nakaz rektora no. 327, ALU, R-119, op. 3, spr. 31, k. 313) along with many employees in lower positions ("lab technicians"). He did not extend Stefania Skwarczyńska's employment (Nakaz rektora no. 366, 29.12.1940, ALU, R-119, op. 31, spr. 3, k. 410). At the same time, all employees and students arrested for their affiliation with the Organization of Ukrainian Nationalists (the so-called Trial of the Fifty-Nine) were removed: lab technician Mykola Vovk (Nakaz rektora no. 329, 20.11.1940, ALU, R-119, op. 3, spr. 31, k. 324), executed four months later (April 14, 1941); a few students, among them Iryna Pyk, a United States citizen, as well as Marta Hrytsai, Liuba Komar, and Ludvika Malashchuk (Nakaz rektora no. 331, 22.11.1940, ALU, R-119, op. 1, spr. 31, k. 329), Kost Berezovsky, Oleh Levytsky, and others. See Taras Hryvul and Ol'ha Oseredchuk, *"Protses-59": pokolinnia bortsiv ta heroiv* (Lviv: LNU, 2011), 65–213.
6   Nakaz rektora no. 325, ALU, R-119, op. 3, spr. 31, k. 305. The tightened regulations required employees who had fallen ill to submit sick notes from a government physician. The university president himself entered the start and end dates of employees' illnesses (the same was true for vacations) in his directives. Today, this strict bureaucratic procedure allows us to reconstruct personnel movements in the academic year of 1940–41.

start of the German-Soviet war.[7] We cannot unequivocally assess whether he did so of his own will or was directed to. If he was following orders, what were they? An assignment from the NKVD or from the party, or an order to return to his post, routine in the first week of the war, when Soviet authorities still refused to consider evacuation? Hugo Steinhaus wrote that the German attack did not perturb Heorhy Bychenko much.[8] The psychologist Tadeusz Tomaszewski noted a rumor circulating at the start of the occupation that Bychenko was an OUN member.[9] A Ukrainian author recalled meeting with the gleeful university president, allegedly delighted that Soviet rule had come to an end. Indeed, he returned to Lviv at a time when the Soviets were forcibly evacuating directors of the medical, polytechnic, and trade institutes.

It is equally likely that Bychenko was a Soviet agent ordered to remain in Lviv, and that he was abetting representatives of the Ukrainian Central Committee who cooperated with the German administration. About his later circumstances we know very little, except two references to his death during the war. In his memoir, Jan Czekanowski mentioned in passing that the university president had supposedly perished in Auschwitz.[10] His name appears first on the list of the murdered Lviv professors, prepared by the Soviet administration in August 1944, but the list also includes an update, probably based on the spoken testimonies of Lvivians, that Bychenko was shot by the Germans in Kyiv in 1943.[11] I consider the second version more plausible: Bychenko departed for Kyiv at the end of September 1941 together with a delegation of the Ukrainian Central Committee, thus at first opportunity to join his family. In any case it is apparent that neither the first nor the second Soviet-appointed president of Lviv University were truly loyal to the Soviet authorities. Their fates after 1941 and some of their actions belie such a claim.

Significantly more sources exist about Mykhailo Marchenko than about Heorhyii Bychenko. The first suffered an absolutely terrible reputation among employees of the former Jan Kazimierz University. Polish memoirists take pleasure in emphasizing his low socioeconomic origin and fume at the fact that he did not hold an academic title. Karolina Lanckorońska reminisced: "He told

---

7 Nakaz rektora no. 184, 27.06.1941, ALU, R-119, op. 3, spr. 52, k. 307.
8 Steinhaus, *Mathematician for All Seasons: Recollections and Notes*, 300.
9 Tomaszewski, *Lwów. Pejzaż psychologiczny*, 90.
10 Jan Czekanowski, *Sto lat antropologii polskiej 1856–1956. Ośrodek lwowski* (Wrocław: Polska Akademia Nauk, 1956), 37.
11 "Spysok zamordovanykh nimtsiami naykovykh robitnykiv," Tsentral'nyi Derzhavnyi Istorychnyi Arkhiv, m. L´viv (TsDIAL), f. 119, op. 1, spr. 4, k. 1.

everybody he was the son and grandson of day-labourers, but nobody could really get much out of him because he was simply not very intelligent."[12] Citing Wincenty Styś, a lawyer and economist, Mieczysław Inglot[13] invokes the even more stinging ideas the cadre of former professors had about Marchenko: he had emerged from the very lowest echelons of society, was entirely devoid of intelligence, and had no feel for acting appropriately in a given situation.

Certainly the academic community valued the university's traditions and its autonomy. But it was also clearly fond of the academic, social, and—last but not least—ethnic hierarchies, hence the outrage at Marchenko's nomination for university president. The title "university president" (rektor) appears in quotation marks in several memoirs, to highlight the discrepancy between Marchenko's position and his rank in the academe.[14] A number of contemporary Polish scholars who research the period of Soviet occupation follow in these footsteps. Even the more recent publications contain imprecise or downright incorrect information, although they postdate the comprehensive studies of Marchenko written by Ukrainian historians. As an example, a biographical entry included in Karolina Lanckorońska's memoir is correct in three facts only: the dates of Marchenko's birth, death, and the year when he became president of Lviv University. A publication devoted to the Department of Law during the occupation states that Mykhailo Marchenko was an activist who owed his career to a high position in the party, when in fact he was merely a rank and file member of the Communist Party of Ukraine.[15] A recently published monograph about Lviv University during the occupation years includes an outdated and derivative blurb, sourced from the English-language *Encyclopedia of Ukraine*.[16]

In contrast to Polish publications, Ukrainian memoirs as well as academic studies that examine the Sovietization of the university treat Marchenko with deference: they refer to him as the first Ukrainian university president (inaccurately so, to mention only Iakiv Holovatsky, president during 1864–66) and credit him with pro-Ukrainian campus policies. A 1941 anonymous statement by a Ukrainian lecturer outlines how Marchenko went about Ukrainizing the institution:

---

12 Lanckorońska, *Michelangelo in Ravensbruck: One Woman's War against the Nazis*, 7.
13 Mieczysław Inglot, ed., *Polska kultura literacka Lwowa lat 1939–1941. Ze Lwowa i o Lwowie. Antologia* (Wrocław: Towarzystwo Przyjaciół Polonistyki Wrocławskiej, 1995), 230.
14 Lanckorońska, *Michelangelo in Ravensbruck: One Woman's War against the Nazis*, 33.
15 Adam Redzik, "Wydział Prawa Uniwersytetu Lwowskiego w latach 1939–1945," *Rocznik Lwowski* 1 (2004), http://www.lwow.com.pl/rocznik/prawo39–45.html; Adam Redzik, "Uniwersytet Jana Kazimierz ma 350 lat," *Kurier Galicyjski*, no. 4, January 27, 2011, 26.
16 Jan Draus, *Uniwersytet Jana Kazimierza we Lwowie 1918–1946. Portret kresowej uczelni* (Cracow: Księgarnia Akademicka, 2006), 76–7.

Right after the Red Army marched in, professor Marchenko, appointed by the Soviet authorities as president of Lviv University, began adding to the university's cadre. There were reasons for joy. He reinstated divisions of Ukrainian language, literature, and history. All students were supposed to learn Ukrainian. The student population tripled. The majority received monthly scholarships, free lodging and inexpensive food, and that is why youth flocked to this temple of education.[17]

Zenon Horodysky was an administrative specialist at the time. Half a century later he speaks to the same facts, albeit not as enthusiastically:

After the first days and weeks of incredible noise around "liberation," "unification," both of which brought "joy to Western Ukrainians," drab days of Soviet reality ensued—constant shortages and worries about tomorrow. But there were rays of sunshine in this grey and strange reality, for instance the opening or the name change of Lviv University from "Jan Kazimierz" to "Ivan Franko National University in Lviv" and the appointment of Kyiv University professor Mykhailo Marchenko, a historian and scholar of early Ukrainian culture, as university president. No doubt it was an important moment, considering the long history of Ukrainians' struggle for a Ukrainian university under the Austrian and then Polish rules, and for access to higher education for Ukrainian youth. And here with one decree this painful problem was solved, and our youth, "sons and daughters of peasants, workers, and working intelligentsia" gained an opportunity for "free education." Many Ukrainian professors were hired, to mention just a few: prof. V. [Vasyl] Simovych, prof. Ivan Krypiakevych, Dr. [Ievhen] Davydiak, prof. [Petro] Mechnyk, Dr. [Oleksandr] Maritchak, Dr. Topolnytsky … It is worth noting that the newly appointed president, prof. M. Marchenko, personally saw to the cadre changes.[18]

The above quote reflects the author's desire to align the actions of a Soviet-appointed university president with the spirit of Ukrainian patriotism. Evidently, he was keen on painting Marchenko as a participant in the bitter, lopsided, all-out struggle between the government of the Polish Republic and

---

17 Milena Rudnyts′ka, *Zakhidnia Ukraina pid bol′shevykamy. Zbirnyk*.
18 Zenon Horodys′kyi, "Nezabutnii epizod iz chasu soviets′koï okupatsiï Halychyny," *Svoboda* 188.

its Ukrainian minority population. Though at the time Mykhailo Marchenko was neither a professor nor even an assistant professor (*kandydat nauk*), Horodysky refers to the president as "prof." Of course such specifics may have not been public knowledge; additionally, the memoirist likely did not realize that directives from the top and not the president's decisions called for Ukrainization of the university. Similarly, he may not have been aware of the formal reason behind Marchenko's termination: under his leadership the numbers of Ukrainian students and classes offered in Ukrainian remained unsatisfactory.

Some Ukrainian émigré authors searched in Marchenko's actions for evidence of disloyalty towards Soviet authorities on the one hand, and of an especially friendly attitude towards the local Ukrainian community on the other. This would attest to his overall Ukrainian patriotism. Iaroslava Demianchuk, then a fourth-year student of Ukrainian philology, recalls rumors that the president would warn his coworkers of impending arrests, was a guest of Metropolitan Sheptytsky at his residence on St. George hill, and when Polish students demanded courses in Polish, he would advise them to enroll at Warsaw University instead.[19] During the occupation Zenon Horodysky briefly served as an administrator of one of the properties nationalized by the Soviets and allocated to the university. After the war, he devoted a series of publications to his relatively fleeting contact with the president, in which he depicted Marchenko as a true patriot who sought to save from destruction whatever could be salvaged.[20] While Polish scholars lost their privileges, Ukrainian professors, earlier blocked from academic positions or driven out of the university, under Marchenko obtained positions, including prominent ones. These substantial transformations lie at the root of the discrepancy: Ukrainian testimonies characterize Lviv University's president favorably, while the old Polish guard view him with disdain.

In the perspective of more than a few Galician emigrants the campus's change under Marchenko helped curtail "Polish chauvinism" and ensure "historical justice." During the war a young historian named Oleksandr Dombrovsky enrolled in a seminar Ivan Krypiakevych taught at the Shevchenko Scientific Society. Twenty years later he did not hide his satisfaction when he recalled that under Soviet occupation Poles were not able to celebrate the 600th

---

19 Iaroslava Demianchuk-Tomych, "Do istoriï L′vivs′koho derzhavnoho universytetu im. Ivana Franka," *Zona* 4 (1993): 189–90.
20 Zenon Horodys′kyi, "Derzhavnyi universytet im. Ivana Franka u L′vovi. Spohad z chasiv soviets′koï okupatsiï v 1939–1941 rokakh," *Svoboda* 23–9 (1989).

anniversary of Rus's conquest by Casimir III the Great (Kazimierz Wielki). In his view the university's new name symbolized a transformation Ukrainians had long been awaiting:

> In the year when a celebration of the six hundred years of Polish reign would have affronted the Ukrainian nation, two events occurred at the university campus which signaled that the wheels of history were returning to the tracks of historical justice. At the turn of 1939 and 1940, "Jan Kazimierz" University changed its name to "Ivan Franko" University, and offices which during the Polish occupation had housed the Chair of Polish History, now belonged to the Chair of Ukrainian History led by Ivan Krypiakevych. It was the same location where under the direction of S. [Stanisław] Zakrzewski, and after his death—[Ludwik] Kolankowski, Polish historians had been crafting a scholarly framework for a phantasmagorical idea of a Poland "from sea to sea," reaching back to the Jagiellonian tradition[21]

Somehow it disturbed neither Horodysky nor Dombrovsky that historic justice would triumph thanks to a third power. Émigré authors did not want to link pro-Ukrainian policies with Soviet rule, because it ran counter to the canon accepted in Ukrainian émigré publications. The trend was to ascribe changes deemed historically desirable to patriotic behavior, typical for the population of Central Ukraine and downright natural for the educated intelligentsia that had emerged from the Ukrainian peasantry. Conversely, any developments Galician Ukrainians viewed unfavorably were chalked up to Sovietization. A recently published memoir by Dombrovsky exemplifies such selective interpretation.[22] Passages referring to the increasing Soviet stronghold in Lviv at the beginning of World War II repeatedly emphasize that Ukrainian newcomers to Lviv displayed instinctive patriotism. The historian does not miss a chance to denounce the Polish rule in Eastern Galicia before the war as "Polish occupation of Western Ukrainian territories."

An inquiry into the legacy of Mykhailo Marchenko showcases extremely divergent perspectives on the early days of Soviet occupation. What was blame

---

21 Dombrovs'kyi, "Do istoriï l'vivs'koho universytetu v 1939–1941 rr. (spohad u 20-ti rokovyny)," 32.
22 Oleksandr Dombrovs'kyi, *Spomyny*, vol. 6 (Ostroh: Ukraïns'ke istorychne tovarystvo, 2009).

in the eyes of some, for others signified merit. Who was Marchenko, then? An obtuse bureaucrat who persecuted Polish scholars in Lviv, as so many authors maintain? A Ukrainian patriot who deep down shared the political views of Galician Ukrainians, respected their achievements, and showed compassion for their plight? A party comrade at the disposal of the authorities, as his biography and a weak academic resume seem to suggest? Did he differ from other high-ranking Soviet civil servants, and how? Or was he a Soviet tyrant who abused his power out of hidden nationalistic motives, ignoring Moscow's moderate policies?

Let us consult Karolina Lanckorońska:

> We at the university witnessed the struggle between Kiev and Moscow over the symbolic, but nevertheless important, matter of the university's name. It all hinged on a single word. Kiev turned to Moscow to approve the following title: "The Ukrainian University of Lwów in honour of Ivan Franko." Seemingly, Moscow had nothing against dedicating the university to a Ukrainian poet, but the center of learning itself should not be qualified by an adjective of nationality. There then appeared notices and announcements attributed to the "University of Lwów in honor of Ivan Franko." We knew, however, that the Ukrainians were not beaten, and that this "decapitated" title continued to annoy them. The matter was referred back to Moscow, with the strong backing of some influential comrades. At last, one fine day, two large notice boards painted crimson appeared at the entrance to the university, with the full title: on one board in Russian and, on the other (in second place, rather than first), in Ukrainian. Kiev had triumphed over the Ukrainian University of Lwów in honor of Ivan Franko.[23]

The author describes campus events of early 1940, though she could not have carried on with her observations as she was forced to flee to German-occupied Poland. Indeed, in early spring 1940 a sign with the adjective "Ukrainian" first appeared, and then, promptly, disappeared. Official correspondence used the university's new name, albeit inconsistently, but abandoned it altogether in June 1940. We can trace the name-related travails via a number of sources, such as the university president's decrees from 1940, preserved in the Lviv University Archives.

If it were not for Marchenko's NKVD files, the questions I raise above would have to remain unanswered. The NKVD investigated him from 1941–43.

---

23 Lanckorońska, *Michelangelo in Ravensbruck: One Woman's War against the Nazis*, 22–3.

Two photos: one side view and one full-face, standard in such cases, reveal a man, no longer young, with a prison shave and a slight hunch. The Soviets apprehended Marchenko on the first day of the German-Soviet war, nearly a year after removing him from the post of university president and charged him with cultivating a counterrevolutionary atmosphere and implementing nationalistic policies on campus. On their face such accusations confirm the opinions of both Poles and Ukrainians: Marchenko's anti-Polish actions and pro-Ukrainian attitudes did not follow Soviet policy. Yet it bears emphasizing how freely the NKVD wielded such allegations. During the Great Purge of 1936–38 they used the same pretense to imprison and execute many party comrades. Most citizens of the Republic of Poland who were arrested in 1939–41 faced similar charges (nationalism, counterrevolutionary ploys), regardless of their ethnicity.

Although the preserved documents include several transcripts of Marchenko's testimonies, their actual validity varies. He signed the first statement the same way he had done many times during his brief tenure as university president. But later testimonies bear a signature of a prisoner tortured so severely that he cannot hold a pen in his hand. To these pages we simply cannot give credence. The first source that we can consider an ego-document is his extensive testimony from 1943, which he wrote in the Soviet prison seeking to clear himself of NKVD's charges. Officially, Marchenko was imprisoned for nationalist deviations from party policies, but in actuality the charges stemmed from a denunciation that originated in his own institute in Kyiv and referenced his 1941 book on the effects of the Khmelnytsky uprising.

OF KHMELNYTSKY'S BATTLES WITH THE POLISH ...

In May 1940, still president of Lviv University, Mykhailo Marchenko defended his dissertation "Russia's and Poland's Struggle for Ukraine in the First Decade after the Incorporation of Ukraine into Russia, 1654–1664" ("Borotba Rosii i Polshchi za Ukrainu u pershe desiatylittia pislia pryiednannia Ukrainy do Rosii, 1654–1664 rr.").[24] To a degree, the title deviated from the norm of the time— any suggestion that Ukraine might be an independent entity was banished—and

---

24 Mykhailo Marchenko, *Borot´ba Rosiï i Pol´shchi za Ukraïnu u pershe desiatylittia pislia pryiednannia Ukraïny do Rosiï, 1654–1664 rr.* (Kyiv: Vydavnytstvo AN URSR, 1941). On April 18, 1941 the Institute of History Academic Council confirmed his position as a senior academic employee. For more on the subject, see Oleksandr Rubl'ov and Oksana Iurkova, *Instytut istoriï Ukraïny Natsional´noï Akademiï nauk Ukraïny. Dokumenty i materialy 19368–1947*, vol. 1 (Kyiv: Instytut istoriï Ukraïny NAN Ukraïny, 2011).

this created a basis for the denunciation. The end of the 1930s saw a shift in Soviet historiography, which until then was ambivalent about the Cossack uprising under the leadership of Bohdan Khmelnytsky. Like Peter the Great or Ivan the Terrible, the hetman evolved from a villain of history (in class terms) into a "collector of Rus's lands."[25] This era also engendered the historical drama *Bohdan Khmelnytsky* by Oleksandr Korniichuk (1938). At first, Soviet critics did not greet it with the same enthusiasm they showed for earlier plays by the father of Ukrainian socialist realism, which had dealt with contemporary issues. But the reviews rapidly changed once Stalin uttered praise for the performance.

After the Red Army seized the Eastern area of the Polish Republic, the Soviets decided to employ Khmelnytsky Uprising in their propaganda, circulating flyers, posters, newspapers, brochures, and other materials invoking the Ukrainian fight for sovereignty. The idea was simple: to rally Ukrainian Soviet public opinion by reviving events from almost 300 years ago:

> The great work of Ukrainian national liberation, which successfully began under Khmelnytsky, was not fully realized, not in his days, nor after his death. ... Capitalizing on the weakness of the young Soviet state, propped by the forces of the Entente, in 1920 Poland incorporated into its territories these Ukrainian and Belarusian lands which for over a hundred years had been part of the Russian State. ... When the Polish-German war [sic] began in September 1939, it fully exposed Poland's internal impotence. ... Two brotherly nations brutally ripped away—Ukrainians and Belarusians—until recently residents of Poland, are returning to the great family of our formerly single nation.[26]

The administration harnessed the visual and performing arts to fulfill similarly politicized tasks. The opera *Bohdan Khmelnytsky* produced by a theater from Zhytomyr was one of the first performances in Soviet-occupied Lviv.[27] In early fall, Korniichuk prepared a film script; the filming began promptly in

---

25 Serhy Iekelchyk devotes his engaging volume to the politics of memory in the Stalin era; the study examines how the figure of hetman Bohdan Khmelnytsky evolved over time from a malefactor to a hero. See Serhii Iekelchyk, *Imperiia pamiati. Rosiis′ko-ukraïns′ki stosunky v radians′kii istorychnii uiavi* (Kyiv: Krytyka, 2008), 44–52.

26 Nikolai Podorozhnyi, *Osvoboditel'naia voina ukrains'kogo naroda (1648–1654 gg.)* (Moscow: Gosudarstvennoe voennoe izdatel'stvo Narkomata oborony SSSR, 1939), 85–6. The brochure's printing was authorized on September 25, 1939, a week after the Soviet annexation.

27 "Hastroli Zhytomyrs'koho teatru im. Shchorsa," *Vil'na Ukraïna*, no. 48, November 19, 1939, 4.

November.²⁸ But the movie arrived in cinemas after more than a year, in March 1941, likely because attention and money migrated to more current issues of social and national oppression. An example are two films made in 1940 in the Kyiv studio: *Liberation* [*Osvobozhdenie*] by Oleksandr Dovzhenko and *Wind from the East* [*Veter s Vostoka*] by Abraham Room, as well as *Dream* [*Mechta*] by Mikhail Romm from the Moscow studio. On the cusp of the German-Soviet war, appeals to Ukrainian patriotism inspired by the Khmelnytsky insurrection resounded again. The film was based on Korniichuk's screen play and directed by Ihor Savchenko. Its screenings were supposed to strengthen the loyalty of Ukrainians living in the occupied territories towards Soviet authorities and to fuel anti-Polish sentiments.²⁹ When describing the audience's reactions to the film *Bohdan Khmelnytsky*, the authors emphasized that the scene in which Cossacks tear Polish flags to pieces stirred up strong emotions. Ukrainians recalled the viewers' enthusiasm, while Poles either did not comment on the subject at all, or voiced deep distaste.

As we can see, Mykhailo Marchenko did not choose his dissertation topic at random. It is notable that the volume could come out in print on the eve of the German-Soviet war. The historian drew on literature accessible in Lviv libraries, above all on the Shevchenko Scientific Society's collection. In his interpretation, Marchenko replaced the notion that Ukrainians formed an alliance with Russia as part of an eternal drive to unite Rus's territories (Rus was, predictably, equated with Russia) with a different vision: the Tsardom of Russia and the First Republic of Poland fought for control of Ukrainian lands. From a lay perspective, the discrepancy appears insignificant, but in the 1930s a nuance of that caliber could cost a life. Marchenko's former colleagues and rivals from the Academy of Sciences denounced him, for their interpretations differed from his, and they harbored longstanding animosity for him. In 1941 they probably felt that the time was right for revenge, sensing the reasons for Marchenko's dismissal from the university. Mykola Petrovsky, Marchenko's accuser, adhered to the Stalinist formula in his scholarship on the Pereiaslav Council, while Marchenko viewed its outcomes for Ukraine far more critically.³⁰ The arrest was just a matter of time; a chance to survive could only come, under

---

28 "Pochalysia ziomky do fil'mu 'Bohdan Khmel'nyt'skyi'," *Vil'na Ukraïna*, no. 47, November 18, 1939, 4.
29 L. [first name unknown] Ostapenko, "Istorychna epopeia," *Vil'na Ukraïna*, no. 45, March 24, 1941, 3.
30 Oleksandr Rubl'ov called attention to this disparity. See his "Malovidomi storinky biohrafii ukraïns'koho istoryka. Mykhailo Marchenko."

favorable circumstances, from changes in interior policy, but none were on the horizon. The outbreak of the war only hastened the course of events, presumably sealing Marchenko's fate.

THE HISTORY OF UKRAINE AS COUNTERREVOLUTION

Marchenko was arrested at 2 am on June 23, 1941, under the pretext that he did not show up at the mobilization point (*voenkomat*). However, the arrest warrant dated June 22, 1941 spells out only the accusation of nationalism:

> The Committee for State Security of the Ukrainian SSR received information that Mikhail Ivanovich expresses nationalistic views and shows tendencies for organized k[counter]-r[revolutionary] struggle against the Soviet Government. Marchenko M. I. is an active Ukrainian nationalist. During his employment as president of the Ivan Franko National University in Lviv, he allowed himself to commit serious distortions of our party's national policy. Instead of clearing the university of fascist-reactionary elements, he defended them; under his care they carried out enemy actions. He maintained close ties to the nationalist element among students and professors and inserted nationalist ideas into his presentations and appearances. He displays terroristic and emigratory sentiments.[31]

In actuality the NKVD imprisoned Marchenko because they suspected him of connections with the Organization of Ukrainian Nationalists.[32] The allegation arose from the testimony of Konstantin Valchyk, leader of the Ternopil OUN district, who had been responsible for planning an insurrection in that region. Arrested in the fall of 1940, the OUN member became a precious source for the NKVD, supplying information about the structure of the organization, its members, and the details of their activities. Soon Valchyk became the NKVD's secret collaborator. In the second half of December 1940, directly following city council elections, his comprehensive depositions helped the NKVD to eliminate the OUN network in Galicia. However, since information relating to Marchenko came from a third-party source, initially it could only be used to further probe his activities:

---

31 Quoted in Rubl'ov and Iurkova, *Instytut istorii Ukraïny Natsional'noï Akademii nauk Ukraïny. Dokumenty i materialy 1936–1947*, 331.
32 Ibid.

> Chief of intelligence of the [OUN] state executive "Kruk"[33] (nom de guerre of Stepan Dumansky) and his envoy Malanchuk [Malashchuk] are in contact with the president of Lviv University Marchenko. ... Marchenko regularly comes to Malanchuk's apartment at 8 Ujejski 8 [4 Ujejski] and in conversations with her and with "Kruk" conveys his anti-Soviet nationalistic beliefs. ... According to the words of "Vorona" (nom de guerre of Myroslav Havrylyshyn) all of Marchenko's practical activities at the university serve to educate youth in the nationalistic spirit, but I do not have direct information relating to his OUN membership.[34]

The OUN activist characterized the work of his organization, which aimed to gain followers among Komsomol members and party functionaries, in great detail. By the time of this deposition, two months had passed since Marchenko had been forced out as university president. Thus any intelligence about meetings between the president and OUN members—even if true—was no longer current. Moreover, the above passage relies exclusively on accounts of others, and this was likely the reason why Marchenko was not apprehended at that time. However, his case still made it among the files of persons investigated on suspicion of counterrevolutionary activities. Half a year later, the NKVD put material harvested from Valchyk's interrogation to use, making it the basis for detaining this so recently trustworthy party member. With the start of the German-Soviet war, the NKVD sought to "neutralize" persons even minimally overshadowed by suspicion, and Marchenko's imprisonment was no exception. May and June 1941 brought mass arrests of anyone suspected of ties to OUN occurred, mainly in the territories of Eastern Galicia and Volhynia. Most of them perished in the NKVD prison massacre in those regions between June 23 and 28.[35] The outbreak of the war did not put a stop to this; in the areas of Soviet

---

33 HDA SBU, f. 16., op. 33, spr. 13, k. 184. The brother of Stepan Dumans'kyi, Mykola, was engaged to Ludvika Malashchuk. In her apartment, the NKVD set a trap and simultaneously arrested four persons: Ludvika and three Dumansky brothers. Two of them (Mykhailo and Stepan) were sentenced to death and the sentence was carried out in spring 1941. The eldest brother, Petro, was transferred to a prison in Berdychiv in late June 1941, from which he attempted to escape. See Hryvul and Oseredchuk, *"Protses-59": pokolinnia bortsiv ta heroiv*, 213.
34 Testimony of Konstantin Ivanovich Valchyk from November 6–7, 1939, HDA SBU, f. 16, op. 33, spr. 63, k. 171–2. See also Spetssoobshchenie operupolnomochennogo kapitana Shaposhnikova v TsK KP(b)U, 12.12.1940, HDA SBU, f. 16, op. 33, spr. 63, k. 81.
35 Oleh Romaniv and Inna Feduschchak, *Zakhidnoukraïns'ka tragediia 1941*, vol. 18 (Lviv: Naukove tovarystvo im. Shevchenka, 2002).

Ukraine not yet seized by the Nazis those apprehended included persons categorized on the NKVD's lists as alleged Ukrainian nationalists, among them the septuagenarian Ahatanhel Krymsky, a notable orientalist.

As evidence in the Marchenko case, the NKVD used books published in Lviv that they found in his Kyiv apartment on the (aptly named) Victims of the Revolution street.[36] The indictment listed the following charges: "From Lviv he brought a sizeable collection of k[counter]-r[evolutionary] literature, and he distributed it among friends of similar ideological inclinations."[37] In the investigators' eyes, Lviv-published volumes from the 1930s, incidentally highly sought after in Lviv bookstores by Ukrainian intelligentsia newly arrived from the USSR, amounted to "counterrevolution" (Iury Shevelov wrote about the process of purchasing items that had been removed from circulation through bookstore backrooms). During the search, the NKVD confiscated, among many other titles, the highly popular *The Great History of Ukraine* [*Velyka istoriia Ukrainy*], printed by the publishing house Tyktor.[38] A few years earlier Marchenko's predecessor in the feudal period division of the Academy of Sciences was sentenced to death for owning this volume. One of the authors of *The Great History of Ukraine* was Ivan Krypiakevych, who before the war had worked as a high school teacher, and the other was the art historian Mykola Holubets. In 1940–41 Krypiakevych worked as director of the Lviv division of the Ukrainian SSR Academy of Sciences Institute of History, which theoretically suggested that he enjoyed the trust of Soviet authorities. Mykhailo Rudnytsky found himself in a similarly ambivalent position; he wrote essays in literary criticism in the volume *From Myrnyi to Khvylovyi* [*Vid Myrnoho do Khvylyovoho*], also confiscated, and in the fall of 1939 became a professor at Lviv University, while simultaneously working for the newspaper *Vilna Ukraina*. After the war the Soviets pressured both Rudnytsky and Krypiakevych to produce statements of "self-criticism," and to follow up by publishing texts that would prove their loyalty to the state. Since 1939 they had belonged to a group of Ukrainian

---

36 For a list of their titles, see Rubl'ov, "Malovidomi storinky biohrafii ukraïns'koho istoryka. Mykhailo Marchenko," 364–5.
37 Quoted in Rubl'ov and Iurkova, *Instytut istorii Ukraïny Natsional'noï Akademii nauk Ukra'ny. Dokumenty i materialy 19368–1947*, 131.
38 Ivan Tyktor created a press corporation "Ukraïns'ka presa," which in the interwar period was the most respected and most profitable Ukrainian publisher, printing daily newspapers (including the paper *Novyi Chas*) as well as literature, popular science, and especially history. Tyktor also published monumental volumes such as *The Great History of Ukraine* [*Velyka istoriia Ukraïny*], *History of Ukrainian Culture* [*Istoria ukraïns'koï kultury*], and *History of Ukrainian Army* [*Istoria ukraïns'koho viis'ka*].

intelligentsia who received clearance to hold official posts, yet behind the scenes the NKVD was working their cases. In July 1941 rumors circulated that the Soviets intended to eliminate Krypiakievich on the strength of a denouncement by two university party activists, Andry Skaba and Oleksandr Dzeverin. But it was too late.[39] As for Rudnytsky, we will follow his story in the chapter "Ukrainian *Hamlet*."

During Marchenko's trial neither the investigator nor the judges took the trouble to connect those volumes he brought from Lviv with OUN activities; the books were deemed nationalistic simply because they had been withdrawn from the shelves. Soviet authorities ran up against a complex obstacle: as the Soviet Union absorbed new territories in the west, it had to face off with both the Polish underground as well as with the Ukrainian independence movement and its intellectual base. It would be impossible to overestimate the influence of the Galician intelligentsia on subsequent transformations in the Ukrainian SSR. For the duration of the Soviet occupation, the river Zbruch served as a line separating the Ukrainian SSR from the newly incorporated districts. The physical border helped restrict the transfer of people and ideas, including literature that in the fall of 1939 was commonly available in Lviv, but categorically forbidden in Kyiv. Even representatives of Kyiv's academic institutions exercised great caution when bringing in books from Lviv, aware that it could provoke the gravest of charges—counterrevolution.[40]

COMMUNISM THROUGH THE EYES OF GRANDFATHER AND GRANDSON

Mykhailo Marchenko spent the next three years in a prison in Tomsk, Western Siberia. Paradoxically, the sentence may have assured his survival. When the German-Soviet war broke out, he was not even forty. A June 22 draft notice called him to active duty. He could have perished at the front, though war survival rates for *politruks* or political officers were generally higher than for soldiers. Certainly, he would have been killed if captured by the Germans.

Released in 1944, Marchenko returned to Kyiv, but not until after the war ended. Initially he taught at the Pedagogical College (a steep demotion), and since 1956 at Kyiv University. Many students who attended the university in

---

39 Tomaszewski, *Lwów. Pejzaż psychologiczny*, 90.
40 By way of example, in a letter from March 12, 1940 to Kyrylo Studyns'kyi, Natalia Polons'ka-Vasylenko requested a package containing *Notes of the Shevchenko Scientific Society*. She resorted to the official mailing path through the Academy of Sciences, as the use of one's private postal address could have triggered political charges. TsDIAL, f. 362, op. 1, spr. 371, k. 14.

the 1960s remembered him for his (uncharacteristic for Soviet society) openness. Correspondence addressed to the First Secretary of the Central Committee of the Communist Party of Ukraine reported at length about Marchenko giving a speech at a 1956 meeting of the university party organization in which he criticized the "cult of the individual." The historian decried the abysmal situation of Ukrainian culture after the Bolshevik revolution.[41] This time, however, Khrushchev's Thaw helped him avoid criminal liability. In 1983, the very elderly Marchenko was severely beaten by unknown assailants and died shortly thereafter.

The assault was not random; his grandson Valery (son of Nina, née Marchenko and Veniamin Umrilov), who died in a labor camp in 1984, had been active in the dissident movement, and had been in the Ukrainian Helsinki Group that fought for human and civil rights in the USSR since 1983. Even in the *Gulag* Valery continued his resistance against the system. Prior to his sentence, Valery and his grandfather had formed a very close bond,[42] so much so that the grandson took on the last name Marchenko. In an open letter from July 1975 he made accusations against the system and particular people. Having grown critical of any compromise, Valery came to fault his grandfather, Mykhailo Marchenko, for not opposing evil and for having helped establish a system founded on captivity. The extensive quote below helps recognize the ethical and ideological conflicts between Valery's generation, which overcame fear and mustered up the courage to defend human rights, and an earlier generation, which had lived utterly demeaned by terror. This document also sheds light onto Mykhailo Marchenko's personal history, an exemplar of the saga of an entire generation of Ukrainian communist activists who embarked on their careers at the turn of the 1920s and 1930s.

> In 1933 you started your studies at the Institute of Red Professors. You remained in Kharkiv, dove into "Karl Hooey Marx," observed party arrangements. Your mother and my great-grandmother saved your children and wife from starvation. The resourceful old lady hid a cow from

---

41 I owe this information to Oleksandr Rubl'ov. See a note by the First Secretary of the Kyiv district party committee Hryhory Hryshko from April 10, 1956, addressed to the First Secretary of the Central Committee of the Communist Party of Ukraine Oleksy Krychenko: Pro provedennia zboriv po pidsumkakh roboty XX z´їzdu KPRS ta pro nepartiini zaiavy i diï okremykh komunistiv u vyshchykh uchbovykh zakladakh i tvorchykh orhanizatsiiakh m. Kyieva, TsDAHO Ukraïny, f. 1, op. 24. spr. 1256, k.14.
42 Their closeness shines through in Valery Marchenko's letters addressed to his grandfather. See Valerii Marchenko, *Lysty do materi z nevoli* (Kyïv: Fundatsia im. O. Ol'zhycha, 1994).

confiscation, while all cereal and cattle were taken away from the rest of the *kolkhoz* and sent in an unknown direction.

Nine million people perished of starvation—the Central Committee of the Communist Party of Ukraine plenum named this number at the same session after which Skrypnyk shot himself. In front of him he laid out Lenin's writings on national issues and shot himself in the head. That is how he summed up the building of socialism in Ukraine.

And you became a historian then. ... Some of my grandfather's scholarly work makes me proud. Your dissertation *Russia's and Poland's Struggle for Ukraine* taught many to love their Motherland. I am one of them. Yet there is one "but:" what of the rest? Scholar and society. Scholar's responsibility for what he created. Who benefits from what you wrote? And here there is much to ponder. ...

Miraculously, in 1937 you escaped death. The party organization secretary at the Institute of History condemned your work and accused you of sneaking in concepts of Ukrainian bourgeois nationalism. As luck would have it, they arrested the secretary the following night. After this development his words were interpreted as ideological sabotage, nothing but slander directed at an honest Soviet scholar.

What outstanding reality! Your family did not starve, they did not execute you, what else could one want? Nothing but to praise the Lord and rejoice in his generous gifts. ...

Galicia—this Ukrainian Piedmont of the last fifty years—awakened national consciousness in many eastern Ukrainians. Without a doubt the liberalism of today's professor of Kyiv University Mykhailo Marchenko took shape precisely during his stay in Western Ukraine. ...

You may not have recognized the injustice of your time. But all of you, Soviet intelligentsia, kept silent, hoping to somehow wait out the era, always shielding yourselves by staying on the sidelines. Meanwhile things were turning from bad to worse. Caution evolved into fear, and fear nested itself in your souls forever. And this animal-like state was considered an advancement of culture and of the individual.

Protecting me from life's storms, not wanting to kindle a taste for revenge in me, you did not teach me to see the true face of the KGB. How useful this knowledge could have been to me! It could have shielded me from many a mistake! ...

For me to negate bolshevism is not a discovery, but a way of existence. You cannot oppose it passively. No one can help us but ourselves.

The only option for every Ukrainian citizen is to demand that all issues be solved democratically.[43]

Strong language. It must have hit the addressee hard, more so because of what he undoubtedly knew: his grandson was right, even though he assessed his grandfather's involvement in establishing the Bolshevik regime too conclusively, in black and white.

Valery Marchenko rests next to his grandfather in their ancestral village of Hatne by Kyiv. Mykhailo Marchenko came from Hatne, collectivized it in the early 1930s, and left it for good to escape hunger and find a better life in the capital of the Ukrainian SSR.

FROM "KARL HOOEY MARX" TO *POLITRUK*

During the "breakthrough year for communism building"—1937—Mykhailo Marchenko was put in charge of the history of feudalism division at the Ukrainian SSR Academy of Sciences Institute of History. The appointment occurred a month after his graduation from the Institute of Red Professors in Kharkiv, a quasi-university which trained communist cadres to replace professors who had been educated in Tsarist Russia. As Oleksandr Rublov writes:

> On August 28, 1937 according to the resolution of the Secretariat of the Central Committee of the Communist Party of Ukraine pertaining to the employment of the Institute of Red Professors' graduates, it was decided in the matter of Mykhailo Marchenko "to assign comrade Marchenko M. I. to work at the Institute of History of the Ukrainian SSR Academy of Sciences." The document bore the Central Committee secretary's signature.[44]

Only party members with more than three years of experience could attend the Institute of Red Professors. The course of study in this smithy of future cadres initially spanned three years; the Soviet system needed to turn out new elites at an accelerated pace. At the time Marchenko already had eight years as a party member under his belt and received good grades in his courses, two factors to which he owed his nomination to the division director at the

---

43 Ibid., 167–70.
44 Rubl'ov, "Malovidomi storinky biohrafii ukraïns'koho istoryka. Mykhailo Marchenko," 108.

Academy of Sciences, signed by First Secretary Stanislav Kosior.[45] He led a section of eight persons, all more senior than he, not only in age, but in scholarly achievements as well. But when it came to party membership, he had the credentials. Of other researchers, the historian and seventeenth-century specialist Mykola Petrovsky became his subordinate, and Oleksandr Ohloblyn and Natalia Polonska-Vasylenko (the widow of Mykola Vasylenko who during the short-lived Ukrainian independence served as president of the Academy of Sciences and therefore suffered repercussions) were moved to positions lower than Marchenko's. And only a few months before he had attended their lectures.

Marchenko began his duties a few months after a purge at the Ukrainian SSR Academy of Sciences Institute of History. At the end of 1936 the NKVD arrested the Institute's director, Artashes Saradzhev; by mid-1937, the director of the feudal period division Trokhym Skubytsky was in prison. Among materials brought in as evidence against Skubytsky was a book already familiar to us, *The Great History of Ukraine*, published in Lviv in 1935.[46] Soon rank and file employees got their turns: Mykola Tryhubenko, Hryhory Slusarenko, Kostia Hrebenkin, and Vasyl Hurystrymba. All were charged with subscribing to nationalist tendencies and shot. In early 1937 the Institute of History got a new director, Sergei Belousov, who specialized in the history of the Communist Party of the Soviet Union and had graduated from another Institute of Red Professors, in Moscow.[47] The cadre selection adhered to the blueprint foreseen by the creators of the network of the Institutes of Red Professors in the USSR: removal of the old, pre-revolutionary personnel and their replacement by young Bolsheviks. In 1937–39 the thirty-five-year-old Marchenko survived a purge of the party ranks; he belonged to a new generation tasked with building the system. That was an advantage over the old guard, which the Soviets eliminated almost entirely.

In 1939, in keeping with the plans of the Ukrainian Academy of Sciences, Mykhailo Marchenko was supposed to finish his dissertation titled "Noble Poland's Failed Intervention of 1664"[48] ("Rozhrom interventsii shlakhetskoi Polshchi v 1664 r.") at breakneck speed. Meanwhile, in early September, he received his draft notice to enlist in the Red Army. He became a political

---

45 Ibid.
46 Ibid., 114.
47 Ibid., 108.
48 The advisors of his thesis "Rozhrom interventsii shlakhets´koï Polshchi v 1664 r." were Marchenko's subordinates—professors Ohloblyn and Petrovsky (Rubl'ov and Iurkova, *Instytut istorii Ukraïny Natsional'noï Akademii nauk Ukrainy. Dokumenty i materialy 19368–1947*, 110–11).

commissar in the propaganda division of the Political Council of the Kyiv Military District (the name changed after September 17 to the Ukrainian Front) and was tasked with waging a propaganda war against "lordly [*shlakhets′ka*] Poland."[49] It was Marchenko who prepared an address modelled on 1917 Bolshevik flyers signed by marshal Semion Timoshenko. The flyers called on Polish soldiers to get rid of officers and surrender to the Red Army, which, it was promised, would look after them: "Soldiers! Fight officers and generals. Do not follow your officers' orders. Drive them out of your country. Go ahead and cross over to our side, to your brothers, the Red Army. Here you shall find attention and care."[50] He also wrote proclamations to the civilian population and articles directed at soldiers of the Red Army, to provide ideological reasons for seizing Western Ukraine.[51] Red Army commanders outlined yet another propaganda item: the military units were expected to impress with their physical appearance as they marched into Poland. While the soldiers complained about a lack of uniforms and dismal sanitary conditions,[52] the commanders' instructions specified that they had to look neat, sing while marching, refrain from smoking, etc. The plan certainly failed: every journal entry speaks to the lamentable image Soviet soldiers projected. To the same propagandist aim, the leadership selected soldiers based on language skills to address civilians at assemblies. Suddenly, millions of flyers, as well as newspapers, were published in Ukrainian, and not in Russian.[53] Conversely, any indoctrination aimed at the Polish population was more of an afterthought, as the Soviets directed their focus to gaining support among "brothers" and discrediting the "Polish lords."

The manifestos penned by Marchenko were nothing out of the ordinary. In September the administration produced and distributed ten million flyers, and a staggering number of posters and portraits. Once the military action ended, the Soviets graduated to softer displays of power—military parades. When it came to propaganda, energy and means were never an issue.

---

49 Rubl'ov, "Malovidomi storinky biohrafii ukraïns′koho istoryka. Mykhailo Marchenko,: 109. The council's Ukrainian name was *Politupravlinnia Kyïvs′koho osoblyvoho viis′kovoho okruhu* (KOVO).

50 Quoted in Grzegorz Mazur, Jerzy Skwara, and Jerzy Węgierski, *Kronika 2350 dni wojny i okupacji Lwowa. 1 IX 1939—5 II 1946* (Warsaw: Unia, 2007), 54.

51 Mykhailo Marchenko, "Zapadnaia Ukraina—zemlia ukrainskikh rabochikh i krest'ian (v sviazi s sobytiiami vossoedineniia Zapadnoi Ukrainy s USSR)," *Krasnaia armiia*. September 18, 1939.

52 Vladyslav Hrynevych, *Nepryborkane riznoholossia: Druha svitova viina i suspil'no-politychni nastroi v Ukraïni, 1939–cherven' 1941* (Kyiv: Lira, 2012), 143.

53 Ibid.

One of the preserved regulations of the Ukrainian SSR's Council of People's Commissars, no. 1190 from October 16, 1939, refers to allocating 206,000 rubles towards "expenses to cover costs incurred by the Ukrainian Kinofikatsia, which had commissioned forty mobile cinemas to serve the people of Western Ukraine."[54] Civilian airplanes brought nearly forty tons of indoctrinating materials: newspapers, posters, portraits of leaders, and films.[55] One after another, film screenings and guest performances by song and dance groups took place. The first one to arrive and conquer the hearts of Western Ukrainians was the Leontovych Choir from Vinnytsia. Kyiv actors followed suit, going straight to Ternopil.[56] Writers came too. The playwright Oleksandr Korniichuk was the first author to come from Soviet Ukraine and recruit the locals. He was the president of the Writers' Association and author of *Bohdan Khmelnytsky*, a drama recently praised by Stalin. Later in September more propagandists joined him: Mykola Bazhan, Andry Malyshko, Natan Rybak, and Anatoly Shyian.[57]

"AN EBULLIENT WELCOME"

As a tip of their hat to Western Ukraine, the Soviets decided to have Stalin's *History of the All-Union Communist Party* translated into Ukrainian (and Polish), a step previously unthinkable in the Ukrainian SSR. They also tasked the team behind the all-union film newsreels with depicting "the population's ebullient welcome of the Red Army."[58] Moscow journalists reported at length on the pitiful economic state of the seized territories and the happiness of the locals at the prospect of Soviet rule. The propaganda push enlisted tried and true comrades, fortified by a new crop of party members, which included the Pole Wanda Wasilewska.

The Polish activist claimed that she first encountered the Soviet authorities at the Bug river. She explained that, like so many others in September 1939, she went east, fleeing the German invasion. Aside from the reminiscences of her comrades, I did not come across any official documents that could provide more clues about this key moment: how did Wasilewska gain the Soviets' trust? What made her so incomparable and untouchable, in contrast with other Polish writers? For one, she

---

54 TsDAHO, f. 2, op. 7, spr. 133, k. 58.
55 *Visti VUTsVK*, October 9, 1939.
56 Ibid., September 21, 1939 and, accordingly, September 23, 1939.
57 Ibid., September 23, 1939 and September 29, 1939.
58 Ibid., September 23, 1939.

received significant material support—10,000 rubles—from the Assistance Fund for Western Ukrainian Intelligentsia (at a time when a pension did not exceed 100 rubles). Second, the Soviets made an exception for her, deviating from the obligatory communist party enrollment procedure; Wasilewska did not have to produce references, and the period between her application and admission took only ten days, though otherwise a waiting period of several years applied.[59] As early as in October 1939, Wasilewska saw her journalistic pieces in print, in mass editions, in Russian, Ukrainian, and Polish. During the same period Soviet-controlled media worked hard to cement the image of locals spontaneously joining in a jubilant welcome for the Red Army. In line with Goebbels's principle, "repeat a lie a thousand times and it becomes the truth," this picture, so obviously far from the truth, became a universally accepted trope in the narrative of the Soviet annexation on September 17, 1939.

In Wasilewska's texts, the notion that the Soviet army received a friendly reception serves an extra purpose: it asserts that Poland's interior policies and its USSR doctrine suffered a crushing defeat. The writer complains about the information blockade, which the Polish authorities allegedly instituted to keep Polish citizens from receiving accurate information about the neighboring state, so that the Republic of Poland could make its anti-Soviet propaganda more effective:

> With extraordinary, mixed feelings, towns were awaiting the Red Army's arrival. There was joy, hope of being saved from the barbarity of the war, but fear as well—what is this army, who is this red soldier?
>
> The towns still remembered the Tsarist army, Cossacks charging at the crowds, the military organizing Jewish pogroms. Now they tensely awaited the Red Army's arrival. ... The powerful machine advanced slowly. Flowers on tanks. Red autumn dahlias, late carnations—like red flag ribbons. A sign of love, with which the people welcomed the Red Army. ... A hundred years of propaganda, a hundred years of recruitment for the USSR could not have achieved as much as meeting those Soviet soldiers.[60]

---

59 Many thanks to Oleksandr Rubl'ov for drawing my attention to this highly important detail.
60 Vanda Vasilevskaia, "Pod krasnym znamenem," typescript in the collection of Tsentral'nyi Derzhavnyi arkhiv-muzei literatury i mystetstva (TsDAMLiM), f. 73, op. 1, spr. 153—zbirka publitsystychnykh tvoriv Vandy Vasylevs'koï 1939–1940, k. 3–5.

This quote exemplifies standard propaganda of the period. But neither Wasilewska nor other propagandist attained the goal intended by the military's Political Directorate; on the pages of contemporaneous personal journals the army looks rather different. Journal entries commonly marvel at the military technology, but depict Soviet soldiers as haggard and fearful, evoking both fear and pity. Ievhen Nakonechny offers a rare account of meeting soldiers and political officers. To learn more about the new system, his father, a Lviv worker, under a ruse invited two Red Army soldiers and a *politruk* for a visit. Soon other tenants from the building, all from proletarian backgrounds, joined the bash. Among them was a communist-leaning Jew, who took to chatting with the *politruk* while the father engaged a soldier from Podilia. The soldier confirmed that the horrific news of the Holodomor, Stalin's man-made Great Famine in Ukraine, was true. A few hours spent conversing with the *politruk* quickly cured the Jewish neighbor of his infatuation with communism: "The next day Musio came by. He looked subdued. 'Until yesterday we lived in a state that allowed everything not forbidden by law. And now we live in a state that forbids everything except what it decrees.' Later father often repeated those words."[61] True, subsequent experiences always color memories committed to paper many decades after the war. While we should not trust them to accurately reflect past climates and attitudes, here the details speak for themselves.

The Soviets retooled their powerful propaganda machine from anti-bourgeoise/anti-fascist to strictly anti-Polish, albeit without making adjustments to techniques or imagery. They encouraged hatred for Poles and the Polish state. At least such was the perception of many inhabitants of the occupied territories:

> All actions of the occupier were steeped in the same objectives. The first was *divide et impera* [divide and conquer] between Poles and Ukrainians, between Poles and Jews, between Jews and Russians. The second was clearly to repeatedly inculcate in all those people an extraordinary hatred for the Polish nation, felt on many levels. Poles were "lords" and should be destroyed along with their state. That is not to say that those other nations remained privileged, they got deported or imprisoned as well.[62]

To aid in the agitprop, Oleksandr Dovzhenko's film *Shchors* was translated into Ukrainian, with 250 copies prepared for distribution. This was the only

---

61 Nakonechnyi, *"Shoa" u L'vovi*, 27.
62 Because it would be impossible to list all testimonies, I limit myself to this poignant passage by Anna Rudzińska from her memoir *O moją Polskę* (Łódź: Lodart, 2003).

The director Oleksandr Dovzhenko campaigned for the Soviet authorities, even as he blistered them in his journal

film produced in a Ukrainian studio shown in the first weeks of the occupation. Its selection was not accidental; the film portrayed a "revolutionary hero," who as commander drove ataman Petliura, "a lackey of the white Poles," out of Ukrainian territories. Other propaganda publications emphasized that the USSR "intervened" out of duty to aid its "Ukrainian and Belarusan brothers." On the other hand, the internal indoctrination intended for the Red Army focused on class revenge on Polish lords and patriotic revenge on Poles for the war of 1920. These tropes featured prominently in the 1935 song *Red Cavalry March*, with lyrics by Aleksei Surkov. The march was part of the Red Army's musical repertoire:

> Let the dog-atamans remember
> Let the Polish lords remember
> The sabers of our Cavalry.

Lev Mekhlis, director of the Red Army's Political Directorate, equated soldiers of the Polish Army with "lords," officers, and settlers in his instructions, and they were to be ruthlessly eliminated.[63] How army officers approached this propaganda is another matter; the nonaggression treaty between the USSR and the Third Reich shocked many of them. Some drafted soldiers compared the Soviet invasion with the German attack on Czechoslovakia, which occurred under a similar pretense—to protect a minority population.[64]

All the same, after 1945 Polish literature on the subject adopted the image of this "joyous welcome." The treachery of Poland's Ukrainian and Jewish citizens emerged as the dominant discourse in journals and studies published in exile. In the last twenty-five years, this version of events gained wider publicity as issues of the prewar eastern borderlands became more popular. Belatedly, Soviet propaganda has triumphed.

TRUSTED COMRADE

On September 17, 1939, Mykhailo Marchenko, part of the Political Directorate, crossed the border into "lordly Poland" alongside Soviet troops. As a political officer he gave speeches at meetings in Galician and Volhynian towns. That is how he caught the attention of his higher-ups; a week later the political commander of the Ukrainian Front, First Secretary of the Central Committee of the Communist Party of Ukraine Nikita Khrushchev assigned a special task to Marchenko: to prepare a report about the seized territory, Western Ukraine. On the same day Marchenko flew to Kyiv to prepare materials about the political and economic situation in Western Ukraine. A few days later he returned to the Political Directorate of the Ukrainian Front, which by then was already stationed in Lviv. Here he made a few appearances at official meetings, such as a rally of Lviv's intelligentsia where he spoke of "bourgeois-nationalistic politics." On October 8 the propaganda secretary of the Central Committee Iosyp Lysenko called him in and with the Second Secretary, Mykhailo Burmystenko, instructed him to take on the position of university president.[65]

---

63 Hrynevych, *Nepryborkane riznoholossia: Druha svitova viina i suspil'no-politychni nastroi v Ukraïni, 1939–cherven' 1941*, 148.
64 Ibid., 368. The author quotes reports preserved in the Russian State Military Archive that pertain to the mood in the Red Army ranks.
65 Official directive of the People's Commissariat for Education (Nakaz Narkoma osvity, TsDAHO, f. 1, op. 6, spr. 513).

In a deposition dated May 30, 1943 Marchenko provided details of that conversation: "'How would I like to be assigned to work at the State University in Lviv and to serve as its president?' Lysenko and I knew each other from Kyiv. At first I hesitated, I had doubts whether I was up to the task, but in the end I agreed. Representatives of the People's Commissariat for Education of the Ukrainian SSR who were in Lviv at the time saw to all formalities."[66]

Such an assignment signaled that the party authorities trusted this young functionary, who fulfilled the task efficiently. The goal was to put the community face-to-face with a fait accompli by swiftly placing a Soviet civil servant in an institution Soviet propaganda considered strategic. At that time Kyrylo Studynsky had returned from a consultation with the All-Soviet Committee for Higher Education in Moscow, where, as we read in the previous chapter, he presented the issue of a Ukrainian university and spoke about the situation of the local intelligentsia. The Deputy People's Commissar for Education V. I. Danylchenko (first name unknown) and the director of the committee Oleksy Filippov arrived in Lviv and took care of formalities there. At the turn of September and October, Soviet authorities were operating on an emergency basis: in the early period of the occupation, very high party functionaries—the First Secretary of the Communist Party of Ukraine Nikita Khrushchev, Second Secretary and director of the Ukrainian SSR's Supreme Soviet Mykhailo Burmystenko,[67] and Iosyp Lysenko—all served in Lviv, painstakingly selecting the "right" cadres for the highest posts.

A month later the committee's deputy director Aleksei Gagarin personally reviewed all Galician Ukrainian candidates for professor positions whose names the new university president had proposed. Gagarin professed that he would adhere to the principle of forgiving people for their prewar activities so long as they proved their loyalty to the Soviet administration. But soon it became clear that his declarations did not match his actions; as their first order of business, the Soviets settled accounts with *poputchiks* or fellow travelers, not with nationalists. One of many examples are the fates of two Ukrainian lawyers

---

66 Quoted in Rubl'ov, "Malovidomi storinky biohrafiï ukraïns'koho istoryka. Mykhailo Marchenko," 120.
67 Mykhailo Burmystenko was a party operative who served in the secret police (*Cheka*) between 1919 and 1920 and was likely responsible for blowing up an apartment building on Kyiv's main street (Khreshchatyk) after the Germans took Kyiv in September 1941. Several thousand civilian tenants were killed. See Il'ia Starinov, "Zapiski diversanta," *Al'manakh "Vympel"* 3 (1997): 201–2; Liudmila Kondratenko and Liudmila Khoinats'ka, "Do 100-richchia vid dnia narodzhennia M. O. Burmystenka," *Ukraïns'kyi istorychnyi zhurnal* 6 (2002): 152–4

who worked at the university in the Department of Law: Volodymyr Starosolsky and Oleksandr Maritchak.[68] Both became famous in the 1930s for defending OUN activists in trials. The socialist Starosolsky went to prison promptly in 1939, while his family was deported to Kazakhstan. Maritchak on the other hand remained in Lviv until the German-Soviet war, and in early July 1941 he took the post of deputy foreign minister in the government of Iaroslav Stetsko.

As was the case with other high ranking Soviet civil servants, Mykhailo Marchenko received privileges in Lviv that were not available to him in Kyiv: a grand office and an elegant apartment for himself, and for the university an almost unlimited budget. The authorities were extremely eager to prove the advantages of the Soviet system to the population of occupied territories and put almost no limitations on funding for higher education. In his testimony from 1943, Marchenko recalls the excellent working conditions he was enjoying in Lviv, for the first (and last) time in his life. Undoubtedly he was aware that the appointment to university president signified a meteoric rise in status. Most likely he also knew that his situation could change at any time, regardless of his merits and high-level connections. Soviet personnel policy followed its own logic: rotations occurred with regularity to prevent civil servants from developing a loyalty to the local community. Nevertheless, Marchenko's world view underwent a significant and lasting transformation; because of the people and books he surrounded himself with, this communist activist morphed into a Ukrainian patriot, although he kept those beliefs close to his chest while serving as university president and wearing a Soviet costume.

At first Marchenko moved into the apartment of Pavlo Kryvutsky, who became director of the Land Mortgage Bank SA in Lviv in September 1939, and had served as an officer in the Ukrainian Galician Army during World War I. For Kryvutsky, as a banker and Prosvita (Ukrainian community organization) activist, providing a place to stay for Marchenko might have felt like an insurance policy, however temporary, against potential reprisals. At the turn of 1939 and 1940, once the Soviets nationalized banks and enterprises, Kryvutsky and his family left for the General Government, having obtained permission because of his wife's German ethnic background. Meanwhile the authorities placed Marchenko in the flat of an apartment building at 11 Supiński (today Kotsiubynsky Street), where several professors lived. The previous tenant, Reverend professor Aleksy Klawek, had close ties to National Democracy. He was a noted biblical scholar, student chaplain and trustee of the Union of Catholic

---

68   ALU, R-119, op. 1, spr. 118.

Students, and an honorary member of the national academic fraternity "Orlęta" ("Eaglets"). When the war broke out, Father Klawek decided to return to his hometown Rogoźna, assuming that the Soviets would target both him, a clergyman and a nationalist activist, and his family members who had fled to Lviv from the Poznań district. In a curious twist, the new president, whom many blamed for eliminating the Department of Theology, took over the home of the department's prominent lecturer.

Thus by year's end Marchenko was living among Lviv's most distinguished scholars. Suddenly the former president Roman Longchamps de Berier, mathematicians Stefan Banach and Eustachy Żyliński, biochemist Jakub Parnas, noted Polonists Juliusz Kleiner and Witold Taszycki, botanist and former president of Jan Kazimierz University Stanisław Kulczyński, physicist Stanisław Loria, classics scholar Jerzy Kowalski (his wife Anna Kowalska was a close friend of the writer Maria Dąbrowska), attorney Ludwik Ehrlich, and philosopher Kazimierz Ajdukiewicz, all became his neighbors. It is striking that none of the reminiscences familiar to me indicate that Marchenko lived next door. Despite the obvious proximity, when Juliusz Kleiner fell ill and needed to contact the university, rather than approaching his neighbor Marchenko, he wrote to Kyrylo Studynsky. Anna Kowalska's sparse notes never mention the new tenant. Only from Marchenko's 1943 testimony do we learn that he had visited Banach multiple times. In contrast to the established academic circle of non-Ukrainians, the old Ukrainian intelligentsia welcomed Marchenko in their homes. The old cadre saw in him a parvenu[69] and, worse yet, an administrator representing the occupier. Most frequently Marchenko socialized with Vasyl Simovych, who became dean of Philosophy in 1940 and lived at 26 Czarniecki, in a building which had housed the now-disbanded Shevchenko Scientific Society.

TO SOVIETIZE, FIRST UKRAINIZE

After his initial speech to university faculty, which outlined "the mission of Soviet research in the territories of Western Ukraine," Marchenko must have realized the complexity of his mission. The ministry tasked him with the duty to transform Jan Kazimierz University into a Soviet institution. Yet he could only rely, at least in the early months, on local personnel, because the government was hardly eager to send down anyone except political commissars, and the

---

69 Lanckorońska, *Michelangelo in Ravensbruck: One Woman's War against the Nazis*, 7.

qualified Soviet academics were not interested in coming to Lviv for longer than a quick work trip so they could acquire "bourgeois" clothes. Simultaneously, according to the directives, Marchenko needed to get rid of persons whom the authorities classified as enemies of the new system. To solve this conundrum, Marchenko followed a Soviet blueprint, firing those who had been arrested and those who did not report to the university in October 1939.[70] Formally, each dean was to supply information related to the personnel in question.

At first Marchenko capitalized on the euphoria of "liberated" Ukrainians who were elated to see their compatriots taking positions in various areas of public life and hopeful at the prospect of a Ukrainian university, a dream rekindled by the Soviets. Immediately he appointed a number of scholars from the Shevchenko Scientific Society (NTSh) as provosts or deans. Former deans, vice presidents, and presidents now participated in admissions committees,[71] served as associate deans or institute directors. Almost from the start, in November 1939, party functionaries showed up on campus to ensure that the new order had taken hold.[72]

---

70 In the fall of 1939, based on the university president's directive, a large group of faculty, as well as administrative and technical employees, lost their jobs. The first wave affected Stanisław Grabski, Ludwik Dworzak, and Tadeusz Kosiński, who were under arrest; associate professors Zdzisław Stahl, Jan Piekałkiewicz, Antoni Dering, Aleksander Raczyński, Piotr Kalwe, Wit Klonowski, Władysław Namysłowski; and assistants Jan Logo-Sobolewski, Józef Fiema, Franciszek Longchamps, Wojciech Bem, Stanisław Serwacki, Franciszek Zbiegień (Nakaz rektora no. 30, 3.11.1939, ALU, R-119, op. 3, spr. 3, k. 24; Nakaz rektora no. 34, 10.11.1939, ALU, R-119, op. 3, spr. 3, k. 34). In October, more employees were "let go": adjuncts in the geophysics and meteorology facility Adam Kochański (Nakaz rektora no. 22, 30.10.1939, ALU, R-119, op. 3, spr. 3, k. 17), Zbigniew Socha (Nakaz rektora no. 38, 5.11.1939, ALU, R-119, op. 3, spr. 3, k. 30); professors Ludwik Kolankowski and Leon Kozłowski; associate professors Olgierd Górka, Zygmunt Kukulski, Stanisław Klimek, Wacław Lipiński, and Łukasz Kurdybach (Nakaz rektora no. 39, 9.11.1939, ALU, R-119, op. 3, spr. 3, k. 31); professor Henryk Arctowski and dr. Adam Kochański; Ernest Styrski, Wiktor Gorzelan, Stefan Drzewicki, Kazimierz Sidorowicz (janitor), and Józef Tomasik (mechanic); drs. Antoni Opolski and Jan Rylski; professors Jan Samsonowicz, and dr. Władysław Getner (Nakaz rektora no. 42, 10.11.1939, ALU, R-119, op. 3, spr. 3, k. 34).

71 See, for example, the university president's directive pertaining to the lineup of the admissions committee for the Department of Mathematics and Natural Sciences (Nakaz rektora no. 31, 3.11.1939, ALU, R-119, op. 3, spr. 3, k. 29); Stefan Biskupsky (chair), professor Stanisław Kulczyński, Fedir Derkach, Paula Festing (representative of the students' committee), Roman Góralko (member of the students' committee).

72 First hired in this capacity was a lecturer on the foundations of Marxism-Leninism, Captain Iakiv Levchenko (Nakaz rektora no. 46, 13.11.1939, ALU, R-119, op. 3, spr. 3, k. 46), then Andry Brahinets, who became vice-president for academic matters, replacing Zenon Khraplyvy (Nakaz rektora no. 32, 3.11.1939, ALU, R-119, op. 3, spr. 3, k. 26).

The first Galician scholar whom Marchenko met was professor Mykhailo Vozniak. Author of a textbook on old Ukrainian literature, Vozniak popularized the works of Ivan Franko and was one of four Galician members of the Academy of Sciences. Thanks to the efforts of Mykhailo Hrushevsky, Vozniak was admitted into the ranks of the real members of the All-Ukrainian Academy of Sciences in 1929.[73] The admission occurred with much fanfare, but in September 1933 he was publicly removed for having "sold out to the Polish landowners," as the charge was initially worded. The scholar welcomed the newcomer Marchenko kindly, opening to him stores of forbidden scholarship. Less than two years later, duplicates from Vozniak's library collection turned into evidence in Marchenko's prosecution. Four years later in a Siberian prison in Tomsk, Marchenko recalled the details of how the two met:

> I remember that one of the first assignments I received was to give a speech at a meeting of the local Lviv intelligentsia on the topic: "Polish bourgeois-nationalist parties—sworn enemies of the people." To prepare for it a bit, I needed to consult the local library holdings. The first library I visited was the library of the Shevchenko Scientific Society in Lviv at 26 Czarniecki. Of the local intelligentsia I first met professor and real member of the Academy of Sciences, Vozniak Mykhailo Stepanovych. Before then I only knew him from numerous studies on the subject of Ukrainian literary history. In the first days of my stay in Lviv I visited that library multiple times, met with professor Vozniak twice or thrice, and he showed me around the collection with which he had been familiar for decades, as well as around the society's ethnographic museum. He gave me a sense of Lviv's scholarly life, which interested me very much. My conversations with professor Vozniak pertained exclusively to academic topics.[74]

As a university president appointed by the Central Committee, Marchenko sought out former Academy of Sciences members, perhaps of his own volition, or perhaps following directives from the top. The decrees from his first weeks in office list the names of all four Galician members of the Academy of

---

73 Resolution of the Council of People's Commissars from April 16, 1929, copies preserved in the collection of Professor Mykhailo Vozniak (LBAN, Voz. 1 p. 1, k. 5–6).
74 Marchenko gave this testimony in Tomsk on May 30, 1943. Quoted in Rubl'ov and Iurkova, *Instytut istorii Ukraïny Natsional'noï Akademii nauk Ukrainy. Dokumenty i materialy 19368–1947*, 379.

Sciences: Kyrylo Studynsky,[75] Vasyl Shchurat,[76] Mykhailo Vozniak,[77] and Filaret Kolessa.[78] In later statements Marchenko mentioned Ivan Krypiakevych[79] and Vasyl Simovych, whom he knew from their publications. He claimed the new hires Mykola Andrusiak, Iaroslav Pasternak,[80] and Mykhailo Rudnytsky[81] were recommended to him. Andrusiak, who in 1939 held a minor position at the NTSh library, remembers the story behind the hirings differently. According to him, at Marchenko's request he prepared materials related to Ukrainian parties in Galicia. Out of gratitude for helping him with the upcoming presentation, the newly appointed president hired Andrusiak as an assistant. Andrusiak's journal emphasizes his role as a go-between, linking the old and the new faculty. He writes that the professors were convinced he had some say in personnel policies and sought his favor, unwilling to accept the fact that nothing was up to him. In mid-December, after the restructuring of the university was completed, the young historian received a reassignment to a rather modest post as a librarian.[82] If we assume his account to be accurate, at the turn of 1939 and 1940 a representative of the Academy of Sciences named Ilia Stebun offered him a job as branch director of the Institute of History, under the condition that

---

75 In October 1939, Marchenko appointed Kyrylo Studynsky to director of the Institute of Ukrainian Literary History (Nakaz rektora no. 2, 18.10.1939, ALU, R-119, op. 3, spr. 3, k. 2).

76 Vasyl Shchurat became professor at the institute (Nakaz rektora no. 7, 24.10.1939, ALU, R-119, op. 3, spr. 3, k. 7). See also Vasyl Shchurat's CV, dated October 22, 1939, in the Lviv University Archives. The following passage merits particular attention:

> I began my academic activity in the fields of history of Ukrainian literature, culture, and ethnography in 1890 (while still in secondary school). Of particular interest to me were connections between Ukrainian culture and Western Europe. Gradually I developed a focus on Shevchenko studies. Based on the treatises I published, in 1933 I was admitted as a real member of the Shevchenko Scientific Society, and later became its chairman. In 1929 I was selected as a member of the All-Ukrainian Academy of Sciences, from which I was removed for reasons unknown to me. (archive.lnu.edu.ua/avtobiohrafiya-vasylya-schurata, accessed May 24, 2013)

77 Nakaz rektora no. 24, 30.10.1939, ALU, R-119, op. 3, spr. 3, k. 25.
78 Nakaz rektora no. 78, 27.11.1939, ALU, R-119, op. 3, spr. 3, k. 96.
79 Krypiakevych was appointed professor of history (Nakaz rektora no. 10, 24.10.1939, ALU, R-119, op. 3, spr. 3, k. 7).
80 Nakaz rektora no. 31, 3.11.1939, ALU, R-119, op. 3, spr. 3, k. 35.
81 Nakaz rektora no. 78, 27.11.1939, ALU, R-119, op. 3, spr. 3, k. 96.
82 Andrusiak was hired as the president's assistant on October 24, 1939 (Nakaz rektora no. 25, 30.10.1939, ALU, R-119, op. 3, spr. 3, k. 20), and reassigned to the library on December 15, 1939 (Nakaz rektora no. 92, 14.12.1939).

Andrusiak renounce his former views and condemn the articles he had published in Dmytro Dontsov's nationalistic *Visnyk*. Given that it was an offer one dared not refuse, Andrusiak resolved to transfer to a safer place—the General Government. The next eighteen months he spent in Cracow, working together with OUN's Melnyk faction and publishing popular brochures on Ukrainian history.[83] Not surprisingly, Marchenko's testimonies emphasize the substantive support he had received from Vozniak, in whom the authorities placed significantly more trust than in Andrusiak. The NKVD became aware of the latter's ties to the nationalist movement no later than in December 1939.

The university president also hired a few lecturers from the USSR.[84] At first they were almost exclusively specialists in Marxism-Leninism. Iakiv Levchenko served as the university's political commissar.[85] On November 28, 1939, deputy director of the USSR's Committee for Higher Education Affairs Aleksei Gagarin assigned Andry Brahinets, a self-proclaimed historian, to Lviv University. His duty was to assure that all transformations at the university, including the personnel selection, follow the Committee's directives. Simultaneously, Brahinets served as dean of History and director of the Marxism-Leninism division. Evidently, this post did not satisfy Brahinets, and he was soon promoted to vice president.[86] At the authorities' request, Marchenko also hired Stefan Rudniański without delay,[87] who, being a communist, was to teach philosophy.

The pro-Ukrainian hiring policy lasted until spring 1940. By mid-April, on the orders of the All-Soviet Committee for Higher Education Affairs, names of half of the university's Academic Council, which had only become active on

---

83 Mykola Andrusiak, "Zhmutok spohadiv u zv'iazku z redahuvanniam d-rom Olehom Kandyboiu 'Zbirnyka Ukraïns'koho naykovoho instytutu v Amerytsi,'" *Ukraïns'kyi istoryk* 1–4 (1976): 110–11.

84 Marchenko hired A. Kulikov and A. Tymofiienko (first names unknown; Nakaz rektora no. 40, 10.11. 1939; no. 41, 9.11.1939). The employment of Iakiv Levchenko was backdated to October 5, 1939 (Nakaz rektora no. 92, 14.12.1939).

85 Hugo Steinhaus writes about Levchenko's contacts with the NKVD. The direct line became evident when a group of professors tried to intervene on behalf of the arrested Stanisław Grabski, as well as when Levchenko set up an impromptu interrogation after Steinhaus requested a pass to the hospital (Steinhaus, *Mathematician for All Seasons: Recollections and Notes*, 244–5).

86 Nakaz rektora no. 78, 28.11.1939, ALU, R-119, op. 3, spr. 3, k. 96.

87 Jan Draus incorrectly refers to the day Rudniański's employment began (May 1940). According to university documents, the Marxist was one of the first to be hired (see: Nakaz rektora no. 8, 23.10.1939, which refers to an immediate hiring and the remuneration for him and more than a dozen other professors, as well as Nakaz rektora no. 63, 17.11.1939).

December 2, 1939, were removed from its rolls. Even the best-known scholars were ousted: Kolessa, Krypiakevych, Rudnytsky, Svientsitsky, Shchurat, and Vozniak (three of the four members of Academy of Sciences).[88] It made no difference that only a month earlier, in March 1940, Kolessa, Vozniak, and Shchurat became deputes to the Supreme Soviet of the Ukrainian SSR. From the moment the university resumed classes, key departments, including law and history, employed a large number of faculty from Moscow and a few Ukrainians. Petro Nedbailo became dean of the law department, while Mykola Pashe-Ozersky led the division of criminal law in the USSR.

To return to the start of Marchenko's tenure and his hiring policy in fall 1939, he generally staffed positions in the president's and the deans' offices with Ukrainian intelligentsia and hired many scholarly members of the Shevchenko Scientific Society as professors. But the prewar, non-Ukrainian faculty did not take their academic rank seriously.[89] Old animosities, stemming from ethnic prejudice and stiff competition for university positions, acquired a new dimension during the Soviet occupation: the new cadres bore the blame for actively supporting Sovietization.

In early November 1939, after a meeting attended by Kyrylo Studynsky, the representative of the delegation of the People's Assembly, the Moscow Committee for Higher Education Affairs obligated the university president to finalize all necessary changes at his institution by December, giving Marchenko barely a month to do so.[90] Marchenko wrote about the planned transformations (really: Sovietization) of the university in the official publication of the Communist Party of Ukraine, the newspaper *Komunist*.[91] Meanwhile the university followed old procedures. The switch to the Soviet system began on January 15, 1940, severely affecting both students and faculty, who saw the new order as

---

88 In the words of a historian of Lviv University, "A clear signal to reverse the course of Ukrainization came from Moscow, in the form of a resolution of the April 15, 1940, from All-Soviet Committee for Higher Education Affairs. It pertained to the makeup of the university's Academic Council. From sixty candidates the committee rejected exactly half—thirty. It suffices to look through the list to understand that Moscow disapproved of Marchenko's collaboration with the local Ukrainian intelligentsia, whom the Soviets continued to approach as 'bourgeois nationalists.'" Volodymyr Kachmar, "Mykhailo Marchenko—rektor L´vivs´koho derzhavnoho ukraïns´koho universytetu v 1939/1940 rr.," *Visnyk l´vivs´koho Universytetu, Seriia Mizhnarodni vidnosyny* 15 (2005): 88.
89 Steinhaus, *Mathematician for All Seasons: Recollections and Notes*, 252.
90 Instructions of the Committee for Higher Education Affairs, DALO, R-119. op. 3, spr. 29.
91 Mykhailo Marchenko, "L'vivs'kyi universytet na novykh shlakhakh," *Komunist*, November 16, 1939.

obtuse bureaucracy: "The People's Commissariat for Education began to bury us in directives, plans, surveys, circulars, etc."[92] The end goal was to subordinate all personnel to central authorities.

Some changes, though radical, had a less acute impact on the restructured units. For instance, when the Department of Medicine broke off and turned into the Medical Institute, it acquired more independence. Conversely, transformations that occurred in the Department of Humanities created much more distress. Its separation into two departments, history and philology, followed the Soviet model. Additionally, the Soviets eliminated the Polish history divisions and gradually replaced them with Soviet academic units: nations of the USSR, dialectical materialism, history of colonized countries. Within a year the administration literally decimated the prewar ranks of historians; of thirty-two only three remained.[93]

Soviet changes at the university dealt the harshest blow to theologians. In fall 1939, they were the very first to go. Here, memoirists condemn Marchenko for eliminating the Department of Theology, assuming that he acted of his own initiative. Yet it is doubtful that he made this decision without getting the authorities' approval. First of all, no Soviet university tolerated theology, and secondly, any university president in the USSR was fully subordinate to his superiors. To be sure, in a statement from 1943, Marchenko himself describes his dislike for clerics who gathered in campus hallways for morning prayer. Still, this does not mean that he could eliminate their department on his own. The decision-making process followed the standards of Soviet hierarchy. For example, Marchenko issued his directive to establish the Medical Institute based on a disposition of the Committee for Higher Education Affairs. Soviet Marxist Anatoly Kosichev attributes the reasons behind eliminating the Department of Theology to a conspiracy theory, referring to the demotion of professor Aleksei Gagarin, Moscow delegation's chairman. According to Kosichev, Gagarin got into a public discussion with Lviv theologians and suffered such a crushing defeat that he was removed from the position

---

92 An anonymous statement by a Ukrainian professor (Rudnyts'ka, *Zakhidnia Ukraina pid bolshevykamy. Zbirnyk*, 186).
93 The following faculty were still teaching in October 1940: art historian Władysław Podlacha (even though in March 1940 he had tried to defend the fired Karolina Lanckorońska), Kazimierz Majewski (medievalist), and Teofil Modzelewski (paleographer). In the academic year of 1940/1941 Edmund Bulanda and Franciszek Bujak were no longer among the lecturers, though they worked there until at least the end of summer 1940.

of deputy minister.⁹⁴ Regardless of what several Polish memoirists and one Soviet author stipulate, their versions do not reflect the realities of Soviet institutions. Both Gagarin, a Moscow delegate, as well as Marchenko, a Kyiv representative, could not dissolve a department without a decision made at the highest level. The campus reorganization plans from late September 1939 foresaw no place for the Department of Theology. Whoever and however may have issued the formal verdict in this matter, there is no doubt that this department could not have survived in a Soviet state. Its existence posed a challenge to the "scientific worldview."

In previous chapters we followed stories of scientists who worked in the Department of Mathematics and Natural Sciences as well as the Department of Medicine. A later chapter will piece together the saga of the former Department of Humanities. Sweeping changes affected the Department of Law.⁹⁵ In January 1940 the curriculum changed to Soviet law. The law of the Republic of Poland, now an occupied country, no longer applied, and, consequently, all related courses were eliminated.⁹⁶ The department relocated to a new facility, which had housed a now-dissolved Greek-Catholic seminary. Luckily, at least part of the seminary's library collection moved to the newly established branch of the library of AN USRS (Academy of Sciences of the Ukrainian SSR). The branch holdings included collections of the Shevchenko Scientific Society and the Ossolineum.⁹⁷ A number of faculty members lost their positions "due to a lack of jobs," while others received demotions (for example Dawid Schorr), but many retained their jobs (among them Kazimierz Przybyłowski, Maurycy Allerhand, and Przemysław Dąbkowski).⁹⁸ Yet others, like Stanisław Ehrlich, a refugee from Cracow, were hired after declaring loyalty and on the strength of colleagues' recommendations.

Mykola Pashe-Ozersky (1889–62), of Tatar ethnicity, son of a Tsarist judge in the Siedlce province, became the main specialist in USSR criminal law. Before the revolution he had studied at St. Volodymyr University in Kyiv,

---

94 Anatolii Kosichev, *Filosofiia, vremia, liudi: vospominaniia i razmyshleniia dekana filosofskogo fakul'teta MGU im. M. Lomonosova* (Moscow: Media Grupp, 2007), 24–6.
95 Nakaz rektora no. 29, 1.11.1939, ALU, R-119, op. 3, spr. 3, k. 23.
96 Żygulski, *Jestem z lwowskiego etapu*, 84.
97 Zenon Horodysky, who at the time worked as administrator of the seminary's dormitory, recalls that the collection was transferred at Mykhailo Marchenko's initiative. Zenon Horodys'kyi, "Derzhavnyi universytet im. Ivana Franka y L'vovi," *Svoboda* 28 (February 14, 1989). In fall 1939 Horodysky was a student member of the admissions committee to the Department of Law (ALU, R-119, op. 3, spr. 3, k. 35).
98 See Redzik, "Wydział Prawa Uniwersytetu Lwowskiego w latach 1939–1945," 112–115.

later specializing in criminal law. In June 1940 Pashe-Ozersky arrived in Lviv.[99] According to a Ukrainian researcher, Ozersky was the NKVD informer "Vishniakov," who allegedly infiltrated the Greek-Catholic clergy (though he only had tangential contacts to this community, which certainly casts doubt on the allegation).[100] In his memoir, Kazimierz Żygulski recounts the absurdities of the Soviet system, focusing in particular on Pashe-Ozersky's lectures. His teachings equipped the students with formal knowledge of the Soviet legal system, providing elaborate analyses of the most famous political trials in the USSR and their legal basis. Ozersky concentrated on the most dangerous article of the penal code ("terrorism and sabotage") and emphasized that based on this article only Soviet citizens could be put on trial on such charges. According to Żygulski, the knowledge helped at least one future accused out of dire straits.[101] Ozersky's role as a lecturer in the Soviet era seems unclear. During the German occupation he remained in Lviv and worked on a German-Ukrainian legal dictionary with the linguist Iury Shevelov, under the auspices of the Ukrainian Central Committee. In the eyes of Soviet law this made him a German collaborator. After the war he briefly served as university president. Arrested in summer 1945, he was cleared of charges in less than a year. It may be that he owed his "freedom" to having been an NKVD agent. Ozersky lost his job at Lviv University in the purge of 1948. In 1954 he defended his habilitation, which, tellingly, centered on circumstances that remove legal liability under Soviet criminal law.

A junior colleague from the division preparing the German-Ukrainian dictionary, the linguist Iury Shevelov, spoke of Pashe-Ozersky unfavorably, referring to him as "Soviet." Yet they had two things in common: firstly, a "wrong" background; secondly, they worked together in German-occupied Lviv. Pashe-Ozersky and Shevelov were both *inorodtsy* (of non-Slavic origin— the first Tatar, the latter German). Both were born in parts of Poland appropriated by Tsarist Russia as sons of high-level Tsarist officials. In Soviet conditions, that alone gave sufficient grounds for reprisals. But not only were they able to avoid repercussions, they even achieved a certain status. Shevelov may have been reacting to Ozersky's decision to stay in the Soviet Union in 1944. Did the attorney indeed look at Galicians with contempt, as was the case for

---

99 Lichnoe delo Nikolaia Pashe-Ozerskogo, ALU, R-119, op. 1, spr. 144, k. 20–30.
100 Vasyl' Bilas, "Ahenturna sprava 'Khodiachye.' NKVD proty UHKTs," *Istorychna pravda*, April 15, 2011, http://www.istpravda.com.ua/articles/2011/04/15/36016, accessed September 2, 2014.
101 Żygulski, *Jestem z lwowskiego etapu*, 79–81.

Soviet officials? Another unknown: which documents may have provided the basis for Shevelov's suggestion that Ozersky worked for the NKVD?[102] Paradoxically, Shevelov categorically rejected suspicions that his friend and mentor, Viktor Petrov, was an NKVD agent, although those accusations were far more substantiated. One thing is certain: Pashe-Ozersky had occasion to take advantage of legal openings in theory as well as in practice.

Let us return to Marchenko's personnel policies at the university. Contrary to the opinions of Polish memoirists, the Soviet university president tried to prevent a complete purge of Polish cadres. While he could not object to the NKVD, he sought to weaken the outcomes of educational policies whose goal was to align the university with Soviet models. The Deputy People's Commissar Ivan Kirsa demanded that Marchenko carry out more extreme measures, for instance dismiss Polish professors. In early May 1940, a special resolution of the Collegium of the People's Commissariat for Education of the Ukrainian SSR noted "an insufficient degree of the university's Ukrainization." In particular, the document pointed out that lectures were still conducted in Polish and it required the president to enforce teaching in Ukrainian by the new academic year.[103] Summing up the academic year at Lviv's higher education institutions on the pages of *Vilna Ukraina*, Iakiv Levchenko, a lecturer in Marxism-Leninism, in actuality an NKVD liaison, indicated that instructors of Ukrainian were too lenient with the students and did all they could to make the examinations in Ukrainian easy. Levchenko did not hesitate to inform the readers of disciplinary measures against permissive faculty. Levchenko was referring to Petro Karmansky, who as a member of the admissions committee gave inflated marks for exams in Ukrainian to persons who did not speak the language fluently enough, so that they could be admitted to the university. This came to light either during a review or because of a denouncement.[104] Levchenko's article did not disclose that Marchenko would also suffer consequences.

Later, to explain how the conflict with the Ukrainian educational administration came about, Marchenko invoked the classic satire of Russian bureaucracy by Mikhail Saltykov-Shchedrin, in which the new mayor of the town Glupov (Stupidville) distinguished himself by riding into town on a white horse, burned

---

102 Iurii Shevel'ov, *Ia—mene—meni (i dovkruhy). Spohady*, vol. 1 (Kharkiv: M. P. Kots', 2001), 365.
103 Vytiah z postanovy ch. 46 Kolehii Narodnoho Komisariatu Osvity URSR, 4.05.1940, Pro stan pedahohichnykh vyshiv zakhidnykh oblastei, TsDIAL, f. 362, op. 1, spr. 43, k. 20.
104 Nakaz rektora no. 225, 8.08.1940, ALU, R-119, op. 1, spr. 30, k. 16.

down secondary schools, and canceled education.[105] Marchenko's use of this literary trope in circumstances far from fiction indicates that he was aware of his own responsibilities and understood the caliber of the academic institution he came to lead. Nevertheless, to Polish observers it seemed that they were dealing with a stolid Soviet bureaucrat; worse yet, a covert nationalist.

The Soviets restructured the university and quickly politicized the campus, turning it into an ideological instrument. The newly appointed president, and with him a number of Ukrainian professors, including Kyrylo Studynsky, took part in hectic preparations for the People's Assembly of Western Ukraine. All faculty participated: they were required to attend meetings and assemblies. The Soviet administration pushed the academic community to lend its authority to the Assembly. (When it comes to organizational support, the authorities relied solely on trusted forces, above all on their own cadres, which arrived in the seized territories in masses: two hundred and fifty party functionaries, nearly one hundred and fifty Komsomol members, and eighty political officers, not counting NKVD officers or the military.[106]) It was a small (or not) matter of a resolution in which university professors expressed support for the People's Assembly, as much of a formality as the telegram to Stalin that was "unanimously" approved at the first meeting on September 28, 1939. This time, a deep rift cut through the community: the newly hired Ukrainian faculty spoke in favor of incorporating into the USSR.[107] Prewar professors also voted in favor, despite feeling that the Soviets had violated them and their community. Soon proponents of "unification" came to realize how the Soviet system operated. It turned out that one of its objectives was to employ Ukrainization to effectively de-Ukrainize. Within those dozen weeks, Soviet administration dismantled the greatest Galician Ukrainian achievements in the public sphere, from political parties to civic organizations, to newspapers, and libraries.

---

105 Deposition from March 6, 1942. Quoted in Rubl'ov, "Malovidomi storinky biohrafii ukraïns'koho istoryka. Mykhailo Marchenko," 123.
106 See resolution of the Central Committee of the Communist Party of Ukraine from October 2, 1939. Quoted in Mykola Lytvyn, Oleksandr Luts'kyi, and Kim Naumenko, *1939. Zakhidni zemli* (Lviv: Instytut ukraïnoznavstva NANU im. I. Kryp'iakevycha, 1999), 111.
107 Steinhaus, *Mathematician for All Seasons: Recollections and Notes*, 242. First *Vil´na Ukraïna* and *Czerwony Sztandar*, and after the session of the Supreme Soviet of the USSR, also *Komunist*, printed official speeches. As noted earlier, they were always subject to strict control. "Pro derzhavnu vladu v Zakhidnii Ukraïni. Dopovid' deputata, doktora medytsyny, profesora M. I. Panchyshyna," *Vil´na Ukraïna*, no. 31, October 28, 1939); "Pro vkhodzhennia Zakhidnoï Ukraïny do skladu Ukraïns´koï Radians´koï Sotsialistychnoï Respubliky. Dopovid' deputata, profesora L´vivs´koho universytetu K.I. Studyns´koho," ibid.

Formally, the Soviet Union incorporated the seized territories on November 1, 1939: At the request of "lawful representatives," Western Ukraine and Western Belarus joined the USSR. Consequently, people, institutions, and the economy fell under the same rules as existed in the USSR. Barely two weeks later a delegation of the All-Soviet Committee for Higher Education Affairs in Moscow showed up on the Lviv campus (this was a supreme organ that oversaw People's Commissariats in the republics, which in the first twenty years of the USSR were equivalent to ministries). The head of the delegation was Aleksei Gagarin, the deputy director and Marxist philosopher. The visitors arrived in order to unify local higher education structures with the Soviet system, with a focus on curricula, the education process, and, of course, on vetting employees and students. Some prewar professors believed that the changes Marchenko implemented were motivated by nationalistic views, prevalent among Kyiv officials, and seized the chance to try and negotiate the future of the university. Ukrainian professors spotted in this strategy typical Polish politics: "make a deal" with the Russians and bypass the Ukrainians. The Moscow delegation had received precise tactical instructions: to display an open and liberal attitude towards the local cadres, but without wavering from the set strategic goal of full integration. Hugo Steinhaus tells the following anecdote on the subject:

> [At the meeting] Kleiner proposed that in addition to the Department of Marxism and Leninism, we should institute a department of the history of philosophy so that the students could find out what the political and philosophical currents had been in Europe prior to the creation by Marx and Lenin of the final philosophical system. But Gagarin responded: "Our students now learn the one true philosophy, and what Comrade Kleiner is proposing is what we call fetid liberalism."[108]

Further on Steinhaus recalls that when professors tried to invoke Gagarin, the university president replied: "Gagarin durak!" (Gagarin is an idiot!).[109] This incident took place after the Committee had already relieved Gagarin of his duties, shortly after his ill-fated visit to Lviv.

In the following academic year, exactly a year after the Red Army marched into Lviv, Marchenko, too, was let go. In Soviet custom his higher-ups pinned

---

108 Steinhaus, *Mathematician for All Seasons: Recollections and Notes*, 255.
109 Ibid.

on him full responsibility for communist policies on campus. One of the most important ones was the formal Ukrainization: at the end of October, Ukrainian became the official language (by then government offices had already formally switched to Ukrainian), the university's name changed,[110] and in early 1940, the new plaque "Ivan Franko Ukrainian National University" stirred extreme, if opposite, emotions among Poles and Ukrainians. Meanwhile, in the first half of the year Marchenko received two reprimands from the party and from the ministry. He had carried out the transition to a Ukrainian university too slowly and permitted too high a percentage of non-Ukrainian students.

In a deposition from 1943, Marchenko recalls a January visit from the Second Secretary of the Central Committee Mykhailo Burmystenko: "In early January the Second Secretary of the Central Committee of the Communist Party of Ukraine M. Burmystenko appeared on campus. ... He called my attention to the fact that names on doors and bulletin boards are still in Polish. He asked me: 'Why have you not emphasized so far that it is a Ukrainian university? Do not be afraid, they will not accuse you of nationalism!'"[111] Though no documents pertaining to Burmystenko's "oral directive" are available, a copy of the Commissariat of Education Collegium's resolution confirms Marchenko's statement.

In continuation of the reprimands, the officials dismissing him cited shortcomings related to introducing the Ukrainian language too slowly and admitting too few students of Ukrainian nationality.[112] Assuming that the report presented on May 4, 1940 at the Collegium of the People's Commissariat of Education reflects the truth, fifty percent of lectures were held in Ukrainian. Trying to heed the demands of the Commissariat, while avoiding accusations by the faculty that he was implementing directives of his own will, the president displayed the Commissariat's directive in the hallway. The document announced an effective date when all activities would switch to Ukrainian:

---

110 In a draft of the statute from December 2, 1939, signed by the People's Commissar of Education of the Ukrainian SSR Fedir Redko (see Rubl'ov, "Malovidomi storinky biohrafii ukraïns'koho istoryka. Mykhailo Marchenko," 105), and approved at the first session of the University Academic Council, the university adopted the name change to Ivan Franko National Ukrainian University in Lviv (see DALO, f. R-119, op. 3, spr. 22, k. 2); whereas in the directive of the All-Soviet Committee for Higher Education Affairs of the USSR from December 1, 1939, the adjective "Ukrainian" did not appear (see DALO, f. R-119, op. 3, spr. 29, k. 1). Marchenko used the new name with the adjective "Ukrainian" in ordinances between April 30 and June 24, 1940 (see ALU, R-119, op. 3, spr. 3).
111 Rubl'ov, "Malovidomi storinky biohrafii ukraïns'koho istoryka. Mykhailo Marchenko," 105.
112 Ibid.

September 1, 1940. The decision to remove Marchenko was probably made in late spring, but certainly no later than in July 1940.[113] In June of next year the NKVD arrested Marchenko on charges quite opposite from what had prompted his dismissal: he submitted to nationalist leanings and implemented nationalist policies at the university.

On Easter Sunday, March 24, 1940, elections to the Supreme Soviets of the Union of Socialist Soviet Republics and the Ukrainian SSR took place, with two Lviv University representatives as candidates: for the Ukrainian position Mykhailo Vozniak, and for the All-Soviet one, Kyrylo Studynsky. Though earlier the administration requested that Marchenko provide information needed to put him forward as a candidate, his name was not among the proposed party member deputies nor professors. This was a clear signal that his star was waning. Conversely Studynsky (along with Wanda Wasilewska) came to represent the local intelligentsia. The authorities spared no effort to create the impression that the deputies were chosen in a free election and that they had a say in decision making.[114] Quite obviously, Marchenko was not removed for the reasons spelled out in the charges. The Soviets had decided his fate in late spring, and by summer, after Stalin dictated a reversal of the anti-Polish strategy, Marchenko came in handy, the ideal scapegoat.

DEPUTIES FROM POLITICAL QUOTA

In elections to the Supreme Soviet of the USSR, the following persons received deputy mandates: chairman of the Lviv Oblast Council Leonid Hryshchuk, Marian Panchyshyn, Kyrylo Studynsky, and Wanda Wasilewska. Simultaneously elections to the Supreme Soviet of the Ukrainian SSR took place, in which Petro Franko (the writer's son), actor Iosyp Stadnyk, and professor Mykhailo Vozniak became representatives of Galician Ukrainians, and Helena Kuźmińska the Polish delegate. Top party officials received the majority of both council seats (Ukrainian SSR's and USSR's—republican and all-Soviet). More Poles

---

113 On August 23, 1940 the Central Committee of the Communist (Bolshevik) Party of Ukraine approved the new university president, Heorhy Bychenko. Marchenko's name was crossed out from a list of university presidents prepared by the Higher Education Board, dated July 1, 1940 (TsDaHO, f. 166, op. 11, spr. 461, k. 1).

114 *Vilna Ukraina* published stories about the election process, including photos of Wanda Wasilewska casting a ballot (*Vil'na Ukraïna*, no. 71, March 25, 1940), of the deputies (*Vil'na Ukraïna*, no. 74, March 28, 1940), and of a conversation between Khrushchev and the deputies to the Supreme Soviet of the USSR, with Studynsky in the foreground (*Vil'na Ukraïna*, no. 81, April 5, 1940).

(approximately 30 %), as well as Jews (circa 20 %) were among local council candidates, especially for the Lviv City Council. In December 1940, city council seats went to professors of the Medical Institute (Oleksandr Makarchenko, Maksym Muzyka, Jakub Parnas, and Jan Tadeusz Lenartowicz), Lviv Polytechnic, Lviv University (Stefan Banach, Stanisław Mazur, Stefan Rudniański, Heorhy Bychenko, and Kyrylo Studynsky) and the local Academy of Sciences branch (Ivan Krypiakevych).[115]

Lviv's Poles did not consider their participation in City Council collaboration, although previously they had applied that label to the all-Soviet and all-Ukrainian elections. Perhaps such a double standard reflected the lesser importance of city administration, but the shift also reveals that the locals were adjusting to the political realities that turned out to be more permanent than would have seemed possible at the start of the war. Apparently, a blanket condemnation only applied to non-Poles who participated in elections (such as Jakub Parnas, as we read in the previous chapter). Anna Kowalska's journal shows that her community indeed adapted; once it came to light that neither she nor her husband, a university professor, took part in the December election, even though they lived in the "professor" apartment building at Supiński and were therefore on the authorities' radar, their friends reacted disapprovingly: "they hold a grudge, are offended, argue that by going to the polls they showed more of a sense of humor than by abstaining. All that Sunday soldiers from the local committee pestered us, ringing the bell and banging on our door."[116]

The psychologist Tadeusz Tomaszewski confirmed that after a year of occupation the community's mood had changed. If the locals attended the May Day demonstration in 1940 most reluctantly, they took part in the anniversary of the October Revolution with mere indifference, no longer objecting, even internally. When the university president gave a speech in the fall of 1940, during which he referred to the Ukrainian SSR as the homeland of Poles too, the university community received his words warmly,[117] although a year earlier it had rejected similar pronouncements as acts of aggression by the occupier. Curiously, personal journals and academic studies have cemented the idea that in the fall of 1940 Soviet policy towards Poles was eased. It is still rare today for

---

115 *Vilna Ukraina* published all candidates' presentations (*Vil'na Ukraïna*, no. 268, November 16, 1940; no. 269, November 17, 1940; no. 271, November 20, 1940; no. 275, November 24, 1940; and no. 276, November 26, 1940).
116 Kowalska, *Dzienniki 1927–1969*, 39.
117 Tomaszewski, *Lwów. Pejzaż psychologiczny*, 36.

The first session of Lviv's Soviet city council, December 31, 1940

a Polish author or scholar to admit that it was in fact the intelligentsia's attitude that had shifted.

When it comes to Wasilewska and Studynsky and their respective roles in the elections, Polish sources judge them rather differently. Wasilewska typically receives a uniformly bad rap, so much so that the label *byvshaia polka* ("a former Pole"), which uses Russian to heighten the irony, stuck to her permanently. The category of *byvshii* ("former") is unique to Soviet policy. It originates from the designation of *byvshie liudi* ("former people")—persons whom the government stripped of various rights (voting, freedom of movement, retirement benefits, and so forth) as punishment for their previously privileged socioeconomic origin. Today the phrase *byvshaia polka* simply connotes a renegade, although during the occupation the Soviets also used the word for former Polish citizens to whom they forcibly issued Soviet passports.[118]

Lviv's Poles interpreted Studynsky's membership in the Supreme Soviet as a political tradeoff: the Ukrainian acquired prominent status in exchange for publicly condemning the bygone Polish rule. Karolina Lanckorońska offers this prickly commentary:

> Photographs of the candidates together with their printed biographies appeared on the house walls. One of the leading representatives of Lwów was Professor Studyns'kyj, who, for distinguished research in the field of Ukrainian literature, had been proclaimed Professor Extraordinary by the Austrians for his outstanding services. When, however, in 1918, the enemy, Poland, emerged triumphant, Studyns'kyj was downgraded to ordinary professor [sic].[119]

Here, the author willingly acknowledged the enmity between Poles and "Ruthenians." Yet she argued that since Ukrainian consciousness emerged only recently,[120] Polish and Ukrainian political rights, sovereignty included, were not comparable. She did not entertain the idea of equal protections for citizens of other ethnicities, including in matters of employment and pension benefits, of which the Polish Republic had stripped Kyrylo Studynsky.

In contrast, Ukrainian memoirists center on the distinctions and honors Studynsky held, while official letters from Soviet citizens addressed to Studynsky praise him as a symbol of liberated "Ukrainian brothers" and of the unwavering resolve of Galician Ukrainians. But, as we are about to learn, this deputy acted in capacities that extended well beyond his official titles.

---

118 See Maria Bruchnalska's letter to Juliusz Kleiner, October 21, 1940, Juliusz Kleiner (Iuliush Klainer) fonds, TsDIAL, f. 716, op. 1, spr. 27, k. 26.
119 Lanckorońska, *Michelangelo in Ravensbruck: One Woman's War against the Nazis*, 13–14.
120 Ibid., 23.

A CONTROVERSIAL MEMBER OF THE ACADEMY OF SCIENCES

The figure of Kyrylo Studynsky triggered strong feelings among Lviv's inhabitants. Various groups accused him of a number of political offenses: he was alternately a nationalist agitator of student youth, a Sovietophile, an NKVD agent, or an agent of Polish counterintelligence. Allegedly he bore responsibility for the 1908 assassination of Andrzej Potocki, the viceroy of Galicia, then orchestrated the breakup of the All-Ukrainian Academy of Sciences in the late 1920s and was implicated in the tragic fate of its vice president, Serhy Iefremov (chief defendant in the 1930 trial of the Union for the Liberation of Ukraine). He was reproached for supporting the Soviets, yet also declared guilty of pressuring the Ukrainian National Democratic Alliance (UNDO) to adopt an overly conciliatory stance against the Polish government during the 1930 Polish repression campaign against the Ukrainian population of Galicia. Lastly, he bore the blame for actively collaborating with the Soviets between 1939–41. Such extreme perspectives originated in diametrically opposing political circles—Polish National Democracy, the Organization of Ukrainian Nationalists, the center-right UNDO, and finally, the Soviet elite. They coincided with the most crucial events and developments for Galician Ukrainians: the Polish-Ukrainian conflict, which intensified at the turn of the nineteenth and twentieth centuries and centered on the demands for a Ukrainian university, the Polish-Ukrainian war of 1918–19, the radicalization of the Ukrainian political movement at the turn of the 1920s and 1930s, and ultimately, the dramatic changes brought on by World War II.

Each of these threads, as well as Studynsky's roles in those events crucial to Ukrainian history, merit separate studies. Yet today he remains a forgotten figure; no thorough biography exists, nor has the scholar's social and political engagement attracted much attention. Among the exceptions are two modest publications, 300 copies each,[121] as well as a selection from his correspondence,[122] every so often a publication in the regional press to mark special occasions, and, recently, an extensive article by the Polish historian Stanisław Stępień.[123] The

---

121 Uliana Iedlins′ka, *Kyrylo Studyns′kyi. Zhyttiepysno-bibliohrafichnyi narys* (Lviv: NTSh, 2006); Andrii Klish, *Kyrylo Studyns′kyi. Zhyttia ta diial′nist′* (Ternopil: Vydavnytstvo TNPU, 2011).

122 Oksana Haiova et al., *U pivstolitnikh zmahanniakh: Vybrani lysty do Kyryla Studyns′koho (1891–1941)* (Kyiv: Naukova dumka, 1993); *Lysty Mykhaila Hrushevs′koho do Kyryla Studyns′koho. 1894–1932*, compiled by Halyna Svarnyk. (Lviv: M. P. Kots', 1998).

123 Stanisław Stępień, "Kyryło Studyńskyj (1868–1941)," in *Złota księga historiografii lwowskiej XIX i XX wieku*, ed. Jerzy Maternicki, Paweł Sierżęga and Leonid Zaszkilniak, vol. 45, bk. 1 (Rzeszów: Wydawnictwo Uniwersytetu Rzeszowskiego, 2014), 219–32.

present study cannot attempt a detailed discussion of Studynsky's life, but instead will focus on moments that are instrumental for an understanding of his conduct during the Soviet occupation.

As was true for most educated Ukrainians coming of age in the late 1800s, Kyrylo Studynsky's father was a Greek-Catholic clergyman. The younger Studynsky was educated in Lviv and Vienna and went on to devote his life to scholarly work and social and political activism. It was thanks to his efforts that Ukrainians gained increased influence on educational issues in pre-1914 Galicia. At the turn of the nineteenth and twentieth centuries he associated with conservative circles; such affiliations helped further many a career in those decades. After working at the Jagiellonian University for a few years he was offered a professorship at Lviv University, and soon joined the Galician Regional School Council in Lviv. In the early twentieth century he was elected vice chairman of the Shevchenko Scientific Society (and in the 1920s, its chairman); a close friendship between Studynsky and his colleague from the Dnipro region, Mykhailo Hrushevsky, developed, and Studynsky became his right-hand man. Polish authorities held him in internment camps (first in Baranów, then in Dąbie) in December 1918, as a member of the Ukrainian National Council in Lviv. Since his internment occurred while the Polish-Ukrainian war was still going on, Studynsky refused to swear allegiance to the Polish state (in his autobiography, he drew an important distinction: he refused to pledge loyalty to the Polish nation).[124] This precluded him from returning to work at the university. In fall 1919, after Ukrainians had lost their fight for sovereignty, Studynsky declared that he was ready to give the oath, but he had already been barred from the academic path. Meanwhile, Mykhailo Hrushevsky, who had emigrated to Vienna, decided to return to Kyiv, where the Soviets put in place a policy of large-scale Ukrainization, aiming to establish a Ukrainian Piedmont in the Ukrainian SSR. In 1924 Studynsky embarked on a cooperation with the All-Ukrainian Academy of Sciences, making multiple trips to Kyiv and Kharkiv (then the capital of the Ukrainian SSR). He participated in the festivities honoring Mykhailo Hrushevsky's sixtieth birthday in 1926, and soon thereafter became one of the best known and most criticized Galician Sovietophiles.[125]

---

124 From Studynsky's autobiography: "When Ukrainian youth stood at Lviv's gates ..., I could not give an oath of allegiance to the Polish nation (such was the oath's initial wording) and was thus stripped of my salary" (TsDIAL, f. 362, op. 1, spr. 3, k. 7).

125 On the topic of Galician Sovietophiles and their tragic lot, see Oleksandr Rubl′ov, *Zakhidnoukraïns′ka inteligentsiia u zahal′nonatsional′nykh politychnykh i kul′turnykh protsesakh 1914–1939 rr.* (Kyiv: Instytut istoriï NANU, 2004); and Oleksandr Rubl′ov and Iurii

In 1928, Studynsky's thirty-fifth work anniversary coincided with his sixtieth birthday. Soviet authorities went to great lengths to recognize both, sending congratulatory cables to Lviv and guaranteeing him the salary he was entitled to as Academy member. At the same time the Second Polish Republic retracted Studynsky's compensation at Lviv's Jan Kazimierz University (until August 1929 he was receiving a basic salary, but could not lecture; then the salary was retracted, and a pension—to which he was formally entitled—was not authorized, based on a regulation stipulating that any former university faculty who had not given the oath could not receive pensions).[126] Across the border, in the Ukrainian SSR, the next years abounded in dramatic events. Soviet policies of superficial Ukrainization came to a halt with the first huge show trial that ended in draconian sentences for alleged and real members of the SVU—Union for the Liberation of Ukraine.[127] The administration ratcheted up the spiral of

---

Cherchenko, *Stalinshchyna i dolia zakhidnoukraïns'koi intelihentsii 20–50-ti roky XX st.* (Kyiv: Naukova dumka, 1994). Among personal testimonies, noteworthy are the reminiscences of Larysa Krushelnytska, the only member of the Krushelnytsky family who survived after moving to the Ukrainian SSR (Larysa Krushel'nyts'ka, *Rubaly lis. Spohady halychanky* [Lviv: L'vivs'ka naukova biblioteka im. V. Stefanyka, 2001]). On a side note, recently published materials explain Anton Krushelnytsky's (1878–37) mysterious decision to move his entire family to the Ukrainian SSR. He prepared detailed reports about Ukrainian political life in Galicia for the Soviet consulate, in which he included intraparty conflicts, providing details about UNDO and its leaders, including Kost and Dmytro Levytsky, as well as Ostap Lutsky, Ivan Kedryn-Rudnytsky, Roman Smal-Stotsky. There can be no doubt that five years later these reports, and other sources of his materials, made it easier for the Soviet occupier to control the newly seized territory, put together proscription lists, and conduct arrests: Nataliia Rubl'ova and Oleksandr Rubl'ov, *Ukraïna i Pol'shcha: dokumenty i materialy 1920–1939* (Kyiv: Dukh i Litera, 2012).

126 See Kyrylo Studynsky's petition to the Finance Ministry, TsDIAL, f. 362, op. 1, spr. 3, k. 7, 36. In his 1939 autobiography, Studynsky offers these details: "In December 1919 together with other Ukrainian civil servants I reported to work. At the time my salary was determined at 90%, but without the activation stipend and a stipend for higher education credentials. I drew the salary (as did Rev. Myszkowski) until August 1929, when my salary was retracted. At that point I applied for a pension, but my request was denied. Attorney Błażkiewicz appealed to the Administrative Tribunal, but I lost. The basis for the decision was a 1923 contract between the Polish government and Austria which declared that persons who did not give an oath forfeited their right to a pension" (Kyrylo Studyns'kyi, Avtobiohrafiia, TsDIAL, f. 362, op. 1, spr. 3, k. 7).

127 For a long time scholars believed that the Union for the Liberation of Ukraine was a pure invention of Soviet security forces. Based on published documents we now know that these forces played a key role in controlling all manifestations of civic life. It may be that the Union in fact existed, but whether it was a phantom organization created much in the vein of "Trest" (operation "Trust")—set up by Soviet agents—is hard to say. The most recent source publication does not dispel such doubts. See Vasyl' Danylenko, *Ukraïns'ka*

retributions, leading to the great purge of 1937–38. Then came the man-made Great Famine—Holodomor—of 1932–33. Today we still struggle to account for its millions of victims. Despite these developments, until the early 1930s Studynsky remained supportive of the Soviet cultural and national policies, or at least his former community of UNDO activists and Christian Democrats saw it that way.[128] His statements in the Lviv newspapers *Novyi Chas* and *Dilo* regarding cultural policies in the Ukrainian SSR de facto conveyed support. Yet Studynsky did not identify as a Sovietophile, though even his private correspondence glorified Soviet cultural achievements:

> Neither the Central Council nor the hetman [commander Pavlo Skoropadsky] created anything; communists came and began building an impressive cultural life, and civic life too. Should we fight them because of that, in the name of anarchy? Must we fight Bolshevism on account of its achievements, such as ending the rule of foreign landowners (Muscovite and Polish) in Ukraine, and lifting up cultural life?[129]

The NKVD skillfully stoked animosities within Kyiv's academic community, and the scholar himself was not above playing tactical games. In the name of his friendship with Mykhailo Hrushevsky, who was in conflict with Serhy Iefremov, the Galician academic publicly took the historian's side, accusing Iefremov of … a pro-Russian hiring policy in the Academy of Sciences. In a series of articles titled "For a Ukrainian Academy of Sciences," Studynsky said: "[The Academy of Sciences] did not become a center of Ukrainian scholarly movement, did not offer a full-time position to scholars outside of Kyiv or from abroad, from Galicia, Volhynia, Carpathian Ruthenia, Bukovyna, etc., and instead surrounded itself with Russian scholars."[130] Iefremov's reply showed off the sharpness of his seasoned journalist's pen. The editors published it on July 25, 1928, and they declined to print Studynsky's retort. Unexpectedly, a leading communist propagandist from the USSR named Andry Khvylia came to Studynsky's aid, seizing a chance to strike out at a political opponent: he accused Iefremov of supporting

---

intelihentsiia i vlada. Zvedennia sekretnoho viddilu DPU USRR 1927–1929 rr. (Kyiv: Tempora, 2012).

128 See testimony of Volodymyr Tselevych, member of the UNDO executive: HDA SBU, f. 16, op. 32, spr. 1, k. 121–2.

129 A letter from Kyrylo Studynsky to Olha Kobylianska. Quoted in Klish, *Kyrylo Studyns'kyi. Zhyttia ta diial'nist'*, 94.

130 *Dilo*, nos. 105, 109, 110, and 111, 1928.

Dilo, a "Polish-Ukrainian fascist [*sic*] newspaper,"[131] in reality the oldest Ukrainian newspaper published in Lviv which, in fact, opposed Polish policies.

Perhaps personal reasons came into play as well. In 1926, the position of a member of the Academy of Sciences went to a Kyiv-affiliated Petersburg philologist named Volodymyr Peretts, and not to Studynsky. Materials of the Ukrainian SSR's State Political Directorate's (GPU) intelligence service mention a conflict between the Hrushevsky group and Iefremov's allies, which centered on positions in the Academy of Sciences:

> In 1926, after the academy member Biliashivsky had died, there was a vacant post for a full-time academy member in the Academy of Sciences. The Hrushevsky group planned to appoint the non-full-time academy member Studynsky. But the Krymsky-Iefremov group gave the position to the non-full-time academy member Peretts. This displeased Hrushevsky's proponents greatly and they tried to at least win the salary equivalent to what a full-time academy member earned for Studynsky.[132]

Serhy Iefremov, at the time the vice chairman of the Ukrainian Academy of Sciences, enjoyed great authority among the old Ukrainian intelligentsia, especially those who remained in Kyiv instead of moving to the first capital of Soviet Ukraine—Kharkiv. Unlike Hrushevsky, allowed to return from emigration on the condition of declaring loyalty to Soviet authorities, Iefremov, who in 1917 had served as vice chairman of the Central Council, second-in-command to Hrushevsky, had no intention of cooperating with this government. Upon the Academy's petition, the literary historian received amnesty and the opportunity to work legally. In 1922 he became the Academy's vice chairman and poured all his energy into academic publishing projects. Iefremov made the noted orientalist Ahatanhel Krymsky his right hand, appointing him as the academic secretary, which, informally, put Krymsky in charge of the entire Academy. After the Soviet Union changed its nativization (*korenizatsiia*) policies and gradually eliminated all institutions that were even partially independent, the Academy of Sciences found itself in the firing line as well. The Soviets' main goal was to replace the Academy's leadership and plant their loyal cadres in the

---

131 Andrii Khvylia, "Pid akademichnym zabralom," *Komunist*, no. 23, September 26, 1928.
132 A weekly information briefing of the secret division of the Ukrainian SSR's State Political Directorate (GPU) for January 1–7, 1927. Quoted in Danylenko, *Ukraïns'ka intelihentsiia i vlada. Zvedennia sekretnoho viddilu DPU USRR 1927–1929 rr.*, 37.

highest positions. In 1928 they succeeded; Mykola Skrypnyk, a narkom sought after in the period of Ukrainization, pushed through the nomination of the microbiologist Danylo Zablotny for chairman. Using all means available, Iefremov fought to resist the Academy's Sovietization, while Hrushevsky believed that concessions were necessary. Reading Natalia Polonska-Vasylenko's memoir we get a glimpse of the strategic quandaries that plagued academic circles during that period.[133]

Iefremov and Hrushevsky, former fighters for Ukrainian independence, had once been close affiliates. Soviet authorities viewed them both as enemies, and they skillfully played on the scholars' ambitions and their mutual dislike. After Iefremov was arrested in 1929, the academic community, already split by the conflict between those two personalities, did not rush to defend the ex-vice chairman. To be sure, the Soviets imprisoned most of Iefremov's proponents, with a few exceptions, such as Krymsky, although they arrested his adopted son to put pressure on the academy member. The others belonged either to the "Hrushevsky wing," or to the new, communist formation which sought to push out the old cadres—those scholars who had joined the academy before the revolution. Most morally objectionable was Studynsky's attack on Iefremov after the latter was already in prison. In his publication Studynsky relied on materials made available by the Soviet consul in Lviv, Hryhory Radchenko, from the mock political trial of the Union for the Liberation of Ukraine, as well as Iefremov's private journal, which the prosecution used as evidence.[134] Soon after destroying Iefremov, the tentacles of repression reached Hrushevsky, and then his daughter and wife.

A true scandal erupted when Kyrylo Studynsky enlisted his authority to disprove the first account from the *Gulag*, published in 1931 by the press "Chervona Kalyna," and written by Vitaly Iurchenko (nom de guerre of Iury Karas-Holynsky), born in the vicinity of Uman. Iurchenko was a former non-commissioned officer of the Ukrainian People's Republic who managed to

---

133 "During the elections of the new chairman, the education commissar Skrypnyk had to face our demonstration of resistance, when instead of selecting his candidate for the meeting chair, we almost unanimously elected the Academy's first chairman, Vladimir Vernadsky. The authorities did not expect such a demonstration of solidarity from the academic community. ... At that moment we were elated and did not allow the thought that this is how we would bury the Academy of Sciences, which the Ukrainian community had worked to create at great sacrifice" (Natalia Polons'ka-Vasylenko, *Spohady* [Kyiv: Vydavnychyi dim Kyievo-Mohylians'ka Akademiia, 2011], 467–68).
134 See Rubl'ov, *Zakhidnoukrains'ka inteligentsiia u zahal'nonatsional'nykh politychnykh i kul'turnykh protsesakh 1914–1939 rr.*, 522–4 for a detailed account.

escape from the camp in 1930 and to make his way to Galicia. To make matters worse, Studynsky provided a photo of the author to the Soviet consul, which gave rise to the accusation that he was a spy for the USSR.[135] The widely read daily *Dilo* published an exchange of opinions between Ivan Kedryn-Rudnytsky and Studynsky. Their interaction ended in a libel suit against the publisher.[136] Studynsky lost and had to step down as chairman of the Shevchenko Scientific Society[137] and withdraw from public life. Not only did Studynsky's prestige plummet, but the reputation of the entire Ukrainian intelligentsia suffered a severe blow. To make matters worse, in 1931 a young member of the Organization of Ukrainian Nationalists' militia beat up Studynsky. This attack occurred in the aftermath of the 1930 Polish repression campaign, during which the scholar supposedly advocated for appeasement. The once-respected academy member found himself in a situation far from enviable.

In the mid-1930s, Studynsky described himself as destitute:

> I worked in Austria from 1895 till 1918, twenty-three years; at the university—four years; together— twenty-seven years, but I have not had an income in nine years. If it were not for the house I bought for my wife while living in Austria, which brings in a very modest profit, I would surely have to beg on the streets or sell out in Kyiv, only to be sent from there to the Solovki prison camp as a counterrevolutionary.[138]

Though he clearly exaggerated his situation, if we compare it to his prewar and interwar financial status or to the position of his Lviv colleagues of similar age and comparable scholarly merit, it becomes obvious that his material status and social standing dropped considerably. The salary allocated to him as a member of the Academy of Sciences of the Ukrainian SSR brought him more harm than good; he was accused of collaborating with the Soviets, who,

---

135 Ibid., 529–30. Another reference to contacts between Studynsky and the Soviet consul Lapchynsky appears in the testimony of Volodymyr Tselevych, member of the UNDO executive (HDA SBU, f. 16, op. 32, spr. 1, k. 121–2).

136 Ivan Kedryn, "Professor Kyrylo Studyns'kyi contra 'Dilo' i 'Chervona Kalyna'," *Dilo*, no. 106, May 17, 1932. A full set of newspaper excerpts is preserved in Studynsky's collection (TsDIAL, f. 362, op. 1, spr. 45).

137 A subsequent chairman of the Shevchenko Society, Ivan Rakovsky, blamed Studynsky's removal on Polish politics, which assumed Bolshevik meddling everywhere it looked: Ivan Rakovs'kyi, "Spomyny pro Naukove Tovarystvo im. Tarasa Shevchenka u L'vovi," *Ukraïns'kyi istoryk* 1–4 (1979): 92.

138 TsDIAL, f. 362, op. 1, spr. 3, k. 7–8.

ironically, owed him more than two years backpay (the compensation went through the Lviv consulate of the USSR).[139]

Despite the *Dilo*'s press campaign urging Galician Academy scholars to give up their membership in protest against the repressions directed at the intelligentsia in the Ukrainian SSR, Studynsky refused, arguing that such a step would a diminish a respected institution. Soon the new management, with Oleksandr Bohomolets as chairman, did it for him. At the request of the Communist Party of Ukraine Central Committee, the Academy of Sciences executive board adopted a resolution removing Galician academics as members.[140] That the Central Committee was able to dictate such decisions to the Academy's board reveals the institution's absolute subordination to the party leadership. Yet even the Central Committee did not act of its own accord, but rather prompted by information, or, more accurately, instructions, from the NKVD. At that time Soviet agencies depicted Studynsky in the worst light. He was allegedly an UNDO representative, an UVO liaison, an agent of the Polish counterintelligence, and a Polish and French spy (his son studied in Paris) who passed on classified information to the Polish consul in Kharkiv. This information he was thought to collect with the help of the Ukrainian National Center (which was an invention of the GPU), supposedly led by Hrushevsky.[141] Likely because of these "revelations," a joint resolution was adopted, and a witch hunt in the press followed. Studynsky had made statements in the Galician press about Soviet reprisals and the Great Famine and those were now used as pretext. The most brutal attack came from Nikolai Bukharin, who accused Studynsky of spying for Polish counterintelligence. Bukharin was one of the best educated Bolsheviks and a co-creator of the Soviet economic policy. A member of the Academy of Sciences, in 1934 Bukharin had stepped up to defend Boris Pasternak.

---

139 "Informatsiine povidomlennia konsula SSSR u L'vovi I. Radchenka shchodo potochnoï sytuatsiï na zakhidnoukraïns'kykh terenakh II Rechi Pospolytoï, 15.04.1932," in Rubl'ova and Rubl'ov, *Ukraïna i Pol'shcha: dokumenty i materialy 1920–1939*, 391; Rubl'ov, *Zakhidnoukraïns'ka inteligentsiia u zahal'nonatsional'nykh politychnykh i kul'turnykh protsesakh 1914–1939 rr.*, 537–40.

140 Pavlo Sokhan', ed., *Istoriia Natsional'noi Akademii nauk Ukrainy, 1929–1933: Dokumenty i materialy* (Kyiv: Naukova dumka, 1993), 294. Quoted in Rubl'ov, *Zakhidnoukraïns'ka inteligentsiia u zahal'nonatsional'nykh politychnykh i kul'turnykh protsesakh 1914–1939 rr.*, 538–9.

141 A disposition passed on by the narkom Serov to the director of the Lviv oblast captain Krasnovov in December 1939 contains an excerpt from the accusation that hung over Studynsky (HDA SBU, f. 16, op. 32, spr. 43, k. 178–83). In the fall the agency began investigating Studynsky and his community under the codename "Westerners." This pejorative term, meaning "hostile Galician element," has enjoyed a long life—it is still in use today.

Five years later, after the Trial of Twenty One—members of an alleged "Bloc of Rightists and Trotskyites"—the Soviets executed Bukharin. In a letter to Stalin, Bukharin wrote: "Standing on the edge of a precipice, from which there is no return, I give you my word, as I await my death, that I am innocent of those crimes which I admitted to during the investigation."[142]

Studynsky followed the events in the USSR very carefully, noting on the first day of Bukharin's trial:

> On March 1 [1938] a new trial against communists began, Bukharin among them. He was the editor of the newspaper *Izvestiia ispolnitelnogo komiteta*, where in 1933 he called me a spy of Polish counterintelligence. I never was one and never will be, but whether Bukharin wasn't one, God only knows. In the end Nemesis always is one step behind people's evil deeds, and perhaps the worst of them is to sully someone's name and honor.[143]

Here Studynsky showed no understanding of the essence of the Soviet system, nor of the logic behind reprisals. This comes as a surprise; after all, he kept in close contact with the intelligentsia in Soviet Ukraine and was certainly aware of politically motivated repressions, which struck his closest friends Mykhailo Hrushevsky and Fedir Savchenko. He even intervened on behalf of the latter. The published selection from Kyrylo Studynsky's correspondence contains a number of letters from the 1930s reflecting the tragic fates of people who found themselves targets of reprisal; from the ethnologist Rev. Ksenofont Sosenko, who wrote in the matter of his son-in-law, arrested by the NKVD; Olha Savchenko, wife of Studynsky's imprisoned friend; Maria, Mykhailo

---

142 Letter from December 10, 1937. Quoted in Grover Ferr and Vladimir Bobrov, *1937. Pravosudie Stalina. Obzhalovaniiu ne podlezhit* (Moscow: Iauza Eksmo, 2010). A mission Bukharin reputedly bestowed on his wife Anna Larina (as a wife of an "enemy of the people," she also suffered reprisals) takes on a different overtone. Legend has it that not until 1956 did she find the courage to put his spoken message on paper, under the title "To a future generation of party leaders" ["Budushchemu pokoleniiu rukovoditelei partii"]: "I am leaving life. I bow my head, but not before the proletarian scythe, which is properly merciless but also chaste. I am helpless, instead, before an infernal machine that seems to use medieval methods, yet possesses gigantic power, fabricates organized slander, acts boldly and confidently" (Anna Larina, *This I Cannot Forget: The Memoirs of Nikolai Bukharin's Widow* [New York: W. W. Norton & Co., 1993], 343).

143 TsDIAL, f. 362, op. 1, spr. 3, k. 25.

Hrushevsky's spouse.[144] Known are two of Studynsky's letters in which the scholar pleaded with the Ukrainian SSR's authorities to reopen Savchenko's case,[145] apparently forgetting that he had joined the smear campaign against Iefremov. If Studynsky had trouble remembering his own dubious role, others did not: in a letter from October 1935, the Hetmanate's (short-lived anti-socialist Ukrainian State of 1918) former Foreign Minister Dmytro Doroshenko did not cut him any slack. When the scholar pressed Doroshenko as to why he would suggest that Studynsky glorified the Soviet government and complained that such stipulations put Studynsky at odds with the Polish authorities, Doroshenko did not back down: "And you, sir, were you aware back then how dangerous your statements were to Iefremov?"[146]

Less than two years later, the Supreme Soviet deputy Studynsky got the opportunity to learn the system firsthand.

PROVIDENTIAL FIGURE

In the eyes of the Ukrainian intelligentsia, and, we can assume, in his own perception as well, Studynsky was the most serious candidate for the position of Lviv University president. As a member of the first Ukrainian delegation to the Soviet government, he soon amassed various honors. For instance, he was asked to open the People's Assembly of Western Ukraine in October 1939. In stark contrast, the doyen of Galician politicians Kost Levytsky, who headed the delegation, was arrested and charged with involvement in counterrevolutionary activities.

The delegation met with the commander of the Red Army division that had seized Lviv and with the chairman of the Provisional City Administration. Following instructions from above, the Soviets acted politely and pledged to the locals that no one would be called to account for their political past, and that any changes would be implemented gradually.

> On September 24, I heard those assurances from the mouths of Soviet notables and, I must admit, I gave them credence. Even though I had been

---

144 Haiova, *U pivstolitnikh zmahanniakh: Vybrani lysty do Kyryla Studyns'koho (1891–1941)*, 630–34.
145 See Rubl'ov, *Zakhidnoukraïns'ka inteligentsiia u zahal'nonatsional'nykh politychnykh i kul'turnykh protsesakh 1914–1939 rr.*, 533–4.
146 Dmytro Doroshenko's letter to Kyrylo Studynsky, October 21, 1935. See TsDIAL, f. 362, op. 1, spr. 290, k. 4. Quoted in Rubl'ov, *Zakhidnoukraïns'ka inteligentsiia u zahal'nonatsional'nykh politychnykh i kul'turnykh protsesakh 1914–1939 rr.*, 649.

on this planet a long time and during my life have seen many changes, until then I never witnessed representatives of an army and a country's government openly and intentionally lie to an official delegation of the local population.[147]

It never occurred to Levytsky that the Soviets would misconstrue his offer of involvement in political life. From the investigation files it appears that the authorities suspected he intended to create a party whose program would be adapted to the new conditions. That, to the NKVD, equaled counterrevolution.[148] The Soviets never appreciated offers of active support, as such propositions implied the desire to participate in governance. After spending a month in prison on Łącki Street, Levytsky, despite having suffered a stroke, was sent to Moscow with a regular prisoner transport,[149] where he spent the next one and a half years in the Lubianka and Butyrka prisons.

Since Studynsky was a delegate to the People's Assembly, Ivan Rakovsky, chairman of the Shevchenko Society, approached him to help save Kost Levytsky, who was eighty years old at the time of his arrest. He urged Studynsky to ask the Assembly to announce amnesty "for all imprisoned and accused of anti-Soviet activities in the years when we were simply slaves of the Polish state, or at least amnesty for those aged sixty or older. ... Such general or even just partial amnesty would be a magnanimous and noble deed, guaranteed to win heartfelt support for Soviet authorities among our Ukrainian masses."[150]

---

147 See Milena Rudnyts'ka, *Zakhidnia Ukraina pid bol'shevykamy. Zbirnyk*, 381.
148 Information by the USSR Deputy People's Commissar of State Security Vsevolod Merkulov and the Ukrainian Commissar of the NKVD Ivan Serov, addressed to the chief of Soviet security Lavrentii Beria, October 3, 1939. See "Spetsopovidomlennia zastupnyka narkoma vnutrishnikh sprav L. Berii pro robotu operatyvnykh chekists′kykh hrup u Zakhidnii Ukraini. Pislia 28 veresnia 1939 r.," in Danylenko and Kokin, *Radians'ki orhany derzhavnoï bezpeky u 1939–1941 r. Dokumenty HDA SB Ukrainy*, 214.
149 Kost Levytsky shared a prison cell with Stanisław Ostrowski, the city's mayor, arrested a few days earlier. Their accounts differ in important details. Ostrowski emphasizes his moral superiority to Levytsky: "It was unpleasant to hear Dr. Kost Levytsky's complaints: that he was innocent, that they held him by mistake as an expert in Ukrainian matters, that he was a noted attorney in Lviv and demanded an unconditional release. These were statements of a person broken by advanced age and the experiences of preceding weeks, and the replies he received were rude, vulgar Soviet nicknames and taunts" (Ostrowski, *Dnie pohańbienia. Wspomnienia z lat 1939–1941. W obronie polskości ziemi lwowskiej*).
150 Ivan Rakovsky's letter from October 27, 1939 to Kyrylo Studynsky. See TsDIAL, f. 362, op. 1, spr. 55, k. 150. Quoted in Haiova, *U pivstolitnikh zmahanniakh: Vybrani lysty do Kyryla Studyns'koho (1891–1941)*, 667.

Rakovsky sent the same letter to Panchyshyn. The chapter "Haven at the Clinic" showed that the delegates, especially Panchyshyn, functioned as mere puppets. Clearly, Rakovsky had not grasped yet that his letters' addressees—the delegates to the People's Assembly—lacked any actual influence, and the entire Galician intelligentsia was in dire straits (six weeks later Rakovsky fled to the German-controlled territories). The Soviets released Kost Levytsky from Lubianka on May 14, 1941. Whether Studynsky's efforts played a part is hard to say.

Many Galician Ukrainians sent similar appeals to Studynsky. The Association of Ukrainian Real Property Owners approached the activist with an official plea "to make every effort to compel the People's Assembly of Western Ukraine to make certain changes to Article 6 and Chapter I of Stalin's Constitution."[151] The Association argued for declaring a ten-year moratorium on all changes to civil and criminal law, as well as to administrative regulations. Other suggestions included retaining the pension structure of all civil servants and private sector employees. The parish priest in the village of Krasne, Rev. Vasyl Navrotsky, sent a letter to the People's Assembly chairman expressing his outrage at those assembly delegates who made dishonest accusations against the Metropolitan Sheptytsky and the entire Greek-Catholic clergy, and at all those in attendance who did not protest such slander.[152]

Such letters demonstrate that at first Ukrainians viewed the Soviet administration similarly to the Tsarist Russian occupation during World War I. On the one hand, it was understood that Soviet governance meant changes to the existing political order. This was common knowledge, especially in Eastern Galicia. On the other hand, customs typical of civic society, traditions of a parliamentary system, and the perceived role of public opinion compelled people such as these letter writers to try to move heaven and earth. Only in 1940 did the totalitarian essence of Soviet rule finally sink in.

The following months delivered multiple blows to the Ukrainian intelligentsia. Studynsky returned from Moscow and Kyiv, where—as he announced in newspapers and at public assemblies, including a session of the Lviv chapters of the Writers' Association—the delegation was received with widespread enthusiasm, and the government welcomed them as guests of the highest rank. But the scholar brought back some unofficial news as well: the Shevchenko

---

151 Lyst Soiuzu Ukraïns'kykh vlasnykiv Real'nosti, holova Iulian Rusyn, sekretar Ivan Oleksyn, TsDIAL, f. 362, op. 1, spr. 43, k. 7.
152 TsDIAL, f. 362, op. 1, spr. 356, k. 3–5.

Society would soon be disbanded. Though Soviet plans for Lviv included establishing a few chapters of the institutes of the Ukrainian SSR Scientific Academy, only "verified" members of the Shevchenko Society could count on employment in those new institutions.[153] On January 13, 1940, one day before the Society "voluntarily" dissolved, its chairman Ivan Rakovsky left for Cracow, thanks to the support of Hans Koch, chairman of the German repatriation commission.[154] The reorganized structures had no use for Rakovsky since the plans assumed the creation of humanities and economics divisions, and Rakovsky was a zoologist and an anthropologist. The possibility that he was in danger of arrest cannot be ruled out.

The NKVD's suspicions followed Studynsky from Moscow and Kyiv. They gleaned displays of nationalism in his public appearances. When, after several years, Studynsky attempted to rekindle contacts with friends who did not perish in the Great Purge, the Soviets suspected it was a ploy to resurrect a network of spies.[155] Officially, however, Studynsky basked in distinctions. In December 1939 he regained the title of academy member (as did Kolessa, Shchurat, and Vozniak), and in early 1940 he was appointed as director of the Linguistics Division in a chapter of the Scientific Academy that replaced the Shevchenko Society. In December, after the young historian Mykola Andrusiak was removed from his position as assistant to the university president, Studynsky's influence over campus personnel policies increased.[156] In January 1940 he became a provost for academic affairs.[157] Yet the post of university president was out of the question—it could only go to a trusted party member.

Though Studynsky got credit for "ukrainizing" Marchenko, no other direct testimonies survive besides the former university president's prison testimonies. The inmate described a circle of people with whom he maintained informal contacts while leading the university. He cultivated a friendship with Studynsky and the two men went on a joint family vacation in Truskavets. For

---

153 Rakovs'kyi, "Spomyny pro Naukove Tovarystvo im. Tarasa Shevchenka u L'vovi," 100.
154 Ibid.
155 See HDA SBU, f. 16, op. 32, spr. 43, k. 182–3.
156 Juliusz Kleiner negotiated with Studynsky on matters of employment in the Department of Polish Philology. See also a December 18, 1939 letter by Marta Rudnytska, wife of professor Mykhailo Rudnytsky, pertaining to the hire of an English specialist, Dr. Lederer (first name unknown; TsDIAL, f. 362, op. 1, spr. 376), and a vacation schedule of lecturers, which includes Lederer's name (Nakaz rektora no. 197, 24.06.1940, ALU, R-119, op. 1, spr. 30, k. 213); Ivan Bryk's letter to Kyrylo Studynsky from December 10, 1939, which shows that the author received an employment offer (TsDIAL, f. 362, op. 1, spr. 251, k.99).
157 Nakaz rektora no. 104 (copy), 4.01.1940, TsDIAL, f. 362, op. 1, spr. 62, k. 5.

obvious reasons the statement in question does not reveal any information about their possibly shared political views. The powerful influence of Galician Ukrainians on newcomers from Kyiv comes to light in the recollections written by Nina Marchenko (the historian's daughter and the dissident's mother).[158] For her, then an eleven-year-old girl, those stays in Lviv and Truskavets brought a discovery of a completely different world—polite manners and ... the ubiquity of Ukrainian language, which one did not hear in Kyiv.[159] We can also draw on Volodymyr Starosolsky's account: "They said of Marchenko that upon his arrival in L'viv he was more a communist than a Ukrainian, and at the time of his departure, more a Ukrainian than a communist."[160] There is also evidence pointing to Marchenko's friendship with the Galician historian Ivan Krypiakevych (in the fall of 1939 Marchenko appointed him as director of the division of Ukrainian history; in 1940 Krypiakevych held this title in combination with a post in the Lviv chapter of the Scientific Academy's history division). Twenty years later Krypiakevych had the occasion to pay back his moral debt, serving as a reader of Marchenko's habilitation thesis.

It is possible, yet far from certain, that Marchenko knew of the NKVD's hunt for Studynsky, which began long before the academy member's death at the start of the German-Soviet war. In the fall 1939 the deputy came under the NKVD's careful surveillance. By early 1940, Serov, irritated with the slow progress, demanded that the head of the NKVD's Lviv oblast section, a Captain Kapiton Krasnov, surround "our front man" with agents and collect detailed information about Studynsky and his circle.[161] We can be sure that such information was supplied, though I did not come across related documents.

A glance at available correspondence between the Supreme Soviet deputy and administrative organs, as well as local NKVD chiefs, makes the functionaries' irritation evident. Regrettably, the equivalent documentation collected by Panchyshyn did not survive, perhaps because, having fortuitously evaded the mandatory Soviet evacuation, he needed to rid himself of anything linking him to the Soviets, as the next occupier would consider it grounds for arrest. No trace remains of Wasilewska's official actions either. Professor Mykhailo

---

158 Vasyl' Ovsiienko, "U borot'bi za syna. Interviu Nadiï Mykhailivny Marchenko Vasyliu Ovsiienku, 16.06.1998," in *Matinka Nina. Spohady pro Ninu Mykhailivnu Marchenko (Smuzhanytsiu)*, ed. Andrii Horbal' and Nataliia Puriaieva (Kyiv: Smoloskyp, 2013), 16–18.
159 Ibid., 18.
160 Uliana Starosol's'ka, ed., *Zapysky NTSh 210: Volodymyr Starosol's'kyi, 1878–1942* (1991): 125–6.
161 Order from February 19, 1940 (HDA SBU, f. 16, op. 33, spr. 71, k. 57).

Vozniak's vast collection includes only one letter to him as a deputy, in which a former university colleague seeks help in dealing with the authorities.[162] I did not locate Petro Franko's letters. Franko became a People's Assembly deputy and a delegate of the Executive Committee to Moscow and Kyiv in November 1939, and subsequently a deputy to the Supreme Soviet of the Ukrainian SSR. In 1936 Franko managed to return to Lviv from Kharkiv, where he had worked since 1931 as a chemist. After returning, he published articles about the Great Famine in Ukraine. Harboring no illusions about the Soviets and their ethnic policies, he did not hide his views:

> At one of the assemblies [at the Lviv Polytechnic] the son of the great Ukrainian poet Ivan Franko, Petro Ivanovych, made a speech; he had just returned from a trip around the USSR, where he was shown the wonders of socialism; in his verbal account the young Franko, with a great dose of humor and somewhat dangerous satire, described the life of Soviet society—what a grand life, with queues everywhere, but they create unlimited opportunities to meet interesting people, and help forge social bonds, exchange ideas; they render buying and reading newspapers superfluous because one can learn everything just standing in these lines.[163]

In all likelihood the Soviets made Petro Franko a deputy so he could adorn the political process as Ukrainian decoration. But Franko held no real sway when it came to helping people whom the NKVD targeted, especially since it was Moscow and not Kyiv that made decisions about key prisoners. If his notable father's name protected Franko Jr., his own biography—he had served in the Ukrainian Sich Riflemen, was a legendary pilot, initiated the scouting movement after World War I, and later published about the Great Ukrainian Famine—made him a persona non-grata in Soviet Ukraine. On June 28, 1941, after a mandatory evacuation, both Franko and Studynsky vanished without a trace.

---

162 Adam Mykolaievych's letter from January 12, 1941 references a denunciation on which the author was arrested as a director of a Soviet school near the former border along Zbruch. The local population boycotted his school (LNB, Boz. 382, p. 100, k. 1–3). Both Studynsky and Panchyshyn intervened on Mykolaievych's behalf. The letter's author approached Vozniak for material support and later confirmed receiving the money (letter from January 29, 1941, LNB, Boz. 382, p. 100, k.5).

163 Popławski, "Okupanci na Politechnice Lwowskiej. Społeczność uczelni w latach 1939–1945," k. 20.

Though in the eyes of the Soviet secret service Studynsky was a suspect, nevertheless, thanks to his prominent position, Soviet functionaries, and even the secret service itself, had to answer his queries. By spring 1940 he had become an institution. For many people his support or advice offered one last chance to avert the worst.

Reading the official speeches of the People's Assembly chairman from the first months of the Soviet occupation leaves us with the impression that he truly believed his dream of a united Ukraine was realized and that he took to heart his grand role in the new administration. In contrast, his correspondence with victims of Sovietization and letters from the prosecutor's office, the secret service, and the commission for exoneration by the USSR Supreme Soviet executive give rise to a different sort of speculation. If Studynsky harbored any hope or illusions about the intentions of the Soviet authorities, he quickly grasped the truth. The only thing he could still accomplish was to attempt to help the ever-increasing scores of people who needed his support, in other words, to mitigate the outcomes. His actions were but a drop in an ocean of great need.

ON THE SURFACE AND IN REALITY

In *Pejzaż psychologiczny*, Tadeusz Tomaszewski mentions that Juliusz Kleiner made it his mission to alleviate the hardships experienced by Polish professors in Lviv and to counteract "Ukrainian intrigues." With this purpose Kleiner approached Wanda Wasilewska.[164] Later, recounting her stay in Lviv, Wasilewska depicted the episode differently; after her conversation with Stalin in July 1940 and corresponding directives "from above," an official meeting between the professors and the oblast authorities took place, but none of those invited dared to raise any issues, let alone share a list of demands.[165]

In *Wszystko, co najważniejsze* [*Everything that is most important*], Ola Watowa attributes the release of her friend and spiritual guide in Soviet exile, the Polonist Stefania Skwarczyńska, to Wanda Wasilewska's intervention at a high level. When telling the Wats' story in *Caviar and Ashes*, Marci Shore quotes Watowa's account as well.[166] From rumors recorded by Tomaszewski we learn about Kleiner's efforts on behalf of Polish professors. Yet Watowa is the only

---

164 Tomaszewski, *Lwów. Pejzaż psychologiczny*, 56–7.
165 Ostrowski, *Dnie pohańbienia. Wspomnienia z lat 1939–1941. W obronie polskości ziemi lwowskiej*, 347.
166 Shore, *Caviar and Ashes*, 188.

Ola (Paulina) Watowa's beauty dazzled the Warsaw literati before the war, 1924

source of speculation that Wasilewska must have mediated with the Soviets to save Skwarczyńska. If we disregard such secondhand conjecture, other information about Wasilewska makes it unlikely that she would go to any trouble in this particular matter, considering that ideologically she and Skwarczyńska had nothing in common. Because of her marriage to an officer of the Polish Army, the Soviets considered the noted Polonist an "enemy of the people." My doubts in this case are all the more serious since Wasilewska, aside from a small amount of money, did not extend any support to Aleksander Wat or his wife when they were deported with their child. Yet as a communist, Wat moved in circles much closer to Wasilewska than Skwarczyńska would have, as the wife of an officer of a right-leaning Polish state. From the Soviet perspective, Skwarczyńska and Watowa were equally tainted: they both belonged to the same category of "wives of enemies of the people." The notion that Wasilewska, a Polish communist activist and author, advocated for those imprisoned or deported appears baseless. It is accurate that the writer, who was comparatively quite well-off, sent packages to persons from her closest circle. But aside from the matter of Broniewski, which we will trace in the next chapter, she did not intervene, or at least no documents confirm that she did. Years after the war Stefan Rudniański's son and Wasilewska's comrade from the Communist Party of Poland (KPP) argued that the activist did nothing, even when her closest colleagues, his father included, pleaded with her for help. Supposedly she kept Rudniański Sr. waiting for hours in the foyer of the villa she occupied.[167]

Wasilewska must have been one of the well-informed insiders, since she got notice of the arrests of Władysław Broniewski, Aleksander Wat, and other writers the very next morning, at 6 am on January 25, 1940. As she said later, she stepped in because it seemed certain that the arrests were a result of a simple error which would soon get cleared up. Still, she left Lviv on the same day, likely to go to Kyiv. The day after, Witold Kolski published a text condemning the arrested "nationalists" in *Czerwony Sztandar*.[168] Though Wasilewska wrote for the paper as well, she was not able to prevent Kolski's article from appearing. Her memoirs mention the arrest of the poets, but she says nothing of trying to influence the situation during her trip. Instead she focuses on her activities in other ideological matters, such as the language of instruction at the university or university tuition. Those entries were not made until the fall of 1940,[169] and their chronology belies the actual timing. Additionally, her published memoir draws on a recording made in 1964, creating understandable inconsistencies. And, lest we forget, the activist would have presented her life story through an ideological filter.

From Wasilewska's memoirs we can surmise that she first made an attempt to speak out in Broniewski's support no earlier than two months after his arrest. In recounting her efforts she mentions Vasyl Serhiienko, but it is not entirely clear whether she turned to him as the NKVD director for the Lviv Oblast (he assumed this post on February 26, 1940, replacing the ineffectual and often reprimanded Kapiton Krasnov) or a year later, when Serhiienko took over for Serov, becoming People's Commissar of Internal Affairs for the Ukrainian SSR. Not until mid-1940 did Wasilewska attempt to mediate the matter with Khrushchev, at least according to Serov's notes. By then Broniewski was outside of Khrushchev's direct range of influence as he was no longer in Lviv or Kyiv, having been transferred to the Lubianka prison in Moscow in May 1940. In September 1940, predicting that Nikita Khrushchev would take this matter to

---

167 Relacja Jarosława Rudniańskiego z 2000 roku, k. 9.
168 Witold Kolski, "Zgnieść gadzinę nacjonalistyczną!," *Czerwony Sztandar*, January 27, 1940.
169 Ostrowski, *Dnie pohańbienia. Wspomnienia z lat 1939–1941. W obronie polskości ziemi lwowskiej*, 346–7.

Stalin, the Internal Affairs Commissar Ivan Serov sent Władysław Broniewski's file to Lavrentii Beria. Its contents show that the NKVD had declared the poet a "Polish nationalist," dangerous to the system.[170]

In contrast to Wasilewska, Petro Panch, chairman of the Writers' Association's Organizational Committee, reacted to the arrests immediately. Though his journal entries are undated, he references the day in his narrative:

> The militia [police] arrested Broniewski, Wat, Skuza, Peiper, and Stern for "hooliganism." They are conducting an investigation.
>
> Today (January 25) six [women] came to see me, all pleading for their husbands and friends:
>
> "But they were completely sober! We were far from cheerful, on the contrary, quite bored."
>
> That night four other writers were apprehended. But this was not the militia. Among them Mrs. Nagler, wife of the chief of Warsaw's military police.
>
> Three more wives came to ask me to intervene on behalf of their husbands.
>
> "The [Writers' Association] Organizational Committee does not control the actions of this organization [NKVD]," I reply when they ask me to find out, "on what basis their husbands were arrested."[171]

The Polish accounts I was able to access do not mention the wives' visits. None say a word about Panch and his efforts, whose support for the arrested Polish writers could have cost him dearly. In a note from April, the Narkom Serov indirectly referenced Kolski's article in *Czerwony Sztandar*, presenting it as a meaningful indicator of the public's pulse. He declared Panch's interest in this matter harmful and later used it to remove Panch from his post. Serov accused the writer of failing to fulfill basic administrative duties, and devoting time instead to issues outside of his responsibilities. Two pages from a secret report addressed to the First Secretary of the Central Committee of the Communist Party of Ukraine enumerate Panch's alleged ideological shortcomings, with a few lines referring to his attempt to rescue the writers: "Lviv's intelligentsia met the reprisals against counterrevolutionary writers—Watt

---

170 HDA SBU, f. 16, op. 33, spr. 58.
171 Petro Panch, "Iz shchodennykovykh zapysiv," *Kul'turne zhyttia v Ukraïni. Zakhidni zemli 1995–1996*, vol. 1, 79.

[*sic*], Broniewski, Peiper, and others, with understanding. However, Panch, instead of presenting the events in the appropriate light to the writer community, ran interference for the purpose of the men's release."[172] Serov supplemented his note with an excerpt from the testimonies of Ukrainian writers shot in the 1930s, which referenced Panch. Thus the NKVD kept "incriminating evidence" against Panch at the ready. In summer of 1940 Panch was removed from his position and replaced by Oleksa Desniak, who knew not to commit similar errors.

While Panch's support is well documented, Wasilewska's statements of her efforts to assist those arrested or deported in 1940 do not match any actual documentation. Yes, Jan Kott tells the story of Wasilewska running down the station platform, assisted by high-ranking NKVD officers, to effect Kott's and Boy-Żeleński's last-chance release from the transport. But an officer "decorated with medals like a Christmas tree" could only appear in an embellished story, and certainly not on a platform from which a prisoner transport departed. Not to mention that Żeleński was not among the deported, and the Soviets freed Kott within less than an hour of his arrest and could not have delivered him to the train station that quickly.

Later, after founding the Union of Polish Patriots, Wasilewska demonstrated her true powers of persuasion, but her efforts, at least until 1943, benefitted only fellow communists. Finally, by 1944, among the people freed from labor camps or prisons were some with no communist ties. To give an example, Emil Sommerstein, recently released from a camp, was coopted in the hasty preparations to create a Polish puppet government. As a prewar Zionist Sejm deputy, like many other Polish Jews, he was not subject to the 1941 Sikorski-Maysky agreement which granted amnesty to tens of thousands of Polish citizens held in Soviet camps. Historians plausibly credit Wasilewska with Sommerstein's release, though no available documents confirm her role.[173]

---

172 Note, April 1940. See HDA SBU, f. 16, op. 33, spr. 58, k. 237.
173 We know little about Emil Sommerstein's fate in the USSR. The only source available today is the memoir of his daughter, who worked as his secretary during his term in the Provisional Government of the Republic of Poland in Lublin. She maintained that her father refused to discuss his prison years then, as well as after emigrating to the US. See Mira Temczyn's account, Jerusalem, March 25, 1979, in Yad Vashem Archives, 03/4167. I would like to thank Samuel Barnai from the Hebrew University in Jerusalem for his assistance in locating Temczyn's narrative.

Stefania Skwarczyńska was deported to Kazakhstan in April 1940.
Thanks to the efforts of Juliusz Kleiner and Kyrylo Studynsky
she returned to Lviv six months later

But let us return to Stefania Skwarczyńska. In April 1940, the Soviets deported her from Lviv as an officer's wife, together with her children and mother-in-law. Half a year later she returned from exile and assumed her prior university position. Her case is unique, the only true happy ending I came across. Most publications attribute this nearly miraculous pardon to the intervention of Juliusz Kleiner, Skwarczyńska's teacher and maven, with Wanda Wasilewska. In fact, the Polonist did seek help for Skwarczyńska, but not from Wasilewska. It is symptomatic of their overall preconceptions that memoir authors and researchers act alike in this instance, consciously or unwittingly following assumptions of solidarity rooted in ethnic bonds. They ignore all other motivations, such as the pull of academic camaraderie. In doing so, they disregard visible inconsistencies, for example Wasilewska's alleged intervention on behalf of the stranger Skwarczyńska, even though the activist showed no interest at all in the plight of her own friends, Aleksander and Ola Wat.

The Soviets could not have discharged Skwarczyńska—be it from exile or a labor camp—informally, without a written order. Though access to archival collections of the special forces is quite difficult, other sources of information

Juliusz Kleiner as the director of the division of Polish at Lviv University looked out for his colleagues

about the prescribed procedures are available, for instance the correspondence between Kleiner and Kyrylo Studynsky, who at the time was serving as academic provost.[174] Those letters focus almost entirely on hiring issues in the Department of Humanities, including the associate professor Skwarczyńska.[175] A few months later Juliusz Kleiner approached Kyrylo Studynsky to intervene in the matter of Stefania Skwarczyńska, deported on April 11, 1940.[176] Indirectly, we also learn of the deputy's energetic efforts from the correspondence of Maria Bruchnalska and Juliusz Kleiner.[177] Studynsky's arbitration was successful, and the NKVD sent out a notification letter addressed to Studynsky,

---

[174] Studynsky became provost right after the new year, as the university began to operate according to the new statute and program (see ordinance no. 104, 4.01.1940).
[175] TsDIAL, f. 362, op. 1, spr. 311, k. 26–49.
[176] The date of her termination from the university indirectly reflects the date of her deportation: April 12, 1940 (Nakaz rektora no. 164, 30.04.1940, ALU, R-119, k. 147).
[177] Maria Bruchnalska's note to Juliusz Kleiner, October 21, 1940 (TsDIAL, f. 716, op. 1, spr. 27, k. 26).

Juliusz Kleiner's doctoral diploma from 1908. His contacts with Kyrylo Studynsky date back to this period

with a copy for Juliusz Kleiner.[178] In the next academic year the distinguished Polonist and literary theorist Stefania Skwarczyńska returned to the university.[179] For the remainder of the war, her work and activism mirrored the paths typical for her community: she joined the resistance, worked for Weigl's Institute, returned to the university in 1944, and once the borders were redrawn after Yalta, left for Poland.

Studynsky succeeded as well in changing the outcome of a case which the former Polish Prime Minister Kazimierz Bartel brought to his attention. As a result of the historian's persistence, the NKVD rescinded their decision to deport Stefania Neyman, mother-in-law of Stanisław Pilat, professor at the Lviv Polytechnic and former director of the Drohobych refinery.[180] In August 1940

---

178 See TsDIAL, f. 362, op. 1, spr. 46, k. 103.
179 Stefania Skwarczyńska regained employment at the Institute of Polish Literature on February 15, 1941 (Nakaz rektora no. 66, 13.03.1941, ALU, R-119, op. 3, spr. 31, k. 149).
180 Kazimierz Bartel's letter to Kyrylo Studynsky, April 18, 1940 (TsDIAL, f. 362, op. 1, spr. 231, k. 10–11).

the NKVD head for the Lviv Oblast Vasyl Serhiienko informed his boss Ivan Serov that Stanisław Pilat's plea in this matter was rejected and requested further instructions;[181] but soon thereafter the order to deport Mrs. Neyman was retracted. Stanisław Pilat was one of the science professors whom the Soviets courted, making him a deputy to the Lviv City Council in December 1940. Half a year later the Nazis murdered him on Wuleckie Hills; his wife Ewa Neyman-Pilat, thirty years his junior, survived him by just four years.

But Studynsky's efforts could affect results only rarely. Most officials replied to his appeals curtly, stating that they found no basis to reverse decisions or lessen sentences. In circumstances comparable (in Soviet eyes) to Stefania Skwarczyńska's, nothing could be done for judge Adolf Slyzh. At first, thanks to Mykhailo Rudnytsky's backing, Slyzh had found work in the dean's office. But his luck turned quickly, and if it were not for the former judge's foresight and Studynsky's persistence, not only Slyzh, but his entire large family would have been deported. For historians, his case is a rare well-documented instance: in addition to the judge's reminiscences,[182] even his correspondence from that period survives,[183] making it possible to reconstruct the details of his case.

On April 12 and 13, 1940 the Soviets carried out mass deportations of persons categorized as relatives of "enemies of the people" (Stefania Skwarczyńska included). In the aftermath, the militia continued to "cleanse" the town of "uncertain elements." As Slyzh reminisced, they called him in for questioning multiple times and asked detailed questions about his biography. This took place after the elections to the Supreme Soviets of the Ukrainian SSR and USSR, when intense preparations for another round of deportations began. Because Slyzh had only presided over civil trials, he was not arrested in fall of 1939. The devout socialist and attorney Volodymyr Starosolsky who had defended nationalists in political trials was not as lucky and ended up in prison. After having managed to secure employment at the university on January 15, 1940, Slyzh may have believed that his situation was stable, especially given his modest class origin. While his political views brought him close to Christian Democrats, he did not engage in politics, devoting himself instead

---

181 HDA SBU, f. 16, op. 33, spr. 55, k. 281.
182 Adolf Slyzh's memoir appeared in print, compiled by Oleh Pavlyshyn (Adol'f Slyzh, *Moï lita. Spohady* [Lviv: Manuskrypt, 2014]). I am grateful to my colleague for sharing with me such invaluable material prior to publication.
183 TsDIAL, f. 362, op. 1, spr. 46, k. 104. Adolf Slyzh's petition, addressed to captain Veriovka, chief of police at 12 Zielona Street, requesting that the headquarters' order to leave Lviv within ten days from April 28, 1940 be annulled.

to civic-educational activism, and focusing on supporting his large family and providing quality education for his children. In the 1930s he purchased a small apartment building in a Lviv suburb, which he paid off right before the war. It was probably this property that triggered the evacuation orders for the Slyzh family. The administrative authorities needed housing for their own employees, many of whom were brought in from the depths of the USSR. Slyzh tried to appeal the decision but was unsuccessful. He recalls that his entire family had to report to the headquarters with their passports. Thankfully, he had enough foresight to notify Studynsky, who, fearing that the judge's family would be arrested on the spot and immediately deported, arrived at the police station together with the judge. There all family members received the "paragraph 11" stamp in their Soviet passports, the deputy's arguments notwithstanding. The protesting supplicants were referred to the head of the Lviv Oblast's NKVD at Pełczyńska Street (probably Vasyl Serhiienko), where Kyrylo Studynsky again accomplished nothing. Though he heard them out, the NKVD chief stated calmly that according to Soviet law, any judge who had been issuing verdicts according to a capitalist legal code was an enemy of the people. Another clause stipulated that "former people" had no right to reside in larger cities, and therefore he could not be of any help. Adolf Slyzh made another attempt to appeal the decision, writing to the chief of militia, but to no avail. He pinned his last hopes on Marchenko, but the university president told him that he could not do anything for him either. At the time, Karolina Lanckorońska[184] found herself in a similar situation. She attributed Marchenko's lack of support to his dislike for Polish aristocrats. In reality, when the NKVD developed an interest in an employee, not only the university president, but even people more powerful could do nothing but wring their hands.

The Slyzhes immediately placed their children with Lviv families, with the exception of their youngest. Adolf and his wife decided to hide out in his brother's parsonage. This solution too was risky—the NKVD was bound to find the fugitives sooner or later. Agents who came to the apartment building to remove the family sealed all rooms and hastily evicted a relative who had stayed behind. After a few weeks, Slyzh, on account of having been a judge, registered with the German repatriation commission. This time his former position turned out to be a life saver: the Germans were glad to approve the repatriation of a rare surviving civil judge, after the Soviets had arrested almost all representatives of the judiciary in the fall. Slyzh left Lviv for Bełżec, where he had practiced years

---

184 Lanckorońska, *Michelangelo in Ravensbruck: One Woman's War against the Nazis*, 33.

before. In fall of 1941 he returned to his house in Lviv, but in 1944 he left it behind, fleeing from the approaching Soviets.

Studynsky intervened not only on behalf of university employees. As a deputy he appealed to various organs in matters of other people who turned to him for help. He did so regardless of their ethnicity or even the severity of their troubles. Only a fraction of his extensive correspondence with Soviet government agencies and private persons survives. He set out to assist prisoners, deportees, persons without a passport who faced deportation, persecuted officials and judges, priests on whom the Soviets levied excessive taxes, people whose pensions were taken away, and various other afflicted community members.[185] A letter regarding deputy mayor Wiktor Chajes, apprehended in late October 1939, helps trace Kyrylo Studynsky's first documented intervention.[186] Studynsky did not seem to expect a positive outcome in this case. If it had not been possible to get Kost Levytsky out of prison, any success in the case of Wiktor Chajes was even less likely: for Soviet authorities he was double the enemy, a high-ranking official of the Polish state, and a deplorable capitalist (he was a banker). During a raid on his home the agents did not take away his personal notes, as they did with Levytsky, for later use as evidence in the investigation. His diary, *Pamiętnik Polaka wyznania mojżeszowego* [*Diary of a Pole of Mosaic faith*], whose last entry from September 22, 1939 read "Long live Poland!," became a symbol of the loyalty of Jewish elites to the Polish state. Studynsky advised Chajes's wife to obtain a letter from his employees as proof of her husband's innocence and assured her he would vouch for Chajes. Neither of these steps accomplished anything.

Likewise there was no helping the arrested UNDO activists[187] once the Soviets declared the party counterrevolutionary. The official grounds for their arrests was an allegation that UNDO politicians had abetted in the persecution

---

185 TsDIAL, f. 362, op. 1, spr. 260.
186 Among Kyrylo Studynsky's correspondence is a copy of a letter from Chajes's wife to the Lviv military prosecutor. Mrs. Chajes invokes Studynsky's name and states that the academic vouched for her husband (TsDIAL, f. 362, op. 1, spr. 46, k. 111).
187 The correspondence includes an August 27, 1940 letter from the deputy secretary of the USSR Supreme Soviet Exoneration Commission, A. (first name unknown) Selanin, addressed to Kyrylo Studynsky, related to the case of Mykhailo Strutynsky, deputy general secretary of the UNDO (TsDIAL, p. 362, op. 1, spr. 46, k. 106). Mykhailo Ostroverkha, who at the time lived in Studynsky's apartment, recalls that Studynsky attempted to save his former political opponents (who probably would have come from the UNDO circles; the UNDO spoke out harshly against Studynsky and alleged he was a Sovietophile). (Ostroverkha, *Na zakruti. Osin' 1939 r.*, 114).

of Ukrainians by the Polish government.[188] The Soviet administration treated people affiliated with legal prewar political parties and with those parties' press organs as enemies of the people. While the government carried out reprisals, the official press mirrored its policies. Public campaigns of hatred intensified on the anniversary of the "liberation" or even on less prominent occasions such as "Day of the Press." The title of an article by the editor in chief of *Vilna Ukraina* speaks to the style of those attacks—"A little on the collaboration of penny-a-liners from the nationalist pack of dogs" ["Deshcho pro spivrobitnytstvo pysak z natsionalistychnoii psarni"].[189]

No efforts could alleviate the situation of imprisoned reserve officers either. The NKVD denied the families permission to provide even the most prosaic comforts such as delivering a change of clothes. The person in question here was Gustaw, the son of a well-known Polonist named Wilhelm Bruchnalski. Wilhelm Bruchnalski, who died before the war, had been Juliusz Kleiner's teacher. His son Gustaw, a popular Lviv dentist, was arrested as a reserve officer, probably on charges of being a member of the Polish resistance. His mother, Maria, approached Studynsky through Kleiner. But here too the "blessed Mr. Studynsky," as Maria Bruchnalska referred to him, accomplished nothing. The prisoner was executed in April 1941.[190]

Not only the inhabitants of Soviet-occupied territories counted on Studynsky's help. Some of his earlier friends from Kyiv pinned great hopes on Kyrylo Studynsky's position. A testament to their beliefs is a letter from Olha Savchenko, wife of Mykhailo Hrushevsky's secretary. Savchenko mailed it on October 28, 1939 from faraway Saratov, where she had followed her arrested husband. Upon hearing the news that Studynsky was a member of the People's Assembly she wrote to him with great enthusiasm:

> Dear Comrade, I could not sleep all night, I was so moved by the radio transmission of Kyrylo Osypovych's speech. I am delighted that you are alive, healthy,

---

188 See informational note by the USSR Deputy People's Commissar of State Security Vsevolod Merkulov and the USSR People's Commissar of State Security Ivan Serov for the chief of Soviet security Lavrentii Beria from October 8, 1939 ("Spetsopovidomlennia zastupnyka narkoma vnutrishnikh sprav L. Berii pro robotu operatyvnykh chekists'kykh hrup u Zakhidnii Ukraïni. Pislia 28 veres'nia 1939 r.," in Danylenko and Kokin, *Radians'ki orhany derzhavnoï bezpeky u 1939–1941 r. Dokumenty HDA SB Ukrainy*, 221–2).
189 Pavlo Zhyvotenko, "Deshcho pro spivrobitnytstvo pysak z natsionalistychnoï psarni," *Vil'na Ukraïna*, 1939–41, no. 140, May 5, 1940, 4.
190 P. T. Tron'ko et al., *Reabilitovani istorieiu. L'vivs'ka oblast'*, vol. 1, 628.

and full of energy. You are experiencing amazing days! You are finally getting to see Ukraine's unification! And it had seemed so unrealistic! It brought me the hope too that soon the day will come when I will be together with my husband, from whom, despite all imaginable efforts, I have had no news since July of last year. I do not know where he is nor whether he is still alive.[191]

The situation did not bode well, which Studynsky perhaps understood. A year after the trials against the SVU (Union for the Liberation of Ukraine), the Soviets accused Fedir Savchenko, a student of Mykhailo Hrushevsky, of being a member of the (made up) Ukrainian National Center, allegedly founded and led by the great historian himself. The chief charge were intelligence contacts with … Studynsky. In 1936, Savchenko, after his release from prison, was exiled to Saratov. Arrested again in 1937, he remained behind bars until the summer of 1938, and then all communication stopped. The sentencing clause "without the right to correspondence" suggests that the NKVD murdered him, probably still before the war. Nevertheless Studynsky attempted to intervene,[192] as he did in the matter of Hrushevsky's daughter Kateryna.[193] As we learn from later correspondence between Kateryna's mother, Maria Hrushevska and the librarian Volodymyr Doroshenko,[194] as well as from painstaking determinations by the literary historian Vasyl Horyn,[195] because of the deputy's appeal the authorities did reexamine Kateryna Hrushevska's case (she was accused of being an activist in the Ukrainian National Center as well), but they upheld her sentence of eight years in labor camps.

---

191 Olha Savchenko's letter to Kyrylo Studynsky from Saratov, October 28, 1939 (TsDIAL, f. 362, op. 1, spr. 430, k. 73). Quoted in Haiova, *U pivstolitnikh zmahanniakh: Vybrani lysty do Kyryla Studyns'koho (1891–1941)*, 667.
192 Kyrylo Studynsky's correspondence with Soviet government agencies includes a copy of Olha Savchenko's complaint, addressed to the chairman of the USSR Supreme Soviet Mikhail Kalinin (TsDIAL, f. 362, op. 1, spr. 46, k. 98–100). Also preserved is Olha Savchenko's letter from December 7, 1939, in which she thanks Studynsky for his intervention (TsDIAL, f. 362, op. 1, spr. 377, k. 44). Quoted in Haiova, *U pivstolitnikh zmahanniakh: Vybrani lysty do Kyryla Studyns'koho (1891–1941)*, 673.
193 Letter from Maria Hrushevska to Kyrylo Studynsky, Kyiv, July 10, 1940 (TsDIAL, f. 362, op. 1, spr. 432, k. 6–7. Quoted in Haiova, *U pivstolitnikh zmahanniakh: Vybrani lysty do Kyryla Studyns'koho (1891–1941)*, 680–81.
194 Mariia Val′o, "Lysty Mariï Hrushevs′koï do Volodymyra Doroshenka (1942–1943 rr.)," *Zapysky L′vivs′koï naukovoï biblioteky im. V. Stefanyka* 12: 464–69.
195 Vasyl′ Horyn′, "Sprava Kateryny Hrushevs′koï u svitli novykh dokumentiv," in *Ukraïna: kulturna spadshchyna, natsional′na svidomist′, derzhavnist′*, vol. 15: *Confraternitas: Iuvileinyi zbirnyk na poshanu Iaroslava Isaievycha*, ed. Mykola Krykun and Ostap Sereda (Lviv: Instytut ukraïnoznavstva im. I. Kryp′iakevycha, 2006–2007), 782–91.

The surviving sources that document Kyrylo Studynsky's efforts to defend persons whom the Soviets imprisoned or otherwise persecuted are the replies of various agencies to his requests and copies of letters from interested parties. The collection does not include copies of Studynsky's official letters.[196] An exception is a draft of a letter addressed to the first secretary Nikita Khrushchev regarding the sentences meted out in the famous trial of OUN activists. The deputy pleaded with Khrushchev to commute the death sentences, at least in the case of the youngest women (some of the sentenced girls were seventeen—eighteen years old). To apply maximum pressure, Studynsky resorted to the riskiest arguments:

> We bow to the sentence of the Soviet authorities, though nevertheless the secrecy surrounding the trial gives rise to doubts, whether the court took under consideration the degree of liability of the defendants. ... We are convinced that the Supreme Court in Kyiv carefully considered these cases and believe that no death sentence will be carried out except for persons who desecrated their lives by killing. We also believe that other severe sentences will be reduced or commuted. However, we, the servants of our nation, feel compelled to turn to You as the First Secretary of the Central Committee of the Communist Party of Ukraine with utmost trust in You as a person and Your sense of responsibility and justice with one and only one plea, that You be willing to request the trial records and to review the indictments against boys and girls separately. On Monday, January 27, a new trial is slated to begin, in which several dozen people will occupy the defendants' benches. We fear that again numerous death sentences will be pronounced, which might create a fresh excuse for international agencies to renew their crazed attacks against the Soviet State. For that very reason, as a Soviet citizen whose heart is fully devoted to the Soviet authorities, I ask that the sentences issued be not only just, but also reflect the high prestige of the strength and power of the Soviet State. I am afraid that someone might come to the conclusion that Poland held mass trials more than once where the charges included murder, but those trials resulted in only one or two death sentences. Such mass trials as those currently held in Lviv have never occurred. I also have quite certain information that death sentences

---

196 Collection 362 in the Central State Historical Archives of Ukraine in Lviv (TsDIAL). In the Central State Archives of Supreme Bodies of Power and Government of Ukraine (TsDAVO) no complaints addressed to the appellate prosecutor have been preserved.

were issued in Stanislau as well. I ask you to verify all these sentences. In my opinion it is not the severity of a sentence, but, on the contrary, its leniency, that serves as the most effective propaganda to induce the deepest commitment to the Soviet State among our local population.[197]

Many thorough studies focus on the "Trial of the Fifty Nine" OUN members and the second OUN Homeland Executive.[198] For our purposes, it suffices to say that the Supreme Court of the Ukrainian SSR upheld the sentence, though the Supreme Court of the USSR, after reviewing the case again, commuted a few of the death sentences. Yet again, Studynsky's political authority turned out crucial.

Omelian Pritsak began his PhD studies under Professor Ahatanhel Krymsky in the fall of 1940; soon he was drafted into the Red Army

The NKVD followed the crumbs laid by testimonies of Konstantyn Valchyk and Stepan Bandera's envoy, Ivan Maksymov, whom they apprehended. Both men gave information about OUN members and alleged sympathizers.

---

197 TsDIAL, f. 362, op. 1, spr. 228, k. 93.
198 See for example: Liuba Komar, *Protses 59-ty* (Lviv: NTSh, 1997); and Hryvul and Oseredchuk, *"Protses-59": pokolinnia bortsiv ta heroïv*.

The Soviet agency then went after identifying ties between certain Kyiv residents and the OUN. Some very prominent people fell into their sights, for instance the chairman of the Academy of Sciences Oleksandr Bohomolets, as well as "figureheads" investigated many years earlier, such as the academy member and distinguished orientalist Ahatanhel Krymsky.[199] At this stage the agents began watching Omelian Pritsak, whom Krymsky admitted to the doctoral program in summer 1940. The NKVD suspected that the young Eastern studies scholar had established contact with the academy member on OUN's orders.[200] Soon the agents isolated Pritsak, and in later October he received his draft card to the Red Army. Initially he served in Bashkir, then in the Kirov oblast of the Russian Federation, and beginning in April 1941, in Bila Tserkva.[201] Paradoxically, serving in the military saved his life; the Soviets arrested nearly every person (approximately 100) whose name appeared in the report and executed those whose OUN connections they proved. At the beginning of the German-Soviet war, Pritsak was captured by the Germans, but as a private he managed to get out of Galicia. In fall 1941 he made his way to Kyiv and tried to locate his former master. At that time Natalia Polonska-Vasylenko placed Krymsky's collection in Pritsak's hands in hopes that Pritsak would be able to save it from destruction. She was right: despite his wartime and postwar travails, Pritsak successfully preserved what remained of Krymsky's archives.[202]

---

199 Information from the Ukrainian State Security Commissar Ivan Serov addressed to the chief of Soviet State Security Lavrentii Beria and the head of counter-intelligence Pavel Fedotov from September 30, 1940 ("Spetsopovidomlennia zastupnyka narkoma vnutrishnikh sprav L. Berii pro robotu operatyvnykh chekists'kykh hrup u Zakhidnii Ukraïni. Pislia 28 veresnia 1939 r.," in Danylenko and Kokin, *Radians'ki orhany derzhavnoï bezpeky u 1939–1941 r. Dokumenty HDA SB Ukrainy*, 317). See also HDA SBU, f. 16, op. 33, spr. 25.

200 In an interview conducted by Andry Portnov, Dmytro Viedienieiev, who researches the history of USSR state security services, repeated this scenario as laid out in Ivan Serov's note to Laurentii Beria without any analysis, and went as far as to suggest that Pritsak had been an NKVD agent: Dmytro Viedienieiev, "Vid dytiachoho sadochka do Instytutu natsional'noï pam'iati. Chastyna 2. Pro 'ahenturni' istoriï Viktora Petrova ta Omeliana Pritsaka, spohady Pavla Sudoplatova i doliu Bohdana Stashyns'koho," www.historians.in.ua/index.php/en/intervyu/695-dmytro--vyedyenyeyev-vid-dytyachoho-sadochka-do-instytutu-natsional-noyi-pamyati-chastyna-2-pro-ahenturni-istoriyi-viktorapetrova-ta-omeliana-pritsaka-spohady-pavla-sudoplatova-i--doliu-bohdana-stashynskoho, accessed July 5, 2013.

201 Taisiia Sydorchuk, "Materialy Ahatanhela Kryms'koho v arkhivi Omeliana Pritsaka," *Ukraïns'kyi arkheohrafichnyi shchorichnyk* 18 (2013): 101–116.

202 Omelian Pritsak transported the collection first to Lviv, and then abroad. For many years the archive was housed at Harvard University, at the Ukrainian Institute which he founded. Eventually, after he passed, the collection returned to Kyiv, and is now part of the Kyiv-Mohyla Academy archive.

BACK INTO GOOD GRACES, BUT NOT FOR LONG

After putting the Union for the Liberation of Ukraine on trial, Soviet authorities removed Ahatanhel Krymsky from high-level responsibilities in the Academy of Sciences. In addition, they took away his salary, as Vladimir Vernadsky, who by then was living in Moscow, mentions in his journal (Vernadsky was also a person people turned to for help in cases of officer families deported from Lviv[203]). Krymsky, who had worked closely with Iefremov, a pre-revolution academic, remained under the NKVD's close watch. His professional situation had improved a bit at the end of the 1930s, when reprisals against the university community eased up. We can surmise that the scholar's strategy evolved as well—at public appearances his statements never diverged from the official line, though he was aware that "whatever I may say, 'they' do not believe me anyway."[204] Doctoral students reappeared, as did opportunities to publish, and after 1939 the Soviet government deemed Krymsky, who welcomed the annexation of Western Galicia, as desirable "export goods." As an academic of the old generation, still well-known to Galician Ukrainians from the pre-World War I era, he was perfectly suited to legitimize Soviet authority among the Galician intelligentsia.

At the start of World War II Krymsky was staying in his home in Zvenyhorodka, where he usually spent the summer months. Unable to leave (all civilians were barred from train travel) for over a month, he kept in contact with Kyiv by mail and cable during his involuntary extended vacation. In a letter to Natalia Polonska-Vasylenko, written a few days after the Red Army invaded the territories of the Second Polish Republic, the scholar could not contain his joy:

> I could not help myself and started reading the papers. It is a historic moment of colossal significance! [Ukrainian bibliographer Fedir] Petrun was in Zvenyhorodka and reminded me that in May I had said to him: "Nothing will come of Moscow's negotiations with England and France, because Poland will never allow the Soviet army on its territories, and that

---

203   Vladimir Vernadskii, *Dnevniki 1935–1941*, vol. 2, *1939–1941* (Moscow: Nauka, 2008). See also engineer Severyn Grabianko's letter from June 1940, preserved in Vernadsky's collection, where the former graduate of Petersburg Polytechnic, working in Lviv, pleads with Verdanskii to help ease the plight of the deported families (ARAN, f. 518, op. 3, d. 455, k. 5–6).
204   Nataliia Polons′ka-Vasylenko, "Akademik Ahatanhel Iukhymovych Kryms′kyi," *Ukraïns′kyi istoryk* 3–4 (1971): 93.

is why the USSR will transfer its favor to Germany." True, I did say something like that to him in May, because my mind was not littered by reading newspapers, it was fresh, not open to other influences. Now, reading the news, I will surely lose my ability to think independently, but what is happening now anyone can understand. A unification of the entire Rus, with Galicia, St. Volodymyr's "Cherven towns," that is something exceptionally splendid. Molotov turned out far more prudent than Litvinov![205]

In his exhilaration Krymsky was not alone; many Kyiv intellectuals shared in these views. But people less connected to Galicia judged the situation with more restraint. Some expressed sympathy for the Polish Republic. We see it reflected in the NKVD's weekly reports on the climate among each of the social classes. In their denunciations, intelligentsia agents quote phrases such as "the fourth partition of Poland" (words of Svitozar Drahomanov, son of Mykhailo—a prominent thinker and socialist activist), and "a predatory attack" (words of writer Arkady Liubchenko). The film director Oleksandr Dovzhenko showed prescience in predicting that this "present from Hitler will cost us dearly."[206]

In January 1940 Krymsky participated in the first celebratory away session of the Academy of Sciences in Lviv. This event was supposed to sweeten a bitter pill—the elimination of the Shevchenko Scientific Society—for those Galician Ukrainians who found work in Lviv's Academy chapters. After the initial trip, the orientalist frequented Lviv, giving presentations at the university, which—according to Pritsak—made an enormous impression on the local faculty (though the notes of the Lviv orientalist Stefan Stasiak,[207] preserved in the archive, do not confirm Pritsak's memory). Since the turn of the nineteenth and twentieth centuries Ahatanhel Krymsky cultivated close relationships with Galician Ukrainians and was a personal friend of Ivan Franko. Not surprisingly, when Soviet authorities, as part of their propagandist Ukrainization in Lviv, decided to publicly honor the anniversary of the poet's death, Krymsky was asked to speak at Franko's grave. The speech appeared in *Vilna Ukraina*; it is one of the rare texts in the newspaper that do not cause disgust.

---

205 Letter from September 22, 1939 (TsDAMLiM, f. 542, op. 1, spr. 175, k. 17).
206 "Spetsopovidomlennia zastupnyka narkoma vnutrishnikh sprav L. Berii pro robotu operatyvnykh chekists'kykh hrup u Zakhidnii Ukraïni. Pislia 28 veresnia 1939 r.," in Danylenko and Kokin, *Radians'ki orhany derzhavnoï bezpeky u 1939–1941 r. Dokumenty HDA SB Ukrainy*, 999, 1030, 1073.
207 Stefan Stasiak's fond, Archiwum PAN in Warsaw, III-197, teczka 32.

Based on preserved letters it appears that the old animosity between Krymsky and Studynsky receded and the two became friends. In early 1940 the director of the Linguistics Institute of the Ukrainian SSR Academy of Sciences Maria Boiko, to whom Studynsky reported as the director of the Lviv chapter, inserted regards from Ahatanhel Krymsky into her official correspondence.[208] Barely a year earlier the situation would have been difficult to picture: the orientalist had been accused of affirming nationalism and relieved of all responsibilities, while the literary historian had fallen under suspicion of being a Polish agent. At the time it was not safe to even mention those two names, let alone admit to personal familiarity.

But by fall 1939 the Soviets changed their attitude towards both scholars, at least officially, as new political circumstances made Krymsky and Studynsky potentially useful. It was all the easier to take advantage of them since both welcomed the annexation of Ukrainian territories of the Polish Republic, believing that their dream of a united Ukraine, divided centuries before, was coming true. The political project of *sobornost*—an idea, born during their youth, that all ethnically Ukrainian areas (under Russian, Austrian, Hungarian, and Rumanian rules) would be united as Ukraine, failed in 1919. Twenty years later it returned in a very different shape, enforced by the Red Army.

At the turn of 1930 and 1940 Ahatanhel Krymsky got *carte blanche* to reactivate the Institute of Oriental Studies, and received permission to hire a doctoral student from Lviv—Omelian Pritsak. In January 1941 lavish official celebrations of his seventieth birthday took place both in Kyiv and at Lviv University. Yet Krymsky was right when he insisted that the Soviets would never trust him. Barely half a year later the NKVD arrested him as a "Ukrainian nationalist." Studynsky, onto whom the Soviet authorities bestowed the highest privileges, also died at the hands of the NKVD. Mykhailo Marchenko, a generation younger, elevated to the honor of a university president, and then accused of nationalism, survived. Had he not attempted to prove his innocence by penning a testimony in 1943, our knowledge of the academic community in Lviv at the start of World War II and the relationships within that community would have been that much more limited.

The last person to see Studynsky alive was Natalia Polonska-Vasylenko. Many years later she recalled their chance meeting at Korolenko Street, near the Academy of Sciences and … the NKVD, as she reminisced about the equally mysterious disappearance of Ahatanhel Krymsky. The NKVD "evacuated"

---

208 Undated letter (TsDIAL, f. 362, op. 1, spr. 247, k. 23).

Krymsky from his native village of Zvenyhorodka in July 1941.[209] We can only roughly estimate that the encounter between Studynsky and Polonska-Vasylenko took place in late June or early July 1941.

Memoirs and available archival documents, such as the testimony of Mykhailo Marchenko,[210] tell of the arrests of the surviving intelligentsia in Soviet Ukraine at the start of the German-Soviet war, but scholarly publications rarely even mention this topic.[211] The fate of people who disappeared in that period remains unknown, mostly because the archival materials are minimally accessible. Moreover, to his day the term "forcibly evacuated" is used in reference to persons who were actually arrested. In light of what we know about how the NKVD operated, any information that the Soviet administration later released to the surviving relatives is not reliable. Depending on the nationality of the missing person, families received either of the two stock answers: their loved ones perished "during a German bombardment of a train transport of evacuated Soviet citizens"[212] or "at the hands of Ukrainian nationalists."[213] It was extremely rare for organs of the NKVD to confirm a prisoner's execution in official documents related to prisoners' deaths. Most victims of the Great Purge vanished "without the right to correspondence," which—according to what historians have been able to determine—typically meant that the said person had been shot. The NKVD often amended the date of death in exoneration documents (these trials took place in the late 1950s and late 1980s) to the war years, as to transfer the responsibility from

---

209 Microfiche from the investigation of Ahatanhel Krymsky in *Skhidnyi svit* 2 (1996): 17–21.
210 Ovsiienko, "U borot'bi za syna. Interviu Nadiï Mykhailivny Marchenko Vasyliu Ovsiienku, 16.06.1998," 17.
211 While much attention has been devoted to the NKVD murders of prisoners in Eastern Galicia, no separate investigation of the NKVD's "preventive actions" in late June and early July 1941 exists to date. Only Rublov and Cherchenko mention it in passing: see *Stalinshchyna i dolia zakhidnoukraïns'koi intelihentsii 20–50-ti roky XX st.*, 208. Vladyslav Hrynevych's study invokes only one reference to the arrest of Mykhailo Donets, the opera singer who played Ivan Karas in the most popular Ukrainian opera *Zaporozhets za Dunaiem* (Hrynevych, *Nepryborkane riznoholossia: Druha svitova viina i suspil'no-polytychni nastroï v Ukraïni, 1939–cherven' 1941*, 420).
212 That was the official account of how Ahatanhel Krymsky died. From declassified investigation files we now know that he was exiled to Kazakhstan, where he died in a prison hospital in Kostanay on January 25, 1942 (see among other sources: Oleksa Musiienko, ed., *Z poroha smerti. Pys'mennyky Ukraïny—zhertvy stalins'kykh represii* (Kyiv: Radians'kyi pys'mennyk, 1991), 280–82.
213 Jarosław Rudniański received this information in response to his search for his father. See Relacja Jarosława Rudniańskiego z 2000 roku, k. 7–8.

the security agencies to war events or to blame the Germans outright. For many decades, the traces of their atrocities remained obscured, and that is why, without access to archives in Moscow, it remains so difficult to establish even the most basic data about persons arrested between late June and early July of 1941.

ON BOTH BANKS OF THE ZBRUCH

Though in the 1930s the ties binding the Ukrainian intelligentsia on both sides of the border river Zbruch grew markedly weaker, they solidified again at the start of the war. A new generation of Soviet Ukrainian intelligentsia, slated to replace the old, pre-revolution cadres whom the Soviets by and large eliminated in the Great Purge, gained patronage and role models among Galician academics. For Soviet authorities this presented an unwelcome side effect of their annexation of Eastern Galicia and Volhynia. They terrorized political party leaders and civic organizations, imposed limitations on movement between the former Ukrainian SSR and the recently incorporated eastern territories of the Polish Republic, applied ideological criteria when issuing travel permits (an appropriate NKVD office reviewed all travel requests). Yet despite all these measures, the "Galician Piedmont," "locus of the Ukrainian irredenta," as Kedryn-Rudnytsky phrased it, though it had suffered harm, still helped shape the identity of Ukrainian intellectuals in the 1940s. Changes to Stalin's ethnic policy affected Soviet Ukraine during the war and directly thereafter. They resulted not only from the German-Soviet war and the need to appeal to patriotic sentiments of Soviet citizens (a topic historians have addressed repeatedly) but also from the annexation of Poland's eastern lands. To date the latter connection has not been thoroughly researched.

To serve the needs of anti-Polish propaganda, an entire arsenal was put into motion. One of the strategies was to appeal to Ukrainian patriotism. In keeping with this trend, Marchenko titled his doctoral thesis, published in the spring of 1941, "Russia's and Poland's Struggle for Ukraine in the First Decade after the Incorporation of Ukraine into Russia, 1654–1664." Not coincidentally, the Soviets decided to use the opera libretto of *Bohdan Khmelnytsky* in a propaganda film (earlier, striving to gauge the reactions of the Lviv community, a dress rehearsal disguised as a theater performance of said piece occurred). In a strange twist, the history of the Cossack wars provided a foundation for a contemporary ethnic identity. At the same time, officials quietly exonerated Hrushevsky's notion of Ukrainian history (though the historian himself remained disgraced), adapting it to propagandistic needs. The historian's surviving Galician disciples, among them Ivan Krypiakevych, were able to secure positions in the Soviet academic world.

None of these developments prevented Galician Ukrainians from grasping the political reality that surrounded them. Even those who gave in to the illusion of a "unified Ukraine," quickly learned their very painful lesson. No influential person from that community became a cog in the Soviet wheel. In contrast to the ascent of activists such as Wanda Wasilewska, Julia Brystygierowa, Jerzy Borejsza, as well as postwar champions of Communism, the few Ukrainian intellectuals who remained in Lviv were all subject to reprisals. After the war they did not play any part as political operatives; the higher-level posts, whether in the government or in academia, were reserved for trusted party members freshly arrived from the USSR.

Even the attitude of those Ukrainian intellectuals who lent their authority to support the Soviets smacks of ambivalence. Studynsky did not become an arm of total oppression; on the contrary, he used a variety of means to mitigate its outcomes. Marchenko, although picked specifically to serve as a cog, as it turns out fell under the spell of Galician professors. As a graduate of the Institute of Red Professors which educated the new Bolshevik generation of young wolves, a political officer in the Red Army, and a trusted member of the Central Committee of the Communist Party of Ukraine, he immediately grasped the magnitude of Galician Ukrainians' intellectual heritage. He went on to—literally and figuratively—share these achievements with friends before his arrest, and later played an important role in shaping the new generation of Ukrainian historians during the Thaw. For his part, Ahatanhel Krymsky, the most distinguished Ukrainian orientalist, a contemporary of Kyrylo Studynsky and friend of Ivan Franko, was used by the Soviet authorities as a pre-revolution intellectual to attest to the high caliber of humanities research in the Soviet Union. Indeed, he made a positive impression on the Ukrainian community and exerted tremendous influence on the scholarly development of Omelian Pritsak, who later founded the Ukrainian Research Institute at the most prestigious university in the US—Harvard.

Polish memoirists, if they note any trace of disloyalty against the Soviets among Ukrainians, twist it to emphasize that their non-Polish colleagues were simply entrenched in (the obviously superior) Polish culture. Karolina Lanckorońska writes: "People reared for generations in a Polish cultural atmosphere—although politically hostile towards us—often came to us in despair, just to confide that this Ukraine that had suddenly taken control of them was unspeakably barbaric and diametrically alien. Such conversations imbued us with the boldest hopes of future concord and understanding."[214] Her words reflect a deep-seated conviction that for centuries Poland has been carrying out a civilizing mission in Ruthenia. On the other hand, wherever Polish influence did not quite reach or where barbarians retained more control, those areas fell into civilizational decline, returning to their original savage state. Indirectly, she expresses the idea that the cultural divide between Galician and Soviet Ukrainians would bring the prodigal son—Galician Ukrainians—back to their father's house, and thus guarantee the resurrection of the Polish Republic within its prewar borders.

Undoubtedly, a commandment of solidarity within the academic community extended beyond ethnic divisions, and it mandated mutual support in the face of a threat. The linguist and pedagogue Iulian Redko, recalling the difficult situation in a school where he worked as an assistant principal in 1940 (a former Polish high school where Juliusz Kleiner once taught), wrote: "Although all teachers were Poles who did not like Ukrainians, often National Democrats, nevertheless they were happy, because they saw in me 'their man,' someone with Western values, who received an education at the same university as they did, and who spoke Polish with them. They were very afraid of the Bolshevik principal Muzyka, who really did hate them as class enemies. They were afraid that he would send them all to Siberia. 'Mr. Redko, but you will defend us!'"[215] When memoirists maintain that the Lviv intelligentsia united in fear of "eastern barbarism," they do not acknowledge the extremely complex motivations that steered actual people's choices.

The authorities Sovietized the occupied territories by a variety of means,[216] but the Sovietization of the university, achieved via an initial

---

214 Lanckorońska, *Michelangelo in Ravensbruck: One Woman's War against the Nazis*, 23.
215 Iulian Red'ko, *Statti, spohady, materialy* (Lviv: LNB, 2006), 169.
216 Here the subject literature is plentiful. Among the most important earlier studies are: in English—Jan Tomasz Gross, *Revolution from Abroad: The Soviet Conquest of Poland's Western Ukraine and Western Belorussia* (Princeton: Princeton University Press, 2002); Ben-Cion Pinchuk, "Sovietization in a Multi-Ethnic Environment: Jewish Culture in Soviet Poland, 1939–1941," *Jewish Social Studies* 48, no. 2 (1986): 163–74; in Polish—Włodzimierz Bonusiak, *Polityka ludnościowa i ekonomiczna ZSRR na okupowanych ziemiach polskich w latach 1939–1941* (Rzeszów: Wydawnictwo Uniwersytetu Rzeszowskiego, 2006); Albin Głowacki, *Sowieci wobec Polaków na ziemiach wschodnich II Rzeczypospolitej w latach 1939–1941* (Łódź: Wydawnictwo Uniwersytetu Łódzkiego, 1997); Grzegorz Hryciuk, "Polacy we Lwowie pod okupacją radziecką i niemiecką"; Grzegorz Mazur, "Polityka sowiecka na 'Zachodniej Ukrainie' 1939–1941. Zarys problematyki," *Zeszyty Historyczne* 130 (1999): 68–95. The most important Ukrainian authors who have

Ukrainization, sparked the strongest emotions. The established professors felt that introducing Ukrainian as the language of instruction and creating Ukrainian academic divisions lowered the university's status. A sense of deprivation, be it actual or perceived, triggers negative reactions in communities that undergo such experiences, and gives rise to prejudice and hostility towards other groups, strangers or competitors alike. The old Ukrainian intelligentsia, driven out of positions in local administration and at the university, and the young generation, educated during the interwar period and denied a chance for advancement, had their own grounds to blame Polish academics for the status quo. At the start of the Soviet occupation, when a number of Ukrainian academics gained privileged access to positions, their Polish colleagues did not even see it as Ukrainian revenge. To see it as such would presuppose that the two sides were somewhat equal. Instead, they decried the loss of privileges to which they were, by definition, entitled.

When formal relationships came under ideological pressures, the resistance against Ukrainization and a dislike for those who were tasked with carrying out the policy grew into a barrier viewed as a civilizational divide. Polish memoirists habitually depict an influx of barbarians from the east, boorish, unfamiliar with the most basic achievements of civilization, and they invoke countless anecdotes to illustrate their point. Though they appear to hold newcomers from the East in uniformly low esteem, in reality it all depended on the persons and their position in the academic milieu. The chapter *Academic Snapshots* mentions cordial relationships, and at times even close friendships between mathematicians from Lviv and from Russia. In contrast, Galician Ukrainians who advanced to leadership positions received a different treatment. Their Polish colleagues accused them of collaboration and criticized their allegedly inferior scholarly record, essentially categorizing local Ukrainians the same as the newly arrived Soviets. To them, both groups represented the occupier (and were boorish dunces). A similar compensatory strategy applied to Ukrainians as did to the Soviets, those savages from the east. Neither group of Ukrainians, Soviet or local, was qualified to hold academic positions. Such sentiments come through in direct statements about the Ukrainian faculty, as well as in symptomatic omissions. One would be hard pressed to identify a Polish memoirist who embarks on a deeper reflection on relations between the Polish and Ukrainian

---

published on this issue are Volodymyr Baran and Vasyl Tokarsky, Oleksandr Lutsky, Oleksandr Rublov.

intelligentsia. Instances of supranational solidarity within that community are omitted, too. Very rarely does a positive comment about newly arrived Ukrainians appear, and only as an exception to the rule. The roles of enlightened scientists from the USSR go to Russians, and, though seldom—to Jews. In this narrative, Ukrainian academics—from either bank of the river Zbruch—play a different part: they are barbarians who have broken into the garden of scholarship.

The band Polish Parade, directed by Henryk Wars, in the Middle East

CHAPTER 5

The Great Journey

When on June 26, 1941 the NKVD burst into Eugeniusz Bodo's apartment in Lviv, the darling of Polish audiences thought that the Soviets were just intent on assuring his safety and had come to evacuate him. After all, he had to run from the Germans once before, in September 1939. Like Hemar, Bodo also had parodied Hitler in prewar cabarets in Warsaw, and starred in the film *Caution—Spy!*, which took aim at the Third Reich. Fearing retribution from the Nazis, the actor left Warsaw in the first days of Poland's German occupation. Three years later, in his 1942 testimony recorded in a NKVD prison, he explained his reasons for escaping from Warsaw: "At the time friends came over and told me how the Germans took Poznań and shot an actor there for having starred in anti-fascist plays. Then my mother talked me into leaving as well, because I also had a part in an anti-fascist movie."[1]

Bodo made his way to Lviv via Białystok and Rivne, which was the most common itinerary for those leaving Warsaw. Approximately seventy percent of those fleeing east were persons of Jewish ethnicity. Some fled because they were afraid of having been marked for extermination. Published in Berlin in 1939, the *Sonderfahndungsbuch Polen* (*Special Prosecution Book—Poland*) specified 61,000 people, although neither Bodo nor Marian Hemar (familiar to us from the chapter "Haven at the Clinic"), nor Ida Kamińska, were among them. All the same, Kamińska's friend, a Warsaw journalist, tipped her off that she too was in this book, and so she immediately took off for the Soviet zone. The Nazis kept their inventory of wanted persons open, with many blank pages; in 1940 they printed a "new, supplemental edition" in Cracow. As for Bodo, when

---

1 Eugeniusz Bodo, confessions. Quoted in: Filip Gańczak, "Szwajcar, czyli szpion," *pamiec. pl.* 10 (2013), https://pamiec.pl/pa/tylko-u-nas/12898,SZWAJCAR-CZYLI-SZPION-artykul-Filipa-Ganczaka.html.

Eugeniusz Bodo was the darling of prewar audiences

the German-Soviet war came, he indeed appeared on a list of people subject to immediate imprisonment. A Soviet one.

"ONLY IN LVIV"

In the fall of 1939, a large group of stage actors arrived in Lviv, among them Eugeniusz Bodo, composer and songwriter Henryk Wars, lyricist Emanuel Szlechter, and singer Gwidon Borucki. The bunch knew each other well. Bodo had worked with Henryk Wars before the war and they promoted many hit songs together. Soon they began performing as the Lviv Tea-Jazz orchestra, a group established by the new authorities. They had stolen the hearts of Polish audiences; now the Soviet public had adopted the artists as their new darlings, applauding them in Moscow, Odesa, Kyiv, Kharkiv, Baku, Tbilisi, Batumi, and Sochi. The tune "Tylko we Lwowi" ["Only in Lviv"], from the 1939 film

Włóczęgi [*The Vagrants*], originally performed by the well-known Lvivian duo Szczepcio and Tońcio, quickly became an earworm. The jazz band would finish each performance by playing its Russian version, sung by Bodo, to convey a cordial good-bye and an invitation to Lviv: "Zhdem vas vo L´vove" ["Lviv awaits you"]. Though the singer enjoyed immense popularity and received top honoraria, after his recordings in Moscow and concerts in Odesa in the spring of 1941, he stopped touring with the orchestra. Instead, he returned to Lviv as soon as he could to wait for the authorities' permission to leave the USSR. Bodo's decision dealt a blow to Henryk Wars, as the eloquent performer was not easy to replace. It was even harder to adjust the band's repertoire—so much so that once Bodo quit, a female singer took over his hit "Umówiłem się z nią na dziewiątą" ["I have a date with her at nine"]. But the Lviv Tea-Jazz, its cast diminished, continued to tour. The outbreak of the German-Soviet war surprised them *en route* and they decided to flee farther east. Despite facing terrible conditions, all survived. All but Bodo.

The Lviv Tea-Jazz orchestra, largely made up of war castaways, set out on their first tour in April 1940.[2] They left Lviv on the eve of the April mass deportations. It is hard to establish today whether the fortuitous timing was entirely coincidental, or whether some friendly Soviet colleagues tipped them off. What we do know is that singers from the Theater of the Opera, and actors from all three dramatic theaters and from the satirical Teatr Miniatiur, appear on the list of the 644 *bezhentsy* (refugees) whom the local Soviet theater administration "reclaimed" from the NKVD, thus saving them from deportation in June 1940. In contrast, the names of our jazz orchestra members, except for Henryk Wars, do not appear on this list. The record mentions neither Eugeniusz Bodo, nor Gwidon Borucki nor any other Warsaw musician turned Tea-Jazz member. Sadly, the vast majority of refugees who had arrived in Lviv from the West were not as lucky.[3]

---

2   "Gastroli lvivs'kykh artystiv po SRSR," *Vil'na Ukraïna*, no. 87, April 12, 1940.
3   The list, presented by the head of the Lviv Oblast NKVD Major Vasyl Serhiienko was approved by the Ukrainian SSR's People's Commissar of State Security Ivan Serov (Spetssoobshcheniia o khode pereseleniia spetskontingenta iz zapadnykh oblastei USSR v vostochnye, n.d., f. 16, op. 33. spr. 33, k. 187–8). Among the artists affiliated with Teatr Miniatiur, nineteen avoided deportation, including the screenwriter, actor, and singer Konrad Tom (real name Konrad Runowiecki, stage name Tim-Tom) and Zofia Terne (real name Wiera Chajter). By that time the Lviv band Tea-Jazz had already been incorporated into the Lviv State Philharmonic Orchestra (whose thirty-three musicians were listed as not subject to deportation).

The Lviv Tea-Jazz on the Potemkin Steps in Odesa

In August 1940, at the peak of vacation season, the band visited Odessa, filling the summer amphitheater. The performances occurred after the USSR had annexed Bukovyna and Bessarabia, as well as the Baltic countries, and after France had fallen. A preserved photo shows the group smiling, arranged on the Potemkin steps; looking at it one would never surmise that there was a war going on, and that these artists were getting a crash course in Soviet survival. In the fall of 1940, after returning from the first USSR tour to Lviv, Bodo continued to work at Teatr Miniatiur, where he played the lead in a show titled *Muzyka na ulicy* [*Music in the Street*], whose plot resembled one of his prewar films—*The Vagrants* [*Włóczęgi*]. The play told an outwardly carefree, but in truth propaganda-charged story of wandering American musicians who, in the midst of the turmoil of the war, had come to Lviv. This peaceful city, freshly liberated from the yoke of capitalism, welcomes them warmly and recognizes them for their artistry.[4] However, the film's plot and the reality of Lviv did not exactly match. Not without reason, Bodo soon began an application process to leave the USSR, indicating the United States as his destination. His itinerary would have been the exact opposite of the musical's plot, in which the main characters arrived in the USSR from America.

---

4   "Muzyka na ulicy," *Czerwony Sztandar*, 1941, no. 47.

In the spring of 1941, forty-three members of the theater group Teatr Miniatiur ventured on yet another tour.[5] They convinced themselves that even in a totalitarian country, the public showed up in droves for the old songs and not for the propaganda. Both sides found sustenance in illusions: the audience believed, or pretended to believe, that the Soviet ideals reflected in the music had truly captivated the troupe's hearts, and the musicians wanted to feel that their artistry was the sole draw. Indeed, the public revered those songs just as much as they loved the hits performed by the Leningrad Tea-Jazz orchestra, for example the tango "Burnt by the Sun" ["Utomlennye solntsem"] (which later provided the musical background for Nikita Mikhalkov's 1994 movie of the same title). In the end the public and the performers wanted nothing more than to forget their plight, even if only for a moment.

After yet another enthusiastic reception in Odesa in the late spring of 1941, Bodo returned to Lviv. The rest of the band stayed to enjoy Odesa's beaches, though not for long; after the German-Soviet war broke out, the artists set out on their Great Journey. They crossed Central Asia, this time without supervision, impresarios, or honoraria, under conditions that were entirely unlike their earlier triumphant tours through the European territories of the USSR. In 1942 they made it to the Middle East with the Anders' Army. Together with others who had survived the horror of *Gulag* or the ravages of the war, they formed a new ensemble. Their music evoked a fighting spirit among the newly minted soldiers, only recently released from labor camps or forced exile.

Though the Lviv Tea-Jazz's musical program relied on prewar hit songs, each had to undergo some ideological retouching, and be in Russian. A Kyiv native, Feliks Konarski (stage name Ref-Ren), translated some of the lyrics. Eugeniusz Bodo became the Russian-language announcer. Under Wars's direction, Bodo, Gwidon Borucki, Renata Bogdańska, Janina Jasińska, Adam Aston, and Albert Harris made up the group's core. At the turn of 1941 and 1942, all the artists, except for Bodo, enlisted in the Anders' Army. During their travels they were joined by Michał Waszyński, released from *Gulag* following the Sikorski-Maysky treaty. (Waszyński, a film director, had been Bodo's business partner before the war; the two made dozens of movies, such as the previously mentioned *Vagabonds*. In cinematic history he is best known for making the 1937 *Dybbuk*, the most distinguished Jewish film to originate from Poland.) In the Middle East Waszyński worked for the Military Office of Propaganda and Education, leading its film division, and gathering many

---

5   "Khronika," *Literatura i mystetstvo* 3 (1941): 51.

stage actors. At the end of the war he made the documentary *Monte Cassino* (1944), as well as a feature film about the Anders' Army titled *The Great Journey* (1946). Renata Bogdańska (stage name of Irena Iarosevych) played one of leads, and her first husband Gwidon Borucki (stage name of Gwidon Gottlieb) performed one of the best known Polish patriotic songs from World War II, "Czerwone maki na Monte Cassino" ["The Red Poppies on Monte Cassino"].[6] Together, they co-created the Anders' Army legend. The film's title reflects the tragedy, heroism, and sacrifice of all those who set out on this great journey from the occupied territories of the Polish Republic through the USSR, the Near East, to Italy, and, finally, after demobilizing, to Great Britain.

For Wars's band, their great journey began in Lviv, where most of the members escaped from Nazi-occupied Warsaw. The Tea-Jazz orchestra emerged shortly after the People's Assembly resolution had passed, allowing the USSR to formally incorporate the seized territory in November 1939. In similar circumstances, a musical ensemble formed in Białystok under the management of the trumpeter Adolf Rosner, known as the "white Armstrong." The group performed in Minsk, Moscow, and Leningrad. Only after the war did the communists declare war on jazz music. Rosner ended up in *Gulag* for attempting to cross the border to return to Poland. Approximately at the same time, at the onset of the Cold War, a ban was placed on the production of jazz records.

The Tea-Jazz artists were a close-knit group, whose professional and personal ties predated the war. At the start of the war Lviv became their haven. As was the case with other institutions nationalized by the Soviets, the Philharmonic, which formally oversaw the band, was managed by a Soviet director (here memoirists mention Mikhailo Potshybitkin, but it seems they got his name wrong). In the first months the actors and musicians, especially those of Jewish ethnicity, did not experience persecution, and the Soviets even doted on a few of them. One example is Ida Kamińska, who arrived in Lviv through Białystok at the Soviet authorities' invitation. She immediately got a contract as a director, and her Yiddish theater acquired the status of a state institution, as did Polish and Ukrainian theaters. She retained her position until late spring, but then a Soviet administrator replaced her. Such reshuffling occurred in other institutions as well. But overall, stage artists enjoyed

---

6   Bogumiła Żongołłowicz, *Jego były "Czerwone maki." Życie i twórczość Gwidona Boruckiego—Guido Lorraine'a* (Toruń: Oficyna wydawnicza Kucharski, 2010).

high status, as we learn from perusing the lengthy lists of people exempted from evacuation, which was otherwise mandatory for refugees. These lists feature 121 artists of the Theater of the Opera, the Philharmonic, the Polish Theater, and the Jewish Theater (almost twenty percent of the total number of 644). This is a sizeable figure, especially when compared to the list of just five academics.

Before the war, most of the artists mentioned in this chapter had enjoyed immense popularity. In the fall of 1939, a twist of fate brought together singer Eugeniusz Bodo, composer Henryk Wars, and lyricist Emanuel Szlechter, co-creators of the hit song "Only in Lviv" ["Tylko we Lwowi"]. It happened in Lviv, of course. But only those who happened to be away from Lviv in June 1941 survived the war.

CAUTION, SPY!

Eugeniusz Bodo quit the band in the late spring of 1941 and returned to Lviv. There he would await permission to depart for the United States. Born in Switzerland, he counted on his Swiss passport to extricate himself from the Soviet embrace. Tragically, Bodo did not realize that the application alone would provoke the NKVD, and his foreign citizenship only made things worse. The notion of a neutral country did not exist in Soviet vocabulary. How did the artist arrive at such a risky decision? Perhaps his vigilance softened after Soviet

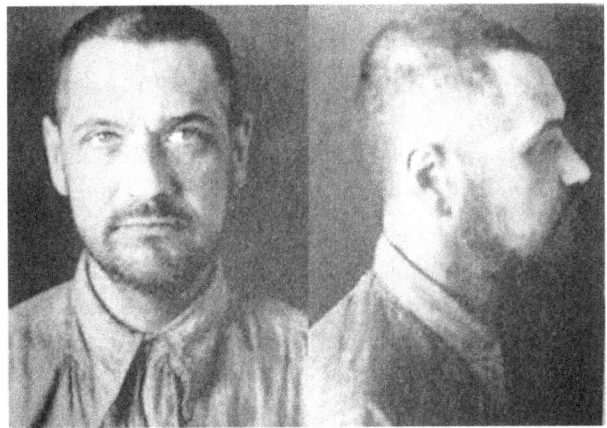

Eugeniusz Bodo was arrested by the NKVD in late June 1941.
He died in a Soviet prison.

authorities went all out to help Wars, extricating Henryk Wars's family from the Warsaw ghetto and bringing them to the USSR. They also rescued Wanda Wasilewska's daughter from Warsaw. Or maybe the singer trusted in the protection his band's popularity afforded him? Or was he so certain of the authorities' faith in him because they had paid him so generously (Bodo and Wars were among the few artists who were classified as belonging to the highest creative category, and were handsomely compensated)? But all those assurances turned out to be illusory. Decades later we finally have confirmation of his arrest, the war transport, prison time in Bashkiria, and finally a *Gulag* sentence in Kotlas, although until the fall of the USSR these events remained a secret, as did the circumstances of his death.[7]

At the start of the German-Soviet war, the NKVD conducted mass arrests of persons they considered potential allies of the enemy. According to the Soviet nomenclature the majority of people arrested in late June fell into two categories: "spies" or "Ukrainian nationalists." In the first days of the war, Lviv's prisons were filled to the brim. Immediately after the war broke out, the NKVD evacuated some of those who had been arrested earlier, and murdered thousands of others. Only a handful survived. Persons whose files the NKVD labeled as "suspect," but also particularly essential because of the positions they held, were evacuated under escort. Not perchance the names of two deputies—Petro Franko and Kyrylo Studynsky—appear on that list. Franko was familiar with Soviet dealings inside and out, having worked at a research institute in Kharkiv. He left there before the Stalinist repressions, ostensibly to care for his widowed mother. Because his late father, the proletarian poet Ivan Franko, had become a cult figure, the authorities could not decline Petro's request to leave for Lviv. The actual percentage of Galician intellectuals who managed to leave the Ukrainian SSR was very low. Most Galician Sovietophiles ended up shot. Originally, they had left Galicia for the Ukrainian SSR out of patriotic motivations, eager to serve Ukraine with their knowledge and expertise. The move also gave them a chance to make a living, since in Polish Galicia educated Ukrainians could not find work commensurate with their qualifications. At the moment of his arrest on June 25, 1941, Petro Franko most likely fully understood what was to come, but there was no way out. One trail of documents suggests that he was "shot during an escape attempt." Like Franko, Studynsky, along with his wife, was deported under the NKVD's escort, though at first he did not realize that this was an arrest and not an

---

7   Ibid.

evacuation. Researchers have not been able to establish where these "evacuees" were executed. Studynsky's colleague from the Academy, the orientalist Ahatanhel Krymsky, whose saga we followed in the previous chapter, was apprehended by the NKVD in his native Zvenyhorodka in Central Ukraine. He understood his situation almost immediately, having seen and experienced plenty of Soviet tactics. Unlike his friends—Petro Franko, whom he first met as a child, and Studynsky with whom he worked so closely—Krymsky lived in captivity for another year, until he died of exhaustion and lack of medical care.

Citizens of Poland took longer to fully grasp their situation if they had not previously been acquainted with the Soviet system. Except for those persons whom the NKVD executed in the first days of the war, they actually stood more of a chance of survival. The caveat was that they had to be ethnic Poles, because Soviet authorities applied a very narrow interpretation to a memorandum added to the Sikorski-Maysky agreement of July 30, 1941. Though the agreement granted amnesty to Polish citizens imprisoned or exiled to Soviet camps, the USSR refused to apply it to prewar Polish citizens of non-Polish nationalities. In fall 1941, Polish ambassador Stanisław Kot began pressing the Soviets to release from captivity prewar representatives and senators, but to no avail. Prominent Ukrainian and Jewish political activists remained in camps or in forced exile to the Soviet frontier (an example was the infamous case of Erlich and Alter, Bundist leaders whom the Soviets briefly let out, only to re-arrest and execute them two months later[8]). Some Jewish and Ukrainian prisoners and exiles managed to regain their freedom in early fall of 1941, if that term is even applicable to their status in the USSR. Joining the Anders' Army presented the only way out, but when it came to nonethnic Poles, and to Ukrainians in particular, the army's leadership feared those recruits would be disloyal and accepted them only reluctantly. Ukrainians who did not pass through the sieve of the draft board tried to go back to Ukraine. A few made their way home but did not get to stay there long. Soon after the war ended, they were sent back to labor camps, this time on collaboration charges; they were not accused of working with the Poles (most indictments of Ukrainian politicians arrested by the NKVD included this designation), but rather with the Germans.

---

8 David Engel, "The Polish Government-in-Exile and the Erlich-Alter Affair," in *Jews in Eastern Poland and the USSR, 1939–46*, ed. Norman Davies and Antony Polonsky (London: Macmillan, 1991), 172–81.

According to the Soviets, Eugeniusz Bodo's Swiss citizenship excluded him from the Sikorski-Maysky treaty. Ambassador Stanisław Kot personally sought Bodo's release, and the first secretary of the Polish embassy Aleksander Mniszek wrote letters to the prisoner and the authorities. All in vain. Such diplomatic intervention only affirmed the NKVD functionaries' certainty that Bodo was an active spy. Absurdly, Bodo's leading role as an agent in the unfinished film *Uwaga—szpieg!* [*Caution, Spy!*]. presented an additional incriminating factor. According to the investigators, he must have known the secrets of the profession inside and out, because a mere actor could never successfully play a spy. This terrible coincidence sealed the artist's fate. Complete isolation and hunger contributed to Bodo's physical demise. In prison and in the *Gulag*, inmates treated the former stage darling Bodo like a leper. Any contact with the foreigner would bring an accusation of espionage, which by default carried the highest penalty. He had no one to help him survive. On October 7, 1943 Bodo died of emaciation in the Kotlas *Gulag*. It took the fall of the USSR half a century later to obtain his rehabilitation.

Who was Bodo? The NKVD functionaries knew every detail of his life from the interrogations. A European, a man of success who effortlessly navigated a number of cultures, languages, and countries. They read his resume according to their own preconceptions—only a spy could cross borders without obstacles. For his part, Bodo, a citizen of the world, never grasped the merciless logic of the Soviet state security apparatus.

Eugeniusz Bogdan Junod was born in Switzerland, lived in Łódź, and after World War I, in Warsaw. He grew up on stage. In the early 1900s, his father opened a cinema in Łódź and the family experienced a financial windfall. Then came another, after Teodor Junod built his Teatr Variété. Later the son adopted the motto "life is a variety show," and justifiably so; in the 1930s he became a movie star, a darling of cabaret audiences, bon vivant and joint owner of a film production company (with Michał Waszyński), and director of *The Vagrants*. As a producer, Bodo frequently traveled to Berlin, which later gave the NKVD another reason to suspect him of spying for the enemy (who, of course, until June 1941 had been a Soviet ally). The actor was fluent in German and Russian. This only added to the suspicions, as the Soviet Union and Germany were now at war (*Caution—Spy!*). He had spoken German since childhood and learned Russian in school, growing up under Tsarist rule. Bodo perfected his Russian skills when he accompanied his father on frequent trips through Western Russia with a traveling cinema. Thirty years later he could entertain Soviet crowds in Russian with ease, emceeing the band's shows and performing the new Sovietized hit "Only in Lviv."

"AN OVERHAUL IS COMING TO LVIV"

Eugeniusz Junod-Bodo's first job in Soviet Lviv was at the Teatr Miniatiur. A performance under the symbolic tile *Od początku* [*From the Beginning*] opened the season in November 1939.[9] In spring 1940, Teatr Miniatiur staged *Zielony karnawał* [*The Green Carnival*],[10] which offered a stark contrast with what the town's inhabitants experienced at that very time: the Soviets deported more than 10,000 persons related to "enemies of the people."

In *Mój wiek* [*My Century*] Aleksander Wat reminisces about theater in those days: "Immediately after the Soviets marched in, right away cabarets emerged. They were extremely supportive, even of jazz."[11] Actually, back then jazz was not yet censored; on the contrary, it was all the rage. As for cabarets, the Soviets opened ... one, Teatr Miniatiur. It was to replace a number of entertainment groups, including *Lviv's Merry Wave* [*Wesoła Lwowska Fala*] with Szczepcio and Tońcio. Thirty years had passed since Wat had lived in Lviv, understandably blurring some details. Yet his assertions also illustrate to what extent subsequent opinions and events distort our image of the past: in the fall of 1939 Lviv did not boast numerous cabarets, nor was jazz music censored. Years after, Wat remembered it differently; the knowledge he acquired later effaced those earlier memories.

The jazz band under Henryk Wars's management came together in late 1939.[12] The composer had been drafted to the Polish Army in late August 1939, and subsequently captured by Germans, but managed to escape from a prisoner transport, and by late fall made his way to Lviv.

---

9   *Czerwony Sztandar*, no. 35, November 2; 1939; *Vil'na Ukraïna*, no. 36, November 3, 1939.
10 Mykhailo Rudnyts'kyi, "Chomu 'Zelenyi karnaval'?" *Vil'na Ukraïna*, no. 108, May 10, 1940.
11 Aleksander Wat, *Mój wiek. Pamiętnik mówiony*, vol. 1 (Warsaw: Czytelnik, 1998), 302.
12 Various sources indicate the wrong date for when the band began—spring of 1940. The Lviv Tea-Jazz was actually formed in the fall of 1939. A direct confirmation comes via Gwidon Borucki in "Polscy artyści w czasie II wojny światowej, cz.1: Przymusowe tournee po Rosji," *Polski Kurier/Polish Kurier: polsko-australijskie czasopismo społeczno-kulturalne* 116–117 (1997): 28–30, http://www.e-teatr.pl/pl/dokumenty/2015_12/69711/g_b__polscy_artysci_w_czasie_ii_wojny_swiatowej__cz__1__polish_kurier__no__116_117__1997.pdf, accessed January 27, 2014. Indirectly, we can surmise that the band had already existed before their program was prepared in spring 1940.

To many refugees, Lviv seemed akin to Noah's Ark, a city which "perhaps had never before welcomed at once such a number of celebrities, who now blended into the street crowd, reduced to the role of disoriented and defenseless ordinary people."[13] Among those who escaped from Warsaw were also former Lviv resident Gwidon Borucki, who had lived there relatively briefly, and the Lviv native Emanuel Szlechter, a well-known songwriter and author of film musical hits such as "Odrobina szczęścia w miłości" or "Umówiłem się z nią na dziewiątą" ["A bit of luck with love," "I have a date with her at nine"], both of which gained fame in Bodo's interpretation. Since the early 1930s, the lyricist had worked together with Warsaw cabaret Małe Qui Pro Quo, though he never cut his ties to Lviv and wrote the lyrics to the popular song "Only in Lviv." Upon returning to his hometown at the start of the war, he was immediately hired as actor and director of the Teatr Miniatiur. Thus began the collaboration of former Warsaw colleagues turned refugees: Henryk Wars, Eugeniusz Bodo, Michał Waszyński. But when half a year later the Tea-Jazz went on tour, Emmanuel Szlechter did not. As a Polish writer, he was not part of the touring ensemble. Someone else was in charge of preparing the now Russian-language repertoire.

Pavel Grigoriev rewrote the lyrics to "Only in Lviv" to fit the new political circumstances. Now the song began with "A major overhaul is coming to Lviv" ["Vo Lvove remont kapitalny idet"]. This simple metaphor for the Soviet order was meant to convince the listeners of the city's sunny atmosphere and hospitality. The Russian version ended with an invitation to Lviv. The town's legendary wealth and beauty still had its powers of attraction, even if the business trip frenzy undertaken by Soviet civil servants to Lviv had slowly subsided. Bureaucrats had been eager to travel to Lviv so they could obtain "luxury" goods, in low supply elsewhere in the Soviet Union, but obtainable for almost nothing here. The new lyrics assured the public that Lviv was happy to share all its riches with visitors—like brothers: "Vse to, chem nash L'vov khorosh i bogat / On vam predostavit, kak brat!" ["Lvov will share all its beauty and riches / fulfilling all your brotherly wishes"] and issued a cordial invitation: "Nam khochetsia s vami uvidet'sia vnov' / Zhdem vas vo L'vove! / Vas vstretit goriachaia nasha liubov', / Prosim vo L'vov!" ["We fancy to see you again and again / Lvov awaits you, my friend / You shall be greeted with heartfelt love / One visit in Lvov just won't be enough!"].

---

13   Michał Borwicz, "Inżynierowie dusz," *Zeszyty Historyczne* 3 (1963): 123.

These words concluded the band's every show. Jubilant artistry was an indispensable ingredient of socialist realist culture. The performers believed that their music moved the audience more than the lyrics did. At first the song sounded merely naive, but one more listen made the active distortion of reality apparent. Were their hopes justified? Probably not. Back in Lviv, the performers as well as their fans must have heard the blatant taunts, the Soviet chutzpah, in these songs.

Often, Lviv's residents updated prewar musical hits into some more risqué, and some seemingly innocent street songs, proving that even in everyday life, the town rejected the Soviet order, including the imposition of "Moscow time": "I have a date with her at nine, / At nine—new time, / She arrived at nine, At nine—old time."[14] These two worlds—the new and the old—like the new and old time, did not fit with each other at all.

A young Lviv poet by the name of Józef Nacht (Prutkowski) wrote this version of the song. Bodo, who sang the original, and Szlechter, who penned the lyrics for Bodo, were forced to live according to the new time (the Soviets put Lviv on Moscow time on the same day they introduced the ruble as the sole currency—on December 23, 1939, a day before Christmas Eve). As for Nacht, he was arrested, and later released from the *Gulag*, though too late to join the Anders' Army. Instead, he returned to Poland with the (Soviet-organized) Kościuszko Infantry division. He did not go back to writing until the Thaw, when he joined the satirical magazine *Szpilki*.

Bodo never left the *Gulag*. If not for Alfred Mirek's account, the fate of Junod-Bodo would have most likely remained unknown. In 1942 Mirek recognized Bodo in a Soviet prison as the artist who sung the "Farewell Song" ["Proshchalna pesenka"] at a concert in Moscow two years before. Mirek's *Zapiski zakliuchennogo* [*Notes of a Prisoner*] appeared in 1989;[15] it offered the first credible information about Eugeniusz Bodo's whereabouts since his return to Lviv in late spring of 1941 and his subsequent arrest.[16] Fifty years later, thanks to the evidence from Mirek's account, a relative of Junod-Bodo obtained through the Red Cross an official confirmation of the actor's death in a Soviet camp. Bodo was posthumously cleared of espionage charges. That is how the Soviets conducted their "major overhaul" in Lviv.

---

14 Borwicz, "Inżynierowie dusz," 157.
15 Alfred Mirek, *Tiuremnyi rekviem. Zapiski zakliuchennogo* (Moscow: Prava cheloveka, 1997), 134–7.
16 Ryszard Wolański, *Eugeniusz Bodo: "Już taki jestem zimny drań"* (Poznań: Rebis, 2012), 336–49.

"THEM OTHERS CAN TRAVEL . . ."

As he wrote the lyrics to the original "Only in Lviv," Emmanuel Szlechter probably had no inkling of where the war would take him:

> Them others can travel wherever they please
> Like they Parisians, Londoners, Viennese,
> But me? Ain't budging from this very stead.
> So what if I make the Lord mad!

The song quickly turned into a favorite among the new generation of Lvivians, and is still popular today, in and far beyond Lviv.

In truth, the lyrics' author had lived in Warsaw since 1932 and rarely visited Lviv. The composer, Henryk Wars, was always hesitant to leave Warsaw. But poetic license allows for playing with language norms, and for embellishing reality. What mattered was the song's appeal to a wide audience. Not everyone was swept off their feet: Roman Tomczyk, a journalist from the right-wing weekly *Prosto z mostu*, displayed zero patience with either the lyricist or the composer and called on all patriots to throw this tango "composed by one Jew to the lyrics of another" in the dumpster: "This seedy group gets its sustenance from 'Polish' cinema (all Jewry!), the Polish Radio (it is nothing but a branch office of a community of the Israelite persuasion), from the so-called 'little theaters' (see crime reports: Bajer) and from society's utter lack of reaction."[17] By the late 1930s neither his way of thinking nor the rhetoric were isolated occurrences, and they were not limited to the right-wing circle of this particular magazine. Poles had a love-hate relationship with their Jewish entertainers Hemar, Wars, and Szlechter.

The war brought both Wars and Szlechter to Lviv (the previous chapter, "Haven at the Clinic," describes how two refugees reacted to Hemar's flight from Poland). Szlechter returned to his hometown, never to leave it again.

Adam Redzik authored a comprehensive publication devoted to this prominent Lviv lyricist. An expert on the town's legal community during the occupation, Redzik maintains that Szlechter refused to accept his Soviet passport as a protest against the occupation (this information is repeated by many other authors). Allegedly this was the reason why Szlechter did not get permission to

---

17 Roman Tomczyk, "Natarczywe melodie. Kilka wspomnień," *Prosto z mostu* 47 (October 30, 1938): 3. I wish to thank Adam Pomorski for directing me to this article, so shocking in its vitriolic hatred.

ПРАВИЛА

1. Лицо, получившее пропуск на в'езд в запретную пограничную зону или пограничную полосу и не могущее по каким либо причинам выехать, обязано: в городах — в течение двух суток, в сельских местностях — трех суток, вернуть пропуск органу РК милиции, его выдавшему.

2. Лица, получившие пропуск на в'езд в запретную пограничную зону или пограничную полосу, обязаны не позднее 24 часов с момента прибытия в пункт, указанный в пропуске, явиться для регистрации пропуска и прописки паспорта в ближайший орган РК милиции, а при выбытии явиться в этот же орган для отметки о выбытии.

3. Если в пункте пребывания лица, получившего пропуск, нет органа РК милиции, пропуск пред'является для регистрации, паспорт для прописки в тот же срок председателю сельсовета по территориальности.

4. По возвращении к месту постоянного жительства, — пропуск подлежит немедленному возвращению органу РК милиции, его выдавшему.

5. Лицо прибывшее в запретную пограничную зону или в пограничную полосу, имеет право проживания только в том населенном пункте запретной пограничной зоны (полосы), который указан в пропуске.

Проживание в других населенных пунктах запретной пограничной зоны или пограничной полосы, а равно передвижение в них может производиться только с разрешения органа РК милиции по месту регистрации пропуска.

При вынужденной остановке, в пути следования в населенном пункте, входящем в запретную пограничную зону или пограничную полосу и невозможности продолжать свой путь по независящим от лица, получившего пропуск обстоятельствам, оно должно немедленно пред'явить свой пропуск органу РК милиции, а при отсутствии его, представителю сельского совета для производства отметок о времени прибытия, причины остановки и времени выбытия.

6. Лицо, утратившее пропуск на в'езд в запретную пограничную зону или пограничную полосу, обязано подать об этом письменное заявление органу РК милиции по месту утраты пропуска с указанием обстоятельств утраты.

7. Лицо, в'ехавшее в запретную пограничную зону и в пограничную полосу без разрешения органов РК милиции, передавшее свой пропуск другому лицу, а равно уклонившееся от регистрации выданного пропуска, — подлежит ответственности по закону от 7 сентября 1937 года, (С. 3. 1937 года № 59 ст. 251).

Облит № 1417, Львов, Тип. „Вильна Украина" № 2.
Заказ № 102, Тираж 10.000 экз.

Regulations for persons staying in the border areas. NKVD instruction, 1940

A pass authorizing Omelian Pritsak to cross the USSR border, 1940

go on tour with Wars's band. He remained in Lviv, where the outbreak of the German-Soviet war caught him by surprise.[18]

We can disregard a certain inconsistency in interpreting the lyricist's patriotic stance—on the one hand he refused Soviet citizenship, on the other, he took part in Tea-Jazz's propaganda shows. Let us look at the facts instead. True, Szlechter did not go on tour, but for different reasons than those mentioned above. A passport served as an identification document within the Soviet Union, but did not authorize the holder to move around freely, let alone to cross the Soviet border. To get past the old border on the river Zbruch, one needed an official trip permit issued by an institution, or an order of employment. Only local authorities could stamp visas on such permits, with the NKVD holding the right of first refusal. Though this procedure applied equally to citizens of Soviet Ukraine as to those from beyond the Zbruch, persons residing in occupied territories rarely received travel authorization, and their institutions had to fight for it. Most certainly Szlechter had a Soviet passport, since as a Jew who had been born in Lviv and had resided there until 1932, he could not refuse the document; the issuance of a passport was mandatory for all inhabitants. On November 29, 1939, a decision of the USSR Supreme Soviet automatically made all non-Poles Soviet citizens. If any refusals occurred, they took place among the *bezhentsy* and carried serious consequences—deportation or imprisonment. Almost all *bezhentsy* without passports were deported in June 1940. For people who did not accept their Soviet passports, their only chance to survive was to go into hiding. Szlechter was neither deported nor did he disappear from public view. On the contrary, he worked for an official institution. It follows that he remained in Lviv not for lack of documents. He was either not "budging from this very stead"—which we know was merely poetic license, since he lived in Warsaw before the war and wrote his song from there, or, more likely, the authorities did not allow him to travel. Firstly, he was not a band member; in addition, the repertoire relied on Russian lyrics, and Szlechter wrote in Polish and in Yiddish (his best-known Yiddish songs were "Srulek" and "Żydowskie wesele"—"The Jewish wedding"). The musicians with whom he had been working for years all went on tour, and "Proshchalnaia pesenka"— the Russian version of "Only in Lviv"—became the anchor of their repertoire.

---

18   Adam Redzik, "Jak twórca szlagierów wszechczasów nie został adwokatem: rzecz o Emanuelu Schlechterze (1904–1943). W 110 rocznicę urodzin i 70 rocznicę śmierci," *Palestra* 1–2 (2014): 254, http://palestra.pl/pdf_pliki/36_redzik_schlechter.pdf, accessed February 9, 2014. Also see Redzik's article "Życie z piosenką," *Kurier Galicyjski*, no. 20, October 29–November 14, 2013, 26.

The original lyricist remained in Lviv. "Them others can travel wherever they please." To Moscow, Baku, or Tashkent.

DEATH TANGO

When Germany attacked the Soviet Union, Emanuel Szlechter was in Lviv. By late 1941 he was forced to move to the ghetto, a fate which the entire Jewish community shared. He perished during the liquidation of the Lviv ghetto in 1943, though the exact date of his death is unknown. Decades later, former and new Lvivians still sing his song.

Adam Redzik retells the story of Szlechter's last months through Simon Wiesenthal:[19] On orders of the SS Untersturmführer Richard Rokita, the poet wrote "The Death Tango." As Wiesenthal writes, an orchestra consisting of renowned Jewish musicians would perform this piece during executions at the

An orchestra at the Janowska Camp. The 1943 photograph, titled "Death Tango," was used as evidence in the Nuremberg trials

---

19 Simon Wiesenthal, *The Sunflower: On the Possibilities and Limits of Forgiveness* (New York: Schocken Books, 1997), 12.

Janowska Camp in Lviv. The story, however established, shows some inconsistencies. Szlechter was not a composer, but a lyricist. The orchestra forced to accompany executions included instrumental musicians, not singers. Cruel as this statement sounds, singing and lyrics would not be heard over the sound of machine guns. . . .

Over time, legends grew around the "Death Tango." During World War II the term referred to any musical piece performed in death camps. Many people associate it with the musical motif of the song "To ostatnia niedzielia" ["The last Sunday"], popular before the war, also called the song of suicides (in the late 1920s the Leningrad Tea-Jazz's repertoire featured a Russian version under the title "Burnt by the Sun"). The song's Argentine roots predate World War I, and many versions exist across Europe. "Death Tango" itself does not refer to a single composition.

Paul Celan was the first to use the metaphors of "death tango" and "grave in the sky" in his poem "Tangoul Mortii," which he included in the May 1947 Rumanian version of *Contemporanul* (later editions and translations use the title "Todesfuge"—"Death Fugue"). This is post-Auschwitz poetry: the twentieth-century *dance macabre*; life and death, music and murder, colliding in the abyss. The title of a recent novel by Iury Vynnychuk borrows Celan's metaphor.[20] Of its four protagonists, friends of different nationalities from the same Lviv courtyard, only a Jewish violinist survives. Till the end of his days he searches for a secret note that will connect the different edges of existence. If you can play it on the violin, the murdered, as if in a ritual of passing, can enter another world to return in a different era, finish things—loves and caresses—they left uncompleted. And give witness, remember things forgotten.

Well before the Holocaust, Emanuel Szlechter wrote about returning to this world: "And if I should be born again some time, then only in Lviv."

We do not know whether he wrote a song titled "Death Tango" while in the ghetto, and Wiesenthal's reminiscence is not sufficient proof. Michał Borwicz, born in Cracow, seven years younger than the lyricist, spent most of the occupation in Lviv. Miraculously, he survived at the Janowska Camp, and committed the rest of his life to documenting the Holocaust. After the war, he edited a poetry anthology devoted to Jews during the war, *Pieśń ujdzie cało* [*The song will escape unharmed*]. His collection does not include a "Death Tango," though he would certainly have wanted such a song to bear witness even if he had heard it

---

20 Iurii Vynnychuk, *Tanho smerti* (Kharkiv: Folio, 2012).

once.²¹ Borwicz, who at the time of the publication headed the Cracow division of the Jewish Historical Commission, mentions a single event that the Nazis authorized at the Lviv ghetto, instructing the musicians to offer actual entertainment to the prisoners. By then Borwicz was already at the Janowska Camp and had heard the story through eyewitness accounts. People, each in their own way, reflected their circumstances; in the face of imminent death, songs offered "a march through a cemetery of prewar customs and sentiments. A last look for those walking towards death."²²

When we weigh the possibility that Szlechter may have written lyrics to a "Death Tango," we must bear this in mind: contrary to the title of Borwicz's anthology, most works created in the ghetto during the war perished alongside their authors. "The cry of bloody silence" is a metaphor Borwicz uses to convey the desolation that follows yet another "action" in the ghetto—fringes of possessions, strewn notes, with no one left to collect them. Many noted writers and their creations, Bruno Schulz's close friend Debora Vogel among them, shared in this fate. The miracle of survival graced only a few and came at a terribly high price.²³

A DREAM

In Poland of the 1930s, one of the best-known composers of film scores was Henryk Wars. He wrote the melody to the cheerful Batiar (hoodlum) waltz "Only in Lviv." Once he reached Lviv, the Soviets hired him to conduct the Lviv Tea-Jazz orchestra. This distinguished creator of popular music quickly began amassing creative triumphs. During the spring and summer of 1940, his band toured the USSR with great success, and soon after he received an offer to write the musical score for *Mechta*. The film's director, Mikhail Romm, was a prominent Soviet filmmaker, and at the time was serving as artistic director of the State Board for the Production of Film and of the studio Mosfilm. In May

---

21   Michał M. Borwicz, *Pieśń ujdzie cało* (Cracow: Centralna Komisja Historyczna, 1947), and Michał Borwicz, *Literatura w obozie* (Cracow: Centralna Żydowska Komisja Historyczna, 1946).
22   Borwicz, *Pieśń ujdzie cało*, 21.
23   Leon Weliczker, *Brygada śmierci (Sonderkommando 105). Pamiętnik*, ed. Rachela Auerbach (Łódź: Wydawnictwo Żydowskiej Komisji Historycznej przy Centralnym Komitecie Żydów Polskich, 1946). Reprinted as Leon Weliczker, *Brygada śmierci (Sonderkommando 105). Pamiętnik*, ed. Rachela Auerbach (Lublin: Ośrodek "Brama Grodzka—Teatr NN," 2012). A complete version appeared after Weliczker emigrated to the West: Leon Weliczker Wells, *The Janowska Road* (New York: Macmillan, 1963).

1940 *Vilna Ukraina* reported that *Dream*'s screenwriters Mikhail Romm and Evgeny Gabrilovich had made it their mission to depict "the harsh and hopeless lives of workers, their dreams of liberation and true existence in the Soviet land" against the backdrop of the "rotting capitalism of former Poland."[24] Romm specialized in propaganda movies, and the "liberation" substantially increased the need for brainwashing.

At the same time as Mikhail Romm began working on the melodrama *Dream*, Abraham Room was filming *Wind from the East*, which celebrated the first anniversary of the Red Army's takeover of Lviv and other Western territories of the Polish Republic. The film was made in a Kyiv studio, with music composed by Vasyl Barvinsky. Wanda Wasilewska was a consultant and helped to weave together the tale of the glory of the Soviet troops and the anxious welcome they received. Yet another related film dates back to the same period: *Liberation* by Oleksandr Dovzhenko, screened in Lviv theaters on September 11 in anticipation of the first anniversary. But soon the film, though ideologically without blemish, vanished from theaters. Perhaps the NKVD's poor opinion of Dovzhenko played a part.[25]

Unlike the Kyiv-produced *Wind from the East*, Romm's Moscow-made *Dream*, with a musical score by Wars performed by the Lviv Tea-Jazz, attracted a sizeable audience. The musical setting may have contributed to its success, but even more importantly, the story took place in Lviv. A few scenes were recorded outdoors, and the majority at the Mosfilm studio. Curiously, the footage did not match the introductory captions which warned that Lviv was "a city of five churches, two prisons, thirty-nine houses of prostitution . . ." Much of the plot played out inside the villa where the protagonists rented rooms. The villa's name, Dream, signaled a contrast with the harsh lives of its inhabitants "in the years preceding the unification of Ukrainian territories." The female lead came to the city like "thousands of people searching for work and happiness," and her plight was supposed to move Soviet viewers to tears. Music played up the ideological divisions in the film. In scenes calculated to turn the audience against the nefarious informer or police chief who persecute the noble protagonists as they carry out illegal communist activities, jazzy tunes resound. They hint at the moral corruption of not just those antiheroes, but by proxy, of the entire local establishment.

---

24 "Film pro kolyshniu Zakhidniu Ukrainu," *Vil'na Ukraïna*, no. 114, May 17, 1940.
25 Dokumenty iz arkhivnoï spravy na Dovzhenka O. P.: Vytiah iz operatyvnoho povidomlennia pro vyslovliuvannia Dovzhenka O. P., 16.12.1939, HDA SBU, f. 68, op. 292, k. 26.

As the director began filming *Dream*, he faced a multitude of circumstances which arrived as a corollary to the "liberation" he so praised. This was neither the first nor the last time he was to deal with these difficulties, though seemingly no filmmaker was more loyal to the Soviet authorities. In 1939, Romm received an award from Stalin for his films about Lenin. But by spring of 1940, he was focusing all energy on saving his relative and namesake Michał, who was a physician and reserve lieutenant in the Polish Army. The Romms were a Jewish family with long-standing ties to Vilnius. In the late nineteenth century they owned the largest publishing house in the "Jerusalem of the North," which published books in Hebrew and Yiddish. The director's father had been sent to Siberia for his engagement in the socialist movement, and Mikhail Romm was born in Irkutsk. His subsequent path reflects the fate of an entire generation born in the early twentieth century; too young to fight in the 1917 Bolshevik revolution, by the interwar period they had to step in for the old Bolsheviks eliminated in the Great Purge. The rest of the family remained in Vilnius; in the fall of 1920 the city became part of the Republic of Poland. Born in Vilnius, younger than Mikhail by a few years, Dr. Michał Romm received his draft card on the eve of the war in 1939. As one of more than 20,000 Polish officers imprisoned by the Soviets, he was slated for execution on Stalin's orders. Thanks to the intervention of his director cousin, who luckily had made Stalin's favorite movie about Lenin, Dr. Romm was at the last minute pulled from the transport of officers traveling from the camp in Ostashkov to Mednoye, the site of the looming atrocity.[26]

Dream did not come to cinemas till the second half of 1943. Officially the war had caused the delay. The production date is listed as 1941; later the director maintained that the filming ended on June 22, and war conditions necessitated a two-year wait. Romm knew how to separate reality and propaganda, and he proved it with one of the most important films from the 1960s thaw. USSR audiences interpreted his 1966 documentary *Obyknovennyi fashizm* [*Ordinary Fascism*], also known to English-speaking audiences under the titles *Triumph over Violence* and *Echo of the Jackboot*, as a critique of totalitarianism. Another indication of Romm's sober outlook on the Soviet system is his 1943 letter to Stalin, published in a collection of his reminiscences *Ustnye rasskazy* [*Stories*

---

26 Aleksander Gieysztor, ed., *Katyń. Dokumenty zbrodni*, vol. 2: *Zagłada (marzec-czerwiec 1940)* (Warsaw: Naczelna Dyrekcja Archiwów Państwowych, 1998), 243–4, 469, 472.

told], but not until the *perestroika* days of 1989, and after his death. In this letter Romm lamented the fate of his film and of other directors' work, including Oleksandr Dovzhenko, who fell into disfavor for his war documentary *Ukraina u vohni* [*Ukraine on fire*].

Did Romm have an inkling as to why his *Dream* stayed on the shelf for two years? Perhaps some idea, but he certainly was not privy to the full spectrum of reasons. Once the Sikorski-Maysky treaty was signed on July 30, 1941, his film could have been "harmful to the alliance." Even before both sides signed the agreement, and soon after the September 17, 1940 festivities commemorating the first anniversary of "liberation," the anti-Polish propaganda had begun to ease up. Though Romm held a high position in the hierarchy of Soviet cinematography (from 1940 until 1943 he was the artistic director with the State Board for the Production of Film), the authorities used various methods to stall *Dream*. Finally the film arrived in theaters in September 1943—a few months after the USSR broke off diplomatic relations with the Polish government-in-exile. Formally the crisis erupted because of the Polish position regarding the Katyn atrocity. In a strange coincidence—Romm's cousin barely escaped the Katyn massacre—the director's troubles with *Dream* stemmed from a directly related political crisis. Could the Soviet director have guessed what end befell the officers? We can imagine that he kept such thoughts at bay. In contrast with another survivor, professor Stanisław Swianiewicz, Romm's cousin, the lieutenant Michał Romm who was yanked from the officer transport at the last minute, did not leave behind any testimony of these dramatic events.

In the fall of 1943 the movie was shown in cinemas. By that point it could again provide ideological support for the Red Army's counteroffensive as the Soviets took back Lviv from the Nazis. By the time Soviet audiences watched *Dream* for the first time, Henryk Wars's band was crossing the Middle East with Anders' Army. Next spring, as the Red Army neared Lviv, the core of the Lviv Tea-Jazz, contributors of the soundtrack to the film, was supporting Polish troops on Monte Cassino.

After the triumph of *The Great Journey* (1946), whose main plot line played out on Monte Cassino, Henryk Wars emigrated to the United States. He continued to write popular music as well as compose film scores. If we use other postwar emigrants as a yardstick, he found success. Yet the American dream proved elusive. In the history of popular music, Wars figures mainly as the creator of Polish popular songs.

Henryk Wars led the Anders' Army band Polish Parade, 1943

"AT THE FIRST FLUTTER OF MY HEART . . ."[27]

The extant albums by the Lviv Tea-Jazz orchestra, recorded in 1941, highlight the director's and the soloists' names. As previously mentioned, Eugeniusz Bodo performed "Only in Lviv," under the title "The Farewell Song." Albert Harris sang "Zapomnienie" ["Forgetting"], translated by the Kyiv-born Ref-Ren (Feliks Konarski), and Renata Iarosevych—the beloved "Na pierwszy znak, gdy serce drgnie" ["At the First Flutter of My Heart"], a piece from the 1933 film *Spy in a Mask* and originally popularized by Hanka Ordonówna. Jarosiewicz was a brand-new addition to the group of famous Warsaw artists. Naturally, she sang in Russian, the lyrics reworked by Pavel Grigoriev. The song became an instant hit.

Who was the new singer? Irena Iarosevych, as that was her actual name, must have truly impressed the Warsaw musicians to be hired as a soloist in an

---

27 I would like to thank Oleh Pavlyshyn for drawing my attention to Bohdan Nahaylo's documentary devoted to Iryna Iarosevych-Anders—*Renata Bogdanska*, vol. 1: *Ukrainian Dimension*, vol. 2: *Polish Dimension* (Ukrainian Institute in London, 2011).

ensemble consisting of noted performers. Her chances to be seen as an equal by the select circle were slim: not only had she never even been near Warsaw, she came of age in Lviv and took her first steps on Ukrainian stages. Surely, to the stars from the capital she would have looked very provincial. Yet she was well-known among the Ukrainian musical circles in Lviv, singing in the jazz band Yabtso with Leonid Jablonsky, Anatol Kos-Anatolsky, Bohdan Vesolovsky, and Myron Eberhart. She also performed popular hits such as "La Paloma" and "Miami Rhumba"—in Ukrainian—and original romantic songs, such as "Choven khytaietsia sered vody" ["A Boat Rocks in The Water"], and numbers composed by Vesolovsky (with whom she was involved at the time).

Iarosevych first opted for the artistic alias "Renata Bogdańska" during the war, as she began singing in the group *Polish Parade*. Before then she had used her maiden name Iarosevych; prewar Ukrainian posters feature her as "Rena Iarosevych," while on sleeves of Soviet records her last name was adjusted to Iarosevich. The later alias "Renata Bogdańska" was meant to suggest Polish identity.

Irena Iarosevych was born in 1917 in Freudenthal (now Bruntál in the Czech Republic), as the third and youngest child of Olena Nyzhankivska and Mykola Iarosevych, a Greek-Catholic priest who had been imprisoned in Talerhof (1914–15) and later served among Ukrainian refugees in Czechia as their chaplain. In the mid-1920s the family settled in Lviv. Irena attended the Lviv high school of the Basilian Sisters. Like most Ukrainian youth from educated families, she was a member of the *Plast* (scouts). The family was musically inclined (her mother's brother was the composer Ostap Nyzhankivsky) and Irena attended music school. She was a classmate of Iury Shukhevych (executed by the NKVD on June 27, 1941)[28] at the Mykola Lysenko Musical Institute. As was common for Ukrainians who came of age in the interwar years, her peers were close to the Organization of Ukrainian Nationalists. Yet Irena's official biography keeps silent about her non-Polish ethnicity or any traces connecting her to the Ukrainian creative milieu of prewar Lviv.

She started performing in the 1930s with the band Yabtso.[29] In 1938, when the group's heart and soul, the composer Bohdan Vesolovsky, joined the Ukrainian units fighting for Transcarpathian Ukraine, Yabtso dissolved. Soon

---

28 "Spysok rozstrilianykh," *Ukraïns'ki shchodenni visti*, no. 1, July 5, 1941.
29 Oleksandr Zelins'kyi, *Bohdan Vesolovs'kyi, Renata Bohdans'ka ta Leonid Iablons'kyi—predstavnyky ukraïns'koï rozvazhalnoï muzyky w Halychyni (1930-ti roky)* (Lviv: Naukovi zapysky NTSh, 2009).

World War II came, and with it, the Soviet "liberation" of Lviv. Iarosevych joined Henryk Wars's group. In Kyiv, at the start of Tea-Jazz's tour, she married her stage partner Gwidon Borucki, who had recruited her to the band in the first place. The two met in the summer of 1939 in the Polish resort town of Zakopane, where they had come to earn some extra money as entertainers. In late 1941 Iarosevych and her husband joined the Polish Army in the USSR and traversed the entire Anders's route through the Middle East to Monte Cassino to Rome. She eventually settled in London.

Irena Iarosevych found success as a singer and a film actress. Soon after the premiere of *The Great Journey*, which took place in Rome in 1946, her affair with General Anders, conspicuous during the Italian campaign, became public knowledge. The couple married in 1948. In postwar London, Irena, now the wife of Władysław Anders, worked with Marian Hemar and Feliks Konarski (Ref-Ren) singing the most beloved songs of Lviv with Hemar's cabaret. Irena, together with Hemar and Ref-Ren, engendered the city's enduring myth, and Iarosevych became an icon of the "vanished Lviv."

Did Irena Iarosevych-Anders choose Polish nationality, or was she merely loyal to her husband? Are the two possibilities intertwined? Her many public statements as well as her foreword to the first edition of her husband's book printed in Poland seem to suggest that both motivations played a role: "I think of my husband, who passed away twenty years ago, with great respect for his stance and his achievements in serving the Nation."[30] As a wife, her duty was to care for his reputation and his place in history.[31] But she went above and beyond those responsibilities, supporting the polonocentric narrative that dominated among the emigrant community and overshadowed or even contested Ukrainian and Jewish perspectives. Did the years before and during the war, the shared fate of Poles, Ukrainians, and Jews, leave an imprint on her? In 1943, the army published a prayer book for soldiers of the eastern rite, thanks to the efforts of Jerzy Giedroyc, director of the Polish Second Corps Military Books and Periodicals division. Did she keep her copy?

We cannot not ask these questions, yet comprehensive answers are beyond our reach. If journals, letters, and memoirs could have shed more light on her life, none are available today. All that remains are documentary films, occasional

---

30 Władysław Anders, *Bez ostatniego rozdziału. Wspomnienia z lat 1939–1946* (Lublin: Test, 1992), 3.
31 Compare the statement from the foreword: "[I]n its importance this volume achieved the status of a textbook of our history in those most difficult World War Two years." Ibid., foreword.

press interviews, and secondhand accounts. Our sole insight into the Ukrainian thread of Iarosevych's past comes from Bohdan Nahaylo's documentary work, especially the *Ukrainian Dimension*.[32]

THE GREAT JOURNEY

Michał Waszyński's film *The Great Journey*, with musical score by Henryk Wars, offers a fictional-documentary take on the story of the Polish Army from the outbreak of the war until its end. The main plotline plays out against the backdrop of the Allied troops fighting to break through the Gustav line. As the protagonist struggles for his life in a field hospital, the film recounts the great journey of Anders' Army soldiers: from the September campaign, through Soviet camps, to the Middle East, and, finally, on to the Italian campaign.

Renata Bogdańska (Irena Iarosevych) in *The Great Journey*, 1946.

---

32 Bohdan Nahaylo, "The Muse of Bloodlands. Reconstructing the concealed biography of Renata Bogdańska-Anders, aka Irena Yarosevych" (paper presentation and documentary at the Ukrainian Institute, London, September 27, 2012), http://ukrainianinstitute.org.uk/news_182/.

The film centers on a single event, the battle of Monte Cassino, and the song "Red Poppies on Monte Cassino" provides its musical background. The hero's beloved, Irena, is played by Renata Bogdańska (Irena Iarosevych), and the film uses her actual first name and her profession (singer), while the rest is fiction: the female lead and her love are sent to Soviet camps. New heroic biographies emerge. The protagonist's diary entries, read by a nurse who has fallen in love with him, drive the plot. To emphasize its historical background, the movie makes use of documentary footage captured by the army's film section, led by Michał Waszyński. The journal (not authentic) serves to further the movie's chief mission: to generate the legend of Anders' Army.

While carrying a message of Polish patriotism, the movie obscured stories of Ukrainian and Jewish soldiers and civilians, left out because they did not fit the Polish national narrative the film sought to fashion. Such was the case even though the director, the composer, and some of the actors were members of other ethnic groups. Some, though not all, made the choice to identify as Polish during their great journey. Those may have been pragmatic choices: to join Anders' Army one had to declare Polish nationality, first and foremost because the Soviet government refused to apply the Sikorski-Maysky agreement to people of Jewish or Ukrainian ethnicity.[33]

Beria, head of the NKVD at the time, informed Stalin that of the almost 400,000 released persons, only half were Polish. As soon as the Soviets realized that the desire to join Anders' Army was spreading like wildfire, they acted to keep non-Poles from enlisting. The November 29, 1939 resolution of the USSR Supreme Soviet Presidium stipulated that they were Soviet citizens and should thus be drafted into the Red Army. Despite the efforts of ambassador Stanisław Kot, the Soviets would not discharge Galician Ukrainians from camps (most former political activists died there in 1941–42, of emaciation and exhaustion). The Soviets strictly controlled the recruitment process by Polish representatives

---

33 Some of the sources of information about the Soviet policy towards former Polish citizens are: Stanisław Kot, *Listy z Rosji do gen. Sikorskiego* (London: Jutro Polski, 1955), 189, 437; Roman Buczek, "Działalność opiekuńcza Ambasady RP w ZSRR w latach 1941–1943," *Zeszyty Historyczne* 29 (1974): 42–115; Zygmunt Bohusz-Szyszko, *Czerwony sfinks* (London: Polski Dom Wydawniczy, 1946), 186; Klemens Rudnicki, *Na polskim szlaku* (London: Gryf, 1957), 200–1. Ambassador Kot reported on the attitude of the army leadership towards persons of Ukrainian and Jewish background particularly critically in his March 1943 memorandum to the Prime Minister Sikorski, in which he listed the most jarring behaviors and named the responsible leadership. See "Stosunki ambasady RP w ZSRR z wojskiem," Polish Institute and Sikorski Museum, zespół Prezydium Rady Ministrów 102/3, k. 5, http://polishinstitute.com/prm/prm102c.pdf, accessed on June 15, 2015.

in the USSR. Consequently, even at the first stage it was paramount to hide one's non-Polish ethnicity. The draft board, which included official representatives of the NKVD, verified the recruits' ethnic background.

But volunteers of backgrounds other than Polish faced more barriers beyond that which Soviet authorities continuously put up. A number of testimonies reveal that the army limited eligibility based on religion and nationality.[34] Of particular significance is a statement Ambassador Kot presented to the Polish government:

> They have not let a single Ukrainian out so far. Only now do I find out Dmytro Lewicki [Levytsky] was in the army in Buzuluk, the old and ailing UNDO commandant, no other politician from the party got released. He took refuge in the care of our army in Buzuluk. The chief of staff received him, but issued no orders to provide for him, nor did he tell the Embassy that such an important figure was in the army's care. Lewicki was even forbidden from dining with noncommissioned officers, and was shipped south with a transport, where he soon died of hunger and fatigue. We had struck gold and then lost it.[35]

Before qualifying to join the Polish Army persons of Jewish descent had to fill out a questionnaire so that their loyalty in the years 1939–41 could be verified.[36] By imposing this requirement, the leadership attempted to exclude from service those who had been open to Soviet rule or were guilty of having supported it in some way. No matter the obstacles, many Jews and Ukrainians found ways to enlist (in contrast, Belarussians did not encounter similar obstacles). Commanders and their officers, especially from the Division of Propaganda, made an effort to create an atmosphere of religious and ethnic

---

34 Ukrainian authors Pavlo Shavel, Bohdan Durbak, and Orest Korchak-Horodysky make references to these criteria in the émigré press. My information stems from Ievhen Matseliukh, "Ukraintsi v Armii Andersa," *Pols'ki studii* 7 (2014): 105–116. Jarosław Rudniański's account, recorded in March and April of 2000, specifies that conscripts had to change their identity from Jewish to Polish and that the board verified religious affiliation by having applicants recite the Lord's Prayer and the Hail Mary. These assertions appear exaggerated and difficult to verify (Relacja Jarosława Rudniańskiego z 2000 roku, 1/1193, k. 17). See also Jerzy Grzybowski, *Białorusini w polskich regularnych formacjach wojskowych w latach 1918–1945* (Warsaw: Oficyna Wydawnicza Rytm, 2007), esp. 225.

35 Kot, *Listy z Rosji do gen. Sikorskiego*, 189.

36 Krzysztof Jasiewicz collected and published almost ninety such documents: Krzysztof Jasiewicz, *Rzeczywistość sowiecka w świadectwach polskich Żydów* (Warsaw: Rytm, 2009).

tolerance, but cases of xenophobia did occur.[37] The Soviets were very attuned to those instances and seized on them in later propaganda communications to dissuade Jews who still remained in the USSR from joining Polish units. Mirroring Soviet denouncements, the Jewish Telegraph Agency disseminated this information in the West.[38] Similarly, the few extant postwar Ukrainian reminiscences focus chiefly on xenophobia.[39] Such perspectives neatly feed into the national narratives that dominate emigrant communities. In order to emphasize martyrdom, it becomes paramount to feature the persecution of one's own nation, without leaving space for examples of inter-ethnic tolerance and support.

In 1941, the Lviv Tea-Jazz, whose core consisted of Polish-Jews, ceased to exist. As part of the Anders' Army a new band was formed under the name of Polish Parade. As Michał Waszyński's path illustrates, the band members changed their national identification. To enlist, the director of *Dybbuk* declared Warsaw as his place of birth, and Roman-Catholicism as his religious affiliation, though he had been born in Kovel into a family of Chassidic tradition.[40] Irena Iarosevych took similar steps. Henryk Wars made a different choice. Born into a Jewish family in Warsaw, after demobilizing in 1947 he emigrated to the United States and became an American composer. 1946 was the last time he wrote a score for a Polish movie. It was *The Great Journey*. In addition to prewar hits, including those from Lviv, the film resounded with other songs which members of Polish Parade got to know during the Soviet occupation. A particularly poignant scene in the film depicts prisoners

---

37 See Anders, *Bez ostatniego rozdziału. Wspomnienia z lat 1939–1946*, 133–4; Iezhy Gedroits', "Pro vidnoshennia do ukraïntsiv," *Visti kombatanta* 31 (1976): 34–5; Ryszard Terlecki, "The Jewish Issue in the Polish Army in the USSR and the Near East. 1941–1944," in *Jews in Eastern Poland and the USSR, 1939–46*, ed. Norman Davies and Antony Polonsky (London: Macmillan, 1991), 161–71. Indirectly, the procedure described by Krzysztof Jasiewicz also speaks to this practice (Jasiewicz, *Rzeczywistość sowiecka 1939–1941 w świadectwach polskich Żydów*, 45–50).

38 Terlecki, "The Jewish Issue in the Polish Army in the USSR and the Near East. 1941–1944," 164.

39 One example is the memoir of an Anders' Army soldier Mykhailo Kozy edited by the OUN activist Zinovy Knysh. See Zinovii Knysh, *Za chuzhu spravu: rozpovid' Mykhaila Koziia z sela Bohdanivka povit Skalat pro ioho pryhody v bol'shevyts'komu poloni i v pol'skyi armii henerala Andresa* (Toronto: Sribna Surma, 1961).

40 Samuel Blumenfeld, *Człowiek, który chciał być księciem* (Warsaw: Świat Książki, 2008). The book focuses on the pre- and postwar years. Details of the director's life in the USSR are unknown; the Russian human rights organization Memorial published a list of people who suffered communist-era repressions, but it did not include Waszyński's name.

working under inhumane conditions in a Soviet labor camp as the NKVD spreads terror. A joyful, pathos-filled song "Shiroka strana rodnaia" ("Vast is the Motherland") provides the musical backdrop. Its chorus asserts "I know of no other such country / Where a man can breathe so freely."

The stories of Irena Iarosevych-Anders and her better-known friends from the band Lviv Tea-Jazz make up only a part of the history of Lviv's artistic milieu. Most often journalists and biographers gravitate toward dramatic trials and tribulations. Few choose to write of the unequivocal choices dictated by survival strategies, of adopted identities. Yet these were totalitarian times, when such decisions carried the weightiest of consequences. They could save or end one's life.

Neither Henryk Wars nor Michał Waszyński, Gwidon Borucki or Irena Iarosevych-Anders left behind journals or memoirs. All four were leading figures in mid-twentieth-century Polish culture. They completed the great journey. Each one—albeit under somewhat different circumstances—elected to self-identify as Polish. The Polish national narrative effaced their non-Polish ethnicities.

"And all the poppies on Monte Cassino will be redder for Poles' blood in their soil."

Portrait of Mykhailo Rudnytsky by Iaroslava Muzyka, 1936

CHAPTER 6

Ukrainian Hamlet

> To be, or not to be, that is the question:
> Whether 'tis nobler in the mind to suffer
> The slings and arrows of outrageous fortune,
> Or to take arms against a sea of troubles
> And by opposing end them. ...
> —Shakespeare, *Hamlet*, 3:1, ll. 56–60.

In popular perception, Hamlet's famed soliloquy, much like the literary character himself, has come to symbolize an indecisive and weak personality. However, the current chapter's title does not draw on this common yet simplistic reading. Adhering to genre principles, Shakespeare arranged for destiny to place his hero in an impossible predicament. The protagonist's tragedy is greater than the choice between suffering silently and resisting evil, between courageously bearing your fate and rebelling against it. Hamlet's ultimate alternatives are life or death. As I weave in Hamlet's monologue and other excerpts from the play throughout the chapter, my goal is not to refresh our memory of Shakespeare's drama, but to suggest ways of rereading it within the framework of a particular place and time: Lviv of 1943. Precisely when Mykhailo Rudnytsky, our current protagonist, finished *Hamlet*'s Ukrainian translation.

Quotes from *Hamlet* serve as counterpoints to this chapter's main narrative current. Mykhailo Rudnytsky translated the play in 1942 and Lviv's Theater of the Opera staged it the following year. In a parallel fashion, I attempt to flesh out a quandary all thinking humans face: the difficulty of exploring truth, which emerges as, inevitably, we encounter ambiguity. At the same time, I wish to call attention to the pathos that defines the protagonist: Hamlet is destined to fail regardless of what choice he makes. To opt for life will cause unbearable suffering and certainly bring calamity onto his loved ones; choosing death will break the commandment "Thou shall not kill."

Mykhailo Rudnytsky's personnel form

Volodymyr Blavatsky and Iosyp Hirniak, two directors at the Lviv Theater of the Opera, on the eve of *Hamlet*'s Ukrainian premiere, 1943

Above all, however, I wish to give the reader a sense of how Ukrainian spectators in Lviv may have received *Hamlet* that year, what additional interpretations this reception yielded, and which connections simply jump out at us as we attempt to decipher the life of Mykhailo Rudnytsky: Shakespeare's translator and this chapter's protagonist.

At the start of the second year of German occupation, on September 21, 1943, the Theater of the Opera in Lviv at Adolf-Hitler Ring staged *Hamlet*'s Ukrainian premiere. Iosyp Hirniak, a student and successor of Les Kurbas (founder of Kharkiv's Berezil Theater) directed the play. Volodymyr Blavatsky, director of the Theater of the Opera, played the leading part. It was at his request that Mykhailo Rudnytsky, poet, translator, and the greatest critic in Lviv and all of Ukraine, prepared a contemporary translation.

Meanwhile, the Red Army was embarking on a counteroffensive. The Dnipro line had not been broken yet, but Lviv sounded air raid alarms with increasing frequency. Rumors circulated that any minute the Red Army would appear on the other bank of the Poltva. Many Lvivians thought the return of the Soviets inevitable. The Ghetto had been liquidated, and most of its residents perished in Bełżec. At the Janowska Camp even those able to work were systematically murdered. In town, roundups intensified. Almost half a million residents of the District of Galicia were sent to Germany to perform forced labor. For several months, Ukrainians were drafted into the SS Division Galizien. More and more Polish refugees from Volhynia, escaping ethnic violence, streamed into the city.

To stage a premiere of *Hamlet* at such a moment meant to spite history's dictum *inter arma silent musae*. How could this performance have come about under the conditions of occupation and censorship? Firstly, in the General Government, Ukrainians were the only group (besides Germans) permitted to conduct cultural activities, though between censorship and modest financial resources, there were limits. Additionally, by the turn of 1942 and 1943, the Third Reich "softened" its restrictions a bit, allowing for works by foreign playwrights to be staged as long as they displayed a "heroic spirit." Shakespeare's plays made the cut.

A young Lviv writer by the name of Ostap Tarnavsky penned a press announcement about the upcoming play, adding (incorrectly) that the translator himself attended the dress rehearsal. Almost half a century later Tarnavsky's memoir was published. His entry on the topic of *Hamlet* names the translator, though the whole of the passage abounds in oblique references:

> *For personal reasons* [during the German occupation; note and typeset O. H.], Mykhailo Rudnytsky did not become active either, though he kept in contact with *certain literary figures* and did not stop working, translating dramatic works for the theater and editing and writing articles for our press and publishing houses, *without, however, signing his name*. It is Mykhailo Rudnytsky to whom we owe *Hamlet*'s first Ukrainian performance in Lviv, as he was the one to translate Shakespeare's work, commissioned by the theater's director Volodymyr Blavatsky.[1]

Tarnavsky's hints imply that Mykhailo Rudnytsky's status during the German occupation was uncertain. Despite that, the many people who kept abreast of his situation could find him without major difficulties, or at least without resorting to conspiracy. In the interwar years Rudnytsky was the most renowned literary critic and at the start of the Soviet occupation he worked as a journalist at the newspaper *Vilna Ukraina*. With this much exposure, what exactly were his circumstances in Nazi-occupied Lviv? Are assertions of

---

1   Ostap Tarnavs'kyi, *Literaturnyi L'viv 1939–1944* (Lviv: Prosvita, 1995), 70.

Polish memoirists accurate that Ukrainians who established ties with either the Soviet or the German regimes were bound by a silent agreement: cover for us now, and we will have your back later? Popular opinion among Poles held that Ukrainian solidarity was based on blood ties, as if in the mafia. During German rule it guaranteed safety to Ukrainians who had served as Soviet functionaries, in return for the alleged protection awarded to nationalists and Germanophiles during the Soviet occupation. Indeed, during the first Soviet occupation, Rudnytsky worked at *Vilna Ukraina* and taught at the university. This would have given the German occupier grounds to classify him as a "Bolshevik agent." Nevertheless, even Tarnavsky's statement above, so conspiratorial in tone, does not suggest that group solidarity played a role in Rudnytsky's case. During the German occupation, the greatest among Lvivian critics remained on the sidelines of cultural activity. Was he hiding from the Germans? If so, why would he attend *Hamlet*'s dress rehearsal? If not, then why did he continue signing even his most blistering pieces, but did not publish his translation, so masterful that the most accomplished translator might envy it? Did he not want to or was he unable to do so? No literary historical source at hand gives us an answer, or even attempts to pose these questions.[2]

Mykhailo Rudnytsky was the only one of his siblings who stayed in Lviv after the Red Army marched in. His wife, Marta Rudnytska (her father Ievhen Olesnytsky, a noted Lviv attorney, had served as a representative to the Polish National Assembly—*Sejm Krajowy*—as well as to the parliament in Vienna in the Austro-Hungarian era), emigrated across the ocean, together with the couple's adult daughter Daryna. While in the US, Marta kept in contact with her husband's siblings, but never saw Rudnytsky again. Could it be that Rudnytsky felt he had no reason to flee from the Soviet administration, since he had never participated in public life during the German occupation, and, in contrast to his younger brother Ivan and sister Milena, did not engage in politics? Perhaps he thought, like so many who lived through the ravages of the war and the Holocaust, that Soviet rule would create opportunities, while fleeing west with the Germans would only put him in danger? Did the need to remain in his own cultural element trump all other considerations? Or was he not determined enough to make a snap decision, and then circumstances decided for him?

---

2   An interesting study devoted to the critic was published by Mykola Ilnytsky: Mykola Il'nyts'kyi, *Krytyky i kryterii. Literaturno-krytychna dumka v Zakhidnii Ukraïni 20–30-ykh rokiv XX st.* (Lviv: VTNL, 1998), 52–78. Oleh Bahan's foreword "Koryfei liberal'noï literaturnoï krytyky" to Mykhailo Rudnyts'kyi, *Vid Myrnoho do Khvyl'ovoho; Mizh ideieiu i formoiu* (Drohobych: Vidrodzhennia, 2009), 3–26, includes a biographical sketch of Rudnytsky.

Was it possibly the most difficult moment of his life, not unlike the predicament Shakespeare had his protagonist face? Or perhaps his choice to stay resulted from an earlier resolution, made back in 1939?

Hamlet's premiere occurred at the height of the war, a dozen or so years after Ukrainian theater in Soviet Ukraine had reached its zenith with legendary performances at Les Kurbas's Berezil Theater. The timing of the premiere seems as improbable as do Rudnytsky's mysterious circumstances and his choice to stay as the Soviets approached. Let us explore the parallels between *Hamlet*'s performance and the saga of this contemporaneous Ukrainian intellectual.

A GALICIAN COSMOPOLITE

> Absent thee from felicity a while,
> And in this harsh world draw thy breath in pain
> To tell my story.
> —Shakespeare, *Hamlet*, 5:2, ll. 310–14

Mykhailo Rudnytsky (1889–1975), the eldest of the Rudnytsky children (other siblings from oldest to youngest: Volodymyr, Milena, Ivan, and Anton), stayed on in Lviv after 1944. In 1907 he enrolled in law at Lviv University, back then named after Emperor Francis I. His father, Ivan, was the first in the family to choose a secular profession—notary; for generations back, the males in the family had heeded the call of Greek-Catholic priesthood. Until his death, his father wandered Galician towns, trying to set up his own notary office. Ivan Rudnytsky died at the age of fifty, leaving behind five children, all under age. Each graduated from the university and went on to achieve a high profile in their respective disciplines. Their mother, Ida Spiegel, ensured that they received an education. Ida came from a family of Jewish merchants and married the son of a Greek-Catholic priest against the wishes of both families, after an engagement that lasted ten years. She was twenty-seven then (the average marrying age for women was nineteen at the time). At her Roman-Catholic baptism she took the name Olga.

In those years Ukrainian-Jewish marriages were quite rare and usually resulted in a split from one's family. In this case, Ivan Rudnytsky married Ida only after his mother, who was vehemently opposed to the union, passed away. Even after World War I, Ukrainian-Jewish couples faced obstacles from immediate families. A case in point are two painters, Roman Selsky and Margit

Ostap Ortwin was the president of the Lviv chapter of the Polish Writers' Union

Reich; their relatives on both sides put up roadblocks, as Selsky related in his memoirs. My mother also told stories about Iaroslava Muzyka and Ludwik Lille, who had to break off their relationship in similar circumstances.

Ivan and Olga (Ida) Rudnytsky felt most at ease in Polish and probably spoke it at home. At the end of the nineteenth century, the era of Galician autonomy, Galician Jews quickly Polonized, and the long-standing Polonization of Greek-Catholic clergy carried on. Many families who chose Ukrainian identity nevertheless spoke Polish at home; in the chapter "Haven at the Clinic" we met Maksym Muzyka who came from such a background; he later became a friend of Rudnytsky.

When he began studying law in 1907, Mykhailo Rudnytsky only had one living parent and could not count on financial support from his immediate family, although relatives on his mother's side helped with housing. Simultaneously Rudnytsky started working at the Polish Bookstore at 3 Akademicka. Its owner, Bernard Połoniecki, was a relative of Olga's and Rudnytsky's guardian. On Połoniecki's recommendation (the man, a Polonized Jew,[3] was a major

---

[3] Maria Konopka, ed., *Bernard Połoniecki, księgarz lwowski: dzienniki, pamiętniki i listy z lat 1880–1943* (Warsaw: Biblioteka Narodowa, 2006).

publisher of the modernist literature of *Young Poland*), Rudnytsky became the secretary to the leading modernist critic Ostap Ortwin, who oversaw the editorial department. At the bookstore, Rudnytsky met the famous modernist poet Leopold Staff. Among the titles he prepared for publication under Ortwin's supervision was Stanisław Brzozowski's *Diary* (1913). Many educated Ukrainians of his generation, including Rudnytsky, fell under the formative influence of Brzozowski's social philosophy. Ortwin persuaded Rudnytsky to change his major to philosophy; during the 1910–1911 semester the future critic studied at the Sorbonne. This period also marks the beginning of his literary activity and of contacts with the group *Moloda Muza* (*Young Muse*), whose name purposely invokes *Young Poland* to emphasize the close ties between both circles. Rudnytsky finished his studies in Lviv on the eve of the war. In July of 1914, he received the degree of Doctor of Philosophy for his thesis *Ivan Franko as a Writer and Critic*. The title issues an open challenge to the academic community, which had barred Franko from a university appointment.

During World War I, Mykhailo Rudnytsky proved luckier than his younger brother Ivan, whose travails we followed in the chapter "Academic Snapshots." Although twenty-five, he evaded being drafted into the Imperial-Royal Army and fighting in the war (on the other hand Ivan, injured in battle, was a prisoner of war for two years). This is not to say, however, that the tumult of war passed him by. In September of 1914, the occupier suspended the activities of the Polish Bookstore. Incidentally, a conflict between the owner, Połoniecki, and the editor, Ortwin, had already shaken up the publishing house. But Rudnytsky immediately found work as a court translator, since he spoke several languages fluently, including those then deemed essential: German, Russian, and Polish.

The Russian occupation of Galicia continued. Before the Austro-German offensive in June of 1915, Rudnytsky evacuated with the rest of the office and spent the remainder of the war in Kyiv. A contemporary scholar seized on that fact to purport that Rudnytsky may have been an informer for the secret service *Okhranka*, and later for the NKVD[4] (to put it in context, Janusz Korczak was in Kyiv at the same time, also forcibly evacuated there as a physician). From 1917 on, Rudnytsky worked as a German teacher at the Second Kyiv Gymnasium. There he befriended Mykola Zerov, who taught Latin and introduced Rudnytsky to a group of poets later referred to as the "neoclassicists." The

---

4   Bahan, "Koryfei liberal'noï literaturnoï krytyky," 22–3.

circle included Maksym Rylsky, Pavlo Fylypovych, Mykhailo Orest, and Iury Klen. Rudnytsky also lectured at St. Volodymyr University. After the 1917 revolution, his brother fled captivity and reached Kyiv, and from 1918 on they both worked for the government of the Ukrainian People's Republic (UNR) in Kyiv, Mykhailo probably as a translator. There he met Vynnychenko, Petliura, and several other politicians active in the Central Council (he knew Hrushevsky from Lviv)[5]. Until summer of 1919 he interpreted for the Ukrainian diplomatic mission at the peace conference of Versailles.[6] After the fall of the UNR, between 1919 and 1922 Rudnytsky lived in France and in Great Britain. Upon returning to Lviv he committed his London observations to paper. Twenty years later, the almanac *Chervona Kalyna* printed his recollections from the peace conference, in which he discussed errors made by the Ukrainian delegations of the UNR—Ukrainian People's Republic—and ZUNR—West Ukrainian People's Republic.

In the second half of 1922 Rudnytsky returned to Lviv, roughly at the same time as his brother Ivan made it back from Vienna. At that time, Polish authorities gave permission to most political emigrants from Galicia to return to what now was Poland. Soon Rudnytsky, who studied English literature during his stay in Great Britain and rekindled connections with the prewar milieu of intellectuals while in France, began teaching French and English literatures at the Lviv Ukrainian Underground University. He and his brother worked for the UNDO newspaper *Dilo*. Mykhailo became the chief cultural contributor to this most influential Ukrainian daily and came to be considered an oracle in literary matters. Yet Rudnytsky was not satisfied; his dream was to start a cultural periodical. In the mid-1920s he initiated the magazine *Svit*, which lasted four years, and then in the mid-1930s the biweekly *Nazustrich*, fashioned after the Polish *Wiadomości Literackie*. Both titles competed with Dontsov's *Visnyk*. Each existed barely four years and faced harsh opposition from the right as well as the left.[7]

During that time Mykhailo Rudnytsky also wrote for the Polish-language Zionist newspaper *Chwila*, edited by Henryk Hescheles. Among *Chwila*'s

---

5   Bohdan Horyn', *Ne til'ky pro sebe. Knyha persha (1955–1965)* (Kyiv: Pul'sary, 2006), 61.
6   Mykhailo Rudnytsky's personnel files, ALU, R-119, op. 1, spr. 244, k. 1–4.
7   After the first issues of the biweekly *Nazustrich* appeared, Dontsov fiercely criticized the new periodical in his column "Z presovoho fil'mu," *Visnyk* 4 (1934): 311. With each month the polemic intensified. Dontsov alleged that the new magazine was directly dependent on the Soviet embassy. In the end the editorial board of *Nazustrich* demanded that *Visnyk* take back its allegations of "veiled Sovietophilia" (Biblioteka Narodowa w Warszawie, Archiwum im. Tarasa Szewczenki, Kolekcja Dmytra Doncowa, t. 5, v. 1, k. 129).

contributors were Debora Vogel and Artur Sandauer; Pesach Stark (who later changed his name to Julian Stryjkowski) first published there. The *Visnyk* circle did not hold back its vitriol in commenting on Rudnytsky's cooperation with the Jewish *Chwila*. Alas, the atmosphere of anti-Semitic excesses in the increasingly volatile political climate of the mid 1930s normalized calling people out on their Jewish provenance, and Dontsov's circle was no exception. (In the chapter "Academic Snapshots" we witnessed similar attitudes through remarks about Tadeusz Hollender and Hugo Steinhaus.) In print, however, the rule seemed to be to refrain from ethnic harassment, though some exchanges could get personal. As an unaffiliated liberal, Rudnytsky presented an easy target for Dontsov, more exposed than leftists from *Novi shlakhy* or the center-right *Meta*, periodicals which had the backing of their political groups.[8]

At that time the Ukrainian liberal community—contrary to today's beliefs—was quite sizeable, with creative types outnumbering politicians. Until the war broke out, the milieu was as diverse as it was typical. It brought together educated central Europeans born at the turn of the nineteenth and twentieth centuries, who adopted broad horizons and a liberal compass and thought past borders and national divisions, even as their formative years fell into the era of nationalism. Vienna ceased to be their capital, and Warsaw turned out to be too provincial, allowing ethnocentrism to triumph. Only Paris held steady—an unchanging compass point on the cultural map of Europe. Rudnytsky played an important role in these circles, contributing a unique framework of reference, enriched by experiences in Kyiv, his contacts with neoclassicists, and a deep knowledge of western European and Polish cultures. In contrast to his brother Ivan, who was strongly rooted in the world of politics, so much so that he came to sign his articles as "Homo Politicus," Mykhailo Rudnytsky existed and found fulfillment through culture.

In the 1930s, the critic grew into one of the most important personalities of Ukrainian cultural life in Lviv. Nicknamed Mephistopheles for his unbridled polemical temperament, Rudnytsky was a man of limitless energy, in his element on the pages of the newspaper *Dilo* and in satirical publications alike, always animating meetings and discussions. Under the auspices of the Society of Writers and Journalists, Rudnytsky organized charitable events. The series of public discussions named "Must Writers Have a Worldview?" gained a wide following, in part because *Visnyk*'s circle fiercely denounced him for propagating

---

8   On the topic of Dontsov's anti-Semitism and anti-liberalism, see Oleksandr Zaitsev, *Ukraïns'kyi integral'nyi natsionalizm (1920-ti-1930-ti roky)* (Kyiv: Krytyka, 2013), 194–201.

"a lack of beliefs." Rudnytsky drew Catholic critics into no less acrimonious disputes. At that time, he published his two most important books: *Between Idea and Form* (1932) as well as *From Myrny to Khvylovy* (1936). The former sketched a theoretical reflection on literature and literary criticism, the latter, fashioned after traditional literary monographs, carried some volatile content; it proclaimed the birth of modern Ukrainian literature. Neither title was published again for the duration of Soviet rule in Ukraine. Nevertheless, the next generation (or its representatives living in exile) adopted Rudnytsky as an exemplary critic. For myself, both books were a true discovery in the early 1980s, offering irrefutable proof that as far back as half a century, Ukrainian critics had been developing modern approaches to literature.

Rudnytsky kept in close contact with the creative circles affiliated with the Association of Independent Ukrainian Artists (ANUM) and shared its goals of bringing the Ukrainian art scene into a European context. He was friends with the group's leaders: the poet and painter Sviatoslav Hordynsky seventeen years his junior, with whom he coedited the bimonthly journal *Nazustrich*, and with his peer, the painter Iaroslava Muzyka, who served as the association's president. The Muzyka couple would spend vacations with Rudnytsky at the

Mykhailo Rudnytsky, Iaroslava Muzyka, Leonty Maksymonko, and Maksym Muzyka; Iaremche, 1930s

trendy resort town Iaremche. In 1936 (the same year *From Myrny to Khvylovy* came out) Iaroslava Muzyka painted a portrait of Mykhailo, which survived the war. The critic frequented exhibits organized by ANUM and contributed to the association's almanac "Mystetstvo—L'Art." Those bonds of friendship with Lviv's creatives allowed him to survive the war and played a vital role during the German occupation.

"FREE UKRAINE"—FOR FIVE KOPEKS

> O, 'tis too true!
> How smart a lash that speech doth give my conscience!
> —Shakespeare, *Hamlet*, 3:1, ll. 57–8

During the first year of the war, Mykhailo Rudnytsky worked at the daily *Vilna Ukraina*. Simultaneously, in late November 1939 he was hired at Lviv University (though earlier, in 1937, the Polish administration had kept him out). He became the chair of Western European Literatures and in January 1940 moved up to assistant dean of Philology (the dean was Vasyl Simovych, a distinguished philologist and structuralist).[9] By October 1939, the critic had joined the Writers' Union organizing committee, alongside his former master Ostap Ortwin as well as a few Polish and Jewish authors.[10] A year later the monthly journal *Literatura i mystetstvo* was established and Rudnytsky published there. If we ignore the first two pieces he wrote for *Vilna Ukraina*, which Mykhailo Ostroverkha justifiably considers disgraceful,[11] the critic's role in the daily (as well as in the literary journal) was entirely comparable with Tadeusz Boy-Żeleński's work for *Czerwony Sztandar* and *Nowe Widnokręgi*. The authorities were laser-focused on recruiting important names who counted in the opinion-formation process, "opinion makers" in today's language. To this aim, the Soviets were willing to turn a blind eye to the critic's past affiliation with the "bourgeois-capitalist" newspaper *Dilo*, whose editor in chief, as we read in the chapter "Academic Snapshots," they arrested in the first weeks of the occupation.

---

9   Mykhailo Rudnytsky's personnel files, ALU, R-119, op. 1, spr. 244, k. 1–4.
10 "U pisarzy polskich," *Czerwony Sztandar*, no. 15, October 10, 1939.
11 Mykhailo Ostroverkha, "Na krutomu zvoroti istoriï Ievropy," Shevchenko Scientific Society Archive, Ostroverkha Papers, box 6, folder 1, k. 105: "Mykhailo Rudnytsky is going all out … settling accounts with 'nationalist swines.' He lists names: who was guilty of 'spitting' at the Stalinist doctrine, at the ideas of the working class."

On Monday, September 25, 1939, Soviet administration representatives Oleksandr Korniichuk and Andry Chekaniuk, editor in chief of the newspaper *The Communist*, met with Ukrainian journalists at the Prosvita offices.[12] The government had called on Chekaniuk as a long-term party member and a 1937 graduate of the Institute of Red Professors to come to Lviv in September 1939 to oversee the creation of the Soviet daily *Vilna Ukraina* and serve as the administrative receiver of *Dilo*'s assets. At the request of the uniformed visitors, on September 23 *Dilo*'s editor in chief Ivan Nimchuk showed them around the editorial office and the print shop, though the night of September 16/17 Polish police had just raided those facilities, leaving them ransacked. Nimchuk hoped that the city interim commander would keep his promises; he had assured the chairman of the Ukrainian delegation Kost Levytsky that the new administration would be supportive of Ukrainian culture. Members of the delegation remained in good spirits, although they did not get a clear answer from the commander when they requested his permission to continue publishing *Dilo* as an independent, nonpartisan daily, which would appear parallel to the Soviet newspaper. In reference to the initial promises, Kost Levytsky remarked that words sounded good, but one had to wait for deeds. As it turned out, the wait was not too long: the next morning, on Sunday, September 24, new owners moved into the editorial office in Prosvita's building at 10 Rynek Square. The Soviet daily's first issue appeared on Monday, September 25. Paperboys advertised it in the typical Lviv tongue-in-cheek manner: "*Vilna Ukraina*—for just five kopeks" (In actuality, this anecdote must have come from a later period since the ruble did not go into effect until October, at first as a currency parallel to the złoty.) For some, the realization that such "freedom" was not even worth half a penny came sooner, for others later.

Korniichuk chaired the meeting with journalists, but the editor Chekaniuk dominated it. He unleashed a frontal attack against Ivan Nimchuk, blaming him for the prewar appeasement policies of the UNDO, which he called "treacherous." Nearly the entire room stood up to defend *Dilo*'s editor: "As a result of this speech those present gradually moved from defending Nimchuk to attacking Chekaniuk and the policy of the USSR toward the Ukrainian nation in Poland."[13] A verbal altercation occurred, with journalists arguing that the actual traitors were not the UNDO politicians, and even less so the

---

12 "Novi perspektyvy plodotvornoï pratsi (na naradi zhurnalistiv L'vova)," *Vil'na Ukraïna*, no. 4, September 28, 1939.
13 Nimchuk, *595 dniv soviets'kym viaznem*, 28–9.

journalists of its press organ (*Dilo*). Rather, the Soviet government bore responsibility for betraying the interests of the Ukrainian nation when it did not come to the defense of their brotherly nation. A Ukrainian gentleman saved Chekaniuk from the predicament by reminding everyone that it was time for dinner. But it was only a fleeting victory.

Nimchuk's detailed account references a well-known Lviv journalist who seconded Chekaniuk, but he does not name him.[14] It is unlikely that it was Rudnytsky who behaved that way. Many journalists participated in the meeting, though he was the only *Dilo* employee hired on the spot for the replacement Soviet paper. His university personnel file lists his date of hire at the newspaper as September 23, 1939, which does not match the actual chronology. The Soviet editors did not come down to Lviv until Sunday, September 24, thus there was nobody who could have physically signed him on the day before.

On Tuesday, September 26, another meeting was called; this time *The Communist*'s editor did not allow for any discussion. At the end of his monologue Chekaniuk suggested to the present journalists that they submit employment applications. Contrary to previous assurances, very few of the nearly eighty Ukrainian journalists working in Lviv got jobs in one of the two Ukrainian-language Soviet newspapers: *Vilna Ukraina* or *Komsomolskaia Pravda*, except the Galician communists Petro Kozlaniuk, Kuzma Pelekhaty, Iaroslav Halan, and Mykhailo Zaiats. Zaiats had just been released from the Bereza Kartuska Prison, but did not get to enjoy his freedom very long—the NKVD arrested him on March 22, 1940 along with nineteen other communists. Mykhailo Rudnytsky joined the editorial office as well, but how or why is hard to piece together. Perhaps the communists backed him, since he kept in contact before the war, or maybe a trade-off occurred: employment in exchange for collaboration. The NKVD began recruiting informers and agents in October.[15] Some journalists (Osyp Nazaruk and Mykhailo Ostroverkha) chose not to disclose their profession and found other work or otherwise made themselves scarce. The latter mentioned cases where the NKVD pressured persons they apprehended and released them on the condition that they become informers.

The new order changed everything: on day one, portraits of Petliura and Mazepa disappeared from the newspaper's office, and staff writers in military uniforms sat at the radio receiver—the next issue would be prepared on the basis of

---

14 Ibid.
15 See reports by Commissar Ivan Serov sent in October and November to Lavrentii Beria: Materialy agenturno-operativnoi raboty UNKVD po L'vovskoi oblasti, HDA SBU, f. 16, op. 32, spr. 33, spr. 70.

Soviet reports. That afternoon *Dilo*'s editor in chief went back to his apartment at Murarska Street with a heavy heart. Two days had passed since the takeover of the newspaper, and barely twenty-four hours since the meeting where those present were encouraged to help restore normalcy and were assured that their old "trespasses" would be forgotten. Late in the afternoon of September 26, agents arrived to search Nimchuk's apartment. In the evening they arrested the editor and took him to the prison at Łącki Street. He only came out 595 days later, and returned to Lviv on May 15, 1941. He was one of only two prominent Ukrainian prisoners who were released; the other was the octogenarian Kost Levytsky. Meanwhile, the new editor, comrade Chekaniuk, announced in the Soviet newspaper *The Communist* that Ukrainians from both banks of the Zbruch, brothers long torn apart by the Polish occupation, had at last been reunited at a historic meeting.[16]

EVIL'S PLEASANT DAWN STINGS AT DUSK

> The Devil hath power
> To assume a pleasing shape.
> —Shakespeare, *Hamlet*, 2:2, ll. 628–629

By late September of 1939, in the aftermath of those initial meetings, the Galician intelligentsia realized that political parties would not survive; most dissolved on Sunday, September 24. Civic organizations and creative associations disbanded as well. The last days of September brought a wave of assemblies at which members in attendance would make a resolution to dissolve their organization. Three days after the memorable journalist meeting, on September 28, the Society of Writers and Journalists was eliminated. A month later, the Society's longtime president Roman Kupchynsky made it to the German side.[17] The newspaper *Vilna Ukraina* printed a slavish appeal to the writers and journalists of the Ukrainian SSR, signed among others by Mykhailo Rudnytsky and Roman Kupchynsky.[18] In secret, professor Vasyl Simovych, the Society's treasurer, withdrew the organization's money; it would later help support colleagues who found themselves destitute. Soon the state took over the Society's sole real property—a villa in Kamin Dovbusha. The first issues of *Vilna Ukraina* and *Czerwony Sztandar* were filled with

---

16 Author "Zustrich brativ (z peredovytsi 'Komunista')," *Vil'na Ukraïna*, no. 4, September 28, 1939.
17 Ostroverkha, "Na krutomu zvoroti istoriï Ievropy," k. 74.
18 "Pryvit pys'mennykam i zhurnalistam Radians'koi Ukraïny vid Spilky ukraïns'kykh pys'mennykiv i zhurnalistiv Zakhidnoi Ukraïny," *Vil'na Ukraïna*, no. 7, October 1, 1939.

collective letters voicing joy at the arrival of the "rescuer and hero, the Red Army." A number of writers were ready to work with the Soviets. The very first issues of both periodicals included new contributions by local poets.

Such publications helped to create the illusion that the local population supported the Soviet administration. In fact, some members of the Communist Party of Western Ukraine could not hide their satisfaction with the end of Polish rule and openly demanded retribution. An article by Petro Kozlaniuk titled "Chas rozplaty nastav" ["The Time Has Come to Settle Accounts"] talks about disarming the Polish police and adorning village homes with red flags.[19] Subsequently, Kuzma Pelekhaty and Kozlaniuk wrote about operations conducted by the Polish police and military against Ukrainian peasants in September 1939.[20] Their purpose was to divert attention from the actual violence on the part of the USSR and redirect it at the representatives of the Polish state who continued persecuting the local population even in the face of the war.

One of the first issues of *Vilna Ukraina* included a poem by the young writer Ostap Tarnavsky, titled "Pryvit Chervonii armii" ["A Welcome for the Red Army"],[21] which Mykhailo Rudnytsky delivered to the editorial office—or this is how Tarnavsky remembers this episode.[22]

A BRIDLED CRITIC

> Something have you heard
> Of Hamlet's transformation. …
> —Shakespeare, *Hamlet*, 2:2, ll. 4–5

Mykhailo Rudnytsky's position at *Vilna Ukraina* was equivalent to the one he had held at *Dilo*—editor of the literary division. In the fall he became a source of information for the NKVD under the pseudonym "Shchel" ["Crevice"].[23] As many others at that time, especially journalists working for Soviet-run newspapers,[24] he probably found himself cornered and decided to game it. Based on

---

19 Petro Kozlaniuk, "Chas rozplaty nastav!," *Vil'na Ukraïna*, no. 5, September 29, 1939.
20 Petro Kozlaniuk and Kuz'ma Pelekhatyi, "Vbyvstva, pozhary i morduvannia," *Vil'na Ukraïna*, no. 7, October 1, 1939.
21 Ostap Tarnavs'kyi, "Pryvit Chervonii armii," *Vil'na Ukraïna*, no. 5, September 29, 1939.
22 Tarnavs'kyi, *Literaturnyi L'viv 1939–1944*, 45.
23 HDA SBU, FP 74893, t. 2, k. 84.
24 Ostroverkha referred to an attempt to recruit an acquaintance on September 29, 1939 (Ostroverkha, "Na krutomu zvoroti istoriï Ievropy," k. 77), and on several occasions described how the NKVD created pressure during interrogations and sowed a climate of fear in Lviv.

available documents it appears that he merely provided information that was public knowledge. It is unlikely that his reports supplied the NKVD with any actual intelligence.[25]

In October he published two articles directed against writers of the *Visnyk* circle: Ulas Samchuk, Sviatoslav Hordynsky, Iury Kosach, and Ievhen Malaniuk. The pieces ruthlessly took them to task for espousing bourgeois worldviews in alignment with their alleged sponsor—the Ukrainian government-in-exile. A separate spot dealt with the publications of the Ukrainian Scientific Institute in Warsaw. The titles adhered to a distinctly Soviet style: "Na literaturnomy bezputti" ["In the Literary Wasteland"] and "Trubadur zoolohichnoho natsionalizmu" ["Troubadour of Zoological Nationalism"][26] Whether Rudnytsky really submitted those pieces is doubtful, but they do bear his name. Some contemporaries, like Mykhailo Ostroverkha, believed that the critic acted out of base motives, having found the right moment to "get even" with nationalists. Ostroverkha was especially incensed that the article named the writers, putting them in peril. Judging from available sources (in particular analyses of various communities and organizations in the Second Polish Republic) and official newspaper publications of the late 1930s, the Soviets readied a list of persons who would come under fire in advance. The file overlapped with a record of persons subject to immediate arrest. We can surmise that the request to pen a piece for *Vilna Ukraina* arrived with this inventory attached. At the time, writers referenced in Rudnytsky's article were out of reach in the German-occupied territories, which the author certainly was aware of (on a side note, he continued maintaining a close relationship with Hordynsky, as coeditor of the periodical *Nazutrich*). Hence Rudnytsky's press contributions could not harm anyone except their author. But from then on, some compatriots saw him as a collaborator (nationalists had long been accusing him of being a Sovietophile and now they seemingly had gotten their proof). In the opinion of Ostroverkha, who was affiliated with the nationalist camp, Rudnytsky was a trusted man of the Soviet administration. Beyond the public denunciation published on the pages of *Vilna Ukraina*, Ostroverkha's circle blamed Rudnytsky for violating the Ukrainian national idea: "soon he stooped so low as to write of a blue-yellow

---

25 HDA SBU, f. 16, op. 32, spr. 70, k. 25.
26 Mykhailo Rudnyts'kyi, "Na literaturnomy bezputti," *Vil'na Ukraïna*, no. 10, October 5, 1939, (this article tears apart "the bourgeois world views" of Ulas Samchuk, Iury Kosach, and Sviatoslav Hordynsky), as well as his article "Trubadur zoolohichnoho natsionalizmu," *Vil'na Ukraïna*, no. 21, October 18, 1939 (an article about Ievhen Malaniuk).

rag."²⁷ In truth, such an insult is nowhere to be found in any of his writings, although, as we saw, the first two pieces Rudnytsky penned for *Vilna Ukraina* certainly smacked of slander.

Ostroverkha viewed Rudnytsky's friendship with Soviet Ukrainian writer Mykola Bazhan with suspicion as well: "Mykhailo Rudnytsky whispers with Mykola Bazhan, who was awarded Stalin's medal. A sneaky facial expression, on the skinny side, dark, bald, fairly well-dressed in a dark new suit, purchased here."²⁸ Here Ostroverhkha is referring to an assembly which took place on October 13, 1939 at the city hall. At that time the Soviets sent Bazhan to Lviv as a representative, in charge of securing cultural heritage and carrying out the requisite organizational changes. Bazhan did what he could to protect cultural collections from plunder by Soviet soldiers. Rudnytsky and Bazhan knew each other from their Kyiv days. What they whispered about we can only stipulate. It is likely that Rudnytsky inquired about the fate of Zerov, whom he considered a friend and teacher (the poet and critic fell victim to the Great Terror and was executed in 1937). But Ostroverkha believed that Bazhan and Rudnytsky were scheming.

Rudnytsky's next contributions for the pages of *Vilna Ukraina* focused on literary projects. At the critic's initiative a museum for Ivan Franko was created; he wrote about the need for such an institution in November 1939.²⁹ After the new year he published several reviews of works by Soviet authors: a volume of poetry *Liubliu* [*I Love*] by Volodymyr Sosiura, stories by Agata Turchynska titled *Urozhai* [*Abundant Harvest*], and the play *Platon Krechet* by Oleksandr Korniichuk.³⁰ Before the March 1940 elections to the Supreme Soviet of the USSR and of the Ukrainian SSR, Rudnytsky wrote vignettes about local Ukrainian candidates: literary historian Mykhailo Vozniak, actor Ivan Rubchak, and veteran of the Ukrainian Galician Army and chemist by profession, Petro Franko.³¹ On the eve of the elections he published the historical sketch "Iak Ivana Franka v parlament obyraly" ["How they elected Ivan Franko to the

---

27 Ostroverkha, "Na krutomu zvoroti istoriï Ievropy," k. 105.
28 Ibid., k. 129.
29 Mykhailo Rudnyts'kyi, "Pamiatky pro velykoho pys'mennyka," *Vil'na Ukraïna*, no. 44, November 15, 1939.
30 Mykhailo Rudnyts'kyi, "Boiova liryka. V. Sosiura, L'ubl'iu," *Vil'na Ukraïna*, no. 5, January 6, 1940; Mykhailo Rudnyts'kyi, "Pisni pro shchastia. Agata Turchyns'ka. 'Urozhai'," *Vil'na Ukraïna* no. 9, January 11, 1940; no. 1, January 1, 1940.
31 "Nashi kandydaty," *Vil'na Ukraïna*, no. 49, February 29, 1940; no. 52, March 4, 1940; "Kandydat do Verkhovnoï Rady URSR Petro Franko," *Vil'na Ukraïna*, no. 54, March 6, 1940.

parliament"][32] as well as a second one, about Franko's adventures with Austrian censorship.[33] In contrast, Iaroslav Halan fell in lockstep with the Soviet propaganda and the accusations that all Ukrainian parties in Poland had supported the "fascist" Polish regime. His pamphlet "Lytsari nasyl'stva i zrady" ["Knights of Violence and Treason"] condemned the Ukrainian Parliamentary Representation, allegedly an ally of "the grand henchman Piłsudski."[34]

In summing up the first six months of Soviet rule, the local media announced the plans of Lviv writers; their vast majority committed to producing works devoted to social and national subjugation or paeans to the liberation (just three months earlier some local literati penned a collective poem celebrating Stalin; later those authors reminisced, as if to excuse their participation, that it amounted to an artistic fiasco). Rudnytsky announced that he would publish comparative studies about Shevchenko's novella *The Artist*, contemporaneous European autobiographical novels,[35] and Ivan Franko's writings.[36] Boy-Żeleński adopted a similar strategy, focusing on studies about Stendhal and a translation of Marcel Proust's *À la recherche du temps perdu* (it appears the censor found the title inadmissible and changed it to the more ideologically appropriate *Chasing Better Times*). Two poets writing in Yiddish, Naum Bomse and Dawid Koenigsberg, also turned to translations—of old Chinese poetry and of Heinrich Heine.[37]

Between spring 1940 and the outbreak of the German-Soviet war, thus over a year's time, Rudnytsky only contributed one piece to *Vilna Ukraina*, to present the figure of Ivan Krypiakevych, a historian who was running for the city council in the December elections. In November, the paper published an anniversary issue dedicated to the Polish Romantic poet Adam Mickiewicz commemorating the eighty-fifth anniversary of his death, with one translation by Rudnytsky. The monthly *Literatura i mystetstvo* printed a few more pieces (review of a poetry volume, a study of Vasyl Stefanyk, a translation of Mickiewicz's "Ode to Youth"). But Rudnytsky did not join the editorial board of the

---

32 Mykhailo Rudnyts'kyi, "Jak Ivana Franka do parlamentu obyraly," *Vil'na Ukraïna*, no. 66, March 20, 1940.
33 Mykhailo Rudnyts'kyi, "Ivan Franko ta avstriis'ka tsenzura (Do istoriï p´iesy 'Ukradene shchastia Ivana Franka')," *Vil'na Ukraïna*, no. 68, March 22, 1940.
34 Iaroslav Halan, "Lytsari nasyl'stva i zrady," *Vil'na Ukraïna*, no. 50, March 1, 1940.
35 "Naukova sesiia u L'vivs'komu derzhavnomu universyteti pro Shevchenka. Do 100-richchia Kobzaria," *Vil'na Ukraïna*, no. 94, April 21, 1940.
36 Mykhailo Rudnyts'kyi, "Zolia i Franko," *Vil'na Ukraïna*, no. 79, April 3, 1940; Mykhailo Rudnyts'kyi, "Franko i svitova literatura," *Vil'na Ukraïna*, no. 124, May 29, 1940.
37 "Tvorchi plany l'vivs'kykh pys'mennykiv," *Vil'na Ukraïna*, no. 67, March 21, 1940.

magazine. If we consider how actively he participated in literary life before the war, his occupation-era output appears quite slim. The imbalance between the number of publications from October 1939 until April 1940 and the next year presents another curious contrast.

It may thus seem that in 1940 and 1941 Soviet authorities left Rudnytsky more or less alone, judging by his neutral publications in the daily *Vilna Ukraina* and the monthly *Literatura i mystetstvo*. Yet we can be certain he remained under careful surveillance. A year before, Rudnytsky had run afoul of Korniichuk at the first writers' assembly on October 13, 1939. He was the only attendee to approach the assembly's chair with a formal request: "Since we have Polish and Jewish writers in the room who do not understand Ukrainian, I would like to briefly summarize for them in Polish what we had discussed."[38] The chairman categorically objected. But instead of retreating, Rudnytsky recapitulated the presentations.[39] Whether this manifestation of politeness toward Polish and Jewish colleagues brought negative consequences we cannot say. But it is likely that Korniichuk provided information to the NKVD about every speaker who exhibited courage or merely an independent spirit. Without access to the agency's documents it is impossible to determine which denunciation served as the basis for the NKVD to detain and interrogate Rudnytsky, as well as recruit him. Rudnytsky was registered as a personal information source under the code name "Crevice" (however, having been issued a code name did not necessarily signify that a person had agreed to collaborate). The NKVD did not trust any locals, not the people whose names adorned front pages of newspapers, and not even their own agents. Rudnytsky was never part of the trusted circle. The secret service directive to surround suspects with agents applied to all public figures, even former communists or persons enlisted to implement the new system. Undoubtedly, along with all prominent Lvivians, the critic was placed under special surveillance even as he was registered as an informer. We know that the NKVD kept tabs on their own agents, let alone on such unreliable individuals as educated locals. The main opportunities for observation were the workplace and the union, and Rudnytsky had two employers—the newspaper and the university—and belonged to the union. No available sources talk about the climate in the offices of *Vilna Ukraina*. We can only surmise that it resembled the atmosphere at *Czerwony Sztandar*, described by Aleksander Wat in *Mój wiek*

---

38 Ostroverkha, *Na zakruti. Osin' 1939 r.*, 94.
39 Ostroverkha, "Na krutomu zvoroti istoriï Ievropy," k. 132 (this detail is omitted in the published version).

[*My Century*] or Julian Stryjkowski in his novel *Wielki strach* [*The Great Fear*]. In that respect, far more is known about the university community, mainly from Polish testimonies (the chapters "Academic Snapshots" and "Barbarian in the Garden" address this subject at length).

DENUNCIATION—THE SHORTEST OF LITERARY GENRES

> Call me what instrument you will, though you
> can fret me, yet you cannot play upon me.
> —Shakespeare, *Hamlet*, 3:2, ll. 401–2

In late November of 1939, Rudnytsky was hired as a professor and director of the Division of Western European Literatures, just a few days after Boy-Żeleński became professor of French literature.[40] While Polish journal authors stay silent about the Ukrainian critic (with one exception, which I'll discuss next), Boy's name comes up quite often.[41] To many, he was a living legend and his lectures enjoyed immense popularity. Jan Kott, attracted by Boy's fame, decided to apply for admission to the doctoral program in Romance languages, albeit unsuccessfully. Boy quipped about his work at Lviv University: at a Ukrainian university I give lectures on French literature to Jews, in Polish. He seemed to view the precarious situation of Polish culture as nearly hopeless; according to Michał Borwicz, Boy said: "I fear that under the new politics my Proust readers will die out." Rudnytsky, though twenty years younger, was now the boss of his former master; no doubt an uncomfortable position, though under different conditions he surely would have considered such cooperation a great honor.

Although the Soviets forced a policy of Ukrainization, at the university— as we read in previous chapters—the rule took hold only incrementally, with no one enforcing the directive. In the philology department, only the divisions of Ukrainian literature and language switched to Ukrainian. Formally all lecturers had to study Ukrainian (Dean Vasyl Simovych assigned the pedagogical duty to an elderly high school professor named Amvrosii Androkhovych, whom colleagues treated with affection, and later added a recent graduate, Myroslav

---

40 Nakaz rektora no. 78, 27.11.1939, ALU, R-119, op. 3, spr. 3, k. 96 (Rudnytsky's hire); Nakaz rektora no. 68, 22.11.1939, ALU, R-119 op. 3, spr. 3, k. 55 (Boy's hire).
41 Barbara Winklowa gives an overview of those reminiscences in *Boy we Lwowie 1939–1941* (Warsaw: Oficyna Wydawnicza Rytm, 1992). Jacek Trznadel counters Winklowa with a fervent critique of Boy's stance in *Kolaboranci. Tadeusz Boy-Żeleński i grupa komunistycznych pisarzy we Lwowie 1939–1941*, 56–105.

Curriculum vitae of Tadeusz Boy-Żeleński,
professor of French literature at Lviv University, 1940

Semchyshyn). A new degree program was created—Ukrainian philology. In practice this major had no admission limits since directives from above dictated that the number of Ukrainian and Jewish students had to increase. Consequently, many refugees of Jewish origin enrolled as Ukrainian majors in the first year of occupation just to avoid deportation. Some tried to transfer to the division of modern languages after a year. The issue of Ukrainian as the language of instruction returned cyclically, after each official audit. In the academic year of 1940/1941 the new university president, adhering to requirements communicated by the Education Narkomat (People's Commissariat), obligated all lecturers to gradually transition to Ukrainian and announced that by next year those who refused would be fired. Though at first the local Ukrainian cadre supported the transition to Ukrainian, their attitude changed over time. Tadeusz Tomaszewski, who worked in the Division of Psychology as an assistant under Mieczysław Kreutz, recalls that Rudnytsky and Iury Poliansky presented a conciliatory position on the issue during a discussion at the academic council meeting on March 6, 1941. By then pressures to force the university to switch to Ukrainian intensified. Apparently Rudnytsky stated that learning a language is a lengthy process and should occur naturally if one is expected to lecture in that tongue.[42] This was half a year after the Soviets had removed Rudnytsky from his position as assistant dean (he then became "assistant to the dean"). The university president's directive does not reference the cause of his demotion.[43] We could attribute the decision to a more general trend in Soviet personnel policy in Galicia to gradually remove local Ukrainians from leadership positions. But an extant note leading us to Ewa Gruber, who before the war was connected to a youth communist cell, suggests otherwise. Gruber was a graduate assistant of the distinguished orientalist Stefan Stasiak. In a note addressed to university president Mykhailo Marchenko, she demanded that a dean who dared to admonish a student be called to account:

> The undersigned persons state that on May 22 in the presence of the director of the orientalism division and its employees, comrade Assistant Dean professor Rudnytsky in a longer speech specifically said: "And in general comrade Szajan is doing the wrong thing by rising to the defense of the socialist realism at the Writers' Club every night. What a pity that he was not present during the evening where [Aleksiei] Tolstoy appeared,

---

42   Tomaszewski, *Lwów. Pejzaż psychologiczny*, 52.
43   Nakaz rektora no. 255, 11.09.1940, ALU, R-119, op. 3, spr. 31, k. 101.

because he would have learned from him that in the Soviet Union, they had given it up a long time ago.[44]

In an atmosphere steeped in fear, Rudnytsky's statement might come as a surprise. The authorities ruthlessly eradicated any deviations from the obligatory party line. Why then did he as a professor and assistant dean not excercise caution in his campus interactions? Why did he go so far as to ridicule a young apprentice of socialist literature (who later became a proponent of the Ukrainian neopagan religion RUN-Wira)? It is doubtful that he felt untouchable—for the NKVD he was but a pawn, a source of information. More likely his unbridled temperament got the better of him and provoked him to voice a long-held contempt for any attempts to ideologize literature. As people active in postwar cultural life reminisce, even at an advanced age and in spite of his Stalin-era soul-crushing experiences, he would continue to cause headaches for apparatchiks from the *obkom* (the oblast party committee).[45]

Ewa Gruber referenced the critic's remark in her report to the university president on June 12, 1940. This was not the first time she demonstrated communist zeal. Another extant document is a draft of Gruber's letter to Stalin from the autumn of 1939, in which, thanking him for the liberation, she pleads with him to also extend his care to those regions of Poland that were currently occupied by the Nazis.[46] Diplomatically speaking, older colleagues from the same division did not hold the assistant in high esteem.[47] Soon thereafter, Gruber was given a time-and-a-half position in the orientalist division,[48] though the university gave many lecturers limited hours or even terminated their jobs altogether. (Gruber had belonged to a communist youth organization; in the mid 1930s, despite the support of her boss, she was removed from the university; by early November 1939 she received a promise of employment from the Soviet university president, which we should attribute to her political engagement.[49])

In all likelihood the administration demoted Rudnytsky from assistant dean to assistant to the dean at the start of the new academic year in response to Ewa Gruber's denouncement. In place of the current dean Vasyl Simovych,

---

44 Stefan Stasiak fonds, III-197, t. 35, k. 1.
45 Bohdan Horyn', *Ne til'ky pro sebe. Knyha persha (1955–1965)*, 59.
46 Stasiak fonds III-197, t. 50 (VI-41), k. 1–2
47 Tadeusz Tomaszewski cites the opinion of philologist Jerzy Kuryłowicz (Tomaszewski, *Lwów. Pejzaż psychologiczny*, 35).
48 Nakaz rektora no. 66, 13.03.1941, ALU, R-119, op. 3, spr. 52, k. 139.
49 Stasiak fonds III-197, t. 51, k. 120.

in late September 1940 they nominated assistant dean Zygmunt Czerny.[50] However, they retained Rudnytsky as a professor, with a relatively high salary, although the authorities would not include him among university or union delegates, made no plans to publish his books or writings, and did not award him any university prizes or stipends from the Writers' Union. With Kyrylo Studynsky's backing, the division of English hired the critic's wife Marta Rudnytska as senior lecturer.[51] She too never received any distinctions. Such treatment signaled that the Soviets did not trust Rudnytsky one bit and felt he had already played out his role.

UNDER A WATCHFUL EYE

> Rightly to be great
> Is not to stir without great argument,
> But greatly to find quarrel in a straw
> When honor's at the stake.
> —Shakespeare, *Hamlet*, 4.4, ll. 56–59

In the fall of 1939, Lviv literati found themselves in the same position as all Soviet writers: fully dependent on the state. According to data from December 22, 1939, the Writers' Club, which the authorities moved to the Bielski Palace with much fanfare, had 162 members.[52] Only those who did not register, and registration was considered obligatory,[53] enjoyed relative freedom. Until the annexation of Poland's Eastern territories was confirmed in November 1939, one could dodge some of the pressures, as we gather from a document in the Ostap Ortwin collection,[54] but the strategy soon turned dangerous. The authorities

---

50 Nakaz rektora no. 276, 30.09.1940, ALU, R-119, op. 3, spr. 31, k. 166. A prior regulation (no. 255, 11.09.1940) references professor Czerny as assistant dean.
51 Marta Rudnytska's letter to dean Kyrylo Studynsky from December 18, 1939, TsDIAL, f. 362, op. 1, spr. 376, k. 1.
52 "Orhkomitet spilky pys'mennykiv," *Vil'na Ukraïna*, no. 74, December 22, 1939.
53 Chairman of the Lviv chapter of the Writers' Union Lviv Petro Panch noted in 1939: "Parpicki [Parnicki]—leader of Catholic youth, did not register. … Maria Dąbrowska is in Brzuchowice." See Petro Panch's note from 1939 ("Vytiah iz shchodennykovykh zapysiv, dorozhnikh notatok Petra Pancha pro literaturne i hromads'ko-politychne zhyttia v Zakhidnii Ukraïni," in *Kul'turne zhyttia v Ukraïni. Zakhidni zemli*, vol. 1, 73–4). The newspaper *Vilna Ukraina* announced the end of registration ("Zakinchennia obliku Orhkomitetom pys'mennykiv," *Vil'na Ukraïna*, no. 39, November 7, 1939.
54 A November 28, 1939 letter from the Writers' Organizational Committee of the city of Lviv to the Writers' Union of the city of Lviv, signed by Petro Panch and the committee's sec-

let this be known on various occasions, for instance when the union of employees of the housing authority called Ortwin. He was doubly vulnerable since he had not registered and owned an apartment building.[55] Any unregistered refugees were deported.

Lviv felt particularly humiliated by certain procedures which regulating the population's official status—confirmation of academic degrees for university faculty, or residency for the *bezhentsy*. Writers had to pass through a double sieve: first, a committee evaluated their literary oeuvre, then the union judged their writings' social value. Only after receiving a positive opinion from both bodies could one join the Soviet writers' organization, which accorded the "privilege" of publishing fees. If the committee took a dislike to one's work and deemed it harmful (such was the case of Wacław Grubiński, who twenty years earlier wrote the comedy *Lenin*; his colleagues—the committee—now declared it slanderous to the revolution's leader), the best possible outcome for the ill-fated writer was a labor camp (Grubiński was first sentenced to death, but the verdict was later changed).

The Soviet playbook dictated that writers participate in evenings organized by the club and publicly discuss each other's work. This awarded the authorities a measure of control over the literati, and an opportunity to further divide a community, already quite fragmented even before social engineering caused further damage. Aside from the various ethnic groups, Lviv's writers fell into the categories of locals versus refugees, who depended much more heavily on assistance available only through the union; the left, which found common ground with the new authorities relatively smoothly; and the rest, which did not wish to or could not fall in line; finally the well-known writers whom the Soviets courted, and those of lesser stature, some of whom raced each other to secure the authorities' favor.

The first year of occupation sowed terror across the entire seized territory, though it was masked as freedom bestowed by the Soviets. The next year, from September 1940 till the end of June 1941, could be described as a period of "minor stabilization." The authority of the Soviets solidified. As the intelligentsia accepted new institutions and submitted to their own lowly roles, the first stage of Sovietization de facto ended. In autumn of 1940 an overall gentler course began, if the adjective is even appropriate. (An earlier chapter describes

---

retary Iaroslav Tsurkovsky, makes a request for free dinners. Likely Ostap Ortwin put together the list of ten Jewish writers; two Ukrainian authors were added afterward (L'vivs'ka natsional'na naukova biblioteka Ukraïny im. Vasyla Stefanyka, Viddil rukopysiv [LBAN], Ort. 119, p. 99, k. 1).

55 Letter from May 6, 1940, LBAN, Ort. 387, p. 20.

mass arrests and death sentences for Ukrainian youth affiliated with the OUN. Simultaneously an impressment was in place; the locals, now official citizens of the USSR, were being forcibly drafted into the Red Army. Most recruits were Ukrainian youth; this was not only a matter of statistics, but an outcome of an earlier policy as well, when repressions disproportionately targeted the Polish population.) Those who came to terms with the status quo became increasingly entangled in working with the administration, not necessarily by choice; the system's logic required ever new gestures of loyalty. Papers printed reports of celebratory commemorations of Mickiewicz and introductions of candidates side by side, featuring representatives of the creative class as candidates in elections to the local government agencies. From today's perspective, the newspapers aptly document an apparent trade-off: acquiescence rewarded with concessions.

An emblematic example comes via the monthly *Literatura i mystetstvo*, where stories related to anniversaries of the great minds intertwined with contributions on "current topics." One of them was a discussion of "Soviet themes in the writings of Lviv authors." Its participants, among them Jerzy Borejsza and Jerzy Putrament, emulated Soviet writers, rushing to critique the shortcomings of literature written after 1939 for insufficiently reflecting the pertinent political transformations. The periodical also introduced works by newly minted members of the Soviet Writers' Union, for example "Lyst komsomolky"[56] ["Letter from a Komsomol Girl"] by the young Ukrainian author Ostap Tarnavsky (Tarnavsky admits that this poem, written from the perspective of a Komsomol girl to Stalin, was a conscious levy, and mentions that the Soviet editor tried to discourage such propagandist pieces by lowering the writer's fee). The announcements of events held at the Literary Club printed in a January issue of the same periodical speak for themselves: on January 10, 1940 a workshop with a Marxism-Leninism lecturer took place (writers were required to participate), on January 16 there was a celebration of the thirtieth work anniversary of Boy-Żeleński (Stanisław Wasylewski presided over the evening, with Mykhailo Rudnytsky among the guests), on January 21 a commemoration of the seventeenth anniversary of Vladimir Lenin's death, and on January 28 a celebration of Pavlo Tychyna's poetry (at the same time a delegation of the Lviv union chapter traveled for Kyiv to participate in the official festivities on the occasion of Tychyna's fiftieth birthday).

Many studies have looked at how the Soviet Writers' Union operated within the system's framework. Polish authors turn their focus to the Lviv chapter

---

56 Ostap Tarnavs'kyi, "Lyst komsomolky," *Literatura i mystetstvo* 4 (1940): 20.

between 1939 and 1941 and report an atmosphere of denunciations, elbowing, and constant struggles to stay afloat.[57] All union members had to attend assemblies and literary evenings, as well as meetings of specific divisions. There was a formal accounting of absences and dues. Such social engineering constantly cajoled local intellectuals to participate in a strictly regulated public life, aiming to control and intimidate as well as filling up individual schedules to ensure that no other activity could occur. Remarkably, none of the Writers' Union members who survived that period kept a journal. The reminiscences that are available were penned years or decades later; they contain contradictions and give voice to animosities, as we previously witnessed within the context of the January 1940 arrest of several literati, Władysław Broniewski and Aleksander Wat among them.

Memoirists who write about the period between September 1940 and June 1941 state that the Soviets liberalized their policy towards ethnic Poles, and yet they continue to focus on the administration's demeaning practices. The anniversary of the "liberation" turned into an opportunity to organize a series of propagandist events, from a military parade and anniversary assemblies, radio shows, and exhibits, to the screening of Dovzhenko's film *Osvobozhdenie*, which I mentioned in the chapter "The Great Journey," and, finally, to press articles. The paper *Vilna Ukraina* published a survey asking representatives of the Ukrainian intelligentsia to respond to the question "what the Soviet rule brought us."[58] In a similar vein, *Czerwony Sztandar* wrote: "On the anniversary of the liberation, from the bottom of our hearts we salute the Red Army for knocking down the walls of our prison."[59] On the one hand, the observance gave the Soviets an opportunity to loudly boast about their conquest, and on the other, to treat local intellectuals charitably. They authorized new literary periodicals, an act which in the eyes of many Polish intellectuals signaled a change in the wind. Indeed, there were reasons to celebrate: the new publications generated a source of income for a broader circle of literati beyond those chosen by the administration who were permitted to publish in the main

---

57 Winklowa, *Boy we Lwowie 1939–1941*; Inglot, *Polska kultura literacka Lwowa lat 1939–1941. Ze Lwowa i o Lwowie. Antologia*; Trznadel, *Kolaboranci. Tadeusz Boy-Żeleński i grupa komunistycznych pisarzy we Lwowie 1939–1941*; Joanna Chłosta, *Polskie życie literackie we Lwowie w latach 1939–1941 w świetle oficjalnej prasy polskojęzycznej* (Olsztyn: Wydawnictwo Uniwersytetu Warmińsko-Mazurskiego, 2000).

58 *Vil'na Ukraïna*, no. 215, September 13, 1940. Statements by ethnographer Filaret Kolessa, economist Volodymyr Kalynovych, and others.

59 Wanda Wasilewska, "Ku nowym dniom," *Czerwony Sztandar*, no. 301, September 17, 1940.

venues. Also at that time, the Soviets bestowed academic titles, recruited students to doctoral programs, and finally began accepting new members into Soviet creative unions, thus opening up paths to publishing royalties.

Earlier, we got a sense of how, from a distance of six months, Mykhailo Ostroverkha related the October 13, 1939 writers' meeting at the city hall. He described at some length presentations by Rudnytsky and a number of other speakers. It must be noted that while his account is certainly biased—he approaches Rudnytsky and as well as Polish and Jewish writers with much hostility—a comparison with a thorough report published in *Vilna Ukraina*[60] shows that Ostroverkha's entry is accurate and that he named all the lead speakers. Indeed, a high number of refugee writers attended the meeting. Ostroverkha writes that Wanda Wasilewska (who arrived late from another meeting), Helena Kuźmińska, Władysław Broniewski (who read the attendees' address to Stalin), as well as Vasyl Pachovsky, along with new arrivals from the Soviet Union: Vasily Lebedev-Kumach, Mykola Bazhan, Petro Panch, and Pavlo Tychyna, were elected to the executive committee. Ostroverkha gives a blow-by-blow description and quotes Wojciech Skuza as saying: "What has happened [Poland's defeat] had to happen, it was easily predictable. ... Under the new conditions we need to create a new life, new values. We need to raise a new generation of Poles."[61] Then he goes on to dismiss Ukrainian presentations as "bleary" and "feeble," and concludes that Polish writers spoke best and most honorably, implying that Ukrainian writers were acting servile.[62]

Oleksandr Korniichuk spoke at the beginning of the writers' assembly held at the city hall, focusing on his favorite topic: the literature of socialist realism, for which Maxim Gorky's work and his formula of the writer's task as "the engineer of the soul" had set an unattainable standard, an ideal derived from Stalin's own thought. According to Ostroverkha, Korniichuk did not mention creative freedom. Roman Kupchynsky gives a similar description of the meeting between the Soviet Writers' Union and the local Ukrainian literati.[63] Both reminiscences differ from Aleksander Wat's later account, in which he paints Korniichuk as practically a rotten liberal: "We will not pressure you in any way,

---

60 "Zustrich pys'mennykiv Radians'koi Ukraïny i Zakhidnoï Ukraïny," *Vil'na Ukraïna*, no. 18, October 14, 1939.
61 Ostroverkha, "Na krutomu zvoroti istoriï Ievropy," Ostroverkha Papers, k. 131.
62 Ibid.
63 Roman Kupchyns'kyi, "Spohady poeta Romana Kupchyns'koho pro pryizd do L'vova hrupy ukraïns'kykh pys'mennykiv z Kyieva voseny 1939 roku," *Iliustrovani visti* 7 (1941): 5–8. Quoted in *Kul'turne zhyttia v Ukraïni. Zakhidni zemli 1939–1953*, vol. 1, 126.

will not subject you to any propaganda. You should come to your own conclusions."⁶⁴ Other Polish authors have similar memories of the meeting; as Jan Brzoza wrote, to the amusement of the entire room, Ortwin asked: "Then can we also write about love and sunsets?"⁶⁵ Supposedly Korniichuk assured the assembled writers that "they can write pieces without a social idea, about regular human passions, about love, hatred, ambition, jealousy … and the Bolshevik government will not hold it against them in the slightest."⁶⁶ Even if the president of the Ukrainian SSR Writers' Union really gave such assurances, no lucid Soviet citizen could take his words seriously. When Wacław Grubiński quoted Korniichuk's statement to an NKVD investigator, the functionary deemed it a lie; the union's president who was also a member of the Ukrainian SSR's Supreme Soviet could not possibly have uttered such absurdities.⁶⁷

Because Polish memoirists wrote about these events much later, their accounts are rarely precise. I will, however, cite one, since it aligns with other memoirs in how it details the process of admittance into the circle of Lviv writers. This event coincided with the anniversary of the "liberation." For that reason alone, it could be seen as demeaning to the national pride of Polish citizens. In addition to humiliation, the selection process evoked fear.

On September 15, 1940 the Soviet Writers' Union convened at a celebratory session. Amongst the executive committee led by Korniichuk sat an array of Soviet authors. Kyrylo Studynsky was recruited as well. As its first order of business, the committee admitted Wanda Wasilewska as its member, and within the next few days, accepted the remaining fifty-eight writers who passed⁶⁸ the verification process. The most notable and distinguished figure in this group was Tadeusz Boy-Żeleński. Twenty years later, Michał Borwicz, a Polish and Jewish writer who survived the Shoah, offered these details:

---

64 Wat, *Mój wiek. Pamiętnik mówiony*, 276.
65 Jan Brzoza, *Moje przygody literackie* (Katowice: Śląsk, 1967), 90.
66 Wacław Grubiński, *Między młotem a sierpem* (London: Stowarzyszenie Pisarzy Polskich, 1948). Quoted in Trznadel, *Kolaboranci. Tadeusz Boy-Żeleński i grupa komunistycznych pisarzy we Lwowie 1939–1941*, 252. For a similar account, see Brzoza, *Moje przygody literackie*, quoted in Trznadel, *Kolaboranci. Tadeusz Boy-Żeleński i grupa komunistycznych pisarzy we Lwowie 1939–1941*, 252, and Wat, *Mój wiek. Pamiętnik mówiony*, 276.
67 Grubiński, *Między młotem a sierpem*, 252.
68 "Pryiom do Spilky pys'mennykiv," *Vil'na Ukraïna* no. 221, September 20, 1940. The issue includes a full list of the admitted writers. See also Inglot, *Polska kultura literacka Lwowa lat 1939–1941. Ze Lwowa i o Lwowie. Antologia*, 33. The researcher gives twenty-one names but leaves out Jewish and Ukrainian writers.

Havryluk held in his hand the curriculum vitae of the author of *Brązownicy* [*The Guilders*] with a bibliography featuring dozens of titles and hundreds of volumes of his translations from French literature. As he asked the "candidate" to rise, he stood up as well and said: "In the presence of a writer who created more works than many have read, I should stand up." The room responded with spontaneous applause. For Boy? Probably. But also for Havryluk: for knowing how to restore a hierarchy of things with this one, in essence plain, sentence, even if just for a moment.[69]

It was a demonstration of solidarity, rare for this community. The writers overcame an ideological barrier as well as an ethnic one too (as a rule, Ukrainian and Jewish writers kept to themselves, each nationality entrenched in its own milieu, and each scrambling for the authorities' favor). Occasionally good will surfaced, as when on October 13 Rudnytsky insisted on translating the presentations for non-Ukrainian speaking participants. But far more often memoirists highlight mudslinging or public criticism. Some colleagues used the denigrating process of admission to the Soviet Writers' Union to obtain strictly regimented royalties, get revenge, or even to eliminate a personal enemy, who at the very moment of a public denunciation would immediately turn into a "class enemy." Boy's attitude stood in stark contrast with such opportunism. Ostap Tarnavsky expresses much admiration for the Polish writer and translator, and not only because of his intellectual stature: Boy proposed organizing a soccer game, a rare event that united the creative circles and was not tainted with ideology.[70]

Thirty years later Ostap Tarnavsky recalled the ritual behind creating a Ukrainian chapter of the Soviet Writers' Union and its member admissions. His description of the new member ceremony in September calls special attention to an incident involving Rudnytsky. As the candidates were being discussed, the committee's secretary, Iaroslav Tsurkovsky, came forward with accusations against Rudnytsky. He had disliked the critic for a while, and now a handy opportunity for revenge presented itself. The animosity stemmed from a review Rudnytsky had written long before, in which he called Tsurkovsky's volume of futuristic poetry derivative. Back then the poet engaged in a fierce polemic with the critic; now was his chance to avenge the setback

---

69 Borwicz, "Inżynierowie dusz," 148. An almost identical description of this event appears in the collection of Beliaev's and Rudnytsky's accusatory pamphlets, where the events are related by Iaroslav Halan: Vladimir Beliaev and Mikhail Rudnitskii, *Pod chuzhimi znamenami* (Moscow: Molodaia gvardiia, 1954), 102.
70 Tarnavs'kyi, *Literaturnyi L'viv 1939–1944*, 107.

from a dozen years ago. Iaroslav Halan rose to the critic's defense; he was the most politically active of the writers who had been members of the Communist Party of Western Ukraine, such as Stepan Tudor, Petro Kozlaniuk, and Oleksandr Havryluk (the latter had served a sentence in the Bereza Kartuska prison). Oleksandr Korniichuk chaired the meeting *ex officio*. The playwright, as always well prepared, had obviously either foreseen this "surprise" or perhaps even arranged for it. He let Tsurkovsky and Halan—Rudnytsky's unexpected ally—speak. Ever the communist writer, Halan went to some trouble to drum up a suitable dialectic proving that the communist system needed a critic with liberal views. As Tarnavsky recalls, after listening to both speakers, the union president took an old volume of Tsurkovsky's poetry out of his pocket and began reading one of the poems, unhurriedly, placing particular emphasis on the verse "Ukraine above all." He then pointed out how it reminded him of "Deutschland über alles." Without letting Tsurkovsky, Rudnytsky, or anyone else recover from the impact, Korniichuk moved to his next line of attack: "Mykhailo Ivanovych, we know you and will admit you to the union, but the Soviet government will never forget about your book *From Myrny to Khvylovy*."[71]

His were not empty promises. Korniichuk was speaking for the authorities. Far from forgiving Rudnytsky for his essays, he brought up the critic's past "sins" to checkmate him. The ideological offense consisted in choosing to write about an author who had committed suicide in protest against the murderous policy of the Soviet Union in Ukraine. Worse yet, the critic elevated Khvylovy to a symbol of his era, and of Ukraine's futile attempts to wrestle away from the embrace of Russian culture and civilization. Curiously, if what Rudnytsky had written was difficult for the Soviets to accept, they had even more trouble with Rudnytsky's programmatically apolitical stance. So did others: before the war, various political camps had eyed the critic with suspicion for that same reason, assuming he must be their opponent's ally.

During the 1930s, the era of extreme ideologies, Rudnytsky consistently rejected a political worldview; to him it placed an unnecessary burden on creative freedom. Instead, he posed the provocative question: "Must a writer have a worldview?" In his bluntness, he had once called Dontsov an "egocentric fascist."[72]

---

71 Ibid., 58.
72 "Ukrainian intelligentsia in Galicia does not read poetry and never understood it. Now the main publication, 'Literaturno-Naukovyi Visnyk,' is helping us unlearn it too. For years its editor has been a politician who judges all creativity from the perspective of egocentric fascism [this is a reference to Dontsov]" (Mykhailo Rudnyts'kyi, "Współczesna literatura ukraińska," *Chwila*, October 1, 1929).

He approached all ideologies of his time with equal disdain and claimed that communism and nationalism were merely two sides of the same coin: "to balance [Ukrainian] communist literature in Galicia and abroad, nationalist messianism was created. Internationalism and nationalism in literature are like two daughters of the same mother who has been stricken with tuberculosis—or agitprop. We have long known their granny too: popular literature that espouses nationalist and social engagement. Like beneficiaries, our writers have been living off her inheritance to this day. ..."[73]

No wonder the Soviets never took a liking to Rudnytsky. Before the war both the left and the right would attack him as well. Dontsov tore him to shreds, sometimes enlisting young friends to fight his battles against the critic. An article "Prymityvna ievropeiizatsiia," published in Dontsov's *Visnyk* and signed as "Zoïl," is attributed to Bohdan Ihor Antonych: "And the editor of *Dilo*, who writes for *Chwila* and *Novi shliakhy*, has become an announcer of these poets, a leader of this latest Ruthenian 'Europeanization,' communist in the vein of *café-chantant*, and oriented towards Moscow. He introduces new 'European' periodicals in programmatical articles, proclaiming a Europe that is too one-sided, a rebellious and skeptical Europe."[74]

Clearly, neither side minced words. Blistering face-offs from before the war lived on in the memories of writers who attended the Union of Soviet Writers' meetings. Political opinions aside, Rudnytsky was an incisive critic and made many enemies that way. Besides Ostap Tarnavsky's record of how Tsurkovsky tried to get even, there were more stories to follow. In Michał Borwicz's words, "those who were envious spelled danger, especially to Lviv writers, the locals. Old grudges that had festered for years were now coming to the surface, and anything anyone ever published was at hand."[75]

A NEW CONSTELLATION

> The great man down, you mark his favourite flies;
> The poor, advanced makes friends of enemies.
> —Shakespeare, *Hamlet*, 3:2, ll. 227–8

At the start of the Soviet occupation, the faces of Lviv's literary community changed. First off, a number of writers from central Poland arrived, second,

---

73 Mykhailo Rudnyts'kyi, "Evropa i my," *My: Literaturnyi neperiodychnyi zhurnal* 1 (1933): 98–9.
74 Zoïl, "Prymityvna ievropeiizatsiia," *Visnyk* 2 (1934): 127–30. Quoted in: Bohdan Ihor Antonych, *Tvory*, ed. Mykhailo Moskalenko and Liubov Holovata (Kyiv: Dnipro, 1998), 494.
75 Borwicz, "Inżynierowie dusz," 147.

many local ones vanished. Some did not return from the war, others were arrested, such as Stanisław Vincenz, previously a frequent visitor in town, Herminia Naglerowa, Józef Nacht, and Teodor Parnicki. The two best-known names from the leftist periodical *Sygnały*, Karol Kuryluk and Tadeusz Hollender, stayed on the sidelines, as did Anna Kowalska, who had close ties to this group. The most interesting figures of Yiddish literature, such as Debora Vogel, kept out of the official currents of literary activity. Others, like Nuchim (Naum) Bomse, joined the Writers' Union, but never played the game (after the war Bomse wrote to Vincenz: "the time I spent in Russia destroyed my poetry"). While several publications examine Polish literary life during the Soviet occupation,[76] a broader picture of the Ukrainian literary community is still needed. The studies available are limited to individual recollections[77] or consider the literary milieu only as part of a larger analysis.[78] One exception is the study *Drama bez katarsysu* [*Drama without Catharsis*] by Mykola Ilnytsky.[79]

The Ukrainian literary map underwent dramatic shifts as well. As the war broke out, the best-known writers affiliated with the *Visnyk* circle were away from Lviv (and Dontsov himself was in Bereza Kartuska prison, serving a political sentence). Other lesser-known figures, like Bohdan Kravtsiv or Mykhailo Ostroverkha, managed to make their way into areas occupied by Germans in the first months of the Soviet occupation. In 1941 some of them returned to the city. In 1939, only the surviving members of the Ukrainian literary left remained in town (the majority had perished in the Soviet Union in the 1930s), and they were now front and center. Soviet authorities bestowed favors onto

---

76 See the aforementioned publications by Polish scholars. Marci Shore's *Caviar and Ashes* is an excellent source as well, with a chapter about the literary community at the start of Lviv's occupation.
77 Tarnavs'kyi, *Literaturnyi L'viv 1939–1944*; Semchyshyn, *Z knyhy Leva*.
78 Rubl'ov and Cherchenko, *Stalinshchyna i dolia zakhidnoukrains'koi intelihentsii 20–50-ti roky XX st.*, 184–210; Volodymyr Baran and Vasyl' Tokars'kyi, *Ukraïna: Zakhidni zemli 1939–1941* (Lviv: Instytut ukraïnoznavstva NAN Ukraïny, 2009), 106–9; Ivanna Luchakivs'ka, *Ukraïns'ka intelihentsiia zakhidnykh oblastei URSR v pershi roky radians'koï vlady (1939–1941 rr.)* (Drohobych: Vidrodzhennia, 1999); Lytvyn, Luts'kyi, and Naumenko, *1939. Zakhidni zemli*; Vasyl' Kovaliuk, "Kultorolohichni ta dukhovni aspekty radianizatsii Zakhidnoi Ukraïny (veresen' 1939—cherven' 1941 r.)," *Ukraïns'kyi istorychnyi zhurnal* 2–3 (1993): 3–17; Oleksandr Luts'kyi, "Intelihentsiia v planakh utverdzhennia radians'koho totalitarnoho rezhymu na zakhidnoukraïns'kykh zemliakh 1939–1941," *Intelihentsiia i vlada. Hromads'ko-politychnyi naukovyi zbirnyk* 1 (2003): 98–104.
79 Mykola Il'nyts'kyi, *Drama bez katarsysu: Storinky literaturnoho zhyttia L'vova druhoi polovyny XX stolittia* (Lviv: Instytut ukraïnoznavstva im. I. Kryp´iakevycha NAN Ukraïny, 2003).

a few of the oldest writers from the group *Moloda Muza*: Mykhailo Iatskiv, Petro Karmansky, and Vasyl Pachovsky; but only Karmansky played a significant role, while the other two stayed out of the limelight. A group of young and relatively average literati replaced the writers who left the scene, such as the aforementioned Tsurkovsky, Ivan Kernytsky (from the liberal circle of the periodical *Nazustrich*), or the firebrand Vasyl Tkachuk. Not many women were left in the community. Sofia Parfanovych limited her literary activity, feeling safer as a physician. Two other female authors, Kostiantyna Malytska (a noted writer and an activist in the women's movement) or Maria Strutynska (her husband Mykhailo, before the war a representative to the Polish parliament and an UNDO member, was arrested in the fall of 1939[80]), gave up on literary activities altogether. Conversely, the Soviets were glad to publish short stories by Iryna Wilde (pen name of Daryna Plakhotniuk), a writer whom Mykhailo Rudnytsky had promoted in the mid-1930s.

In the first weeks of the occupation, writers, scholars, doctors, and lawyers, having recuperated from the shock of Poland's defeat, all tried to figure out a *modus vivendi*. Lviv's best-known literati joined the organizational committee of the Writers' Union. The general assembly included Maria Kasprowiczowa and Ostap Ortwin.[81] After the election to the People's Assembly, and once the USSR officially incorporated Poland's Western territories, the situation changed. In November 1939 the unification with the USSR proceeded full steam. Some writers, the president of the local chapter of the prewar Writers' Association among them, completely withdrew from literary activity. Nevertheless, Ortwin continued to look out for others; among his papers is a letter from the president of the Organizational Committee to the Writers' Union requesting free lunches for twelve writers, ten of them Jewish.[82] In the fall of 1939 Ortwin probably headed the union (*profsoiuz*), which managed the cafeteria and could provide verification of membership. Gustaw Herling-Grudziński recalled Ortwin's help with deep gratitude, though he only stayed in Lviv for a short time (after crossing the border he fell into Soviet hands and was sent to the *Gulag*, but was released in accordance with the Sikorski-Maysky agreement; he narrated his *Gulag* experiences in *A World Apart*). Because of his young age he had little

---

80   Stanisław Stępień, "Strutyński Michał (1888–1941)," in *Polski Słownik Biograficzny*, vol. 46, bk. 4 (Warsaw: IH PAN, 2007), 488–90.
81   "Komitet organizacyjny pisarzy," *Czerwony Sztandar* no. 20, October 15, 1939.
82   Letter from the Organizational Committee of Lviv Writers to the Lviv Writers' Union from November 28, 1939, signed by director Petro Panch and secretary Iaroslav Tsurkovsky, LNB, Ort. 119, p. 99, 28.11.1939.

grasp of the situation, but neither his short stay in Lviv nor his lack of experience prevented him from passing judgment. As he reminisced about Lviv half a century later, Herling-Grudziński drew simplistic distinctions between writers who preserved their dignity and stuck with Ortwin, and deserters who joined the Soviet Writers' Union. Herling-Grudziński's message sent from a labor camp in the Arkhangelsk oblast, as well as the abovementioned official letter, are the only extant documents that reflect Ortwin's moral stance (indirectly, correspondence from fall 1941 also attests to his conduct; the senders thank Ortwin for safeguarding their manuscripts and ask for their return).[83]

Journal writers rarely discuss cases of cooperation with the authorities. It is difficult to obtain a broader picture, as those ego-documents tend to focus on their authors' own community and pass over writers from other circles, especially groups defined by nationality. I found almost no comments about authors who did not frequent the Writers' Club and kept out of official literary activity, though there were plenty of such people, be they locals (Ostap Ortwin, Tadeusz Hollender, Anna Kowalska) or refugees (Maria Dąbrowska).

An exception is the figure of Tsurkovsky, whose name frequently appears in the memoir narratives. Evidently, he made an indelible mark on many people's minds, though aside from his public denunciation of Rudnytsky his chief offense seems to be the position he held. As Tarnavsky maintained, the honor should have gone to one of the leftist writers, such as Halan, Tudor, or Havryluk. Indeed, in the 1930s Tsurkovsky was not active as a writer. His rebellious years were behind him, and he moved to Katowice where he worked as a psychologist. But he arrived in Lviv at the start of the occupation—according to his biography only because he came to visit family in August 1939. If we believe Tarnavsky, Kyrylo Studynsky backed his nomination to become the club's secretary.[84] Servile with the authorities, he was disloyal to colleagues. Once the Nazis marched in, he quickly adjusted his politics. While literati who remained active during the German occupation glossed over his flip-flopping, others—Ukrainians as well as Poles—declared it a disgrace.[85] Polish writers

---

83 Gustaw Herling-Grudziński's letter from December 16, 1940 (LNB, Ort. 241, p. 17); Stanisław Obrzud's letter from Cracow, November 2, 1941 (LNB, Ort. 357, p. 20); Janina Brzostowska's letter from Warsaw, November 4, 1941 (LNB, Ort. 196, p. 16).

84 See Tarnavs'kyi, *Literaturnyi L'viv 1939–1944*, 56 and Tsalyk and Selihei, *U pivstolitnikh zmahanniakh: Vybrani lysty do Kyryla Studyns'koho (1891–1941)*, 670.

85 "Z vystupu Iaroslava Halana na rozshyrenomu plenumi Spilky pys'mennykiv Ukraïny (29.06.1944)," in *Kul'turne zhyttia v Ukraïni. Zakhidni zemli*, vol. 1, 194; "Poiasnennia Petra

saw Tsurkovsky's case as the rule, and not the exception ("there were many like him"[86]). In July of 1941, Michał Borwicz was looking to shelter at a gardener's home in a Lviv suburb and ran into Tsurkovsky; in stark contrast, the former secretary was there with an official delegation (though it is curious how this mission brought him to a gardening plot).[87]

By July 1941 Tsurkovsky again secured a leadership position in the Literary and Artistic Club, this time as its vice president.[88] That is when the matter of Mykhailo Rudnytsky fell into his hands, which did not bode well. Jan Brzoza mentions that during the Nazi occupation Tsurkovsky held a high official post—director of the Psychotechnical Institute at the Health Department in Lviv. A psychologist by profession, Tsurkovsky worked at the Institute of Psychology in Katowice before the war. Simultaneously, professor Mieczysław Kreutz along with junior colleagues sought the approval of German authorities to create the institute in Lviv.[89] Yet the director's role fell to Tsurkovsky; given that the Nazis purged all persons who held any leadership positions during the Soviet occupation, this was considered proof that Tsurkovsky had secretly harbored pro-German sentiments. Some even speculated that he was a German agent, although his Ukrainian ethnicity alone could have been a sufficient factor for the Germans to favor him over Kreutz.

In her reminiscences, Maria Savchyn, an underground OUN activist, paints Tsurkovsky as an extremely disloyal person. When she decided to quit her job, the director placed her on a list of people wanted by the police. But another testimony shows him in a very different light. Iury Vintiuk, author of the most comprehensive biographical article about the psychologist, quotes a statement according to which, at the same time he reportedly put Savchyn in danger, Tsurkovsky hired a physician by the name of Izaak Aks at the institute. After all Jews were ordered to move to the ghetto, he set up a hiding place for Aks in the building's attic. The doctor hid there till March 1944, when suddenly the German military staff took over the building. Yet Aks was saved. After the war he testified in favor of Tsurkovsky, whom the Soviets accused and convicted

---

Karmans'koho deiakikh momentiv z ioho tvorchosti (25.01.1945)," in *Kul'turne zhyttia v Ukraïni. Zakhidni zemli*, 2:785.
86 Brzoza, *Moje przygody literackie*, quoted in Trznadel, *Kolaboranci. Tadeusz Boy-Żeleński i grupa komunistycznych pisarzy we Lwowie 1939–1941*, 106.
87 Borwicz, "Inżynierowie dusz," 161–2.
88 *Nashi dni* 1 (December 1941): 14–15. Quoted in *Kul'turne zhyttia v Ukraïni. Zakhidni zemli*, vol. 1, 133.
89 Tomaszewski, *Lwów. Pejzaż psychologiczny*, 83.

of collaborating with the Nazis in 1946; the testimony made it possible for the psychologist to return to Lviv in 1949. Iury Vintiuk writes that Boris Dorfman passed Aks's testimony on to Yad Vashem,[90] but does not cite any sources, nor does he reference Dorfman's evidence, making it difficult to verify his narrative. There is no Aks on the 1939 member roster of Lviv's chamber of physicians, and his name is not listed in the local phone book from 1939. The story itself is not necessarily false; perhaps there was an error in the doctor's name or he did not have a local practice.

In the eyes of Polish writers, Tsurkovsky came to embody the attitudes of the Ukrainian intelligentsia, who merely feigned a friendly disposition towards the Soviet authorities, while deep down they favored the Germans. Those same writers completely gloss over the role of Pole Stanisław Wasylewski, a popular literary figure in Lviv, who wrote historical books and was friends with Juliusz Kleiner and Kornel Makuszyński. During the Soviet occupation Wasylewski had an office in the Writers' Club at the Bielski palace on Kopernika Street and exercised a range of duties there; in sum he enjoyed a position and benefits not unlike Tsurkovsky's. Wasylewski published in *Czerwony Sztandar*, arranged a Mickiewicz showcase in November 1940, and then, during the German occupation, worked at *Gazeta Lwowska*. Yet memoirists (Wat excepted) never mention any of this, and researchers claim that Wasylewski acted on orders from the Polish underground, a questionable assertion.[91]

THE NEW GUILDERS

> But virtue, as it never will be moved,
> Though lewdness court it in a shape of heaven,
> So lust, though to a radiant angel link'd,
> Will sate itself in a celestial bed,
> And prey on garbage.
> —Shakespeare, *Hamlet*, 1:5, ll. 60–4

Within Lviv's cultural institutions, the Soviets created the appearance of an equilibrium between ethnicities, albeit with special oversight. Separate theaters, for example, did not foster contacts outside one's own culture. Official

---

90 Iurii Vintiuk, *Iaroslav Tsurkovs'kyi: osobystist' i vchenyi. Polytychna psykholohia. Naukovyi zbirnyk* (Lviv: Vydavnychyi tsentr LNU im. Ivana Franka, 2002), 242

91 See Grzegorz Hryciuk, *"Gazeta Lwowska" 1941–1944* (Wrocław: Wydawnictwo Uniwersytetu Wrocławskiego, 1996), 213–14.

celebrations and anniversaries presented the only opportunity for stage artists of different nationalities to come together. Over the two years of Soviet occupation, Lviv commemorated the October Bolshevik revolution and Stalin's constitution, saluted the workers on May 1, and celebrated the first anniversary of the "liberation." The latter event occasioned the founding of a Ukrainian periodical titled *Literatura i mystetstvo* [*Literature and Art*]. Oleksa Desniak, chairman of the Lviv union chapter, became its editor in chief; the editorial board included Wanda Wasilewska, Elżbieta Szemplińska, Stepan Tudor, and Petro Karmansky. Soon after, the Polish magazine *Nowe Widnokręgi* [*New Horizons*] was established. These magazines printed original works as well as translations, including some produced by Lviv writers. Nearly every issue published texts related to certain literary observances, the most important of which were the eighty-fifth anniversary of Adam Mickiewicz's death, the seventieth birthday of Lesia Ukrainka, the twenty-fifth anniversary of Ivan Franko's death, and the eightieth anniversary of the death of Taras Shevchenko. All such celebrations were necessarily steeped in propaganda. A standard way to inject maximum ideology into the festivities was to reinterpret the literary works themselves. The classics were carefully reread to spot kernels of revolutionary or internationalist ideas. Just as importantly, an appropriate constellation was needed: a new classic embraced by the Soviet canon should always be preceded by a prior canonized classic, ideally a Russian one. Hugo Steinhaus offers an acerbic outline of the rules that governed such aesthetic selections:

> Many of our great national figures, literary and otherwise—such as Mickiewicz and Kościuszko—were assimilated into the Soviet canon, but, conversely, Peter the Great and Suvorov were now to be admitted as "ours." In the same breath as Mickiewicz one now had to mention Pushkin, as well as various minor poets of national significance, such as Lesya Ukrainka or the Kazakh poet Jambyl Jabayev, close to a hundred years old, who wrote rather naive little poems. All such representatives of local culture had to be lumped together and extravagantly praised, so as to make it clear that nationality doesn't matter, that poets of all stripes form a single cooperative, reciting their verses in the manner of a massed choir singing *The Internationale* in Russian, to the deafening accompaniment of a gigantic orchestra.[92]

---

92 Steinhaus, *Mathematician for All Seasons: Recollections and Notes*, 276.

The ritual behind anniversaries also extended to celebrating Mickiewicz. Jerzy Borejsza, one of the administration's trusted people, announced on the pages of *Czerwony Sztandar* how the poet's oeuvre is to be interpreted. He ended with a quote from Mickiewicz, taken out of context: "I was and am a socialist."[93] Wiktor Grosz and Zofia Dzierżyńska also wrote in a similar vein, while articles by Boy and Julian Przyboś contrasted with the prescribed approach. Since internationalism constituted an inseparable aspect of communist ideology, a special place was alloted to (commissioned) translations into the languages of Soviet nations (in fall of 1939, the Polish language gained this status as well; on personal data forms in the column "foreign languages" and "languages of the USSR nations," Polish figured in the second category, regardless of the nationality of the person submitting the form). These celebrations took place in most prestigious venues (Theater of the Opera, university auditorium, theaters) and were scripted at the highest level, as evidenced by the participation of delegates from the capital of the republic and the Soviet Union. The press devoted much space to the internationalist message of the observances. If we were to trust the reporting, we might surmise that finally a long-awaited moment had arrived; bigotry had stepped back to make room for a brotherly friendship between Poles, Ukrainians, and Jews, all owing to the wise policies of the Soviet leadership, and especially to the most enlightened of leaders of all times and nations, Joseph Stalin. *Czerwony Sztandar* reported from a rally at St. Mary's Square: "Yesterday at noon members of the committee commemorating the great poet gathered at the feet of Mickiewicz's monument, guests from Moscow, Leningrad, and Kyiv arrived for the celebrations, as well as Lviv writers. They approached the monument in a dense parade, carrying a splendid wreath to pay homage to the bard of freedom and brotherhood of the people."[94]

Three months earlier, on August 17, 1940, the Nazis destroyed Mickiewicz's monument in Cracow. No doubt the Lviv community heard about it; for the intelligentsia it would have been a pivotal moment in their perception of Nazi policies. The war on all Polish symbols in the General Government contrasted with Soviet policies in the occupied territories. In Lviv the administration limited itself to changing some street names, but they retracted, for instance, a decision to rename Mickiewicz Street to Voroshylov Street. Monuments were left untouched; not only Mickiewicz, Aleksander Fredro, or Jan

---

93 Iurii Boreisha, "Adam Mickiewicz," *Vil'na Ukraïna*, no. 229, September 29, 1940.
94 *Czerwony Sztandar*, no. 326, November 26, 1940.

The festivities commemorating Adam Mickiewicz in Lviv in November 1940 resembled propaganda rallies

Kiliński remained in place, but even King Jan III Sobieski (some visitors confused it with the monument to Khmelnytsky in Kyiv).

It should be noted that the authorities decided to organize the festivities honoring Mickiewicz in late August of 1940, thus after the Germans destroyed the poet's statue in Cracow. True, a three-volume anniversary edition of the poet's works in Russian had been planned before, at latest in July of 1940,[95] but the directive to arrange for a series of commemorative events came a month later. At that time *Czerwony Sztandar* published an article by Julian Przyboś,[96] followed by other pieces that strictly adhered to the new interpretation of Mickiewicz referenced above. The November anniversary lasted several days, culminating in a commemoration held at the Theater of the Opera and transmitted live on the radio, with high-ranking Soviet delegates in attendance. The State Polish Dramatic Theater staged a show titled *Mickiewicz's Book*, based on a script by Stanisław Wasylewski. On October 12, the Writers' Club hosted a festive evening devoted to the poet; Boy and Juliusz Kleiner presented papers, and actors from Polish, Jewish, and Ukrainians theaters—Jan Kreczmar, Dawid Koenigsberg, and Volodymyr Blavatsky—recited poems.[97]

Mieczysław Inglot was able to thoroughly recreate all the events comprising the anniversary celebration from preserved archival materials: a rally, a commemoration, an exhibit at the library of the Academy of Sciences (Ossolineum), a scholarly conference at Lviv University, and an evening at the Lviv branch of the Writers' Union.[98] In his interpretation, the festivities signaled that the Soviets were reversing their policy towards Poles. Public personas who stood with the new administration also felt that the wind was changing. According to Jerzy Putrament, the celebrations finally enabled unanimous cooperation among Polish intellectuals: "This was the first—since September [1939]—demonstration of the unity of the Polish left and of Polish culture with Soviet causes."[99] Indeed, the Mickiewicz anniversary committee consisted of Oleksa Desniak, chairman of the Lviv chapter of the Writers' Union who

---

95 "Within four days Gembarowicz and I are supposed to prepare eighty illustrations for the Russian three-volume selection from Mickiewicz's works" (Dziennik Stanisława Ossowskiego, podporucznika WP w 1939 roku, 27.08.1939–22.07.1941, k. 16).
96 Julian Przyboś, "Mickiewicz jako poeta i działacz społeczny," *Czerwony Sztandar*, no. 287, August 31, 1940.
97 "Khronika," *Literatura i mystetstvo* 2 (1940): 47
98 Inglot, *Polska kultura literacka Lwowa lat 1939–1941. Ze Lwowa i o Lwowie. Antologia*, 124–57.
99 Jerzy Putrament, *Pół wieku. Wojna* (Warsaw: Książka i Wiedza, 1984), 87.

was present *ex officio*, and those who in the fall of 1939 had immediately sided with the Soviet authorities and were now selected to the committee along party lines—Wanda Wasilewska and Jerzy Borejsza.[100] Other writers who had thus far tried to remain neutral joined as well: Tadeusz Boy-Żeleński, Julian Przyboś, Juliusz Kleiner, Petro Karmansky, and Dawid Koenigsberg.

Yet in November 1940 the Polish intelligentsia treated the ceremony with ambivalence, as we read in Tadeusz Tomaszewski's memoir: "The verdict on how to approach these festivities is relatively unclear. The number of absent professors hints at a rather negative attitude. Some speak of this Mickiewicz cult with a smirk: 'They are making him into a Bolshevik.' But that is nonsense. Poles should take advantage of any opportunities they find in the new conditions to present and broaden their culture. Sulking is the worst method."[101] Tomaszewski named only a few academics, Witold Taszycki, Adam Fischer, and Zdzisław Stieber (then an assistant). Juliusz Kleiner did not attend, blaming his absence on illness. Three writers are mentioned: two leftists (Karol Kuryluk and Jan Kott) as well as the popular writer Stanisław Wasylewski, a generation older. The psychologist concluded that the academic milieu boycotted the celebrations, while the writers joined in. His opinion was perhaps swayed by such high caliber speakers as Boy and Przyboś, but just as probably the author wanted to show, if subconsciously, that he and his university community distanced themselves from an event that stirred controversy among Poles.

The memoirist also quoted Przemysław Zwoliński, then an assistant in the division of Polish language and literature, who made wary remarks about Boy. The famed writer-translator himself gave introductory remarks during the commemorations at the Theater of the Opera and at the university conference: "it may have been nice in the *News*, but here, in these circumstances, it did not make a good impression." Tomaszewski commented: "Yet it made a good impression on others."[102] In fact, Boy's position had sparked controversy since the fall of 1939. It would seem that with the passage of time, Boy's conduct would have received a balanced assessment, but this was not to be. The issue of Boy has stirred strong emotions for many decades. Jacek Trznadel, whose *Hańba domowa* [*Disgrace at Home*] at one time presented a high-profile attempt to

---

100 Mieczysław Inglot maintains that Borejsza was not part of the committee and considers that fact striking, since Borejsza initiated the celebration in the first place. However, *Vil'na Ukraïna*, no. 202, August 29, 1940 ("Iuvileinyi komitet") lists a lineup different from what *Czerwony Sztandar* had printed; Borejsza's name is included, next to Boy's.
101 Tomaszewski, *Lwów. Pejzaż psychologiczny*, 44.
102 Ibid.

settle accounts with communism, devoted a separate book to Boy. The title *Kolaboranci* [*Collaborators*] could not make his perspective more clear. Trznadel argued that the writer crossed the line of collaboration, and went after Boy for participating in the Mickiewicz festivities.[103] Yet if we compare Boy's essay and Przyboś' article against the standard anniversary publications printed by the Soviet press (from *Czerwony Sztandar* and *Vilna Ukraina*, to the literary periodicals *Nowe Widnokręgi* or *Literatura i mystetstvo*, to union papers), we can see that both writers held a respectable distance from ideological clichés.

The authorities required that all official festivities espouse Soviet propaganda and did not permit any unofficial celebrations (extant notes of schoolchildren show that some of them organized events in Mickiewicz's honor of their own accord). A rigid canon mandated that worthy literary works be revolutionary and internationalist. In Mickiewicz's case, the focus fell on "brotherhood among peoples," an aspect of his work that coincidentally helped obscure his patriotic message. It is possible that authors of such articles stuck to directives, but more likely the pieces were finished off in the editor's office. Excerpts from Boy's presentation published in *Czerwony Sztandar*, in which the writer highlights "new opportunities which the Soviet authorities offer to researchers who strive to illuminate Mickiewicz's life and activism,"[104] show no tangible affinity with the author's writing style.

To increase the emphasis on the internationalist dimension of Mickiewicz's poetry, the authorities exercised great care in selecting the organizational committee, putting together the official guest list and arranging for telegrams sent from everywhere in the USSR. Scholars who worked to reconstruct this peculiar "Mickiewicz cult," typically examined publications from the time,[105] but rarely consulted reminiscences penned by participants. Only Mieczysław Inglot refers to an individual testimony, which leads him to consider how the general public regarded the festivities. Evidently the audience had been waiting for a sign, a beacon of hope, and became quite animated when a Russian writer proclaimed: "as immortal as Mickiewicz's poetry is, so is the Polish nation!" Spontaneous applause erupted. Inglot, relying on the

---

103 Trznadel, *Kolaboranci. Tadeusz Boy-Żeleński i grupa komunistycznych pisarzy we Lwowie 1939–1941*, 146–7.
104 *Czerwony Sztandar*, no. 325, November 25, 1940.
105 See Chłosta, *Polskie życie literackie we Lwowie w latach 1939–1941 w świetle oficjalnej prasy polskojęzycznej* (Olsztyn: Wydawnictwo Uniwersytetu Warmińsko-Mazurskiego, 2000), 123–45.

testimony of Marian Jakóbiec, credits Pavel Antokolsky[106] with this expression of solidarity. According to *Czerwony Sztandar*, the statement was made by Lev Nikulin.[107]

Similar gestures by Ukrainians from Kyiv did not earn gratitude from the Polish public. Poles considered Ukrainian speeches as a minor part of the ceremonies and did not feel compelled to listen for a special message. The Polish community received Russian declarations differently from those conveyed by Ukrainian guests. From the Ukrainian point of view, Poles were looking to secure an ally among high authorities. Conversely Poles believed that Kyiv Ukrainians showed hostility to anything Polish. Popular opinion held that Galician Ukrainians entered an alliance with representatives of the Kyiv government to retaliate for the prewar years, and only Russians could keep them at bay. But if Polish observers had been more attuned to the Ukrainian side, at least one of the official Ukrainian writer delegates should have made a positive impression, yet he remains almost entirely unnoticed in witness accounts. Maksym Rylsky had translated Mickiewicz's epic poem *Pan Tadeusz*, a project reported on by the Polish pre-1939 press. The volume appeared a dozen years earlier and was considered the most distinguished translation into a Slavic language (very likely it was the best translation of *Pan Tadeusz* into any language). Among Rylsky's output were also numerous articles devoted to his favorite poet. (Subsequent editions of his rendition of *Pan Tadeusz* published after the war reflect a gradual increase in censorship; for instance, the derogatory term "Muscovites" disappears.)

For Rylsky, translating Mickiewicz's poetry in the atmosphere of the Stalinist Terror of the 1930s presented the only opportunity for creative freedom. After being accused of participating in the fictitious Union for the Liberation of Ukraine and spending several months in 1931 in the harsh Lukianivska prison in Kyiv, the former neoclassicist, faced with a new wave of repressions, wrote a "Song about Stalin," in hopes it would become his "insurance policy."[108] Though he never received honors comparable to what the Soviets bestowed on Bazhan or Tychyna, among the neoclassicists he alone emerged from the repressions of the 1930s alive. Between the 1920s and the start of the German-Soviet war, NKVD documents consistently characterized Rylsky as a "nationalist."

---

106 Ibid., 132.
107 *Czerwony Sztandar*, no. 327, November 27, 1940.
108 Stanislav Tsalyk and Pylyp Selihei, *Taiemnytsi pys'mennyts'kykh shukhliad. Detektyvna istoriia ukraïns'koï literatury* (Kyiv: Nash chas, 2010), 57–9.

Informers also reported on his reaction to the invasion of the Polish territories by the Red Army, which the poet saw as dishonorable and unjust.[109] In January 1940, after returning from Lviv, Rylsky said that the population in those annexed territories was far from delighted.[110] To compare, Mykola Bazhan, who was in Armenia when the war broke out, both publicly and privately expressed satisfaction at the "unification of Ukrainian lands."[111] Immediately upon his return to Kyiv, Bazhan became part of an official delegation to Lviv, where he supervised the takeover of libraries.

Regardless of his personal convictions, Rylsky (his father Tadeusz came from Polish nobility and was of one the ideologists of the Ukrainian civic association Hromada of Kyiv) understood that he could not count on a warm welcome in Lviv. On the contrary, he expected to be treated as a renegade.[112] For those who attended the celebration at the Theater of the Opera, Rylsky was even less, just a basic Soviet *apparatchik*. His speech was merely part of the abominable ritual. Stanisław Ossowski's diary provides the most details:

> In the evening a commemoration at the theater. First the official part. On stage, sixteen flags of the sixteen republics and huge profiles of Lenin and

---

109 HDA SBU, f. 16, op. 32, spr. 54, k. 126. Quoted in Hrynevych, *Nepryborkane riznoholossia: Druha svitova viina i suspil'no-politychni nastroï v Ukraïni, 1939—cherven' 1941*, 108.

110 Danylenko and Kokin, *Radians'ki orhany derzhavnoi bezpeky u 1939–1941 r. Dokumenty HDA SB Ukraïny*, 1111.

111 This is how Mykola Bazhan's wife, Nina, remembered those days: "In September we traveled to Armenia to a writers' gathering devoted to the millennium of the epic folk poem *David of Sassoun*. ... On September 17, Radio Ierevan reported that the government of the USSR had decided to offer support to Western Ukrainian regions. Mykola spoke at a meeting called to show solidarity. He stated he wanted to return to Ukraine to be together with the people in the liberated land of his brothers. We returned to Kyiv via Georgia, and just a few days later Mykola went on a work trip to Lviv. 'I am terribly tired'—he wrote from there. 'Prior to the People's Assembly the work was feverish and insane. I slept four–five hours a night. Now it is night and I'm sitting here and preparing this very important document. I just came back from the first day of the Assembly—from the opening. Never have I seen and experienced anything like it. There is a lump in my throat. People were crying. ... What an amazing nation, how proud and happy am I to call myself this nation's son. I am witnessing great events. May I make even the tiniest contribution from the bottom of my soul'" (*Karbovanykh sliv volodar. Spohady pro Mykolu Bazhana* [Kyiv: Dnipro, 1988], 40–41).

112 "Spetspovidomlennia zastupnyka narkoma vnutrishnikh sprav URSR M. Horlyns'koho sekretariu TsK KP(b)U M. Khrushchovu pro reahuvannia naselennia Ukraïny na vstup viis'k RSChA v Zakhidnu Ukraïnu i Zakhidnu Bilorusiiu ta na ukladennia dohovoriv iz Nimechchynoiu ta prybaltiis'kymy derzhavamy," in Danylenko and Kokin, *Radians'ki orhany derzhavnoi bezpeky u 1939–1941 r. Dokumenty HDA SB Ukraïny*, 1072.

Stalin. Above the stage a portrait of Mickiewicz illuminated by spotlights. The committee consists of dozens of people. Opening speech. Boy's presentation. A string of speeches from various institutions in Ukraine and in Russia. One Leningrad professor allegedly spoke in Polish (he whispered, so I did not hear it). The speeches make Mickiewicz into an official representative of Polish culture in the USSR. Next to Pushkin, Shevchenko, Rustaveli, and Jambyl. There is talk of how Mickiewicz is immortal and so is the Polish nation. Rylsky gives a shoutout in honor of a) Mickiewicz, b) the great Polish nation, c) the great Ukrainian nation, d) the leader of nations, Stalin. They talk of Stalin's "friendship of peoples," Mickiewicz's dream come true.[113]

At the time Ossowski worked in the manuscript room of the Academy of Sciences Library (Ossolineum) and together with Mieczysław Gębarowicz took part in preparations for the anniversary exhibit. He had a keen sense of observation and excellent analytical ability. Though Ossowski did not harbor ethnic prejudice, even he was not attuned to Rylsky's message. All he could see was Soviet ritual. The future philosopher of culture did not read much into the translations that resounded from the stage. Curiously, his account does not mention the Ukrainian translation at all (the only ones he brings up are into Russian and Yiddish): "The concert part—in four languages—came out weak. The 'Improvisation' in [Jan] Kreczmar's interpretation was at an appropriate level, though the abbreviations bothered me—mostly in the first part. Good recitation of Jewish translation of 'The Watch' and 'The Three Budrys.' Upon her entrance, [Wanda] Siemaszkowa received a prolonged standing ovation. The liveliest applause went to: Siemaszkowa, Boy, Kreczmar, one of the Russian orators, and an artist of the Jewish theater."[114]

Ossowski noticed the Russian speaker and Polish artists but omitted the name of a Russian representative (probably Nikulin), as well as the Jewish theater actress. It was Ida Kamińska herself,[115] who, like Ossowski, had been connected with Warsaw (where she led the Jewish Theater until the war). Yet earlier, describing the commemoration at the library, the sociologist referred to Dawid Koenigsberg's translation of an excerpt from *Pan Tadeusz*. Thirty years

---

113 Dziennik Stanisława Ossowskiego, podporucznika WP w 1939 roku, 27.08.1939–22.07.1941, k. 28.
114 Ibid., k. 28–9.
115 Tetiana Stepanchykova, *Istoriia ievreis'koho teatru u L'vovi: kriz' terny, do zirok!* (Lviv: Liha Pres, 2005), 205.

Ida Kamińska, actor, in 1939–41 director at the State Jewish Theater in Lviv

later the actress reminisced about that evening at the Theater of the Opera, where she recited the passage Ossowski referenced (though she may have mixed up the details) and received compliments from Boy-Żeleński.[116]

The new Soviet guilders attempted to pare the bard's poetry to better fit the mold of communist ideology. Regardless of those reinterpretations, the Polish public reacted well to the celebrations. The particularities of the new cult mattered less; far more crucial was that the authorities officially promoted Mickiewicz (the anniversary of his death was not a round one and, absent political will, it could have been conveniently overlooked). For the Polish community, it carried the promise that the rights of Poles would be restored.

Based on available contemporaneous accounts, the public completely ignored the internationalist intent behind the festivities. A few Russian presentations were interpreted as a gesture of solidarity with Poles, but other speeches— by local Ukrainians and Jews or visitors from Kyiv—simply went unnoticed. This still holds true today: literary historians skip over the participation of Ukrainian or Jewish writers and actors in these celebrations. The translations

---

116 Ida Kaminska, *My Life, My Theater* (London: Macmillan, 1973), 129.

are also forgotten. Yet the presence of Ukrainian and Jewish literati gave the anniversary its very poignance; even the official speakers credited Mickiewicz's work with having played a formative role in their intellectual development.

TRANSLATION AS A BY-PRODUCT OF INTERNATIONALIST FRIENDSHIPS

> The king doth wake to-night and takes his rouse,
> Keeps wassail, and the swaggering up-spring reels;
> And, as he drains his draughts of Rhenish down,
> The kettle-drum and trumpet thus bray out
> The triumph of his pledge.
> —Shakespeare, *Hamlet*, 1:4, ll. 9–13

Festivities honoring poets were part of the Soviet playbook. Their actual purpose was to reinterpret their writings as well as winning over the intelligentsia. This strategy worked with a limited success; the educated class rejected the supranational aspect of this ideological practice, or, as they sneered, this "cult." The elaborate internationalist entourage, prepared with much effort and expense, made no impression. Indifferent to the ideological push, the public appropriated anniversary celebrations held between November and December 1940—whether Mickiewicz's, Tolstoy's, Franko's, or Isaac Leibush Peretz's, as tributes due to their nation's eminent writers. Contrary to the authorities' expectations, other ethnic groups did not embrace such opportunities to get to know the culture next door. A look at the table of contents in *Literatura i mystetstvo* illustrates the extent of those orchestrated efforts for each issue, one third (or more) of the magazine's pages were taken up by new translations from the Polish and Yiddish. It was openly acknowledged that official cultural commemorations served a larger, internationalist agenda.[117]

Among such events, celebrations honoring Mickiewicz resounded with an especially festive tone. Besides an evening at the Theater of the Opera, transmitted on the radio, a series of related ceremonies took place at all cultural and academic institutions, schools, and state-run companies in October and November. Their scale put them on par with the anniversary of the October Revolution. In contrast, neither of the Ukrainian authors—not Shevchenko nor Franko—merited observances of a similar scope. The system did not eulogize other Polish writers, though a few got their own rituals. The Writers'

---

117 Mykhailo Rudnyt'skyi, "Tychyna ukraïns'koiu movoiu," *Literatura i mystetstvo* 2 (1941): 51.

Union decided to honor Boy and organized an evening celebrating three decades of his creative engagement. Aside from a presentation by Stanisław Wasylewski, the anniversary must have seemed low-key in comparison with the festivities that commemorated Tychyna's combined fiftieth birthday and thirtieth anniversary of literary work.[118] Overall, celebrations in honor of living writers occurred on a reduced scale, serving as a reminder that to attain the status of a living classic, such as was awarded to Tychyna, and to a lesser degree to Boy, one had to fully submit to the authorities. *Noblesse oblige*.

The official galas fêting Ukrainian writers—Taras Shevchenko, Lesia Ukrainka, Mykhailo Kotsiubynsky, Olha Kobylianska, Vasyl Stefanyk, Volodymyr Sosiura, and Pavlo Tychyna—presented ideologically curated portraits to the public. Their effect was to incorporate these authors into the artificially promoted canon of internationalism. But the framework had a side effect; it prevented potential Polish readers from experiencing the literary value of those works, prompting them to reject those writings on principle as part of Soviet culture. We could deem this process "Sovietization through Ukrainization," though the Ukrainian scholar Vladyslav Hrynevych formulated the paradox even more aptly as "De-ukrainization in Ukrainian." A similar tactic could not affect Poland's national bard Mickiewicz. No matter how much "they made a Bolshevik out of him," the absurdity was apparent to everyone. Yet the same healthy scepticism did not apply to the reinterpretation of Ukrainian classics, whether because Poles were utterly unfamiliar with Ukrainian literature, or because they shrugged off a culture they considered inferior.[119]

Polish authors affiliated with the Soviet Writers' Union got actively involved in the publishing projects of the Natsmenvydav, or, to be more precise— the Polish division of the Ethnic Minorities Press, led by Adolf Bromberg, a member of the Communist Party of Western Ukraine before the war. In 1940–41, the local press announced Natsmenvydav's publishing agenda, which encompassed textbooks, propaganda literature, as well as belles-lettres. On the list were a few volumes by certain Polish writers whom the Soviet authorities deemed progressive, as well as selections from Ukrainian poetry in Polish translation (by Shevchenko, Tychyna, Sosiura, and others). After the war Polish poets passed over the translation projects they completed during their Lviv period in embarrassed silence; in contrast, proponents of Polish-Soviet friendship

---

118 Ibid., 52.
119 See comments on Lesia Ukrainka's poetry and Iryna Wilde's prose in Steinhaus, *Mathematician for All Seasons: Recollections and Notes*, 213.

extolled the blessed outcomes of this "Lviv episode."[120] Without access to the few lone reminiscences, especially by Ostap Tarnavsky,[121] we might have assumed that scripted ceremonials as well as state-licensed translation projects made no discernible mark on the local community.

Between propaganda-laden commemorations and poetry selections redacted by censors, the status of Ukrainian poetry was marred and its reception so deformed that it hampered contact with another culture.[122] Jan Kott, admitted to the Writers' Union Lviv chapter in September 1939, tells a story that exemplifies this detrimental outcome. Union membership came with a number of privileges, chief among them royalties for publications. Those opportunities were strictly regimented; unaffiliated writers or translators could not get their work published (though in rare instances, professional solidarity helped circumvent this prohibition). After arriving in Lviv, Kott held various jobs, as a rule all poorly paid: an archivist, a book keeper's assistant, a proofreader. But after he joined the union and owing to his friendship with Mieczysław Jastrun, his opportunities for well-compensated work expanded. To Kott as well as to his colleagues, the Soviet-commissioned literary work was merely a source of income, this attitude conveyed through a crass conversion:

> During the second winter of the war or perhaps only the spring of 1941, work began on a huge edition of Polish translations of Ukrainian poets, ancient and modern. The editors were Adam Ważyk and Mieczysław Jastrun. Mieczysław distributed the texts among his friends and I got my share. ... The pay was by the verse, that is to say by the line, and it was very generous. Frozen sturgeon ... was arriving in Lvov; for four lines of Sosiora or Rylski, a translator could buy two pounds of very good beluga sturgeon at the department store. The most profitable work, of course, was to translate poems written in "tiers," according to Mayakovsky's system. But most of the poems, unfortunately, were traditional, with rhymes, though so plentiful that Mieczysław distributed them by the yard. At the door he would cry: "Get to work! Poems! And more poems!" I got half a yard of Bazhan and a yard and a half of Sosiora.[123]

---

120 For this development, see my "Modyfikovana retseptsiia. Vydavnycha praktyka komunistychnoï Pol'shchi ta ukraïns'ka kul'tura," *Ukraïna Moderna* 16 (2010): 183–97.
121 Tarnavs'kyi, *Literaturnyi L'viv 1939–1944*, 85–6.
122 Olia Hnatiuk, "Modyfikovana retseptsiia. Vydavnycha praktyka komunistychnoï Pol'shchi ta ukraïns'ka kul'tura," 183–97.
123 Kott, *Still Alive: An Autobiographical Essay*, 43.

This embarrassing passage sheds light on the powerful barrier that impeded intellectual exchanges betwen educated Lvivians: some of the city's non-Ukrainian elites treated Ukrainian culture with utter disdain. No one criticized the mediocre results that emerged from the above commissions, as the cause was readily apparent. Before the war, public schools required that pupils learn Ukrainian, while private schools in the Ternopil, Stanislau, and Lviv voivodships introduced the subject at the founders' discretion. But it was en vogue for high school pupils to neglect the study of Ukrainian. A lack of familiarity with Ukrainian literature did not diminish an educated person's credentials. The same was true for literary works in Yiddish, perhaps with the exception of Szymon Ansky and of Debora Vogel's *Akacjes blien* [*Acacias Are Blooming*]—her volume was translated into Polish within a year of its publication. (Even Polish Jews themselves regarded works in Yiddish as too simple. Hilel Halkin referred to this cultural conflict as the period of the great Jewish language war.[124] Polish-speaking Jews took the side of Hebrew, effectively bolstering the opposition to Yiddish as a literary language.) The war only deepened such prejudice. Yet it was a foregone conclusion that other ethnic groups would show an interest in Polish culture. Simply put, Polish culture formed the center of gravity; the cultural output of other tangential ethnicities merited no attention.

Perhaps yet another, subconscious, factor contributed to Jan Kott's scorn for Ukrainian poets. His writer colleagues disliked him (they felt the same about other leftist authors) for his participation in Soviet-orchestrated literary activities. Some manifested their sentiment directly, others hid it under a mask of indifference. Many drew a connection between leftist politics and Jewish ethnicity. In her *Journals* [*Dzienniki*] the writer and Romanist Anna Kowalska noted with distaste that Polish literati fought over translation commissions from journals and publishers,[125] going so far as to point out the high incomes and mocking the Writers' Union as a "union of prostitutes." In another passage she voiced her antipathy for a poet connected with the Skamander circle, her peer Mieczysław Jastrun, who worked as an editor for the State Ethnic Minorities Press during the Soviet occupation: "Jastrun does not like me, though he hardly knows me. I hate him for this new face, for jumping at the opportunity, for being faithless to Poland, for selling out spiritually in return for Jewish equality."[126] The note dates back to March 14, 1941. At the time, half a year had

---

124 Hilel Halkin, "Wielka żydowska wojna językowa," *Scriptores* 2 (2003): 57.
125 Kowalska, *Dzienniki 1927–1969*, 53.
126 Ibid., 47.

passed since the group of writers was admitted to the union and it had been eighteen months since the occupation began. Of the editorial staff for the Lviv leftist literary periodical *Sygnały*, where Kowalska worked, only Halina Górska, who co-organized the 1936 Lviv Anti-Fascist Congress of Cultural Workers, was accepted. Left out were Karol Kuryluk, Tadeusz Hollender, and Kowalska herself. Though the *Journals'* author showed little fondness for Górska, at least she did not blaim Górska's political leanings on her ethnicity or call her a renegade. But, as we have seen, she was quick to condemn another colleague when it was a Jewish writer.

Let us return to translations of Ukrainian poetry, which the Natsmenvydav press published on a large scale, abiding by the alleged change in attitude towards Poles. The idea that Ukrainian literature in Polish would count towards the readings made available for the Polish minority must have provoked objections from Polish readers. As for original works, only pieces by "progressive authors" such as Wanda Wasilewska, Elżbieta Szemplińska, or Leon Pasternak could get published. Galician Ukrainian intelligentsia did not revel in these developments; their earlier *Schadenfreude* receded, and a soberer outlook took hold: an increasing awareness that Soviet censorship held Ukrainian culture in its firm grip. Mykhailo Rudnytsky sensed it too. As he discussed a Polish-language selection of Tychyna's poems,[127] the critic managed to convey between the lines what a Kyiv publishing house would not have let slip out; under the guise of analyzing the translations of Tychyna's most difficult poems, he extoled the high caliber of Tychyna's early work, and dismissed the "mature" Tychyna, including his "engaged" poetry, with perfunctory generalities. Indeed, when it comes Tychyna's later creative phase, his poem titles alone could scare readers away: "The Party Leads," "A Song for the Red Army," and "Felix Dzerzhinsky." In reference to specific selections made by Oleksandr Havryluk and Adam Ważyk (and undoubtedly revised by censors from the General Directorate for the Protection of State Secrets in the Press—*Glavlit*), Rudnytsky had the audacity to suggest that if the translators had some say in the process, they would have omitted more than one poem. In all fairness, the collection contained over a dozen poems from the volumes *Soniashni klarnety* and *Viter z Ukrainy*, even though at the time other editions of Tychyna's work could not feature those titles. This was Tychyna as an export product. Rudnytsky refrained from dissecting these collective translations, penned by such high caliber literati as Mieczysław Jastrun and Julian Przyboś, as well as Adam Ważyk, Stanisław Jerzy Lec, the

---

127 Mykhailo Rudnyt'skyi, "Tychyna pols'koiu movoiu," *Literatura i mystetstvo* 1 (1941): 51–2.

satirist Józef Nacht, and Jan Kott. His reticence speaks volumes; the translation project amounted to a creative failure. Yet the author did not think it appropriate to fault the translators for their lack of skill; instead he preferred to carefully trace the causes: a random selection of translators, an ideologically motivated choice of poems, and, lastly, no foreword for the benefit of Polish readership. In sum: external political conditions undermined the basic tenets of editorial culture.

Beside many translations into Polish, of varying quality, the dictate of forced internationalist friendship called for Ukrainian translations from Polish literature as well. The authors to be translated included Lviv colleagues, many of them refugees from the west (Boy-Żeleński's essays, and stories by Jalu Kurek and Adolf Rudnicki). Most pieces appeared in the monthly *Literatura i mystetstvo*, and the newspaper *Vilna Ukraina* made space for shorter contributions. Individual works—by Jalu Kurek, Halina Górska, and, predictably, Wanda Wasilewska—came out as well. On the anniversary of Mickiewicz's death, besides journalistic tributes, Rudnytsky's translation of Mickiewicz's poem "To My Muscovite Friends" was also published (the potentially pejorative "Muscovite" altered to "Russian"). *Literatura i mystetsvo* paid special attention to celebratory publications on officially promoted anniversaries, adhering to Soviet practice.

An issue of *Literatura i mystetsvo* devoted to Mickiewicz printed several translations by Ukrainian poets, among them excellent interpretations of two Crimean Sonnets by Mykola Matviiv Melnyk and "Ode to Youth" translated by Mykhailo Rudnytsky. Petro Karmansky, the best-known member of *Moloda Muza*, shared his poem "In Memory of Adam Mickiewicz." Karmansky openly expressed his debt to Mickiewicz, declaring that without *Forefathers' Eve* and "Ode to Youth" he would never have become a poet. But Polish colleagues were unimpressed by Karmansky's masterful work or his very personal homage. Perhaps it seemed meaningless to them, just another public tribute, part of an empty political ritual; after all, that is how some Polish writers approached their translations from Ukrainian. And yet both these *Moloda Muza* members viewed Polish culture as their most important reference point; it was part of their identity, though they were at home in a number of cultures. Karmansky had spent several years in Brazil but his longing for Lviv brought him back. Rudnytsky, a scholar of Romance and English literatures, took his first steps as Ostap Ortwin's secretary, and as a critic he emulated Boy. Ukrainian elites publically pledged their affiliation when Polish culture came under threat, but Polish colleagues did not take note.

Both Karmansky and Rudnytsky stayed in Lviv after 1944, and soon became targets of repressions. Each had to fight for survival. Under such conditions even private correspondence easily turned into evidence; it was surely a self-preservation strategy to leave no diaries behind. What we know of their war years comes via fellow cultural actors and … Soviet investigators. Their friendship began in the early twentieth century but did not last through the German occupation. During the Soviet occupation they were forced to move within the same circles, but they had parted way long before. The strategy they chose was similar: to participate in public affairs and use the opportunities for publishing royalties and academic work to survive. Still, their true intentions and motivations show through even in official publications. Both Karmansky and Rudnytsky were closely affiliated with Franko's circles. The fact that they were open to celebrating Mickiewicz's genius merits special recognition, considering the influential iconoclastic anti-Mickiewicz pamphlet "Poet of Treason" that Ivan Franko published in 1897.

After the war, in November 1945, another anniversary of Adam Mickiewicz's death came around. It was Mykhailo Rudnytsky who commemorated it with an article devoted to the bard, but also to the murder of Boy. He published it in *Czerwony Sztandar*.[128] What choice did he have?

ON A WHITE HORSE

> Our thoughts are ours, their ends none of our own.
> —Shakespeare, *Hamlet*, 3:2, l. 236

Earlier, I wrote about the jubilant mood that greeted Germans marching into Lviv, a reaction not at all limited to Ukrainians. At first it seemed that this occupier would favor Ukrainians too, using them as a counterweight to the Polish population. But within a month Ukrainian hopes for autonomy laid in shambles. As for Jewish people—the first few days of the occupation quickly proved wrong any delusions that in Eastern Galicia things would go differently than in the General Government or in the Reich. In July, two pogroms filled the city with horror (historians still argue about the exact number of the dead, but it was in the thousands). The Nazis set out to exterminate the Jewish intelligentsia. In contrast to the murder of Lviv professors, where we know each victim

---

[128] Michał Rudnicki, "Adam Mickiewicz 1855–1945. Piewca wolności i braterstwa ludów," *Czerwony Sztandar*, no. 195, November 25, 1945.

by name, here the identities of most casualties are unknown. Under penalty of death, every Jew was required to wear a badge with the Star of David.

Without permission from the Nazi administration, activists in both factions of the Organization of Ukrainian Nationalists followed in the footsteps of the German divisions and entered Lviv. Initially, the supporters of Stepan Bandera from the OUN-R faction took over. In July backers of Andry Melnyk also began arriving in Lviv. They were late to the competition for power and control over minds, yet were utterly convinced of their mission and their rationale, sentiments to which Ulas Samchuk's reminiscences *Na bilomu koni* [*On a White Horse*] give voice.

On June 30, 1941, from the former Prosvita office on the Rynek Square, Iaroslav Stetsko issued a proclamation renewing the Ukrainian state. Soon Stetsko and Bandera were arrested, along with many OUN members (a second, large-scale wave of arrests occurred on September 15, 1940). Stetsko nominated to his government several Ukrainian activists not affiliated with OUN, although without their agreement. Now the Germans enlisted those persons in city administration (the chapter "Academic Snapshots" follows Dr. Panchyshyn and professor Poliansky; another figure important in this context was Kost Pankivsky). Their service was temporary; once civil servants arrived, Germans replaced Ukrainians. But even a brief stint sufficed to brand them as collaborators.

Ukrainian intelligentsia assumed that the new occupier would reinstate former cultural institutions. They energetically began to lay the foundations, organizing various creative associations. In July and August of 1941 their activities were not yet regimented. But soon it turned out that the German administration had no intention to reopen cultural or academic facilities, nor did they plan on returning property that the previous occupier had nationalized. All unions were incorporated (as chapters) into the Ukrainian National Committee, headed by Kost Pankivsky (in February of 1942 this administrative body became subordinate to the Ukrainian Central Council in Cracow, led by Volodymyr Kubiyovych).

In circumstances not exactly conducive to literary meetings, towards the end of July the president of the reactivated Association of Writers and Journalists Mykola Holubets and vice president Iaroslav Tsurkovsky sent invitations to a meeting with three Ukrainian authors visiting from the General Government. The guests, freshly arrived from Cracow, were Olena Teliha, Oleh Shtul, and Ulas Samchuk. On July 23, 1941, in the cramped Prosvita quarters, a discussion ensued between Ukrainian literati from both occupation zones. The event ended in a scandal—Bandera's affiliates obstructed presentations by Teliha and

Samchuk, who were associated with the Melnyk circles.[129] Yet the causes of the rift ran deeper still.

Ulas Samchuk and Olena Teliha had demanded that their OUN-M supervisor Oleh Olzhych, one of the best-known poets of the interwar period, organize the meeting. Holubets suggested that the time was not right for such gatherings, but they took this as an affront. Later, when Samchuk reminisced about the evening, he did not focus on the provocative questions posed by the Bandera-affiliated youth, but on "representatives of culture and the arts" who tried to share with the visitors their experiences from the Soviet occupation. Samchuk spoke on his favorite topic, the imperative to move away from Romantic revolutionary notions and engage in the organic work of setting up local administrative and educational structures. Teliha brought up heroism. A few attendees advised it was at best insensitive to lecture the locals. Either nobody filled in Teliha on the scale of the Soviet terror, or she simply lacked empathy. She contrasted the anti-Soviet struggle of writers in Eastern Ukraine with the actions of Lviv's writers, who put up no resistance at all, and charged: "where are your Khvylovys? You did not fight; instead, you simply bowed to regime!"[130] Small wonder then that the atmosphere in the room turned icy, as Samchuk described in *On a White Horse*. Samchuk used the public's reaction to retaliate against those who during the Soviet occupation acted—in his opinion—as the regime's "loyal servants." The writer concluded that his Lviv colleagues used the political divisions in the room to discredit the guest speakers and turn attention away from their own conduct.[131] Here he meant not just Tsurkovsky, who indeed had served as secretary of the local chapter of the Soviet Writers' Union, but also Mykola Holubets, journalist and historian of culture, who, unlike Tsurkovsky, had been a mere librarian under the Soviets. A different version comes via Ostap Tarnavsky: "the club's leadership did not want to get involved in the divisions, imported from the west by people who used to be members of the same organization."[132] The memoirist did not mention how the visitors reproached the locals for not standing up to the Soviets; he himself would have been implicated.

Certainly, friction between visitors from the General Government and the Lviv community was inevitable. Echoes of similar disputes sound in

---

129 Tarnavs'kyi, *Literaturnyi L'viv 1939–1944*, 80.
130 Ulas Samchuk, *Na bilomu koni—na koni voronomu* (Ostroh: Vydavnytstvo Natsional'noho universytetu Ostroz'ka Akademiia, 2007), 82.
131 Ibid., 81.
132 Tarnavs'kyi, *Literaturnyi L'viv 1939–1944*, 120.

accounts by Polish authors, who emphasize that those who lived through the German occupation tended to underestimate the communist regime and its system of repressions. In the first weeks of the German-Soviet war, Lviv was reeling from the cruelty and scope of the NKVD prison murders. Anyone who was spared must have found Samchuk's and Teliha's attitudes especially jarring. But the OUN activists were not interested in the tragedy, their eyes were on obtaining power and taking control of the locals. Activist groups making their way east, including Samchuk, Shtul, and Teliha, could not set direct political goals; for that they were too weak. Instead they sought to rule people's hearts and minds by any means available. Before the German crew arrived, they pursued the maximum number of posts in the civil administration to secure their influence; even spots at the lowest levels of the government were desirable should the higher ones slip out of reach. The Galician intelligentsia reacted skeptically. Of particular interest in this respect are notes from an unpublished diary by Maria Strutynska. While she was not a figure central to the community of educated Ukrainians (it would not have been easy for a woman to play such a role), she certainly had some stature, or else the community would not have entrusted her with the job of editing *Nashi dni*, the only Galician cultural periodical published during the German occupation. Strutynska saw the face of Soviet rule up close and she doubted very much that the Melnyk group, who was proceeding east, could understand the locals' experience of communist terror: "they all seemed to me removed from the earth—some superstructure suspended in the air. They would have to be here with us for some time, see a little of Ukraine submerged in Bolshevik reality, to understand that with those people, exhausted from years of hunger, of malnourishment, terror and rigid control, you need to speak in a completely different language."[133] Survivors of the Soviet occupation knew that only after they recoiled from the omnipresent subconscious fear, could there be talk of gaining independence. Even the most beautiful shibboleths could not restore their faith; as recent citizens of Soviet Ukraine they knew the value of political slogans all too well.

It is possible that his narrow focus on a political goal prevented Samchuk from taking in the events Lviv had witnessed between late June and early August: Soviet murders of prisoners, Jewish pogroms, arrests, executions. But we should not rule out that he may have consciously excluded those tragedies

---

133 Note from September 21, 1941 (Mariia Strutynska Papers, Diary 1941–1947, box 1, folder 20, k. 9).

from his memoirs. In reference to the divisive meeting, Samchuk goes on about a table laden with food, a well-lubricated meal, and his conversations with the local literati. He expounds on a later attempt to contact Bandera's group, and mentions meetings with the Metropolitan Sheptytsky, the interim university president Vasyl Simovych, the writer and activist Maria Strutynska, and the editor of the newspaper *Ukrainski shchodenni visti*, Osyp Bodnarovych. But his interest is singular: how to get to Kyiv as soon as possible and start a newspaper that will reach the hearts and minds of the Dnipro brothers. Not a word about the tragedy of the Soviet-occupied population, though had he leaned in a little, he could have grasped their perspective better. Nothing about the constant funerals for victims of atrocities. Yet he met with Simovych repeatedly—they had been introduced in Prague before the war. Surely the interim university president, a philologist and structuralist very highly regarded in the community, had a lot to say about Soviet times and the concerns of his Kyiv colleagues. Strutynska continued looking for her husband, Mykhailo Strutynsky, a well-known activist arrested at the start of the Soviet occupation. She kept on hoping that instead of perishing in the Lviv prison, he would have been transported by the NKVD deep into the USSR. Till the very end of the war she believed she would find him among the survivors, against all odds and in spite of news from fellow prisoners.[134] Strutynska's friend, who also spent many days searching for her husband's body, published a description of her efforts in Bodnarovych's *Ukrainski shchodenni visti*. Undoubtedly Samchuk was privy to these reports. And yet he did not hear them.

It would be pointless to look for even a mere reference to Lviv's Polish or Jewish inhabitants in the memoir *On a White Horse*. Between the Sunday dinner in late July at the Prosvita, which he described so attentively, and a different Sunday event—a theater performance in early August (*A Cossack beyond the Danube*—*Zaporozhets za Dunaiem*, directed by Volodymyr Blavatsky), another pogrom took place on July 25–7, 1941. More than 1,000 people of Jewish ethnicity were murdered. Samchuk must have also witnessed violence against the Jewish population on his daily walks. He and Teliha were staying in an apartment abandoned by an NKVD major at 65 Tarnawski, a bit away from the city center, and would walk to Akademicka Street, the base of the Melnyk group, or to the Rynek Square. Samchuk also visited Metropolitan Sheptytsky.

---

134 Witness reports were published in *Ukraïns'ki shchodenni visti*, no. 6, July 12, 1941: "On Tuesday evening, twice the NKVD called [from our cell] three prisoners each—Ukrainians. The first group included editor Strutynsky, the second, director Radlovsky."

Maria Strutynska kept a diary throughout the entire occupation, despite her husband's arrest

Getting around town, he must have noticed the compulsory registration, and posters announcing that Jews must wear badges with the Star of David. But he steers clear of those topics (similarly, he did not address the anti-Polish operation in Volhynia). Only once do we come across a reference to other ethnicities:

> Lviv in these anxious times was a mixture of old Poland, the not-so-old Soviets, our revolution, and the German occupation. Our flags proudly adorned buildings and our trident emblems glistened, yet store signs still spoke in "glavkharchprom" [Russian acronym for the Soviet food distribution network] and in the language of Mickiewicz underneath. But Ukrainian newspapers were being published, one could hear the sound of Ukrainian radio, Ukrainian theater was operating, navy-blue uniforms of policemen wearing Mazepa caps with tridents appeared. ... And, of course, plenty of grey reich uniforms and cars.[135]

This description is striking in its the juxtaposition of "top-bottom:" Soviet-Polish. The metonymy allows the reader to realize that most Lvivians use

---

135 Samchuk, *Na bilomu koni—na koni voronomu*, 74.

Polish. Samchuk implies, though vaguely, that there is a connection between what is Soviet and what is Polish: the Polish streets live in subjugation yet provide quiet support. The passage is not far removed from propaganda pieces appearing in the German Ukrainian-language press, which claimed that Poles had backed Soviet rule. The present time is dominated by the adjective "Ukrainian." "German" makes no appearance, except for the Reich, for some reason in lower case letters.

It is helpful to place this passage in the context of contemporaneous events and read it side by side with a *Lvivski visti* [*Lviv News*] article from August 1941, titled "Out with Jewish signs."[136] The piece demanded that the city administration install "appropriate signage in Lviv." The title could not be clearer; the text itself drew a similar parallel to prove a Polish-Jewish connection and by doing so took aim at Polish placards as well: "old Polish-Jewish signs such as 'Słowo polskie' or 'Sokół i macierz' have not disappeared yet." Two weeks earlier the outraged Maria Strutynska, who worked for *Ukrainski shchodenni visti* (*Daily News*; the paper was closed in late August of 1941; from then on *Lvivski visti* remained the only publication permitted), condemned the actions of the

Sviatoslav Hordynsky, Ulas Samchuk, Arkady Liubchenko, respectively inhabitants of Lviv, Volhynia, and Kharkiv, and the émigré Ievhen Malaniuk, met up in Lviv in 1943

---

136 "Het' z zhydivs'kymy napysamy," *L'vivs'ki visti*, no. 18, August 29, 1941, 4.

barbaric occupiers for setting synagogues on fire in mid-August, and she decried the loss of the Golden Rose.[137]

Ulas Samchuk's perspective is a fair representation of the ideology espoused by the Ukrainian émigré circles with ties to the nationalist movement: convinced of the righteousness of their cause, willing to force it onto all Ukrainians, lacking a sense of their positions or the realities of their existence. In contrast, Lviv Ukrainians, especially the older generation, approached Stetsko's government skeptically, as evident from the memoirs they penned as emigrants (for instance Kost Pankivsky). Despite holding a privileged position, Ukrainians experienced the German occupation as a continuation of the war, which was growing increasingly more cruel. Samchuk was outraged that Mykola Holubets, the president of the Literary and Artistic Club, gave his Cracow group the cold shoulder. Ostap Tarnavsky, a dozen or so years Samchuk's junior and a generation younger than Holubets, criticized Samchuk's ideas as well. Publications in the occupation press, as well as later reminiscences of persons affiliated with either of the OUN factions, simply do not paint an accurate or a complete picture of the spectrum of attitudes toward the German occupation and the situation of Ukrainians in Galicia. Yet all too often those memories are assumed to represent the community and stand as proof of its collaboration or, at the very least, of its quiet support for Nazi policies towards Poles and Jews.

ON THE PRECIPICE

> For who would bear the whips and scorns of time,
> The oppressor's wrong, the proud man's contumely,
> ....
> The insolence of office and the spurns …
> —Shakespeare, *Hamlet*, 3:1, ll. 78–81

In July 1941 two gatherings took place at the Literary and Artistic Club; the first one was called to restart the club and exchange information; we are familiar with the second one from the preceding passages. A new registration of writers and journalists was in progress. The Ukrainian intelligentsia expected that some of the prewar organizations would be revived and the creative unions set up by

---

137 Entry from August 16, 1941 (Mariia Strutynska Papers, Diary 1941–1947, box 1, folder 20, k. 4). The journal begins on August 10, 1941. On that day, Maria Strutynska ceased her daily searches for her husband's body in the Lviv prison and returned to more regular journal notes.

the Soviets would be reorganized.[138] Unaware that he was putting himself in peril, Mykhailo Rudnytsky also came to the club at 3 Podwalna. At the door he ran into an acquaintance who talked him out of applying for membership. He warned that Petro Karmansky, a former friend from the *Moloda Muza* group, had denounced Rudnytsky as a person of Jewish ethnicity.[139]

Karmansky and Rudnytsky parted ways back in the 1930s, when Karmansky, in his memoir of the first years of the 1900s, called the critic "a self-proclaimed literary oracle." In *From Myrny to Khvylovy*, Rudnytsky responded in kind, subjecting Karmansky's poetry to biting remarks. Now Karmansky, if the warning was to be believed, used Rudnytsky's half-Jewish origins to have him banished from literary activity.

Karmansky himself described the July gathering differently—he was the victim there. According to the poet, Tsurkovsky, as the former secretary of the Soviet Writers' Union, and now the vice president, directed him and other writers to report to the inaugural meeting. As it turned out, both Karmansky and Rudnytsky were precluded from joining the reestablished association. In a note presented to the Soviets, the poet does not say why, but decries the harsh outcome—he was left without any way to support himself. According to him, Rudnytsky was better off financially and thus able to disappear from Lviv, but Karmansky had no such option.[140] This was certainly untrue. The Soviets had given privileges to Karmansky, but not to Rudnytsky; in fact, the critic's income was not high at all since he no longer worked at *Vilna Ukraina* and lived on a university salary plus the occasional royalties from a press article here and there. In contrast, the poet lectured at the university, was on the editorial staff at *Literatura i mystetsvo*, and received fees for published poems as well as a recent poetry volume. As other sources indicate, colleagues disapproved of Karmansky because he had participated in official life during the Soviet occupation. In truth they disliked him far more for receiving a sizeable stipend of 25,000 rubles[141] than for

---

138 Kost' Pan'kivs'kyi, *Vid Derzhavy do Komitetu (Lito 1941 roku u L'vovi)* (Toronto: Kliuchi, 1970), 34.
139 "Lyst professora Mykhaila Rudnyts'koho zastupnykovi zaviduvacha viddilu propahandy TsK KP(b)U Ivanovi Zolotoverkhvomu (24.01.1945)," in *Kul'turne zhyttia v Ukraïni. Zakhidni zemli*, vol. 2, 781.
140 "Poiasnennia poeta Petra Karmans'koho deiakykh momentiv svoho zhyttia ta tvorchosti," in *Kul'turne zhyttia v Ukraïni. Zakhidni zemli*, vol. 2, 785.
141 Oleksandra Stasiuk, "Zhyttievyi shliakh Petra Karmans'koho (hromads'ko-politychnyi aspekt)," in *Ukraïna: kul'turna spadshchyna, natsionalna svidomist', derzhavnist'. Zakhidno-Ukraïns'ka Narodna Respublika: do 90-richchia utvorennia* (Lviv: NAN Ukraïny, Instytut Ukraïnoznavstva im. Ivana Kryp'iakevycha, 2009), 541.

his public statements, which merely toed the prescribed line. Diarists are eager to emphasize the difference between the two poets Karmansky and Pachovsky. The first turned out reliable, attended functions, made appearances, published; the other never let the authorities appropriate his name for their purposes.

Two young writers with posts in the reopened association—Iaroslav Tsurkovsky and Volodymyr Shaian—were Rudnytsky's sworn enemies. Now came their opportunity to get even with the critic, their former contender for literary benefits. Under Soviet rule they tried and failed to get Rudnytsky removed from the union. A change of circumstances suddenly made it possible to get rid of the disliked critic using his "non-Aryan origin." Karmansky writes that in the aftermath, Mykhailo Rudnytsky fell seriously ill. He decided to disappear from public life, yet he needed to find other legal employment now that he was not able to register as a writer. Falling back on work experience acquired in the previous war, he applied to the translation agency run by his university colleague Bolesław Czuruk. He did not work there long; by 1942, just being seen on the street spelled danger for Rudnytsky, and so he vanished from Lviv.[142]

Today we know that Rudnytsky's Lviv friends directed him to Andry Terpyliak near Halych (before the war the brothers Terpyliak owned a horticulture farm in Zalukva, well known across Galicia; they hosted many emigrants from the Petliura camp), who gave the critic shelter.[143] There he worked as a private tutor, probably less so to make a living than to legalize his stay. In reality he sustained himself on fees from editing and from literary translations for the theater (among them such "minor" projects as *Hamlet* and Gogol's *The Government Inspector*). The "Ukrainian Press" ["Ukrainske vydavnytsvo"] commissioned translations from him as well. Rudnytsky's friends knew where he lived; in the wider circles it was understood that he was "holing up in the countryside." But from time to time he could be seen—either at the theater in Lviv, or at the healing spa in Morshyn.

By the end of the occupation Rudnytsky had returned to the translation office. The owner, Bolesław Czuruk, was a Slavist who had worked as a lecturer of Russian and as a sworn translator before the war and then had opened his own translation agency at 1 Akademicki Square. During the Soviet occupation Czuruk continued as a Russian lecturer at Lviv University, but had to shut down

---

142 *Kul'turne zhyttia v Ukraïni. Zakhidni zemli*, vol. 2, 796.
143 Dovidka upravlinnia NKVD L'vivs'koï oblasti obkomovi KP(b)U pro profesora Mykhaila Rudnyts'koho, 10.07.1945, DALO, f. P-3, op. 1, spr. 238, k. 29–30 (*Kul'turne zhyttia v Ukraïni. Zakhidni zemli*, vol. 2, 795–7). See also Ivan Dziuba, *Spohady i rozdumy na finishnii priamii* (Kyiv: Krynytsia, 2008), 775.

his business, restarting it under the German administration. Beside official translations, the agency ran a parallel line of "business," legalizing false documents. This allowed Czuruk to save the lives of several dozen Jews. In 2010 he was posthumously honored as Righteous Among Nations. Today we cannot say whether Rudnytsky was also involved; as a person with Jewish blood he needed help himself, but that is not to say that he did not assist others.

During this period, Mykhailo's brother Ivan Kedryn-Rudnytsky worked for the Cracow Ukrainian-language paper *Krakivski visti*. He rarely came to Lviv, especially following an incident that occurred in 1941. In the aftermath of the Soviet occupation, Kedryn arrived in his home town and went to see what he could still recover from his old apartment; he had left on September 22, 1939 with one briefcase and a change of underwear. He discovered that an old friend, a former officer of the Ukrainian Galician Army, had moved in. The "friend" greeted Kedryn with "Heil Hitler!" and continued the conversation in German.[144]

In late August 1941, as Mykhailo receded from the public view, Milena Rudnytska, a resident of the General Government, was visiting in Lviv. Before the war Milena had served as a deputy to the Polish Sejm and had delivered sharp critiques of Polish policy toward the Ukrainian minority both in the parliament as well as on the international scene. She was a familiar face in Lviv. Very little is known of her war experiences. We can only guess that the Gestapo forced her to forgo any political activity; they did so with other Ukrainian politicians who escaped from the Soviet-occupied territories, for instance Vasyl Mudry. Rudnytska even withdrew from the assistance committee—the Ukrainian Central Committee set up in Cracow under the leadership of Volodymyr Kubiyovych. Based on reminiscences and documents accessible today it is impossible to determine how Milena, Ivan, and their mother avoided being found out as Jewish. They were a prominent family with plenty of enemies eager to turn them in. It is possible that colonel Alfred Bisanz from a mixed (German-Ukrainian) Galician family was their protector. During World War I he had served as an officer in the Ukrainian Galician Army, and now during World War II he worked in the Abwehr and was put in charge of Ukrainian issues, on which he reported to governor Hans Frank. He was in direct contact with the Ukrainian Central Committee and had been its representative in the District of Galicia since August 1941; in 1944 he became a liaison officer of Division Galizien. Although Kedryn's memoir makes no reference to the

---

144 Ivan Kedryn, *Zhyttia—podii—liudy*, 361.

German colonel, the Rudnytskys most certainly knew Bisanz, who acted as a liaison between the Abwehr and the Ukrainian Military Organization UVO.

Did the siblings get together in Lviv in the summer of 1941? All signs suggest so, but there is no written record. Most of what we know about Milena Rudnytska's trip to Lviv comes by way of the writer Maria Strutynska and her journal entries.[145] Rudnytska stayed with her mother Olga (Ida Spiegel) at the downtown Hotel Europa on St. Mary's Square. How was she not afraid of being turned in? Before the war she had lived in Lviv. Now, like her brother, she could not return to her apartment as a "non-Aryan," though we have no information who was living there in 1941. As a former deputy and president of the Union of Ukrainian Women, and one of the most energetic activists of the National Committee for Relief to Starving Ukraine (established in Lviv during the Great Ukrainian Famine in 1933), she was easily recognizable in town. In the early 1930s, after she had carried out an information campaign to broadcast to the international community the suppression of Ukrainian villages in Galicia, the Polish administration deemed her hostile to the Republic of Poland. In 1938 the Union of Ukrainian Women was dissolved. In response Rudnytska founded a new organization, the Corps of Princess Olha (*Druzhyna Kniahyni Olhy*).

It was not a secret in Lviv that the Rudnytsky siblings were half-Jewish. Most certainly there were locals who viewed Milena as an enemy of Poles, a Ukrainian nationalist. Yet she made no attempt to hide; on the contrary, upon arrival she immediately threw herself into activism. Did she feel safe as a Ukrainian? That is doubtful. Nevertheless, she renewed contacts with former colleagues from the Union of Ukrainian Women's board, who witnessed the immense suffering of civilians and prisoners of war after the German invasion. In response they established the organization Women's Service to Ukraine to assist those in need, with a focus on prisoners. The group worked together with Polish friends and affiliates, in particular with Maria Bartlowa. But restarting the Union of Ukrainian Women was out of the question—in a conversation with Maria Strutynska, Rudnytska said that in these circumstances she could not reactivate the union and serve as its president.[146] Most likely she could foresee what was to come and knew that her own position was uncertain. She was right: under the guise of reorganization, Women's Service disbanded after a few months. At that time the Ukrainian National Council became subordinate

---

145 Entry from September 5, 1941 (Mariia Strutynska Papers, Diary 1941–1947, box 1, folder 20, k. 5).
146 Entry from September 14, 1941 (Mariia Strutynska Papers, Diary 1941–1947, k. 7).

to the Ukrainian Central Committee in Cracow, the General Government's capital.

Like her brothers, Milena Rudnytska operated on the precipice of safety. Today it is still a mystery how the entire family, their Jewish mother included, survived without having to hide. After the war this question mark prompted the Bandera circles to insinuate that the Rudnytsky's survival was shameful. A campaign of slander against Rudnytska lasted until at least the late 1940s, not that its initiators went to the trouble of making coherent or plausible arguments. The former parliamentary deputy was accused of being a Gestapo agent, and an NKVD snitch, though both these secret police agencies ruthlessly persecuted politicians of her rank. Milena Rudnytska had adopted a highly critical position towards the Bandera circles, especially against Stetsko's proclamation of the Ukrainian state, and voiced it both during the war and after. Her vocal dissent triggered a witch hunt (coincidentally the Bandera group needed to divert attention from their own actions during World War II and to shed their complicity in Nazi war crimes). As laughable as the allegations seem, the Ukrainian émigré community gradually isolated Rudnytska. She conveyed her sorrow in a letter to the Prime Minister of the Ukrainian People's Republic-in-exile.[147]

Rudnytska came to Lviv in late summer of 1941. She decided to collect and publish accounts of the Bolshevik terror.[148] Perhaps she was compelled by reports in *Krakivski visti* and *Lvivski shchodenni visti* about the mass murders committed by the NKVD in prisons in Lviv and other Soviet-occupied territories, or—more likely—by direct accounts, perhaps also what she learned through of her brother Mykhailo. Ostap Tarnavsky, possibly recommended by Mykhailo, assisted Milena in her efforts.[149] The former president of the Union of Ukrainian Women understood what OUN activists did not: the task of documenting Soviet crimes should not be entrusted to the new occupier. Collecting oral history was a methodology she had used ten years earlier, when she gathered eyewitness reports of the brutal repressions perpetrated by Poles on Ukrainian populations during the pacification of Eastern Galicia in order to present evidence to the international community. Now, under occupation, she resorted to the same method, convinced that it was the only way to preserve such accounts. Thanks to her initiative and energetic efforts, Kost Levytsky's reminiscences were written down. The sage Ukrainian

---

147 Lyst Mileny Rudnyts′koï do Panasa Fedenka, Zheneva, 4 zhovtnia 1948, Arkhiv UVAN, kolektsiia Mileny Rudnyts′koï.
148 Notes from a September 5, 1941 conversation (Mariia Strutynska Papers, Diary 1941–1947, box 1, folder 20, k. 5).
149 Tarnavs′kyi, *Literaturnyi L′viv 1939–1944*, 126.

politician spent over eighteen months in prison before his death in November of 1941. Most reports remained anonymous, as they could have harmed the contributors or their families. None of these accounts, not even the statements of Metropolitan Sheptytsky, were published in the German propaganda press. In early 1942 the volume was ready for print and Rudnytska passed it on to the Prague publisher Iury Tyshchenko. Until the end of 1944, the German censorship office would not permit its publication. In the spring of 1945, an edition numbering 5,000 copies fell into the hands of Prague's Soviet "liberators." Finally, twelve years later, the book appeared in New York.[150] It retained the value of an almost direct witness account, in contrast to news stories from the same period, which were steeped in German propaganda.

Portrait artist Semen Gruzberg (Hruzbenko) survived the occupation in Lviv thanks to friends, among them Ostap Tarnavsky

---

150 Rudnyts'ka, *Zakhidnia Ukraïna pid bol'shevykamy*, passim.

On September 15, 1941, three weeks into collecting these materials, Milena Rudnytska and her aide Ostap Tarnavsky were arrested. The Nazis were casting a wider net; the operation was not connected to Rudnytska's project, but rather it targeted Ukrainian political activists. The next day, after the intervention of the president of the Ukrainian National Council Kost Pankivsky, all detained women were set free.[151] Soon the German authorities released most of the arrested men, including Tarnavsky. The Germans decided to limit their repressions to OUN members only. It is possible that this incident convinced Rudnytska to become more cautious. Her elderly mother's life depended on Milena (the family destroyed Ida Spiegel's old baptism certificate at this point; a Cracow clergyman and friend of the family, the reverend Demian Lopatynsky, issued a falsified new one[152]). Rudnytska left Lviv, first stopping in Cracow, then Prague, and then Berlin.

HAMLET

> ... they are the abstract and brief chronicles of the time.
> —Shakespeare, *Hamlet*, 2:2, l. 550

It is time to finally ask the question only implied at the start of this chapter: how was it possible to legally stage *Hamlet* in Ukrainian during the Nazi occupation, and if this were not enough, to use a translation prepared by someone with Jewish roots? All this at a time when all Polish cultural activities moved underground and persons participating in any form of legal entertainment were ostracized? "Legal" connoted "sanctioned by the occupier," and that smacked of collaboration. The Polish slogan "Tylko świnie siedzą w kinie" ["Only pigs sit at the flicks"] aptly illustrates attitudes towards official entertainment. Jewish cultural life nearly completety vanished, eliminated by the Nazis; any residual instances spoke to the artists' and their audience's courage and will to live.

The occupier regimented all goods, including cultural products and events. As a result, the German administration controlled public events and changed the principles of distribution. Ethnic Germans had unconditional first priority, then came other nationalities, in nesting order. The General

---

151 Strutynska wrote that on September 16, 1941, the Germans released Malytska, Horbachova, Tsisykova, Polianska, and Rudnytska (Mariia Strutynska Papers, Diary 1941–1947, box 1, folder 20, k. 8).
152 Milena Rudnyts'ka, *Statti. Lysty. Dokumenty*, ed. Myroslava Diadiuk and Marta Bohachevs'ka-Khomiak (Lviv: Misioner, 1998), 49.

Government imposed a hierarchy of nationalities, according to which a *Kennkarte* with the letter "U" (which certified documented Ukrainian origin) entitled its carrier to more than a card with a "P" (that is, of Polish ethnicity), while the Jewish population was completely stripped of all rights. Though formally Poles, Ukrainians, and Jews had similar self-governance structures, only Ukrainians could conduct a wider range of activity beyond humanitarian aid. Contrary to popular opinion, the more privileged status of Ukrainians did not reward their readiness to collaborate or their alleged loyalty to the occupier, but rather reflected Nazi policies. For instance: a Ukrainian could attend college in the Reich, but a Pole could not. Ukrainians were permitted to listen to the radio, but for Poles owning one was punishable by death. A *Kennkarte* with the letter "U" came with slightly larger food allotment than a "P" one (not to mention the starvation rations Jews were "entitled" to). Such better treatment resulted from administrative regulations implemented by the occupier to stoke enmity between population groups. The locals themselves held no sway in deciding the rules and permissions. Even Ukrainians arriving from Kyiv, a city within the Reichskommisariat Ukraine, were amazed at the rights their compatriots in District Galizien enjoyed: "Although officially the German occupying authority existed and operated, Lviv lived like a real Ukrainian city. It was hardly comparable to what we experienced in Kyiv."[153] While Lviv could boast several chapters that functioned as cultural associations, in Kyiv all organizations were forbidden, as were all meetings. The Nazis executed Kyiv writers affiliated with the periodical *Litavry*, including Olena Teliha, at Babi Yar.

Aid committees operated within the legal framework. In the case of Ukrainians, such activities were not limited to assisting those in need but allowed for substantial cultural endeavors as well.[154] Kost Pankivsky, president of the Ukrainian National Council during the German occupation, published his memoirs at the turn of the 1950s and 1960s. The three volumes attempt to reconstruct the specific areas in which the various committee divisions operated. His collection of documents at the Ukrainian Free Academy of Sciences includes extensive correspondence with multiple persons about their various

---

153 Hryhorii Kostiuk, *Zustrichi i proshchannia*, vol. 1 (Edmonton: Canadian Institute of Ukrainian Studies, 1998); 2nd ed. (Kyiv: Smoloskyp, 2008), 102.
154 See theses by Natalia Antoniuk and Kostiantyn Kurylyshyn: Natalia Antoniuk, *Ukraïns′ke kul′turne zhyttia v "Heneral′niy Hubernii" (1939–1944 rr.). Za materialamy periodychnoï presy* (Lviv: NANU—L′vivs′ka naukova biblioteka im. V. Stefanyka, 1997); Kostiantyn Kurylyshyn, *Ukraïns′ke zhyttia v umovakh nimets′koï okupatsiï (1939–1944): za materialamy ukraïnomovnoï lehal′noï presy* (Lviv: NANU—LNBL: L′vivs′ke viddilennia Instytutu ukraïns′koï arkheohrafiï ta dzhereloznavstva, 2010).

areas of activity, ranging from medical to cultural. Though his access to the extant materials helped the author paint a panoramic view of the Ukrainian social and cultural life in the District Galizien, his recollections lost the value only direct reminiscences can contribute. Additionally, Pankivsky needed to defend his own position, and thus felt compelled to omit or skirt a number of difficult issues. Referring to cultural activities, he stated: "during the German occupation publishing matters were not an aspect in which we did better than we had under Poland. ... Under the Germans any printed word in the Reich as in all occupied territories was at the authorities' disposal. Freedom of speech did not exist. ... Though our situation was not good, it was better, and our options were broader than those of other nations [Poles and Jews]."[155]

While Germans controlled the Literary and Artistic Club, as was true for all organizations, in this case their grip was not as tight. During the Nazi occupation the club's headquarters, first located at Podwalna Street where the editorial office of the Zionist journal *Chwila* had operated, and then moved to May Third Street (the street name was changed to June 29, the day the Germans marched into Lviv), evolved into a cultural hub for creative circles. Discussion evenings—perhaps the only forum not subject to censorship, though with eyes and ears always present—were very well attended, and visitors from Central and Eastern Ukraine drew the strongest interest. In contrast to the publishing domain, restricted by censorship, theatrical activities fell directly under the propaganda division, led by Herbert Knorr. Of course, limitations existed here as well; above all the minders prescribed the repertoire, set performance dates, as well as approved the cast. The Theater of the Opera alternated shows for Ukrainians with those for Germans; the latter audience always took priority.

Kost Pankivsky stated that Ukrainian theater experienced a revival during those occupation years, and Lviv figured at its center.[156] In addition to the Theater of the Opera, the Merry Lviv Theater [Veselyi Lviv] was founded, at first under a name reminiscent of the early Soviet occupation: Theatrical Jazz in Lviv.[157] It is certainly appropriate to probe the moral dimension of this cultural initiative, and at least some Lviv intellectuals have asked that question.[158] Without actually crossing the line, the activities of the Theater of the Opera

---

155 Pan'kivs'kyi, *Roky nimets'koï okupatsi'*, 343. See publishing catalogue: Larysa Holovata, *Ukraïns'ke vydavnytstvo u Krakovi—L'vovi 1939–1945*, vol. 1 (Kyiv: Krytyka, 2010).
156 Pan'kivs'kyi, *Roky nimets'koi okupatsii*, 351.
157 T. [Ostap Tarnavs'kyi], "Veselyi L'viv. Vidkryttia Teatral'noho Dzhazu u L'vovi," *L'vivs'ki visti*, no. 280, December 8, 1942.
158 Krushel'nyts'ka, *Rubaly lis. Spohady halychanky*, 170.

verged on collaboration. Valery Haidabura, a scholar of theater history of the occupation years, wrote: "In 1941–1944 Ukrainian theater was not a manifestation of collaboration, it did not broadcast fascist ideas from the stage. On the contrary, many performances demonstrated the artists' non-conformist stance."[159] Haidabura's book shows that Ukrainian stage artists enjoyed more creative freedom under this administration than under the Soviets. After the war all actors and directors who were employed during the period were subject to repressions.[160] Some bought their freedom by presenting the activities of their former friends in a false light.[161]

On July 19, 1941, in the early days of the German occupation, Lviv's Theater of the Opera put on *A Cossack beyond the Danube*, directed by Iosyp Stadnyk, and gradually broadened its repertoire in the following months. As part of the push to publicize atrocities committed by the NKVD, in early February 1942 the theater produced a play by Kostiantyn Hupalo called *Triumph of Prosecutor Dalsky*, which met with a passionate reception. (The author, originally from Kyiv, worked as a Russian lecturer at Lviv University during the Soviet occupation. Before returning to Kyiv, he gave the play's manuscript to Blavatsky.) The performance had a strong impact on the Kharkiv-native Iury Shevelov, who had encountered Stalinist terror in the 1930s. This was his first time seeing a stage production that addressed the Soviet apparatus of coercion and its brutal investigative methods.[162] Similarly, the play deeply affected the seventeen-year-old Bohdan Kokh, who had miraculously escaped from the Janowska concentration camp and would join Blavatsky's cast in 1943. (After the war Kokh served a *Gulag* sentence, but eventually went on to a notable acting career in Lviv.) Between 1942 and 1943 the *Triumph* emerged as the most frequently performed script in Lviv (as well as in Ternopil, where Ivan Kohutiak directed the play), a pivotal event in the city's consciousness. The performance became a subject of public debate at the Literary and Artistic Club, taking the form of a mock trial.[163] Much was written about the *Triumph*, and the critics extolled Volodymyr Blavatsky's acting (he portrayed the main character—the

---

159 Valerii Haidabura, *Teatr mizh Hitlerom i Stalinym* (Kyiv: Fakt, 2004), 11.
160 Svitlana Maksymenko, "Tvorcha diial'nist' 'Ukraïns'koho teatru mista L'vova—L'vivs'koho opernoho teatru' (1941–1944 rr.) v konteksti istoriï natsional'noho stsenichnoho mystetstva," PhD diss., Instytut mystetstvoznavstva, fol'klorystyky ta etnolohiï im. M. T. Ryl's'koho NAN Ukraïny, 2008.
161 Lesia Kryvyts'ka, *Povist' pro moie zhyttia* (Kyiv: Mystetstvo, 1965).
162 Iurii Shevel'ov, *Ia—mene—meni (i dovkruhy). Spohady*, 381.
163 "Pravda peremohla!," *Nashi dni* 6 (April 1942): 13.

Soviet prosecutor). Although the play denounced the Soviet regime, we can assume that the audience interpreted it more broadly, given the readily recognizable parallels between the NKVD and the Gestapo. The public knew what befell Ukrainian writers associated with the nationalist underground, including the playwright himself—they perished at Babi Yar.[164] Recent events in Lviv offered plenty of analogies too.

In the first weeks of the German occupation Iosyp Stadnyk was ousted as literary director of the Theater of the Opera. The institution's collective faulted him for not defending Ukrainians arrested by the NKVD and denounced him for collaborating with Soviet authorities. Of the prominent Ukrainians who had served as communist deputies, Marian Panchyshyn, Mykhailo Vozniak, and Stadnyk were now the lone survivors. While the occupying authorities did not arrest Stadnyk, they removed him from his post as theater director (at the same time they fired Petro Soroka and Andry Petrenko, the administrative director; the latter was probably dismissed for protecting an employee of Jewish ethnicity by the name of Stahl. Paradoxically, Petrenko and Soroka worked with Blavatsky to get Stadnyk dismissed). At first Blavatsky took over for Stadnyk. But by July 1942 the Viennese conductor Fritz Weidlich had become the artistic director. The occupiers trusted him more; as an Austrian he implicitly guaranteed an appropriate repertoire and control over personnel. Until mid-1942 Iosyp Stadnyk continued to work as an actor and director, staging classics without avant-garde ambitions, from *A Cossack beyond the Danube* to the *Gypsy Baron*. If his testimony is correct, he was let go on orders from the Stadthauptmann in June of 1942. Six months later he became a theater director in Drohobych (in 1947, based on the testimony of Herbert Knorr, whom the Soviets arrested, the seventy-year-old Stadnyk was accused of being an agent and sentenced to ten years of *Gulag* for passing on information about the theater's season schedule;[165] Andry Petrenko[166] and Petro Soroka[167]—the latter worked as administrator of the Theater of the Opera during the German occupations—faced the same charges; and even though their efforts led to the dismissal of the

---

164 See Maria Strutynska's journal entry from March 1942 (Mariia Strutynska Papers, Diary 1941–1947, box 1, folder 20, k. 20).
165 Haidabura, *Teatr mizh Hitlerom i Stalinym*, 126–34.
166 Svitlana Maksymenko, "Frahmenty kryminal'noi spravy Andriia Petrenka—pershoho dyrektora ukrains'koho teatru mista L'vova—L'vivs'koho opernoho teatru (1941–1942)," *Studii mystetstvoznavchi* 2 (2008): 67–79.
167 Svitlana Maksymenko, "'Kliuchi' Petra Soroky (epizody zhyttia i tvorchosti myttsia)," *Prostsenium* 2–3 (2006): 14–21.

most distinguished Ukrainian theater director, the Soviets condemned all three under the same charge, as German collaborators).

Early in 1942 two actors from Les Kurbas's Berezil Theater in Kharkiv, Iosyp Hirniak and his wife Olimpia Dobrovolska, joined the Lviv ensemble. Residents of the Reichskommissariat Ukraine rarely received permission to move. The German administration treated persons arriving from Eastern Ukraine as potential Soviet agents, much the same as the Soviets had done with refugees from German-occupied territories. But the couple managed to overcome all obstacles and made it to Lviv. Their arrival changed Lviv's theater culture. German directives mandated that the majority of performers be Ukrainian. Most of them would have been provincial actors, as direct reports indicate and research in theater history confirms; parallels with the Jewish theater suggest so as well. Until 1939, neither Ukrainian nor Jewish theaters received any support from the Polish state; consequently, their only source of income could be shows performed for provincial audiences. Thanks to Hirniak, Lviv theaters would adopt a more ambitious repertoire, enriched with plays from the Berezil Theater, such as *Myna Mazailo* by Mykola Kulish.

The arrival of the artist pair from Kharkiv signified a larger trend. After the Germans seized Soviet Ukraine and created the Reichskommissariat Ukraine, the first winter showed that one's chances of survival were minimal. More and more educated Ukrainians from Central and Eastern Ukraine began turning up in Lviv, if they were able to overcome multiple administrative road blocks, with Hirniak, who had improbably survived a *Gulag* sentence, among them.

In 1933, Kurbas postponed preparations to stage *Hamlet* with Iosyp Hirniak in the leading role, in order to focus on the social drama *Maklena Grasa*, Mykola Kulish's last play. The topic—a worldwide crisis in capitalist countries—seemed safe, yet within three days of the premiere Soviet critics had declared it subversive. In December 1933, the NKVD arrested the play's author, its director, and the lead actor. They executed Kulish and Kurbas in 1937. Only Hirniak survived. In August of 1940 he obtained permission to return from Soviet exile together with his wife, Olimpia Dobrovolska, who had also been convicted. The following year both found jobs at a Kyiv theater. In the summer of 1941 they were evacuated with their troupe but managed to make themselves scarce during a train stop. Hirniak and Dobrowolska came to Lviv in the spring of 1942.[168] Soon Iosyp Hirniak became the

---

168 Bohdan Kozak was able to establish the date of their arrival in Lviv as March 1942. See Bohdan Kozak, "Palimpsest ukraïns'koho 'Hamleta': pereklad i prapremiera 1943 r.," *Visnyk L'vivs'koho universytetu, Seria Mystetstvo* 3 (2003): 54.

second-ranking director of Lviv theater, after Blavatsky, as Stadnyk and Soroka slipped into obscurity. Within eighteen months Hirniak and Blavatsky realized Kurbas's dream: *Hamlet* on a Ukrainian stage. The idea first emerged from a discussion of Iury Kosach's speech[169] at the Literary and Artistic Club. Irena Makaryk and Bohdan Kozak have reconstructed how the performance came to be authorized.[170] The rehearsals, which British and French POWs were permitted to attend,[171] lasted several months. *Hamlet*'s premiere was expected to become the season's main event, hence the meticulous preparations. In connection with the upcoming performance, Ostap Tarnavsky created a brochure with illustrations by Semen Hruzbenko (Semen Gruzberg), yet another artist of Jewish ethnicity who found a safe haven within the Theater of the Opera.[172]

Hamlet was not the first of Shakespeare's titles translated by Mykhailo Rudnytsky. Twenty years earlier, shortly after returning from London, he rendered *Othello* into Ukrainian for Volodymyr Blavatsky's theater. But this time around his process was necessarily different; the critic had no access to a dictionary or his extensive library. Many years later, in a letter to Hryhory Kochur, Rudnytsky would criticize the result as "a dismal translation."[173] But his contemporaries were in awe: "His translation has a light rhythm, the language is exquisite, literary, it brilliantly reflects the word play of the original, making it poetic, alive, at times incisive, sarcastic, witty, and thus well-suited for the stage."[174]

Rudnytsky took part in the first reading. At that time, he also had implemented corrections to his work.[175] It was important to him to perfectly render the flow of the dialogue. The critic also held lecture-like talks introducing the actors to the secrets of Shakespeare's writing and to *Hamlet*'s various interpretations. He attended rehearsals as well. These preparations occurred in spring and

---

169 Ibid., 56.
170 Irena Makaryk, "Nichyina zemlia: 'Hamlet'. L'viv, 1943," in *Zapysky Naukovoho Tovarystva imeni T. Shevchenka, Pratsi Teatroznavchoï komisiï* 245 (2003): 315; Kozak, "Palimpsest ukraïns'koho 'Hamleta': pereklad i prapremiera 1943 r.," 56.
171 Pan'kivs'kyi, *Roky nimets'koï okupatsiï*, 351.
172 Semen Borysovych Gruzberg (1918–2000) was born in Kamianets-Podilsky. He was captured at the start of the German-Soviet war but escaped. In 1942 he worked in Buchach in the brigade of Mykhailo Kozyk, restoring Orthodox churches, and lived in Lviv beginning in 1943. After the war Gruzberg created a series of Jewish writers' portraits, Perets Markish and Sholem Aleichem among them.
173 Quoted in Kozak, "Palimpsest ukraïns'koho 'Hamleta': pereklad i prapremiera 1943 r.," 63.
174 Ivan Nimchuk, "Vystava 'Hamleta' u L'vovi," *Nashi dni* 23 (September 1943): 9.
175 Tarnavs'kyi, *Literaturnyi L'viv 1939–1944*, 159. See also by the same author: *Vidome i pozavidome* (Kyiv: Chas, 1999), 526–7.

Semen Gruzberg's (Hruzbenko's) illustrations for the performance of *Hamlet* were published in the magazine *Nashi dni* in 1943

summer of 1943,[176] meaning that at least a few times between the start of the year and the end of summer Rudnytsky showed up in Lviv.

Since the press referred to the play's brilliant translation in January of 1943, even before *Hamlet* was performed, Rudnytsky must have finished it at the turn of 1942 and 1943. We know his authorship was not a secret, since his name was mentioned by the press and at the premiere as well. It appears that Rudnytsky began the work at the hospitable quarters of the Terpyliak brothers in late summer of 1942, completing it in 1943 around New Year's. In a letter to Blavatsky he recalled the project as a blessing. There was no need to explain; to him, creative work offered refuge and respite. During those years many others clung to creativity, a thin thread still connecting them to life even when they no longer harbored any hope of survival.

At that time Michał Borwicz (Maksymilian Boruchowicz), mentioned previously, was imprisoned at the Janowska camp. A few years later he recalled how poetry could emerge in such circumstances: "An icy January in 1943. … Cutting through ice, snow removal in Lviv, this time at Zamarstynowska Street. During this labor, verses of an increasingly clear poem began to afflict me. … For a while this is more or less how literary pieces came into being in the camp. Shrouded in tight secrecy or communicated only to those closest to us, they would perish along with their authors."[177]

Between mid-year of 1942 and 1943, the Nazis first carried out the Blitz Aktion in Lviv, and then, in August 1942, the so called "Große Aktion" in the ghetto. Of the nearly 160,000 people residing within the closed-off ghetto, no more than 60,000 were left. During the next stage, the ghetto area was decreased and transferred directly to the Gestapo's command. The *Judenlager* (Julag) was created. Gradually prisoners of the Janowska camp were murdered as well, with executions taking place either on site or at the Bełżec extermination camp. In June 1943 the Nazis liquidated the ghetto altogether, and by November proclaimed the city of Lviv *Judenrein*. Those subsequent operations claimed the lives of Rudnytsky's colleagues from *Chwila*—Debora Vogel with her family and Adolf Rothfeld. (Henryk Hescheles, *Chwila*'s editor in chief, incarcerated by the Soviets for almost a year, was murdered on prison grounds during a Jewish pogrom immediately after the Germans seized Lviv.) Colleagues from the Writers' Union perished too: Dawid Koenigsberg (mentioned earlier as the translator of *Pan Tadeusz* into Yiddish), Jankiel Schudrich, Sania Friedman, Alter Kacyzne, and from the theater and art circles—Fryc Kleinman.

---

176 Kozak, "Palimpsest ukraïns′koho 'Hamleta': pereklad i prapremiera 1943 r.," 59.
177 Borwicz, *Literatura w obozie*, 11–12.

Right before the premiere on September 21, 1943, Rudnytsky vanished from Lviv. In a letter to Volodymyr Blavatsky, who led the theater and directed the play, as well as playing the lead, the critic gave a prosaic explanation: "I could not attend the premiere mostly because this historic day was terribly rainy, windy, and so an early departure was out of the question. On top of that I did not feel too well."[178] Nothing in the letter hints at the vexing cause of his disappearance. Just a minor thing, unpleasant fall weather and an aging man not up to leaving the house that day.

Rudnytsky indicated that he abandoned the ensemble during the most intensive rehearsals, which leads us to believe that he left Lviv in haste, prompted by grave circumstances. The theater historian Bohdan Kozak, who published the letter, surmises that Rudnytsky was referring to mid-September. The timing is suggested by the dates of subsequent letters and a journal entry made by a patient at the Morshyn spa, where Rudnytsky arrived. It is certain that Lviv was not the safest place for the prominent critic. But as we are about to learn, neither was Morshyn. In late September the translator decided to return for one of the performances, since it was such a high-profile theatrical event. Writing to Blavatsky on October 1, after he saw the play, Rudnytsky starts off with (fairly nebulous) reasons explaining why he did not come by before or after the show. Then he goes on to give his impressions from the performance. The letter takes on the form of a theater review—a genre he did not relinquish even during the Soviet occupation, and now practiced in private correspondence. Bohdan Kozak has thoroughly analyzed Rudnytsky's detailed commentary. My own interest lies in uncovering why Rudnytsky did not meet with Blavatsky, if just a few weeks earlier he had not hestitated to participate in rehearsals. "During the performance and even more so later, there was no time to stop by. Having arrived in the countryside, I once more recapitulate my impressions and wish to express a heartfelt admiration for this performance. As you well know, I have never been generous with compliments, and thus would have no reason to butter you up now."[179]

All the signs indicate that Rudnytsky wished to remain incognito, and he would have inevitably encountered a larger group had he come to see the director and lead actor. It is possible the critic knew that the theater's administration was obligated to file monthly reports regarding the repertoire and the ensemble's lineup with the Sicherheitsdienst at Pełczyńska Street.[180] Even if the

---

178 Kozak, "Palimpsest ukraïns′koho 'Hamleta': pereklad i prapremiera 1943 r.," 64.
179 Mykhailo Rudnytsky's letter to Volodymyr Blavatsky, October 1, 1943. Quoted in Kozak, "Palimpsest ukraïns′koho 'Hamleta': pereklad i prapremiera 1943 r.," 66.
180 Svitlana Maksymenko, "Sprava ioho zhyttia (frahmenty kryminal′noï spravy I. Stadnyka)," *Prostsenium* 1 (2001): 20–35.

controlling organs had not registered his earlier visits, at a moment when the play was gaining publicity and his name was featured on the posters, a denunciation was to be expected. It is thus likely that Rudnytsky decided any continued stay in Lviv and a public appearance at the theater carried too much risk.

By late 1943 Lviv was *Judenrein*. Throughout 1942 the occupier systematically murdered Jews—those residing in the ghetto as well as others who had thus far succeeded in finding shelter somewhere in the occupied city. In 1943 the murderous work was done; now came time for the *Untermenschen*. The Nazis intensified street roundups and transports to labor camps in the Reich and carried out hostage executions on a frequent basis. They were concerned that an enemy front might emerge, and military actions by Ukrainian and Polish guerilla groups posed such a danger for the German troops. Sydir Kovpak's raid on German forces delivered a serious threat; in July 1943 Kovpak's units were able to cross the border from the Reichskommissariat Ukraine into District Galizien. The occupier wanted to prevent any kind of cooperation among the locals; they had their hands full with the German losses on the Eastern front.

The strategy of divide and conquer, consciously and consistently implemented by Hans Frank, relied on racial segregation, placing Germans at the top of the pyramid (Reichsdeutsche and Volksdeutsche in the appropriate order), then Ukrainians, after them Poles; right below the category of those *Untermenschen* were the Jews. 1943 became a crucial phase of Frank's policy. Within District Galizien the Germans conscripted Ukrainians (some compulsory) into the Division "Galizien," putting a patriotic cover on amassing more soldiers for the front. In a parallel move, they drafted certain groups of Poles (Silesians and Kashubians) into the Wehrmacht, as citizens of the Third Reich. Simultaneously in Volhynia, located within the boundaries of Reichskommissariat Ukraine, Erich Koch ruthlessly exploited and exterminated any "undesirable elements." In 1943, as policemen of Ukrainian ethnicity joined the Ukrainian Insurgent Army (UPA), the administration began replacing them with Poles. In August the program extended to Lviv.[181] In July of 1943 ethnic conflicts in Volhynia reached their highest point with Ukrainian nationalists murdering Polish civilians on a mass scale. The (Polish) police carried out retributive operations. Though Volhynia and Galicia belonged to separate administrative units subject to different ethnic policies, Polish and Ukrainian civilian populations, as well

---

181 Mazur, Skwara, and Węgierski, *Kronika 2350 dni wojny i okupacji Lwowa. 1.IX.1939–5.II.1946*, 362.

as paramilitary resistance groups, carefully tracked any changes, positive or negative, interpreting them as a privilege for the "other" side, to be contested immediately. Information traveled fast, and as news from Volhynia filtered into Lviv and thousands of refugees gave direct reports, the scale of Polish-Ukrainian hostilities in Lviv increased. In his pastoral letter "Thou Shall Not Kill," Metropolitan Sheptytsky attempted to put a stop the violence, but to no avail. Even less effective was an appeal from the president of the Ukrainian Central Committee, Volodymyr Kubiyovych. In early September the Nazis eliminated remnants of the Janowska camp. With the ever-increasing roundups in the streets, even "good papers" no longer assured protection. The Polish Home Army's militia unit murdered Dr. Andry Lastovetsky. At the funeral of the dean of medical courses, shouts "death to Polacks" sounded in the background. Both Ukrainians and Poles outperformed each other in promises of revenge and threats against two renowned and highly respected physicians—the Pole Adam Gruca and the Ukrainian Marian Panchyshyn.

TAKING THE CURE

> ... if it be now, 'tis not to come; if it be not to come,
> it will be now; if it be not now, yet it will come.
> —Shakespeare, *Hamlet*, 5:2, ll. 234–36

In mid-September Mykhailo Rudnytsky suddenly left Lviv and traveled to the sanitorium in Morshyn. He did so on the eve of the play's premiere, for which he had previously often put his safety at risk. The spa town turned out to be a dubious shelter. As the facility served the Ukrainian Central Committee, persons referred there for health reasons necessarily represented various opinions and pedigrees. A few days after Rudnytsky arrived, other faces, all too familiar to Rudnytsky, showed up as well: the sculptor Serhy Lytvynenko (from the Petliura immigration circles) and two writers who associated with the nationalists: Rostyslav Iendyk and Iaroslav Tsurkovsky. Two years earlier, at the start of the German occupation, Tsurkovsky had forced Rudnytsky to retreat from public life and keep a low profile. Now the spa became the scene of their unexpected encounter. As for Iendyk, before 1939 he was openly fascinated with fascism and authored a biography of Hitler published by the *Visnyk* library. But in Morshyn he kept Rudnytsky company—evidently putting aside the prewar clashes between *Visnyk* and the critic. Iendyk's pals could not bear such a demonstration of solidarity and attacked him for affiliating himself with a "turncoat and Ukrainophobe."[182] None of this was good news for Rudnytsky; he had hoped the spa town would allow him to wait out the worst in relative safety, conveniently shaded by the Ukrainian Central Committee's umbrella.

If minor events such as these coincidental encounters were reason enough to stay out of sight, the major ones certainly made it urgent. Upon returning to Zalukva, the critic resolved to remain there until the end of 1943. However, he began to feel unsafe there, too. Ethnic cleansing conducted by the Ukrainian Insurgent Army (UPA) spread to Eastern Galicia. More and more frequently Polish civilian self-defense groups sought revenge and the Polish Home Army (AK) carried out acts of organized violence against Ukrainians. Rudnytsky's hosts, the Terpyliaks, were too well known and too well off to not attract attention. Thus in early 1944 Rudnytsky returned to Lviv. Now the city seemed to offer a safer cover than what he could find in the no-longer-quiet countryside.

The reference to encounters between Rudnytsky and members of the Literary and Artistic Club in Morshyn comes from the journal of Arkady Liubchenko. Liubchenko watched the critic from afar, without engaging in conversations, or so his journal makes it seem. The two men did not know each other well, though they may have met before—at a literary reading Liubchenko held during the first Soviet occupation. Rudnytsky must have recognized the tremendous talent of this illustrious prose writer affiliated with the circle of Mykola Khvylovy. In spring of 1943, after countless travails, Liubchenko finally made his way from Kharkiv via Kyiv to Lviv. There he received a warm welcome from the club regulars. Some literati, for instance Ostap Tarnavsky or Sviatoslav Hordynsky, remembered his 1940 reading. To Lviv writers, he represented the only surviving witness of the 1920s "Executed Renaissance" and thus was a living legend. His essay devoted to Mykola Khvylovy titled "His Secret" ["Ioho taiemnytsia"], published on the tenth anniversary of the writer's death in a special May 1943 issue of the monthly *Nashi dni* made an indelible impression on readers. Writer colleagues drummed up support for Liubchenko from the Ukrainian Central Committee and sent him to the sanitorium in Morshyn. The gravely ill Liubchenko mostly remained at the spa, rarely coming to Lviv. In his journal, the writer recorded his experiences and impressions from the Nazi occupation with exceptional exactitude, beginning at the moment when German troops entered Kharkiv in November 1941 until the very end of his life when he was hospitalized in Germany in early 1945. The journal provides a

---

182 *Shchodennyk Arkadiia Liubchenka* (Lviv: Vydavnytstvo M. P. Kots', 1999), 167.

personal chronicle of the occupation, seen through the eyes of a resident of Eastern Ukraine, initially swept up by a sense of euphoria. His first words:

> Ukraine is risen. Amongst war ruins, fires, it emerges as if a phoenix from the ashes.
>
> Almost half of Kharkiv burnt down by the Bolsheviks, destroyed. I saw it all. How many dramatic experiences in the last month! And how many still await—hunger as well as cold, and poverty, and blood. … But my nation, having survived this terrifying cauldron, will see a better life. However things were, Ukraine, which twenty-five years ago stepped onto the path to sovereignty, through storms, torture, repressions, and exploitation, is not losing its statehood and is entering a new stage of self-determination.
>
> Away from Moscow!—can you hear this, Mykola? [in reference to Khvylovy and his famous call].[183]

From behind the pathos a fervent hope peers out, arising after a time of deep despair. In the following notes the writer's pathos makes way for bitterness and a fear of the Germans. After six months in Nazi-occupied Kharkiv, Liubchenko was able to procure a permit to go to Kyiv, and from there, after another half a year, to Lviv. It seemed to the author that he extracted himself from a death trap.

Arkady Liubchenko's journal appeared in print more than half a century after his death. Beyond the usual reports about wartime conditions, the volume contains personal confessions, some very intimate, some quite brutal. His is one of the most controversial ego-documents in Ukrainian literature I have ever read. It presents an unusual mix: a show of exceptional talent, demonstrations of sensitivity towards some people and utter indifference about the fate of others, gentleness and cruelty, patriotism and xenophobia. Even though fifty years had passed between Liubchenko's writing of the journal and its publication, the volume stirred up fierce emotions. Accusations abounded, with immorality (numerous erotic adventures) among the lightest charges, and antisemitism and Russophobia among the gravest. Until Ukraine became independent in 1991, Liubchenko remained a forbidden writer. Alongside many other intellectuals of his generation, he was deemed a collaborator. Yet his journal provides absolute proof that the author, arrested by the Gestapo twice on the same charges ("a Bolshevik agent"), not only did not collaborate, but never harbored pro-German

---

183   Ibid., 7.

sentiments. And yet he tended to approve of repressions aimed at other ethnicities. The pieces he published in *Nashi dni* and a volume of stories *The Puppet Show* [*Vertep*] printed in 1943 by the Ukrainian publishing house "Ukrainske vydavnytstvo" may have fueled suspicions of collaboration.

Of Liubchenko's work, his portrait of Mykola Khvylovy titled "His Secret" (a recollection of their journey together through the starving Eastern Ukrainian villages in the spring of 1933) appeared particularly damaging to the Soviets. But there was more: the Soviets knew that it was Liubchenko who had preserved the archive of VAPLITE—the legendary Free Academy of Proletarian Literature. It is possible that Viktor Petrov, an NKVD operative (or perhaps a double agent, Soviet and German) supplied the intelligence, or maybe it came from another source. Thus Liubchenko had good reason to be afraid. The eight years that passed between Khvylovy's suicide and the outbreak of the war spanned a period known as the Great Terror, a period in which Liubchenko himself lived in great fear. Until his death, the trepidation never left him. Even more than of the Gestapo, he was terrified of being surrounded by Soviet agents. One of his journal entries refers to a nightmare featuring Oleksandr Korniichuk. One look from Korniichuk suffices to make Liubchenko believe that he is in grave danger and decide it is time to flee.[184]

In the fall of 1943, after a six-month stay in Lviv and Morshyn, Liubchenko came to view Galician Ukrainians with increasing criticism. Those were the same colleagues who took such care of him and supplied him with generous loans and royalties, perks which enabled him more than just bearable survival, at least in comparison with his living conditions in Kharkiv and in Kyiv. The writer describes in detail his meetings with other literati, both local and visiting, and his few visits to the Literary-Artistic Club and the theater. I will omit Liubchenko's personal attacks and instead focus on his impressions from the performance at the Theater of the Opera in November 1943, when he left Morshyn to spend a few days in Lviv. He had certainly heard about *Hamlet*'s premiere from his club friends back in September 1943, and perhaps also read about it in the press. Without a doubt he must have been interested, since ten years earlier the play had been announced in Kharkiv. Incidentally, he did not travel to Lviv to see *Hamlet*, but to deliver a commissioned script to director Blavatsky and to secure another writing fee.

As I had mentioned, Liubchenko came from the circles of VAPLITE and was well familiar with Kurbas's theater from Kharkiv. He had met Iosyp Hirniak

---

184 Ibid., 27 (entry from May 19, 1942).

Arkady Liubchenko and Ivan Kernytsky in Morshyn, 1943

many times. Nevertheless, or perhaps for those very reasons, he evaluated the show very critically, and declared it weak: "*Hamlet* is provincial, in spots even wooden, in spots creaking, sometimes too naïve. Not there, not there at all is the high tone in which *Hamlet* is supposed to sound. Not a surprise. Quite the opposite, I wonder how I. Hirniak managed to achieve as much as he did with this backwater, provincial, motley ensemble. The whole thing is salvaged by Hamlet himself—Blavatsky."[185]

Another Kharkiv transplant, Iury Shevelov (after the war one of the most distinguished Ukrainian critics and essayists) issued an even more venomous verdict.[186] But local intelligentsia thought otherwise and was in awe: *Hamlet*'s premiere at the Theater of the Opera seemed a dream come true. Liubchenko (like Shevelov) had a different perspective. He measured the performance against the standard of Kharkiv's Berezil Theater.

Barely four days after Liubchenko went back to the spa, a grey car drove up to the sanitorium's "Maraton" building where he was staying. Unsuspecting, the patient watched it out the window and went about his day. Upon returning, he engaged in a salon conversation; not for a minute did he think he had reason to worry. A moment later an agent took him aside and suddenly the writer was

---

185 Ibid., 185–6.
186 Shevel'ov, *Ia—mene—meni (i dovkruhy). Spohady*, 381.

under arrest. The fee Liubchenko was paid at the theater for his script turned into incriminating evidence against the alleged Bolshevik spy. Why else would he be in possession of such a large sum? He was transported to Lviv, where the suspicions continued (the deciding factor was that he had the same last name as the late Ukrainian SSR Prime Minister Panas Liubchenko). Clearly the Gestapo had placed him under observation, although they had not followed him closely. They noted his departure from Morshyn, assuming that it was related to the movements of Kovpak's guerilla troops. After three months in prison the writer was released in February of 1944.

It seems like a paradox that Liubchenko, who was not at all politically active, and whom Soviet rule taught to take all manner of precaution in expressing opinions, was arrested and came close to being executed. On the other hand, Mykhailo Rudnytsky, who despite his many enemies neither went into hiding nor changed his name, survived and was never once arrested, not even at the start of the occupation when the Nazis locked up Ukrainian intelligentsia *en masse*.

Hamlet was the last performance Liubchenko saw before his arrest. As it turned out, also his last one before he fled Galicia and wound up in a hospital in Bad Kissingen, Germany. He died on February 25, 1945. A month earlier Mykhailo Rudnytsky, who authored a study of Mykola Khvylovy as well, gave a lengthy explanation to the Soviet authorities about his activities during the period of German occupation. He believed their interest in him was erroneous. In truth the NKVD pursued Rudnytsky for his publication on Khvylovy and his independent opinions.

The final scene was cut because the actor who portrayed Fortinbras was deathly ill. Hence the play ended on the duel between Hamlet and Laertes and with the words: "The rest is silence." Only the corpses of the main characters are left on stage.[187] Bohdan Kozak attempted to reconstruct the show and its relevance to the viewers, perhaps interpreting the director's message too literally: "The spectator, watching the play, equated his life with the protagonist's. The first act of the tragedy of those who sat among the audience began in September 1939, in 1941—the second act came, and in 1943 the third one played out; they would still face act four—the arrival of Soviet troops—and five, the reprisals."[188]

Zbigniew Herbert followed a similar path in his poem "Elegy of Fortinbras" ["Tren Fortynbrasa"]. Fortinbras appears when the tragedy nears its end; death unites the main characters and solves all conflicts. The poet is interested in

---

187 Haidabura, *Teatr mizh Hitlerom i Stalinym*, 120.
188 Kozak, "Palimpsest ukraïns′koho 'Hamleta': pereklad i prapremiera 1943 r.," 69.

what will occur a moment later, and makes Shakespeare's supporting character his lyrical protagonist. Herbert has Fortinbras say: "The rest is not silence but belongs to me." From then on, it will be Fortinbras who will become the engine and interpreter of events.

UNDER FOREIGN FLAGS

> one has to take the city by the neck and shake it a bit
> —Zbigniew Herbert, "Elegy of Fortinbras"[189]

As precarious as Rudnytsky's situation was during the German occupation, soon after the second Soviet "liberation"[190] it took a turn for the worse. His book *From Myrny to Khvylovy* (especially the Khvylovy essay) certainly helped trigger an assault on Rudnytsky, but writing aside, the NKVD simply thought quite ill of him. Initially they attempted to accuse the critic of collaborating with the Nazis, though the strategy was soon abandoned. We can only trace Rudnytsky's troubles based on documents extant in Lviv's archives, since the critic's personal collection is not accessible to the public. It is questionable whether its contents would allow us to reconstitute his situation in the 1940s more precisely. Caution would have dictated destroying it all.

When the university restarted its activities in the fall of 1944, Rudnytsky took on the post of Dean of Philology. In January 1945 the NKVD began its offensive against Petro Karmansky after his anti-Soviet articles in the occupation press came to light. In keeping with the Soviet playbook, his fall from grace occurred at an "active members' meeting"; the accused had to give a public explanation on the spot. Rudnytsky probably worried that his absence might be read as a gesture of solidarity and penned a lengthy letter to the deputy director of the Central Committee's propaganda department. In it he specifically addressed the fateful, dangerous incident connected with the writers' registration in July 1941. In conclusion the author suggested that the addressee—a high-ranking party official—in consideration of the possible solutions allow the poet Karmansky to repent for his infractions with ... translations (the critic certainly knew about the Ukrainian rendition of Dante's *Divine Comedy* which Karmansky worked on during the German occupation). The letter reveals an

---

189 Zbigniew Herbert, "Elegy of Fortinbras," trans. Czesław Miłosz and Peter Dale Scott, *The Collected Poems: 1956–1998* (New York: Harper Collins, 2007),186.
190 Rubl'ov and Cherchenko, *Stalinshchyna i dolia zakhidnoukraïns'koï intelihentsiï 20–50-ti roky XX st.*, 228–30.

obvious naïvité, while also shedding light on the author's high (at least in his own perception) standing.

Meanwhile the NKVD was busy putting together Rudnytsky's file. In a top secret note dated July 1945, the investigators accused Rudnytsky of anti-Soviet and nationalist leanings, and of defending and whitewashing "Ukrainian nationalists of professor Krypiakevych I. P.'s sort."[191] His most severe offense—aside from contacts with "nationalists"—according to the NKVD, were family affiliations: his brother Ivan and sister Milena. Aside from considerations specific to Rudnytsky, it was the overall Soviet policy towards the local intelligentsia that provided the main impetus behind such interest in Rudnytsky. The authorities had no intention of courting the Ukrainian intelligentsia as they did in the fall of 1939. This time they decided to grab them by the neck. Persons who survived the German occupation were presumed Nazi collaborators. If the facts did not quite align, other excuses would be found to justify reprisals. "Bourgeois nationalist" turned out a handy threat. Since it was considered a certainty that nationalists collaborated with the Third Reich, the charge of nationalism equaled an accusation of collaboration. The term itself had a separate history; the fight against bourgeois nationalists began more than a dozen years before the war, and in one of its phases the Soviets disbanded the school of Mykhailo Hrushevsky (via a trial against the fictitious Ukrainian National Center; the majority of those accused, including the historian's daughter, were executed). A handful of Hrushevsky's students remained in Lviv and during the first Soviet occupation were initially favored, then tolerated. However, after the war, the authorities resolved to crush the group lest their ideas spread throughout newly unified Ukraine.

Early 1946 marked the start of the operation. As part of the all-Soviet policy of eradicating nationalist leanings, the spiral of reprisals against Galician intelligentsia was set in motion. A team from the Central Committee sent in to scrutinize university cadres, especially Hrushevsky's disciples,[192] as well as

---

191 Dovidka upravlinnia NKVD L'vivs'koï oblasti obkomovi KP(b)U pro profesora Mykhaila Rudnyts'koho, 10.07.1945.
192 Iaroslav Dashkevych quotes the informational note ("Dokladnaia zapiska o kadrakh professorsko-prepodavatel'skogo sostava kafedr obshchestvennykh nauk i kachestve prepodavaniia v L'vovskikh vuzakh") in his study of the stages and methods used to eradicate Hrushevky's students. See Iaroslav Dashkevych, "Borot'ba z Hrushevs'kym ta ioho shkoloiu u L'vivs'komu universyteti za radians'kykh chasiv," in *Mykhailo Hrushevs'kyi i ukraïns'ka istorychna nauka. Materialy konferentsii*, ed. Iaroslav Hrytsak and Iaroslav Dashkevych (Lviv: Instytut istorychnykh doslidzhen' L'vivs'koho derzhavnoho universytetu imeni Ivana Franka, 1999), 32–94.

the activities of the local party organization,[193] prepared informational notes for the Politburo. In October of 1946, based on those notes, at a session of the Politburo of the Central Committee of the Communist (Bolshevik) Party of Ukraine the following resolution was adopted: "On the necessity of increasing mass-political and ideological work in the state's western oblasts." An ideological attack on the periodical of the Lviv chapter of the Writers' Union *Radianskyy Lviv* followed. The party-affiliated critic Mykhailo Parkhomenko crushed Olha Duchyminska's novel *Eti*, which depicted the fate of a Jewish woman hiding out in a Ukrainian village. Three years later the NKVD arrested Duchyminska, then sixty-six years old, in connection with the assassination of Iaroslav Halan (a Ukrainian communist writer murdered by the OUN, Halan maligned the institution of the church, the clergy, the hierarchy of the Greek-Catholic church eliminated by the Soviets in 1946, as well as the Ukrainian underground and prewar activists who had campaigned for sovereignty) and after a two-year investigation sentenced her to twenty-five years in *Gulag*.

Mykhailo Rudnytsky would hardly count among the circle of Hrushevky's disciples. In the summer of 1946 he published an article in *Vilna Ukraina* urging for a break with the past.[194] Yet it did not stop the authorities from accusing the critic of cultivating nationalist tendencies. Still, in October 1946, the oblast-level party committee leadership issued a positive opinion regarding the critic's current and past activities (under the Nazi occupation),[195] even as the Kyiv press launched an attack on him (Iaroslav Dashkevych attributes the article to Mykhailo Parkhomenko, a Soviet writer and lecturer at Lviv University).[196] But the Central Committee's resolution changed everything. In spring 1947, when the Obkom Chairman Ivan Hrushetsky submitted a thorough report on the Lviv intelligentsia to the secretary of the Central Committee of the Communist Party of Ukraine Lazar Kaganovich, the air around Rudnytsky thickened. Hrushetsky's statement singled out Rudnytsky's actions as an example of classic

---

193 Dokladnaia zapiska o sostoianii ideologicheskoi raboty v partiinoi organizatsii L'vovskoi oblasti [no earlier than July 14, 1946; the editors established the date based on other documents], TsDAHOUf. 1, op. 70, spr. 459, k. 6–27 (quoted in *Kul'turne zhyttia v Ukraïni. Zakhidni zemli*, vol. 2, 814–25).

194 Mykhailo Rudnyts'kyi, "Rishuche porvaty z prokliatym mynulym," *Vil'na Ukraïna*, no. 191, August 16, 1946.

195 Dovidka l'vivs'koho obkomu KP(b)U pro pys'mennykiv l'vivs'koï orhanizatsiï Spilky radians'kykh pys'mennykiv, iaki perebuvaly vid okupatsieiu, 18.10.1946, DALO, f. P. 3, op. 68, spr. 100, k. 175 (quoted in *Kul'turne zhyttia v Ukraïni. Zakhidni zemli*, vol. 1, 355).

196 Dashkevych, "Borot'ba z Hrushevs'kym ta ioho shkoloiu u L'vivs'komu universyteti za radians'kykh chasiv," 86.

ideological dodging; rather than exposing "bourgeois nationalists,"[197] Rudnytsky's tactic helped cover for them. Late June brought a reckoning to Rudnytsky. Even though Iaroslav Halan himself once again rushed to the critic's defense, this time the Obkom chairman refused to listen and demanded categorically that Rudnytsky issue a clear declaration and speak out against his former friends.[198] The next month Halan did not back Rudnytsky anymore and called on the critic to "come to his senses": "What liberal approach could be considered towards them, I ask you, Mykhailo Ivanovych (he turns to prof. Rudnytsky)? We should attack them frontally and eradicate them! Yes or no—Mykhailo Ivanovych?"[199]

These developments followed the Deputy Premier of the Ukrainian SSR Dmytro Manuilsky's address to the Lviv intelligentsia at a meeting on July 24, 1947. Manuilsky was a local (Kyiv-based) apparatchik tasked with carrying out Stalin's new policies towards the educated class. He criticized Rudnytsky, Karmansky, and others harshly. Halan got an earful too, and that caused him to retreat. Manuilsky's presentation was titled "The Fight against Ukrainian Bourgeois Nationalism" ["Borotba z ukrainskym burzhuazyinym natsionalizmom"]. Commentators maintained that he declared the intelligentsia responsible for having pushed Ukrainian youth to join the Insurgent Army. They had better make amends for their corrupting influence and convince Ukrainian guerilla troops to stop fighting, thus proving loyalty to the Soviet authorities. Manuilsky's speech triggered a wave of reprisals that affected Ukrainian intelligentsia in Lviv and in Kyiv, with approximately 200 persons arrested. The persecution lasted—intermittently—until 1955, but reached its absolute peak after Halan was killed in October 1949. The Ukrainian underground carried out the murder under strange circumstances (shortly before the assassination the authorities took away Halan's security protection, along with his gun). As the most politically outspoken journalist whose publications targeted the Ukrainian underground and "Vatican's spies," Halan made an easy target. For the Soviets too. He was an inconvenient witness, as was the reverend Havryil Kostelnyk, murdered in September 1948. Kostelnyk opted to join in eliminating the

---

197 Dovidka l'vivs'koho obkomu KP(b)U DLIA TsK KP(b)U shchodo suspil'no-politychnoï kharakterystyky l'vivs'koï intelihentsii, 5.04.1947, TsDAHOY, f. 1, op. 23, spr. 4558, k. 1–34 (quoted in *Kul'turne zhyttia v Ukraïni. Zakhidni zemli*, vol. 1, 399).

198 Stenohrama narady pys'mennykiv m. L'vova, 30.06.1947, DALO f. P—3, op. 2, spr. 104, k. 68–9 (quoted in *Kul'turne zhyttia v Ukraïni. Zakhidni zemli*, vol. 1, 411).

199 Stenohrama narady aktyvu intelihentsiï m. L'vova, 27.07.1947, DALO f. P—4, op. 1, spr. 155, k. 62–6 (quoted in *Kul'turne zhyttia v Ukraïni. Zakhidni zemli*, vol. 1, 423).

Greek-Catholic Church and helped organize the 1946 "Reunion Sobor," which gave the appearance that the Uniate Church voluntarily agreed to be absorbed into the Ukrainian Orthodox Church. The trial of Halan's killers deepened the suspicions surrounding his death, giving rise to the idea that his murder was in some way connected to the NKVD; after the sentencing one of the defendants reportedly shouted at the prosecutor: "That is not what we had agreed on!".[200]

Six weeks after the fateful speech in Lviv, a larger plenary board session of the Writers' Union took place in Kyiv, attended by the chairman of the Lviv chapter Petro Kozlaniuk, a rare surviving prewar Lviv communist. Now he criticized Karmansky and Rudnytsky, repeating almost verbatim the words Hrushetsky had uttered six months earlier, and giving them a sinister undertone: "It is time to cleanse our benches of those who do not wish to accompany us on our way to the common goal!"[201]

Two months later, at a meeting of the Lviv chapter, Karmansky and Rudnytsky were removed from the union. A number of Kyiv writers contributed harsh critiques; Oleksandr Korniichuk boomed angrily. He was not one to make idle threats. Two prewar books supplied the chief accusations against Rudnytsky: the first one focused on the philosophy of literary works, the second on Ukrainian writers of the late nineteenth century to the 1920s. Korchiichuk reminded the critic of his volume *From Myrny to Khvylovy*, published more than a decade before, following up on a threat he had made at the September 17, 1940 meeting. When Leonid Novychenko and Maksym Rylsky found enough courage to speak up for Rudnytsky and Karmansky, Korniichuk steadied his crosshairs on them: "the literary community will demand an explanation why they were defended and whose activities were steeped in the enemy's bourgeois-nationalist perspective."[202]

After the expulsion, a true witch hunt for Rudnytsky ensued. The weekly *Literaturna hazeta* [*Literary News*] called for casting bourgeois nationalists into the garbage heap of history, their language reminiscent of the Great Terror. As repulsive as the article is, a glance at the below excerpt is necessary; paraphrasing would not do it justice:

> Rudnytsky stands shoulder to shoulder with Piłsudski's gendarmes and Polish intelligence agents. Instead of a seven-shooter and a pistol,

---

200 Anatolii Dimarov, "Prozhyty i rozpovisty," *Berezil'* 3–4 (1998): 68.
201 *Literaturna hazeta*, October 2, 1947 (quoted in Rubl'ov and Cherchenko, *Stalinshchyna i dolia zakhidnoukraïns'koï intelihentsiï 20–50-ti roky XX st.*, 229).
202 Ibid.

Rudnytsky reaches for a pen. In 1932 he publishes a book titled *Between Idea and Form*, in which from the first pages he attempts to malign Marxism … [in his book *From Myrny to Khvylovy*] following in Khvylovy's footsteps he attempts to direct literature towards a "psychologizing Europe," actively promoting the theory of "pure art." … During the German occupation M. Rudnytsky actively participates in editing the nationalist organ *Vechirnia hodyna*, which printed anti-Soviet invectives.[203]

Even the article's title was a call for symbolic violence ("Bourgeois Nationalists to the Garbage Heap of History"). Titles and dates are the only accurate pieces of information in this slanderous piece. From this point forward any member of the intelligentsia could be accused of nationalism. Neither facts nor ideological stances mattered in the least. The Writers' Union forced Rudnytsky out, disregarding a show of solidarity from his colleagues (Iryna Vilde issued a challenge to the nomenclature: "since you are throwing out Rudnytsky, you had better throw all of us out"). Things went so far that even Vladimir Beliaev, who arrived in Lviv in August 1944 as a war correspondent and published materials documenting the bestialities committed during the Nazi occupation, decided to appeal the decision and seek justice in Moscow as a member of the communist party.

Plans were underway to remove Rudnytsky from the university as well. Not by coincidence "pseudo-scholar" was among the insults hurled by the local press. On April 15, 1948 Rudnytsky gave a presentation at a philology department meeting. Its title announced his forthcoming act of public penance: "The Reactionary Bourgeois-Nationalist Concepts in Ukrainian Literary Scholarship of the Former Galicia." Witnesses to the spectacle, such as Roman Lubkivsky, state that Rudnytsky acted with dignity and credit him with showing a measure of courage in defending his views. While Rudnytsky's new university colleagues owed nothing to him, the opposite was true of their obligations to the authorities. They attacked the critic for his prewar essays on the philosophies of Nietzsche, Freud, Schopenhauer, and Bergson, for allegedly slandering Marxist philosophy, for his review of Ilko Borshchak's book about the peace conference in Versailles (Rudnytski had praised the volume even though it contained a reference to the "traitors of the Ukrainian nation").[204] By then twenty years had passed since Versailles, and

---

203 "Burzhuaznykh natsionalistiv—na smitnyk istorii," *Literaturna hazeta*, November 20, 1947 (quoted in *Kul'turne zhyttia v Ukraïni. Zakhidni zemli*, vol. 1, 483).

204 I. [first name unknown] Cherednychenko, V. Lesyk, "Proty burzhuazno-natsionalistychnykh perekruchen' v literaturoznavstvi," *Za radians'ku nauku* no. 11, April 15, 1948 (quoted in *Kul'turne zhyttia v Ukraïni. Zakhidni zemli*, vol. 1, 547–8).

ten since the Borshchak review. *From Myrny to Khvylovy* appeared in 1936 and the volume under special scrutiny—*Between Idea and Form*—in 1932. Both books had already been removed from libraries and could no longer be purchased. Thus even if Rudnytsky's ideas were harmful as alleged, they no longer posed a threat. Instead the objective at hand was to demean Rudnytsky. His self-criticism did not satisfy the authorities. Rudnytsky was devastated and confessed to the communist writer Petro Kozlaniuk that he was on the brink of suicide. Mykhailo Parkhomenko, a member of the executive committee and one of the engines behind the witch hunt, prepared a note for the Central Committee of the Communist Party of Ukraine reporting on the mood among Lviv writers. He warned against firing Rudnytsky and expressed a concern that the authority of the Soviets would sustain unpredictable damage should the critic take his life.[205] In the end the administration

---

205 See Parkhomenko's note (M. Parkhomenko, "Dopovidna zapyska literaturnoho krytyka M. Parkhomenka TsK KP(b)U pro L'vivs'ku organizatsiiu Spilky radians'kykh pys'mennykiv, 15.12.1947," in *Kul'turne zhyttia v Ukraïni. Zakhidni zemli*, vol. 1, 501–3.):

> All members of the Lviv chapter of the Soviet Writers' Union who were not in the party received the removal of M. Rudnytsky negatively. Iryna Vilde immediately announced to everyone concerned: "In that case throw all of us out!" Further she declared that she would organize a collective protest letter addressed to the KTs KP(b)U [Central Committee of the Communist (Bolshevik) Party of Ukraine]. She intended to enlist not only writers, but the Lviv intelligentsia, too. Iaroslav Halan supported her. But this did not happen, thanks to comrade Nechaieva, editor in chief of the Lviv publishing house, who argued against, using good party logic. But if such a letter came to be, it would have been signed. Why? Well, because under the German occupation all local writers and many within the intelligentsia committed far more sins than Rudnytsky did. They viewed the blow aimed at Rudnytsky as just the first one, to be followed by more, this time directed at them. An excuse for the protest was the stated cause of Rudnytsky's removal from the union: he collaborated with the Germans, in particular by working in the editorial office of the nationalist paper *Vechirnia hodyna*. Rudnytsky easily proved that the paper was published not in Lviv, but in Cracow, and that not he (M. R.), but Iaroslav Rudnytsky (a person with the same last name) was the editor. Under the Germans Rudnytsky published translations (*Faust* and works by Hoffman, the latter in the newspaper *Vechirnia hodyna*). We have information that in Lviv only his obituary for M. Holubets appeared. … The writers claim that during the occupation Rudnytsky, being half-Jewish, was hiding from Germans, and consider the accusations against him slander. Differences of opinions also surfaced within the party organization. Communist Vladimir Beliaev announced that he was leaving for Moscow to file a complaint against the decision of the Writers' Union with the KTs VKP(b) [Central Committee of the All-Soviet Communist Party]. He justifies it as follows: since 1939

opted to just push Rudnytsky to the sidelines and control the content of his lectures.

Not much is known about Rudnytsky's fate between 1948 and 1956, the year when the arrests and reprisals finally stopped. It is evident that he paid for his freedom by allowing his name to be added to Vladimir Beliaev's *Under Foreign Flags* [*Pod chuzhimi znamenami*], a collection of calumnious pieces directed at the church, clergy, and nationalists, printed in Moscow in 1954 in a sizeable edition of 90,000 copies. Iaroslav Hrytsak reviewed the correspondence of Ivan Lysiak-Rudnytsky with his uncle Mykhailo and asserts that the critic's sole contribution to Beliaev's volume was a piece about the professors executed on Wuleckie Hills.[206] Yet to this day Lviv cannot forgive Rudnytsky for co-authoring the book, even if nothing implicates him beside his name on the cover. In my opinion at most Rudnytsky served as Beliaev's consultant supplying details or personal information. Below I will discuss the premises that led me to this conclusion.

In early 1947 Beliaev wrote a letter to Ivan Hrushetsky, the Lviv Obkom's secretary of the Central Committee of the Communist Party of Ukraine. He reproached the local and national party leadership for disregarding his study *Under Foreign Flags*, which he had sent to a Lviv publisher a year earlier. The book, Beliaev complained, cost him "over ten months of intense work, poring over archival documents etc."[207] This means that Beliaev began preparing the publication at the end of 1944 or, at the latest, in early 1945. The complaint

> Rudnytsky had declared himself on the side of the Soviet authorities and many times appeared in the Soviet press (in reality he published trifle pieces), and abroad published numerous articles speaking out against Germans (about the occupier's atrocities) and nationalists. Nationalist organs in Canada and in the United States refer to Rudnytsky as *Cheka* claiming that he sold out to the Bolsheviks. In Lviv many people view Rudnytsky (in Beliaev's opinion) as a man who sided with the Soviet authorities. To exclude Rudnytsky from the Writers' Union means to take revenge for the past, since after 1939 Rudnytsky did nothing to discredit himself. ... In addition, I wish to inform you that they intend to fire Rudnytsky from Lviv University. In my opinion this should not be done. ... Rudnytsky told Kozlaniuk and many people at the university that he is on the brink of suicide. We cannot reject the possibility that he might do so in a difficult moment. Within a community of people who are hesitant, have not been entirely reeducated, such an incident would resonate in ways very unfavorable for us.

206 Ivan Lysiak-Rudnyts'kyi, *Istorychni ese*, vol. 1 (Kyiv: Osnovy, 1994), 488.
207 See Vladimir Beliaev's letter to the Lviv obkom's secretary: Z lysta pys'mennyka V. Beliaeva do sekretaria l'vivs'koho obkomu KP(b)U I.S. Hrushets'koho pro obstavyny vydannia knyhy *Pid chuzhymy praporamy*, DALO, f. P-3, op. 2, spr. 234, k. 25–6. Quoted in *Kul'turne zhyttia v Ukraïni. Zakhidni zemli*, vol. 1, 371.

does not mention a co-author, and it states that a large portion of the book was accepted for publication by the All-Slavic Committee (Oleksandr Korniichuk and Wanda Wasilewska represented the Ukrainian SSR) which assisted in getting specific chapters published in a foreign "progressive press." Thus *Under Foreign Flags* sat on the publisher's shelf from 1946, and the Soviets would not authorize its printing.

What caused the several-year-long delay? Why was a second author added? Again, official documents point us to an indirect answer. Without getting too far ahead: a propaganda campaign directed against nationalists began in 1947. Soon after Stalin's death Beria redirected his ideological assault at the local cadres. But there were other, more pragmatic reasons as well.

In a report prepared in the first half of 1954 outlining his organization's activities for the last decade, chairman of the Writers' Union Lviv chapter Petro Kozlaniuk shared some successes in ideological work. His praise went to Iaroslav Halan's lampoons, a brochure by Petro Karmansky, and Beliaev's articles. However, the same document discloses that not all in the community were fully engaged in ideological progress: "until now writers of the older generation such as M. Rudnytsky and M. Iatskiv were not included in this important task. They had directly observed the broad-reaching activity of ideologues of Ukrainian bourgeois nationalism like Hrushevsky, Barvinsky, Romanchuk, Levytsky, and other traitors of the Ukrainian nation from the nationalist camp. The Lviv chapter considers it one of its most important tasks to write precisely such works."[208]

The solution was right there: all it would take was to convince the writer to lend his name. Undoubtedly the effect would have been more powerful had the book not featured Beliaev's name at all, but that was inevitable; some pieces from the collection had been published earlier and the truth would have come to light fast. By late September 1950 Rudnytsky's membership in the Soviet Writers' Union was reinstated. The Ukrainian historian Oleksandr Rublov claims that the authorities rewarded the critic for adding his name to the series of crusading lampoons.[209] Likely so. In Karmansky's case the order was opposite: only after his pamphlet *Vatican—A Stronghold of Ignorance and World Reactionaryism* [*Vatykan—natkhnennyk mrakobissia i svitovoi reaktsii*] came out

---

208 Zvit L'vivs'koi organizatsiï Spilky radians'kykh pys'mennykiv pro robotu v 1943–1953 rr., DALO, f. R-2009, op. 1, spr. 53, k. 48–51. Quoted in *Kul'turne zhyttia v Ukraïni. Zakhidni zemli*, vol. 1, 686.
209 Rubl'ov and Cherchenko, *Stalinshchyna i dolia zakhidnoukraïns'koï intelihentsiï 20–50-ti roky XX st.*, 230.

could he rejoin the Writers' Union.²¹⁰ Immediately he was pressured to churn out more tributes.

Another question remains unanswered: why did it take four more years to publish the volume? *Under Foreign Flags* puts on trial the tradition of the Ukrainian independence movement, the Greek-Catholic clergy, the prewar elites, the nationalist activists, the emigrant community, as well as the alleged traitors. Beliaev based his book and its subsequent expanded editions on NKVD documentation, including files doctored for political trials which took place in Lviv at the turn of the 1940s and 1950s, such as the trial against Vasyl Barvinsky. The entire chapter devoted to the massacre on Wuleckie Hills relies on witness testimonies (Melnyk and Bandera are accused of providing the list of professors ²¹¹). Beliaev and Rudnytsky, or more accurately Beliaev along with a "curating" team, claim that reports relating the murder of the Lviv professors were penned or presented specifically at the authors' request.²¹² But in fact they were prepared from testimonies given by Franciszek Groër and Tomasz Cieszyński to a special Soviet commission created in the fall of 1944 to investigate Nazi atrocities. Another chapter targeted the brothers Barvinsky, who were referred to as spies. Vasyl was an eminent composer, and Oleksandr a well-known physician. Their father, Oleksandr Barvinsky, had belonged to the political elite in the Austro-Hungarian era. Beliaev's book branded him a renegade and issued the same pronouncement on Barvinsky's grandsons, who had joined the SS Division Galizien. In 1956, after Vasyl Barvinsky returned to Lviv, Beliaev complained that the government made a terrible error in permitting the freshly released composer to return to his hometown, since he attracted "anti-Soviet elements."²¹³ Eight years later Barvinsky was posthumously cleared of the crimes. Friends from the Composers' Union insisted on his rehabilitation, though in the Soviet Union it did not mean much. As the chairman of the Union's Lviv chapter, Anatoly Kos-Anatolsky petitioned the censorship agency *Glavlit* to remove the book *Under Foreign Flags* from libraries, reading rooms, and bookstores, since it slandered the Barvinsky family.²¹⁴

---

210 Ibid.
211 Beliaev, Rudnitskii, *Pod chuzhimi znamenami*, 91–2.
212 Ibid., 94.
213 Informational note from January 5, 1957: Z informatsiï l'vivs'koho obkomu KPU TsK KPRS pro politychnu robotu sered naselennia, DALO, f. P-3, op. 6, spr. 82 (quoted in *Kul'turne zhyttia v Ukraïni. Zakhidni zemli*, vol. 2, 234).
214 Petition to clear the name of Vasyl Barvinsky from June 6, 1964: Lyst pravlinnia l'vivs'koï oblasnoï Spilky kompozytoriv Holovlitu URSR pro reabilitatsiiu kompozytora Vasylia Barvins'koho, 6.06.1964, DALO, f. R. 18884, op. 1, spr. 124. Ibid., 616.

How Rudnytsky gave in to the ruse of joint authorship will remain the NKVD's and Beliaev's secret. We know a bit more about the events that pushed Petro Karmansky to publish his incendiary pamphlet *Vatican—A Stronghold of Ignorance and World Reactionaryism* in 1951. Between 1944 and 1946 Karmansky worked as director of the Ivan Franko Museum in Lviv. By early 1945, when the NKVD discovered the archives of the Ukrainian radio station in Cracow, they began "working" the poet. At every step they would bring up poems Karmansky wrote during the German occupation in which he cursed communism. Soon he was fired, and his work could no longer be published.

During the Directorate of Ukraine (1918–20) Karmansky served as the ambassador to the Vatican, so naturally the Soviet propaganda machine identified him as the most effective means of combat. The poet's health deteriorated to the point that he could no longer write, but the pamphlet was nevertheless prepared and published—by a team from the propaganda office, as one of its members reminisced years later.[215] Halan, who had penned blasphemous lampoons directed against the Pope and Metropolitan Sheptytsky, was no longer alive, and so Karmansky's "supervisors" decided to print a new edition of "Karmansky's" virulent publication, with an additional section mocking the Metropolitan. In a letter to Karmansky, the assistant editor from the State Press for Political Literature specified the changes to be made, which affected three-fourths of the text.[216] They left the author no choice; he had to accept this book as his own. As it were not enough, the poet was forced to publish a collection of poems with a title meant to unequivocally proclaim his correct political alignment: *On a Clear Path*. The man—old, stricken by dementia and partially paralyzed—was unable to write anymore, and yet the Soviets menaced him until the end of his life.[217]

Between 1946 and 1956 Mykhailo Rudnytsky made his way through several circles of hell. Though many of his colleagues and friends experienced prison and *Gulag*, including the painter Iaroslava Muzyka, physician Oleksandr Barvinsky, composer Vasyl Barvinsky, and others, Rudnytsky escaped their fate. For that he paid a high price. It is no wonder that he did not leave behind

---

215 M. (first name unknown) Hryhorovych, "Zhandarmy z obkomu," *Literaturna Ukraïna* (June 4, 1992), quoted in Il'nyts'kyi, *Drama bez katarsysu*, 453.
216 Lyst Derzhpolitvydavu URSR do Petra Karmans'koho, 22.04.1952, Arkhiv Instytutu ukraïnoznavstva NANU, f. 1, op. 1, spr. 12, k. 38 (quoted in *Kul'turne zhyttia v Ukraïni. Zakhidni zemli*, vol. 1, 675–6).
217 Stasiuk, "Zhyttievyi shliakh Petra Karmans'koho (hromads'ko-politychnyi aspekt)," 542.

any testimony. Just short fictionalized biographies of writers from a list permitted by censors. Though his handsome portraits *Writers Up Close* [*Pysmennyky zblyzka*, 1956–59] do not adhere to the manner of socialist realism, they were manipulated both by censors and self-censorship and tell us little about the author himself. In cultural history Rudnytsky survives as the author of *From Myrny to Khvylovy*. The history of Lviv's intelligentsia stubbornly faults him for libel against those whom the communists blacklisted.

The Soviet government did everything possible to prove to its opponents that it acted on the will of the people, and the strongest argument possible was to have the old Galician intelligentsia on your side. As during the first occupation, the Soviets strove to rob the community of authorities. Two eminent figures of Ukrainian literary life began parting ways in the interwar years, and their rift deepened during the war. But the return of communism brought them under a common denominator. Neither Karmansky nor Rudnytsky were given a chance to provide an account of those times. To paraphrase Herbert's "Elegy of Fortinbras:" The victor claimed the rest.

ANUM members and guests at an exhibit in Lviv

CHAPTER 7

Artists from Café de la Paix

Iaroslava Muzyka never had much interest in politics; instead, she was engrossed in art. Equally fascinated with modernity and tradition, Muzyka tried a variety of techniques: from simple drawing to oil, icons, painting on glass, restoration, and finally mosaic and enamel, first known as *schmelz*. Over the years, her studio at 26 Czarniecki Street in Lviv had welcomed famous tenants: first the impressionist Ivan Trush, then Mykhailo Boichuk, an avant-garde artist from a slightly younger generation. Both were graduates of the Academy of Fine Arts in Cracow where they had studied with Leon Wyczółkowski. Both are counted among the most distinguished twentieth-century Ukrainian painters.

As a teenager, Iaroslava Muzyka venerated Boichuk's formal experiments, which emerged from his contact with Picasso in Paris and combined icon painting and primitive art with modernity. Shortly before World War I Boichuk received an invitation to join a restoration team working on a Baroque Orthodox church in Lemeshi by Chernihiv. He asked Muzyka to look after his studio in his absence, but as it turned out he would never return. When the war broke out, Russian authorities interned him as an Austro-Hungarian citizen. As was true for many other Galician Ukrainians who found themselves within Russian borders, after the Bolshevik Revolution Boichuk ended up in Kyiv. He lectured at the Fine Arts Academy, and in the mid-1920s founded the Association of Revolutionary Art of Ukraine (Asotsiatsia revolutsyinoho mystetstva Ukrainy, ARMU). Iaroslava Muzyka's fortuitously timed visit to Kyiv occurred before the purge of 1928.[1] During the repressions the monumental art of the Boichukists drew Bolshevik ire. The Great Terror claimed the artists and their creations; Boichuk and his wife, the Łódź native Zofia Nalepińska, were shot, as were their friends Ivan Padalka and Vasyl Sedlar. Their work was systematically hunted down and destroyed by the Soviet government.

---

1   Olena Ripko, *U poshukakh strachenoho mynuloho. Retrospektyva mystets'koï kul'tury L'vova XX stolittia* (Lviv: Kameniar, 1996), 160.

The manuscript of Iaroslava Muzyka's recollections

Perhaps unwittingly, it was at this point that Iaroslava Muzyka took on the first of several challenges later deemed anti-Soviet actions. In the early 1930s, while the Soviet Ukraine waged a war on artistic independence, the painter and her friends founded the Association of Independent Ukrainian Artists (ANUM), its name a nod to Boichuk's ARMU. At the start of the Soviet occupation ANUM members entered the NKVD's field of vision, chiefly as devotees of Boichukism. Muzyka's personal answer to the reprisals against Boichuk and his school was to collect and document all that remained of his work in Galicia. Fate made sure that during the war and thereafter custody of Galician avant-garde art fell to Muzyka: as local artists were leaving in droves, they would deposit their works with her for safekeeping. Their pieces were in good hands, since Muzyka made a living from painting restoration. Somehow, through the war, the years in prison and in the *Gulag*, the countless NKVD searches—the agents had requisitioned all her possessions, including the art—Muzyka was able to safeguard some of Boichuk's legacy. But in the end, when the artist transferred her friends' paintings to the Lviv National Art Gallery, they were destroyed in the early 1950s, falling victim to an ideological campaign condemning formalism and nationalism. In the 1990s, Muzyka's collection, or what was left of it, reignited an interest in Boichuk and inspired attempts to locate any

Iaroslava Muzyka and family during World War I

remaining works.² Somewhat later Ukrainians came to rediscover the Galician avant-garde.³

Iaroslava Muzyka ran afoul of the Soviet administration for the second time when she remained in German-occupied Lviv. As we read in the chapter "Haven at the Clinic," at the start of the German-Soviet war, the Soviets forcibly evacuated her husband, Maksym Muzyka, a doctor and microbiologist. She stayed. Formally employed as a museum conservator, she got by on a little sewing and sales of icons in Byzantine style. Despite her own precarious circumstances during the war she helped Ukrainians, Jews, and Poles. Little did she know that one day the Soviets would accuse her of collaborating with the Germans.

Iaroslava Muzyka challenged the Soviets' authority for the third time, again unintentionally, right after the second "liberation." Though she still cared little for politics, by then politics had developed an interest in her. A string of events turned the painter into an intermediary between the Ukrainian resistance groups and the Soviet government. Through a friend (or so she thought) who became the director of Lviv's District Health Care Division, she relayed a message from Roman Shukhevych that the Ukrainian underground was ready to enter into talks with the Soviet administration. At that moment she stepped into the crosshairs of the NKVD. Had the thaw not come, she would have not been able to get her sentence of twenty-five years in the *Gulag* reduced. As it was, she served seven years, first in prison, then in a labor camp.

Her fate contrasts with the trajectories of her colleagues. After 1945 most of Muzyka's Ukrainian, Polish, and Jewish friends who survived the war were scattered far from Lviv. But before and during the war the Lviv avant-garde artists knew each other well, meeting up at exhibits and in cafés on social and professional occasions.

ARTISTS FROM CAFÉ DE LA PAIX

Tadeusz Hollender, a poet and translator, titled his first report from Lviv for the Polish *Wiadomości Literackie* [*Literary News*] "Artists from Café de la

---

2 Mykhailo Boichuk, *Al'bom-kataloh zberezhenykh tvoriv*, compiled by Vita Susak (Lviv: Oranta-Druk, 2010), 22; Iaroslav Kravchenko, "Iaroslava Muzyka u tvorchii doli Mykhaila Boichuka; novovyiavleni maliunky l'vivs'koho periodu," *Visnyk LAM* 21 (2010): 361–6.

3 Vita Susak, *Ukrainian artists in Paris 1900–1939* (Kyiv: Rodovid, 2010), esp. 36–46, 144–53, 180–89.

Paix."[4] His story focused on the literary-artistic milieu of Lviv Ukrainians who frequented a café located on Mickiewicz Square: "On traditional Thursdays you can encounter here the best of whatever the local Ukrainian world has to offer. In the evenings, columnists and poets, painters and journalists, musicians and literati, politicians and graphic artists, parliamentary representatives and humorists, sit around till late. ... And only from looking at the various groups clustered around the mushroom-shaped tables can we surmise that political constellations do influence these table planetariums."

This journalistic group portrait from the summer of 1935 depicts an interesting mosaic: a variety of political views; locals and immigrants; proponents of engaged art from the *Visnyk* circle and adepts of pure art (the so-called Parisian group) organized around the biweekly *Nazustrich*, itself modeled on *Wiadomości Literackie*; others who veered right in reaction to the repressions in Soviet Ukraine and, to a lesser extent, in the Republic of Poland. Hollender's journalistic collage did not match the stereotype advanced by the Polish contemporaneous press, which lumped the Ukrainian intelligentsia and nationalists together. Hollender wrote about the Ukrainian literati's close ties to Polish culture. He often focused on Mykhailo Rudnytsky as its leading critic; in spite of the age difference between them (a generation), Rudnytsky was Hollender's favorite companion. The journalist did not seek to conceal the tensions that charged Polish-Ukrainian relations. Instead, he tried to convey to *Wiadomości Literackie*'s readers what seemed an obvious truth: the Polish side held the key to solving the Polish-Ukrainian conflict, an enmity which continued to erupt with frequency. A contemporary of Hollender's, Sviatoslav Hordynsky, became the journalist's most frequent interlocutor. Hordynsky was a Ukrainian artist with an intellectual biography that reflected the lives of an entire generation of younger Ukrainians who had entered adulthood during the interwar period: first, in the 1920s, a brief fascination with Soviet Ukraine, followed by a turn to the right. Hollender attributed their political views to defensive nationalism.

It is important to realize that Hollender's contacts with Ukrainians necessitated openness, good will, and a significant effort, as the two sides did not trust each other. Worse yet, Lviv ostracized intellectuals who dared to issue public calls for bridging barriers instead of fueling hostilities. The Ukrainian *Visnyk* excelled at the latter; it vehemently criticized the liberal worldview, which formed the core of the philosophy of reconciliation. It did so in the name of fighting against a "national androgyny":

---

4   Tadeusz Hollender, "List ze Lwowa. Artyści z Kawiarni Pokoju," *Wiadomości Literackie*, no. 32, August 8, 1935, 2.

in our far from joyful reality, there are young and not-so-young people who cultivate in their holy simplicity these anachronist "Parises" (at Café De La Paix); with the pathos of naively sincere snobbism they proclaim a "new" (!) art, they tinker with exotic monographs with a fervor worthy of a better cause, they create some kind of suspicious carefree little world (a cross between a Gypsy caravan and a Jewish shtetl), a world in which a system of peculiar canons and criteria exists, as well as an equally curious hierarchy of values.[5]

The text's author, Ievhen Malaniuk, was targeting Rudnytsky. Malaniuk was undoubtedly right about one thing: a number of pre-World War II artists continued to live and work under the spell of Paris, as they had before 1914. Café de la Paix, at the corner of Mickiewicz Square and Kopernik Street, a coffeehouse that had replaced an earlier Café Avenue, evoked the classic Parisian artists' café. Paris served as an important reference point for intellectuals grouped around *Nazustrich*. To both Rudnytsky and Hordynsky, their stays in the city of lights represented formative chapters of their creative lives.

Not unlike the Ukrainian *Visnyk*, Polish national democrats also denounced these "coffee-house politicians," smelling a betrayal of their interests and the potential of losing the firm foothold Poland had been able to wrangle in Galicia. In contrast, those interested in true dialogue between ethnic groups that went beyond just a friendly chat made an effort to listen to their adversary. This certainly required a highly developed culture of political discourse, as we can infer from reading the notecards Hollender made during conversations with Sviatoslav Hordynsky (the two would communicate on paper because Hordynsky was deaf).

Hordynsky's poem "Do polskykh poetiv" ["To Polish Poets"], which Hollender translated into Polish, served as a counterpoint to Hollender's essay "Artists from Café de la Paix." Sensing the inevitable conflict, certain that human fate has been dominated by history, and convinced that Poles became its subject but Ukrainians were its mere object, the poet poses a poignant question:

> How shall we dare hide ourselves in the despairing rhythms and rhymes,
> How shall we dare button the holster full of words that are ready to shoot?
> The most terrifying thing is that above us lingers
> The unchanging beauty, cruel and always the same

---

5   Ievhen Malaniuk, *Knyha sposterezhen'. Proza* (Toronto: Homin Ukraïny, 1962), 157.

It remains the same even when the train of history rushes forward
And we will feel the cold weight of metal in our hands again.[6]

To Hordynsky, poetry and beauty, existing despite and against the hard reality, offered a platform that made rapport possible. Yet Tadeusz Hollender yearned for more. He had just left *Sygnały*'s [*Signals'*] team after his friend Karol Kuryluk took over as editor and shifted the periodical to the left. Hollender was looking for his own path. The seminal experience he carried away from *Sygnały*—a search for amity with fellow citizens in culture and through culture—inspired him to focus his inventiveness on this very issue. Aside from creative writing and literary essays (also for *Wiadomości Literackie*) Hollender turned to translation (he published Ulas Samchuk's novel *Volhynia* in Polish).[7] Together with his peer and friend from Jan Kazimierz University, Bohdan Ihor Antonych, they prepared an anthology titled *Fifty from Both Banks of the Zbruch* [*Pięćdziesięciu z tej i z tamtej strony Zbrucza*].[8] After the sudden death of the twenty-seven-year-old poet Antonych, Hollender urged *Sygnały*'s editorial team, with whom Antonych had worked, to honor the memory of the deceased. But ideological obstacles won out and *Sygnały* never published the obituary. Likewise, the anthology was not published.

Two years before the war Tadeusz Hollender had moved to Warsaw. He returned to Lviv just as the first Soviet occupation began. Anna Kowalska's journals reveal that he steadfastly refused to get involved in official literary activities under the Soviets and never joined the Soviet Writers' Union. His name does not come up in memoirs dealing with the first year of the occupation and the activities of the Writers' Union Organizational Committee. After the Nazis marched in, Hollender made his way back to Warsaw. There he joined the anti-Nazi resistance, working in underground publishing. Apprehended by the Nazis, he was executed in Warsaw's infamous Pawiak prison in 1943.

Sviatoslav Hordynsky went a different way; like many other members and sympathizers of the OUN, in September 1939 he vanished from the Soviet-occupied city of Lviv and reappeared in Cracow. After the Germans seized Lviv, he returned and became active in the Literary-Artistic Club. Despite his disability, Hordynsky exuded boundless energy. Before the war Hordynsky had been

---

6 Many thanks to the poet Oksana Lutsyshyna for translating these verses from the Ukrainian original.
7 Ulas Samchuk, *Wołyń*, trans. Tadeusz Hollender (Warszawa: Rój, 1938).
8 I wrote about this never-published anthology in *Prolog, nie epilog. Poezja ukraińska w polskich przekładach pierwszej połowy XX wieku* (Warszawa: SOW, 2002), 51–2.

Oleksandr Archipenko was the most famous of Ukrainian avant-garde artists

the driving force behind the artist group ANUM, and now he led the Association of Ukrainian Artists. The Ukrainian Publishing House hired him as a graphic artist; he also edited poetry collections of the Kyiv neoclassicists and made public appearances as a critic. In 1944 he emigrated, first to Germany, then to the United States.

Hollender's essay "Artists from Café de la Paix" presented sketches about Ukrainian writers who frequented the café; his brief write-ups help to create a map of literary life in interwar Lviv. Although at first glance the title of Hollender's essay suggested a focus on visual arts. He directed his spotlight to writers instead, since, as he admitted, art was outside of his expertise. All the same, he felt that if the output of the Ukrainian literary world could hardly dazzle Polish writers, Ukrainian art would certainly impress Polish visual artists. Curiously, Hollender only referenced Oleksandr Archipenko, who, after emigrating in the 1920s, had quickly achieved international renown. It is notable that the journalist searched for modern art developments outside the Lviv city limits; according to the opinions of contemporaries it was a town of tastes too provincial for an artist to succeed. On a side note, a year earlier, Hollender helped open up the pages of *Sygnały* to Ukrainian art.

RETURN FROM PARIS. AMONG PAINTERS FROM *ARTES* AND ANUM

Hordynsky, Hollender's Ukrainian connection, was above all an artist, though occasionally he turned to poetry. In 1932, shortly after returning from Paris, Hordynsky initiated the founding of ANUM, a group that brought together a whole galaxy of eminent painters. Most often they socialized at the Café de la Paix, a coffeehouse whose Parisian inspiration shone through in its name and atmosphere. Iaroslava Muzyka, the association's president, recalled that the idea for ANUM first emerged in the cafe.[9] While ANUM painters worked within the city's larger artistic scene, ambition motivated them to assert their own distinctiveness.

In the 1930s Lviv emerged from the economic crisis of the previous decade and its creative current gained much vigor. In 1932 members of the avant-garde groups *Artes*, ANUM, the New Generation, and the Association of Ten, established the Lviv Professional Union of Visual Artists. Its roster offers a historical tour of interwar modern art. In chapters "Girl with a Dog," "Haven at the Clinic," and "Academic Snapshots," we met three of the artists: Iaroslava Muzyka, Ludwik Lille, and Leon Chwistek. The current chapter expands this circle by a few new names: Otto Hahn, Jerzy Janisch, Fryc Kleinman, Volodymyr Lasovsky, Margit and Roman Selsky, Henryk Streng, and Stanisław Teisseyre. Apart from Kleinman, who had stronger ties to Vienna, the others had a shared fascination with the Parisian avant-garde; as Jerzy Janisch declared, true painting, no matter what school, only occurred in Paris. Some, like Lille, Roman Selsky, and Streng (who would soon change his name to Marek Włodarski to evade persecution by the Nazis), were inspired by Fernand Léger and turned to post-cubism and surrealism. Others, such as Otto Hahn, shifted toward surrealism. Critics had their day, branding the artists as blinded by pseudomodernist ideas. The *Artes* association (1929–35) encompassed avant-garde artists of varying ethnicities (Polish, Jewish, Ukrainian, and Armenian), all affiliated with Lviv. Exhibitions organized by *Artes* showcased visual innovations from beyond their group as well, for instance pieces

---

9 L'vivs'ka natsional'na halereia mystetstv (LNHM), Iaroslava Muzyka fonds, op. 2, Spomyny, k. 3. Collection of papers and correspondence, unpaginated.

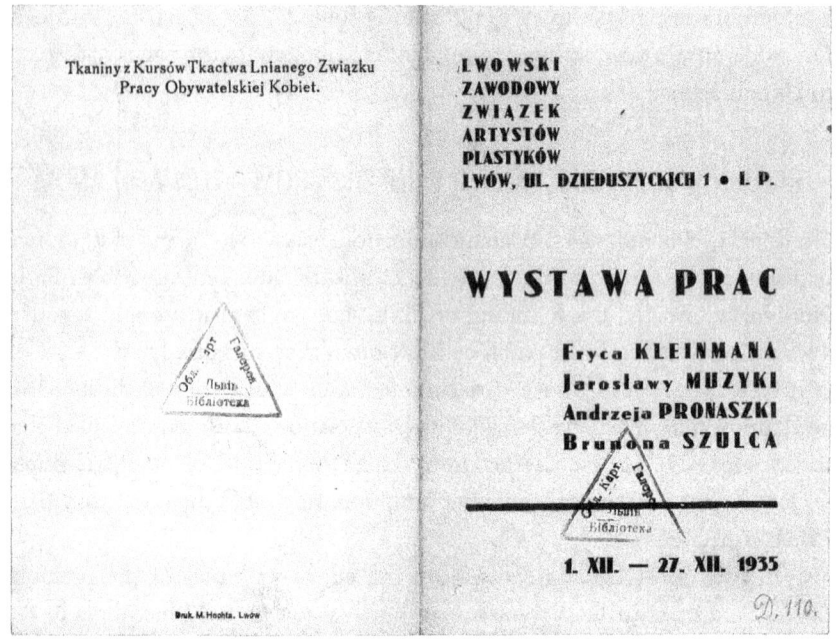

Invitation to an exhibit of works by Fryc *Kleinman*, Iaroslava Muzyka, Andrzej Pronaszko, and Bruno *Schulz*, 1935

by the stylistically close Pavlo Kovzhun. Since *Artes* did not have a separate magazine, at times its members published programmatic texts in ANUM's organ *Mystetstvo* [*Art*][10]—in Ukrainian. Despite the ambitions of Ludwik Lille and Otto Hahn, *Artes* failed to create a theoretical platform, and art historians believe this caused the association to dissolve by the mid-1930s. Conversely, ANUM, despite its diverse composition, lived on until the Soviet occupation. Judging from the fragmentarily preserved correspondence between Iaroslava Muzyka and Ludwik Lille—they continued writing each other after he moved to Paris—the circle's members became close friends. They met up not only in Lviv or at joint exhibitions in Warsaw, but also in Paris; they debated issues in person, and corresponded about the latest events or developments. In one of her letters, Lille related the successes of Sofiia Levytska, his talks with Roman Turyn, and inquired about Osinchuk and Kovzhun.[11]

---

10   Otto Han, "Konstruktyvizm, nadrealizm i shcho dali," *Mystetstvo* 2–3 (1932): 47–8; Liudvik Lill', "Suddi ta pidsudni," *Mystetstvo* 4 (1933): 98–9.

11   Letter from Ludwik Lille to Iaroslava Muzyka, undated [spring 1938], Iaroslava Muzyka fonds, op. 2.

The Lviv Professional Union of Visual Artists succeeded in what the smaller groups it encompassed could not effect: thanks to the support of Lviv's mayor Stanisław Ostrowski it acquired a suitable location in the Museum of Artistic Industry. The gallery was inaugurated in early 1935; within the next two years it would host more than a dozen exhibits. Among the first ones was a December 1935 event that showcased works by Fryc Kleinman, Iaroslava Muzyka, Andrzej Pronaszko, and Bruno Schulz. The reviewers attended to its artistic quality and singled out the difficult technique of painting on glass, mastered by Iaroslava Muzyka. She presented a few of her most recent pieces, created during her travels to France and Italy.[12] Yet perhaps only the young critic Karol Kuryluk recognized the exhibit's uniqueness: "The Union of Visual Artists accomplished something unheard of: in its gallery rooms it brought together artists of three nationalities: Polish, Ukrainian, and Jewish."[13]

Was this truly such a noteworthy achievement? In her memoir devoted to the *Artes* painters, Izabella Czermakowa argued that their circle paid no attention to ethnicity, whether in friendships or debates.[14] While there is no reason to doubt her testimony, it should be remembered that it originated from within the artistic community. Public life adhered to a different set of rules. In Lviv the Union's name alone irked the public because it did not feature the adjective "Polish." The other side erected barriers as well: ANUM's first exhibition, organized by Hordynsky and Kovzhun in 1931 at the Lviv Museum of Ukrainian Art, showcased 120 Ukrainian, French, Italian, and Belgian pieces, but none by Polish artists. All the same, *Mystetstvo*'s editors were happy to open its pages to all artists and critics irrespective of their ethnicity. The Ukrainian-language magazine printed contributions by members of the group *Artes*, and covered art events, especially those associated with ANUM or *Artes*.

The Spring Salon was the group's last prewar exhibit; its participants included Leon Chwistek, Otto Hahn, Jerzy Janisch, Fryc Kleinman, Iaroslava Muzyka, Margit and Roman Selsky, Henryk Streng, Marian Wnuk, and others. We can conclude that to a certain degree the collective gave rise to a community. Soon the friendships binding many of its members would make it

---

12 Mykhailo Rudnyts'kyi, "Maliarka z temperamentom i kholodni ryby," *Nazustrich* 124 (1935): 4; Mykhailo Rudnyts'kyi, "Vystava prats' Iaroslavy Muzyki," *Dilo*, no. 321, December 1, 1935.
13 Karol Kuryluk, "Życie kulturalne we Lwowie," *Tygodnik Ilustrowany*, no. 5, February 2, 1936, 96.
14 Izabella Czermakowa, "Dom na Krasuczynie," in *Czarownik przy zielonej skale: Marek Włodarski—Henryk Streng*, ed. Józef Chrobak, Justyna Michalik, and Marek Wilk (Poznań: Galeria Piekary, 2009), 23.

possible to save the lives of two artists of Jewish descent: Henryk Streng and Margit Selska (née Reich).

KORNIICHUK'S TAKE ON A BRIGHT FUTURE

In the fall of 1939 Lviv's various artistic circles fell under the shared auspices of restrictive ideology. The enforced egalitarianism or *uravnilovka* began with the Soviet press molding the city's public discourse. On September 28, *Vilna Ukraina* published a text that culminated in "Long live our comrade Stalin!" The letter, addressed to "the art workers of Soviet Ukraine," had been signed by members of the local artistic elite: Olena Kulchytska, Iaroslava Muzyka, Mykhailo Osinchuk, Mykola Holubets, Serhy Lytvynenko, Ivan Ivanets, Volodymyr Lasovsky, Edward Kozak.[15] Similar pieces appeared in *Czerwony Sztandar*.

In parallel fashion the administration called meetings of "collectives." On the afternoon of September 28, the Ukrainian Association of Writers and Journalists passed a resolution to disband. The next morning, on September 29, at an ANUM meeting held in the offices of the Shevchenko Scientific Society, Oleksandr Korniichuk gave a speech. He was greeted by Mykhailo Osinchuk, who was stepping in for the association's president, Iaroslava Muzyka. In attendance were ANUM members, as well as Mykhailo Ostroverkha, whom Osinchuk had invited the day before when the two ran into each other at the Viennese Café (Kawiarnia Wiedeńska). Ostroverkha recounted the meeting in detail, stating poignantly:

> At a certain moment of his [Korniichuk's] speech I whispered to Sofiia Valnytska to ask about M. [Mykhailo] Boichuk and others. She went:
> "Comrade academy member! What do artists like Mykh[ailo] Boichuk, Padalka, and others create now? Be so kind as to tell us!"
> "You know, comrades," Korniichuk turned a little sheepish, though not for long, "some of Ukraine's artists let themselves be sucked into counterrevolution. For instance, Padalka colluded with A.[ndry] Khvyla, who on his end colluded with elements harmful to the Soviet Union. And Khvyla was a baron, and another one [here Korniichuk said a name which I forgot], a German. He was shot, and Padalka is in the Solovki [prison camp], M. Boichuk is somewhere in the north of the Union ..."

---

15 "Do robitnykiv mystetstva Radians'koi Ukraïny," *Vil'na Ukraïna*, no. 3, September 28, 1939.

The comrade academy member ended his speech. All present exchanged meaningful looks: "great prospects!"¹⁶

In reality Boichuk, Padalka, and Sedlar had been executed in Kyiv in 1937, and Andry Khvyla in 1938. Korniichuk lied on purpose. What is more, he took note of both the inquiry and the questioner herself—Sofiia Valnytska—and made a point of passing it on to state security. A month later, most likely not of her own free will, the NKVD integrated Valnytska into their network of informers. Ostroverkha described the Soviets' methods of breaking people during recruitment;¹⁷ he had heard about them secondhand the day of Korniichuk's speech. Curiously, it never crossed his mind that a few hours before he had contributed to Valnytska's impeding recruitment when he suggested she probe Korniichuk.

Korniichuk's assignment went beyond mere reconnaissance. At all official assemblies his communiques sounded similar: the organization should dissolve, and its members need to register in the new Soviet organization as part of an all-Soviet structure. Attendees protested: the few Ukrainian painters would drown in the sea of Polish and Jewish visual artists. Korniichuk countered: "let Poles and Jews register with you! After all you are the hosts of this land! I see that you are browbeaten, you do not even have the courage to think that you are becoming the center of artistic life."¹⁸ His words once again confirm that Soviet authorities manipulated the Ukrainian intelligentsia in the first weeks of the occupation, duping them with the illusion that they were gaining legal rights. Ostroverkha was not the only one who sensed this lie. The ANUM artists tended to keep their distance from ideology, and they did not want to get involved this time either. True, they attended official meetings, but continued to convene privately. Soon they would learn that the Soviets allowed no space for the private sphere.

IN THE NEW UNION

After a series of meetings sponsored by Korniichuk came the next step: establishing an organizational committee for the Artists' Union. Soon the Soviets sent Mykhailo Dmytrenko, a painter and the Union's president, down from

---

16 Ostroverkha, "Na krutomu zvoroti istoriï Ievropy," k. 108. As in previous chapters, I use quotes from the memoir's manuscript when the details differ from the self-published version published nearly twenty years later.
17 Ibid., k. 109.
18 Ostroverkha, *Na zakruti. Osin' 1939 r.*, 76–7.

Kyiv. At first the authorities proposed representatives of the three ethnicities for seats on the executive committee: Roman Selsky (Ukrainian), Henryk Streng (Jewish), and Marian Wnuk (Polish). Most likely they were not consulted, or so it appears from Roman Selsky's reminiscences.[19] They were all *Artes* members who just a few months earlier held a joint exhibit. Once the war broke out, they were no longer able to focus on art; instead, they directed their energies to assisting refugees, arranging for a canteen, and looking for means of survival.[20] The organizational committee set up its headquarters at 9 Mickiewicz Square (formerly St. Mary's Square), and began the registration procedure, which ended in early spring of 1940. Seventy artists registered.[21] The committee's roster changed: the three *Artes* members were replaced by senior artists Ivan Trush, Olena Kulchytska, and Osyp Kurylas. In keeping with Korniichuk's pronouncement, all were Ukrainians. Exhibits were hastily put together—first graphic arts, then painting; participation was compulsory for all registered artists.

As one of Milena Rudnytska's sources recalled: "on the rubble of several prewar artistic alliances and associations, the occupier established one professional union in Lviv, herding into its cage painters and sculptors of varying ethnicities, seniority, and creative predilections."[22] The induction to the Artists' Union differed from the procedure the writers underwent, but only a few details. In fall of 1939 the Soviets began to "tame" the literati by commissioning poems hailing Stalin; acceptance to the Artists' Union was conditional on one's participation in the collective exhibit; there, representatives or the Soviet Artists' Union would separate the wheat from the chaff.

"THE INDEPENDENTS"

By late September artist brigades began showing up to promote Soviet art, first in Ternopil, then in Lviv. They also carried out practical assignments: their task was to implement the visual rhetoric in the "liberated" territories. The next team prepared decorations for the People's Assembly in late October 1939. Union members sent to Lviv and the party functionaries who assisted them as minders related their interactions with local artists. Based on those reports the NKVD would build cases against individual persons or entire groups.

---

19 Roman Sels'kyi and Ivan Hrechko, "Sel'skyi pro Sel'skoho. Rozmovliav Ivan Hrechko," in *Roman Sels'kyi. Tvory z pryvatnykh zbirok*, ed. Agnesa Bachyns'ka-Sels'ka (Lviv: Instytut kolektsionerstva pry NTSh, 2004), 26.
20 Ripko, *U poshukakh strachenoho mynuloho*, 108.
21 "Orhkomitet khudozhnkiv," *Vil'na Ukraïna*, no. 52, March 4, 1940.
22 Rudnyts'ka, *Zakhidnia Ukraina pid bol'shevykamy. Zbirnyk*, 222.

Immediately after the People's Assembly ended, a Kyiv visual artist named Oleksandr Pashchenko and a party functionary Tolkachov (first name unknown) submitted a report about the ANUM community to the Lviv oblast NKVD. They characterized the organization, which had dissolved a month earlier, as nationalist, and branded its members as Ukrainian fascists.[23] Alleged proof were ANUM's ties to the Boichukists, who had been executed in 1937 as agents of fascist intelligence.[24] The denouncement smacks of Soviet rhetoric from the 1930s. Once the Soviet Union signed the Molotov-Ribbentrop Pact, terms such as "fascist" were forbidden in official publications so as not to offend their new ally, though security dispatches still made use of it. According to the document, the Lviv artists conducted conversations in an unceremonious and rude manner ["vedut sebia otkryto i naglo"]. Unaccustomed to open debate and the mistrust of propaganda they witnessed in the city, Soviet artists who came to Lviv reacted in the only way they knew—by sending in denunciations.

The NKVD had been lying in wait: in a report from late October the bureau informed Moscow that it was short on agents and asked Moscow to solve the problem. The very next day security officers set up cases and files for the most important ANUM artists: the former president Iaroslava Muzyka, Mykhailo Osinchuk, and Volodymyr Lasovsky. Three days later they enlisted the forty-five-year-old artist Sofiia Valnytska to infiltrate the entire community; the group was assigned the alias of "Samostiinyki" (The Independents). For reasons not quite clear, Valnytska wrote particularly negative reports on Muzyka.[25] Under the code name "Kistrin" she supplied information about former ANUM members for a year; after that she was removed from the network of agents, officially due to an illness, but more likely because the intelligence did not prove useful. Two informers recruited after Valnytska—"Shchel" (Mykhailo Rudnytsky) and "Khudozhnik" (I was not able to identify who this alias belonged to)[26]— used avoidance tactics. "Shchel" said Iaroslava Muzyka lacked any understanding of politics and characterized her as an honest and straightforward person. His reports lacked any specifics. The case review summary concluded with the statement that since 1941 matter was not investigated further;[27] evidently, it turned out turned out to be too trivial. Pashchenko's denunciation from late October and Valnytska's report from early November 1939 conveyed a

---

23 Kryminal'na sprava Iaroslavy Muzyki, HDA SBU, FP 74893, t. 2, k. 78.
24 Ibid., k. 79.
25 Ibid., k. 85. Decoding of agent's personal information: ibid., k. 159.
26 Ibid., k. 100.
27 Ibid., k. 75.

potentially serious charge: the community strove to retain its separate status and its representatives continued to gather privately at the home of the former president of the association. "Kistrin" did not mention that the circle had regularly met at Iaroslava Muzyka's before the war too, for no other reason than the large size of her apartment.

An overview of the Lviv press confirms that the former ANUM members disengaged from official actions. They participated in artistic life to a very limited extent, in an exhibit that offered a summary of the Lviv visual art scene. But all those present at the meeting with Korniichuk declared their readiness to join the organizational committee (except Muzyka and Ostroverkha, though he tried to register as a singer). The artists were allotted a space where they met regularly to discuss the work of their colleagues. What that entailed under ideological pressure is easy to extrapolate from how writers were exorcised, as we read in the previous chapter. In addition to compulsory attendance at these meetings, the community was plagued by ideological trainings and lectures about socialist realist art. Lecturers—some of them prominent, like Aleksandr Gerasimov, president of the All-Soviet Artists' Union, but most often inconsequential—expounded on the differences between naturalism and socialist realism. They condemned all experiments, reducing them to formalism or, best case scenario, decadence, and extoled those artists who, adjusting quickly, transformed their craft in the spirit of socialist realism.[28]

"POSLEDNII ZAL—POSLEDNII RAZ!"

It was easiest for traditional figurative artists to fall in line with the requirements of socialist realism. A case in point is the art of Stanisław Batowski, whose work the Soviet press was glad to reproduce despite his "wrong" class origin (he came from the landed gentry). Artists with leftist views happened to produce the most experimental art. They only adapted to the new terms with difficulty, and, consequently, suffered the most devastating criticism. Among them were prewar communists along with a number of visual artists from the *Artes* group. Half a century later a member of that circle, Stanisław Teisseyre, recalled this paradoxical situation with a dose of humor:

> They hung those paintings, put up the sculptures. They called us all and gave a big speech. "Oh, the first room, that is the best. It is maybe a little too

---

28 L. Hutman, "Khudozhnyky radians'koho L'vova," *Vil'na Ukraïna*, no. 222, September 21, 1940.

naturalist"—because they supposedly condemned naturalism—"maybe too naturalistic, but this is the direction to go in." After that: "there it is, worse, worse, and *poslednii zal—poslednii raz!*" The last room, for the last, ha ha, the last time. Mostly communists found themselves there, ha ha. … It was a coincidence, because they were not just leftists, but leftists in art, too. Well, and of course they did not tolerate abstractionism. The truth is they brought things that were not abstract, yet depicted so little that they were categorically told right away: "poslednii zal—poslednii raz."[29]

The attendees likely relished the irony of the situation, too: the last room displayed paintings by leftist artists. The exhibit took place in 1940 at the headquarters of the Artists' Union on Mickiewicz Square. The first real test of the milieu's loyalty came with the anniversary of the "liberation." Union membership depended on applicants' active participation in state-sponsored events; once admitted, the artists could count on commissions. One hundred and twenty artists presented five hundred pieces within the exhibit titled "Red Army Warriors Liberate Western Ukraine."[30] Among them were Poles (such as Adam Styka, son of Jan Styka, co-creator of the famed monumental "Panorama Racławicka"), Ukrainians (Volodymyr Lasovsky), and Jews (Mendel Schmierer Reif); the newspaper *Vilna Ukraina* pronounced Reif's picture "A Red Army Soldier Tells a Jewish Family about Life in the USSR" the event's showpiece.[31] The catalogue prepared by Leonid Rechmedin, the newspaper's editorial secretary whose job was to make sure the publication toed the party line, lists all the artists' names and works. Among the painters on display were *Artes* and ANUM affiliates, as well as the aforementioned elders, and even Kazimierz Sichulski, a famous representative of Young Poland who had fought in the Polish Legions—a biography that did not quite fit the exhibition's message.

As part of promoting the "liberation" and its success stories, exhibits opened in Kyiv, Kharkiv, and Moscow. Their focus fell especially on showcasing works by the older and younger generations, such as Jakub Glasner, Olena Kulchytska, Ludwik Tyrowicz, and Józefa Kratochwila-Widymska,[32] as well as

---

29 Jarosław Maszewski, "Rozmowa ze Stanisławem Teisseyre'm," *Zeszyty Artystyczne* 19 (2012): 3–16.
30 "Vikdryvaiet'sia u chervni vystavka khudyzhnykiv 'Zvilnennia Zakhidnoï Ukraïny doblesnoiu Chervonoiu Armiieiu,'" *Vil'na Ukraïna*, no. 123, May 28, 1940.
31 "Khudozhnyky L'vova do pershykh rokovyn vyzvolennia," *Vil'na Ukraïna*, no. 155, July 5, 1940.
32 L. Vladych, "Vystavka l'vivs'kykh hrafikiv u Kyievi," *Vil'na Ukraïna*, no. 155, July 5, 1940.

presenting a retrospective of Lviv painters. In June, an exhibition of Lviv artists was organized in Kyiv; a separate room showcased art from Łódź. Local creatives commented on the event: "they will not permit an exhibit like that again."[33]

The task of summarizing the first year of Soviet rule as reflected in the local art scene fell ex officio to Mykhailo Dmytrenko, the president of the Lviv Union of Visual Artists. His article, published in the monthly *Literatura i mystetstvo*, announced "Blyskuchi tvorchi perspektyvy" ["Splendid Creative Prospects"]. The magazine's issue appeared three months before Lviv artists would travel to Moscow for their exhibit. Although on the surface the article resembles other propaganda pieces, Dmytrenko managed to devote a lengthy passage to the Parisian roots of Lviv's creatives: "Paris, which for decades has dictated the fashion in creative work, had a tremendous influence on artists from former Poland: they lived its colors, its attitudes, and, most importantly, its formalist art, emulating both realist impressionists as well as extreme abstractionists. ..."[34] An eye accustomed to reading between the lines will immediately catch the intimation. Conversely, a person who grew up without censorship will not even register the difference between propagandist stencils and Dmytrenko's cautious attempt to break through them. The author, educated under the modernist painter Fedir Krychevsky, came to the Kyiv Fine Arts Institute back in the era of Mykhailo Boichuk and Mykola Burachek. Certainly he had heard that Paris was the Mecca of artists before the Lviv artists arrived; still, meeting them gave him a chance to loosen his ideological corset. Dmytrenko was not alone among transplants from Soviet Ukraine who tried to seize the opportunity that came with living in Lviv and fulfill goals beyond their own artistry. Prior chapters reference the writers Petro Panch and Maksym Rylsky, as well as the historian Mykhailo Marchenko, in a similar context. But Dmytrenko's story stands out because his seemingly insignificant reference to Paris, made in connection with the Moscow exhibit, sheds light on his strategy and his motivations.

A ROW IN MOSCOW

Mykhailo Dmytrenko obtained authorization for a large group of Lviv artists to travel to Moscow, Leningrad, and Kyiv. It appears he was a capable organizer.

---

33   Sels'kyi and Hrechko, "Sel'skyi pro Sel'skoho. Rozmovliav Ivan Hrechko," 26.
34   Mykhailo Dmytrenko, "Blyskuchi tvorchi perspektyvy," *Literatura i mystetstvo* 1 (1940): 27–8.

The retrospective of Lviv paintings was sent to the capital in December 1940. A month later, a party of twenty-eight artists led by Dmytrenko departed from Lviv.[35] Forty years later Stanisław Teisseyre recalled that the group consisted of Polish, Jewish, and Ukrainian artists, each ethnicity comprising one-third of the group respectively. In addition to Teisseyre himself and others he mentioned— Dmytrenko, Roman Turyn, Oleksandr Vynnytsky, and Artur Nacht—I was able to establish that Roman Selsky[36] and Marian and Józefa Wnuk[37] came as well (although I cannot explain why Teisseyre would not have included the names of his close friends). Mrs. Wnuk's recollections keep silent about the exhibit of Lviv art and refer to the trip as an "excursion" of sorts, whose participants daringly criticized socialist realist art.[38] Overall her account trivializes the period of Soviet occupation, telling a story of relatively carefree times. Her husband, the sculptor Marian Wnuk, retained his position as professor at the School of Fine Arts, and she and her friends earned income from generating massive propaganda portraits of Soviet leaders in large numbers. Those pieces were known as *wcierki* (rub-ins) because they relied on replicating small images or photos by rubbing oil paint onto a canvas grid.

However we might judge the artists' engagement, the exhibit hosted by the State Museum of New Western Art in the Soviet capital was not a minor event. Stanisław Teisseyre devoted several pages of his reminiscences to the art show. To be sure, his account contains some inaccuracies and exaggerations, yet the "pictures at the exhibition" he presents tell us quite a bit about the relationships between the Lviv and Moscow artist communities. Teisseyre erroneously calls the Museum of Modern Western Art "Gallery Shchukin" and spins a story of the merchant's foresight and Soviet humanitarianism toward him. Teisseyre's assertion that the authorities permitted Shchukin to stay on as the curator of his own museum is incorrect. Sergei Shchukin was one of the wealthiest Moscow art collectors at the turn of the twentieth century; in contrast to Tretiakov, a collector of domestic art with a focus on the Wanderers, Shchukin accumulated Western art, above all French impressionists and postimpressionists. After he emigrated in 1918, the collection met a predictable fate; Lenin decreed that the art, along with

---

35 "Khronika," *Literatura i mystetstvo* 1 (1941): 49.
36 Piotr Łukaszewicz, *Roman i Margit Sielscy. Obrazy z kolekcji Piotra Wojno i z innych zbiorów polskich. Katalog wystawy* (Wrocław: Muzeum Narodowe we Wrocławiu, 2004), 28.
37 Józefa Wnukowa, "Długie życie upartej dziewczynki. Z profesor Józefą Wnukową rozmawia Henryka Dobosz," interview by Henryka Dobosz, in Chrobak, Michalik, and Wilk, *Czarownik przy zielonej skale: Marek Włodarski—Henryk Streng*, 203.
38 Ibid., 203–4.

Shchukin's mansion, be nationalized. Gradually the holdings were dispersed; the young Soviet government needed money and monetized works of art: not only icons, those "superfluous objects of a religious cult," but Western avant-garde pieces too. Then came Stalinism, and with it, socialist realism. As part of their battle against formalism in art, the Soviets systematically reduced the collection each time they put on exhibits of contemporary art. And so it was that by January 1941, at the time of the art show, part of Shchukin's early twentieth century collection of French paintings was removed from the Museum of New Western Art. Most likely the pieces never made it back; each new show provided a convenient excuse to get rid of the "formalists." Since it was a style that the Lvivians grew up with, as they perused the gallery, they clashed with the Moscow painter Fyodor Bogorodsky (Stanisław Teisseyre incorrectly lists his name as Blagorodsky). Bogorodsky was a former sailor of the Russian cruiser Aurora and, of course, had been a member of the Bolshevik party since 1917. A van Gogh painting remaining on display attracted the Lviv visitors' attention. Being a true Bolshevik, the brave sailor yearned to send the postimpressionist piece to the garbage heap of history. Words were exchanged. In a militant mood he entered the joint gathering of Moscow and Lviv artists.

Prior to the meeting, Dmytrenko, who was in charge of the Lviv delegation, suggested that the artist should express themselves as they did in Lviv. Perhaps he hoped it would relax the obligatory rules of socialist realism? It might have seemed easier for Lvivians to breach that wall, since the regime showed far more tolerance towards them than it did with its own artists. A kind Moscow host, the president of the Soviet Artists' Union Aleksandr Gerasimov, Stalin's favorite, began by criticizing the Lvivians who "dressed up like the French." After him others spoke, each along the same lines. Then Artur Nacht-Samborski, who had come to Lviv as a refugee from Cracow and who usually kept to himself, issued a challenge, paying no regard to the dangerous consequences. As a former Capist (a painter affiliated with the Paris Artists' Committee) he probably could not stand the tenor of those speeches, or perhaps his adrenaline won out—after all he was also a boxer. He started off with a parody of a self-critique, and then moved on to a short lecture on the history of European art.

> Gentlemen, I confess; confess to what this colleague said in the beginning, kind of figuratively, as a metaphor, that we dressed up in French costumes. Indeed, I confess. I am under the influence of twentieth-century French art. Yes—as all of Europe in the course of the fifteenth century was under the influence of the Italian Renaissance. And Velázquez was not ashamed

of being under the influence of the Italian Renaissance, the Dutch were not ashamed, the French were not ashamed, Poussin was not ashamed that he was under such an influence—because, in that era—it was the leading art. As in the present moment, in the twentieth century, French art is the leading art. On the other hand, I must tell my Soviet colleagues that I have seen here your contemporary paintings, your exhibition, to which you took us. It is—forgive me—German art of the mid-1800s.[39]

Now Bogorodsky, who was sitting somewhere back, had had enough. He boomed his truth across the room: you have brought us counterrevolutionaries! Though in his pre-1917 youth he had been in awe of cubism and suprematism, later he devoted himself exclusively to revolutionary themes and helped create the canon of socialist realist painting. As the director of the painting division at the Moscow Institute of Cinematography and a party member with a nearly twenty-five-year tenure, he made for a dangerous opponent. After the meeting concluded, he almost threw a punch at Dmytrenko.

This public scandal spelled peril for all the members of the Lviv delegation, and especially so for Dmytrenko. The situation called for immediate action. On the following evening the artists were already scheduled to meet with Oleksandr Korniichuk, who was acquainting Stalin with the script for his play *Bohdan Khmelnytsky*, and would thus have a chance to put out the fire. That same day Mykhailo Dmytrenko suggested a visit to the suburban dacha (more of a mansion) of the sculptor Sergei Merkurov, a personal friend of Lenin's. Merkurov had studied in Kyiv in the early 1900s, and in the 1930s participated in prominent commissions (in 1933, he designed the Shevchenko monument in Kaniv with Vasyl Krychevsky). Still sentimental, and not just about Kyiv, he got emotional reminiscing about his old love—Olga Boznańska—and his university years in Munich and Paris. When told what had happened the day before, he offered to take care of the matter. He kept his word. At dinner with Korniichuk—if we can trust Roman Selsky's memory, it was New Year's Day (probably according to the Julian Calendar)—Bogorodsky also showed up. After yet another toast he stood up and stunned everyone by apologizing to the Lviv artists. Certainly not everyone understood what had occurred: it was impossible that the party line had changed, thus the matter must have taken such an unexpectedly fortuitous turn thanks to Merkurov. Korniichuk did nothing to smooth over the situation, even though he was the host.

---

39 Maszewski, "Rozmowa ze Stanisławem Teisseyre'm," 14.

The inadvertent culprit of this commotion, Mykhailo Dmytrenko, in contrast to other trusted comrades who were sent to Lviv at the start of the war, retained his post until the outbreak of the German-Soviet conflict. He remained in Lviv during the German occupation, and in his reminiscences, Stanisław Teisseyre did not miss the chance to chide him, claiming that Dmytrenko "was remade by Ukrainian nationalists." The Kyiv artist was able to survive the subsequent years with support of colleagues from the Artists' Union (he had been its director only a few months earlier), especially the sculptor Serhy Lytvynenko and the painter Mykhailo Osinchuk. Dmytrenko led a division affiliated with the Folk Art Institute.[40] During that time he only published one article, in the newspaper *Lvivski visti*, where, while ostensibly praising a supposedly successful exhibit of Ukrainian artists, he reached back to 1918 and discussed the achievements of Heorhy Narbut.[41] Again a reader accustomed to reading between the lines would be able to intuit the author's assessment of the exhibit itself, and of the political situation. In 1944 Dmytrenko left Lviv together with a whole group of Ukrainian artists.

BERIA'S FOUR EYES

Promotional exhibits did not occur all too often and they were not much of a source of income. Daily life in Lviv differed vastly from the idyllic image painted by political commissars and agitators—the grand life of a Soviet painter. To make a living an artist had to work with Stakhanovite speed; fortunately, the USSR had developed a ravenous appetite for portraits and monuments. Within a month of the Soviets entering Lviv the first mass commissions came in. Around the corner were "elections" to the People's Assembly, then its festive session, after that the anniversary of the October revolution, and in December the anniversary of Stalin's constitution. All these events needed to be framed in a suitable manner. Posters and other materials were printed on a mass scale and sent to the occupied territory from Kyiv or Moscow, but outsized portraits of leaders or monuments were another matter. Thus a brigade of Soviet visual artists was sent down to "decorate" the city. They worked at breakneck speed.

The town's look changed, its decor gradually coming to resemble other USSR cities. Memoirists describe the omnipresent redness, emanating from

---

40 "Studiia ta zaochni kursy mystets'koï osvity," *L'vivski visti*, no. 179, August 11, 1942.
41 Mykhailo Dmytrenko, "Obrazotvorche mystetsvo. Z nahody vystavy Spilky obrazotvorchykh mysttsiv," *L'vivski visti*, no. 11, January 21, 1942.

Artists from Café de la Paix | **421**

The monument to Stalin's Constitution

flags, posters, slogans, and portraits too. On December 5, 1939, the third anniversary of Stalin's constitution, a monument to the Stalinist Friendship of Nations was erected at Wały Hetmańskie/Hetman Bulwarks (today Prospekt Svobody/Freedom Avenue), designed by Mykhailo Dmytrenko and Serhy Lytvynenko (a Petliura émigré and the best-known Ukrainian sculptor in Lviv).[42] Allegorical figures of a Red Army soldier, a worker, a mother with her child, and an old Hutsul, with signage in Polish, Ukrainian, and Yiddish, represented the allegedly democratic character of the constitution and the blessed outcomes of the Soviet invasion. It was the first Soviet monument in town, created by Ievhen Dzyndra and Andry Koverko, and the first to be knocked down by the Germans two years later. After six months, when a state factory for sculpture was opened at 26 Mączna, the mass production of busts and statues began. On the anniversary of the annexation, the boulevard Wały Hetmańskie, by then renamed May First Street, acquired another monument—the "Liberation."

If a vast number of monuments and busts filled the city and its public buildings, portraits of revolutionaries and state leaders were produced in even larger quantities. Of course, those were not individual commissions. Artists worked through "Khudozhnik," a cooperative created specifically for that purpose. Jonasz Stern of the Cracow Group led the cooperative, and Henryk Streng from *Artes* became its associate director.[43] The authorities trusted Stern and Streng because of their prewar political engagement: both had been affiliated with the Communist Party of Western Ukraine and the International Red Aid. The co-op brought together former *Artes* members and many other visual artists, among them the aforementioned Oleksandr Vynnytsky, Józefa Wnuk, and Artur Nacht.

Visual artists—surrealists and traditionalists alike—returned to their schoolday technique of reproduction, generating the rubbed-in *wcierki*. The only persons who had a chance to make money were those who could adjust to the conditions of the authorities' full control over art and were efficient copyists at that, though even those skills did not guarantee one's safety. As in newspapers, in art, too, employees shuddered at the thought of overlooking an error in communist keywords and names (editors recalled that their nightmares would feature typos in the name "Stalin"); likewise, a mistake in copying the visage of revolutionary chiefs and USSR leaders could cause serious problems. Artur Nacht was supporting his entire family and had little choice but to take up such mass productions.

---

42 "Vstanovlennia skul'ptury 'Stalins'ka druzhba narodiv'," *Vil'na Ukraïna*, no. 61, December 5, 1939.

43 Józef Chrobak, "Henryk Streng / Marek Włodarski. Kalendarium," in Chrobak, Michalik, and Wilk, *Czarownik przy zielonej skale: Marek Włodarski—Henryk Streng*, 112.

While transferring a portrait of Lavrentii Beria to a canvas, he made a mistake in the enlargement and moved the image by one grid. The miscalculation left the chief of state security with two sets of eyes. The gigantic portrait hung at second-story level along the trajectory of the May First rally and peered down onto the crowds with redoubled attention. The party's leadership would not accept any explanations and accused the artist of sabotage. Thankfully, in the course of the investigation, the school's employees were able to convince the authorities that no sabotage had occurred, and the error had merely been a technical glitch.[44]

Eyes and ears were everywhere indeed. By late October and early November of 1939, the Lviv NKVD had started 190 case files; the agency investigated twenty-nine different groups.[45] The case file names are telling, though ultimately they say far less about the persons targeted than about the NKVD officers' way of thinking. For instance, "Enemies" (Petliura emigration), "Emigrants" (alleged German spies who arrived in Lviv as part of the population exchange from territories occupied by the Third Reich), and "Independents" (the ANUM milieu). After individuals known for their political engagement (who had been arrested in the first weeks of Soviet occupation), average citizens too became objects of interest if their activities stood out in some way. Notes from investigative work specify Iaroslava Muzyka as the leader of the Ukrainian artists' community.[46] In fact, though Muzyka led their organization (ANUM), the association's heart and soul had been Sviatoslav Hordynsky, who defected from Lviv in September. Another important figure was Mykhailo Osinchuk. The group's name referred to "independent artists;" its mere existence and name sufficed to prompt an investigation. When it comes to the *Artes* group, I did not come across similar documents. It is hard to say whether those artists caught the NKVD's eye as well, or if perhaps they escaped the agency's attention on the strength of their community's "progressive" reputation.

In the subsequent months of the occupation, the circle of Soviet terror widened gradually. Small wonder then that artistic activity died down. In the aforementioned official publication, Mykhailo Dmytrenko suggested that the exhibit commemorating the first anniversary of the "liberation" seemed makeshift because the timeframe was too short to create larger-scale works. For all we know no one believed him. Rumors of the approaching war, instead of

---

44 Tadeusz Łodziana, "Lwów, Sopot, Warszawa," *Cracovia Leopolis* 2–3 (2001), http://www.cracovia-leopolis.pl/index.php?pokaz=art&id=939, accessed July 10, 2014.
45 Spravka o sostoianii agenturno-operativnoi raboty L´vovskogo obupravlenia NKVD, HDA SBU, f. 16, op. 32, spr. 70, k. 24.
46 Spravka po agenturnomu delu "Samostiiniki," HDA SBU, f. 16, op. 32, spr. 70, k. 38.

frightening the population, sparked hope among native Lvivians and transplants alike: "Whatever it may be, the devil himself is better than a Soviet paradise."[47] But one month under Nazi occupation gave Lviv plenty of time to take in the extent of Soviet atrocities and to awaken to the true face of National Socialism.

THE TIME OF TRIAL

As street crowds took revenge on the symbols of Soviet rule, stomping on portraits, demolishing monuments (which did not turn out all that durable; as it happened, their plaster construction destined them for transience), a collection of the most recent art, housed in the headquarters of the Artists' Union at 9 St. Mary's Square, also sustained damage. The Nazis waged war on formal experiments with more force than even the Soviets did, fulfilling a directive to destroy "degenerate art," created by—who else—Jews. It is hard to establish today how many pieces and by which artists were burned in the courtyard at St. Mary's Square, since after the war the Soviets followed suit and cleansed Lviv's museum collections of any remnants of capitalist art. Flames claimed works by Henryk Streng, Jonasz Stern, Otto Hahn, and who knows how many others. There was no committee; the action was plainly another pogrom, but this time its target was art. Available reminiscences are too scant to estimate the scale of these burnings; memoirists were simply preoccupied by other tragic events; as the Soviet occupier retreated and a new one entered, first the mass atrocities by the NKVD were discovered, then Stetsko proclaimed the rebirth of the Ukrainian state, and next the Jewish population fell victim to a pogrom lasting several days.

The Nazis enforced a division within the creative community according to ethnicity, excluding Jewish artists and—to an extent—Poles, whose ability to organize was limited in comparison with Ukrainians. However, the *Artes* and ANUM milieus kept in contact, though now they adopted new goals, or really only one: survival. *Artes* members Margit Selska, Jerzy Janisch, Henryk Streng, as well as Artur Nacht (a non-Lvivian who befriended the group during the Soviet occupation) and most of his large family, made it through thanks to colleagues. None of them left testimonies with stories of their rescue. Just as little is known about those who perished as Jews: Otto Hahn, Aleksander Riemer, and Fryc Kleinman (the latter connected with the group through the Lviv Professional Union of Visual Artists). Those who helped save lives left very sparse

---

47 Krushel'nyts'ka, *Rubaly lis. Spohady halychanky*, 155, 162–9.

reports as well, if they even found the courage to write. We have next to no information about the human chain that formed to save twelve-year-old Janina Hescheles, daughter of *Chwila*'s editor in chief. Her father perished in a pogrom after having been released from a Soviet prison just a few months before. Similarly, little is known about the people who saved or tried to save the lives of the artists. An exception are brief accounts by Józefa Wnuk and Volodymyr Lasovsky. Wnuk undertook helping Jonasz Stern and Artur Nacht and his family.[48] Lasovsky assisted Hahn until the summer of 1942 by procuring food (Bohdana Pinchevska provides more details based on correspondence between Lasovsky and a Wrocław art historian[49]), though in vain; Hahn was arrested, likely apprehended somewhere on the street. Shot and injured while escaping from a transport to the Bełżec death camp, he died in Lviv. We do not know who helped him hide in this condition or where he is buried.

In December 1942 the Council for Aid to Jews (*Żegota*) was founded. After a delay, in May 1943, the Lviv *Żegota* branch finally became active. During the preceding two years the majority of Lviv's Jewish population (estimated at over 160,000 persons) had been murdered. The executions took place outside the city, near Vynnyky and in Piaski, in the ravine behind the Janowska Camp, and in death camps. A little information about the Lviv *Żegota* is available, and so we know the basics: Władysława Larysa Choms led the organization, and Stanisław Teisseyre and Marian and Józefa Wnuk were among its activists. Even less is known about the efforts other artists undertook trying to save their

---

48 Józefa Wnukowa, "Długie życie upartej dziewczynki. Z profesor Józefą Wnukową rozmawia Henryka Dobosz," interview by Henryka Dobosz, in Chrobak, Michalik, and Wilk, *Czarownik przy zielonej skale: Marek Włodarski—Henryk Streng*, 205–7.

49 Piotr Łukaszewicz wrote a monograph on the group *Artes*. Pinchevska, a Ukrainian researcher, quotes Lasovsky's letter to Łukaszewicz from the collector's private archive:

> During the German occupation Otto visited me often. He was constantly hungry, I helped him as my modest opportunities allowed. But one day he did not come. When he did not appear for the next few days, I began searching for information about him. I cannot remember anymore who told me that he had jumped from a German transport probably headed for a concentration camp, the escorting guards shot at him from the train. Severely wounded, he reached the Lviv suburbs where he died. ... He did not leave his paintings with me for safekeeping. I could not retrieve any belongings left in his apartment because after arresting him and his family (father and sister), the Germans sealed the apartment. It was impossible to get in there. (Bohdana Pinchevs'ka, "Tvorcha biohrafiia Otto Hana ta osoblyvi vyvchennia tvorchoho spadku ievreis'kykh khudozhnykiv Skhidnoï Halychyny," *Judaica Ukrainica* 1 [2012]: 273)

colleagues. A few crumbs of information helped me reconstruct Iaroslava Muzyka's desperate attempts to rescue others. The task is challenging since no witness accounts except my grandmother's exist, although even she did not leave behind written testimony.

After her husband was forcibly evacuated, in June 1941 the Nazi occupation put Muzyka in dire circumstances. She was without work, and, even worse, being the spouse of a Soviet deputy to the city council and assistant director of the Medical Institute put her in peril. In contrast to her community, Iaroslava Muzyka had not gotten involved in the Artists' Union or participated in exhibits, and had refrained from publishing. Owing to her husband's status, under the Soviets she did not need to worry about basic survival. The Muzykas were even allowed to keep their spacious apartment instead of being forced to vacate it or to share it with Soviet civil servants, although such classy accommodations were certainly a fat prize. Now, as the German-Soviet war began, the artist found herself without financial or emotional support. She could still count on friends, but her only close relation, her sister Anna Rudnytska, was herself supported by her librarian husband, and the artist's nephew Lev Stefanovych lived with her and had only just begun his medical studies.[50] One of her friends, Mykhailo Osinchuk, was a neighbor. Another old friend of her brother's, turned ANUM colleague, Mykola Fediuk, lived by Lviv in Vynnyky. Neither Osinchuk or Fediuk could do much. Even less help could come from the couple's friend Mykhailo Rudnytsky, living under constant threat because of his Jewish roots. Yet he would visit; the two became each other's support system.

Like Rudnytsky, Iaroslava Muzyka did not register in the new association, at the time led by her friend and neighbor Osinchuk. In comparison with Ukrainian writers and actors, the artists organized relatively late, in early October 1941. Twenty-four members attended the general meeting of the Union of Ukrainian Visual Artists (SUOM). Initially Mykhailo Osinchuk chaired the SUOM, with Ivan Ivanets as his deputy director, while Roman Turyn led the internal audit committee, and Mykhailo Dmytrenko, who had been director during the Soviet occupation, took on the position of production director.[51] If we were to apply the standard set by the Soviets, the need for a production director of a sculpture facility could be explained by the increased demand for portraits, busts, and sculptures of Ukrainian activists. Much like the Communists, the Nazis also attended to visual propaganda, as evident from the extant photographs, but not

---

50 TsDIAL, f. 309, op. 1, spr. 2889, k. 7.
51 "Spilka ukraïns'kykh obrazotvorchykh myttsiv," *L'vivs'ki visti*, no. 56, October 12–13, 1941.

quite on the same mass scale. As for Dmytrenko, only the first installments of his long essay about visual arts appeared in print, which tells us that his standing must have turned precarious.[52] His friends arranged for employment papers—not a guarantee of safety, but at least a chance at it. Dmytrenko worked as a lecturer, teaching external courses at the Folk Art Institute, where senior artists Osyp Kutylas and Olena Kulchytska as well as a few younger painters and the sculptor Serhy Lytvynenko[53] also found employment.

But Iaroslava Muzyka chose not to follow this path, though together with her friends Mykhailo Osinchuk, Roman Selsky, and Roman Turyn she joined two exhibitions. The first was organized by the Artists' Union and opened in December 1941 in the organization's former space on St. Mary's Square. In publications and discussion, the Literary-Artistic Club pushed the organization's interest in battle scenes and war themes, but without much success. Muzyka displayed her still lifes.[54] The second exhibit took place a year later; its purpose was to deepen the national character of art. Again, the artist, probably deliberately, sent a landscape with willows.[55] There she met Bohdana Svitlyk, an intelligent young woman interested in art; their encounter would indirectly determine the painter's postwar destiny. Muzyka had an extensive library and lent books to her new friend, not an odd behavior when the libraries were shuttered. Probably unbeknownst to the painter, the young art enthusiast was a member of the Organization of Ukrainian Nationalists. By chance they met again in the fall of 1944, and it is possible that the coincidence inspired OUN to use Muzyka and her husband, who had recently returned to Lviv, to enter negotiations with Soviet authorities. This turn of events would lead to the painter's arrest in 1948.

Did Muzyka consistently stay away from politics or did Osinchuk advise her against joining the Artists' Union? At the time Osinchuk warned the Selskys that they were in peril and urged them to remain in the shadows. Given that in September 1941 Muzyka declined Milena Rudnytska's request for an article, probably on the topic of women's lives during the Soviet occupation,[56]

---

52 Mykhailo Dmytrenko, "Obrazotvorche mystetsvo. Z nahody vystavy Spilky obrazotvorchykh mysttsiv," *L′vivs′ki visti*, no. 11, January 21, 1942, 2.
53 Mykhailo Dmytrenko, "Studiia ta zaochni kursy mystets′koï osvity pry Instytuti Narodnoï Tvorchosti," *L′vivs′ki visti*, no. 179, August 11, 1942, 3.
54 Mykhailo Daragan, "Vystavka Spilky ukraïns′kykh obrazotvorchykh myttsiv," *Nashi dni* 1 (December 1941): 9.
55 Mykhailo Daragan, "Tretiia vystavka Spilky ukraïns′kykh myttsiv," *Nashi dni* 2 (February 1943): 8.
56 Protokol doprosa, 13.01.1949, HDA SBU, FP. 74893, t. 1, k. 119.

the first explanation seems more plausible. But she needed to obtain some sort of employment. Probably thanks to her husband's old connections, in the summer she was hired to work in the city administration's housing division. It is not clear whether she was involved in allocating apartments directly or only indirectly. In any case, the job allowed her to help the Selskys. Naturally she had to keep Margit's Jewish ethnicity a secret. "When Margit and I were evicted from Nad Jarem Street [today Enerhetychna], our friend, Mrs. Muzyka, who at the time worked in the housing division, arranged for new quarters for us."[57]

Roman Selsky referred to those days extremely rarely and reluctantly. His reminiscences, taken down by Ivan Hrechko in a forester's lodge in Bystrytsia in 1985, are the only testimony of this remarkable artist couple's war years. Seven years later (the painter had already passed), Hrechko showed me around this little-known corner in the Hutsulshchyna; today I still remain under its spell. At the time Hrechko did not mention his connection to Selsky, or perhaps I was more interested in Vincenz's *On the High Uplands* and did not ask about the war? More than a dozen years would go by till the reminiscences were published, and another ten until I came across them.

Iaroslava Muzyka did not last long in the city administration. We can only guess when and why she left a workplace that secured her at least minimal safety. Once the Nazis announced they would set up the ghetto and resettle Jews there, working in the housing office became morally dubious. Yet she needed a job. The new occupier took care of "antisocial elements" even faster than the Soviets had.

The Soviets reorganized the Ukrainian National Museum, where Iaroslava Muzyka had worked before the war under director Ilarion Svientsitsky, subordinating it to the Art Gallery. After taking Lviv, the Nazis shut it down. Svientsitsky became the institution's administrative receiver. No activity was permitted until further notice. His daughter Vira Svientsitska, the collection's custodian, described the situation in an article for the monthly *Nashi dni*: "A lack of adequate funds, the cold, the number of employees limited to a bare minimum, do not allow us to begin operating."[58] Only after the museum's status was restored in 1942 was Muzyka hired for a quarter-time position, likely so she could obtain a certificate of employment.[59]

---

57 Sels'kyi and Hrechko, "Sel'skyi pro Sel'skoho. Rozmovliav Ivan Hrechko," 28.
58 Vira Svientsits'ka, "Dumky nad zbirkamy Natsional'noho Muzeiu," *Nashi dni* 2 (January 1942): 6.
59 Protokol doprosa, 24.11.1948, HDA SBU, FP 74893, t. 1, k. 68.

The Selskys had to vacate their apartment at the start of the German occupation.
Roman Selsky, *Door*, 1932

The museums permitted to operate—the Natural History Museum and the Museum of Artistic Industry—could not hire all of the artists looking to survive. Yet their employees tried, within their limited ability, to protect not only the collections, but the people, too. One example were the efforts of museum administrators Ilarion Svientsitsky, Ksawery Piwocki (Museum of Artistic Industry director) and Julian Leszczyński (its curator), with the support of Iury Poliansky (Natural History Museum director) and Mykola Holubets (president of the Literary-Artistic Club) to save the most distinguished collector of Jewish art, Maximilian Goldstein, and his family.[60] An in-depth account of the ill-fated efforts to save Goldstein comes to us by way of the scholar Faina Petriakova.[61] It was a constant struggle because work permits expired after three months. But in the end, nothing could avert the family's tragic fate. In December 1941 they were forced to move to the ghetto, to Panieńska Street. They vacated their apartment at 5 Nowy Świat, which even the Soviets had been eyeing, though at the time Svientsitsky had been able to protect the Goldsteins. For almost all of 1942 an ever-expanding circle of people kept Maximilian Goldstein afloat, but each intervention required increasingly higher protection. On August 20, 1942, during the so called Große Aktion in the Lviv ghetto, the collector penned a letter to the director of the General Government's Department of Culture and Education, seeking permission to continue his employment at the Municipal Museum of Arts and Crafts.[62] Most certainly the museum's administration and other appropriate authorities of the District Galizien supported his letter, otherwise the request would have stood no chance. The permit was issued. A certificate of employment and a pass allowing Goldstein to move around the city are the last documents indicating that, until September 1942, the collector worked at the museum. After that Goldstein and his family disappear without a trace. The extant documents give the impression that for Maximilian Goldstein the preservation of his collection took precedence over his own survival.

During this period Iaroslava Muzyka worked at the museum only sporadically. When a German friend of hers, Anna Załużna, a physician's wife, encouraged Muzyka to open a tobacco kiosk, she accepted the assistance, though likely without much enthusiasm, since she had no experience with retail. She

---

60 DALO, f. 35, op. 1, spr. 146, k. 23, quoted in Taisiia Sydorchuk, "Maksymilʹian Golʹdshtein: ostanni roky zhyttia kolektsionera i muzeieznavtsia (za dokumentamy Derzhavnoho arkhivu Lʹvisʹkoï oblasti)," *Ukraïnsʹka orientalistyka* (2011): 364.
61 Faina Petriakova, "Maksymilʹian Golʹdshtein. Storinky biohrafiï," *Ï* 51 (2008), http://www.ji.lviv.ua/n51texts/petryakova.htm.
62 DALO. f. 35-R, op. 12, spr. 249, k. 33–5. Quoted in Petriakova, "Maksymilʹian Golʹdshtein."

hired a clerk to run the kiosk, and so the income was minimal. The interrogation records show that Załużna passed licenses procured from the German administration onto wives of physicians when they fell on hard times.[63] The investigator conducting the questioning in 1948 made every effort to find proof that Iaroslava Muzyka had collaborated with the Nazis and seized on this thin thread. At first the NKVD insisted that the license was procured with the agreement of German counterintelligence;[64] subsequent investigators erected an entire plot around the little tobacco kiosk: supposedly it was a trap the Abwehr had set for Soviet citizens. How it could have worked, even an NKVD investigator could not explain, but they did not give up. In the next stage of the investigation the kiosk served as a base for subversive OUN activities; a fighter injured while blowing up a German train was supposed to have hidden there; the kiosk allegedly became storage for underground publications as well as medicine needed by OUN's combatants.[65] By the time the investigation ended, the kiosk had grown in size to accommodate a warehouse storing former Jewish property. Every version looked just as improbable, because the kiosk's dimensions were so disproportionate to a storehouse or even just a place large enough to hide an injured person. The last insinuation, that Muzyka had profited from Jewish assets, is particularly despicable. Yet Captain Guzeev, the head of the investigation department in the Ukrainian SSR's Ministry of State Security who took over the case, did not bother with such trifling matters as probability. He was authorized to use "special means" during interrogations by general Serhy Savchenko and stopped at nothing to get what he wanted.

In late 1941 Iaroslava Muzyka met my grandmother through Fryderyka Lille, who was hiding out in my grandmother's house under the "Aryan" name of Irena Szyszkowicz. Iaroslava Muzyka had known the Lille family for at least twenty years. Bonds of decades-long friendship connected her to Ludwik Lille. Before emigrating to Paris in 1937, the artist entrusted part of his collection to her; in addition to prints, he left with her an extensive correspondence related to the upcoming exhibit of Jewish arts and crafts, as well as a collection of textile print patterns (*drykiery*). For almost the entire next year my grandmother and Muzyka would venture out into the ghetto to help Fryderyka Lille's sister and Muzyka's artist and doctor friends. We know next to nothing about the

---

63 Protokol dopytu, 26.11.1948, HDA SBU, FP 74893, t. 1, k. 72.
64 Ibid., 74.
65 Protokol doprosa, 24.01.1949, HDA SBU, FP 74893, t. 1, k. 126; Protokol doprosa, 23.02.1949, k. 194.

persons whom the women assisted. We can only guess—perhaps Fryc Kleinman, with whom Muzyka held a joint exhibit a few years earlier? Jerzy Janisch or Aleksander Riemer, whom she knew from the Lviv Professional Union of Visual Artists? Jewish doctors, friends of her husband? The two women faced a formidable challenge: to somehow get their hands on the most urgently needed items—food and medication. Most memoirists recall that of all the years of World War II, spring of 1942 brought the worst hunger. Iaroslava Muzyka would procure medicines, likely through her nephew who worked in the hospital (he was an OUN member), and it is possible that Dr. Roman Osinchuk and Mykhailo Terletsky, who had owned the pharmacy "Pod Czarnym Orłem" before the war, helped too. At the start of the Soviet occupation my grandmother had amassed much experience in trading goods at the Lviv bazaar Krakidaly where she sold whatever she could to survive; now exchanged clothing and more valuable items for food. But times were different; whereas the Soviets tolerated trade, if only because they too profited from it, the Germans treated it as a dangerous crime.

A petite blonde approaching fifty, Iaroslava Muzyka, and a tall, strong brunette in her late twenties, Eufrozyna Lewkowska, the first with a *Kennkarte* "U," the latter with a "P," both fluent in Ukrainian, Polish, and capable of some German, attracted the interest of the *Hilfspolizei* many a time. Somehow they always escaped trouble. Family legend has it that this was thanks to my grandmother's nerve; in dangerous situations she would turn into a bossy street vendor and bellow at the police. At that time the Nazis hunted for Jews who had not moved to the ghetto. Iaroslava Muzyka was not Jewish, but the terror she felt whenever they ventured out to the ghetto meant she was frequently stopped. My grandmother's presence was reassuring, even though theoretically as a Ukrainian Muzyka should have felt safer than Grandmother, a Pole. The NKVD investigation files state that at some point the Gestapo had searched the painter's apartment. Thanks to the warning relayed by Dr. Andry Lastovetsky they found nothing.

In 1942, during similar apartment searches, the Nazis arrested Margit Selska and sent her to the Janowska camp. They confiscated all paintings, most likely destroying them.[66] They also took Izaak Reich, Margit's father, from the apartment the Selkys had moved to with Iaroslava Muzyka's help at the start of the German occupation. He vanished without a trace, as did

---

66 Evstakhiia Shymchuk, "Foreword," in *Margit Sels'ka. Exhibit Catalogue*, ed. Taras Lozyns'kyi (Lviv: Instytut kolektsionerstva pry NTSh, 2005), 12.

Margit's uncle Scharf and his son. Margit Selska's friends immediately formed a chain of assistance and within less than twenty-four hours managed to pull her out of the camp. Roman Selsky's reminiscences mentioned Ivan Ivanets and the father of Maurycy Axer, but the latter reference appears inaccurate. If anyone could accomplish something, it would not have been the attorney's father, but rather the son, Erwin Axer, who knew the SS Hauptsturmführer Stiasny.[67] Like Margit Selska, the attorney's brother and Erwin's uncle Otto Axer belonged to the Professional Union of Visual Artists before the war, hence their connection. In the spring of 1942 Ivanets took over after Osinchuk as the director of the Union of Ukrainian Visual Artists. In the early days of the German occupation he looked after Henryk Streng, who later sheltered with the ANUM member Volodymyr Lasovsky,[68] and then with Janina Brosch.[69] At the end of the war Ivanets was arrested in Cracow by the Soviet counterintelligence body SMERSH and executed in 1946.

Who supplied Margit with the false documents that allowed her to get out of Lviv we do not know. By then purchasing a birth certificate bordered on a miracle and Żegota was not in place yet. The formal path to procure a *Kennkarte* led through an aid committee—Polish or Ukrainian—which issued certificates that were to confirm the authenticity of a birth record. A faster but more risky method was to counterfeit the *Kennkarte*. I am aware of only one place where Selska could have gotten ahold of some type of document making her travel possible: it was the office of Bolesław Czuruk, where Selska's friend Mykhailo Rudnytsky still worked. It is but a hypothesis.

Margit made it to Cracow, where an old friend from *Artes*, Tadeusz Wojciechowski, lived. From there she found her way to Warsaw; for a while she stayed at the home of Ponisch (first name unknown), an architect. She seized every chance to send a sign of life to her husband and counted the days of their separation.[70] Equipped with "Aryan papers," she returned to Lviv after several months. Her sister directed her to the village where Roman Selsky and

---

67 Zenon Andrzejewski, "Adwokat dr. Maurycy Axer (1886–1942)," *Palestra* 11–12 (2012), http://palestra.pl/old/index.php?go=artykul&id=1451, accessed July 16, 2014.
68 Selsky's reminiscences name Ivanets, and Muzyka's NKVD deposition—Lasovsky. Lasovsky himself talked about it as well in a letter to the art historian Piotr Łukaszewicz. See Sels'kyi and Hrechko, "Sel'skyi pro Sel'skoho. Rozmovliav Ivan Hrechko," 27; Protokol doprosa, 2.02.1949, HDA SBU, FP 74893, t. 1, k. 162.
69 Janina Brosh-Włodarska, "[O Marku Włodarskim]," in Chrobak, Michalik, and Wilk, *Czarownik przy zielonej skale: Marek Włodarski—Henryk Streng*, 9.
70 Selsky family archives, Margit Selska's letters. Quoted in Shymchuk, "Foreword," 12.

his friends stayed and worked. She reached the tiny hamlet of Vyzhniany; there in the local church her husband and Stanisław Teisseyre painted frescos and Marian Wnuk sculpted St. Joseph. (At that time both Teisseyre and Wnuk were involved in the underground activities with *Żegota*.) Next they worked in the Dominican church in Chortkiv, but by late 1943 the area was no longer safe. After that, for at least eight months Margit Selska subsisted in Lviv, staying and working in Oleksandr (Oleksa) Vynnytsky's studio. In that space, located near the Selsky's former apartment, she found physical and emotional refuge.[71] Many years later Roman Selski still wondered how Margit was ever able to paint under those conditions. He himself could not.

Iaroslava Muzyka hardly painted either. The kiosk did not bring a profit, since she hired a sales person. She turned to selling icons and … sewing hats. In spring of 1942 the art school resumed its activity, with separate arrangements for Poles and Ukrainians in a shared building on Snopkowska Street. Muzyka did not work there, though many friends and acquaintances did (at first Osinchuk was the director; Mykola Fediuk taught in the painting division; other friends also took jobs in the parallel Polish school).[72] Marian Wnuk and Stanisław Teisseyre, active in *Żegota* since the summer of 1943, taught in the Polish section of the *Kunstgewerbeschule*.

Like Selsky and Teisseyre, Muzyka waited out the most perilous period in the countryside, painting icons in a church. Semen Gruzberg (during the occupation he took the name Hruzbenko) survived part of the occupation in the same way, creating frescos alongside his former teacher Mykhailo Kozyk. Later, in 1943, he found safe haven at the Theater of the Opera (as the previous chapter mentions, he designed the playbill for *Hamlet*), evading danger thanks to his artist friends. His adventures in the company of the sculptor Ievhen Dzyndra could have ended badly when the two were stopped by the police, but Dzyndra took off running. The cops went on a chase and Gruzberg calmly walked away. Nothing happened to Dzyndra; merely searched and chided, he got off without being arrested.

During the war artists found their opportunities for creative work very limited, except for those working or studying at the *Kunstgewerbeschule*—they

---

71 Sels'kyi and Hrechko, "Sel'skyi pro Sel'skoho. Rozmovliav Ivan Hrechko," 28–9.
72 Antonina Strutyns'ka, "Shkola pid opikoiu muz," *Nashi dni* 7 (June 1942); Karlo Zviryns'kyi, "Mystets'ko-promyslova shkola u L'vovi: spohad," *Visnyk L'vivs'koi Akademii mystetstv* 5 (1995–96): 89–96; Krushel'nyts'ka, *Rubaly lis. Spohady halychanky*, 162–9; Tadeusz Łodziana, *Wspomnienia: Państwowy Instytut Sztuk Plastycznych 1937–1943 we Lwowie* (Wrocław: Sudety, 2003), 38.

had access to paint, canvases, and other materials.[73] A climate of fear and terror presented the biggest obstacle of all. During that time the Union of Ukrainian Visual Artists organized three exhibitions. The first one, hastily put together, opened in December 1941 and centered on the Dnipro painters. The next exhibit presented a retrospective of four late masters: Oleksa Novakivsky, Ivan Trush, Pavlo Kovzhun, and Petro Kholodny Sr. The last took place in 1943; it answered the call for a national art style. A newspaper reproduction of Muzyka's landscape with a willow, her painting included in the third exhibit, remains the only physical trace of Iaroslava Muzyka's artistic presence in wartime Lviv.[74]

Over the course of the Nazi occupation Iaroslava Muzyka somehow again became a curator, as had happened once before, during World War I. Artists looking to safeguard their works would leave them in her care. Soon after the Red Army marched in for the second time and the artist's husband returned to Lviv, the couple made a decision, probably jointly, to transfer this valuable collection to the most trusted of institutions with which they had cultivated ties for many years: the Museum of Ukrainian Art and the former library of the Shevchenko Scientific Society. In 1949 Iaroslava Muzyka would testify that she had "planted" some documents and books in the library shelves, but since nobody would have believed the same about paintings, Muzyka admitted to transferring them to Vira Svientsitska. Ilarion Svientsitsky's daughter had been arrested a few days before Muzyka, and charged with a more serious crime: prewar OUN membership.[75] Three years after those arrests, as part of a "purge," the Soviets conducted a thorough review of the collections at the Museum of Ukrainian Art, the former Shevchenko Scientific Society, as well as the Ossolineum.[76] Soon thereafter a committee led by Vasyl Liubchuk the museum's director, burnt more than five thousands works of art, including pieces by Archipenko (two paintings and two sculptures), Boichuk (fourteen paintings), Mykola Fediuk (two paintings), Hordynsky (six paintings), Dmytrenko (portrait of Maria Zarembianka), Ivanets (seventeen works), Osyp Kurylas (forty portraits of Sich riflemen), Volodymyr Lastovsky (three works), Iaroslava

---

73 Proof of this was the opening of a student exhibit in the summer of 1942. "Vidkryttia vystavky prats´ uchniv Derzhavnoï mystets´ko-promyslovoï shkoly u L´vovi," L´vivs´ki visti, no. 183, August 15, 1942.
74 Mykhailo Dragan, "Tretia vystavka Spilky obrazotvorchykh myttsiv," Nashi dni 2 (January 1943): 9.
75 Postanovlenie na arrest, 5.11.1948, HDA SBU, FP 76466, k. 3–4.
76 "Korotki vidomosti pro khudozhnykiv, tvory iakykh peredano u spetsfond (spysok nepovnyi), 1952 r.," in Kul'turne zhyttia v Ukraïni, vol. 2, 297–302.

Muzyka (seven works), Oleksandr Vynnytsky (number of works unknown), to mention only names pertinent to this chapter.[77] All the works of art Iaroslava Muzyka had managed to keep safe throughout the war but had eventually transferred to the museums perished as well. Marcin Kitz also entrusted his paintings to Muzyka; their fate remains unknown. The artist himself perished, probably in Bełżec, killed for hiding Jews.[78]

"MUSICIANS" FROM LVIV

In late July 1944, Maksym Muzyka returned to Lviv. Soviet authorities tasked him with reopening the Medical Institute. Along with Muzyka, Dr. Iulian Kordiuk returned as well (both had been forcibly evacuated), assuming his former position as the assistant director of the District Health Care Division. But there was no going back to a normal life. As Soviet civil authorities restarted some institutions, the NKVD and the military systematically combed through both the forests and the archives. They dealt with participants of the Polish paramilitary operation "Tempest" ["Burza"] at once, but an ongoing bloody conflict with the Ukrainian resistance tied up some of the Soviet troops in the liberated territories as they were badly needed on the battlefront. The Soviets were keen on eliminating the underground war, but that could only happen by reaching a truce—of course on conditions dictated by the occupier. They were looking for a temporary solution until the war ended. Though by fall of 1944 it was a foregone conclusion that the war would end, peace remained a relatively distant prospect. The Soviets began probing their Ukrainian adversary.

The first signal that the Ukrainian underground was ready to begin talks came from an unexpected direction. On November 19, 1944 Iaroslava Muzyka came to Dr. Kordiuk and announced that a friend with ties to the OUN requested that she contact a representative of the authorities. She trusted Kordiuk—he was her husband's colleague. He was also the only lower-level

---

77 For the first time a list of the works destroyed was published in the Ukrainian exile periodical *Suchasnist*: Vasyl' Iedynak [Ivan Hrechko], "Nasha zabud'kuvatist' abo prohramne tlumlennia boliu," *Suchasnist'* 11 (1988): 47–58.
78 The United States Holocaust Memorial Museum, Photo Archive, #21350, digitalassets.ushmm.org/phptparchives/detail.aspx?id=1162032, accessed on July 16, 2014. Galina Glembotskaia, a scholar of Jewish art in Galicia in the first half of the twentieth century, relates a strange story: allegedly Kitz procured food for his charges in return for their paintings. She did not cite her source. Galina Glembotskaia, *Evreiskie khudozhniki Galitsii, pogibshie v gody fashistskoi okkupatsii* (Kyiv: Arkhiv Tsentru Iudaiky, 2003), 1–23.

official she knew. Two days later the physician related their conversation to the NKVD.[79] After consultations at least at the Kyiv-level the decision was made to pass back a message to the Ukrainian underground that the Soviets were ready to negotiate. The role of intermediary fell to Iaroslava Muzyka.

In late November 1944 the NKVD launched a Khrushchev-approved operation by the codename "Shchos" ["Something"], whose objective was to locate the underground leaders.[80] Its active phase began with the meeting arranged at Muzyka's apartment on February 17, 1945, attended by Iulian Kordiuk (agent "Gusev"), Bohdana Svitlyk ("Svitlana") and Serhy Danylenko (code name "Karin"), whom his superiors equipped with a story: he introduced himself as a representative in charge of communicating with the Orthodox Church.[81] Danylenko was an experienced agent; his career had begun back in 1921 with the *Cheka*. He proved himself early in the operation "Tiutiun" (1923), which was similar to "Trest" (the best-known action of the Soviet counterintelligence, described in Lev Nikulin's novel and depicted in the film *Trest*; its crux was that the GPU set up a phantom organization to entrap true monarchists and opponents of the Bolshevik government). Early on he played a role in cracking the staff of general Tiutyiunnyk and contributed to the failure of the Ukrainian National Army's winter 1921 campaign. Arrested during the Great Terror, he was released in October 1939. During the German-Soviet war he again served in the NKVD. In 1943 he became the deputy chief of the fourth division at the Ministry of State Security (NKBG). Danylenko arrived in Lviv in October 1944. According to an article in *Hazeta 2000* his superiors tasked him with a special assignment: to establish contact with the Ukrainian underground.[82] He most certainly did not limit himself to this one objective and also carried out actions to discredit the Greek-Catholic church, in particular Metropolitan Sheptytsky.

Soon after the meeting at the Muzykas', "Svitlana" relayed two possible dates and places where the Soviet representatives would attend talks. In late February 1945 Danylenko once again paid Iaroslava Muzyka a visit, to clarify

---

79 Spetsial'noe soobshchenie po materialam agenturnogo dela "Muzykanty," 2.02.1945, kopiia 12.06.1954, HDA SBU, FP 74893, t. 2, k. 125–6.
80 Spravka (agenturnoe delo "Shchos'"), 4.06.1954, HDA SBU, FP 74893, t. 2, k. 123–4.
81 See also: Protokol doprosa, 8.11.1948, HDA SBU, FP 74893, t. 1, k. 64.
82 Oleg Rosov, "Operatsiia 'Perelom.' Maloizvestnye podrobnosti grazhdanskogo konflikta v Zapadnoi Ukraine," *Hazeta 2000*, no. 51, December 19–25, 2000. The authors blame the failed operation "Perelom" on the OUN-Provid and his involvement in the Cold War on the side of Western security agencies.

why the arranged meeting had not taken place. Muzyka did not know the answer, but said she was certain that it would occur on the alternate date, which indeed happened on the night of February 28/March 1, 1945. A decision was made to continue the negotiations. "Karin" pressed the Ukrainian Insurgent Army (UPA) negotiators Iakiv Busel and Dmytro Maievsky (both would be killed a few months later) to stick with Iaroslava Muzyka as the intermediary and with her apartment at 26 Czarniecki (by then Radianska Street) as the point of contact. "Karin" came by several more times; he left a letter retrieved by a liaison on March 22.

Although it did come to negotiations between the parties, they ended in failure when the OUN discontinued the meetings. Shukhevych's envoys became certain that they were talking not with government representatives, but with NKVD agents.[83] It is likely they realized that the Soviet side was not really after an agreement or even a cease-fire; they merely pretended to negotiate to get to the underground leaders and eliminate them. Document sources make it crystal clear: the ultimate phase of the two operations "Shchos" and "Berloga" ("Lair;" General Lieutenant Savchenko approved a plan for this action on November 12, 1944), was to hunt down the UPA leader. After both missions failed a new one commenced, under the code name "Vovk" (Wolf). Meanwhile, "Karin" was pushed aside. In 1947 he retired and turned to writing. His books he slandered the clergy, the emigration circles, and the Ukrainian underground.

"OWL"?

Meanwhile, Iaroslava Muzyka joined the Lviv chapter of the Artists' Union, now led by Roman Turyn, who had discovered the celebrated naïve painter Nikifor. Muzyka was getting ready for the Exhibit of Ukrainian Soviet Art in Lviv. The next destination for the exhibit would be the capital. One of her paintings from this period, "Girl with a Dog" (1946), a portrait of my mother, would be shown in Kyiv, though not for another eleven years. The city's visage changed; terror raged on. The only link to the former world was one's harrowingly shrunken circle of friends; it afforded some measure of emotional equilibrium. But even private contacts seemed suspect to the authorities. Iaroslava Muzyka, along with most educated Ukrainians who stayed in Lviv, became a

---

83 Ihor Marchuk, "Perehovory mizh predstavnykamy ukraïns´koho vyzvol´noho rukhu ta radians´koï vlady vnochi z 28 liutoho na 1 bereznia 1945," volyn.rivne.com/ua/arhive/ 2012-02-03/1759, accessed on July 20, 2014.

person of interest for the NKVD. In October of 1947 they searched her apartment for the first time. The officers arrived with an arrest warrant, but as they rummaged through the room, they received a "signal from above"[84] and left the artist alone. The worst had passed, it seemed. A year later the Writers' Union referred Muzyka to the creative artists' facility in Hurzuf, Crimea. Though she should have been thrilled, she had an ominous feeling:

> Rarely does it happen that I receive all documents with such obliging courtesy; even though I did not do anything to initiate the matter, I am being pushed out to Crimea, to Hurzuf.
>
> Strange! I love traveling, but in this case, I would be pleased if an obstacle materialized. Papers were delivered to my house for signature, I organized a farewell party, S. H., I. W., and others were there.
>
> Maks and Tekla walked me to the station, he put me on the train, asked the ticket inspector to look after me, Tekla made the sign of the cross, and I became afraid.[85]

Suddenly, after a two-week stay, she was arrested. The charge sounded absurd: while living in Hurzuf at the home for artists, she painted landscapes and took photographs of landscapes. After transporting her to a prison in Kyiv, the NKVD promptly forgot about the accusation. All circumstances point to a ploy to snatch Muzyka from under someone's protection. Perhaps at that time the Soviets still considered her husband someone to reckon with? Evidently her guardian's wings did not reach beyond Lviv. After a harsh investigation lasting several months, the fifty-five-year-old woman was sentenced to twenty-five years in the *Gulag*. The prosecution found her guilty of OUN membership and of collaborating with the Nazis.

Almost half a century later the historian of special services, Dmytro Viedienieiev, wrote the most sensational episode of Iaroslava Muzyka's life—her role in the negotiations between the Ukrainian underground and Soviet authorities—into the story of the last years of Roman Shukhevych ("Taras Chuprynka"), the Ukrainian Insurgent Army's (UPA) leader. In 2007, a presidential decree posthumously awarded the title of Ukraine's Hero to Shukhevych. The same event also propelled Iaroslava Muzyka into fame as a protagonist in a heroic narrative of the nation's history. The researcher, using restricted

---

84 Protokol doprosa, 8.11.1948, HDA SBU, FP 74893, t. 1, k. 43.
85 Serhii Bilokin', "Tabirnyi zoshyt Iaroslavy Muzyky," *Studii mystetstvoznavchi* 4 (2011): 146.

archival documents of security forces, concluded that the artist had been ... Shukhevych's connection, operating under the nom de guerre "Sova" (Owl). Viedienieiev first wrote about this in 2000, returning to this thread multiple times in scholarly and popular publications alike.[86]

Subsequent stages of Viedienieiev's "investigation" aligned Muzyka with Shukhevych ever closer: from the mysterious "Sova" she gradually turned into a "trusted person of the UPA leader," even an expert on geopolitics. He offers this quote from Muzyka: "the war between the US and USSR is near; it may lead to Ukraine's occupation by Western countries. ... I doubt that as a result it would become independent, [more likely—comment by D.V.] it will become 'a sort of US colony.'"[87] It merits attention that the researcher only quotes snippets from the letter and does not footnote the source. Although he claims that the letter writer's identity was ascertained through handwriting analysis, here the reference is missing as well.

Viedienieiev's publications gradually shifted the narrative: initially it was "Sova" who called for reconciliation; in later versions, closer to 2007 when the Ukrainian government honored the UPA leader as a national hero, it is "the leader of the resistance Roman Shukhevych [who] makes every effort to effect a consultation with the leadership of Soviet Ukraine about the conditions of armistice."[88] After 2010 (when Viktor Yanukovych came to power) the story suddenly changes course. A special issue of the periodical *Halytska brama*, devoted to the memory of Iaroslava Muzyka, assigns the heroic part to Serhy Danylenko ("Karin"), an "agent-humanist" who supposedly pushed for rapprochement. An expanded version of this article made it to the official page of the Foreign Intelligence Service of Ukraine.[89]

The story spread through popular sources and even through academic circles—historians who study the Ukrainian resistance movement, museologists,

---

86 Quoted in Dmytro Viedienieiev and Serhii Shevchenko, "'Sova' prizyvala k primireniiu," *Zerkalo nedeli*, July 15, 2000; Dmytro Viedienieiev and Serhii Shevchenko, "Mirotvortsy tainoi voiny," *Kievskii telegraf*, September 3, 2001; Serhii Shevchenko and Dmytro Viedienieiev, *Ukraïns'ki Solovky* (Kyiv: EksOb, 2001), 172; Dmytro Viedienieiev, "Kontrrazvedchik-gumanist," in *Ukrainskii front v voinakh spetssluzhb: Istoricheskie ocherki* (Kyiv: K.I.C., 2008); Dmytro Viedienieiev, "Kontrrozvidnyk-humanist," *Halyts'ka brama* 1–2 (2010): 19–21.
87 Dmytro Viedienieiev and Hryhorii Bystrukhin, *Dvobii bez kompromisiv. Protyborstvo spetspidrozdiliv OUN ta radians'kykh syl spetsoperatsii. 1945–1980-ti roky* (Kyiv: K.I.C., 2007), 134.
88 Ibid., 133.
89 Dmytro Viedienieiev, "Kryvavyi perelom," www.szru.gov.ua/index_ua/index.html%3Fp=1846.html, accessed July 26, 2014.

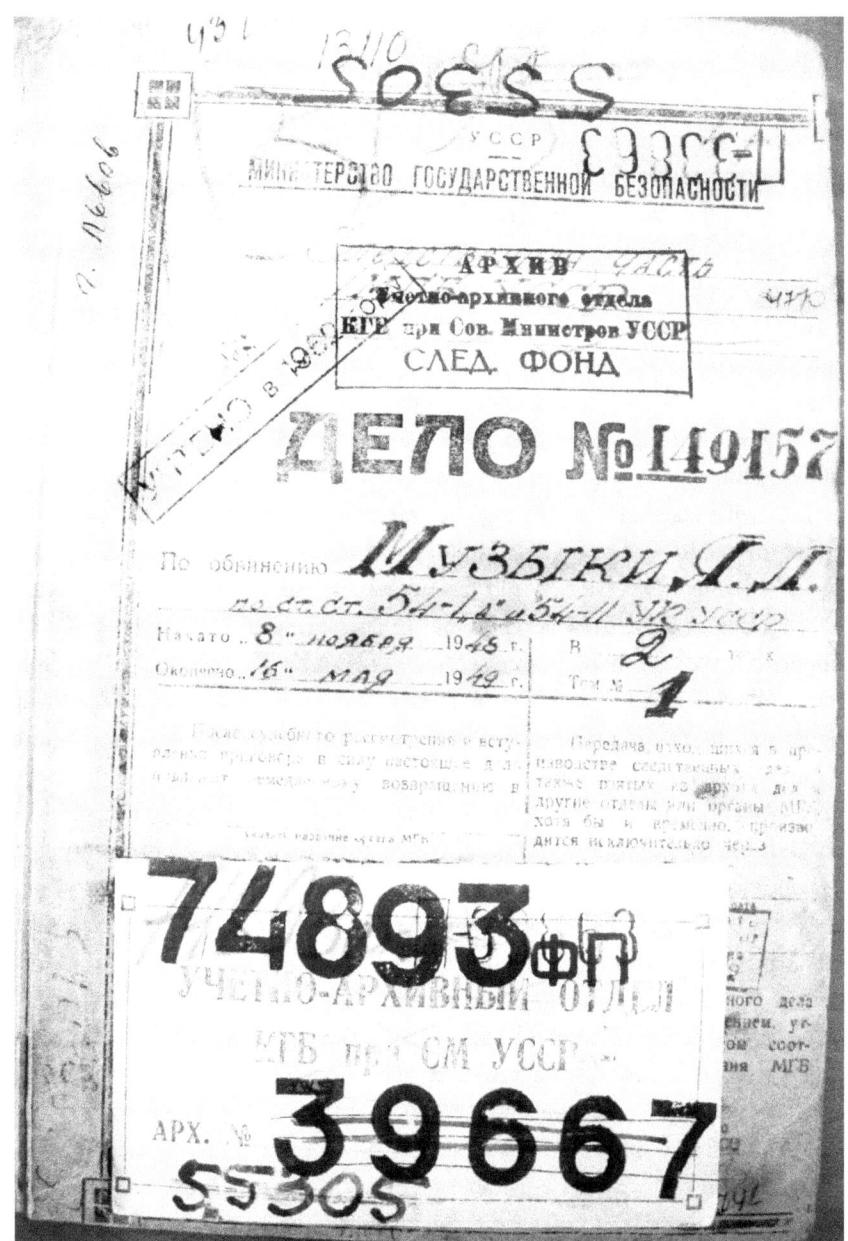

Files from the investigation against Iaroslava Muzyka

and art historians. Iaroslava Muzyka became known not as an artist or collector of the Ukrainian avant-garde's legacy, but as a key member of the Organization of Ukrainian Nationalists.

As attractive as this speculation is, psychologically it is unlikely. Muzyka was devoted to her friends, supported her nephew for almost twenty years, and, last but not least, helped Jews during the Nazi occupation, all actions that show the painter to have been a deeply moral person who possessed personal courage. Her patriotic outlook is beyond doubt as well. It is apparent that the artist consistently sidestepped participation in public life; she even avoided statements that could be perceived as expressions of political activity. Personal choices aside, the political climate of interwar Lviv is significant in this context as well: Muzyka's generation of Ukrainian intelligentsia who came of age in the traditions of parliamentarism and political pluralism approached OUN's actions with reservations. During the war, most of them remained skeptical about the agendas of both OUN factions.

Viedienieiev's version would have been difficult to verify without access to the archives of security services, but in late spring of 2014 I was given an opportunity to visit them. Iaroslava Muzyka's criminal files encompass two volumes, filling nearly 800 pages. As with the vast majority of cases from the era of Stalinism, the reading makes for a mournful experience. Granted, in contrast with investigations that took place in the late 1930s and that resulted in death penalties (Boichuk and his painter friends mentioned early in the chapter suffered this fate), Muzyka's saga "only" concludes with a sentence of twenty-five years in the *Gulag*, a verdict equivalent to the one given to Kateryna Zarytska, daughter of the mathematician Myron Zarytsky, both familiar from the chapter "Academic Snapshots." Zarytska, nom de guerre "Moneta," had been Shukhevych's connection since 1945. When the NKVD apprehended her, she was armed and killed an agent in self-defense. Muzyka was convicted from the same article of the penal code. If we were to trust the Soviet justice system, Viedienieiev's version could seem plausible. Articles 54-1a and 54-2[90] meant that she was charged with two offenses: treason against the homeland and participation in armed insurrection, both punishable with death by firing squad, forfeiture of all property, and loss of citizenship. Such procedures were most often applied against OUN members and persons suspected of ties to the underground resistance. But the majority of intellectuals arrested in the late 1940s had

---

90 Vypiska iz protokola Osobogo Soveshchaniia pri MGB SSSR, 18.06.1949, HDA SBU, FP 74893, k. 264.

nothing to do with the OUN, yet they were prosecuted under the articles mentioned above. Any and all contact with the Ukrainian resistance, even accidental, was interpreted as an affiliation. The prosecution used investigative methods unchanged since the 1930s: entrapment and torture.

Maksym Muzyka attempted to appeal his wife's sentence, but his request was rejected. After Stalin died, Iaroslava Muzyka filed two complaints with the head of the Ministry of Internal Affairs Lavrentii Beria (on May 20 and June 9 of 1953); the second letter reached Moscow after Beria had been executed.[91] The amnesty of 1953 affected criminal prisoners only. The artist's complaint was found to be baseless. In her letter Muzyka had explained what intentions guided her decision to help connect the Soviet authorities and the Ukrainian resistance: "if I can be accused of something, it is that on account of my lack of orientation in politics I attempted to be a broker between the Ukrainian nationalists and the communists. Personally, I had no connection to the Banderist movement, but guided by humanitarian motivations to stop the bloodshed, I agreed to the proposition of my friend B. Svitlyk to introduce her to Dr. Iulian Kordiuk, who had communist friends."[92]

The prisoner listed the brutal interrogation methods the NKVD had subjected her to: she was beaten, demeaned, psychologically abused. The NKVD even staged a jailbreak, supposedly carried out by the Ukrainian underground, to obtain additional testimony from her. The attempt prolonged the investigation and imprisonment by another year before she even began serving her sentence. On orders of General Major Viktor Drozdov, the head of department 2-H and simultaneously vice minister of Internal Affairs, and of Colonel Ivan Shorubalka, the assistant chief of the fourth department, V. Pleshevtsev (first name unknown) orchestrated the "getaway," with the participation of agent "Burievoi." The operation succeeded in confirming that "nationalist sentiments permeate the Ukrainian intelligentsia."[93] Did it really require a special operation to come to this conclusion?

Muzyka wanted the trial to be over as fast as possible and admitted to all charges. By way of an example: the painter's nephew lived with her, so the investigators included this fact under charges of "sustaining a conspiratorial location," even though they never proved that Stefanovych was an OUN member; the

---

91 Muzyka Iaroslava L'vovna, Zhaloba na metod vedeniia sledstviia i pros'ba o peresmotre dela, 20.05.1953, HDA SBU, FP 74893, k. 277–9.
92 HDA SBU, k. 279.
93 Spravka zamestitelia nachal'nika otdeleniia 4 Upravleniia MVD USSR, st. leitenanta V. Pleshevtseva, 5.10.1953, HDA SBU, t. 2, k. 27–9.

mere presumption sufficed. The indictment named friends whom she helped save as victims of her denunciations to the Nazis. In her complaint the prisoner pointed out that many persons in Lviv could confirm that she had assisted Jews. Only in 1955 did the investigators call in a few neighbors (those whom Muzyka had allegedly denounced) for questioning; after their testimonies the charge was reversed. Once the painter was released from the *Gulag*, she tried to make contact with the Lille family; in her letters to my mother she inquired about the fate of her old friend, Ludwik Lille, as well as Fryderyka and Jan.

The authorities followed up neither on Muzyka's grievance about the investigative methods nor on her request to review the case again until, on February 18, 1954, she wrote another letter, addressed to Kliment Voroshilov, then the presidium chairman of USSR's Supreme Soviet.[94] In mid-1955, after many witnesses were questioned, the decision to release Iaroslava Muzyka was issued. The only confirmed charge against her was her role as an intermediary in contacts with the Ukrainian resistance. Predictably, none of the investigators was held even minimally responsible. Six years had passed since her arrest. It took more than a year to verify the validity of the complaint. In 1955 her crime was reclassified ("anti-Soviet propaganda and incitement") and the punishment reduced to time already served.[95] Still, the accused waited another six months to be freed. The files of that investigation included copies and excerpts from cases coded as "Muzykanty" and "Shchos," from denunciations by informers, and interrogations of persons who appeared throughout the case. Since their detailed analysis merits a separate study, I will limit myself to a summary.

Immediately after Iaroslava Muzyka had relayed the message that the Ukrainian underground was interested in meeting with the Soviets, the NKVD began working the artist and her closest circle. They named the operation "Muzykanty," and targeted the artist along with her husband and friends from ANUM: Mykhailo Rudnytsky, Mykhailo Dragan, the pharmacist and philanthropist Mykhailo Terletsky, who had financed many ANUM events before the war, as well as Antonina Strutynska and Iulian Kordiuk.[96] Mykhailo Matviichuk, the director of the Museum of Ethnography sent down from Kyiv, and

---

94   HDA SBU, k. 52–6.
95   Zakliuchenie voennogo prokurora ot 5.04.1955. Vypiska iz protokola zasedaniia Tsentral'noi Komisii po peresmotru del lits, osudzhennykh za kontrrevoliutsionnye prestupleniia, soderzhashchikhsia v lageriakh, koloniiakh i tiur'makh MID SSSSR i nakhodiashchikhsia v ssylke na poselenii, HDA SBU, FP 74893, k. 287–92, k. 293.
96   The NKVD began building the case on January 20, 1945. Obzor po arkhivnomy agenturnomu delu nr 107 "Muzykanty," 1.05.1954, HDA SBU, t. 2, k. 102–4.

Iaroslava Muzyka finished the portrait of Antonina Strutynska before her arrest in 1947

Ivan Iavorsky, entered the NKVD's field of vision also. Three people supplied information: "Gusev" (Iulian Kordiuk[97]), "Autor" and, though rarely, "Futuryst," but their reports did not confirm Muzyka's involvement with the underground.[98] The story of each person whose name appears in the agency's investigations deserves separate attention. Suffice it to say that soon thereafter, a long-term employee of the Museum of Ukrainian Art, Mykhailo Dragan, as well as Dr. Kordiuk, died in the prime of their lives, and Iavorsky committed suicide in prison. Antonina Strutynska, arrested in 1948, spent seven years in the *Gulag*. A decision to deport Maksym Muzyka into Soviet exile was reversed; his service in the Red Army might have saved him. In the last chapter we witnessed the

---

97 Spravka 10.05.1954, HDA SBU, FP 74893, t. 2, k. 121 and 121 3B.
98 Obzor po arkhivnomy agenturnomu delu no. 107 "Muzykanty," 1.05.1954, HDA SBU, FP 74893, t. 2, k. 102–4.

reprisals that befell Rudnytsky. In contrast with the first Soviet occupation and the case of "Samostiinyky," this time it did not matter much that the evidence the NKVD had collected did not indicate connections with the underground. It was simply enough that the case existed.

After the negotiations failed, the NKVD placed the victim under systematic surveillance (an activity coded with the letter "N:" *nabliudenie*) between December 1945 and March 1946.[99] They did not obtain any additional information; nevertheless, General Lieutenant Serhy Savchenko's note of explanation stated that their suspicions had been confirmed: Muzyka was a person trusted by the OUN Provod.[100] Particularly cynical was the accusation that Muzyka organized a meeting with the resistance in her apartment. The allegation was based on Muzyka's testimony and the confession of Kateryna Zarytska, Shukhevych's connection, who did not have firsthand knowledge of the matter. In fact, it was the NKVD and its representative Danylenko "Karin" who inspired the event in question. From a rational point of view the investigation was entirely unnecessary, since both the security services and the oblast committee already knew all the pertinent information. Moreover, they themselves had contributed to the situation by organizing the encounter. The NKVD officers insisted that Muzyka remain in contact with the underground. The only explanation for why three and a half years later they imprisoned the painter and subjected her immediate circle to reprisals is that instructions from above directed the agency to tighten its hold on the local population.

None of the sources—not conclusions from the investigation, not the verdict from June 18, 1949, nor materials from the investigative procedure (an extensive correspondence between the various departments at the Ministry of State Security from 1954–55) nor the court's decision to amend the charges name Iaroslava Muzyka as the personal connection of Roman Shukhevych. The OUN did not confirm this accusation either. After the court reviewed Muzyka's case, it stayed the following charges: before 1939 the painter had been a member of the Union of Ukrainian Women, kept books and periodicals (in other words, a personal library), and in early 1945 set up a meeting between representatives of the Soviet authorities and the OUN. The only, and at that, flimsy, basis for Viedienieiev's thesis that it was indeed Muzyka who hid behind the alias "Sova," may have been the handwriting analysis of her 1948 letter to the

---

99 Spravka 27.04.1954, HDA SBU, FP 74893, t. 2, k. 127.
100 Soobshchenie gen. leitenanta S. Savchenka t. Sokolovu V. G., MVD Moskva, 23.03.1954, HDA SBU, FP 74893, t. 2, k. 41.

obkom secretary Ivan Hrushetsky. But was it carried it out? The historian does not cite any references.

Available documents do not corroborate the tale of Iaroslava Muzyka as Roman Shukhevych's liaison. We are left wondering what purpose this hoax could serve. It does not seem that Viedienieiev intended to remake our artist's biography into a heroic story. His research focuses on Soviet security forces, and not on cultural history; the heroes his publications feature have been operatives of the *Cheka*, the NKVD, and the OUN, not artists. Most plausibly, the historian sought to depict brave *Cheka* officers, in this case "Karin," as people who represented certain important rationales and to artificially separate them from the murderous regime they abated. Viedienieiev buries Danylenko's role before and after this operation, in particular his attempts to discredit Metropolitan Sheptytsky and to browbeat his successor, Iosyf Slipy.[101] Iaroslava Muzyka's character merely serves as a backdrop against which to spin a story of a lone *Cheka* agent who attempted to bring about reconciliation, an offer the Ukrainian resistance spurned.

SKOVORODA'S SYMBOLS

In late 1955 the artist returned to Lviv. Another five years passed until, after she went to court, her status as a felon stripped of civil rights was reversed[102] (an actual rehabilitation occurred only in 1994, once Ukraine became independent, on the hundredth anniversary of the painter's birth). Following the Thaw, she regained her freedom, as much as the word is even applicable to life in the USSR, as well as the chance to gradually rejoin official and unofficial cultural activities. In spite of her compromised health, Muzyka's social life slowly returned to normal. She began corresponding with old friends who lived abroad, compensating for the years spent in isolation. Some letters are moving: the artist took an interest in new trends in the arts, but also in fashion, especially hats, which had disappeared from Lviv's streets after the Soviets

---

101 Reporting on a conversation with Metropolitan Iosyf Slipy, "Karin" described the insinuation tactic he used: the NKVD alleged that Slipy was Metropolitan Sheptytsky's illegitimate son. See "Raport i zapysy besid zastupnyka nachal'nyka 4-ho Upravlinnia NKDIu URSR S. Karina z predstavnykamy UHKTs, 30–31 sichnia 1945," in *Likvidatsiia UHKTs [1939–1946]. Dokumenty radians'kykh orhaniv derzhavnoï bezpeky* (Kyiv: KNU, Tsentr Ukraïnoznavstva, Instytut istoriï NANU, DA SBU, 2006), vol. 1, 332.
102 "Opredelenie Narodnogo suda Shevchenkovskogo r-na g. L´vova, 7.02.1961," in *Kul'turne zhyttia v Ukraïni. Zakhidni zemli*, vol. 2, 491–2.

established their rule; hat-wearers came under suspicion of belonging to the capitalist class.

Correspondence of persons who had been imprisoned was subject to inspection, and every letter from abroad was presumed subversive. Thus letters to Iaroslava Muzyka do not convey particularly interesting information, especially about the past. Instead, they focus on current personal matters and reflections about art. The majority of correspondence came from old friends who had emigrated to the United States after the war. Next in terms of numbers are letters from Poland, including my mother's, from whom the artist learned of her old friend Ludwik Lille's passing.[103] Vague hints suggest that the artist tried to hand over a few lone extant graphics by Polish friends, especially Ludwik Lille, to people abroad, believing their art had a higher chance to be recognized there. Irena (Fryderyka) and Jan Lille served as intermediaries. We do not know if any pieces were actually smuggled abroad because Ludwik's last letter from Paris available in the archive is dated before the war. Perhaps something made it to Wrocław, to be incorporated into the National Museum collections—at least it seems that way from the letters Piotr Łukaszewicz, who curated the first postwar exhibition of Lille's work, sent to Muzyka, conveying his deep gratitude and respect. Of course, the transfer of works of art would have occurred in utmost secrecy, because the Soviets did not permit art to be sent abroad and they controlled all sales. The artist gifted the remainder of the collection not seized in the searches of her apartment (in 1949, at the request of the investigator, a committee supervised the destruction of her confiscated collections, notes, and correspondence) or burnt during the purge of museum holdings in 1952 to the Lviv National Art Gallery (the former Lviv State Picture Gallery). In this way the institution came into Lviv's richest collection of graphic arts with Jewish themes and woodblock-printed fabrics (so-called "vybiiky") from the Lille collection, as well as items of ritual purpose.[104]

Iaroslava Muzyka participated in a few exhibits, which allowed her to renew her membership in the Artists' Union; an artist not affiliated with the organization had no ability to earn money. In 1957 her paintings, including

---

103 Letter from Halina Lewkowska to Iaroslava Muzyka, June 14, 1957, Iaroslava Muzyka fonds, op. 2.
104 Halyna Hlembots'ka, "Iudaïka. Z istoriï pryvatnoho ta muzeinoho kolektsionerstva u L'vovi," in *Obrazy znykloho svitu: Ievreï Skhidnoï Halychyny (seredyna XIX–persha tretyna XX stolittia). Kataloh vystavky*, ed. Halyna Hlembots'ka and Vita Susak (Lviv: Tsentr Ievropy, 2003), 15–22.

"Girl with a Dog," were presented in Kyiv (upon reading the news, my mother became as excited as a child; the artist enclosed the press review). By then Muzyka was seventy-four.

In the 1960s *samvydav* [samizdat] changed the cultural landscape in Soviet Ukraine, offering an alternative to state-sanctioned publication. In the same decade, Iaroslava Muzyka became an authority for the *Shistdesiatnyky* [the 60s' generation], a group centered around the independent circuit. During that period Ihor Kalynets, my mother's contemporary, joined Muzyka's circle of friends. The last poetry volume which he wrote outside of prison, *Spohad pro svit* [*A Remembrance of the World*], was illustrated with a cycle of Muzyka's final graphics, titled *Symvoly Skovorody* [*Skovoroda's Symbols*]. Kalynets gave the same name to a cycle of poems included in his volume, published outside of official circulation. In summer of 1972, Kalynets was arrested for distributing his work through the *samvydav*. Once more, the seventy-eight-year-old Iaroslava Muzyka entered KGB quarters to be interrogated. She died a year later.

The period of World War II and the postwar years were a difficult trial for the Lviv artistic milieu. Those who made it through were scattered around the world. Few Jewish artists survived. Some former ANUM members emigrated (Edvard Kozak, Volodymyr Lasovsky, Serhy Lytvynenko, Antin Malutsa, Mykhailo Osinchuk). From Lviv's avant-garde circles, besides Iaroslava Muzyka only the Selkys and Leopold Levytsky, who had been part of the Cracow group before the war, stayed. Poles and most Jewish artists who did not perish left for Poland. They scattered around the country, settling in Warsaw, Cracow, and Gdańsk (the Sopot School). The vast majority of art collections was wiped out, much of it during the war, as the Nazis burnt "degenerate art," and the rest suffered destruction after the war, when Stalinists set out on a similar purge in Lviv. The stories behind any art that survived are no less gripping than the fates of the artists themselves. The Nazis destroyed almost the entire oeuvre of Otto Hahn, and most paintings by Jerzy Janisch and Margit Selska. Not much remains of the art by Ludwik Lille, Iaroslava Muzyka, Sviatoslav Hordynsky, or Fryc Kleinman.

My attempts to reconstruct the relationships among Lviv's avant-garde artists turned out to be especially difficult. Only a few memoirs relate their war experiences and the information is very scant. No personal journal has survived; correspondence, if preserved, remains in private hands (the Selsky archive). The NKVD decimated the rich Muzyka collections, including the archives of the ANUM and their periodical *Mystetstvo*. We cannot fully rely on other available sources such as Iaroslava Muzyka's interrogation records. The artist did her best to not name names; when absolutely necessary, she only pointed to people who were dead or had escaped beyond the Iron Curtain. But even the very fragmentary accounts I was able to uncover demonstrate that bonds of friendship allowed at least some artists to survive the war, even though the solidarity and support they extended each other in those harrowing times did not save everyone. Likewise, most works of art could not be rescued. The crumbs left to us evoke a deep sadness: the world of multicultural Lviv has disappeared. Yet something remains. Something that merits deep respect—the faithful friendships that helped trump fear.

Index of Names

The names are accompanied by short biographical notes, with the exception of widely known persons. In some cases, it was not possible to establish certain details such as names and dates of birth. Persons mentioned only by first names are not included. Index does not extend to footnotes.

Explanations of acronyms and less commonly used abbreviations:
Cheka: The All-Russian Extraordinary Commission for Combating Counter-Revolution and Sabotage
Gulag: Main Management of [Soviet prison] Camps, here standing in for the camps in general.
UJK: Jan Kazimierz University
UL: Lviv University
SSR: Soviet Socialist Republic
SMERSH: Soviet military counter-intelligence, active 1943–1946
USSR: Union of Soviet Socialist Republics

A

Adenauer, Konrad (1876–1967): first postwar Chancellor of the Federal Republic of Germany
Ajdukiewicz, Kazimierz (1890–1963): philosopher and logician, representative of the Lviv-Warsaw school of philosophy, professor at UJK
Aks, Izaak: speech therapist, after World War II director of the Institute of Phoniatrics in Lviv
Albert, Zygmunt (1908–2001): physician, historian of medicine, assistant at UJK and the Medical Institute; moved to Wrocław after World War II; emigrated in 1981
Aleksandrov, Pavel (1896–1982): Russian mathematician, member of the Academy of Sciences, president of the Moscow Mathematical Society
Allerhand, Maurycy (1868–1942): lawyer, professor at UJK and UL
Alter, Wiktor (1890–1943): Bund leader, member of the executive committee of the Second International, arrested by the NKVD in September 1939

An–sky/Ansky, Szymon (Shloyme Zanvl Rapaport, 1863–1920): Jewish writer and ethnographer

Anders, Irena (née Iarosevych, alias Renata Bogdańska, 1917–2010): second wife of General Władysław Anders; singer and film actress; during World War II member of the bands Lviv Tea–Jazz and Polish Parade

Anders, Władysław (1892–1970): general, commander of Polish Army in the USSR, commander of the Polish 2nd Corps

Androkhovych, Amvrosii (1879–1943): Ukrainian lawyer and philologist, member of the Shevchenko Scientific Society, lectured at LU

Andrusiak, Mykola (1902–85): Ukrainian historian, member of the Shevchenko Scientific Society, fought for Ukrainian independence in 1918–20, emigrated in 1944

Antokolsky, Pavel (1896–1978): Russian poet and translator

Antonych, Bohdan Ihor (1909–37): Ukrainian poet

Archipenko, Oleksandr (1887–1964): Ukrainian avant-garde artist, worked in Paris since 1908, after World War I in the United States

Arem, Samuel: entrepreneur, uncle of Fryderyka Tennenbaum (Irena Lille)

Aston, Adam (Adolf Loewinsohn, 1902–93): singer, performed in Polish, Hebrew, and Yiddish, actor, fought in the battle of Monte Cassino

Auerbach, Marian (Majer Auerbach, 1882–1941): classical philologist, taught at UJK and UL

Axer, Erwin (1917–2012): theater director, in 1939–41 at the Polish Dramatic Theater in Lviv

Axer, Maurycy (1886/7–1942): Lviv lawyer, defense attorney in the famous Gorgonowa trial

Axer, Otto (1906–83): painter

B

Bakals: a married couple who hid children of Jewish ethnicity in their home in the Warsaw district of Żoliborz

Balik, Olga (married name Gürtler): biochemist

Banach, Łucja (née Braus, 1897–1954): wife of Stefan Banach

Banach, Stefan (1892–1945): mathematician, one of the creators of the Lwów School of Mathematics and Philosophy, professor at UJK and UL

Banach, Stefan, Jr.: son of Stefan Banach

Bandera, Stepan (1909–59): faction leader of the Organization of Ukrainian Nationalists (OUN)

Bartel, Kazimierz (1882–1941): mathematician, politician, prime minister in five governments of the Second Polish Republic

Bartlowa, Maria (also Bartel, 1881–1969): president of the League of Women, Camp of National Unity (*Obóz Zjednoczenia Narodowego*, OZON), senator during the Second Polish Republic

Barvinsky, Oleksandr, Sr. (1847–1926): historian, political activist, deputy to the Austrian *Reichsrat*

Barvinsky, Oleksandr, Jr. (1890–1957): physician, taught at the Ukrainian Underground University (1923–25), appointed to Director of the Health Department in April 1941, from 1943 personal physician of the Metropolitan Andrei Sheptytsky; *Gulag* prisoner 1947–57

Barvinsky, Vasyl (1888–1963): son of Oleksandr Sr., composer and conductor; from October 1939 deputy to the People's Assembly of Western Ukraine, in 1939–41 Director of the Lviv Conservatory and president of the Lviv chapter of the Union of Soviet Composers; *Gulag* prisoner 1948–58

Batowski, Stanisław (1866–1946): painter of war scenes (schools of realism and neoromanticism)

Baworowski, Michał (1868–1940): aristocrat, relative of Wiktor Baworowski—founder of the Baworowski Library incorporated into the Ossolineum collection in 1940

Bazhan, Mykola (1904–83): poet and translator, member of the "Executed Renaissance" generation; from 1940 member of the All-Union Communist Party (Bolshevik), 1943–49 deputy director of the Council of People's Commissars; deputy to the Verkhovna Rada (parliament) of the Ukrainian SSR

Beck, Józef (1894–1944): politician and diplomat, 1914–17 officer of the Polish Legions, then member of the Polish Military Organization (POW); from 1932 foreign minister of the Second Polish Republic

Beliaev, Vladimir (1909–90): Russian and Ukrainian Soviet writer and journalist, authored incendiary pamphlets, received the Stalin Prize (1952) and the Order of Polonia Restituta (1967)

Belousov, Sergei (1897–1985): historian, member of the VKP(b), employed at the Institute of History of the Academy of Sciences of the Ukrainian SSR

Berdychowska, Bogumiła (b. 1963): activist for Polish-Ukrainian reconciliation

Bergson, Henri (1859–1941): philosopher, received the Nobel Prize in literature, creator of intuitionism

Beria, Lavrentii (1889–1953): director of the NKVD, responsible for Stalinist atrocities; 1946–1953 premier of the USSR

Berling, Zygmunt (1896–1980): arrested by the NKVD in October 1939, imprisoned in the Starobilsk camp; 1943–44 commander of the Polish 1st Kościuszko Infantry Division

Bernacki, Ludwik (1882–1939): historian, director of the Ossolineum

Beyer, Hans Joachim (1908–71): German historian and sociologist, one of the ideologues of racism; Hauptsturmführer of the SS; in July 1941 part of Einsatzgruppe C responsible for the massacre of Lviv professors (among other crimes)

Biber, Leopold: Lviv physician

Bielski, Eleonora (1884–1977) and **Juliusz** (1862–1941): owners of the palace at Kopernik Street in Lviv, deported in 1940 to the Semipalatinsk (Semey) district

Biliashivsky, Mykola (1867–1926): archeologist, ethnographer, cofounded the All-Ukrainian Academy of Sciences (VUAN)

Bilewicz, Stanisław: Jan Lille's driver

Biłyk, Alfred (1899–1939): lawyer, voivode of the Ternopil and Lviv districts, infantry major in the Polish Army

Birnbaum, Zygmunt William (Wilhelm, 1903–2000): Polish and American mathematician, Hugo Steinhaus's student

Bisanz, Alfred (1890–1951): colonel in the Ukrainian Galician Army, from 1941 chief of the Ukrainian section in the governor's office of District Galizien, organized recruitment into the Galician Waffen-SS Division, in 1946 arrested in Vienna by SMERSH, died in the Lubyanka prison

Biskupsky, Stefan (Stepan): Ukrainian geographer, in 1939 dean at UL

Blavatsky, Volodymyr (Tracz, 1900–1953): director at the Zahrava theater, student of Les Kurbas, emigrated in 1944

Bloch, Maurycy: entrepreneur, Hugo Steinhaus's student

Blumenfeld, Stanisława and Ignacy: Lviv Jewish intellectuals

Błaszczyk, Zofia: English-Polish translator

Bochenek, Bronisław (1912–73): communist activist; went into hiding after the Germans seized Lviv, then left for Warsaw; his wife Maria was honored as Righteous Among the Nations

Bocheński, Aleksander (1904–2001): political publicist, translator, contributor to *Bunt Młodych* and *Polityka*, expert on Ukrainian issues

Bodnarovych, Osyp (1895–1944): journalist, theater critic, politician; editor in chief of the newspapers *Lvivski visti* and *Ukrainski shchodenni visti*

Bodo, Eugeniusz (Eugeniusz Bogdan Junod; 1899–1943): actor and film producer; died in the *Gulag*

Bogatko, Marian (1906–40): worker, activist in the socialist movement, husband of Wanda Wasilewska, came to Lviv in October 1939; murdered by the NKVD

Bogoliubov, Nikolai (1909–92): Russian mathematician and theoretical physicist, professor, member of the Academy of Sciences of the Ukrainian SSR, from 1956 director of the Institute for Nuclear Research in Dubna

Bogorodsky, Fedor (1895–1959): Russian painter, in his youth a futurist, later helped create the canon of socialist-realist art, received the Stalin Prize

Bohachevsky–Chomiak, Marta (b. 1938): American historian, researches the Ukrainian women's movement and Ukrainian church history

Bohomolets, Oleksandr (1881–1946): physician, president of the Academy of Sciences of the Ukrainian SSR, deputy to the Supreme Soviet of the USSR

Boianivska, Marta (b. 1963): medievalist, translator

Boichuk, Mykhailo (1882–1937): avant-garde painter, created the neo-Byzantine style, from 1917 taught at the Fine Arts Academy in Kyiv, leader of the Association of Revolutionary Art of Ukraine (ARMU), arrested by the NKVD and charged with espionage, executed in 1937

Boiko, Maria (1902–86): worked at the Academy of Sciences of the Ukrainian SSR, Institute of Linguistics; Komsomol activist

Boloboiarinov (first name unknown): colonel in the Red Army

Bomse, Naum (Nuchim, 1906–54): Jewish poet writing in Yiddish, with ties to Warsaw, spent 1939–41 in Lviv, from 1941 in the Red Army; from 1946 in Poland, emigrated in 1947, first to France, then to the US

Bonusiak, Włodzimierz (b. 1942): historian of World War II

Borejsza, Jerzy (Beniamin Goldberg, 1902–52): communist activist and writer; from November 1939 till February 1940 director of the Ossolineum, from 1940 editor of Soviet school textbooks in Polish; co-founded the Union of Polish Patriots; after the war one of the most influential members of the communist administration in Poland

Borshchak, Ilko (Illia Barshak, 1892–1959): historian and publicist, emigrated to Paris after the fall of the Ukrainian People's Republic

Borucki, Gwidon (Gwidon Gottlieb, 1912–2009): singer and actor, first husband of Irena Iarosevych, soldier in Anders' Army, emigrated to Australia after World War II

Borwicz, Michał (Maksymilian Boruchowicz, 1911–87): writer and publicist, 1942–43 imprisoned in the Janowski Camp, after the war director of the Cracow division of the Jewish Historical Commission, emigrated in 1947

Boznańska, Olga (1865–1940): painter affiliated with Young Poland

Brahinets, Andry (1903–63): Marxist philosopher, member of the All-Union Communist Party (Bolsheviks), 1939–41 dean of History at UL and director of the Marxism-Leninism division; after the war dean and provost at UL

Bretschneider, Zygfryd: physician

Bristiger, Michał (1921–16): son of Julia Brystygier, musicologist, critic, essayist, and translator; author of recollections about the war and his survival of the Shoah; 1940–41 student at the Medical Institute in Lviv

Bromberg, Adolf Adam (1912–93): publisher, before World War II member of the Communist Party of Western Ukraine (KPZU), 1940–41 editor at the Polish division of the Ethnic Minorities Press (part of the Council of People's Commissars of the Ukrainian SSR); 1941–43 in the Red Army; 1943–45 political officer in the Polish 1st Kościuszko Infantry Division, from 1946 Leon Kasman's right-hand man; in charge of publishing policy, removed after 1968; emigrated in 1970

Broniewski, Władysław (1897–1962): poet and translator, soldier in the Polish Legions, fought in the Polish-Soviet War, then a communist activist; from

September 1939 until January 1940 in Lviv; arrested by the NKVD, released from the Lubyanka prison in August 1941; joined the Anders' Army, returned to Poland in 1945

Brosch, Janina (1912–95): painter, 1943–44 sheltered Henryk Streng (Włodarski), marrying him after the war

Bruchnalska, Maria: activist in the women's movement, popularized Polish patriotic traditions; wife of Wilhelm and mother of Gustaw

Bruchnalski, Gustaw: dentist, soldier of the Polish Legions, in 1940 arrested by the NKVD, murdered in June 1941

Bruchnalski, Wilhelm (1859–1938): literary historian, publisher of Polish classics, professor at UJK, member of the Polish Academy of Arts and Sciences (PAU)

Bruski, Jan Jacek (b. 1969): historian, professor at the Jagiellonian University in Cracow

Brystygier, Julia (Brystygierowa, née Prajs, 1902–75): communist activist, member of the Communist Party of Western Ukraine and the International Red Aid; during World War II member of the Executive Committee of the Union of Polish Patriots, after the war worked for the security apparatus of the People's Republic of Poland, responsible for Stalinist atrocities

Brzoza, Jan (1900–1971): writer and publicist, communist activist; memoirist

Brzozowski, Stanisław (1878–1911): philosopher, writer affiliated with Young Poland, leftist publicist

Bukharin, Nikolai (1888–1938): Soviet economist, member of the Central Committee of the All–Union Communist Party (Bolshevik) Politburo, opposed collectivization; accused on Trotskyism in 1937, executed in 1938

Bukowski, Kazimierz (1899–1945): journalist, editor of the Lviv daily *Wiek Nowy*, lived in Cracow during World War II

Burachek, Mykola (1871–1942): impressionist painter, co-founded and lectured at the Fine Arts Academy in Kyiv, from 1927 in Kharkiv

Burachynsky, Tyt (1880–1968): physician at the People's Clinic in Lviv, Ukrainian civic activist

Burmystenko, Mykhailo (1902–41): member of the Central Committee of the Communist Party (Bolshevik) of Ukraine Politburo, 1938–41 Second Chairman of the Central Committee, from July 1941 organized Soviet guerilla troops on German-occupied Ukrainian territories

Busel, Iakiv (1912–45): student at UJK (1932–33), activist in the Organization of Ukrainian Nationalists, from 1943 member of its executive council Provod and political referent; in the first half of 1944 commander of Ukrainian Insurgent Army (UPA)-North; participated in OUN's negotiations with Serhy Danylenko "Karin"

Bychenko, Heorhy (Iury, 1900–1942): historian, 1940–41 UL rector and head of the Chair of Colonial and Occupied States

C

Casimir III The Great (Kazimierz Wielki, 1310–70): king of Poland
Celan, Paul (Paul Antschel, 1920–70); German-language poet of Jewish background, author of the famous poem "Die Todesfuge" ("Death Fugue")
Chaikivsky, Iosyp: member of the Shevchenko Scientific Society
Chajes, Wiktor (Widger Chajes, 1875–1940): banker, civic activist, deputy mayor of Lviv, victim of the Katyn atrocity; memoirist
Chaplin, Charlie (1889–1977): actor and director
Chekaniuk, Andry (1906–92): communist activist, graduated from the Institute of Red Professors (1937), editor of the newspaper *The Communist* (from 1943 *Radianska Ukraina*)
Chiger, Ignacy (1906–75): Jewish entrepreneur in Lviv, father of Krystyna Chiger; diarist
Chiger, Krystyna (b. 1935): dentist, author of the memoir *The Girl in the Green Sweater*
Chmiel, Jan: student at the Professional Medical Courses in Lviv
Chomsowa, Władysława Larysa (Choms, 1891–1966): civic activist, from 1843 president of the Lviv district Council for Aid to Jews "Żegota"
Chwistek, Leon (1884–1944): logician, painter, art theorist, cofounded the Formist group, professors at UJK and UL
Ciepielowska, Wanda: physician
Cieszyński, Antony (1882–1941): dentist, professor at UJK and the Medical Institute, killed by the Nazis on Wuleckie Hills
Cieszyński, Tomasz (1920–2010): surgeon, oncologist, son of Antoni Cieszyński
Cuming, Cecylia (Bessie Cecylia Cuming, married name Groër, 1887–1971): daughter of an Anglican bishop, wife of Franciszek Groër
Cygielstrejch, Mara (Mina Pistyner): daughter of Jakub and Berta Pistyner; memoirist, witness in the trial against Pieter Nicolaas Menten
Czarnik, Leszek (1905–41): physician, scoutmaster (harcmistrz), arrested by the NKVD in March of 1940, murdered in 1941
Czekanowska, Anna (b. 1929): ethnomusicologist, daughter of Jan Czekanowski; memoirist
Czekanowski, Jan (1882–1965): anthropologist, professor at and president of UJK (1934–36), founded the Polish school of anthropology
Czermakowa, Izabella (1898–1964): translator, memoirist
Czerny, Zygmunt (1888–1975): Romanist, professor at UJK and UL, dean of Philology (1940–41), organized underground courses (1942–44)
Czortkower, Salomon (1903–43): anthropologist, died in the Lviv Ghetto
Czuruk, Bolesław (1881–1950): translator, high school teacher, lectured at UJK and UL, after the war arrested by the Polish secret police; in 2010 posthumously honored as Righteous Among The Nations

D

Dan, Aleksander (Aleksander Weintraub, 1897–1843): writer, communist activist, worked for the Lviv leftist magazine *Sygnały*, during the Soviet occupation journalist at *Czerwony Sztandar*; perished at the Janowska Camp

Dante Alighieri (1265–1321): poet

Danylchenko, V. I. (first name unknown): Deputy People's Commissar for Education

Danylenko, Serhy (code name "Karin," 1898–1985): agent of the Cheka, then of the NKVD, in the 1930s foreign resident agent; worked on the cases of the Ukrainian People's Republic general Iury Tiutiunnyk, and the Ukrainian Insurgent Army general Roman Shukhevych; memoirist

Dashkevych, Iaroslav (1926–2010); historian, son of Roman Dashkevych and Olena Stepaniv

Dashkevych, Roman (1892–1975): lawyer, civic and political activist; founded the paramilitary organizations "Sich" and "Luhy;" army general in the Ukrainian People's Republic; emigrated after the war

Davydiak, Ievhen (1879–1962): lawyer, president of the Ukrainian Underground University in Lviv, lectured at UL

Dąbkowski, Przemysław (1877–1950): lawyer, professor at UJK and UL, member of the Polish Academy of Arts and Sciences (PAU); during the German occupation worked at the Institut für Deutsche Ostarbeit, simultaneously involved in teaching underground courses

Dąbrowska, Maria (1889–1965): Polish writer

Debré, Robert (1882–1978): pediatrician

Demianchuk-Tomych, Iaroslava: student at UL 1939–41; memoirist

Derkach, Fedir (1911–14): officer in the Red Army

Desniak, Oleksa (Oleksiy Rudenko, 1909–42): writer, communist activist, president of the Lviv division of the Soviet Writers' Union of Ukraine (1940–41), editor in chief of *Literatura i mystetstvo*

Dickman, Giza: biochemist, friend of Fryderyka Tennenbaum (Irena Lille), emigrated to Israel after the war

Dmytrenko, Mykhailo (1908–97): painter, studied under Fedir Krychevsky, director of the Lviv chapter of Soviet Artists' Union of Ukraine (1939–41), emigrated after the war

Dobrovolska, Olimpia (1892–1990): actor, wife of Iosyp Hirniak, performed in the Berezil Theater; lived in Lviv during the German occupation; emigrated in 1944

Dobrzaniecki, Władysław (1897–1941): physician, Deefender of Lviv in 1918, professor at UJK, director of St. Sophia's Hospital; murdered by the Nazis on Wuleckie Hills

Dombrovsky, Oleksandr (b. 1914–2014): historian, member of the Shevchenko Scientific Society; 1940–41 lecturer of Ukrainian at the Lviv Polytechnic;

1941–42 librarian at the City Archive; 1942–44 at Ukrainian Free University in Prague; emigrated to the US after the war

Dontsov, Dmytro (1883–1973): political activist, publicist, ideologue of Ukrainian integral nationalism; emigrated in 1939

Dorfman, Boris (b. 1923): Jewish writer, publicist, researcher, in Lviv since 1949; founded the association of Jewish culture in Lviv (1990)

Doroshenko, Dmytro (1882–1951): political activist, diplomat, publicist, foreign minister of the Ukrainian People's Republic; emigrated in 1920; founded the Museum of Ukraine's Struggle for Independence in Prague

Doroshenko, Volodymyr (1879–1963): librarian, director of the Shevchenko Scientific Society's library, emigrated in 1944

Dovzhenko, Oleksandr (1894–1956): film director, soldier of the Ukrainian People's Republic 1918–19; sent with a film crew to areas occupied by the USSR 1939–40; diarist and memoirist

Dragan, Mykhailo (1899–1952): art historian, fought in the Ukrainian Galician Army; studied at the Ukrainian Underground University; student of the painter Oleksa Novakivsky; worked at the Ukrainian National Museum

Drahomanov, Svitozar (1884–1958): son of the socialist activist Mykhailo Drahomanov; translator, publicist, worked in the Department of Labor of the Ukrainian People's Republic 1918–1919; left Kyiv for Lviv in 1943, emigrated after the war

Drozdov, Viktor (1902–66): member of the All-Union Communist Party (Bolshevik), NKVD officer, from 1945 general; in charge of eliminating the Ukrainian underground

Dubovy, Mykhailo (1908–95): physician; military doctor during the 1939 campaign; 1939–40 physician at the Medical Institute's clinic; arrested by the NKVD in 1940; 1940–45 deported to Uzbekistan, after the war professor at the Medical Institute

Duchyminska, Olha (née Reshetylovych, 1883–1988): writer, translator, teacher; worked at the Lviv Museum of Ethnography (1939–41); arrested in 1949, sentenced to twenty-five years; released in 1958

Dudykevych, Bohdan (1907–72): historian, communist activist, studied at UL 1939–41, served in the Red Army from 1941; after the war vice president of the Lviv City Council, director of the Historical Museum and the Lenin Museum

Dumansky, Stepan (1918–41, nom de guerre "Kruk"), studied at the Medical Institute, member of the Organization of Ukrainian Nationalists, arrested by the NKVD in 1940, executed

Dunin-Borkowski, Piotr (1890–1949): aristocrat, political activist, Lviv voivode (1927–28), spokesman for Polish-Ukrainian reconciliation

Dzeverin, Oleksandr: pedagogue, worked at UL 1940–41

Dzierżyńska, Zofia (1882–1968): communist activist, editor at *Nowe Widnokręgi*, wife of Feliks Dzierżyński (Dzerzhinsky)

Dzyndra, Ievhen (1913–83): sculptor

E

Eberhart, Myron: Ukrainian singer, member of the band Yabtso

Ehrlich, Ludwik (1889–1968): lawyer, member of the Polish Academy of Arts and Sciences, professor at the Jagiellonian University and UL; judge at the International Court of Justice at the Hague; terminated from UL in 1940; after the war worked with the International Military Tribunal in Nuremberg

Ehrlich, Stanisław (1907–97): lawyer, lectured at UL 1939–41

Ehrlichowa, Helena: physician

Empress Elisabeth (1837–98): Empress of Austria

Erlich, Henryk (1882–1942): lawyer, politician, Bund leader, member of the executive of the Second International; arrested by the NKVD in October 1939, released in August 1941, arrested again and executed by the NKVD

F

Fediuk, Mykola (1885–1962): painter, ANUM member

Fedyk, Oleksandra: mother of Eufrozyna (married name Lewkowska)

Feuerman, Eleasar Jerzy (b. 1919): physician, emigrated to Israel after the war; memoirist

Figol, Atanazy (1908–93): Ukrainian civic and political activist, member of the Shevchenko Scientific Society; 1941–45 member of the Ukrainian Central Committee within the Third Reich's territory

Filippov, Oleksy (1902–55): chairman of the All-Soviet Committee for Higher Education, deputy minister of education of the Ukrainian SSR (1944–55)

Finberg, Leonid (b. 1948): publisher, director of the Judaica Center at the Kyiv-Mohyla Academy

Fischer, Adam (1889–1943): ethnologist, professor at UJK and UL

Fleck, Ludwik (1896–1961): biologist, physician, philosopher of science; during the German occupation first in the Lviv Ghetto, then in extermination camps in Auschwitz and Buchenwald; emigrated to Israel in 1957

Frank, Hans (1900–1946): lawyer, Hitler's adviser, governor of the General Government, war criminal

Franko, Ivan (1856–1916): writer, translator, journalist, scholar, civic and political activist

Franko, Petro (1890–1941): son of Ivan Franko, chemist, civic and political activist, pilot in the Ukrainian Galician Army, in 1919 interned in the POW camp in Dąbie, 1931–36 worked at the Institute of Chemistry in Kharkiv; teacher

1936–39; in October 1939 deputy to the People's Assembly; from March 1940 deputy to the Supreme Soviet of the Ukrainian SSR; in April 1941 arrested by the NKVD under the guise of evacuation and murdered

Franz Joseph I (1830–1916): Emperor of Austria

Freud, Sigmund (1856–1939): neurologist and psychiatrist, founder of psychoanalysis

Friedman, Filip (Fischel, Jeroham, 1901–60): historian; 1939–41 worked at the Lviv chapter Academy of Sciences of the of the Ukrainian SSR, after the war director of the Central Jewish Historical Commission; emigrated in 1946; witness in the Nuremberg Trials; authored the first study of the Holocaust of Lviv's Jews

Friedman, Sania: Jewish poet from Lviv

Fryze, Stanisław (1885–1964): engineer, professor at the Lviv Polytechnic

Fuliński, Benedykt (1881–1942): biologist, professor at UJK and UL, member of the Polish Academy of Arts and Sciences (PAU), Defender of Lviv (1918), during the German occupation involved in underground teaching

Fylypovych, Pavlo (1891–1937): poet and translator from the Neoclassicist group, arrested by the NKVD in 1935, murdered in the *Gulag*

G

Gabrilovich, Ievgeny (1899–1993): Soviet author and screen writer, recipient of the Stalin Prize; memoirist

Gagarin, Aleksei (1895–1960): Marxist philosopher, 1937–41 vice chairman of the USSR Committee for Higher Education

Ganszyniec, Ryszard (Gansiniec, 1888–1958): classics philologist and Germanist; professor at UJK, led the division of classical philology at UJ; memoirist

Gertner, Lejzor (Elizar, 1884–1942): owned a roadhouse in Żabie, chairman of the Jewish borough, his collection of Hutsul art was transferred in 1940 to the Ethnographic Museum in Lviv

Gerasimov, Aleksandr (1881–1963): Soviet painter, one of the founders of socialist realism, president of the Soviet Artists' Union

Gębarowicz, Mieczysław (1893–1984): art historian, professor at UJK and UL, curator of the Ossolineum Library collections

Gierczycka, Zofia: lab technician, godmother of Halina Lewkowska

Giedroyc, Jerzy (1906–2000): political thinker; editor in chief of *Bunt Młodych, Polityka, Kultura*, spokesman for Polish-Ukrainian reconciliation

Giżycki (first name unknown): German owner of the insurance company "Silesia"

Glasner, Jakub (Libidowski, 1879–1942): artist, refugee

Gluziński, Antoni (1856–1935): physician, professor at UL

Głąbiński, Stanisław (1862–1941): politician, lawyer, publicist, professor at UJK, National Democracy leader; arrested by the NKVD in November 1939, died in prison in Kharkiv

Gnoińska, Hanna (b. 1938): physician, daughter of Regina Tennenbaum (married name Gnoińska)
van Gogh, Vincent (1853–90): painter
Goldstein, Maximilian (1880–1942): banker, collector, founder of the Jewish Museum in Lviv
Gorky, Maxim (1868–1936): writer, founder of socialist realism
Górska, Halina (née Endelman, 1898–1942): writer, leftist activist, editor at the *Sygnały* magazine, member of the Soviet Writers' Union of Ukraine; executed by the Nazis
Grabowski, Witold (1902–63): physician, lectured at UJK and the Medical Institute
Grabski, Stanisław (1871–1949): politician, economist, professor at UJK; author of the *Lex Grabski* education reform eliminating schools for national minorities; arrested by the NKVD in 1939, released in August 1941
Grek, Jan (1875–1941): physician, professor at UJK and the Medical Institute; murdered by the Nazis on Wuleckie Hills
Grigoriev, Pavel (Gorinstein, 1895–1961): wrote lyrics to Soviet propaganda songs
Grishchenko: Soviet functionary assigned to the apartment of Fryderyka and Jan Lille
Groër, Franciszek (1887–1965): physician, professor at UJK and the Medical Institute
Groër, Maria (1920–2008): daughter of Franciszek Groër, physician, collector
Gross, Jan Tomasz (b. 1947): historian and sociologist
Grosz, Wiktor (1907–56): publicist, communist activist, journalist at *Czerwony Sztandar*; co-organizer of the Union of Polish Patriots, of the Polish 1st Kościuszko Infantry Division, and after 1944 of the state security apparatus in Poland
Gruber, Ewa (1908–?): orientalist, worked at UJ and UL
Grubiński, Wacław (1883–1973): writer and critic; arrested in January 1940 by the NKVD, released in August 1941; worked at the Polish embassy in Kuibyshev; emigrated after the war; memoirist
Gruca, Adam (1893–1983): physician, professor at UJK and the Medical Institute; 1939–41 clinic director, during the German occupation lectured at the Professional Medical Courses
Gruszecka, Katarzyna (Hollender): mother of Józef Hollender (Piotr Smolnicki)
Gruzberg, Semen (Hruzbenko, 1918–2000): painter; during the German occupation created portraits under the name Hruzbenko; sheltered by his teacher Mykhailo Kozak
Grzędzielski, Jerzy (1901–41): physician, murdered by the Nazis on Wuleckie Hills
Gürtler, Alojzy: lawyer, prosecutor, from 1939 in the General Government
Gürtler, Olga: *see* Balik, Olga
Guzeev (first name unknown): NKVD captain, in the 1950s head of the investigation department in the Ukrainian SSR's Ministry of State Security, thereafter in Moscow

H

Hahn, Otto (1904–42): painter, art theorist, member of *Artes*

Haidabura, Valery (b. 1937): theater historian

Halan, Iaroslav (1902–49): writer and columnist, communist activist; 1939–41 editor at the newspaper *Vilna Ukraina*; evacuated into the depths of the USSR in 1941; 1945–46 correspondent for the newspaper *Radianska Ukraina* at the Nuremberg trials; author of propagandist pamphlets, murdered by nationalists

Halkin, Hillel (b. 1939): Jewish writer and translator, scholar of Zionism

Handzy (first name unknown): UL student

Harasymchuk, Roman (1900–1976): ethnographer, researched the Hutsulshchyna

Harris, Albert (Aaron Hekelman, 1911–74): singer and composer, performed with the Lviv Tea-Jazz

Hartman, Stanisław (1914–92): mathematician; memoirist

Havryluk, Oleksandr (1911–41): poet, member of the Communist Party of Western Belorussia; imprisoned in Bereza Kartuska, member of the Soviet Writers' Union of Ukraine; killed by a German bomb

Havrylyshyn, Myroslav (nom de guerre "Vorona," 1923–?), high school student, arrested by the NKVD in 1940, one of the minors sentenced in the Trial of the Fifty-Nine

Heine, Heinrich (1797–1856): poet and writer

Hemar, Marian (Jan Maria Hescheles, 1901–72): poet, song writer

Hepner, Benedykt: chemist working in Warsaw, from 1939 Jakub Parnas's assistant

Herbert, Zbigniew (1924–98): poet and essayist

Herling-Grudziński, Gustaw (1919–2000): writer and essayist; arrested by the NKVD in 1940; released in 1942; described his *Gulag* experiences in *A World Apart*

Herzberg, Jan (1908–41): mathematician, student of Leon Chwistek's; communist activist

Hescheles, Henryk (1886–1941): journalist and intellectual, editor in chief of the Zionist newspaper *Chwila*, arrested by the NKVD in 1939, released in 1940; murdered during a pogrom in the Brygidki prison courtyard

Hescheles, Janina (b. 1931, married name Altman): chemist, daughter of Henryk Hescheles; memoirist

Heydrich, Reinhard (1904–42): chief of the Reich Main Security Office; one of the architects of Nazi policies, organized the Wannsee conference, responsible for the Holocaust, created the Einsatzgruppen

Himmler, Heinrich (1900–1945): one of the main leaders of Hitler's Germany, created and led the SS and the Gestapo; Nazi war criminal

Hirniak, Iosyp (1895–1989): theater director and actor, soldier in the Ukrainian Galician Army; from 1920 in Kyiv, from 1926 in Kharkiv, worked at the Berezil Theater; arrested by the NKVD in 1933, released in 1940, from 1942 in Lviv, emigrated in 1944; memoirist

Hirszfeld, Hanna (Hirszfeldowa, née Kasman, 1884–1964): physician, 1944–45 head of the children's hospital in Lublin

Hirszfeld, Ludwik (1884–1954): physician, founder of the immunological school; instrumental in establishing the Marie Curie-Skłodowska University in Lublin; memoirist

Hitler, Adolf (1889–1945): Führer of the Third Reich

Hladky (first name unknown); office director at the Department of Health in Lviv

Hollender, Józef (Piotr Smolnicki): inhabitant of Lviv, Jewish policeman; military prosecutor after the war, responsible for Stalinist repressions

Hollender, Tadeusz (1910–43): poet, translator, publicist, editor at the *Sygnały* magazine; from 1941 in Warsaw, active with the Home Army Operational Command's Office of Information and Propaganda (BiP KG AK); arrested by the Gestapo, executed

Holoborodko, Pavlo (1895–?): surgeon, from 1940 division director at the Medical Institute; after the war in Lviv and Ivano-Frankivsk

Holovatsky, Iakiv (1814–88): Ukrainian writer, historian, UL president

Holubets, Mykola (1891–1942): art historian, publicist, soldier in the Ukrainian Galician Army; co–founded the Association of Independent Ukrainian Artists (ANUM); during the German occupation co-founder of the Literary-Artistic Club

Hordynsky, Sviatoslav (1906–93): poet, translator, and artist; studied in Berlin and Paris; co-founded the Association of Independent Ukrainian Artists (ANUM); emigrated in 1944

Horodysky, Zenon: member of the Organization of Ukrainian Nationalists-M (Melnyk faction); memoirist

Horyn, Vasyl (b. 1936): historian of literature

Hrebenkin, Kostiantyn (1902–37): communist activist, member of the WKP(b), historian, graduated from the Institute of Red Professors, worked at the Academy of Sciences of the Ukrainian SSR; editor at the journal *Istoryk-bilshovyk*; arrested by the NKVD, executed

Hrechko, Ivan (b. 1929): engineer, art collector, secular activist for the revival of the Greek-Catholic Church

Hrushetsky, Ivan (1904–82): communist activist, general; 1944–62 chairman of the Lviv regional Communist Party Committee (KPU)

Hrushevska, Kateryna (1900–1943): daughter of Mykhailo Hrushevsky, ethnologist, sociologist, member of the Shevchenko Scientific Society; arrested by the NKVD in 1938, died in the *Gulag*

Hrushevska, Maria (1868–1948): wife of Mykhailo Hrushevsky, teacher, translator

Hrushevsky, Mykhailo (1866–1934): Ukrainian historian and politician

Hruzbenko, Semen: *see* Gruzberg, Semen

Hryciuk, Grzegorz (b. 1965): Polish historian

Hrynevych, Vladyslav (b. 1959): Ukrainian historian
Hryshchuk, Leonid (1906–60): communist activist; 1939–41 chairman of the Lviv regional Party Committee; from 1940 member of the Communist Party (Bolshevik) of Ukraine
Hrytsak, Iaroslav (b. 1960): Ukrainian historian
Hubert, Stanisław (1905–83): lawyer, lectured at UJK and UL; during the German occupation organized underground courses
Humeniuk, Petro (b. 1957): painter
Hupalo, Kostiantyn (1907–42): writer, 1940–41 director of the Russian language division at UL; executed by the Nazis at Babi Yar
Hurystrymba, Vasyl (1899–1937): historian, arrested by the NKVD in 1937 and executed

I

Iablonsky, Leonid (1908–66): violinist, member of the band Yabtso
Iarosevych, Irena: *see* Anders, Irena
Iarosevych, Mykola (1873–1957): Greek Catholic priest, military chaplain during World War I, father of Irena Iarosevych-Anders
Iarosevych, Olena (née Nyzhankivska, 1878–?): mother of Irena Iarosevych-Anders
Iaroslavsky, Emelian (1878–1943): communist activist, prominent Soviet publicist, awarded the Stalin Prize
Iatskiv, Mykhailo (1873–1961): writer, member of the group *Moloda Muza*
Iefremov, Serhy (1876–1939): historian of literature, publicist, vice president of the All-Ukrainian Academy of Sciences (VUAN); arrested by the NKVD as the alleged leader of the Union for the Liberation of Ukraine; diarist
Iendyk, Rostyslav (1906–74): anthropologist, poet, publicist, member of the Shevchenko Scientific Society, nationalist activist
Ieremenko, Fedir: Soviet commander of Lviv
Ilnytsky, Mykola (b. 1934): historian of literature, translator
Ilovaiska, Iekaterina: buried next to Jan Lewkowski, probably in Sara Lille's resting place
Indruch, Jadwiga (née Skorska, 1887–1977): wife of Rudolf Indruch
Indruch, Rudolf (1892–1927): architect, designed the monument commemorating the Lviv Eaglets (Orlęta Lwowskie)
Inglot, Mieczysław (b. 1931): historian of literature
Ironside, Edmund (1880–1959): British chief of the Imperial General Staff
Iurchenko, Vitaly (Iury Karas-Holynsky, 1900–1943): soldier in the army of the Ukrainian People's Republic, arrested in 1929, escaped from the *Gulag* in 1930; memoirist

Iusimov (first name unknown): officer of the Red Army, Soviet commissar in Lviv in 1939
Ivan the Terrible (1530–84): Russian tsar
Ivanets, Ivan (1893–1946): painter and photographer, during World War I served in the legion of Ukrainian Sich Riflemen; during the German occupation member of the Association of Ukrainian Pictorial Artists; arrested in Cracow by the Soviet counter-intelligence SMERSH, perished in the *Gulag*

J

Jabayev, Jambyl (1846–1945): Kazakh poet, recipient of the Stalin Prize
the Jagiellonians: dynasty
Jahn, Alfred (1915–99): geographer, lectured at UL; memoirist
Jakóbiec, Marian (1910–98): Slavist, historian of literature; memoirist
Jałowy, Bolesław (1906–43): physician, dean at the Medical Institute, during the German occupation lectured at the Professional Medical Courses; murdered by Ukrainian nationalist insurgents
Janczak (first name unknown): UL student
Janisch, Jerzy (1901962): painter, photographer, founder of *Artes*
Jasieński, Bruno (Wiktor Zysman, 1901–38): writer, futurist poet
Jasińska, Janina (1920–?): singer in the band Lviv Tea-Jazz
Jastrun, Mieczysław (1903–83): poet and translator, affiliated with the Skamandrites; 1939–41 in Lviv, member of the Lviv chapter of the Soviet Writers' Union of Ukraine
Jaworski, Ivan: member of the Lviv intelligentsia, part of Iaroslava Muzyka's circle
Jeleński, Szczepan (1881–1949): author of books on popular mathematics
Jodłowski, Stanisław (1902–79): linguist, lectured at UJK
Juhn, Otto: director of the insurance company "Silesia"

K

Kachanov, Nikita (1898–?): director of the Medical Institute's Marxism-Leninism division
Kacyzne, Alter (1885–1941): writer, publicist, photographer, member of the Soviet Writers' Union of Ukraine, Lviv chapter
Kaganovich, Lazar (1893–1991): Soviet politician; responsible for Stalinist crimes, including the Katyń atrocity
Kalynets, Ihor (b. 1939): poet and translator, dissident
Kamińska, Ida (1899–1980): actor and director, director at the State Jewish Theater in Lviv in 1940; memoirist
Karas-Holynsky, Iury: *see* Iurchenko, Vitaly

Karmansky, Petro (1878–1956): poet and translator, member of the group Moloda Muza, diplomatic representative of the Ukrainian People's Republic in the Vatican, lectured at UL, member of the Soviet Writers' Union of Ukraine, Lviv chapter

Kasman, Leon (1905–84): communist activist in the International, 1939–41 in Lviv; 1944–45 department of propaganda director in the Central Committee of the Polish Workers' Party in Lublin

Kasprowiczowa, Maria (née Bunin, 1887–1968), wife of the poet Jan Kasprowicz; memoirist

Kedryn-Rudnytsky, Ivan: *see* Rudnytsky, Ivan

Kernytsky, Ivan (1913–84): writer and journalist; emigrated in 1944

Khimenko, Ivan: president of the Institute of Soviet Trade in 1939

Khmelnytsky, Bohdan (1595–1657): Cossack Hetman

Kholodny, Petro (1876–1930): impressionist and neobyzantine painter, member of the Ukrainian Central Council, emigrated to Poland in 1920

Khomenko, Iakiv (1909–43): Secretary of the Komsomol's Central Committee 1938–43; member of the Communist Party (Bolshevik) of Ukraine 1940–43

Khomiak, Mykhailo (Michael Chomiak, 1905–84): lawyer, journalist, 1940–44 editor in chief of the newspaper *Krakivski visti*, emigrated to Canada in 1944

Khrushchev, Nikita (1894–1971): from 1918 member of the All-Union Communist Party (Bolsheviks), from 1939 Chairman of the Communist Party (Bolshevik) of Ukraine; 1953–64 general secretary of the Central Committee of the Communist Party of the Soviet Union

Khvylia, Andry (1898–1938): writer, journalist, director of the Propaganda Division of the Communist Party (Bolshevik) of Ukraine, targeted Mykola Khvylovy and the Free Academy of Proletarian Literature (VAPLITE); arrested and executed by the NKVD

Khvylovy, Mykola (1893–1933): writer, political activist, member of the Communist Party (Bolshevik) of Ukraine, founded the Free Academy of Proletarian Literature (VAPLITE), key representative of the Executed Renaissance; committed suicide in protest against communist policies

Kiernicki, Rafał (1912–95): Catholic clergyman, arrested by the NKVD in 1940, escaped from prison in June 1941; arrested again in 1944, released in 1947, thereafter priest in Soviet Lviv

Kikh, Mariia (1914–79): youth cell member of the Communist Party of Western Ukraine, deputy to the People's Assembly of Western Ukraine in October 1939; deputy to the Supreme Soviet of the Ukrainian SSR

Kirsa, Ivan: Deputy Commissar of Education of the Ukrainian SSR

Kitz, Marcin (1891–1943): painter, 1940–41 member of the Soviet Artists' Union of Ukraine; in 1943 arrested and executed by the Gestapo for helping to shelter Jews

Kladochny, Rev. Iosyp (1906–94): Greek Catholic clergyman, chaplain at the Bereza Kartuska internment camp; in December 1939 Metropolitan Andrei Sheptytsky's envoy to the Vatican; 1942–43 liaison between the Ukrainian and the Polish resistance; 1943–44 chaplain of the Galician Waffen-SS Division; continued to serve as a priest after the Greek Catholic Church was delegalized

Klawek, Aleksy (1890–1969): Catholic clergyman, professor at UJK, member of the Polish Academy of Arts and Sciences (PAU)

Kleiner, Juliusz (1886–1957): historian of literature, Professor at UJK and UL, member of the Soviet Writers' Union of Ukraine

Kleinman, Fryc (Fryderyk, 1897–1943): painter, graphic artist and set designer, worked for the newspaper *Chwila* and the magazine *Sygnały*

Klen, Iury (Osvald Burghardt, 1891–1947): poet and translator from the Neoclassicist group; emigrated in 1931

Kluczkowski, Jacek (b. 1953): journalist, civil servant, diplomat, ambassador of the Polish Republic in Kyiv 2005–10

Klymiv, Ivan (nom de guerre "Lehenda," 1909–42): activist in the Organization of Ukrainian Nationalists (OUN)

Knaster, Bronisław (1890–1983): mathematician, 1939–41 professor at UL

Knoop, Hans (b. 1943): journalist, spokesman for the denazification of the Netherlands

Knorr, Herbert (1908–?): SS-Hauptsturmführer in Lviv

Kobylianska, Olha (1863–1942): writer, activist in the women's movement in the Bukovyna

Koch, Erich (1896–1986): Nazi party member, Reich Commissioner of Ukraine, war criminal

Koch, Hans (1894–1959): German intelligence officer; in 1918 served in the Ukrainian Galician Army; during World War II liaison between the Organization of Ukrainian Nationalists (OUN) and the German administration

Kochur, Hryhory (1908–94): translator and civic activist, 1943–53 *Gulag* prisoner

Kohutiak, Ivan (1893–1968): actor and theater director

Kokh, Bohdan (1925–96): theater actor, memoirist; in 1943 imprisoned in the Janowska Camp, and 1946–54 in the *Gulag*

Kolankowski, Ludwik (1882–1956): historian, professor at UJK, member of the Polish Academy of Arts and Sciences (PAU)

Kolessa, Filaret (1871–1947): folklorist and musician; in October 1939 deputy to the People's Assembly; professor at UL (1939–41), director of the Museum of Ethnography in Lviv (1940–41)

Kolski, Witold (1902–43): member of the Communist Party of Poland (KPP), 1939–41 deputy editor in chief of the newspaper *Czerwony Sztandar*

Konarski, Feliks (stage name Ref-Ren, 1907–91): poet, actor, singer, creator of the revue in Lviv in 1934; 1939–41 member of the Lviv Tea-Jazz; 1941–45 in the Anders' Army, emigrated in 1945

Konovalets, Ievhen (1891–1938): activist for Ukrainian independence, colonel; organized the Sich Riflemen, led the Ukrainian Military Organization (UVO) and the Organization of Ukrainian Nationalists (OUN); assassinated in Rotterdam by the NKVD agent Pavel Sudoplatov

Kordiuk, Iulian (1894–1947): physician, member of the Shevchenko Scientific Society, 1941–44 in the depths of the USSR; from 1944 deputy Commissar of the Health Department in Lviv

Korniichuk, Oleksandr (1905–72): writer and communist activist, one of the founders of the socialist realist style; chairman of the Soviet Writers' Union of Ukraine (1938–43), member of the Communist Party (Bolshevik) of Ukraine, People's Commissar for Foreign Affairs (1944), chairman of the Supreme Soviet of the Ukrainian SSR (1947–53), member of the Academy of Sciences of the Ukrainian SSR; husband of Wanda Wasilewska

Korolewicz, Michał: *see* Lille, Jan

Kos-Anatolsky, Anatoly (1909–83): composer, in the 1930s member of the band Yabtso, memoirist

Kosach, Iury (1908–90): writer, nephew of Lesia Ukrainka, 1943–44 editor at the newspaper *Lvivski visti*

Kosichev, Anatolii (1914–2014): Marxist philosopher, professor at Moscow University

Kosior, Stanislav (1889–1939): communist activist, Secretary General of the Communist Party (Bolshevik) of Ukraine, responsible for the Terror-Famine in Ukraine

Kossak, Karol (1896–1975): painter, grandson of Juliusz Kossak and nephew of Wojciech Kossak

Kostelnyk, Havryil (1886–1948): Greek Catholic clergyman, originally from the Serbian Vojvodina; 1939–41 subjected to reprisals (among them his son's murder at the hands of the NKVD); in 1946 during the so-called "Reunion Sobor" spoke out in favor of abolishing the Greek Catholic Church and absorbing it into the Orthodox Church; murdered, most likely by the NKVD

Kościuszko, Tadeusz (1746–1817): general, commander in chief of the Polish uprising against Russia in 1794

Kot, Stanisław (1885–1975): political activist affiliated with the People's Movement; vice premier in the government of Władysław Sikorski; 1941–42 ambassador of the exiled Polish government to the USSR

Kotsiubynsky, Mykhailo (1864–1913): writer, civic and political activist

Kotsylovsky, Iosafat (1876–1947): Greek Catholic clergyman, Bishop of Peremyshl (Przemyśl), arrested by the Polish authorities and handed over to the USSR; died in prison in Kyiv

Kott, Jan (1914–2001): literary critic

Kott, Lidia (née Steinhaus, 1919–2000): essayist, daughter of Hugo Steinhaus, wife of Jan Kott

Koval, Oleksandr (1913–71): dentist, 1939–44 head of the dental clinic in Lviv

Kovba, Zhanna (1939–2018): historian

Koverko, Andriy (1893–1967): sculptor and restorer of religious art; participated in exhibitions of the Association of Independent Ukrainian Artists (ANUM)

Kovpak, Sydor (1887–1967): member of the Communist Party (Bolshevik) of Ukraine, commander of the Soviet guerilla troops; raided German units in the occupied territories; memoirist

Kovzhun, Pavlo (1896–1939): painter and art historian; member of the Association of Independent Ukrainian Artists (ANUM), editor in chief of *Mystetstvo*

Kowalska, Anna (née Chrzanowska, 1903–69): writer, diarist; wife of Jerzy Kowalski

Kowalski, Jerzy (1893–1948): classical philologist, professor at UJK, member of the Polish Academy of Arts and Sciences (PAU)

Kozak, Bohdan (b. 1940): director, actor, theater historian

Kozak, Edvard (artistic alias: Eko 1902–92): caricaturist, painter, member of the Association of Independent Ukrainian Artists (ANUM)

Kozlaniuk, Petro (1904–65): writer, communist activist, member of the Soviet Writers' Union of Ukraine; evacuated from Lviv with the Soviets in 1941, returned in 1944

Kozyk, Mykhailo (1879–1947): painter, lectured at the Art Institutes in Kyiv and Kharkiv; during the German occupation taught at the Lviv Art and Industrial School; honored as Righteous Among the Nations

Königsberg, Dawid (1889–1942): Jewish poet and translator

Krasnov, Kapiton (1902–61): NKVD officer, member of the All-Union Communist Party (Bolsheviks); from September 1939 till February 1940 head of the NKVD's Lviv oblast section

Kratochwila-Widymska, Józefa (1878–1965): painter, member of the Soviet Artists' Union of Ukraine

Kravtsiv, Bohdan (1904–75): writer, translator, activist of the Ukrainian Military Organization (UVO) and the Organization of Ukrainian Nationalists (OUN)

Krechowiecki, Adam (1913–91): physician, lectured in the Medical Institute, during the German occupation adjunct at the Professional Medical Courses; memoirist

Kreczmar, Jan (1908–72): actor; memoirist

Kreutz, Mieczysław (1893–1971): psychologist, professor at UJK and UL

Krukowska, Helena (Wasilkowska, 1895–1982): physician, wife of Włodzimierz Krukowski, edited a collection of reminiscences about Franciszek Groër

Krukowski, Włodzimierz (1887–1941): engineer, professor at the Lviv Polytechnic, murdered by the Nazis on Wuleckie Hills

Krushelnytska, Larysa (b. 1928–2017): archeologist, daughter of Ivan Krushelnytsky, rescued from the Soviet Union in 1937, director of the Stefanyk Library; memoirist

Krychevsky, Fedir (1879–1947): painter, student of Gustav Klimt; chairman of the Soviet Artists' Union of Ukraine

Krychevsky, Vasyl (1873–1952): painter, architect, and film set designer, brother of Fedir; considered the founder of modern Ukrainian architecture; lived in Lviv during the German occupation, emigrated in 1944; most of his works, including film, were destroyed after the war once the author was declared a traitor

Krymsky, Ahatanhel (1871–1942): poet, translator, orientalist; organizer and permanent secretary of the All-Ukrainian Academy of Sciences (VUAN); arrested by the NKVD in July 1941, died in prison in Kustanay

Krypiakevych, Ivan (1886–1967): historian, professor at UL, member of the Shevchenko Scientific Society and the Academy of Sciences of the Ukrainian SSR; lectured at the Ukrainian Underground University, 1939–41 director of the Department of History in the Lviv chapter of the Academy of Sciences of the Ukrainian SSR; during the German occupation editor at "Ukrainske vydavnytstvo"

Kryvutsky, Pavlo (?–1963): soldier in the Ukrainian Galician Army, director of the Land Mortgage Bank SA in Lviv, in 1939 made his way to the German-occupied territories; emigrated in 1944

Krzemicka, Zofia (1887–1943): Lviv historian and popularizer of history; died in the Pawiak prison in Warsaw

Krzemieniewski, Seweryn (1871–1945): biologist, professor and president of UJK and UL

Kubicz, Stanisław (1908–86): physician; memoirist

Kubiyovych, Volodymyr (1900–1985): geographer, political activist, member of the Shevchenko Scientific Society, served in the Ukrainian Galician Army; 1940–44 head of the Ukrainian Central Committee; emigrated in 1944; memoirist

Kugel (first name unknown): wife of the building administrator where Jan and Fryderyka Lille lived

Kuhn, Thomas (1922–96): philosopher of science, historian

Kulchytska, Olena (1877–1967): painter

Kulczyński, Stanisław (1895–1975): botanist, political activist, professor and president of UJK and UL, member of the Polish Academy of Arts and Sciences (PAU)

Kulish, Mykola (1892–1937): playwright, worked with the Berezil Theater; member of the Executed Renaissance generation, arrested by the NKVD in 1934, executed

Kunynets, Stefania (married name Fedorovych, 1916–2002): secretary at the Lviv Health Department in 1939–41; emigrated after 1944

Kupchynsky, Roman (1894–1976): writer, civic and political activist; served in the Sich Riflemen and the Ukrainian Galician Army during World War I, journalist at *Dilo*; 1939–44 in Cracow, emigrated in 1944; memoirist

Kurbas, Les (Oleksandr, 1887–1937): theater director, founded the avant-garde theaters Molody Teatr and Berezil; arrested by the NKVD in 1934, executed

Kurchaba, Leonid: physician, Prosvita activist, member of the Organization of Ukrainian Nationalists (OUN); in July 1941 head of the Ukrainian Red Cross in Lviv; arrested by the Gestapo, died in the Montelupich prison in Cracow

Kurek, Jalu (Franciszek, 1904–83): writer, representative of the Cracow avant-garde, 1939–40 in Lviv, illegally smuggled into German occupied territory

Kurovets, Ivan (1863–1931): physician, civic and political activist, in charge of the Health Department in the cabinet of the Western Ukrainian People's Republic (ZUNR); dean of Medicine at the Ukrainian Underground University

Kurtyka, Janusz (1960–2010): historian, 2005–10 president of Poland's Institute of National Remembrance (IPN)

Kurylas, Osyp (1870–1951): painter; graduate of the Cracow Fine Arts Academy; served in the legion of the Ukrainian Sich Riflemen during World War I

Kuryluk, Karol (1910–67): journalist, political activist; editor in chief of the magazine *Sygnały*, during the Soviet occupation editor at the newspaper *Czerwony Sztandar*; honored as Righteous Among the Nations

Kuryłowicz, Jerzy (1895–1978): linguist, professor at UJK and UL, National Party activist

Kuźmińska, Helena: communist activist, worker, in 1940 assistant director in a factory; 1940–47 deputy to the Supreme Soviet of the Ukrainian SSR

L

Lanckorońska, Karolina (1898–2002): art historian, lectured at UJK, member of the Polish Academy of Arts and Sciences (PAU); during World War II active in the Union for Armed Struggle (ZWZ) and the Home Army (AK); emigrated after the war; memoirist; wrote an account of the massacre of Lviv professors

Landberg, Marian (during the war Zbigniew Isalski, 1932–89): nephew of Irena Lille

Landberg, Stanisław: Irena Lille's brother-in-law

Langner, Władysław (1896–1972): general, commander of Lviv's defense in 1939

Lasovsky, Volodymyr (1907–75): painter, art critic, member of the Association of Independent Ukrainian Artists (ANUM); employed at the Folk Art Institute during the German occupation, emigrated in 1944

Lastovetsky, Andry (1902–43): physicist, member of the Shevchenko Scientific Society; 1939–41 at the Medical Institute, 1941–43 dean of the Professional Medical courses; murdered by the Home Army

Lebed, Mykola (1909–98): activist in the Organization of Ukrainian Nationalists (OUN), responsible for the assassination of Bronisław Pieracki; head of the insurgent intelligence service SB OUN (1940–41), second in command to Stepan Bandera; member of the Ukrainian Supreme Liberation Council (UHVR), emigrated after the war

Lebedev-Kumach, Vasily (1898–1949): poet and author of Soviet propaganda songs; recipient of the Stalin Prize

Lebesgue, Henri Léon (1875–1941): mathematician, received an honorary doctorate from UJK

Lec, Stanisław Jerzy (de Tusch-Letz, 1909–66): poet, aphorist, member of the Soviet Writers' Union of Ukraine, prisoner at the Janowska Camp

Lem, Stanisław (1921–2006): writer

Lenartowicz, Jan Tadeusz (1877–1959): physician, professor at UJK, the Medical Institute, and the Professional Medical Courses

Lenin, Vladimir Ilyich (Ulyanov, 1870–1924): first leader of the Soviet state

Leszczyński, Julian: during the German occupation curator at the Museum of Artistic Industry in Lviv

Levchenko, Iakiv: NKVD functionary at UL (1939–40)

Levytska, Sofia (1874–1937): painter, lived in France from 1905

Levytsky, Borys (Lewytzky, 1915–84): publicist, political scientist and activist; until 1941 member of the Organization of Ukrainian Nationalists (OUN); founded the Ukrainian Revolutionary-Democratic Party (URDP); in the fall of 1939 made his way from Lviv to Cracow; emigrated to Germany after the war; contributor to Jerzy Giedroyc's *Kultura*

Levytsky, Dmytro (1877–1942): lawyer, civic and political activist, leader of the Ukrainian National Democratic Alliance (UNDO), chief of the Ukrainian delegation within the Polish Parliament (1928–35), arrested by the NKVD in September 1939, released in 1941, rejected as a recruit to the Anders' Army

Levytsky, Kost (1859–1941): politician, representative to the Austrian Parliament and the Galician Provincial Diet; chief of government of the Western Ukrainian People's Republic; headed the Ukrainian community's delegation to the Soviet authorities; arrested in September 1939, released in the spring of 1941; memoirist

Levytsky, Leopold (1906–73): painter, leftist activist; representative of the Cracow avant-garde

Levytsky, Volodymyr (1872–1956): mathematician, lectured at the Ukrainian Underground University, 1939–41 professor at UL, member of the Shevchenko Scientific Society

Lewin, Jecheskiel (1897–1941): rabbi of the Progressive Synagogue in Lviv, murdered by German troops in the Lviv Brygidki prison in 1941

Lewin, Kurt (1925–2014): son of rabbi Jecheskiel, saved by the Metropolitan Andrei Sheptytsky and his brother, prior of a Studite monastery; memoirist

Lewkowska, Eufrozyna (née Fedyk, 1913–91): nurse, grandmother of the author, honored as Righteous Among the Nations

Lewkowski, Jan (1880–1942): secretary at the Appellate Court in Lviv, grandfather of the author

Léger, Fernand (1891–1955): French painter and sculptor

Lille, Irena (Fryderyka Tennenbaum, assumed name Irena Szyszkowicz, 1903–89): hematologist; memoirist

Lille, Jan (assumed name Michał Korolewicz, circa 1900–1981): lawyer; husband of Irena Lille

Lille, Ludwik (1897–1957): surrealist painter, art critic; member of *Artes*, emigrated in 1937

Lille, Sara (assumed name Barbara Mikoś, "Granny," ?–1943): mother of Jan and Ludwik, sheltered by Eufrozyna Lewkowska

Lindenfeld, Kazimierz (1897–?): biochemist, graduate of Warsaw University, 1939–41 worked together with Jakub Parnas

Lipl, Helena (née Tennenbaum, assumed name Maria Różycka), sister of Irena Lille

Litvinov, Maxim (1876–1951): communist activist, 1930–39 People's Commissar for Foreign Affairs of the USSR

Liubchenko, Arkady (1899–1945): writer, member of the Free Academy of Proletarian Literature (VAPLITE), from 1943 in Lviv, then abroad; diarist (1941–45)

Liubchenko, Panas (1897–1937): communist activist, member of the KP(b)U, one of the executors of the Terror-Famine in Ukraine

Liubchyk, Vasyl: after World War II Assistant Director of the Museum of Ukrainian Art in Lviv, destroyed the collections of modern art in Lviv in 1952

Liudkevych, Stanislav (1879–1979): composer, member of the Shevchenko Scientific Society, from 1939 professor at the Lviv Conservatory

Longchamps de Berier, Roman (1883–1941): lawyer, professor, president of UJK, lectured at UL; murdered by the Nazis on Wuleckie Hills

Lopatynsky, Demian (1866–1951): Greek Catholic clergyman, member of the Ukrainian National Democratic Alliance (UNDO) and of the publishing partnership *Dilo*, from 1938 in Cracow, emigrated after 1944

Loria, Stanisław (1883–1958): physicist, professor at UJK and UL

Lubkivsky, Roman (1941–2015): writer, politician, diplomat

Lukianchikov, Ivan: Deputy People's Commissar of Health

Lusternik, Lazar (1899–1981): mathematician, professor at Moscow University

Lysenko, Iosyp (?–1941): communist activist, member of the Communist Party (Bolshevik) of Ukraine, 1939–41 chaired the Central Committee's Department of Propaganda and Agitation

Lysiak, Pavlo (1887–1948): husband of Milena Rudnytska; attorney, activist for Ukrainian independence, served as a Ukrainian National Democratic Alliance (UNDO) representative to the Polish Parliament

Lysiak-Rudnytsky, Ivan (1919–83): historian, essayist, son of Pavlo Lysiak and Milena Rudnytska; emigrated in 1939

Lytvynenko, Serhy (1899–1964): sculptor, officer in the army of the Ukrainian People's Republic, studied at the Fine Arts Academy in Cracow, from 1930 in Lviv; emigrated in 1944

Ł

Łomnicki, Antoni (1881–1941): mathematician, professor at the Lviv Polytechnic, murdered by the Nazis on Wuleckie Hills

Łozynska, Pelagia (Kazimiera Poraj, 1905–?): wife of Juliusz Szparber; diarist; honored as Righteous Among the Nations

Łukaszewicz, Piotr (b. 1940): art historian

M

Maievsky, Dmytro (nom de guerre "Taras"): activist in the Organization of Ukrainian Nationalists (OUN) and member of its executive Provod, general in the Ukrainian Insurgent Army (UPA), participated in the negotiations with Serhy Danylenko or "Karin"

Makarchenko, Oleksandr (1903–1979): neurologist; 1939–41 director of the Medical Institute; 1942–53 deputy minister of Health; 1962–1963 vice chairman of the Academy of Sciences of the Ukrainian SSR

Makaryk, Irena (b. 1951): literary and theater scholar

Maksymenko, Oksana (née Kokh, b. 1962): librarian; daughter of Bohdan Kokh

Maksymiv, Ivan (1913–1941): member of the Organization of Ukrainian Nationalists (OUN), referent of the Home Executive; arrested by the NKVD in 1940, charged in the Trial of the Fifty-Nine, executed

Maksymonko, Leonty (1893–1965): physician, served in the Ukrainian Galician Army (UHA), lectured at the Ukrainian Underground University; chairman of the Lviv Chamber of Physicians; 1942–44 head of the Ophthalmological Clinic, lectured at the Professional Medical Courses; emigrated in 1944

Makuszyński, Kornel (1884–1953): writer and publicist, author of popular children's books

Malaniuk, Ievhen (1897–1968): poet, essayist; officer in the army of the Ukrainian People's Republic, published in Dmytro Dontsov's *Visnyk* and in the *Biuletyn Polsko-Ukraiński*; 1929–44 in Warsaw; emigrated in 1944

Malashchuk, Ludvika (1915–?): student at UL; member of the Organization of Ukrainian Nationalists (OUN); arrested by the NKVD in 1940, sentenced to death; sentence commuted to fifteen years; later details unknown

Maliutsa, Antin (1908–70): painter, art critic, student of Ludwik Tyrowicz, set designer in Volodymyr Blavatsky's theater; during the German occupation deputy director of the Lviv Art and Industrial School; emigrated in 1944

Malyshko, Andry (1912–70): poet, translator, lyricist, awarded the Stalin Prize

Malytska, Kostiantyna (1872–1947): writer, lyricist, activist in the women's movement

Manteuffel, Jerzy (1900–1954): historian and classical philologist, 1939–41 lectured at UL

Manuilsky, Dmytro (1883–1959): communist activist, chairman of the Soviet delegation to the Comintern, secretary of the Communist Party (Bolshevik) of Ukraine, foreign minister of the Ukrainian SSR (1944–52); initiated the campaign against "bourgeois nationalism" among the Ukrainian intelligentsia

Marchenko, Mykhailo (1902–83): historian, member of the Communist Party (Bolshevik) of Ukraine, graduated from the Red Professors Institute in Kharkiv; from October 1939 until September 1940 president of UL; arrested by the NKVD in June 1941, released in 1944

Marchenko, Nina (first married name Umrilova, second married name Smuzhanytsia, 1929–2011): daughter of Mykhailo Marchenko, mother of Valery; teacher, lectured at a pedagogical university

Marchenko, Valery (1947–84): philologist, dissident, member of the Ukrainian Helsinki Group, twice imprisoned in Soviet labor camps

Maritchak, Oleksandr (1887–1981): attorney, political activist, member of the Ukrainian National Democratic Alliance (UNDO); lectured at the Ukrainian Underground University

Martyniv, Stepan (1910–96): physician, professor at the Medical Institute

Marx, Karl (1818–83): German philosopher, theoretician and ideologue of Marxism

Matviichuk, Mykhailo (1904–93): ethnographer; 1947–51 director of the Lviv Museum of Ethnography

Matviiv-Melnyk, Mykola (1890–1947): writer, journalist, soldier in the Ukrainian Galicia Army, member of the Soviet Writers' Union of Ukraine, lectured at the Institute of Soviet Trade; emigrated in 1944

Mayakovsky, Vladimir (1893–1930): Russian poet, futurist, playwright, communist activist

Maysky, Ivan (1884–1975): Soviet diplomat, 1932–43 Soviet ambassador to Great Britain

Mazepa, Ivan (1639–1709): Cossack Hetman

Mazur, Stanisław (1905–81): mathematician, lectured at the Lviv Polytechnic, worked at the Academy of Sciences of the Ukrainian SSR; 1940–41 Lviv council member; after the war member of the Polish United Workers' Party (PZPR), Sejm representative

Mechnyk, Petro (1885–1953): educator, director of the Ukrainian Secondary School

Meisel, Henryk (1894–1981): microbiologist, student of Rudolf Weigl; during the German occupation worked at Weigl's Institute until 1943, then sent to Auschwitz

Meisel, Paula (née Rossberger): microbiologist, wife of Henryk Meisel

Mekhlis, Lev (1889–1953): communist activist, general; 1937–40 chief of the Red Army's Political Directorate

Melnychuk, Petro (1913–?): pharmacist, assistant dean at the Medical Institute

Melnyk, Andry (1890–1964): officer in the army of the Ukrainian People's Republic, active in the Ukrainian Military Organization (UVO), led the OUN-M faction of the Organization of Ukrainian Nationalists 1938–41

Menten, Pieter Nicolaas (1899–1987): entrepreneur, collector, Nazi war criminal; before the war owned an estate and a company near Stryi; arrested by the NKVD, after his release in December 1939 in Cracow; took receivership of Jewish rare book stores; in July 1941 joined the Einsatzgruppe C; responsible for murders and plunder of Polish and Jewish estates

Merkulov, Vsevolod (1895–1953): Soviet activist, NKVD general, Beria's trusted man

Merkurov, Sergei (1881–1952): Soviet sculptor, studied in Kyiv and Munich; director of the Pushkin Museum in Moscow; received the Stalin Prize

Mickiewicz, Adam (1798–1855): poet
Mikhalkov, Nikita (b. 1945): Soviet and Russian film director
Mikhoels, Solomon (1890–1948): actor and theater director, chairman of the Jewish Antifascist Committee; assassinated on the eve of Stalin's antisemitic purges
Mikoś, Barbara: *see* Lille, Sara
Miłobędzki, Adam: captain in the Polish Army, friend of Stanisław Vincenz
Minc, Hilary (1905–74): communist activist, economist, after the war minister and vice premier of the Polish People's Republic, responsible for Stalinist repressions
Mirek, Alfred (1922–2009): musicologist, *Gulag* prisoner; memoirist
Mniszek, Aleksander (1904–72): director of Władysław Sikorski's secretariat; diplomat, 1941–43 secretary of the Polish embassy in the USSR
Modzelewska, Maria (1903–97): actress
Molotov, Viacheslav (1890–1986): Soviet politician, Chairman of the Council of People's Commissars of the USSR (1930–41), foreign minister, a close associate of Stalin's
Morgenstein (first name unknown): student at UL
Mudry, Vasyl (1893–1966): politician and journalist, (1935–1939), chairman of the Ukrainian National Democratic Alliance (UNDO), editor in chief of *Dilo*; 1939–41 in Cracow, 1941–44 in Lviv, emigrated thereafter
Muzyka, Iaroslava (née Stefanovych, 1893–1973): wife of Maksym Muzyka; painter, student of Stanisław Batowski; art restorer; chairman of the Association of Independent Ukrainian Artists (ANUM); arrested in 1948, released from the *Gulag* in 1955
Muzyka, Maksym (1889–1972): microbiologist; during World War I army doctor, dean of the Ukrainian Underground University; chairman of the Ukrainian Medical Association; 1939–41 and 1944–48 deputy director of the Medical Institute

N

Nacht, Artur (Samborski, 1898–1974): painter, professor at the Fine Arts Academy in Warsaw; member of the Paris Committee, until 1939 in Paris, 1939–41 in Lviv, 1941–42 in the Lviv Ghetto; hid out in Warsaw after his escape
Nacht, Józef (Prutkowski, 1915–81): poet and satirist; arrested in 1940 and sent to the *Gulag*; joined the Kościuszko Infantry Division in 1943
Naegeli, Otto (1871–1938): Swiss hematologist
Naglerowa, Herminia (1890–1957): writer and publicist, from 1939 in Lviv; arrested by the NKVD in 1940, released in August 1941, from 1941 in the Women's Auxiliary Service of Anders' Army; emigrated after the war; memoirist
Nahaylo, Bohdan (Nahajlo, b. 1953): historian, journalist, analyst, worked for Radio Svoboda 1984–2004

Nakonechny, Ievhen (1931–2006): historian; arrested by the NKVD in 1949, released in 1955; memoirist

Nalepińska, Zofia (1884–1937): painter and graphic artist, wife of Mykhailo Boichuk; taught at the Fine Arts Academy in Kyiv; arrested and by the NKVD; executed

Narbut, Heorhy (1886–1920): painter and graphic artist; heraldist; president of the Fine Arts Academy in Kyiv

Navrotsky, Vasyl (1864–1941): Greek Catholic clergyman, parish priest in Krasne by Lviv, father of Maria Strutynska

Nazaruk, Osyp (1883–1940): journalist and politician; during World War I served in the Sich Riflemen and Ukrainian Galician Army; emigrated to the US in the 1920s; in the 1930s editor in chief of *Nova zoria*; memoirist

Nedbailo, Petro (1907–74): lawyer, lecturer and dean at UL; 1941–45 worked for the Soviet Military Prosecutor's Office

Neyman, Stefania: mother of Ewa Neyman-Pilat

Neyman-Pilat, Ewa (1909–45): chemist, wife of Stanisław Pilat

Nietzsche, Friedrich (1844–1900): philosopher and writer

Nikifor (Epifany Drovniak, 1895–1968): primitivist painter

Nikliborc, Władysław (1889–1948): mathematician; fought in the Polish-Bolshevik war; lectured at UJK, professor at the Lviv Polytechnic, also during the occupation

Nikulin, Lev (1891–1967): Soviet writer, communist activist, awarded the Stalin Prize

Nimchuk, Ivan (1891–1956): journalist, civil and political activist, member of the Ukrainian National Democratic Alliance (UNDO), editor in chief of *Dilo*; memoirist

Novakivsky, Oleksa (1872–1935): neoimpressionist painter, student of Jan Matejko and Jan Stanisławski; dean of the Ukrainian Underground University; founded the Novakivsky Art School in Lviv

Novychenko, Leonid (1914–96): literary historian, critic

Nowicki, Witold (1878–1941): physician, murdered by the Nazis on Wuleckie Hills

Nyzhankivsky, Ostap (1863–1919): composer and conductor

O

Oberlander, Theodor (1905–98): officer in the Abwehr and politician; member of the NSDAP and the CDU, minister in Konrad Adenauer's government; during World War II liaison officer for the Nachtigall Battalion, then joined Andrey Vlasov's Russian Liberation Army

Ohloblyn, Oleksandr (1899–1992): historian, political activist; in the 1930s led the archives and worked at the Academy of Sciences of the Ukrainian SSR; in

September–October 1941 chairman of the Kyiv City Council; thereafter director of an archive collecting documentation of Stalinist crimes; emigrated in 1944

Olesnytsky, Ievhen (1860–1917): lawyer, politician, leader in the cooperative movement, served as a representative to the Polish National Assembly and to the Parliament in Vienna; father of Marta Rudnytska

Olzhych, Oleh (1907–44): poet, archeologist, active in the Organization of Ukrainian Nationalists (OUN), member of the executive council Provod of the Melnyk faction (OUN-M)

Opania, Marian (b. 1943): actor, also in cabaret roles

Opieńska-Blauth, Janina (1895–?): biochemist; 1939–41 worked in Lviv at the Medical Institute, in Jakub Parnas's division; during the German occupation lectured at the Professional Medical Courses

Ordonówna, Hanka (Anna Maria Tyszkiewiczowa, née Pietruszyńska, stage name Ordonka, 1902–50): singer and actress, performed in the cabaret Qui pro Quo; from 1940 in Vilnius; arrested by the NKVD, released from the *Gulag* in August 1941

Orest, Mykhailo (1901–63): poet of the Neoclassicist circle, brother of Mykola Zerov; *Gulag* prisoner, released in 1941; 1942–44 in Lviv, emigrated after the war

Orlicz, Władysław (1903–90): mathematician, member of the Lwów School of Mathematics

Ortwin, Ostap (Oskar Katzenellenbogen, 1876–1942): lawyer and literary critic, part of Young Poland; chairman of the Lviv chapter of the prewar Polish Writers' Union

Osinchuk, Mykhailo (1890–1969): painter, graphic artist, member of the Shevchenko Scientific Society, founder of the Association of Independent Ukrainian Artists (ANUM), editor at *Mystetstvo*; soldier of the Ukrainian Galician Army and the army of the Ukrainian People's Republic; 1939–41 lectured at the Art Institute; emigrated in 1944

Osinchuk, Roman (1902–91): brother of Mykhailo Osinchuk, physician, lectured at the Medical Institute, emigrated after 1944

Ossowski, Stanisław (1897–1963): sociologist and culture theorist; 1939–41 worked in Lviv at the library of the Academy of Sciences of the Ukrainian SSR; diarist

Ostern, Paweł (1904–41): biochemist, lectured at UJH and the Medical Institute, murdered by the Nazis in July 1941

Ostroverkha, Mykhailo (1897–1979): writer, journalist, political activist; officer in the Ukrainian Galician Army and the army of the Ukrainian People's Republic; in the 1920s correspondent for *Dilo*, on a fellowship in Italy; in November 1939 made his way to the German-occupied territories, then to Rome; 1941–44 in Galicia, editor at the weekly publication *Do peremohy* for soldiers of the SS Division "Galicia," emigrated in 1944; memoirist

Ostrowski, Stanisław (1892–1982): physician, political activist, representative to the Sejm elected from the Nonpartisan Bloc for Cooperation with the Government (BBWR), last Polish mayor of Lviv, 1972–79 president of the Polish Republic in exile; arrested by the NKVD in September 1939, released in August 1941; physician in the Anders' Army; memoirist

Ostrowski, Tadeusz (1881–1941): physician, professor at UJK and the Medical Institute; chief of the Institute of Surgery; murdered by the Nazis on Wuleckie Hills

P

Pachovsky, Vasyl (1878–1942): poet, member of the group *Moloda Muza*, taught at UJK, lecturer of Ukrainian at UL

Padalka, Ivan (1894–1937): avant-garde artist, art theorist, student of Mykhailo Boichuk, executed by the NKVD

Panch, Petro (Panchenko, 1891–1978): writer, member of the Free Academy of Proletarian Literature (VAPLITE), officer in the army of the Ukrainian People's Republic, 1939–40 chaired the Lviv division of the Soviet Writers' Union

Panchyshyn, Marian (1882–1943): physician, professor at the Ukrainian Underground University, chairman of the Ukrainian Medical Association, director of the People's Clinic, deputy to the Supreme Soviet of the USSR

Pankivsky, Kost (1897–1973): lawyer, political activist, from 1941 General Secretary of the Ukrainian National Council in Lviv, emigrated in 1944; memoirist

Parfanovych, Sofia (1898–1968): physician and writer, emigrated in 1944; memoirist

Parkhomenko, Mykhailo: writer, communist activist

Parnas, Jakub (1884–1949): biochemist, professor at UJK and the Medical Institute; in 1941 ordered to evacuate into the depths of the USSR; Academy member, awarded of the Stalin Prize; died in prison or murdered during an investigation

Parnicki, Teodor (1908–88): writer; arrested by the NKVD in January 1940; released in August 1941, joined the Anders' Army; returned to Poland in 1967

Pashchenko, Oleksandr (1906–63): graphic artist, member of the All-Union Communist Party (Bolsheviks), 1940–44 head of the Soviet Artists' Union of Ukraine

Pashe-Ozersky, Mykola (1889–1962): lawyer, professor at Kyiv University and UL; legal counsel for the Ukrainian Central Committee; during 1942–43 editor of German-Ukrainian legal dictionary; arrested by the NKVD in 1945, released in 1946

Pasternak, Iaroslav (1892–1969): archeologist; served in the Ukrainian Galician Army, member of the Shevchenko Scientific Society; professor at UL, emigrated in 1944

Pasternak, Leon (1910–69): poet, communist activist, editor in chief of *Czerwony Sztandar*, evacuated into the depths of the USSR in 1941, member of the Polish Committee of National Liberation (PKWN)

Pavlenko, U. (first name unknown): NKVD officer at the Medical Institute
Pavlyshyn, Oleh (b. 1961): historian
Peiper, Tadeusz (1891–1969): poet, member of the Cracow avant-garde, arrested in 1940 by the NKVD, released in 1943; member of the Union of Polish Patriots
Pelekhaty, Kuzma (1866–1952): writer, communist activist; member of the Communist Party of Western Ukraine, editor in chief of the newspaper *Vilna Ukraina*, member of the communist underground
Pelensky, Zenon (1902–79): politician, member of the Ukrainian Military Organization, the Ukrainian National Democratic Alliance (UNDO), and the Organization of Ukrainian Nationalists (OUN); emigrated after the war
Peretts, Volodymyr (1870–1935): philologist, publisher of historical Ukrainian manuscripts; member of the Academy of Sciences of the Ukrainian SSR
Peretz, Isaac Leib (1852–1915): writer, classical author of Yiddish literature
Peter I the Great (1672–1725): tsar of Russia
Petliura, Symon (1879–1926): politician, President and commander in chief of the Ukrainian People's Republic, assassinated in Paris
Petrenko, Andry (1881–1957): soldier in the army of the Ukrainian People's Republic and member of its diplomatic mission; in Lviv from 1921, during the German occupation managing director of the Theater of the Opera and administrative employee of the Ukrainian Central Committee; arrested in 1947, released in 1956
Petriakova, Faina (1931–2002): art historian, in the 1990s scholar of Jewish culture
Petrov, Viktor (pen name V. Domontovych, 1894–1969): writer, critic, and archeologist, affiliated with the Neoclassicists; during the German occupation first in Kharkiv, then in Berlin; moved to the USSR in 1949
Petrovsky, Mykola (1894–1951): scholar of Cossack history, member of the Academy of Sciences of the Ukrainian SSR; during World War II evacuated to Ufa; wrote a denunciation of Mykhailo Marchenko (and Oleksandr Ohloblyn); 1942–47 director of the Institute of History at the Academy of Sciences of the Ukrainian SSR
Petrun, Fedir (1894–1963): historian, geographer, orientalist
Picasso, Pablo (1881–1973): painter, graphic artist, sculptor
Pilat, Stanisław (1881–1941): chemical engineer, inventor of oil technologies, professor at the Lviv Polytechnic, worked at the Academy of Sciences of the Ukrainian SSR; murdered by the Nazis on Wuleckie Hills
Piłsudski, Józef (1867–1935): First Marshal of Poland
Pinchevska, Bohdana (b. 1977): art historian
von Pirquet, Clemens (1874–1929): Austrian pediatrician
Pistyner, Fryda: wife of Izaak Pistyner, one of the victims of Pieter Nicolaas Menten
Pistyner, Izaak: Jewish entrepreneur, one of the victims of Pieter Nicolaas Menten

Piwocki, Ksawery (1901–74): art historian, ethnologist, from 1938 director of the Museum of Artistic Industry in Lviv; after the war in Warsaw

Pleshevtsev, V. (first name unknown): NKVD functionary

Podolynsky, Oleksandr (1889–1943): physician, assistant director at the People's Clinic; led the obstetrical clinic at the Professional Medical courses

Poliansky, Iury (1892–1975): geographer, officer in the Ukrainian Galician Army, 1920–1922 commander of the Ukrainian Military Organization, high school teacher; lectured at the Ukrainian Underground University, professor at UL, in July 1941 acting mayor of Lviv

Poliuha, Ivan (1897–1973): soldier in the Ukrainian Galician Army, civic activist

Polonska-Vasylenko, Natalia (1884–1973): historian, professor at the All-Ukrainian Academy of Sciences (VUAN) and Kyiv University; from 1943 in Lviv, emigrated thereafter; memoirist

Połoniecki, Bernard (Pordes, 1862–1943): publisher, owned the Polish Bookstore in Lviv; diarist

Ponisch: Warsaw architect, sheltered Margit Selska

Popper, Karl (1902–94): philosopher

Potocki, Andrzej (1861–1908): Polish aristocrat, politician, Viceroy of Galicia (1903–8); shot by a Ukrainian assassin

Potshybitkin, Mikhail (actual last name unknown): director of the State Jewish Theater in Lviv

Poussin, Nicolas (1594–1665): painter of the classical French Baroque style

Pritsak, Omelian (1919–2006): historian, orientalist, student of Ahatanhel Krymsky; 1943–45 studied in Berlin; founded the Harvard Ukrainian Research Institute

Progulski, Stanisław (1874–1941): pediatrician, professor at UJK, murdered by the Nazis on Wuleckie Hills

Prokopiv, Ivan (1901–?): accountant, teacher, collector; memoirist

Pronaszko, Andrzej (1888–1961): avantgarde artist, member of the Formist group

Proust, Marcel (1871–1922): French writer; his works were translated into Polish by Tadeusz Boy-Żeleński

Prus, Edward (1931–2007): historian, publicist, communist activist; soldier in one of the istrebki paramilitary security units created by the NKVD

Przyboś, Julian (1901–70): poet and translator; Defender of Lwów in 1918 and 1920; from 1939 in Lviv, worked at the Ossolineum Library; member of the Union of Soviet Writers' of Ukraine

Przybyłowski, Kazimierz (1900–1987): lawyer, professor at UJK and UL; organized underground courses; arrested in 1945 by the NKVD; after his release moved to Cracow

Putrament, Jerzy (1910–86): writer and communist activist, member of the Union of Soviet Writers' of Ukraine; in 1941 departed Lviv to evacuate into the depths of the USSR, member of the Union of Polish Patriots

R

Radchenko, Hryhory (1890–1940): physician, diplomat, communist activist, 1930–33 Soviet consul in Lviv; arrested by the NKVD in 1935, died in the Soviet labor camp in Kolyma

Rajszer (first name unknown)

Rakovsky, Ivan (1874–1949): biologist, teacher, editor in chief of *The Ukrainian General Encyclopedia*; president of the Shevchenko Scientific Society; from 1940 in the General Government, emigrated in 1944

Rechmedin, Leonid: journalist, communist activist, political officer in the Red Army

Redko, Iulian (1905–93): educator, philologist; studied at the Ukrainian Underground University, then at UJK; after the war worked as researcher; memoirist

Redlich, Fryderyk (Franciszek, 1896–1964): pediatrician

Redzik, Adam (b. 1977): lawyer and historian

Reich, Izaak: engineer, father of Margit Reich-Selska

Reich-Selska, Margit (1903–80): avant-garde artist, member of *Artes*; wife of Roman Selski

Rencki, Roman (1867–1941): physician, professor at UJK, member of the Polish Academy of Arts and Sciences (PAU), president of the Lviv Medical Association; head of the Morshin sanatorium; arrested in 1939 by the NKVD; murdered by the Nazis on Wuleckie Hills

Rettinger, Ludwika (Wichuna, ?–1939): wife of Mieczysław Rettinger

Rettinger, Mieczysław (1890–1944): literary critic associated with Młoda Polska, political activist; during World War II active in the resistance; arrested by the Gestapo, executed in Sachsenhausen

Reymont, Władysław (1867–1925): writer, Nobel Prize laureate

von Ribbentrop, Joachim (1893–1946): foreign minister of the Third Reich, Nazi party member, war criminal

Riemer, Aleksander (1899–1943): painter, student of Kazimierz Sichulski, member of *Artes*

Rokita, Richard: SS Sturmbannführer, Deputy Commandant of the Janowska Camp, war criminal

Romanchuk, Iulian (1842–1932): civic and political activist, founded the newspaper *Dilo*, representative to the Galician Provincial Diet; along with Kost Levytsky and Ievhen Olesnytsky leader of Galician Ukrainians before World War I

Romm, Mikhail (1901–71): film director, received the Stalin Prize; memoirist

Romm, Michał (1907–?): physician, reserve officer of the Polish Army, saved from the Katyn massacre by his uncle Mikhail Romm

Room, Abraham (1894–1976): film director, received the Stalin Prize; communist activist

Rosenberg (first name unknown): student

Rosner, Adolf (stage name Eddie Rosner, 1910–76): jazz trumpet player and composer, "White Armstrong"; husband of Ruth Kamińska, Ida Kamińska's daughter; orchestra conductor in Western Belarus; arrested by the NKVD in 1946, released in 1954

Rothfeld, Adolf (1886–1942): lawyer, publicist, Zionist activist, city council member; head of the Lviv Judenrat

Rowecki, Stefan (nom de guerre Grot, 1895–1944): general, 1942–1943 first Commander of the Home Army

Rubchak, Ivan (1874–1952): actor and opera singer, delegate to the People's Assembly in 1939

Rubel, Ludwik (1897–1958): journalist, political editor of the daily *Ilustrowany Kurier Codzienny*, representative to the Sejm (1930–1935), emigrated to Great Britain in 1940

Rubinowicz, Wojciech (1889–1974): physicist, professor at UJK

Rublov, Oleksandr (b. 1957): historian

Rudenko, Roman (1907–81): general prosecutor of the USSR; communist activist

Rudniański, Jarosław (1921–2008): psychologist, educator, son of Stefan Rudniański

Rudniański, Stefan (Rubinrot, 1887–1941): educator, philosopher, communist activist

Rudnicki, Adolf (1912–1990): writer

Rudnicki, Klemens (1897–1992): division general; arrested by the NKVD in 1939, released in September 1941; joined the Anders' Army, lived in London after the war; memoirist

Rudnytska, Anna (née Stefanovych): sister of Iaroslava Muzyka

Rudnytska, Daryna: daughter of Mykhailo and Marta

Rudnytska, Marta (née Olesnytska): wife of Mykhailo Rudnytsky

Rudnytska, Milena (1892–1976): political activist, leader in the women's movement; publicist, president of the Union of Ukrainian Women; Sejm deputy in the Second Polish Republic; after 1939 lived in Cracow, Berlin, Prague, Geneva, and Munich

Rudnytska, Olga (born Ida Spiegel, 1862–1950): mother of Milena, Ivan, Mykhailo, Anton, and Volodymyr

Rudnytsky, Anton (1902–1975): musician; brother of Milena, Ivan, Mykhailo, and Volodymyr

Rudnytsky, Ivan (pen name Kedryn, 1896–1995): journalist, political activist, member of the Central Committee of the Ukrainian National Democratic Alliance (UNDO), press secretary of the Ukrainian Parliamentary Representation to the Sejm of the Second Polish Republic; member of the Shevchenko Scientific Society, from 1939 in Cracow, after the war in Austria and in the US; memoirist

Rudnytsky, Mykhailo (1889–1975): writer, literary critic, translator, professor at UL

Rudnytsky, Volodymyr (1890–1974): lawyer
Rudzińska, Agnieszka: historian, deputy director of the Public Education Office at the Polish Institute of National Remembrance (IPN), vice-president of IPN (2011–16)
Rustaveli, Shota (1172–1216): Georgian poet
Ruziewicz, Stanisław (1889–1941): mathematician, professor at UJK at the Lviv Polytechnic; vice-president of the Lviv Institute of Soviet Trade; murdered by the Nazis on Wuleckie Hills
Rybak, Natan (1913–78): socialist realism writer, received the Stalin Prize
Rydz-Śmigły, Edward (1886–1941): military and political leader, officer of the Polish Legions; commander in chief of the armed forces of the Second Polish Republic
Rylski, Tadeusz (1841–1902): civic activist, one of the founders of the Kyiv Hromada, father of Maksym Rylsky
Rylsky, Maksym (1895–1964): poet and translator; member of the Neoclassicist group; member of the Academy of Sciences of the Ukrainian SSR
Rysiewicz, Adam (1918–44): political activist, in Cracow during the war

S

Saks, Stanisław (1897–1942): mathematician, wrote an algebra textbook, professor at UL; fought in the September 1939 campaign, in Warsaw from 1942
Saltykov-Shchedrin, Mikhail (Mikhail Saltykov, pen name N. Shchedrin, 1826–89): classic Russian writer, satirist
Samchuk, Ulas (1905–87): writer and journalist, member of the Organization of Ukrainian Nationalists (OUN), after defecting lived in Prague; during the German occupation editor at a Ukrainian newspaper in Rivne (Reichkomisariat Ukraine), emigrated after the war
Sandauer, Artur (1913–89): literary historian, critic, memoirist
Saradzhev, Artashes (1898–1937): director of the History Institute at the Academy of Sciences of the Ukrainian SSR; arrested by the NKVD in 1936 and executed
Savchenko, Fedir (1892–1937?): historian, member of the All-Ukrainian Academy of Sciences, Mykhailo Hrushevsky's secretary; arrested by the NKVD in 1931 and sentenced to five years, sentenced again in 1937, executed most likely in the same year
Savchenko, Ihor (1906–50): film director, recipient of Stalin prizes
Savchenko, Olha: wife of Fedir Savchenko
Savchenko, Serhy (1904–66): *Cheka* and NKVD functionary, general; from 1940 chief of the NKVD's foreign intelligence, from 1941 Deputy People's Commissar of State Security of the Ukrainian SSR
Savchyn, Maria (nom de guerre Marichka, 1925–2013): intelligence service (SB) liaison of the Organization of Ukrainian Nationalists (OUN); memoirist

Schaff, Adam (1913–2006): Marxist philosopher, communist activist, UJK graduate; 1941–48 at Radio Moscow; main ideologue of the Polish United Workers' Party (PZPR)

Schauder, Juliusz Paweł (1899–1943): mathematician, professor at UL and the Academy of Sciences of the Ukrainian SSR; 1919–20 soldier in Haller's Army; during the German occupation in hiding, arrested in September 1943, shot while escaping from a transport to death camps

Schmierer Reif, Mendel (1910–43): illustrator, caricaturist, satirist

Schopenhauer, Arthur (1788–1860): philosopher

Schorr, Dawid (1889–1941?): attorney

Schöngarth, Karl Georg Eberhard (1903–46): SS general, commandant of the Einsatzgruppe C in Galicia; participated in the Wannsee Conference in 1942; Nazi war criminal

Schudrich, Jakub (1906–43): Yiddish writer, arrested in 1932 as a communist activist; member of Soviet Writers' Union (Lviv branch), killed during an attempt to organize an uprising in the Janowska Camp

Schulz, Bruno (1892–1942): writer, painter, and graphic artist

Schulze, Karl (1905–66): head of the Professional Medical Courses in Lviv during the German occupation

Sedliar, Vasyl (1899–1937): painter, graphic artist, member of the Association of Revolutionary Artists of Ukraine (ARMU); arrested by the NKVD in 1936, executed in Kyiv

Selska, Margit: *see* Reich-Selska, Margit

Selsky, Roman (1903–90): painter, member of *Artes*, the Lviv Professional Union of Visual Artists, and the Association of Independent Ukrainian Artists (ANUM)

Semchyshyn, Myroslav (1910–99): literary historian; member of the Shevchenko Scientific Society, until December 1939 lecturer of Ukrainian at UL, then at the Pedagogical Institute; during the German occupation employed at the Telepress news agency; memoirist

Sempoliński, Ludwik (1899–1981): actor and director

Serhiienko, Vasyl (1903–82): NKVD general, NKVD director for the Lviv oblast and Deputy People's Commissar of Internal Affairs of the Ukrainian SSR (1940–1941), from 1941 People's Commissar of Internal Affairs of the Ukrainian SSR

Serov, Ivan (1905–1990): *Cheka* and NKVD functionary; in the 1930s worked in Stalin's secretariat; September 1939–February 1940 People's Commissar of Internal Affairs of the Ukrainian SSR; from 1941 Deputy Commissar of State Security of the USSR; head of the Soviet KGB; among the operations he led were the Katyn massacre of Polish officers (1940) and expulsion of Crimean Tatars and Kalmyks (1943–44); from 1945 Deputy Commander of the Soviet counter-intelligence agency SMERSH

Shaian, Volodymyr (1908–74): writer, orientalist; ideologue of the Neopagan religion RUN-Vira; during the occupation member of the Union of Soviet Writers of Ukraine

Shakespeare, William (1564–1616): poet, playwright

Shchukin, Sergei (1854–1936): Russian merchant, collector of French modernism, established an art gallery

Shchurat, Vasyl (1871–1948): modernist poet, translator, literary historian, professor at UL

Sheparovych, Iulian (1886–1949): officer of the Ukrainian Galician Army and the army of the Ukrainian People's Republic; participated in the defense of Lviv in 1920; organized the Ukrainian cooperative movement; long-term director of Tsentrosoyuz

Sheptytsky, Andrei (born Roman Szeptycki, 1865–1944): Greek Catholic Archbishop of Lviv and Metropolitan of Halych

Shevchenko, Taras (1814–61): Ukrainian Romantic poet and painter

Shevelov, Iury (George Y.) (né Schneider; pen names Iury Sherekh, Hr. Shevchuk, 1908–2002): essayist, linguist, literary scholar; after leaving Kharkiv in 1924 first in Kyiv, then in Lviv; emigrated in 1944; professor at Harvard, then at Columbia; president of the Ukrainian Free Academy of Arts and Sciences

Shklarski, Liuger: translator

Shore, Marci (b. 1972): essayist and historian of ideas

Shorubalka, Ivan (1917–91): Soviet counter-intelligence (SMERSH) functionary; from 1946 in security forces; specialized in fighting the Ukrainian underground, involved in operations to eliminate general of the Ukrainian Insurgent Army Roman Shukhevych; memoirist

Shtul, Oleh (nom de guerre Zhdanovych, 1917–77): member of the Organization of Ukrainian Nationalists (OUN), from 1943 imprisoned in the Sachsenhausen camp; after the war in France, editor at the newspaper *Ukrainske slovo*

Shukhevych, Iury: brother of Roman Shukhevych, member of Plast and the Organization of Ukrainian Nationalists (OUN)

Shukhevych, Roman (1907–50): member of the executive Provod of the Organization of Ukrainian Nationalists (OUN), 1943–1942 commander of the Nachtigall Battalion. 1943–50 commander of the Ukrainian Insurgent Army

Shyian, Anatolii (1906–89): writer; during the war editor at Soviet frontline newspaper

Sichulski, Kazimierz (1879–1942): painter affiliated with Young Poland; founded an art school in Lviv

Siemiaszkowa, Wanda (1867–1974): actress

Sienkiewicz, Henryk (1846–1916): writer, Nobel Prize laureate

Sieradzki, Włodzimierz (1870–1941): physician, murdered by the Nazis on Wuleckie Hills

Sierpiński, Wacław (1882–1969): mathematician, one of the founders and editors of the journal *Fundamenta Mathematicae*, member of the Polish Academy of Arts and Sciences (PAU), chairman of the Polish Mathematical Society

Sikorski, Władysław (1881–1943): military and political leader; commander in chief of the Polish armed forces, premier of the Polish government in exile; died in a plane crash

Silber (first name unknown): geographer, lectured at UL 1940–41

Simovych, Vasyl (1880–1944): linguist, member of the Shevchenko Scientific Society; during World War I in the Union for the Liberation of Ukraine; 1923–33 professor at the Pedagogical University in Prague, from 1933 in Lviv, in the society Prosvita, 1939–41 professor at UL, during the German occupation editor at the Ukrainian Publishing House (Ukrainske vydavnytstvo)

Siwak, Eugeniusz (1929–2014): engineer, inventor, the author's father

Siwak, Halina (née Lewkowska, 1939–2007): lawyer, the author's mother

Siwak, Leoniła (née Maznica, 1896–1974): wife of Teodor Siwak, the author's grandmother

Siwak, Teodor (Fedir Syvak, 1893–1948): farmer from the vicinity of Hrubieszów; deported three times (1915 into the depths of the USSR; 1945 to the Ukrainian SSR; 1947 to the Recovered Territories); the author's grandfather

Skaba, Andry (1905–86): communist activist, member of the Academy of Sciences of the Ukrainian SSR; 1940–41 led the Contemporary History division at UL

Skoropadsky, Pavlo (1873–1945): political and military leader; Hetman of Ukraine (1918), after 1918 abroad, mostly in Berlin

Skrypnyk, Mykola (1872–1933): communist activist, People's Commissar of Education, led the policy of Ukrainization; committed suicide

Skrzypek, Stanisław (1911–2007): lawyer, historian, and economist; nationalist activist (All-Polish Youth and the National Party), arrested by the NKVD in 1939, released in 1941; joined the Anders' Army; emigrated after the war; memoirist

Skubytsky, Trokhym (1901–37): historian, worked at the Academy of Sciences; member of the Ukrainian history textbook committee; arrested by the NKVD in 1937, executed in Kyiv

Skuza, Wojciech (1908–42): writer, leftist agrarian leader, arrested by the NKVD in 1940, released in 1941, joined the Anders' Army, died in Iran

Skwarczyńska, Stefania (1902–88): literary theorist and historian; lectured at UJK and higher education institutions in Łódź; from 1939 at UL; in April 1940 deported to Kazakhstan, returned to Lviv in October 1940; active in the resistance from 1941; edited poetry anthologies; from 1945 in Łódź

Slipy, Iosyf (Slipyj, Josyf, 1892–1984): Greek Catholic clergyman, Archbishop and Metropolitan of Ukrainian Greek-Catholic Church, 1929–39 president of the

Theological Academy; 1944–84 Metropolitan; arrested by the NKVD in 1945, released from the *Gulag* after eighteen years, from 1963 in the Vatican

Sliusarenko, Hryhory (1904–37): historian, worked at the Academy of Sciences of the Ukrainian SSR, executed by the NKVD

Slyzh, Adolf (1889–1971): Lviv lawyer, judge; emigrated in 1944; memoirist

Słonimski, Antoni (1895–1976): writer and critic; member of the literary group Skamander, contributed to *Wiadomości Literackie*, wrote for the cabaret; during the war abroad; returned to Poland in 1951; affiliated with the anti-communist opposition

Smal-Stocki, Roman (1893–1969): linguist; political activist, member of the Shevchenko cientific Society; ambassador and minister of the Ukrainian People's Republic (1921–23); lived in Warsaw1926–39; secretary of the Ukrainian Scientific Institute in Warsaw, leader in the Promethean movement; during the war in Prague, emigrated thereafter

Smolnicki, Piotr: *see* Hollender, Józef

Snyder, Timothy (b. 1969): historian and public intellectual

Sobolev, Sergei (1908–89): mathematician, member of the Academy of Sciences of the USSR

Sołowij, Adam (1859–1941): physician, professor at UJK, murdered by the Nazis on Wuleckie Hills

Sommerstein, Emil (1883–1957): attorney and politician, affiliated with the Zionist movement; Sejm representative in the Second Polish Republic; arrested by the NKVD in 1939, released in 1944; member of the Polish Committee of National Liberation (PKWN); chaired the Central Committee of Polish Jews (1944–46); emigrated to the US in 1946

Soroka, Bohdan (1940–2015): graphic artist, son of Mykhailo Soroka and Kateryna Zarytska; memoirist

Soroka, Mykhailo (1911–71): member of the Organization of Ukrainian Nationalists (OUN), from 1940 member of its national executive Provod; arrested by the NKVD in 1940; spent thirty-four years in Soviet labor camps; co-organized a prisoner uprising in the Kengir labor camp

Soroka, Petro (1891–1950): stage actor and director; managing director of the Lviv Theater of the Opera (1941–42); arrested by the NKVD in 1947, died in labor camp

Sosenko, Rev. Ksenofont (1861–1941): Greek Catholic clergyman; ethnologist

Sosiura, Volodymyr (1898–1965): poet; served in the army of the Ukrainian People's Republic; member of the literary groups Pluh and the Free Academy of Proletarian Literature (VAPLITE), following their dissolution joined the Union of Soviet Writers' of Ukraine; after the war subjected to harsh attacks for writing patriotic lyrical poetry

Sosnowska, Danuta (b. 1962): scholar of Polish and Slavic studies; historian of ideas

Spiegel, Ida: *see* Rudnytska, Olga

Stadnyk, Iosyp (1874–1954): theater director and actor; 1939–41 artistic director of the State Ukrainian Theater; deputy to the Supreme Soviet of the Ukrainian SSR; during the German occupation director of the Lviv Theater of the Opera and the Drohobych Theater; arrested by the NKVD in 1947; released in 1954

Staff, Leopold (1878–1957): poet, representative of Young Poland, translator, essayist; member of the group Płanetnicy; after World War I in Warsaw; vice-chairman of the Polish Academy of Literature

Stahl, Zdzisław (1901–87): economist, lectured at UJK, activist in the National Democracy and the Camp of National Unity (Obóz Zjednoczenia Narodowego OZON); editor in chief of *Dziennik Lwowski* and *Gazeta Polska*; arrested by the NKVD in 1939; released in 1942, joined the Anders' Army; emigrated after the war

Stalin, Joseph (born Ioseb Besarionis dze Jughashvili, 1878–1953): Soviet dictator

Stark, Marceli (1908–74): lectured at UJK and UL; Stefan Banach's assistant; during the German occupation in the Warsaw Ghetto; concentration camp survivor; after the war worked at Wrocław University and the Polish Academy of Sciences; memoirist

Stark, Pesach: *see* Stryjkowski, Julian

Starosolsky, Stanislav (1889–?): lawyer and diplomat (First Secretary of the Ukrainian People's Republic in Switzerland), cousin of Volodymyr Starosolsky

Starosolsky, Volodymyr (1878–1942): lawyer, leader of the Ukrainian Social Democratic party; member of the Shevchenko Scientific Society; during World War I joined the Sich Riflemen Division; 1918–19 held in the Dąbie internment camp; defense attorney in political trials, including trials against members of the Organization of Ukrainian Nationalists (OUN); arrested by the NKVD in December 1939; died in prison

Stasiak, Stefan (1884–1962): orientalist, professor at UJK and UL

Stebun, Ilia (Ilia Katsnelson, 1911–2005): leading Stalinist literary critic, editor of literary periodicals

Stefanovych, Lev (1919–45?): physician, active in the Ukrainian underground; nephew of Iaroslava Muzyka

Stefanyk, Vasyl (1871–1936): expressionist writer; civic and political activist; deputy to the Austrian Parliament

Steinhaus, Ewelina (née Lipschitz, 1855–1948): mother of Hugo Steinhaus

Steinhaus, Hugo (1887–1972): mathematician; founded the Lwów School of Mathematics; memoirist

Steinhaus, Stefania (1896–1983): wife of Hugo Steinhaus

Stempowski, Jerzy (1893–1969): essayist

Stendhal (Marie-Henri Beyle, 1783–1842): writer

Stern, Anatol (1899–1968): writer, literary critic, translator; founder of Polish Futurism; from 1939 in Lviv; arrested by the NKVD in January 1940; released in 1941; joined the Anders's Army; returned to Poland from Palestine in 1948

Stern, Jonasz (1904–88): artist, member of the Cracow Group, from 1926 in the Communist Party of Poland; incarcerated in Bereza Kartuska in 1938; participated in exhibits in Moscow and Kharkiv in 1940

Stetsko, Iaroslav (1912–86): member of the Organization of Ukrainian Nationalists (OUN), from 1941 Stepan Bandera's second in command; incarcerated by the Germans in Sachsenhausen in July 1941 after proclaiming the Ukrainian State; after the war led the Anti-Bolshevik Bloc of Nations

Stępień, Stanisław (b. 1952): historian; publisher; director of the South-Eastern Research Institute in Przemyśl

Stiasny (first name unknown): SS Hauptsturmführer

Stieber, Zdzisław (1903–80): linguist, Slavic scholar, active in the Home Army in 1941–44; memoirist

Stieglitz, Józef: seller of antique books in Cracow

Streng, Henryk (from 1942 Marek Włodarski, 1903–60): artist, student of Kazimierz Sichulski, from 1929 in Lviv, member of *Artes* and *Neoartes*, vice-president of the Soviet Artists' Union of Ukraine, from 1944 in Warsaw

Struk, Evstakhiy (1909–41): member of the Organization of Ukrainian Nationalists (OUN); administrative director of the Medical Institute, saved fifty of its students from arrest; murdered by the NKVD

Strutynska, Antonina (1907–78): teacher, journalist, during the German occupation proofreader at the magazine *Nashi dni*; arrested by the NKVD in 1949; released in 1957

Strutynska, Maria (née Navrotska, pen name Vira Marska, 1897–1978): writer, civic activist; wife of Mykhailo Strutynsky; during the German occupation editor at the magazine *Nashi dni*; diarist and memoirist

Strutynsky, Mykhailo (1888–1941): civic and political activist, member of the Ukrainian National Democratic Alliance (UNDO); arrested by the NKVD in 1939 and murdered

Stryjkowski, Julian (Pesach Stark, 1905–96): writer, member of the Communist Party of Western Ukraine, editor in chief of the newspaper *Czerwony Sztandar*, member of the Union of Polish Patriots; from the 1960s affiliated with the anti-communist opposition; author of autobiographical prose and memoirist

Studynsky, Kyrylo (1868–1941): Slavist; civic and political activist; chairman of the Shevchenko Scientific Society (1923–33); professor at and vice-president of UL; deputy to the People's Assembly (in September 1939) and to the Supreme Soviet of the USSR (1940–41); murdered by the NKVD

Stur, Jan (Hersz Feingold, 1895–1923): poet, literary critic

Styka, Adam (1890–1959): painter, son of Jan Styka, emigrated after the war

Styka, Jan (1858–1925): one of the painters of *Panorama Racławicka*

Styś, Wincenty (1903–60): economist, agrarian activist; professor at UJK and the Lviv Polytechnic

Surkov, Aleksei (1899–1983): poet, wrote lyrics to Soviet official songs (among them "The Cavalry Song"); communist activist; recipient of Stalin prizes

Susak, Vita: art historian

Suvorov, Aleksandr (1729–1800): military commander of the Russian Empire, ordered the murder of civilian population in conquered cities, including the Praga district of Warsaw

Svientsitska, Vira (1913–91): daughter of Ilarion Svientsitsky; art historian; member of the Organization of Ukrainian Nationalists; arrested by the NKVD in 1947, released in 1956

Svientsitsky, Ilarion (1876–1956): philologist, curator, member of the Shevchenko Scientific Society; 1905–52 director of the Ukrainian National Museum in Lviv

Svitlyk, Bohdana (nom de guerre Svitlana, pen name Maria Dmytrenko, 1918–48): writer, member of the Organization of Ukrainian Nationalists, liaison of the Ukrainian Insurgent Army; killed in a skirmish with an NKVD unit

Swianiewicz, Stanisław (1899–1997): economist, lawyer, Sovietologist; professor at Vilnius University; among the handful saved from the Katyn massacre; memoirist

Szałajko, Kazimierz (1912–2003): mathematician, student of Stefan Banach

Szczepcio (stage name of Kazimierz Wajda, 1905–55): radio actor, co-created the show *Wesoła Lwowska fala* [*Lviv's merry wave*]

Szemplińska, Elżbieta (1910–91): writer and communist activist

Szlechter, Emanuel (1904–43?): song- and screen writer; Defender of Lwów during the Polish-Bolshevik war in 1920; from 1932 in Warsaw, from September 1939 in Lviv; perished in the Janowska Camp

Szpilrajn, Edward (after the war Marczewski, 1907–76): mathematician

Szyszkowicz, Irena: *see* Lille, Irena

Ś

Śladecka, Magdalena: graphic artist, works at the Public Education Office of the Polish Institute of National Remembrance

T

Tarnavsky, Ostap (1917–92): writer, translator; member of the Soviet Writers' Union; during the German occupation editor at the newspaper *Lvivski visti*; emigrated in 1944; memoirist

Taszycki, Witold (1898–1979): professor at UJK, member of the Polish Academy of Arts and Sciences (PAU), director of the Division of Linguistics at UL; initiated the Mickiewicz dictionary (1940); during the German occupation involved in vocational education and underground teaching

Teisseyre, Stanisław (1905–88): painter, member of *Artes* and the Soviet Artists' Union of Ukraine; during the German occupation involved with Żegota; after the war president of the Fine Arts academies in Gdańsk and Poznań
Teliha, Olena (1906–42): poet, member of the Organization of Ukrainian Nationalists; executed by the Nazis at Babi Yar
Tennenbaum, Chaia: *see* Urim, Chaia
Tennenbaum, Fryderyka: *see* Lille, Irena
Tennenbaum, Helena: *see* Lipl, Helena
Tennenbaum, Henryka (Maria Kwiatkowska): sister of Fryderyka (Irena) Lille
Tennenbaum, Izaak: father of Fryderyka (Irena) Lille
Tennenbaum, Regina (Gnoińska): sister of Fryderyka (Irena) Lille
Terletsky, Mykhailo (1886–1966): Lviv pharmacist, owner of the pharmacy "Pid chornym orlom" (today the Pharmacy Museum), supporter of the arts and philanthropist
Terpyliak, Andry: owner of a horticultural farm, supporter of the arts
Tetmajer, Kazimierz Przerwa (1865–1940): poet and writer affiliated with Young Poland
Timoshenko, Semyon (1895–1970): career military, from 1940 Marshal of the Soviet Union
Tiutiunnyk, Iury (1891–1930): military man, army general of the Ukrainian People's Republic; emigrated in 1920—first to Poland, then to Romania; arrested by the *Cheka* as part of the special operation "Tiutiun" while crossing the border to USSR; executed in Moscow
Tkachuk, Vasyl (1916–44): writer, member of the Soviet Writers' Union of Ukraine, from 1941 in the Red Army
Tolkachov (first name unknown): party functionary
Tolstoy, Aleksei (1883–1945): writer, recipient of Stalin prizes
Tolstoy, Leo (1828–1910): Russian writer and thinker
Tomaszewski, Tadeusz (1910–2000): psychologist, lectured at UJK and UL, 1938–39 received a Polish government scholarship to Paris; 1944–45 representative of the Polish Committee of National Liberation (PKWN) for repatriation; involved in establishing the Maria Curie-Skłodowska University in Lublin; diarist
Tomczyk, Roman (1909–79): writer, rightwing journalist
Tońcio (stage name of Henryk Vogelfänger, 1904–90): radio actor, co-created the show *Wesoła Lwowska Fala* [*Lviv's Merry Wave*]
Toperman, Fryderyk (after the war Topolski): engineer, in June 1941 evacuated into the depths of the USSR; member of the Union of Polish Patriots and the Polish Committee of National Liberation (PKWN); emigrated in 1968; memoirist
Topolnytsky (first name unknown): Lviv physician

Torańska, Teresa (1944–2013): journalist, worked for Jerzy Giedroyc's *Kultura*, and after 1989 for *Gazeta Wyborcza*; conducted investigative interviews with representatives of the establishment of the Polish People's Republic

Trehub, Hnat: chief of the Lviv Department of Health, after the war deputy to the Lviv City Council

Trehubenko, Mykola (1902–37): member of the All-Union Communist Party (Bolsheviks); graduated from the Institute of Red Professors; historian, worked at the Academy of Sciences of the Ukrainian SSR; executed by the NKVD

Tretiakov, Pavel (1832–98): merchant; patron of Russian art, founded a gallery

Trush, Ivan (1869–1941): painter

Trznadel, Jacek (b. 1930): writer and publicist; political activist

Tsurkovsky, Iaroslav (1904–95); avantgarde poet, psychologist, studied at the Ukrainian Underground University, then at the Ukrainian Free University in Prague, 1939–41 secretary of the Lviv chapter of Soviet Writers' Union of Ukraine; during the German occupation Director of the Psychotechnical Institute

Tudor, Stepan (1892–1941): writer, member of the Communist Party of Western Ukraine and the Soviet Writers' Union

Turchynska, Agata (1903–72): writer, member of the literary group Western Ukraine and the Soviet Writers' Union of Ukraine

Turyn, Roman (1900–79): painter, member of the Soviet Artists' Union of Ukraine, discovered the naïve painter Nikifor

Tuwim, Julian (1894–1953): poet, member of the literary group Skamander, worked for *Wiadomości Literackie*, emigrated during World War II

Tychyna, Pavlo (1891–1967): poet, political activist; received the Stalin Prize

Tyktor, Ivan (1896–1982): publisher, political activist; officer in the Ukrainian Galician Army; owned the largest Ukrainian publishing conglomerate; from 1939 in Cracow, emigrated after the war

Tyrowicz, Ludwik (1901–58): graphic artist, member of *Artes*

Tyshchenko, Iury (1880–1953): publisher, editor at the newspaper *Svoboda*; during World War II in Prague

U

Ukrainka, Lesia (Larysa Kosach-Kvitka, 1871–1913): modernist poet and playwright

Ulam, Adam (1922–2000): historian, Sovietologist, professor at Harvard University

Ulam, Józef: father of Adam and Stanisław Ulam

Ulam, Stanisław (1909–84): mathematician, one of the developers of the atomic bomb; from 1935 in the US

Umrilov, Veniamin (1926–?): husband of Nina Marchenko, father of Valerii Marchenko

Urim, Chaja (née Arem): mother of Irena Lille
Utzig, Franciszka: first wife of Jan Lewkowski, the author's grandfather

V

Valchyk, Konstantin: member of the Organization of Ukrainian Nationalists, arrested by the KNVD in 1940
Valnytska, Sofiia (née Krasińska, 1896–1964): painter
Vasylenko, Mykola (1866–1935): historian, civic and political activist; member of the Central Council of Ukraine; chairman of the Academy of Sciences; arrested by the NKVD in 1924
Velázquez, Diego (Diego Rodríguez de Silva y Velázquez, 1599–1660): Baroque painter
Vernadsky, Vladimir (Volodymyr, 1863–1945): philosopher of science, biologist, one of the founders of the All- Ukrainian Academy of Sciences; member of the Academy of Sciences of the Ukrainian SSR; diarist
Verstiuk, Vladyslav (b. 1949): historian, vice-chairman of the Ukrainian Institute of National Remembrance between 2008–10
Vesolovsky, Bohdan (1915–71): composer of popular music, conductor; during World War II in Vienna, emigrated after the war
Viedienieiev, Dmytro (b. 1967): historian, lecturer at the National Academy of the Security Service of Ukraine (SBU), vice-chairman of the Ukrainian Institute of National Remembrance between 2010–14
Vilde, Iryna (pen name of Daryna Polotniuk, née Makohon, 1907–82): writer, member of the Soviet Writers' Union of Ukraine
Vincenz, Stanisław (1888–1971): writer, eulogist of the Hutsulshchyna, memoirist
Vintiuk, Iury (b. 1960): psychologist
Vogel, Debora (1902–42): poet and essayist writing in Yiddish and Polish, friend of Bruno Schulz; affiliated with *Artes*
Volodymyr the Great, St. (ca. 960–1015): Kyiv prince
Voroshilov, Kliment (1881–1969): communist activist, career military; 1934–40 People's Commissar of Defense of the USSR, responsible for Stalinist repressions; Marshal of the USSR
Vozniak, Mykhailo (1881–1954): literary historian, member of the Shevchenko Scientific Society and the Academy of Sciences of the Ukrainian SSR; deputy to the Supreme Soviet of the Ukrainian SSR
Vynnytsky, Oleksandr (after the war Aleksander Winnicki-Radziewicz, 1911–2002): artist, graduated of the Fine Arts Academy in Cracow, member of the Cracow Group, after the war in Lublin (Association of Polish Artists and Designers) and Warsaw

Vynnychenko, Volodymyr (1880–1951): writer, political activist, prime minister of the Ukrainian People's Republic; emigrated in 1919

Vynnychuk, Iury (b. 1952): writer and journalist

W

Wars, Henryk (Warszawski, 1902–77): conductor, popular music composer, from 1942 headed the theatre group of the Polish Armed Forces, from 1947 in Hollywood

Wasilewska, Wanda (1905–64): writer, communist activist, wife of Marian Bogatko (1936–40), and of Oleksandr Korniichuk (from 1941); deputy to the Supreme Soviet of the USSR; from 1941 in the All-Union Communist Party (Bolsheviks), chair of the Union of Polish Patriots, vice-chair of the Polish Committee of National Liberation (PKWN); editor at the publications *Czerwony Sztandar* and *Nowe Widnokręgi*, administrative director at the State Polish Theater in Lviv; memoirist

Wasylewski, Stanisław (1885–1953): writer, author of popular history books, member of the Soviet Writers' Union of Ukraine, during the German occupation editor at *Gazeta Lwowska*; memoirist

Waszyński, Michał (1904–65): film director; in September 1939 in Lviv; deported to Siberia; joined the Anders' Army in 1941; emigrated after the war

Wat, Aleksander (Chwat, 1900–1967): writer and translator; from September 1939 in Lviv, editor at the newspaper *Czerwony Sztandar*; arrested by the NKVD in January 1940; released in November 1941; emigrated in 1959; memoirist

Watowa, Ola (Paulina Wat, née Lew, 1903–91): writer, translator, wife of Aleksander Wat: in 1940 deported to Siberia; memoirist

Ważyk, Adam (Ajzyk Wagman, 1905–1982): writer and translator; from September 1939 in Lviv, editor at the newspaper *Czerwony Sztandar*, member of the Soviet Writers' Union of Ukraine; evacuated into the depths of the USSR in 1941, active in the Union of Polish Patriots; after 1956 affiliated with the anti-communist opposition

Weidlich, Fritz (1898–1952): Austrian conductor, during the German occupation director of the Lviv Theater of the Opera

Weigl, Rudolf (1883–1957): microbiologist, invented the typhus vaccine, director of the Institute for the Study of Typhus and Virology

Weinrich, Max (1894–1969): linguist

Wierzyński, Kazimierz (1894–1969): writer, member of the literary group Skamander; during World War I member of the Polish Military Organization, emigrated in 1939

Wiesenthal, Simon (1908–2005): Jewish activist; during World War II prisoner at the Janowska Camp; co-founded the Jewish Historical Documentation Center, hunted down many fugitive Nazi war criminals; memoirist

Witkacy (Stanisław Ignacy Witkiewicz, 1885–1939): writer and painter; art theorist; formist

Witkowska, Maria: owned a bed and breakfast in Slavske

Wittlin, Józef (1896–1976): writer, member of the literary group Skamander; memoirist

Wnuk, Marian (1906–67): sculptor; during World War II involved with *Żegota*

Wnuk, Rafał (b. 1967): historian, worked at the Polish Institute of National Remembrance and the Museum of World War II in Gdańsk

Wnukowa, Józefa (Józefa Wnuk, 1911–2000): painter, from 1938 in Lviv, wife of Marian Wnuk; memoirist

Wojciechowski, Tadeusz (1918–82): painter, architect, stained-glass artist, member of *Artes*

Wojdysławski, Menachem (1918–42): mathematician, studied at Warsaw University; from 1939 at UL in the Division of Geometry led by Stanisław Mazur; murdered in the Częstochowa Ghetto

Wolchuk, Roman (1922–2014): engineer; from 1941 in Vienna, emigrated to the US after the war; memoirist

Wolski, Jerzy: medical student, *Gulag* prisoner, emigrated after the war

Wóycicki, Kazimierz (b. 1949): political scientist, publicist, active in the anti-communist opposition

Wreciona, Ievhen (1905–75): member of the executive Provod of the Organization of Ukrainian Nationalists (OUN); organized a militia in Lviv in 1941; co-founded the Ukrainian Insurgent Army in 1942

Wyczółkowski, Leon (1852–1936): painter

Y

Yanukovych, Viktor (b. 1950): 2010–14 president of Ukraine

Z

Zabolotny, Danylo (1866–1929): microbiologist, chairman of the Ukrainian Academy of Sciences (VUAN)

Zaiats, Mykhailo (1889–1941): communist activist; member of the Communist Party of Western Ukraine and the Ukrainian Peasants' and Workers' Socialist Alliance (Sel-Rob), arrested by the NKVD in 1939, murdered in prison

Zajączkowski, Mariusz (b. 1974): historian, worked at the Lublin division of the Office of Public Education

Zakrzewski, Stanisław (1873–1936): historian, professor at UJK, member of the Polish Academy of Arts and Sciences (PAU); political activist; senator from the

Nonpartisan Bloc for Cooperation with the Government (BBWR) in the in the Second Polish Republic

Załużna, Anna: wife of a Lviv physician

Zarembianka, Maria (1897–1957): actress

Zarytska, Kateryna (1914–86): daughter of Myron Zarytsky and wife of Mykhailo Soroka; member of the Organization of Ukrainian Nationalists; arrested by the NKVD in 1940; during the German occupation organized the Ukrainian Red Cross; from 1944 liaison for Roman Shukhevych

Zarytsky, Myron (1889–1961): mathematician, member of the Shevchenko Scientific Society and the Polish Mathematical Society, professor at UL

Zerov, Mykola (1890–1937): poet, literary scholar, leader of the Kyiv Neoclassicists

Zhuravliov, Viktor (1914–69): physicist, division director at the Medical Institute

Zierhoffer, August (1893–1969): geographer, professor at UJK and UL

Zimińska, Mira (Marianna Zimińska-Sygietyńska,1901–97): actress and director

Zwoliński, Przemysław (1914–81): linguist, Slavist, lectured at UL

Ż

Żaba, Jarosław (1915–83): communist activist, emigrated after World War II

Żeleński, Tadeusz (pen name Boy, 1874–1941): writer, critic, translator of French literature, liberal publicist, medical school graduate, member of the Polish Academy of Literature; 1939–41 professor at UL, murdered by the Nazis on Wuleckie Hills

Żeleński, Władysław (1903–2006): lawyer, historian, publicist; emigrated in 1939; worked for Jerzy Giedroyc's *Kultura* and for *Zeszyty Historyczne*

Żeromski, Stefan (1864–1925): writer; first chairman of the Polish Pen Club

Żygulski, Kazimierz (1919–2012): cultural historian, sociologist; memoirist

Żyliński, Eustachy (1889–1954): mathematician, professor at UJK and UL, during the German occupation organized underground education

Bibliography

PRINTED BOOKS AND ARTICLES

Albert, Zygmunt. "Kaźń profesorów lwowskich." http://www.lwow.com.pl/albert/.

———. *Lwowski wydział lekarski w czasie okupacij hitlerowskiej, 1941–1944.* Wrocław: Zakład Narodowy im. Ossolińskich, 1975.

Anders, Władysław. *Bez ostatniego rozdziału. Wspomnienia z lat 1939–1946.* Lublin: Test, 1992.

Andrusiak, Mykola. "Zhmutok spohadiv u zv'iazku z redahuvanniam d-rom Olehom Kandyboiu 'Zbirnyka Ukraïns′koho naukovoho instytutu v Amerytsi'," *Ukraïns′kyi istoryk*, no. 1–4 (1976): 110–13.

Andrzejewski, Zenon. "Adwokat dr Maurycy Axer (1886–1942)." *Palestra* 11–12 (2012). Accessed July 16, 2014. http://palestra.pl/old/index.php?go=artykul&id=1451.

"Anonymous report of a young escapee from Warsaw." In *Archiwum Ringelbluma. Konspiracyjne Archiwum Getta Warszawy*, edited by Andrzej Żbikowski, vol. 3: *Relacje z Kresów*. Warsaw: Żydowski Instytut Historyczny, 2000.

Antoniuk, Natalia. *Ukrains′ke kul′turne zhyttia v "Heneral′niy Hubernii" (1939–1944 rr.). Za materialamy periodychnoï presy* (Lviv: NANU—L′vivs′ka naukova biblioteka im. V. Stefanyka, 1997.

Antonych, Bohdan Ihor. *Tvory*, edited by Mykhailo Moskalenko and Lubov Holovata. Kyiv: Dnipro, 1998.

Axer, Erwin. *Z pamięci*. Warsaw: Iskry, 2006.

Bahan, Oleh. "Koryfei liberal′noï literaturnoï krytyky." Foreword to Mykhailo Rudnyts′kyi, *Vid Myrnoho do Khvyl′ovoho; Mizh ideieiu i formoiu*. Drohobych: Vidrodzhennia, 2009.

Baran, Volodymyr, and Vasyl′ Tokars′kyi, *Ukraïna: Zakhidni zemli 1939–1941*. Lviv: Instytut ukraïnoznavstva NAN Ukraïny, 2009.

Bartlowa, Maria. "Pamiętnik Marii Bartlowej." *Zeszyty Historyczne* 81 (1987): 34–65.

Bazhan-Lauer, Nina Volodymyrivna, ed. *Karbovanykh sliv volodar. Spohady pro Mykolu Bazhana*. Kyiv: Dnipro, 1988.

Beliaev, Vladimir. "Losy uczonych lwowskich." *Nowe Widnokręgi* 23–4 (1944): 11.

Beliaev, Vladimir, and Mikhail Rudnitskii. *Pod chuzhimi znamenami*. Moscow: Molodaia gvardiia, 1954.

Bilas, Vasyl′. "Ahenturna sprava 'Khodiachye.' NKVD proty UHKTs." *Istorychna pravda*, April 15, 2011. http://www.istpravda.com.ua/articles/2011/04/15/36016.

Bilokin′, Serhii. "Tabirnyi zoshyt Iaroslavy Muzyky." *Studii mystetstvoznavchi* 36, no. 4 (2011): 144–50.

Blumenfeld, Samuel. *Człowiek, który chciał być księciem*. Warsaw: Świat Książki, 2008.

Boberski, Jan, Stanisław Marian Brzozowski, Konrad Dyba, Zbysław Popławski, Jerzy Schroeder, Robert Szewalski, and Jerzy Węgierski, eds. *Politechnika Lwowska 1844–1945*. Wrocław: Wydawnictwo Politechniki Wrocławskiej, 1993.

Bohusz-Szyszko, Zygmunt. *Czerwony sfinks*. London: Polski Dom Wydawniczy, 1946.

Boichuk, Mykhailo. *Al′bom-kataloh zberezhenykh tvoriv*, compiled by Vita Susak. Lviv: Oranta-Druk, 2010.

Bolianovs′kyi, Andrii. *Ubyvstvo pols′kykh uchenykh u L′vovi v lypni 1941 roku: fakty, mify, rozslidu-vannia*. Lviv: Vydavnytstvo Lvivs′koï politekhniky, 2011.

Bonusiak, Włodzimierz. *Kto zabił profesorów Lwowskich?* Rzeszów: Krajowa Agencja Wydawnicza, 1989.

——— . *Polityka ludnościowa i ekonomiczna ZSRR na okupowanych ziemiach polskich w latach 1939–1941*. Rzeszów: Wydawnictwo Uniwersytetu Rzeszowskiego, 2006.

Borucki, Gwidon. "Polscy artyści w czasie II wojny światowej, cz.1: Przymusowe tournee po Rosji." *Polski Kurier/Polish Kurier: polsko-australijskie czasopismo społeczno-kulturalne* 116–117 (1997): 28–30. http://www.e-teatr.pl/pl/dokumenty/2015_12/69711/g_b____polscy_artysci_w_czasie_ii_wojny_swiatowej__cz__1__polish_kurier__no__116_117__1997.pdf.

Borwicz, Michał M. "Inżynierowie dusz." *Zeszyty Historyczne* 3 (1963): 121–63.

——— . *Literatura w obozie*. Cracow: Centralna Żydowska Komisja Historyczna, 1946.

———, ed. *Pieśń ujdzie cało*. Cracow: Centralna Komisja Historyczna, 1947.

Bruski, Jan Jacek. "Nieznane polskie dokumenty na temat Hołodomoru. Efekty rekonesansu archiwalnego w Moskwie." *Nowa Ukraina* 5–6 (2008): 64–76.

Brystygier, Mykhail. "Mykele, Maikl, Michel′, Mykhel′ … Beseda Nykolaia Rasheeva s Mykhailom Brystyherom." Interview by Nykolai Rasheev. *Iehupets'* 22 (2013): 385–413.

Brzoza, Jan. *Moje przygody literackie*. Katowice: Śląsk, 1967.

Buczek, Roman. "Działalność opiekuńcza Ambasady RP w ZSRR w latach 1941–1943." *Zeszyty Historyczne* 29 (1974): 42–115.

Chiger, Ignacy. *Świat w mroku. Pamiętnik ojca dziewczynki w zielonym sweterku*. Warsaw: PWN, 2011.

Chłosta, Joanna. *Polskie życie literackie we Lwowie w latach 1939–1941 w świetle oficjalnej prasy polskojęzycznej*. Olsztyn: Wydawnictwo Uniwersytetu Warmińsko-Mazurskiego, 2000.

Chodorowski, Jerzy. "Lwowskie zderzenie cywilizacji. Ze wspomnień o Profesorze Wincentym Stysiu," *Nowy Przegląd Wszechpolski* 11–12 (2005): 11–15.

Chruszczow, N. S. "Fragmenty wspomnień N. S. Chruszczowa." *Zeszyty Historyczne* 132 (2000): 109–92.

Ciesielska, Maria. "Ludwick Fleck—profesor mikrobiologii i filozof (1896–1961)." http://lwow.eu/fleck/fleck.html.

Cieślikowa, Agnieszka. *Prasa okupowanego Lwowa*. Warsaw: Neriton, 1997.

Cieszyński, Tomasz. "Działalność Wydziału Lekarskiego UJK we Lwowie w czasie II wojny światowej od września 1939 do sierpnia 1944 roku." *Archiwum Historii i Filozofii Medycyny* 58. 2 (1995): 141–52.

——— . "O profesorze Jakubie Parnasie na tle Lwowa z lat 1938 do 1945." *Archiwum Historii i Filozofii Medycyny* 61. 2 (1997).

Cohen, Robert S., and Thomas Schnelle, eds. *Cognition and Fact—Materials on Ludwik Fleck,\.* Boston: D. Reidel Publishing Company, 1986.

Czarnik, Oskar Stanisław. "Leszek Czarnik—jeden z 'Argonautów'. Z dziejów konspiracji na Ziemiach Wschodnich, 1939–1941." *Zeszyty Historyczne* 141 (2002): 177–92.

Czekanowska, Anna. *Świat rzeczywisty—świat zapamiętany. Losy Polaków we Lwowie 1939–1941.* Lublin: Norbertinum, 2010.

Czekanowski, Jan. *Sto lat antropologii polskiej 1856–1956. Ośrodek lwowski.* Wrocław: Polska Akademia Nauk, 1956.

Czermakowa, Izabella. "Dom na Krasuczynie." In *Czarownik przy zielonej skale: Marek Włodarski—Henryk Streng,* edited by Józef Chrobak, Justyna Michalik, and Marek Wilk, 21–4. Poznań: Galeria Piekary, 2009.

Danylenko, Vasyl', and Serhii Kokin, eds. *Radians'ki orhany derzhavnoï bezpeky u 1939–1941 r. Dokumenty HDA SB Ukraïny.* Kyiv: Vydavnychyi dim "Kyievo-Mohylians'ka Akademiia," 2009.

Danylenko, Vasyl'. *Ukraïns'ka intelihentsiia i vlada. Zvedennia sekretnoho viddilu DPU USRR 1927–1929 rr.* Kyiv: Tempora, 2012.

Dashkevych, Iaroslav. "Borot'ba z Hrushevs'kym ta ioho shkoloiu u L'vivs'komu universyteti za radians'kykh chasiv." In *Mykhailo Hrushevs'kyi i ukraïns'ka istorychna nauka. Materialy konferentsiï,* edited by Iaroslav Hrytsak and Iaroslav Dashkevych. Lviv: Instytut istorychnykh doslidzhen' L'vivs'koho derzhavnoho universytetu imeni Ivana Franka, Instytut ukraïns'koï arkheohrafiï ta dzhereloznavstva im. Mykhaila Hrushevs'koho; NAN Ukraïny, L'vivs'ke viddilennia, 1999.

———. *Postati. Narysy pro diiachiv istoriï, polityky, kul'tury.* Lviv: Piramida, 2007.

Demianchuk-Tomych, Iaroslava. "Do istoriï L'vivs'koho derzhavnoho universytetu im. Ivana Franka." *Zona* 4 (1993): 188–95.

Dimarov, Anatolii. *Prozhyty i rozpovisty. Povist' pro simdesiat lit.* Kyiv: Dnipro, 1998.

Dokumenty XX veka. Vsemirnaia istoriia v Internete. http://doc20vek.ru/node/2301.

Dombrovs'kyi, Oleksandr. "Do istoriï l'vivs'koho universytetu v 1939–1941 rr. (spohad u 20-ti rokovyny)." *Kyiv* 2 59 (1960): 31–5.

———. *Spomyny,* vol. 6. New York: Ukraïns'ke istorychne tovarystvo, 2009.

Dorabialska, Alicja. *Jeszcze jedno życie.* Warsaw: PAX, 1972.

Dovhopolyi, Iaroslav. "Piter Menten i lvivs'ki rozstrilni spysky." *Zaxid.net* (June 12, 2012). https://zaxid.net/piter_menten_i_lvivski_rozstrilni_spiski_n1272557.

Draus, Jan. *Uniwersytet Jana Kazimierza we Lwowie 1918–1946. Portret kresowej uczelni.* Cracow: Księgarnia Akademicka, 2006.

Duda, Roman. *Lwowska Szkoła Matematyczna.* Wrocław: Wydawnictwo Uniwersytetu Wrocławskiego, 2007.

Dziuba, Ivan. *Spohady i rozdumy na finishnii priamii.* Kyiv: Krynytsia, 2008.

Engel, David. "The Polish Government-in-Exile and the Erlich–Alter Affair." In *Jews in Eastern Poland and the USSR, 1939–46,* edited by Norman Davies and Antony Polonsky, 172–82. London: Macmillan, 1991.

Ferr, Grover, and Vladimir Bobrov. *1937. Pravosudie Stalina. Obzhalovaniiu ne podlezhit.* Moscow: Iauza Eksmo, 2010.

Feuerman, Eleasar J., and Laurence Weinbaum. "My Lost Professors of Medicine in Lvov: Remembering the Early Victims of the Nazis." *Dermatopathology: Practical & Conceptual* 7, no. 4 (2001). https://www.derm101.com/dpc-archive/october-december-2001-volume-7-no-4/dpc0704a07-my-lost-professors-of-medicine-in-lvov-remembrance-of-early-victims-of-the-nazis/.

Filippov, Sergei. *Deiatel´nost´ organov VKP(b) v zapadnykh oblastiakh Ukrainy i Belorussii v 1939–1941 gg.*, vol. 1: *Represii protiv poliakov i pol´skikh grazhdan. Istoricheskie sborniki "Memoriala."* Moscow: Zven´ia, 1997.

Fleck, Ludwik. "Pathology of the Holocaust." http://www.ludwik-fleck-kreis.org/uploadfiles/documents/2801_002803_070404-LF-PathologyoftheHolo(3).pdf.

———. *Entstehung und Entwicklung einer wissenschaftlichen Tatsache*. Basel: Benno Schwabe & Co., 1935.

Friedman, Filip. *Zagłada Żydów lwowskich*, vol. 4. Łódź: Wydawnictwo Centralnej Żydowskiej Komisji Historycznej przy Centralnym Komitecie Żydów Polskich, 1945.

Gałęzowski, Marek. *Na wzór Berka Joselewicza. Żołnierze i oficerowie pochodzenia żydowskiego w Legionach Polskich*. Warsaw: Instytut Pamięci Narodowej, 2010.

Gańczak, Filip. "Szwajcar, czyli szpion," *pamiec.pl*. 10 (2013). https://pamiec.pl/pa/tylko-u-nas/12898,SZWAJCAR-CZYLI-SZPION-artykul-Filipa-Ganczaka.html.

Gedroits´, Iezhy. "Pro vidnoshennia do ukraïnt´siv." *Visti kombatanta* 31 (1976): 34–5.

Gleichgewicht, Bolesław. *Widziane z oddali*. Wrocław: Wydawnictwo Dolnośląskie, 1993.

Glembotskaia, Galina. *Evreiskie khudozhniki Galitsii, pogibshie v gody fashistskoi okkupatsii*. Kyiv: Arkhiv Tsentru Iudaiky, 2003.

Głowacki, Albin. *Sowieci wobec Polaków na ziemiach wschodnich II Rzeczypospolitej w latach 1939–1941*. Łódź: Wydawnictwo Uniwersytetu Łódzkiego, 1997.

Gogol, Bogusław. *"Czerwony Sztandar." Rzecz o sowietyzacji ziem Małopolski Wschodniej: wrzesień 1939–czerwiec 1941*. Gdańsk: Wydawnictwo Uniwersytetu Gdańskiego, 2000.

Gross, Jan Tomasz. *Revolution from Abroad: The Soviet Conquest of Poland's Western Ukraine and Western Belorussia*. Princeton: Princeton University Press, 2002.

———. *Studium zniewolenia. Wybory październikowe 22.X.1939*. Cracow: Universitas, 1999.

Grubiński, Wacław. *Między młotem a sierpem*. London: Stowarzyszenie Pisarzy Polskich, 1948.

Grzybowski, Jerzy. *Białorusini w polskich regularnych formacjach wojskowych w latach 1918–1945*. Warsaw: Rytm, 2006.

Haidabura, Valerii. *Teatr mizh Hitlerom i Stalinym*. Kyiv: Fakt, 2004.

Halkin, Hillel. "Wielka żydowska wojna językowa." *Scriptores* 2 (2003): 56–63

Hanitkevych, Iaroslav. "Istorychni etapy naistarshoho v Ukraini L'vivs'koho Natsional'noho medychnoho universytetu im. Danyla Halyts'koho." http://ntsh.org/content/ganitkevich-yaroslav-istorichni-etapi-naystarshogo-v-ukrayini-lvivskogo-nacionalnogo.

Hartman, Stanisław. *Wspomnienia (lwowskie i inne)*. Wrocław: Leopoldinum, 1994.

Hescheles, Janina. *Oczyma dwunastoletniej dziewczynki*. Cracow: Wojewódzka Żydowska Historyczna, 1946.

Hirszfeld, Ludwik. *The Story of One Life*. Translated and edited by Marta A. Balińska and William H. Schneider. Rochester: University of Rochester Press, 2010.

Hlembots′ka, Halyna. "Iudaïka. Z istoriï pryvatnoho ta muzeinoho kolektsionerstva u L′vovi." In *Obrazy znykloho svitu: Ievreï Skhidnoï Halychyny (seredyna XIX–persha tretyna XX stolittia). Kataloh vystavky*, edited by Halyna Hlembots′ka and Vita Susak, 15–22. Lviv: Tsentr Ievropy, 2003.

Hnatiuk, Ola and Katarzyna Kotyńska, eds. *Prolog, nie epilog. Poezja ukraińska w polskich przekładach pierwszej połowy XX wieku.* Warsaw: SOW, 2002.

Hnatiuk, Ola. "Modyfikovana retseptsiia. Vydavnycha praktyka komunistychnoï Pol′shchi ta ukraïns′ka kul′tura," *Ukraïna Moderna* 16 (2010): 183–97.

———. "Piotr Dunin-Borkowski." *Zeszyty Historyczne* 155 (2006): 188–225.

Holovata, Larysa. *Ukraïns′ke vydavnytstvo u Krakovi—L′vovi 1939–1945*, vol. 1. Kyiv: Krytyka, 2010.

Homo Politicus [Ivan Kedryn-Rudnyts′kyi]. *Prychyny upadku Pol′shchi*. Cracow: Ukraïns′ke vydavnytstvo, 1940.

Horodys′kyi, Zenon. "Derzhavnyi universytet im. Ivana Franka u L′vovi. Spohad z chasiv soviets′koi okupatsii v 1939–1941 rokakh." *Svoboda* 23–29 (1989).

———. "Nezabutnii epizod iz chasu soviets′koi okupatsii Halychyny." *Svoboda* 188 (1987).

Horyn′, Bohdan. *Ne til′ky pro sebe. Knyha persha (1955–1965)*. Kyiv: Pul′sary, 2006.

Horyn′, Vasyl′. "Sprava Kateryny Hrushevs′koï u svitli novykh dokumentiv." *Ukraïna: kulturna spadshchyna, natsional′na svidomist′, derzhavnist′* 15: *Confraternitas: Iuvileinyi zbirnyk na poshanu Iaroslava Isaievycha* (2006–2007): 782–91.

Hryciuk, Grzegorz. "Całkiem dobre miejsce na przetrwanie wojny." In *Ukraiński polonofil. Pamięci Bohdana Osadczuka*, edited by Iwona Hofman, 111–22. Lublin: UMCS, 2012.

———. *"Gazeta Lwowska" 1941–1944*. Wrocław: Wydawnictwo Uniwersytetu Wrocławskiego, 1996.

———. "Polacy we Lwowie pod okupacją radziecką i niemiecką." Ph.D. dissertation. Wrocław: Instytut Historii Uniwersytetu Wrocławskiego, 1993. Summary in *Dzieje Najnowsze* 3 (1997): 179–82.

———. *Przemiany narodowościowe i ludnościowe w Galicji Wschodniej i na Wołyniu w latach 1931–1948*. Toruń: Wydawnictwo Adam Marszałek, 2005.

Hrynevych, Vladyslav. *Nepryborkane riznoholossia. Druha svitova viina i suspil′no-politychni nastroï v Ukraïni, 1939–cherven′ 1941 rr.* Dnipropetrovsk: Lira, 2012.

Hryvul, Taras, and Ol′ha Oseredchuk. *"Protses-59": pokolinnia bortsiv ta heroïv.* Lviv: LNU, 2011.

Iedlins′ka, Uliana. *Kyrylo Studyns′kyi (1868–1941). Zhyttiepysno-bibliohrafichnyi narys.* Lviv: Naukove tovarystvo im. Shevchenka, 2006.

Iedynak, Vasyl′ [Ivan Hrechko]. "Nasha zabud′kuvatist′ abo prohramne tlumlennia boliu." *Suchasnist′* 11 (1988): 44–58.

Iekel′chyk, Serhii. *Imperiia pamiati. Rosiis′ko-ukraïns′ki stosunky v radians′kii istorychnii uiavi.* Kyiv: Krytyka, 2008.

Il′nyts′kyi, Mykola. *Krytyky i kryterii. Literaturno-krytychna dumka v Zakhidnii Ukraïni 20–30-ykh rokiv XX st.* Lviv: VTNL, 1998.

———. *Drama bez katarsysu: Storinky literaturnoho zhyttia L′vova polovyny XX stolittia.* Lviv: Instytut ukraïnoznavstva im. I. Kryp′iakevycha NAN Ukrainy, 2008

Inglot, Mieczysław, ed. *Polska kultura literacka Lwowa lat 1939–1941. Ze Lwowa i o Lwowie. Antologia*. Wrocław: Towarzystwo Przyjaciół Polonistyki Wrocławskiej, 1995.

Ironside, Edmund. *Time Unguarded: The Ironside Diaries*. New York: McKay, 1963.

Istoriia Natsional'noi Akademii nauk Ukrainy, 1929–1933: Dokumenty i materialy, edited by Pavlo Sokhan'. Kyiv: Naukova dumka, 1993.

Jahn, Alfred. *Z Kleparowa w świat szeroki*. Wrocław: Ossolineum, 1991.

Jasiewicz, Krzysztof. *Rzeczywistość sowiecka 1939–1941w świadectwach polskich Żydów*. Warsaw: Rytm, 2009.

Kachmar, Volodymyr. "Mykhailo Marchenko—rektor L´vivs´koho derzhavnoho ukraïns´koho universytetu v 1939/1940 rr." *Visnyk l´vivs´koho Universytetu, Seriia Mizhnarodni vidnosyny* 15 (2005): 81–90.

Kalbarczyk, Sławomir. "Kazimierz Bartel pod okupacją sowiecką we Lwowie." *Przegląd Historyczny* 82, no. 2 (1991): 277–300.

———. *Polscy pracownicy nauki ofiary zbrodni sowieckich*. Warsaw: Instytut Pamięci Narodowej, 2001.

Kałuża, Roman. *Stefan Banach*. Warsaw: Wydawnictwo GZ, 1992.

Kaminska, Ida. *My Life, My Theater*. New York: Macmillan, 1973.

Katyń. Dokumenty zbrodni, vol. 2: *Zagłada (marzec-czerwiec 1940)*, edited by Aleksander Gieysztor. Warsaw: Naczelna Dyrekcja Archiwów Państwowych, 1998.

Kaźń profesorów lwowskich—lipiec 1941, edited by Zygmunt Albert. Wrocław: Wydawnictwo Uniwersytetu Wrocławskiego, 1989.

Kedryn, Ivan. "Pol'shcha vpala i nas zadavyla." *Novyi shliakh*, September 29, 1979.

———. *Zhyttia—podii—liudy. Spomyny i komentari*. New York: Chervona Kalyna, 1976.

Kharkevych, Myroslav. *Ia vas ne zabuv. Spomyny 1939–1945*. New York: Ukraïns'ko-amerykans'ka fundatsia "Volia," 1997.

Khonigsman, Iakov. *Katastrofa evreistva Zapadnoï Ukrainy*. Lviv: n.p., 1998.

Klish, Andrii. *Kyrylo Studyns'kyi. Zhyttia ta diial'nist'*. Ternopil: Vydavnytstvo TNPU, 2011.

Knoop, Hans. *The Menten Affair*. New York: Macmillan, 1978.

Knysh, Zinovii. *Za chuzhu spravu: rozpovid' Mykhaila Koziia z sela Bohdanivka povit Skalat pro ioho pryhody v bol'shevyts'komu poloni i v pol's'kii armii henerala Andersa*. Toronto: Sribna Surma, 1961.

Komar, Liuba. *Protses 59-ty*. Lviv: NTSh, 1997.

Kondratenko, Liudmila, and Liudmila Khoinats'ka. "Do 100-richchia vid dnia narodzhennia M. O. Burmystenka." *Ukraïns'kyi istorychnyi zhurnal* 6 (2002): 152–4.

Konopka, Maria, ed. *Bernard Połoniecki, księgarz lwowski: dzienniki, pamiętniki i listy z lat 1880–1943*. Warsaw: Biblioteka Narodowa, 2006.

Kosichev, Anatolii. *Filosofiia, vremia, liudi: vospominaniia i razmyshleniia dekana filosofskogo fakul'teta MGU im. M. Lomonosova*. Moscow: Media Grupp, 2007.

Kostiuk, Hryhorii. *Zustrichi i proshchannia*, vol. 1. Edmonton: Canadian Institute of Ukrainian Studies, 1998. 2nd edition: Kyiv: Smoloskyp, 2008.

Kot, Stanisław. *Listy z Rosji do gen. Sikorskiego*. London: Jutro Polski, 1955.

Kott, Jan. *Still Alive: An Autobiographical Essay*. New Haven: Yale University Press, 1994.

Kovaliuk, Vasyl'. "Kultorolohichni ta dukhovni aspekty radianizatsiï Zakhidnoï Ukraïny (veresen' 1939–cherven' 1941 r.)." *Ukraïns'kyi istorychnyi zhurnal* 2–3 (1993): 3–17.

Kovba, Zhanna. *Liudianist' u bezodni pekla. Povedinka mistsevoho naselennia Skhidnoï Halychyny v roky "ostatochnoho rozviazannia ievreis'koho pytannia."* Kyiv: Biblioteka Instytutu Iudaïky, 2000.

Kowalska, Anna. *Dzienniki 1927–1969*. Warsaw: Iskry, 2008.

Kozak, Bohdan. "Palimpsest ukrains'koho 'Hamleta': pereklad i prapremiera 1943 r." *Visnyk L'vivs'koho universytetu* 3 (2003): 52–75.

Kravchenko, Iaroslav. "Iaroslava Muzyka u tvorchii doli Mykhaila Boichuka: novovyiavleni maliunky l'vivs'koho periodu." *Visnyk LAM* 21 (2010): 361–6.

Krukowska, Helena, ed. *Franciszek Groer. Życie i działalność. Zbiór wspomnień*. Warsaw: PZWL, 1973.

Krushel'nyts'ka, Larysa. *Rubaly lis. Spohady halychanky*. Lviv: L'vivs'ka naukova biblioteka im. V. Stefanyka, 2001.

Kryvyts'ka, Lesia. *Povist' pro moie zhyttia*. Kyiv: Mystetstvo, 1965.

Kulczyńska, Maria. "Raport Karli Lanckorońskiej." *Odra* 4 (1977): 7–18.

Kurylyshyn, Kostiantyn. *Ukraïns'ke zhyttia v umovakh nimets'koï okupatsiï (1939–1944 rr.). Za materialamy ukraïnomovnoï lehal'noï presy*. Lviv: NANU, 2010.

Kuzyk, M. "Vidvidyny u d-ra Maksyma Muzyky." *Likars'kyi visnyk* 21, no. 2 (April 1974): 67–70.

Lanckorońska, Karolina. *Michelangelo in Ravensbruck: One Woman's War against the Nazis*. New York: Da Capo, 2008.

Larina, Anna. *This I Cannot Forget: The Memoirs of Nikolai Bukharin's Widow*. New York: W. W. Norton & Co., 1993.

Lewickyj, Borys. "Einsatzgruppen der Sicherheitspolizei." *Kultura* 150 (1960): 87–90.

Lill', Liudvik. "Suddi ta pidsudni." *Mystetstvo* 4 (1933): 98–9.

Liubchenko, Arkadii. *Shchodennyk Arkadiia Liubchenka*. New York: Kots', 1999.

Luchakivs'ka, Ivanna. *Ukraïns'ka intelihentsiia zakhidnykh oblastei URSR v pershi roky radians'koï vlady (1939–1941 rr.)*. Drohobych: Vidrodzhennia, 1999.

Luts'kyi, Oleksandr. "Intelihentsiia v planakh utverdzhennia radians'koho totalitarnoho rezhymu na zakhidnoukraïns'kykh zemliakh 1939–1941." *Intelihentsiia i vlada. Hromads'ko-politychnyi naukovyi zbirnyk* 1 (2003): 98–104.

Lysiak-Rudnyts'kyi, Ivan. *Istorychni ese*, vol. 1. Kyiv: Osnovy, 1994.

Lysty Mykhaila Hrushevs'koho do Kyryla Studyns'koho. 1894–1932, compiled by Halyna Svarnyk. New York: Kots', 1998.

Lytvyn, Mykola, Oleksandr Luts'kyi, and Kim Naumenko. *1939. Zakhidni zemli*. Lviv: Instytut ukraïnoznavstva NANU im. I. Kryp'iakevycha, 1999.

Łodziana, Tadeusz. "Lwów, Sopot, Warszawa." *Cracovia Leopolis* 2–3 (2001). http://www.cracovialeopolis.pl/index.php?pokaz=art&id=939.

———. *Wspomnienia: Państwowy Instytut Sztuk Plastycznych 1937–1943 we Lwowie*. Wrocław: Sudety, 2003.

Łukaszewicz, Piotr. *Roman i Margit Sielscy. Obrazy z kolekcji Piotra Wojno i z innych zbiorów polskich. Katalog wystawy*. Wrocław: Muzeum Narodowe we Wrocławiu, 2004.

Mahl′ovanyi, Anatolii and Vasyl′ Novak. "Do 100-richchia vid dnia narodzhennia profesora Stepana Mykhailovycha Martyniva". Zhurnal Akademiï medychnykh nauk Ukraïny 16, no. 1 (2010): 177–80.

Makarchuk, Vladimir, *Gosudarstvenno--territorial′nyi status zapadno-ukrainskikh zemel′ v period Vtoroi mirovoi voiny. Istoriko-pravovoe issledovanie*. Moscow: Fond sodeistviia aktual′nym istoricheskim issledovaniiam, 2010.

Makaryk, Irena. *Nichyina zemlia: "Hamlet". L′viv, 1943*, vol. 245. Lviv: Zapysky Naukovoho Tovarystva imeni T. Shevchenka; Pratsi Teatroznavchoï komisiï, 2003.

Maksymenko, Svitlana. "Frahmenty kryminal′noï spravy Andriia Petrenka—pershoho dyrektora ukraïns′koho teatru mista L′vova—L′vivs′koho opernoho teatru (1941–1942)," *Studii mystetstvoznavchi* 2 (2008): 67–79.

———. "'Kliuchi' Petra Soroky (epizody zhyttia i tvorchosti myttsia)." *Prostsenium* 2–3 (2006): 14–21.

———. "Sprava ioho zhyttia (frahmenty kryminal′noï spravy I. Stadnyka)." *Prostsenium* 1 (2001): 20–35.

———. "Tvorcha diial′nist′ 'Ukraïns′koho teatru mista L′vova—L′vivs′koho opernoho teatru' (1941–1944 rr.) v konteksti istoriï natsional′noho stsenichnoho mystetstva," PhD diss., Instytut mystetstvoznavstva, fol′klorystyky ta etnolohiï im. M. T. Ryl′s′koho NAN Ukraïny, 2008.

Malaniuk, Ievhen. *Knyha sposterezhen′. Proza*. Toronto: Homin Ukraïny, 1962.

Maligranda, Lech, and Jarosław Prytuła. "Przesłuchania Stefana Banacha z 1944." *Wiadomości Matematyczne* 48, no. 1 (2012): 51–72.

Marchenko, Mykhailo. *Borot′ba Rosiï i Polshchi za Ukraïnu u pershe desiatylittia pryiednannia Ukraïny do Rosiï, 1654–1664 rr.* Kyiv: Vydavnytstvo AN URSR, 1941.

"Marchenko, Mykhailo." *Internet Encyclopedia of Ukraine*. www.encyclopediaofukraine.com.

Marchenko, Nadiia, and Vasylii Ovsiienko. "U borot′bi za syna. Interviu Nadiï Mykhailivny Marchenko Vasyliu Ovsiienku, 16.06.1998." In *Matinka Nina. Spohady pro Ninu Mykhailivnu Marchenko (Smuzhanytsiu)*, edited by Andrii Horbal′ and Nataliia Puriaieva, 16–18. Kyiv: Smoloskyp, 2013.

Marchenko, Valerii. *Lysty do materi z nevoli*. Kyiv: Fundatsiia im. O. Ol′zhycha, 1994.

Maszewski, Jarosław. "Rozmowa ze Stanisławem Teisseyre'm." *Zeszyty Artystyczne* 19 (2012): 3–16.

Matseliukh, Ievhen. "Ukraïntsi v Armiï Andersa." *Pols′ki studiï* 7 (2014): 105–16.

Mazur, Grzegorz. "Polityka sowiecka na 'Zachodniej Ukrainie' 1939–1941. Zarys problematyki." *Zeszyty Historyczne* 130 (1999): 68–95.

———. "Zamach na marszałka Józefa Piłsudskiego." *Annales Universitatis Mariae Curie-Skłodowska*, Sectio F: *Historia* 60 (2005): 407–17.

Mazur, Grzegorz, Jerzy Skwara, and Jerzy Węgierski. *Kronika 2350 dni wojny i okupacji Lwowa. 1.IX.1939–5.II.1946*. Warsaw: Unia, 2007.

Michalski, Stanisław, and Seweryn Dziamski. *Filozoficzne i pedagogiczne poglądy Stefana Rudniańskiego*. Warsaw: Książka i Wiedza, 1980.

Microfiche from the investigation of Ahatanhel Krymsky. *Skhidnyi svit* 2 (1996): 17–21.

Mirek, Alfred. *Tiuremnyi rekviem. Zapiski zakliuchennogo*. Moscow: Prava cheloveka, 1997.

Motyka, Grzegorz, and Rafał Wnuk. *Pany i rezuny. Współpraca AK-WiN i UPA 1945–1947*. Warsaw: Volumen, 1997.

Movchan, Iulian. "Dvadtsat' piat' rokiv tomu (u 25-ti rokovyny smerty d-ra M. Panchyshyna)." *Likars'kyi visnyk* 15 4 (1968): 50–3.

———. "Studiï medytsyny u L'vovi za nimets'koï okupatsiï." *Likars'kii zbirnyk. Medytsyna i biolohia. Nova seriia* 17 (2010): 228–41.

Musiienko, Oleksa, ed. *Z poroha smerti. Pys´mennyky Ukraïny—zhertvy stalins´kykh represii*. Kyiv: Radians´kyi pys´mennyk, 1991.

Muzyka, Maksym, and Fryderyka Lille. "Sprawa związku pomiędzy szybkością opadania krwinek a grupami krwi." *Wiadomości Lekarskie* 12 (1932): 3–6.

Nahaylo, Bohdan. "The Muse of Bloodlands. Reconstructing the concealed biography of Renata Bogdańska-Anders, aka Irena Yarosevych." Presentation at the Ukrainian Institute in London. ukrainianinstitute.org.uk/news_182/.

Nakonechnyi, Ievhen. *"Shoa" u L'vovi*. Lviv: Piramida, 2006.

Nazaruk, Osyp. *595 dniv soviets'kym viaznem*. Toronto: Vydavnytstvo i drukarnia oo. vasyliian, 1950.

———. *Ucieczka ze Lwowa do Warszawy. Wspomnienia ukraińskiego konserwatysty z pierwszej połowy października 1939 r*. Przemyśl: Południowo-Wschodni Instytut Naukowy, 1999.

Niurnbergskii protsess. Sbornik materialov v 8 tomakh, vol. 5. Edited by A. M. Rekunkov et al. Moscow: Iuridicheskaia literatura, 1991.

Olesiak, Zbigniew. "O lwowskim środowisku akademickim podczas wojny." *Kwartalnik Historii Nauki i Techniki* 46, no. 2 (2001): 35–63.

Osinchuk, Roman. "Mar'ian Panchyshyn i Maksym Muzyka—profesory ukrains'koho (taiemnoho) universytetu (1920–1924)." *Likars'kii zbirnyk. Nova seriia* 4 (1996): 138–40.

———. "Orhanizatsiia okhorony zdorov'ia u l'vivs'kii oblasti (1939–1941 rr.)." *Likars'kii zbirnyk. Medytsyna i biolohiia. Nova seriia* 18 (2010): 191–226.

Ostroverkha, Mykhailo. *Nova imperiia: Italiia i fashyzm*. Lviv: Dorohy, 1938.

———. *Na zakruti. Osin' 1939 r*. New York: self-published, 1958.

Ostrowski, Stanisław. *Dnie pohańbienia. Wspomnienia z lat 1939–1941. W obronie polskości ziemi lwowskiej*. Warsaw: Pokolenie, 1986.

Pan'kivs'kyi, Kost'. *Roky nimets'koï okupatsiï*. New York: Kliuchi, 1965.

———. *Vid Derzhavy do Komitetu (Lito 1941 roku u L'vovi)*. Toronto: Kliuchi, 1970.

Pavlovs'kyi, Mykhailo. *Na skhreshchenykh dorohakh zhyttia Sofii Parfanovych. Do 100-richchia ULT u L'vovi*. Lviv: KOS, 2010.

Petriakova, Faina. "Maksymil'ian Gol'dshtein. Storinky biohrafiï." *Ï* 51 (2008). http://www.ji.lviv.ua/n51texts/petryakova.htm.

Pinchevs'ka, Bohdana. "Tvorcha biohrafiia Otto Hana ta osoblyvosti vyvchennia tvorchoho spadku ievreis'kykh khudozhnykiv Skhidnoï Halychyny." *Judaica Ukrainica* 1 (2012): 264–84.

Pinchuk, Ben-Cion. "Cultural Sovietization in a Multi-Ethnic Environment: Jewish Culture in Soviet Poland, 1939–1941." *Jewish Social Studies* 48, no. 2 (1986): 163–174.

Plichko, Anatolii and Iaroslav Prytula. "Do 60-richchia publikatsii ukrains'koho perekladu knyhy S. Banakha." *Matematychni studii* 30, no. 1 (2008).

Podorozhnyi, Nikolai. *Osvoboditel'naia voina ukrainskogo naroda (1648–1654 gg.)*. Moscow: Gosudarstvennoe voennoe izdatel'stvo Narkomata oborony SSSR, 1939.

Polons'ka-Vasylenko, Nataliia. "Akademik Ahatanhel Iukhimovych Kryms'kyi 1871–1941." *Ukraïns'kyi istoryk* 3–4 (1971): 90–98.

———. *Spohady*. Kyiv: Kyievo-Mohylians'ka Akademiia, 2011.

Popielski, Bolesław, and Wanda Wojtkiewicz-Rok. "Dzieje Wydziału Lekarskiego Uniwersytetu Jana Kazimierza we Lwowie 1939–1944." In *Lwowskie środowisko naukowe w latach 1939–1945*, edited by Irena Stasiewicz-Jasiukowa, 58–83. Warsaw: Polska Akademia Nauk, 1993.

Poraj, Kazimiera. "Dziennik lwowski." *Biuletyn Żydowskiego Instytutu Historycznego* 52 (1964): 79–106.

Prus, Edward. *Herosi spod znaku tryzuba*. Warsaw: Instytut Wydawniczy Związków Zawodowych, 1985.

Putrament, Jerzy. *Pół wieku. Wojna*. Warsaw: Książka i Wiedza, 1984.

Rakovs'kyi, Ivan. "Spomyny pro Naukove Tovarystvo im. Tarasa Shevchenka u L'vovi." *Ukrains'kyi istoryk* 1–4 (1979): 91–101.

Reabilitovani istoirieiu. L'vivs'ka oblast', vol. 1, edited by P. T. Tron'ko et al. Kyiv: Astroliabiia, 2009.

Red'ko, Iulian. *Statti, spohady, materialy*. Lviv: LNB, 2006.

Redzik, Adam. "Jak twórca szlagierów wszechczasów nie został adwokatem: rzecz o Emanuelu Schlechterze (1904–1943). W 110 rocznicę urodzin i 70 rocznicę śmierci." *Palestra* 1–2 (2014): 245–55. http://palestra.pl/pdf_pliki/36_redzik_schlechter.pdf.

———. "Wydział Prawa Uniwersytetu Lwowskiego w latach 1939–1945." *Rocznik Lwowski* 1 (2004): 91–125. http://www.lwow.com.pl/rocznik/prawo39–45.html.

Rembiszewska, Dorota, ed. *Zdzisław Stieber (1903–1980). Materiały i wspomnienia*. Warsaw: Slawistyczny Ośrodek Wydawniczy, 2013.

Ripko, Olena. *U poshukakh strachenoho mynuloho. Retrospektyva mystets'koï kul'tury L'vova XX stolittia*. Lviv: Kameniar, 1996.

Romaniv, Oleh, and Inna Feduschchak. *Zakhidnoukraïns'ka tragediia 1941*, vol. 18. New York: Naukove tovarystvo im. Shevchenka, 2002.

Rubl'ova, Nataliia, and Oleksandr Rubl'ov, eds. *Ukraïna i Pol'shcha: dokumenty i materialy 1920–1939 rokiv*. Kyiv: Dukh i Litera, 2012.

Rubl'ov, Oleksandr. "Malovidomi storinky biohrafiï ukraïns'koho istoryka. Mykhailo Marchenko." *Ukraïns'kyi istorychnyi zhurnal* 1 (1996): 106–18.

———. "Ternystyi shliakh ukrains'koho vchenoho-patriota: M. I. Marchenka." In Mykhailo Marchenko, *Kyïvs'ka Rus' u borot'bi z kochovykamy do monhol'skoï navaly; Monohrafiia*, 144–190. Kyiv: Promin', 2012.

———. *Zakhidnoukraïns'ka inteligentsiia u zahal'nonatsional'nykh politychnykh i kul'turnykh protsesakh 1914–1939 rr.* Kyiv: Instytut istoriï NANU, 2004.

Rubl'ov, Oleksandr, and Iurii Cherchenko. *Stalinshchyna i dolia zakhidnoukraïns'koï intelihentsiï 20–50-ti roky XX st.* Kyiv: Naukova dumka, 1994.

Rubl'ov, Oleksandr, and Oksana Iurkova, eds. *Instytut istoriï Ukraïny Natsional'noi Akademii nauk Ukraïny. Dokumenty i materialy 1936–1947*, vol. 1. Kyiv: Instytut istorii Ukraïny NANU, 2011.

Rudnicki, Klemens. *Na polskim szlaku*. London: Gryf, 1957.

Rudnyts'ka, Milena. *Statti. Lysty. Dokumenty*, edited by Myroslava Diadiuk and Marta Bohachevs'ka-Khomiak. Lviv: Misioner, 1998.

———, ed. *Zakhidnia Ukraïna pid bol'shevykamy. Zbirnyk*. New York: Shevchenko Scientific Society, 1958.

———. "Zhyttiepys Mileny Rudnyts'koï." *Vidnova* 1 (1984): 125–28.

Rudzińska, Anna. *O moją Polskę*. Łódź: Lodart, 2003.

Samchuk, Ulas. *Na bilomu koni—na koni voronomu*. Ostroh: Vydavnytstvo Natsional'noho universytetu Ostroz'ka Akademiia, 2007.

———. *Wołyń*, translated by Tadeusz Hollender. Warsaw: Rój, 1938.

Schaff, Adam. *Pora na spowiedź*. Warsaw: BGW, 1993.

Schenk, Dieter. *Der Lemberger Professorenmord und der Holocaust in Ostgalizien*. Bonn: J. H. Dietz, 2007.

Schramm, Hilary. *Kronika Uniwersytetu Jana Kazimierza we Lwowie za rok akademicki 1929/30*. Lviv: Uniwersytet Jana Kazimierza, 1931.

Sels'kyi, Roman, and Ivan Hrechko. "Sel'skyi pro Sel'skoho. Rozmovliav Ivan Hrechko." In *Roman Sels'kyi. Tvory z pryvatnykh zbirok*, edited by Agnesa Bachyns'ka-Sels'ka, 22–9. Lviv: Instytut kolektsionerstva pry NTSh, 2004.

Semchyshyn, Myroslav. *Z knyhy Leva: Ukraïns'kyii L'viv dvadsiatykh-sorokovykh rokiv: spomyny*. Lviv: Naukove tovarystvo im. Shevchenka NTSh, 1998.

Serhiichuk, Volodymyr, Serhii Bohunow et al., eds. *Likvidatsiia UHKTs [1939–1946]. Dokumenty radians'kykh orhaniv derzhavnoï bezpeky*. Kyiv: KNU, Tsentr Ukraïnoznavstva, Instytut istoriï NANU, DA SBU, 2006, vol. 1.

Shevchenko, Serhii, and Dmytro Viedienieiev. *Ukraïns'ki Solovky*. Kyiv: EksOb, 2001.

Shevel'ov, Iurii. *Ia—mene—meni (i dovkruhy). Spohady*, vol. 1. New York: Kots', 2001.

———. "Zhyttia i pratsia Vasylia Simovycha." *Slovo* 23 (1991): 6–7.

Shore, Marci. *Caviar and Ashes: A Warsaw Generation's Life and Death in Marxism, 1918–1968*. New Haven: Yale University Press, 2006.

Shymchuk, Evstakhiia. Foreword to *Margit Sel's'ka: Al'bom*, exhibit catalogue, edited by Taras Lozyns'kyi, 5–12. Lviv: Instytut kolektsionerstva pry NTSh, 2005.

Siemiradzki, Józef. *Kronika Uniwersytetu Jana Kazimierza we Lwowie za rok akademicki 1926/27*. Lviv: Uniwersytet Jana Kazimierza, 1928.

Shchurat, Vasyl'. "Avtobiohrafiia." archive.lnu.edu.ua/avtobiohrafiya-vasylya-schurata.

Slyzh, Adol'f. *Moi lita. Spohady*. Lviv: Manuskrypt, 2014.

Skrzypek, Stanisław. *Rosja, jaką widziałem. Wspomnienia z lat 1939–1942*. Newtown, MT: Montgomeryshire Printing, 1949.

Slyvka, Iurii, Tamara Halaichak, and Oleksandr Luts'kyi, eds. *Kul'turne zhyttia v Ukraini: Zakhidni zemli*. Vol. 1: *1939–1953* and vol. 2: *1953–1966*. Kyiv: Naukova Dumka, 1995.

Sobolew, Siergiej. "Przemówienie wygłoszone na uroczystości ku uczczeniu pamięci Stefana Banacha." *Wiadomości Matematyczne* 4 (1961): 261–64.

Soroka, Bohdan. *Hrafika*. Lviv: Kolir-PRO, 2011.

Sosnovs'ka, Danuta. *Universytet na rozdorizhzhi istrorii*. Kyiv: Smoloskyp, 2011.

Starinov, Il'ia. *Zapiski diversanta*. Moscow: Al'manakh "Vympel" 3 1997.

Stark, Marceli. *A jednak żyję i czuję …* Warsaw: Instytut Pamięci Narodowej, 2013.

Starosol's'ka, Uliana, ed. *Volodymyr Starosol's'kyi, 1878–1942*. Lviv: Zapysky NTSh 1991, vol. 210.

Stasiuk, Oleksandra. "Zhyttievyi shliakh Petra Karmans'koho (hromads'ko-politychnyi aspekt)." *Ukraïna: kul'turna spadshchyna, natsionalna svidomist', derzhavnist'. Zakhidno-Ukraïns'ka Narodna Respublika: do 90-richchia utvorennia. Zbirnyk naukovych prats´* 1 (2009): 535–43.

Steinhaus, Hugo. *Mathematician for All Seasons: Recollections and Notes*. Birkhäuser: Cham, 2015.

Stepanchykova, Tetiana. *Istoriia ievreis'koho teatru u L'vovi : kriz' terny, do zirok!* Lviv: Liha Pres, 2005.

Stepaniv, Olena. *Suchasnyi Lviv*. Lviv: Ukraïns'ke vydavnytstvo, 1943.

Stępień, Stanisław. "Strutyński Michał (1888–1941)." In *Polski Słownik Biograficzny*, vol. 46, bk. 4, (183) 488–90. Warsaw: IH PAN, 2007.

———. "Kyryło Studyńskyj (1868–1941)." In *Złota księga historiografii lwowskiej XIX i XX wieku*, edited by Jerzy Maternicki, Paweł Sierżęga, and Leonid Zaszkilniak, vol. 45, bk. 1, 219–32. Rzeszów: Wydawnictwo Uniwersytetu Rzeszowskiego, 2014.

Stets'kiv, Ievhen. "Studiï u L'vivs'komu Medychnomu Instytuti v roky Druhoï svitovoï viiny 1939–1944." *Narodne zdorov'ia* 11–12 (2009): 248–49.

Stets'ko, Iaroslav. *30 chervnia 1941. Proholoshennia vidnovlennia derzhavnosty Ukraïny*. Toronto: Liga Vyzvolennia Ukraïny, 1967.

Stuchły, Zbigniew, ed. *Zwyciężyc tyfus. Instytut Rudolfa Weigla we Lwowie. Dokumenty i wspomnienia*. Wrocław: Sudety, 2001.

Susak, Vita. *Ukrainian Artists in Paris 1919–1939*. Translated by Serhii Synhaiivsky and Anna Susak. Kyiv: Rodovid, 2010.

Sydorchuk, Taisiia. "Materialy Ahatanhela Kryms'koho v arkhivi Omeliana Pritsaka." *Ukraïns'kyi arkheohrafichnyi shchorichnyk* 18 (2013): 101–16.

Syzdek, Eleonora. Foreword to *Wanda Wasilewska we wspomnieniach*, edited by Eleonora Syzdek. Warsaw: Książka i Wiedza, 1982.

Szałajko, Kazimierz. "Wspomnienia o Stefanie Banachu na tle Lwowa i lwowskiej szkoły matematycznej." *Zeszyty Naukowe Akademii Górniczo-Hutniczej im. S. Staszica, Opuscula Mathematica* 1522, no. 13 (1993): 45–54.

Tarnavs'kyi, Ostap. *Literaturnyi L'viv 1939–1944. Spomyny*. Lviv: Prosvita, 1995.

———. *Vidome i pozavidome*. Kyiv: Chas, 1999.

Terlecki, Ryszard. "The Jewish Issue in the Polish Army in the USSR and the Near East. 1941–1944." In *Jews in Eastern Poland and the USSR, 1939–46*, edited by Norman Davies and Antony Polonsky, 161–71. London: Macmillan, 1991.

Tokarev, Vasilii. "Stalin i Vanda Vasilevskaia: limitirovannyi dialog (1940)." *Przegląd Rusycystyczny* 1, no. 117 (2007): 39–57.

Tomaszewski, Tadeusz. *Lwów. Pejzaż psychologiczny*. Warsaw: Wydawnictwo Instytutu Psychologii Polskiej Akademii Nauk, 1996.

Torańska, Teresa, et al. *Śmierć spóźnia się o minutę, Trzy rozmowy Teresy Torańskiej. Michał Bristiger. Michał Głowiński. Adam Daniel Rotfeld*. Warsaw: Agora, 2010.

Trznadel, Jacek. *Kolaboranci. Tadeusz Boy-Żeleński i grupa komunistycznych pisarzy we Lwowie 1939–1941*. Komorów: Antyk, 1998.

Tsalyk, Stanislav, and Pylyp Selihei. *Taiemnytsi pys'mennyts'kykh shukhliad. Detektyvna istoriia ukraïns'koï literatury*. Kyiv: Nash chas, 2010.

U pivstolitnikh zmahanniakh: Vybrani lysty do Kyryla Studyns'koho (1891–1941), compiled by Oksana Haiova, Uliana Iedlins'ka, and Halyna Svarnyk. Kyiv: Naukova dumka, 1993.

Ulam, Adam B. *Understanding the Cold War: A Historian's Personal Reflections*. New Brunswick, NJ: Transaction Publishers, 2000.

Urbankowski, Bohdan. *Czerwona msza, czyli uśmiech Stalina*. Warsaw: Alfa, 1998.

Val'o, Mariia. "Lysty Marii Hrushevs'koï do Volodymyra Doroshenka (1942–1943 rr.)." *Zapysky L'vivs'koi naukovoï biblioteky im. V. Stefanyka* 12 (2004): 464–94.

Vernadskii, Vladimir. *Dnevniki 1935–1941*, vol. 2: *1939–1941*. Moscow: Nauka, 2008.

Viedienieiev, Dmitrii. "Kontrrazvedchik-gumanist." *Ukrainskii front v voinakh spetssluzhb: Istoricheskie ocherki*. Kyiv: K.I.C., 2008.

———. (as Viedienieiev, Dmytro.) "Kontrrozvidnyk-humanist." *Halyts'ka brama* 1–2 (2010): 19–21.

———. (as Viedienieiev, Dmytro.) "Kryvavyi perelom." www.szru.gov.ua/index_ua/index.html%3Fp=1846.html.

———. (as Viedienieiev, Dmytro.) "Vid dytiachoho sadochka do Instytutu natsional'noi pamiati. Chastyna 2. Pro 'ahenturni' istoriï Viktora Petrova ta Omeliana Pritsaka, spohady Pavla Sudoplatova i doliu Bohdana Stashyns'koho." www.historians.in.ua/index.php/en/intervyu/695-dmytro--vyedyenyeyev-vid-dytyachoho-sadochka-do-instytutu-natsionalnoyi-pamyati-chastyna-2-pro-ahenturni-istorii-viktorapetrova-ta-omeliana-pritsaka-spohady-pavla-sudoplatova-i--doliu-bohdana-stashynskoho.

Viedienieiev, Dmitrii, and Serhii Shevchenko. "Mirotvortsy tainoi voiny." *Kievskii telegraf*, September 3, 2001.

———. "'Sova' prizyvala k primireniiu." *Zerkalo nedeli*, July 15, 2000.

Viedienieiev, Dmytro, and Hryhorii Bystrukhin. *Dvobii bez kompromisiv. Protyborstvo spetspidrozdiliv OUN ta radians'kykh syl spetsoperatsii. 1945–1980-ti roky. Monohrafiia*. Kyiv: K. I. C., 2007.

Vincenz, Stanisław. *Dialogi z Sowietami*. Cracow: Oficyna Literacka, 1986.

Vintiuk, Iurii. "Iaroslav Tsurkovs'kyi: osobystist' i vchenyi." *Politychna psykholohia. Naukovyi zbirnyk*. Lviv: Vydavnychyi tsentr LNU im. Ivana Franka, 2003: 234–38.

Volchuk, Roman. *Spomyny z peredvoiennoho L'vova ta voiennoho Vidnia*. Kyiv: Krytyka, 2002.

Vynnychuk, Iurii. *Tanho smerti*. Kharkiv: Folio, 2012.

Wasilewska, Wanda. *Wspomnienia Wandy Wasilewskiej*, vol. 7. Warsaw: Archiwum Ruchu Robotniczego, 1981.

Wat, Aleksander. *Mój wiek. Pamiętnik mówiony*. Vol. 1. Warsaw: Czytelnik, 1998.

Weliczker, Leon. *Brygada śmierci (Sonderkommando 105). Pamiętnik*, edited by Rachela Auerbach. Łódź: Wydawnictwo Żydowskiej Komisji Historycznej przy Centralnym Komitecie Żydów Polskich, 1946. Reprinted edition: Lublin: Ośrodek "Brama Grodzka—Teatr NN," 2012.

———. *The Janowska Road*. New York: Macmillan, 1963.

Wiertlewska-Bielarz, Jadwiga, and Ludwik Fleck. *Polska szkoła filozofii medycyny. Przedstawiciele i wybrane teksty źródłowe*, edited by Michał Musielak and Jan Zamojski. Poznań: Wydawnictwo Naukowe Uniwersytetu Medycznego im. K. Marcinkowskiego w Poznaniu, 2010.

Wiesenthal, Simon. *The Sunflower: On the Possibilities and Limits of Forgiveness*. New York: Schocken Books, 1997.

Więsław, Witold. "Listy Wacława Sierpińskiego do Stanisława Ruziewicza." *Roczniki Polskiego Towarzystwa Matematycznego. Seria 2: Wiadomości Matematyczne* 40 (2004): 139–67.

Winklowa, Barbara. *Boy we Lwowie 1939–1941*. Warsaw: Rytm, 1992.

Wnukowa, Józefa. "Długie życie upartej dziewczynki. Z profesor Józefą Wnukową rozmawia Henryka Dobosz," interview by Henryka Dobosz. In *Czarownik przy zielonej skale: Marek Włodarski—Henryk Streng*, edited by Jozef Chrobak, Justyna Michalik, and Marek Wilk. Poznań: Galeria Piekary, 2009.

Wolański, Ryszard. *Eugeniusz Bodo: "Już taki jestem zimny drań."* Poznań: Rebis, 2012.

"Wystawa." *Wortal Stefana Banacha*. Accessed April 21, 2013. http://kielich.amu.edu.pl/Stefan_Banach/jpg/wystawa/nbp7.pdf.

Yones, Eliyahu. *Smoke in the Sand: The Jews of Lvov in the War Years 1939–1944*. New York: Gefen, 2004.

Zaitsev, Oleksandr. *Ukraïns'kyi integral'nyi natsionalizm (1920-ti-1930-ti roky). Narysy intelektual'noï istoriï*. Kyiv: Krytyka, 2013.

Zakrynychna, Iryna. "Istoriohrafiia vyvchennia naukovoï tvorchosti Mykhaila Marchenka." *Spetsial'ni istorychni dystsypliny: Pytannia teoriï ta metodyky. Zbirnyk naukovykh prats'* 13, no. 2 (2006): 127–38.

Zashkil'niak, Leonid. "Mykhailo Marchenko." In *Istorychnyi fakul'tet L'vivs'koho natsional'noho universytetu im. Ivana Franka (1940–2000). Iuvileina knyha do 60-ty richchia istorychnoho fakul'tetu*, edited by O. Vynnychenko and O. Tseluiko. Lviv: Vydavnychyi tsentr L'vivs'koho universytetu, 2000.

Zelins'kyi, Oleksandr. "Bohdan Vesolovs'kyi, Renata Bohdans'ka ta Leonid Iablons'kyi—predstavnyky ukraïns'koi rozvazhalnoï muzyky v Halychyni (1930-ti roky)." *Zapysky NTSh* 258 (2009).

Zvyryns'kyi, Karlo. "Mystets'ko-promyslova shkola u L'vovi: spohad." *Visnyk L'vivs'koi Akademiï mystetstv* 5 (1995–1996).

Żeleński, Władysław. "Podroże lwowskich profesorow do Moskwy w r. 1940." *Wiadomości* 23 (1975).

Żongołłowicz, Bogumiła. *Jego były "Czerwone maki." Życie i twórczość Gwidona Boruckiego—Guido Lorraine'a*. Toruń: Oficyna wydawnicza Kucharski, 2010.

"Życiorys." *Wortal Stefana Banacha*. http://kielich.amu.edu.pl/Stefan_Banach/zyciorys.html.

Żygulski, Kazimierz. *Jestem z lwowskiego etapu*. Warsaw: Instytut Wydawniczy PAX, 1994. Accessed September 7, 2014. lwow.home.pl/zygulski/zygulski.html.

Żyndul, Jolanta "Zajścia antyżydowskie w Polsce w latach 1935–1937: geografia i formy." *Biuletyn Żydowskiego Instytutu Historycznego* 3 (1991): 159.

ARCHIVAL SOURCES

Archives of the Ivan Franko National University in Lviv (Arkhiv L'vivs'koho natsional'noho universytetu im. Ivana Franka, ALU)

Nakazy rektora
Osobovi spravy pratsivnykiv L'vivs'koho derzhavnoho universytetu imeni Ivana Franka

Archives of the Judaica Institute, Kyiv (Arkhiv Tsentru Iudaïky)

Galina Glembotskaia fonds, Evreiskie khudozhniki Galitsii, pogibshie v gody fashistskoi okkupatsii

Archives of the National University of Kyiv-Mohyla Academy (Arkhiv Natsional'noho universytetu Kyievo-Mohylians'ka Akademiia)

Omelian Pritsak fonds

Archive of the Polish Academy of Sciences, Warsaw (Archiwum Polskiej Akademii Nauk w Warszawie, Archiwum PAN)

Seweryn Krzemieniewski fonds
Stefan Stasiak fonds
Wacław Sierpiński fonds
Hugo Steinhaus fonds

Archives of the Polish Institute and Sikorski Museum, London (pism.co.uk)

Council of Ministers collection: Polish armed forces

Archives of the Ukrainian Academy of Arts and Sciences in the US

Kost Pankivsky Papers
Sofija Parfanovych Papers
Milena Rudnytska Papers
Rostyslav Yendyk Papers

Author's Private Collection

Lewkowski family collection
Lille, Irena. Correspondence (1945–1988)
Lille, Irena. *Moje życie* [*My Life*]. Manuscript, Saint Cloud (France), January 1981

Central State Archive-Museum of Literature and Art, Kyiv (Tsentral′nyi derzhavnyi arkhiv-muzei literatury i mystetstva, TsDAMLiM)

Natsional′na Spilka Pys′mennykiv Ukraïny
Oleksandr Korniichuk fonds
Mykola Vasylenko fonds (collection of Natalia Polonska-Vasylenko)
Vanda Vasylevska fonds

Central State Historical Archives of Ukraine in Lviv (Tsentral′nyi Derzhavnyi Istorychnyi Arkhiv, L′viv, TsDIAL)

Mykola Andrusiak fonds
Volodymyr Doroshenko fonds
Petro Franko fonds
Maximilian Goldstein fonds
Juliusz Kleiner fonds
Ivan Krypiakevych fonds
Naukove Tovarystvo im. Shevchenka
Narodni Zbory Zakhidnoï Ukraïny
Osyp Nazaruk fonds
Roman Osinchuk fonds
Kost Pankivsky fonds
Spysok zamordovanykh nimtsiamy naukovykh robitnykiv
Volodymyr Starosolsky fonds
Lev Stefanovych fonds
Kyrylo Studynsky fonds
Oleksandr Tysovsky fonds

East Archive of KARTA Center (Archiwum Wschodnie Ośrodka KARTA, OK AW)

Czarnik, Oskar Stanisław. Wspomnienia, rękopis z 1991 roku

Hartman, Stanisław. Wspomnienia Stanisława Hartmana

Krechowiecki, Adam. Wspomnienia Adama Krechowieckiego. Okupacja sowiecka we Lwowie w latach od wejścia Armii Czerwonej we wrześniu 1939 do wkroczenia wojsk niemieckich w czerwcu 1941

Ossowski, Stanisław. Dziennik Stanisława Ossowskiego, podporucznika WP w 1939 roku

Popławski, Zbysław. Wspomnienia Zbysława Popławskiego. Okupanci na Politechnice Lwowskiej. Społeczność uczelni w latach 1939–1945

Rudniański, Jarosław. Relacja Jarosława Rudniańskiego z 2000 roku

Topolski, Fryderyk. Materiały, vol. 1: Wspomnienia i ludzie—Kronika wydarzeń, vol. 2: Korespondencja i materiały osobiste

Zieliński, Zdzisław. Wspomnienia Zdzisława Zielińskiego Lwowskie okupacje

Haluzevyi Derzhavnyi Arkhiv Sluzhby Bezpeky Ukraïny (HDA SBU)

Delo po obvineniiu Geshelesa Genrika Ben'iamovicha

Delo po obvineniiu Marchenko Mikhaila Ivanovicha

Delo po obvineniiu Muzyki Iaroslavy L'vovny

Delo po obvineniiu Sventsitskoi Very Ilarionovny

Delo po obvineniiu Strutinskoi Antoniny Kazimirovny

Dokladnye zapiski i soobshcheniia ob agenturno-operativnoi rabote sredi tserkovnikov

Dokladnye zapiski i spravki na ukrainskikh natsionalistov

Dokladnye zapiski o vskrytii v Zapadnoi Ukraine kontrrevoliutsionnykh organizatsii, 1940 g.

Dokladnye zapiski o reagirovaniiakh naseleniia USSR na sobytiia mezhdunarodnoi i vnutrennei zhizni, 1939 g.

Dokladnye zapiski ob operativnoi rabote, provedennoi NKVD USSR pri prisoedinenii zapadnykh oblastei USSR

Dokladnye zapiski po vskrytiiu i likvidirovaniiu organami NKVD USSR ounovskikh organizatsii, 1940 g.

Dokladnye zapiski NKVD zapadnykh oblastei i protokoly doprosov ukrainskikh natsionalistov, 1940 g.

Materialy agenturno-operativnoi raboty UNKVD po L'vovskoi oblasti 28.10–29.11.1939

O khode razrabotki operativno-chekistskikh grupp Zapadnoi Ukrainy

Perepiska TsK KP(b)U

Protokoly doprosov Tselevicha, Levitskogo, Ianushaitisa i drugikh chlenov politotdela UVO

Spetssoobshcheniia i dokladnye zapiski o vskrytykh i likvidirovannykh organami NKVD USSR kontrrevoliutsionnykh organizatsii pol'skikh natsionalistov, 1940 g.

Spetssoobshcheniia o vskrytii natsionalisticheskogo podpol'ia OUN, 1940 g.

Spetssoobshcheniia o khode pereseleniia spetskontingenta iz zapadnykh oblastei USSR v vostochnye

Spravki o khode pasportizatsii v zapadnykh oblastiakh USSR, 1940 g.

Svedeniia o sostoianii operativnoi raboty UNKVD L'vovskoi oblasti, 1940 g.

Jewish Historical Institute Archives, Warsaw (Archiwum Żydowskiego Instytutu Historycznego)

Department of Documentation of Yad Vashem Distinctions (Dział Dokumentacji Odznaczeń Yad Vashem)

Collection of Memoirs of Holocaust Survivors (Zbiór pamiętników Żydów Ocalałych z Zagłady)

Lviv National Art Galery (L'vivs'ka Natsional'na Halereia Mystetstv im. B. H. Voznyts'koho, LNMH)

Iaroslava Muzyka fonds

Ossolineum Library, Manuscript Division, Wrocław (Biblioteka Ossolineum, Dział Rękopisów)

Steinhaus, Hugo. Wspomnienia z lat 1920–1964
Stieber, Zdzisław. Lwowskie wspomnienia z lat 1937–1944

National Library of Poland in Warsaw (Biblioteka Narodowa w Warszawie)

Shevchenko Scientific Society Archives (Arhiwum Naukowego Towarzystwa im Tarasa Szewczenki), Dmytro Doncow fonds.

Shevchenko Scientific Society Archives, New York

Ivan Kedryn-Rudnytsky Papers
Hryhor Luzhnytsky Papers
Mykhailo Ostroverkha Papers
Sofia Parfanovych Papers
Iryna Radlovska-Shcherbaniuk Papers
Ivan Shkvarko Papers
Maria Strutynska Papers

State Archives of Lviv Region (Derzhavnyi Arkhiv L'vivs'koï oblasti, DALO)

Fond L'vivs'koho natsional'noho universytetu im. Ivana Franka
Fond L'vivs'koho oblasnoho komitetu KP(b)U
Fond Universytetu im. Iana Kazymyra

United States Holocaust Memorial Museum (ushmm.org)

Cygielstrejch, Mara. Mara Cygielstrejch Reminiscences
Rogowsky, Janet. Janet Rogowsky Memoir

University of Washington

Zygmunt William Birnbaum Papers, University Libraries, University of Washington. http://www.lib.washington.edu/specialcollections/collections/exhibits/spotlight-on-zygmunt-william-birnbaum-papers/images/19TELEGRAMsml.jpg.

Vasyl Stefanyk National Scientific Library of Ukraine in Lviv, Manuscript Division (L'vivs'ka natsional'na naukova biblioteka Ukraïny im. Vasylia Stefanyka, LBAN)

Juliusz Kleiner fonds
Ivan Krypiakevych fonds
Ostap Ortvin fonds
Spohady Ivana Prokopova [Reminiscences of Ivan Prokopov]
Shchodennyk Oleksandra Prusevycha [Journal of Oleksandr Prusevych]
Mykhailo Vozniak fonds

Warsaw University Library (Biblioteka Uniwersytecka w Warszawie, BUW), Manuscript Division (Dział Rękopisów)

Archive of the Home Army Office for Information and Propaganda (Archiwum Biura Informacji i Propagandy Komendy Głównej Armii Krajowej)
Dąbrowska, Maria. Correspondence collection.

NEWSPAPERS AND PERIODICALS

Chwila
Czerwony Sztandar
Dilo
Do peremohy
Gazeta Lwowska
Komunist
Krakivs'ki visti
Krasnaia armiia
Kultura (Paris)
Kurier Galicyjski
Literaturna hazeta
Literatura i mystetstvo
Literaturna Ukraïna
L'vivs'ki visti
Nashi dni
Novyi shliakh
Nowe Widnokręgi
Prosto z mostu
Suchasna Ukraïna
Svoboda

Tygodnik Ilustrowany
Ukraïns'ki shchodenni visti
Vil'na Ukraïna
Visnyk
Visti Vseukraïns'koho Tsentral'noho Vykonavchoho Komitetu (VUTsVK)
Wiadomości
Wiadomości Literackie

Index

Adenauer, Konrad, 42, 44
Ajdukiewicz, Kazimierz, 31, 211
Aks, Izaak, 337–338
Albert, Zygmunt, 41n33, 49–50, 56, 60, 79n115, 80
Aleksandrov, Pavel, 172
Allerhand, Maurycy, 218
Alter, Wiktor, 277
An-sky/Ansky, Szymon, 352
Anders, Irena, 273–274, 292–296, 298–299
Anders, Władysław, 139, 169, 292, 273–274, 277, 281, 291, 294–296, 298
Androkhovych, Amvrosii, 123, 321
Andrukhovych, Yuri, ix
Andrusiak, Mykola, 214–215, 240
Antokolsky, Pavel, 345
Antonych, Bohdan Ihor, 333, 405
    Fifty from Both Banks of the Zbruch, 405
Archipenko, Oleksandr, vii, 406, 435
Arem, Samuel, 27
Aston, Adam, 273
Auerbach, Marian, 45, 173n205
Axer, Erwin, 47, 109, 433
Axer, Maurycy, 109, 433
Axer, Otto, 433

Bakals, 87
Balik, Olga (married name Gürtler), 67, 69, 72

Banach, Łucja, 111, 177
Banach, Stefan, 31, 33, 46–48, 93, 95, 99, 111, 114, 120, 150–151, 155n161, 158, 163–168, 170–178, 211, 225
    Analiza Funkcjonalna, 175
Banach, Stefan Jr., 111, 178
Bandera, Stepan, 4, 80, 257, 356–357, 359, 367, 395
Bartel, Kazimierz, 44–46, 119, 150n143, 174–175, 250
Bartlowa, Maria, 150, 366
Barvinsky, Oleksandr, Sr., 395
Barvinsky, Oleksandr, Jr., 58, 80, 176–178, 394–397
Barvinsky, Vasyl, 131n90, 395–397
Batowski, Stanisław, 414
Baworowski, Michał, 69, 71, 84, 86
Bazhan, Mykola, 57, 147, 204, 318, 329, 345–346, 351
Beck, Józef, 99
Beliaev, Vladimir, 42, 46–47, 331n69, 391–396
    Under Foreign Flags, 393–396
Belousov, Sergei, 202
Berdychowska, Bogumiła, 144n129
Bergson, Henri, 391
Beria, Lavrentii, 142n124, 145n132, 238n148, 246, 254n188, 258n199, 296, 314n15, 394, 423, 443
Berling, Zygmunt, 14

Bernacki, Ludwik, 44
Beyer, Hans Joachim, 46
Biber, Leopold, 45
Bielski, Eleonora and Juliusz, 325, 338
Biliashivsky, Mykola, 232
Bilewicz, Stanisław, 73, 85
Biłyk, Alfred, 40
Birnbaum, Zygmunt William, 119–120
Bisanz, Alfred, 365–366
Biskupsky, Stefan, 133–134, 138, 166
Blavatsky, Volodymyr, 303–304, 342, 359, 372–373, 375, 377–378, 383–384
Bloch, Maurycy, 119–120
Blumenfeld, Stanisława and Ignacy, 110
Błaszczyk, Zofia, 1
Bochenek, Bronisław, 136
Bocheński, Aleksander, 109, 110n44
Bodnarovych, Osyp, 359
Bodo, Eugeniusz (Eugeniusz Bogdan Junod; 1899–1943), xi, 269–273, 275–276, 278–281, 292
Bogatko, Marian, 146–147
Bogoliubov, Nikolai, 172
Bogorodsky, Fedor, 418–419
Bohachevsky–Chomiak, Marta, xiii, 369n159
Bohomolets, Oleksandr, 235, 258
Boianivska, Marta, xiii
Boichuk, Mykhailo, 399, 401–402, 410–411, 413, 416, 435, 442
Boiko, Maria, 261
Boloboiarinov, 69, 72
Bomse, Naum (Nuchim), 319, 334
Bonusiak, Włodzimierz, 50, 265n216
Borejsza, Jerzy (Beniamin Goldberg), 264, 327, 340, 343
Borshchak, Ilko (Illia Barshak), 392
Borucki, Gwidon (Gwidon Gottlieb), 270–271, 273–274, 279n12, 280, 294, 299

Borwicz, Michał (Maksymilian Boruchowicz), 287–288, 321, 330, 337, 377
Boznańska, Olga, 419
Brahinets, Andry, 172n202, 173n206, 212n72, 215
Bretschneider, Zygfryd, 40
Bristigier, Michał, 72
Bromberg, Adolf Adam, 350
Broniewski, Władysław, 112–113, 132, 147, 244–247, 328–329
Brosch, Janina, 433
Bruchnalska, Maria, 249, 254
Bruchnalski, Gustaw, 254
Bruchnalski, Wilhelm, 254
Bruski, Jan Jacek, 147
Brystygier, Julia (Brystygierowa, nee Prajs), 136
Brzoza, Jan, 330, 337
Brzozowski, Stanisław, 308
Bukharin, Nikolai, 235–236
Bukowski, Kazimierz, 109
Burachek, Mykola, 416
Burachynsky, Tyt, 80
Burmystenko, Mykhailo, 208–209, 223
Busel, Iakiv, 438
Bychenko, Heorhy (Iury), 152, 163, 177, 185–186, 224n113, 225

Casimir III The Great (Kazimierz Wielki), 190
Celan, Paul (Paul Antschel), 287
Chaikivsky, Iosyp, 145
Chajes, Wiktor (Widger Chajes), 128, 253
Chaplin, Charlie, 28
Chekaniuk, Andry, 116, 313–315
Chiger, Ignacy, xvi, 67n92, 75
Chiger, Krystyna, 67n92
Chmiel, Jan, 62
Chomsowa, Władysława Larysa (Choms), 425

Chwistek, Leon, 31, 150n144, 158–159, 166n190, 167, 173n205, 407, 409
Ciepielowska, Wanda, 86
Cieszyński, Antony, 81
Cieszyński, Tomasz, 41, 56–57, 61–62, 395
Cuming, Cecylia, 37
Cygielstrejch, Mara (Mina Pistyner), 51
Czarnik, Leszek, 33
Czekanowska, Anna, 129n81
Czekanowski, Jan, 128–129, 186
Czermakowa, Izabella, 409
Czerny, Zygmunt, 325
Czortkower, Salomon, 45
Czuruk, Bolesław, 364–365, 433

Dan, Aleksander (Aleksander Weintraub), 27
Dante Alighieri, 386
 Divine Comedy, 386
Danylchenko, V. I., 209
Danylenko, Serhy (Karin), 437–438, 440, 446–447
Dashkevych, Iaroslav, 74n103, 387n192, 388
Dashkevych, Roman, 100, 108
Davydiak, Ievhen, 121, 188
Dąbkowski, Przemysław, 218
Dąbrowska, Maria, 109, 110n44, 211, 325n53, 336
Debré, Robert, 21, 68
Demianchuk-Tomych, Iaroslava, 189
Derkach, Fedir, 134, 212n71
Desniak, Oleksa (Oleksiy Rudenko), 247, 339, 342
Dickman, Giza, 30, 37
Dmytrenko, Mykhailo, 411, 416–420, 422–423, 426–427, 435
Dobrovolska, Olimpia, 374
Dobrzaniecki, Władysław, 48, 81

Dombrovsky, Oleksandr, 129, 131, 150, 189–190
Dontsov, Dmytro, 97, 104, 215, 309–310, 332–334
Dorfman, Boris, 338
Doroshenko, Dmytro, 237
Doroshenko, Volodymyr, 145, 255
Dovzhenko, Oleksandr, 194, 206–207, 260, 289, 291, 328
Dragan, Mykhailo, 444–445
Drahomanov, Svitozar, 260
Drozdov, Viktor, 443
Dubovy, Mykhailo, 60, 131n91
Duchyminska, Olha (nee Reshetylovych), 388 *Eti*, 388
Dudykevych, Bohdan, 128
Dumansky, Stepan, 196
Dunin-Borkowski, Piotr, 100, 109, 161
Dzeverin, Oleksandr, 198
Dzierżyńska, Zofia, 340
Dzyndra, Ievhen, 422, 434

Eberhart, Myron, 293
Ehrlich, Ludwik, 211
Ehrlich, Stanisław, 118, 155n161, 218
Ehrlichowa, Helena, 40
Empress Elisabeth, 66
Erlich, Henryk, 277

Fediuk, Mykola, 426, 434–435
Fedyk, Oleksandra (Lewkowska), 8–9
Feuerman, Eleasar Jerzy, 40, 115
Figol, Atanazy, 108
Filippov, Oleksy, 209
Finberg, Leonid, xiii
Fischer, Adam, 343
Fleck, Ludwik, 31–37, 52
Frank, Hans, 365, 379
Franko, Ivan, 25, 37, 124, 151, 191, 213, 242, 260, 264, 276, 308, 318–319, 339, 349, 355, 396

Franko, Petro, 224, 242, 276–277, 318
Franz Joseph I, 66
Freud, Sigmund, 391
Friedman, Filip (Fischel, Jeroham), 154
Friedman, Sania, 377
Fryze, Stanisław, 142–143
Fuliński, Benedykt, 94, 159
Fylypovych, Pavlo, 309

Gabrilovich, Ievgeny, 289
Gagarin, Aleksei, 124, 209, 215, 217–218, 222
Ganszyniec, Ryszard (Gansiniec), 118
Gerasimov, Aleksandr, 414, 418
Gertner, Lejzor (Elizar), 111
Gębarowicz, Mieczysław, 77, 347
Gierczycka, Zofia, 67, 86
Giedroyc, Jerzy, 294
Giżycki, 85
Glasner, Jakub (Libidowski), 415
Gluziński, Antoni, 56
Głąbiński, Stanisław, 113
Gnoińska, Hanna, 1, 12, 23, 65
Goebbels, Joseph, 205
Gogol, Nikolai, 4, 364
    The Government Inspector, 364
    Taras Bulba, 4
van Gogh, Vincent, 418
Goldstein, Maximilian, 430
Gorky, Maxim, 329
Górska, Halina (nee Endelman), 353–354
Grabowski, Witold, 82, 103
Grabski, Stanisław, 133, 212n70, 215n85
Grek, Jan, 41, 48, 62, 82
Grigoriev, Pavel (Gorinstein), 280, 292
Grishchenko, 73
Groër, Franciszek, 12, 18, 30–33, 36–41, 48–52, 55, 57, 59, 62, 67–69, 79–81, 83, 86–87, 395
Groër, Maria, 33, 50

Gross, Jan Tomasz, xi, 126
    Neighbors, 126
    Revolution from Abroad, xi, 126
Grosz, Wiktor, 340
Gruber, Ewa, 323–324
Grubiński, Wacław, 326, 330
Gruca, Adam, 55, 57, 80, 380
Gruszecka, Katarzyna (Hollender), 14
Gruzberg, Semen (Hruzbenko), 368, 375–376, 434
Grzędzielski, Jerzy, 81
Gürtler, Alojzy, 69
Gürtler, Olga: *see* Balik, Olga
Guzeev, 431

Hahn, Otto, 407–409, 424–425, 449
Haidabura, Valery, 372
Halan, Iaroslav, 135, 314, 319, 331n69, 332, 336, 388–390, 392n205, 394, 396
Halkin, Hillel, 352
Handzy, 128
Harasymchuk, Roman, 145
Harris, Albert (Aaron Hekelman), 273, 292
Hartman, Stanisław, 76, 85, 150, 168
Havryluk, Oleksandr, 331–332, 336, 353
Havrylyshyn, Myroslav (nom de guerre "Vorona,"), 196
Heine, Heinrich, 319
Hemar, Marian (Jan Maria Hescheles), 25–28, 269, 282, 294
Hepner, Benedykt, 60
Herbert, Zbigniew, 33, 385–386
    Barbarian in the Garden, 181
    "Tren Fortynbrasa," 385–386
Herling-Grudziński, Gustaw, 335–336
Herzberg, Jan, 160, 162–163, 173n208
Hescheles, Henryk, 27–28, 309, 377
Hescheles, Janina (b. 1931, married name Altman), 425
Heydrich, Reinhard, 46

Himmler, Heinrich, 50
Hirniak, Iosyp, 303, 374–375, 383–384
Hirszfeld, Hanna (Hirszfeldowa, nee Kasman, 1884–1964), 35, 88
Hirszfeld, Ludwik, 35–36, 88
Hitler, Adolf, 26, 28, 76n108, 77, 84, 99, 101, 108, 119, 160, 260, 269, 303, 365, 380
Hladky, 59
Hollender, Józef (Piotr Smolnicki), 14–15
Hollender, Tadeusz, 14–15, 96–97, 310, 334, 336, 353, 402–406
Holoborodko, Pavlo, 58
Holovatsky, Iakiv, 187
Holubets, Mykola, 131n90, 197, 356–357, 362, 392n205, 410, 430
Hordynsky, Sviatoslav, 311, 317, 361, 381, 403–405, 407, 409, 423, 435, 449
Horodysky, Zenon, 188–190
Horyn, Vasyl, 255
Hrebenkin, Kostiantyn, 202
Hrechko, Ivan, 428
Hrushetsky, Ivan, 165, 388, 390, 393, 447
Hrushevska, Kateryna, 255
Hrushevska, Maria, 255
Hrushevsky, Mykhailo, 213, 229, 231–233, 235–237, 254–255, 263, 309, 387, 394
Hruzbenko, Semen: *see* Gruzberg, Semen, 368, 375, 434
Hryciuk, Grzegorz, 144
Hrynevych, Vladyslav, 160, 350
Hryshchuk, Leonid, 224
Hrytsak, Iaroslav, 387n192, 393
Hubert, Stanisław, 95
Humeniuk, Petro, 18
Hupalo, Kostiantyn, 372
Hurystrymba, Vasyl, 202

Iablonsky, Leonid, 293
Iarosevych, Irena (stage name Renata Bogdańska, also performed as Rena Jarosiewicz), *see* Anders, Irena
Iarosevych, Mykola, 293
Iarosevych, Olena (nee Nyzhankivska), 293
Iaroslavsky, Emelian, 137
Iatskiv, Mykhailo, 335, 394
Iefremov, Serhy, 228, 231–233, 237, 259
Iendyk, Rostyslav, 380
Ieremenko, Fedir, 115
Ilnytsky, Mykola, 334
  Drama without Catharsis, 334
Ilovaiska, Iekaterina, 13
Indruch, Jadwiga (nee Skorska), 94
Indruch, Rudolf, 94
Inglot, Mieczysław, 187, 342, 343–345
Ironside, Edmund, 101
Iurchenko, Vitaly (Iury Karas-Holynsky), 233
Iusimov, 142
Ivan the Terrible, 193
Ivanets, Ivan, 131n90, 410, 426, 433, 435

Jabayev, Jambyl, 347
the Jagiellonians, 190
Jahn, Alfred, 113, 150, 154
Jakóbiec, Marian, 345
Jałowy, Bolesław, 33, 55, 57, 61–63, 80–81, 163
Janczak, 128
Janisch, Jerzy, 407, 409, 424, 432, 449
Jasieński, Bruno (Wiktor Zysman), 159
Jasińska, Janina, 273
Jastrun, Mieczysław, 158, 351–353
Jaworski, Ivan, 445
Jeleński, Szczepan, 91 *Lilavati*, 91
Jodłowski, Stanisław, 3
Juhn, Otto, 85–86

Kachanov, Nikita, 59
Kacyzne, Alter, 377
Kaganovich, Lazar, 388
Kalynets, Ihor, 449
Kamińska, Ida, 269, 274, 347–348
Karas-Holynsky, Iury: see Iurchenko, Vitaly
Karmansky, Petro, 220, 335, 339, 343, 354–355, 363–364, 386, 389–390, 394, 396–397
Kasman, Leon, 88
Kasprowiczowa, Maria (nee Bunin), 335
Kedryn-Rudnytsky, Ivan: see Rudnytsky, Ivan
Kernytsky, Ivan, 335, 384
Khimenko, Ivan, 134
Khmelnytsky, Bohdan, 192–194, 342
Kholodny, Petro, 435
Khomenko, Iakiv, 115–116
Khomiak, Mykhailo (Michael Chomiak), 109
Khrushchev, Nikita, 37, 54, 57, 145–147, 199, 208–209, 224n114, 245, 256, 437
Khvylia, Andriy, 231
Khvylovy, Mykola, 332, 357, 381–383, 385–386
Kiernicki, Rafał, 81
Kikh, Mariia, 136
Kirsa, Ivan, 220
Kitz, Marcin, 436
Kladochny, Rev. Iosyp, 109
Klawek, Aleksy, 210–211
Kleiner, Juliusz, 155n161, 211, 222, 240n156, 243, 248–250, 254, 265, 338, 342–343
Kleinman, Fryc (Fryderyk), 377, 407–409, 424, 432, 449
Klen, Iury (Osvald Burghardt), 309
Kluczkowski, Jacek, xiv
Klymiv, Ivan (nom de guerre "Lehenda"), 44

Knaster, Bronisław, 113, 166n190, 167–169, 173n205, 178
Knoop, Hans, 50–51 *The Menten Affair*, 50
Knorr, Herbert, 371, 373
Kobylianska, Olha, 350
Koch, Erich, 379
Koch, Hans, 240
Kochur, Hryhory, 375
Kohutiak, Ivan, 372
Kokh, Bohdan, 372
Kolankowski, Ludwik, 190, 212n70
Kolessa, Filaret, 214, 216, 240
Kolski, Witold, 245–246
Konarski, Feliks, 273, 292, 294
Konovalets, Ievhen, 100
Kordiuk, Iulian, 58, 63, 131n91, 436–437, 443–445
Korniichuk, Oleksandr, 116, 118, 121, 124, 128, 130, 139, 147–148, 150n144, 174, 193–194, 204, 313, 318, 320, 329–330, 332, 383, 390, 394, 410–412, 414, 419
  Bohdan Khmelnytsky, 139, 193, 204, 263, 419
  Platon Krechet, 318
Korolewicz, Michał: see Lille, Jan, 12, 18, 22, 85, 87–88
Kos-Anatolsky, Anatoly, 293, 395
Kosach, Iury, 317, 375
Kosichev, Anatolii, 217–218
Kosior, Stanislav, 202
Kossak, Karol, 112
Kostelnyk, Havryil, 389
Kościuszko, Tadeusz, 120, 169, 281, 339
Kot, Stanisław, 277–278, 296–297
Kotsiubynsky, Mykhailo, 350
Kotsylovsky, Iosafat, 3
Kott, Jan, 25, 95, 110, 112–113, 150, 158, 247, 321, 343, 351–352, 354
Kott, Lidia (nee Steinhaus), 95, 110, 112

Koval, Oleksandr, 60
Kovba, Zhanna, 33–34, 74n103
Koverko, Andriy, 422
Kovpak, Sydor, 379, 385
Kovzhun, Pavlo, 407–409, 435
Kowalska, Anna (nee Chrzanowska), 185, 211, 225, 334, 336, 352–353, 405
Kowalski, Jerzy, 211
Kozak, Bohdan, 374n168, 375, 378, 385
Kozak, Edvard (artistic alias: Eko), 131n90, 410, 449
Kozlaniuk, Petro, 135n104, 314, 316, 332, 390, 392–394
Kozyk, Mykhailo, 375n172, 434
Königsberg, Dawid, 319, 342–343, 347, 377
Krasnov, Kapiton, 146n135, 235n141, 241, 245
Kratochwila-Widymska, Józefa, 415
Kravtsiv, Bohdan, 115, 334
Krechowiecki, Adam, 52, 76
Kreczmar, Jan, 342, 347
Kreutz, Mieczysław, 25, 33, 162, 323, 337
Krukowska, Helena (Wasilkowska), 12, 86–87
Krukowski, Włodzimierz, 12, 174
Krushelnytska, Larysa, xvi, 230n125
Krychevsky, Fedir, 416
Krychevsky, Vasyl, 419
Krymsky, Ahatanhel, 197, 232–233, 257–262, 264, 277
Krypiakevych, Ivan, 145, 152, 155, 172, 188–190, 197, 214n79, 216, 225, 241, 264, 319, 387
Kryvutsky, Pavlo, 210
Krzemicka, Zofia, 97, 99, 104, 106
Krzemieniewski, Seweryn, 129–131, 164
Kubicz, Stanisław, 40
Kubiyovych, Volodymyr, 356, 365, 380
Kugel, 79
Kuhn, Thomas, 31
  The Structure of Scientific Revolutions, 31
Kulchytska, Olena, 131n90, 410, 412, 415, 427
Kulczyński, Stanisław, 134, 160, 163, 173, 177, 211, 212n71
Kulish, Mykola, 374
Kunynets, Stefania (married name Fedorovych), 54
Kupchynsky, Roman, 131, 315, 329
Kurbas, Les (Oleksandr), 303, 374
Kurchaba, Leonid, 80
Kurek, Jalu (Franciszek), 354
Kurovets, Ivan, 72
Kurtyka, Janusz
Kurylas, Osyp, 412, 435
Kuryluk, Karol, 334, 343, 353, 405, 409
Kuryłowicz, Jerzy, 129, 324n47
Kuźmińska, Helena, 224, 329

Lanckorońska, Karolina, xvi, 47, 115, 117–118, 130, 150, 186–187, 191, 217, 227, 252, 264
Landberg, Marian (during the war Zbigniew Isalski), 12, 65, 87
Landberg, Stanisław, 86
Langner, Władysław, 108
Lasovsky, Volodymyr, 131n90, 407, 410, 413, 415, 425, 433, 449
Lastovetsky, Andry, 56–58, 63, 380, 432
Lebed, Mykola, 44
Lebedev-Kumach, Vasily, 329
Lebesgue, Henri Léon, 119
Lec, Stanisław Jerzy (de Tusch-Letz), 354
Lem, Stanisław, 175
Lenartowicz, Jan Tadeusz, 225
Lenin, Vladimir Ilyich, 222, 290, 346, 417, 419
Leszczyński, Julian, 430
Levchenko, Iakiv, 133, 212n72, 215, 220

Levytska, Sofia, 408
Levytsky (Levytzkyj), Borys, 44, 473
Levytsky, Dmytro, 154, 230n125, 297
Levytsky, Kost, 125, 237–239, 253, 313, 315
Levytsky, Leopold, 449
Levytsky, Volodymyr, 145
Lewin, Jecheskiel, 154
Lewin, Kurt, xvi
Lewkowska, Eufrozyna (nee Fedyk), 3, 7–19, 70, 73, 86–87, 432
Lewkowski, Jan, 8–14, 19, 70, 73
Léger, Fernand, 407
Lille, Irena (Fryderyka Tennenbaum, assumed name Irena Szyszkowicz), xi, 12–16, 18–27, 29–32, 35–37, 40–41, 52, 59, 64–73, 79, 81–88, 120, 431
  My Life, 65
Lille, Jan (assumed name Michał Korolewicz), 12–14, 18–19, 21–23, 36, 69–70, 73, 79, 82–86, 88, 448
Lille, Ludwik, 22–23, 27, 36, 69, 72, 307, 407–408, 431, 444, 448–449
Lille, Sara (assumed name Barbara Mikoś, "Granny,"), 12–14, 19, 69–70, 79, 86
Lindenfeld, Kazimierz, 60
Lipl, Helena (nee Tennenbaum, assumed name Maria Rożycka), 87
Litvinov, Maxim, 260
Liubchenko, Arkady, 260, 361, 381–385
Liubchenko, Panas, 385
Liubchyk, Vasyl
Liudkevych, Stanislav, 131n90
Longchamps de Berier, Roman, 115, 129, 182, 211
Lopatynsky, Demian, 369
Loria, Stanisław, 58, 166n190, 211
Lubkivsky, Roman, 391
Lukianchikov, Ivan, 53

Lusternik, Lazar, 172
Lysenko, Iosyp, 208–209
Lysenko, Mykola, 293
Lysiak, Pavlo, 108
Lysiak-Rudnytsky, Ivan, 393
Lytvynenko, Serhy, 131n90, 380, 410, 420, 422, 427, 449

Łomnicki, Antoni, 95
Łozynska, Pelagia (Kazimiera Poraj), 48
Łukaszewicz, Piotr, 425n49, 433n68, 448

Maievsky, Dmytro (nom de guerre "Taras"), 438
Makarchenko, Oleksandr, 52–53, 63, 225
Makaryk, Irena, 375
Maksymenko, Oksana (nee Kokh, b. 1962), 18
Maksymiv, Ivan, 257
Maksymonko, Leonty, 80, 311
Makuszyński, Kornel, 338
Malaniuk, Ievhen, 317, 361, 404
Malashchuk, Ludvika, 185n5, 196n33
Maliutsa, Antin, 449
Malyshko, Andry, 204
Malytska, Kostiantyna, 335, 369n151
Manteuffel, Jerzy, 153
Manuilsky, Dmytro, 389
Marchenko, Mykhailo, xi, 142, 163, 170, 173n205, 177, 180, 182–192, 194–203, 208–218, 220–224, 240–241, 252, 261–264, 323, 416
Marchenko, Nina (first married name Umrilova, second married name Smuzhanytsia), 199, 241
Marchenko, Valery, 199, 201, 241
Maritchak, Oleksandr, 188, 210
Martyniv, Stepan, 60
Marx, Karl, 39, 58, 122, 141, 160, 162, 199, 201, 212n72, 215, 217, 220, 222, 327, 391

Matviichuk, Mykhailo, 444
Matviiv-Melnyk, Mykola, 354
Mayakovsky, Vladimir, 351
Maysky, Ivan, 247, 273, 278, 291, 296, 335
Mazepa, Ivan, 314, 360
Mazur, Stanisław, 130, 166n190, 171–173, 225
Mechnyk, Petro, 188
Meisel, Henryk, 34–35
Meisel, Paula (nee Rossberger), 34–35
Mekhlis, Lev, 208
Melnychuk, Petro, 57, 60
Melnyk, Andry, 215, 356–359, 395
Menten, Pieter Nicolaas, 48–51
Merkulov, Vsevolod, 133, 238n148, 254n188
Merkurov, Sergei, 419
Mickiewicz, Adam, 152, 319, 327, 338–344, 347–350, 354–355, 360
   Pan Tadeusz, 345, 347, 377
Mikhalkov, Nikita, 273
Mikhoels, Solomon, 61
Mikoś, Barbara, *see* Lille, Sara
Miłobędzki, Adam, 111
Minc, Hilary, 18, 22, 36, 88
Mirek, Alfred, 281
   Notes of a Prisoner, 281
Mniszek, Aleksander, 278
Modzelewska, Maria, 25
Molotov, Viacheslav, 24, 103, 127, 160, 260, 413
Morgenstein, 128
Mudry, Vasyl, 107, 365
Muzyka, Iaroslava (née Stefanovych), xi, xiv, xviii, 2, 6, 14–17, 63, 71–72, 86, 131n90, 300, 307, 311–312, 397, 399–402, 407–410, 413–414, 423, 426–428, 430–449
Muzyka, Maksym, 16, 32, 41, 52–53, 57–58, 60, 62–63, 67, 71–72, 80, 131n91, 265, 307, 311, 402, 426, 436, 443, 445
Mysko, Emmanuel, 44

Nacht, Artur (Samborski), 417–418, 422, 424–425
Nacht, Józef (Prutkowski), 281, 334, 354
Naegeli, Otto, 68
Naglerowa, Herminia, 334
Nahaylo (Nahajlo), Bohdan, 292n27, 295
Nakonechny, Ievhen, 75, 206
Nalepińska, Zofia, 399
Narbut, Heorhy, 420
Navrotsky, Vasyl, 239
Nazaruk, Osyp, 105, 108, 314
Nedbailo, Petro, 121, 173n206, 216
Neyman, Stefania, 250–251
Neyman-Pilat, Ewa, 251
Nietzsche, Friedrich, 391
Nikifor (Epifany Drovniak), 438
Nikliborc, Władysław, 113–114
Nikulin, Lev, 345, 347, 437
Nimchuk, Ivan, 101, 116, 128, 313–315
Novakivsky, Oleksa, 435
Novychenko, Leonid, 390
Nowicki, Witold, 60n78, 81
Nyzhankivsky, Ostap, 293

Oberlander, Theodor, 42
Ohloblyn, Oleksandr, 202
Olesnytsky, Ievhen, 305
Olzhych, Oleh, 357
Opania, Marian, 28
Opieńska-Blauth, Janina, 60
Ordonówna, Hanka (Anna Maria Tyszkiewiczowa, nee Pietruszyńska, stage name Ordonka), 292
Orest, Mykhailo, 309
Orlicz, Władysław, 166, 172

Ortwin, Ostap (Oskar Katzenellenbogen), 307–308, 312, 325–326, 330, 335–336, 354
Osinchuk, Mykhailo, 131n90, 408, 410, 413, 420, 423, 426–427, 433–434, 449
Osinchuk, Roman, 56, 58, 63–64, 80, 432
Ossowski, Stanisław, 77, 346–348
Ostern, Paweł, 45
Ostroverkha, Mykhailo, 55, 97–99, 103–107, 110, 112, 115, 119, 131–132, 136, 144, 253n187, 312, 314, 316n24, 317–318, 329, 334, 410–411, 414
Ostrowski, Stanisław, 128, 238n149, 409
Ostrowski, Tadeusz, 48, 62, 82

Pachovsky, Vasyl, 329, 335, 364
Padalka, Ivan, 399, 410–411
Panch, Petro, 114, 246–247, 325n53, 329, 335n82, 416
Panchyshyn, Marian, 30, 52–58, 60, 62, 64, 65n89, 79–81, 124, 131n91, 152, 155, 177, 224, 239, 241, 242n162, 356, 373, 380
Pankivsky, Kost, 356, 362, 369–371
Parfanovych, Sofia, 58, 131, 335
Parkhomenko, Mykhailo, 388, 392
Parnas, Jakub, 57–58, 60–64, 67, 163–166, 178, 211, 225
Parnicki, Teodor, 325n53, 334
Pashchenko, Oleksandr, 413
Pashe-Ozersky, Mykola, 216, 218–220
Pasternak, Boris, 235
Pasternak, Iaroslav, 145, 214
Pasternak, Leon, 137–138, 353
Pavlenko, U., 59
Pavlyshyn, Oleh, xiv, 251n182
Peiper, Tadeusz, 246–247
Pelekhaty, Kuzma, 135n104, 314, 316

Pelensky, Zenon, 107
Peretts, Volodymyr, 232
Peretz, Isaac Leib, 349
Peter I the Great, 193, 339
Petliura, Symon, 100, 207, 309, 314, 364, 380, 422–423
Petrenko, Andry, 373
Petriakova, Faina, 430
Petrov, Viktor (pen name V. Domontovych), 220, 258, 383
Petrovsky, Mykola, 194, 202
Petrun, Fedir, 259
Picasso, Pablo, 399
Pilat, Stanisław, 250–251
Piłsudski, Józef, 69, 319, 390
Pinchevska, Bohdana, 425
von Pirquet, Clemens, 37
Pistyner, Fryda, 51
Pistyner, Izaak, 51
Piwocki, Ksawery, 430
Pleshevtsev, V., 443
Podolynsky, Oleksandr, 56, 63
Poliansky, Iury, 145, 152–155, 166n188, 172n202, 173n207, 323, 356, 430
Poliuha, Ivan, 60
Polonska-Vasylenko, Natalia, 198n40, 202, 233, 258–259, 261–262
Połoniecki, Bernard (Pordes), 307–308
Ponisch, 433
Popper, Karl, 31
Potocki, Andrzej, 228
Potshybitkin, Mikhail, 274
Poussin, Nicolas, 419
Pritsak, Omelian, 129, 257–258, 260–261, 264, 284
Progulski, Stanisław, 41, 67, 81
Prokopiv, Ivan, 39, 54, 59, 80
Pronaszko, Andrzej, 408–409
Proust, Marcel, 319, 321
 A La Recherche du Temps Perdu, 319
Prus, Edward, 44 Heroes of the Trident, 44

Przyboś, Julian, 340, 342–344, 353
Przybyłowski, Kazimierz, 218
Putrament, Jerzy, 327, 342

Radchenko, Hryhory, 233
Rajszer, 142
Rakovsky, Ivan, 145, 234n137, 238–240
Rechmedin, Leonid, 415
Redko, Iulian, 265
Redlich, Fryderyk (Franciszek), 40
Redzik, Adam, 187, 282, 286
Reich, Izaak, 432
Reich-Selska, Margit, 306, 407, 409–410, 424, 427–429, 432–434, 449
Rencki, Roman, 27, 46–48, 66, 81
Rettinger, Ludwika (Wichuna), 111
Rettinger, Mieczysław, 109–110
Reymont, Władysław, 97
Riabchuk, Mykola, 181
von Ribbentrop, Joachim, 24, 99, 103, 127, 160, 413
Riemer, Aleksander, 424, 432
Rokita, Richard, 286
Romanchuk, Iulian, 394
Romm, Michał, 290–291
Romm, Mikhail, 194, 288–290
Room, Abraham, 194, 289
Rosenberg, 128
Rosner, Adolf (stage name Eddie Rosner), 274
Rothfeld, Adolf, 377
Rowecki, Stefan (nom de guerre Grot), 109
Rubchak, Ivan, 318
Rubel, Ludwik, 120
Rubinowicz, Wojciech, 58, 166n190
Rublov, Oleksandr, 201, 262n211, 266n216, 394
Rudenko, Roman, 47, 55
Rudniański, Jarosław, 136–137, 262n213, 297n34

Rudniański, Stefan, 137, 162, 215, 225, 245
Rudnicki, Adolf, 354
Rudnicki, Klemens, 129, 296n33
Rudnytska, Anna (nee Stefanovych), 426
Rudnytska, Daryna, 305
Rudnytska, Marta (nee Olesnytska), 240n156, 305, 325
Rudnytska, Milena, 102, 365–369
    Twenty Years of Polish Lawlessness in Western Ukraine, 102
Rudnytska, Olha (born Ida Spiegel), 306, 366–367
Rudnytsky, Anton, 306
Rudnytsky, Ivan (pen name Kedryn), 97–103, 105, 107–110, 147, 158, 230, 234, 263, 365–366 *The Causes of Poland's Fall*, 101–102, 109
Rudnytsky, Mykhailo, xi, 131, 197–198, 216, 240, 251, 263, 300–312, 314–321, 323–325, 327, 329, 331–333, 335–337, 353–355, 363–367, 375, 377–381, 385–397, 403–404, 413, 426, 433, 444, 446
    Between Idea and Form, 311, 391–392
    From Myrny to Khvylovy, 311–312, 332, 363, 386, 390–392, 397
Rudnytsky, Volodymyr, 306
Rudzińska, Agnieszka, xiv, 206
Rustaveli, Shota, 347
Ruziewicz, Stanisław, 96–97
Rybak, Natan, 204
Rydz-Śmigły, Edward, 101
Rylski, Tadeusz, 346
Rylsky, Maksym, 309, 345–347, 390, 416
Rysiewicz, Adam, 142

Saks, Stanisław, 113, 166n190, 167–168, 169n198, 173n205

Saltykov-Shchedrin, Mikhail, 220
Samchuk, Ulas, 317, 356–362
    On a White Horse, 356–357, 359
Sandauer, Artur, 310
Sands, Philippe, xi
Saradzhev, Artashes, 202
Savchenko, Fedir, 236–237, 255
Savchenko, Ihor, 194
Savchenko, Olha, 236, 254
Savchenko, Serhy, 431, 438, 446
Savchyn, Maria (nom de guerre Marichka), 337
Schaff, Adam, 137
Schauder, Juliusz Paweł, 114, 166n190, 173
Schmierer Reif, Mendel, 415
Schopenhauer, Arthur, 391
Schorr, Dawid, 218
Schöngarth, Karl Georg Eberhard, 48, 50
Schudrich, Jakub, 377
Schulz, Bruno, 288, 408–409
Schulze, Karl, 56, 80
Sedlar, Vasyl, 399, 411
Selska, Margit, *see* Reich-Selska, Margit
Selsky, Roman, 306–307, 407, 409, 412, 417, 419, 427–429, 432–434, 449
Semchyshyn, Myroslav, 75, 124, 321, 323
Sempoliński, Ludwik, 28
Serhiienko, Vasyl, 245, 251–252, 271n3
Serov, Ivan, 32, 142n124, 145n132, 146, 170n199, 235n141, 238n148, 241, 245–247, 251, 254n188, 258n199, 271n3, 314n15
Shaian, Volodymyr, 364
Shakespeare, William, 3–4, 301, 303–304, 306, 375, 383, 386
    Hamlet, 301, 303–306, 312, 315–316, 321, 325, 333, 338, 349, 355, 362, 364, 369, 374–377, 380, 383–386, 434
    Othello, 375

Shchukin, Sergei, 417–418
Shchurat, Vasyl, 173n206, 214, 216, 240
Sheparovych, Iulian, 59
Sheptytsky, Andrei (born Roman Szeptycki), vii, 56, 107, 109, 154, 176–177, 189, 239, 359, 368, 380, 396, 437, 447
Shevchenko, Taras, 214, 319, 339, 347, 349–350, 419
Shevelov, Iury (George Y.) (né Schneider; pen names Iury Sherekh, Hr. Shevchuk), 197, 219–220, 372, 384
Shklarski, Liuger, 175
Shore, Marci, 243
    Caviar and Ashes, 243
Shorubalka, Ivan, 443
Shtul, Oleh (nom de guerre Zhdanovych), 356, 358
Shukhevych, Iury, 293
Shukhevych, Roman, 6, 176, 293, 402, 439–440, 446
Shyian, Anatolii, 204
Sichulski, Kazimierz, 415
Siemiaszkowa, Wanda, 347
Sienkiewicz, Henryk, 97
Sieradzki, Włodzimierz, 81
Sierpiński, Wacław, 95–97, 175
Sikorski, Władysław, 169, 247, 273, 277–278, 291, 296, 335
Silber, 154
Simovych, Vasyl, 124, 152–153, 172n202, 173n206, 188, 211, 214, 312, 315, 321, 324, 359
Siwak, Eugeniusz, 2, 5–7
Siwak, Halina (nee Lewkowska), xiii–xiv, xviii, 1–9, 12–14, 17–19, 23, 65, 67, 177, 448n103
Siwak, Leoniła (nee Maznica), 5–6
Siwak, Teodor (Syvak, Fedir), 5–7
Skaba, Andry, 198
Skoropadsky, Pavlo, 231

Skrypnyk, Mykola, 200, 233
Skrzypek, Stanisław, 113, 175
Skubytsky, Trokhym, 202
Skuza, Wojciech, 246, 329
Skwarczyńska, Stefania, 33, 185n5, 243–244, 248–251
Slipy, Iosyf (Slipyj, Josyf), 447n101
Sliusarenko, Hryhory, 202
Slyzh, Adolf, 251–252
Słonimski, Antoni, 28
Smal-Stocki, Roman, 108, 230n125
Smolnicki, Piotr, *see* Hollender, Jozef
Snyder, Timothy, x, xiii
Sobolev, Sergei, 172
Sołowij, Adam, 47–48, 82
Sommerstein, Emil, 27n6, 247
Soroka, Bohdan, 175
Soroka, Mykhailo, 176
Soroka, Petro, 373, 375
Sosenko, Rev. Ksenofont, 236
Sosiura, Volodymyr, 318, 350
  I Love, 318
Sosnowska, Danuta, xiii, 122
Spiegel, Ida, *see* Rudnytska, Olha
Stadnyk, Iosyp, 224, 372–373, 375
Staff, Leopold, 308
Stahl, Zdzisław, 114, 212n70, 373
Stalin, Joseph (born Ioseb Besarionis dze Jughashvili), x, 5, 23, 84, 88, 115, 129, 132, 133n96, 138, 142, 146, 159n171, 174, 193–194, 204, 206, 221, 224, 236, 239, 243, 246, 263, 290, 296, 312n11, 318–319, 324, 327, 329, 339–340, 345–347, 372, 389, 394, 410, 412, 418–422, 442–443, 449
Stark, Marceli, 161–162, 169n198
Stark, Pesach, *see* Stryjkowski, Julian
Starosolsky, Stanislav, 121–122
Starosolsky, Volodymyr, 210, 251
Stasiak, Stefan, 260, 323

Stebun, Ilia (Ilia Katsnelson), 214
Stefanovych, Lev, 426, 443
Stefanyk, Vasyl, 319, 350
Steinhaus, Ewelina, 99, 112
Steinhaus, Hugo, xi, 31–32, 39, 91–99, 103–104, 110, 112–116, 118–120, 123, 125, 130, 133–134, 143, 148–153, 156–170, 172, 173n205, 175, 177n224, 178, 186, 215n85, 222, 310, 339
  Mathematical Snapshots, 91–92, 175, 178
Steinhaus, Stefania, 93–96, 98, 106–107, 110, 112, 119, 159
Stempowski, Jerzy, 110–111
Stendhal (Marie-Henri Beyle), 319
Stern, Anatol, 246
Stern, Jonasz, 422, 424–425
Stetsko, Iaroslav, 63n86, 80, 152, 210, 356, 362, 367, 424
Stępień, Stanisław, xiii, 228, 335
Stiasny, 433
Stieber, Zdzisław, 133n99, 153, 343
Stieglitz, Józef, 50
Streng, Henryk (from 1942 Marek Włodarski), 407, 409–410, 412, 422, 424–425, 433
Struk, Evstakhiy, 57, 60
Strutynska, Antonina, 444–445
Strutynska, Maria (nee Navrotska, pen name Vira Marska), 335, 358–361, 366, 369n151
Strutynsky, Mykhailo, 253n187, 335, 359
Stryjkowski, Julian (Pesach Stark), 310, 321
  The Great Fear, 321
Studynsky, Kyrylo, 54–55, 124, 138, 144–146, 155, 159, 209, 211, 214, 216, 221, 224–243, 248–257, 261–262, 264, 276–277, 325, 330, 336

Stur, Jan (Hersz Feingold), 27
Styka, Adam, 415
Styka, Jan, 415
Styś, Wincenty, 130, 187
Surkov, Aleksei, 207
Susak, Vita, 18
Suvorov, Aleksandr, 339
Svientsitska, Vira, 428, 435
Svientsitsky, Ilarion, 428, 430, 435
Svitlyk, Bohdana (nom de guerre Svitlana, pen name Maria Dmytrenko), 427, 437, 443
Swianiewicz, Stanisław, 1, 291
Szałajko, Kazimierz, 168
Szczepcio, 271, 279
Szemplińska, Elżbieta, 339, 353
Szlechter, Emanuel, 270, 275, 280–282, 285–288
Szpilrajn, Edward (after the war Marczewski, 1907–76), 167, 169
Szyszkowicz, Irena, *see* Lille, Irena
Śladecka, Magdalena, xiv

Tarnavsky, Ostap, xvi, 75, 304–305, 316, 327, 331–333, 336, 351, 357, 362, 367–369, 375, 381
Taszycki, Witold, 3, 118, 177, 211, 343
Teisseyre, Stanisław, 407, 414, 417–418, 420, 425, 434
Teliha, Olena, 356–359, 370
Tennenbaum, Chaia: *see* Urim, Chaia
Tennenbaum, Fryderyka: *see* Lille, Irena
Tennenbaum, Helena: *see* Lipl, Helena
Tennenbaum, Henryka (Maria Kwiatkowska), 15, 66, 86–87
Tennenbaum, Izaak, 66
Tennenbaum, Regina, 66
Terletsky, Mykhailo, 444
Terpyliak, Andry, 364, 377, 381
Tetmajer, Kazimierz Przerwa, 97
Timoshenko, Semyon, 54, 203
Tiutiunnyk, Iury, 437

Tkachuk, Vasyl, 335
Tolkachov, 413
Tolstoy, Aleksei, 323
Tolstoy, Leo, 349
Tomaszewski, Tadeusz, 25, 29, 33, 49, 54, 57, 62, 76–77, 94n1, 150, 152–155, 162, 174n210, 176, 179, 186, 225, 243, 323, 343
  Pejzaż Psychologiczny, 25n3, 94n1, 179, 243
Tomczyk, Roman, 282
Tońcio (stage name of Henryk Vogelfanger), 271, 279
Toperman, Fryderyk (after the war Topolski), 135–137, 139n120
Topolnytsky, 188
Torańska, Teresa, 72
Trehub, Hnat, 30–31, 53, 59–60, 72
Trehubenko, Mykola, 202
Tretiakov, Pavel, 417
Trush, Ivan, 399, 412, 435
Trznadel, Jacek, 159n171, 321n41, 343–344
  Collaborators, 344
  Disgrace at Home, 343
Tsurkovsky, Iaroslav, 326n54, 331–333, 335–338, 356–357, 363–364, 380
Tudor, Stepan, 332, 336, 339
Turchynska, Agata, 318
  Abundant Harvest, 318
Turyn, Roman, 408, 417, 426–427, 438
Tuwim, Julian, 26, 28
Tychyna, Pavlo, 327, 329, 345, 350, 353
Tyktor, Ivan, 197
Tyrowicz, Ludwik, 415
Tyshchenko, Iury, 368

Ukrainka, Lesia (Larysa Kosach-Kvitka), 339, 350
Ulam, Adam, 120, 169
Ulam, Józef, 120, 169
Ulam, Stanisław, 91, 111, 120, 169, 177

Umrilov, Veniamin, 199
Urim, Chaja (née Arem), 66
Utzig, Franciszka, 9, 12

Valchyk, Konstantin, 195–196, 257
Valnytska, Sofiia (nee Krasińska), 410–411, 413
Vasylenko, Mykola, 202
Velázquez, Diego, 418–419
Vernadsky, Vladimir, 233, 259
Verstiuk, Vladyslav, xiii, xiv
Vesolovsky, Bohdan, 293
Viedienieiev, Dmytro, 258, 439–440, 442, 446–447
Vilde, Iryna (pen name of Daryna Polotniuk, nee Makohon, 1907–82), 335, 350n119, 391–392
Vincenz, Stanisław, 95, 110–111, 114, 334, 428
  Dialogues with the Soviets, 114
  On the High Uplands, 428
Vintiuk, Iury, 337–338
Vogel, Debora, 288, 310, 334, 377
  Acacias Are Blooming, 352
Volodymyr the Great, 260
Voroshilov, Kliment, 444
Vozniak, Mykhailo, 213–216, 224, 240, 242, 318, 373
Vynnychenko, Volodymyr, 309
Vynnychuk, Iury, 287
Vynnytsky, Oleksandr (after the war Aleksander Winnicki-Radziewicz), 417, 422, 434, 436

Wars, Henryk (Warszawski), 268, 270–271, 273–276, 279–280, 282, 285, 288–289, 291–292, 294–295, 298–299
Wasilewska, Wanda, 130, 136, 145–148, 150n144, 159, 174, 204–206, 224, 226, 241, 243–248, 264, 276, 289, 329–330, 339, 343, 353–354, 394

Wasylewski, Stanisław, 327, 338, 342–343, 350
Waszyński, Michał, 273, 278, 280, 295–296, 298–299
Wat, Aleksander (Chwat), xvi, 132, 146–147, 244–246, 248, 279, 320, 328–329, 338
  My Century, 279, 320
Watowa, Ola (Paulina Wat, nee Lew), 243–244, 248
Ważyk, Adam (Ajzyk Wagman), 351, 353
Weidlich, Fritz, 373
Weigl, Rudolf, 32–35, 41, 170, 177, 250
Weinrich, Max, 157
Wierzyński, Kazimierz, 25–27
Wiesenthal, Simon, 286–287
Witkacy (Stanisław Ignacy Witkiewicz), 26–27
Witkowska, Maria, 113
Wittlin, Józef, x, 27
Wnuk, Marian, 409, 412, 417, 434
Wnuk, Rafał, 58n72
Wnukowa, Józefa (Jozefa Wnuk), 422, 425
Wojciechowski, Tadeusz, 433
Wojdysławski, Menachem, 160, 167, 173n208
Wolchuk, Roman, 44–45
Wolski, Jerzy, 169
Wóycicki, Kazimierz, xiii
Wreciona, Ievhen, 44
Wyczółkowski, Leon, 399

Yanukovych, Viktor, 440

Zabolotny, Danylo, 233
Zaiats, Mykhailo, 314
Zajączkowski, Mariusz, xiv
Zakrzewski, Stanisław, 190
Załużna, Anna, 430–431
Zarembianka, Maria, 435

Zarytska, Kateryna, 176, 442, 446
Zarytsky, Myron, 152, 166–167, 170, 172n201, 173n206, 175–177, 442
Zerov, Mykola, 308, 318
Zhuravliov, Viktor, 58
Zierhoffer, August, 133–134, 166
Zimińska, Mira, 28
Zwoliński, Przemysław, 343

Żaba, Jarosław, 136, 139n120
Żeleński, Tadeusz (pen name Boy), 41, 46–48, 82, 159, 174, 247, 312, 319, 321–322, 327, 330, 343, 348, 354
Żeleński, Władysław, 46–47
Żeromski, Stefan, 97
Żygulski, Kazimierz, 113, 150, 219
Żyliński, Eustachy, 166n190, 168, 211

www.ingramcontent.com/pod-product-compliance
Lightning Source LLC
Chambersburg PA
CBHW061922220426

43662CB00012B/1776